KT-159-416

COUNTRY LIVING
M A G A Z I N E

GUIDE TO RURAL ENGLAND

THE HEART OF ENGLAND

AUTHORISED: WITHDRAWN FROM STOCK

NORTH EAST LINCOLNSHIRE LIBRARIES

By David Gerrard

© Travel Publishing Ltd.

Published by:
Travel Publishing Ltd
7a Apollo House, Calleva Park
Aldermaston, Berks, RG7 8TN
ISBN 1-902-00784-0
© Travel Publishing Ltd

Country Living is a registered trademark of The National
Magazine Company Limited.

First Published: 2003

COUNTRY LIVING GUIDES:

East Anglia	The South East of England
Heart of England	The South of England
Ireland	Wales
Scotland	The West Country

PLEASE NOTE:

All advertisements in this publication have been accepted in good faith by Travel Publishing and they have not necessarily been endorsed by *Country Living* Magazine.

All information is included by the publishers in good faith and is believed to be correct at the time of going to press. No responsibility can be accepted for errors.

Editor: Peter Long

Printing by: Scotprint, Haddington

Location Maps: © Maps in Minutes ™ (2003)   © Crown Copyright, Ordnance Survey 2003

Walks: Walks have been reproduced from the Jarrold Pathfinder Guides
                  © Jarrold Publishing

Walk Maps: Reproduced from Ordnance Survey mapping on behalf of the
                  Controller of Her Majesty's Stationery Office, © Crown Copyright.
                  Licence Number MC 100035812

Cover Design: Lines & Words, Aldermaston

Cover Photo: Holy Trinity Church and the River Avon, Stratford upon Avon,
               Warwickshire: © www.britainonview.com

Text Photos: Text photos have been kindly supplied by the Britain on View photo library
               © www.britainonview.com

This book is sold subject to the condition that it shall not by way of trade or otherwise be lent, re-sold, hired out, or otherwise circulated without the publisher's prior consent in any form of binding or cover other than that which it is published and without similar condition including this condition being imposed on the subsequent purchase.

Foreword

Britain is an explorer's paradise - the variety of landscape, wildlife and cultural attractions promise days of energetic walking and breathtaking sights, or quiet contemplation in awe-inspiring countryside. From the North York Moors to the Dorset coastline, nothing beats Britain's extraordinary, natural beauty.

Each month, *Country Living Magazine* celebrates the richness and diversity of our countryside with features on rural Britain and the traditions that have their roots there. So it is with great pleasure that I introduce you to the *Country Living Magazine Guide to Rural England* series. Packed with information about unusual and unique aspects of our countryside, the guides will point both fair-weather and intrepid travellers in the right direction.

This book provides a fascinating tour of the Heart of England, from the Malvern Hills to the Peak District, Melton Mowbray to Shrewsbury. Whether it's the history and heritage of Sherwood Forest that sparks your enthusiasm, or the literary world of Shakespeare's birthplace, Stratford upon Avon, that appeals to your cultural senses, this area has hugely contrasting counties and towns to enjoy.

I hope this guide will help make your visit a rewarding experience and that you will return inspired, refreshed and ready to head off on your next countryside adventure.

Susy Smith

Susy Smith

PS To subscribe to *Country Living Magazine* each month, call 01858 438844

NORTH EAST LINCOLNSHIRE COUNCIL	
54073000304362	
Browns Books	05/01/04
914.20486	9.99

B37668569 6

Introduction

This is the second *Country Living Magazine* rural guide edited by David Gerrard who was a full-time television documentary director and scriptwriter before becoming a full-time travel writer. He has published more than 30 titles covering many areas of Britain and Ireland. As with the Ireland edition David has ensured that The *Country Living Magazine Guide to England - The Heart of England* is packed with vivid descriptions, historical stories, amusing anecdotes and interesting facts on hundreds of places in the traditional countryside of Herefordshire, Worcestershire, Shropshire, Staffordshire, Derbyshire, Nottinghamshire, Lincolnshire, Leicestershire, Rutland, Northamptonshire, Warwickshire and the West Midlands.

The coloured advertising panels within each chapter provide further information on places to see, stay, eat, drink, shop and even exercise! We have also selected a number of walks from Jarrold's Pathfinder Guides which we highly recommend if you wish to appreciate fully the beauty and charm of the varied rural landscapes of the Heart of England.

The guide however is not simply an "armchair tour". Its prime aim is to encourage the reader to visit the places described and discover much more about the wonderful towns, villages and countryside of the Heart of England. Whether you decide to explore these counties by wheeled transport or by foot we are sure you will enjoy the experience.

We are always interested in receiving comments on places covered (or not covered) in our guides so please do not hesitate to use the reader reaction form provided at the rear of this guide to give us your considered comments. This will help us refine and improve the content of the next edition. We also welcome any general comments which will help improve the overall presentation of the guides themselves.

Finally, for more information on the full range of travel guides published by Travel Publishing please refer to the details and order form at the rear of this guide or log on to our website at www.travelpublishing.co.uk

Travel Publishing

Locator Map

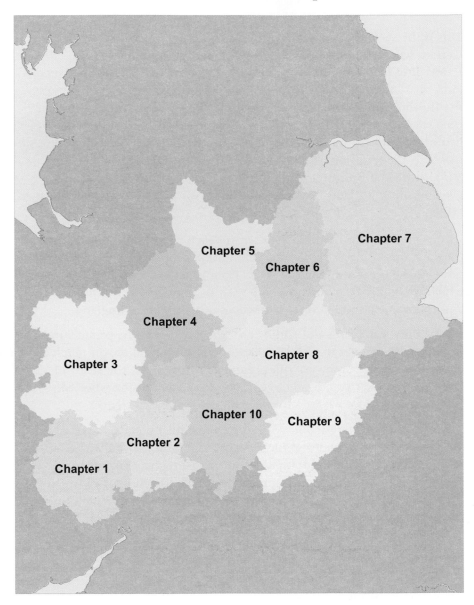

Contents

1 HEREFORDSHIRE

"Wherever one goes, there will not be a mile that is visually unrewarding." Sir Nikolaus Pevsner was clearly impressed, and today's visitors will also find delights at every turn in the rolling landscape, the pretty villages and the charming market towns. Herefordshire had few natural resources, so the industrial scars that spoil many counties are mercifully absent; the beauty remains relatively intact, so too the peace, and motorists will generally find jam-free roads. Apples and hops are the traditional crops of Herefordshire, and the cider industry is still a thriving one. The days when almost every farm produced its own cider are long gone, but many of the old mills are preserved on the farms or in museums. Large areas (over 9,500 acres) of the county are given over to cider orchards, and 63 million gallons of cider are produced here each year - well over half the UK total.

Symonds Yat

In western Herefordshire perry is something of a speciality, the drink being made on similar lines to cider but with pears instead of apples. Hops have been cultivated in the county since the 16th century and once provided late summer work for thousands of pickers, mainly from the Black Country and South Wales. The industry is considerably smaller than before, and mechanisation has greatly reduced the need for human effort. The poles and wires are a less common sight than previously, but they can still be seen, along with the occasional kiln for drying the hops - the Herefordshire equivalent of Kent's oast houses. Among the animals, sheep and cattle are a familiar sight; Hereford cattle still abound, and their stock are now to be found in many parts of the world, particularly the Americas.

Industry was never developed to any great extent, partly through the remoteness of the location and the poverty of communications, and the visible traces of the county's heritage are confined largely to castles (this is

Winter Landscape, Herefordshire

Border territory) and churches. The castles were mainly of the straightforward motte and bailey variety, the motte being a tower-topped earthen mound surrounded by a small court, the bailey a larger yard with the stables and workshops and accommodation. Skirmishes with the Welsh were a common occurrence for many centuries, and one of the county's best-known landmarks, Offa's Dyke, was built in the 8th century as a defence against the marauders.

ADVERTISERS AND PLACES OF INTEREST

LOCATOR MAP

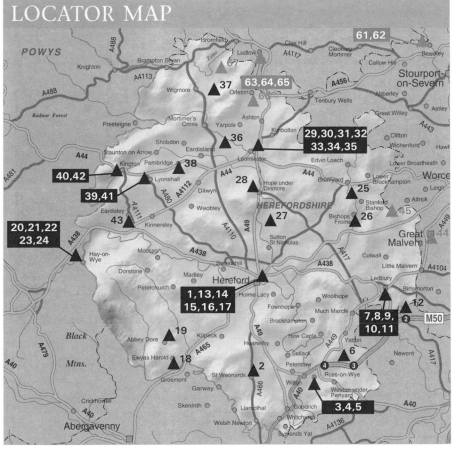

HEREFORDSHIRE COUNCIL

50-51 Broad Street, Hereford HR4 9AR
Tel: 01432 260182

FOR ACCOMMODATION VISIT: www.visitorlinks.com

HEREFORD CONTEMPORARY CRAFT FAIR

Tel: 01432 260129

As part of Hereford's initiative to be branded as the City of Living Crafts, Church Street and Capuchin Yard are being developed as a crafts quarter with street furniture, signage and layout all being revised to reflect local crafts. This enterprise reaches its high point each year with the **Hereford Contemporary Craft Fair**, which in 2003 will take place between November 21st and 23rd. From its humble beginnings in 1993 in Hereford Town Hall, it has flourished to become

Sarah Monk

one of the leading events of its kind in the West Midlands. The Fair now draws some 3000 visitors over the three days and has helped to raise the profile of design-led crafts in the county.

The Fair attracts some of the best designer makers in the UK and the comprehensive range of crafts includes glass, jewellery, furniture, textiles, metals, ceramics and leather. Visitors have the opportunity of viewing, buying or commissioning a wide choice of contemporary crafts in a variety of materials and disciplines, direct from the maker. Promoted by Herefordshire Council's Cultural Services as part of its Creative Industries programme, the Fair provides a fascinating showcase for some of the country's most exciting and innovative craftspeople.

VISIT: www.craftsguide.org.uk

HEREFORD ART WEEK

Tel: 01544 370637

The first **Hereford Art Week** took place in 2002 and this major new visual arts event was an instant success. As well as providing a wonderful opportunity to explore one of the UK's most beautiful counties through its art, the event enables visitors to meet artists in their studios, talk to them about what inspires them, see them in action, browse their work – or buy it. Almost all of the county's galleries take part by showing the work of local artists and craftsmakers – many of them arrange additional

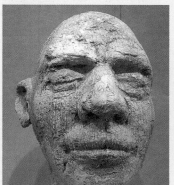

meet-the-artist events as well. At the hub of the week is the h.Art Open Exhibition in the Gwynne Warehouse Studio at Hereford's Left Bank Village. Here visitors can see the work of 21 selected artists and get a flavour of the exciting quality and range of the art being created in the county.

The open exhibition also provides up-to-date information on Art Week events, more details on individual artists and suggestions as to how to plan your art tour around the county. An informative brochure details every exhibition, venue, gallery and studio, and bright pink signs on roads and streets guide visitors to h.Art venues. In 2003, Art Week takes place from Saturday 13th to Sunday 21st September.

VISIT: www.h-art.org.uk

Richard Gilbert

Supported by financial contribution from the European Development Fund and Advantage West Midlands.

SOUTH HEREFORDSHIRE

The River Wye rises in the Plynlimon mountains east of Aberystwyth, near the spot where the Severn also has its source. The Wye enters England by Hay-on-Wye and winds its way through some of the most delightful scenery in the whole land, changing mood and direction from time to time and finally joining its original neighbour at the Severn Estuary. The whole of its length offers great touring and walking country, and the Wye Valley Walk, waymarked with the logo of the leaping salmon, follows the river closely for 112 miles, almost half of which are in

Symonds Yat

Herefordshire. The valley was designated an Area of Outstanding Natural Beauty (AONB) in 1971, and the river itself was the first to be recognised as a Site of Special Scientific Interest (SSSI). The salmon logo is, of course, wholly appropriate, as the Wye is a mecca for anglers, with salmon the king of a realm that also includes perch, pike, tench, roach and eels. In the 18th century artists, poets and the leisured classes enjoyed the Wye Tour, a highly agreeable alternative to the European Grand Tour, and two centuries later the car, train and bicycle have brought the charm of the valley within the reach of all.

SYMONDS YAT

5 miles NE of Monmouth off the A40 and B4164

Travelling upstream, a journey through the southern part of the county starts at the beauty spot of Symonds Yat, an inland resort to which visitors flock to enjoy the views, the walks, the river cruises, the wildlife (peregrine falcons nest at Coldwell Rocks), the history and

the adventure. Into the last category fall canoeing - rushing down the Wye gorge south of the village - and rock climbing. Symonds Yat (yat means pass) is divided into east and west by the Wye, with no vehicular bridge at that point. Pedestrians can make use of the punt ferry, pulled across the river by chain, but the journey by car is 4.5 miles. Walking in the area is an endless delight, and at **The Biblins** a swaying suspension bridge provides vertiginous thrills across the river. Notable landmarks include the **Seven Sisters Rocks**, a collection of oolitic limestone crags; **Merlin's Cave**; King Arthur's Cave, where the bones of mammoths and other prehistoric creatures have been found; **Coldwell Rocks** and **Yat Rock** itself, rising to five hundred feet above sea level at a point where the river performs a long and majestic loop. Also on the Symonds Yat walkabout is a massive boulder measuring 60ft by 40ft, one of the largest in the country.

Other entertainment in the area is

TREAGO CASTLE COTTAGES

St Weonards, Herefordshire HR2 8QB
Tel/Fax: 01981 580208
e-mail: fiona.mynors@cmail.co.uk

Treago Castle Cottages offer superb self-catering accommodation in the peaceful grounds of Treago Castle, deep in the unspoilt countryside of south Herefordshire. The castle itself, some 500 years old, stands in beautiful parkland and has been lived in by the Mynors family for 15 generations. Sir Richard and Lady Fiona Mynors are the present incumbents.

The castle's 5 acres of garden include an arboretum and a vineyard producing quality wines for sale. Guests have the use of a 34ft heated indoor swimming pool, incorporating a high quality de-humidification system, which is open throughout the year.

Originally built in the 1800s as stables, the attractive stone-built property has been imaginatively converted into 3 well-equipped cottages. All are provided with night storage heaters, electric blankets (double beds), garden furniture, barbecues, washing machines, tumble dryers, wood burning stoves, cots and high chairs. Bed linen and tea towels are provided; electricity by meter reading.

The Looseboxes is an extremely comfortable property that has 5 bedrooms and sleeps 10 plus 2 cots. It has a magnificent sitting/ dining room with exposed beams, wood burning stove, grand piano, colour TV and video. The large modern fitted kitchen is equipped with dishwasher, fridge-freezer and microwave. French windows lead to a private fenced garden with patio and barbecue.

The Coach House has 2 bedrooms, a sofa bed for 2, and a cot is also available. Similarly equipped to The Looseboxes, the Coach House also has French windows opening on to a garden.

Hollyhock House is a meticulously converted and very comfortable 4-bedroom wing of the stable block. It has two double bedrooms, 1 twin bedded room, a single room with an additional bed stowed under, and there's also a sofa bed in the spacious dining room. The open-beamed sitting room has a wood burning stove, colour TV and video, and there are French doors to the garden.

Looseboxes and the Coach House are accessible by wheelchair lift and these properties, with or without Hollyhock House, can be interconnected for a large group. Dogs are welcome (£20 per week) but please note that all the cottages are non-smoking. Within half a mile of the cottages there's a very good village shop.

Located only 9 miles from Exit 4 of the M50, the cottages are within easy reach of Hereford with its glorious Cathedral and Chained Library housing the medieval Mappa Mundi. A few miles to the southeast stretches the Royal Forest of Dean, one of Britain's few remaining ancient woodlands; a similar distance to the west rise the splendidly scenic Black Mountains.

provided by the **Jubilee Maze**, an amazing hedge puzzle devised by brothers Lindsay and Edward Heyes to celebrate Queen Elizabeth's 1977 Jubilee. On the same site is a museum of mazes and a puzzle shop. In the **Jubilee Park**, at Symonds Yat West, is **The Splendour of the Orient**, with Oriental water gardens, Chinese furniture, gifts from the Orient and a tea room and restaurant. Another major attraction in the Park is a garden centre with an extensive range of plants plus garden furniture and a gift shop. The church in Symonds Yat, built in the 14th century, is dedicated to St Dubricius, a local who converted the area to Christianity and who, according to legend, crowned King Arthur.

WHITCHURCH

4½ miles NE of Monmouth off the A40

Just north of Symonds Yat, in the shadow of the Rock, lies the village of Whitchurch, where at the **World of Butterflies** visitors can experience the warmth of a tropical hothouse with butterflies flitting freely about their heads. A little further up, and off, the A40, is **Kerne Bridge**, a settlement which grew around a bridge built in 1828, where coracles are still made, and from where the energetic walker can hike into history at the majestic **Goodrich Castle** in a commanding position above the Wye. Built of red sandstone in the 11th century by Godric Mapplestone, the castle is now ruined but still magnificent. It was the last bastion to fall in the Civil War, attacked by 'Roaring Meg', a siege gun cast in Whitchurch which could hurl a 200lb ball and which can now be seen in Hereford. The siege lasted four and a half months and marked the end of the castle's 'working life'. English Heritage maintains the ruins in excellent condition, and the 12th century keep and elements from the next two centuries are

well worth a visit, to walk the ramparts or just to imagine the glorious sight it once presented.

Torwood, near Whitchurch, is an interesting cottage garden by the village school, specialising in shrubs, conifers and herbaceous plants. Private visits welcome.

GOODRICH

6 miles NE of Monmouth off the A40

Goodrich village is notable for the landmark 14th century broach spire of its parish church. The vicar at a critical point in the Civil War was one Thomas Swift, grandfather of Jonathan Swift, author of *Gulliver's Travels*. This staunch Royalist hid some of the church's treasures, including a superb silver chalice, from the marauders, and, it is said, sewed 300 pieces of gold into his waistcoat to take to the King.

WELSH NEWTON

4 miles N of Monmouth on the A466

The village lies right on the A466, and just off it stands **Pembridge Castle**, now in use as a private house. In the village churchyard of St Mary the Virgin lies the body of John Kemble, a Roman Catholic who was executed in 1679 for daring to hold a mass in the castle. A plain slab commemorates this martyr, who was 80 years of age when he met his violent end.

Several more castles along the River Monmow are further reminders that this pretty part of the world was once very turbulent.

ST WEONARDS

9 miles N of Monmouth on the A466

This little hilltop village is named after an obscure Welsh saint who is portrayed in the church named after him in early-16th century stained glass. Most of the church is of that period but a 13th century doorway in the porch has survived.

About 3 miles north of St Weonards, at Wormelow, the **Violette Szabo GC Museum** (free) celebrates the bravery of the young woman who was parachuted into Nazi-occupied France to work with the Maquis. While trying to save a key agent, using single-handedly a sten gun, she was captured, imprisoned, tortured and shot in January 1945. The 1950s film *Carve Her Name With Pride*, with Virginia McKenna in the title role, tells her dramatic story. The museum, opened in June 2000, contains memorabilia of this remarkable woman and is open from April to October.

LLANROTHAL
6 miles NW of Monmouth off the A466

Standing in isolation at the end of a lane by the river is the Church of St John the Baptist, built in the 12th and 13th centuries and restored from almost total ruin in the 1920s.

SKENFRITH
7 miles NW of Monmouth on the B4521

A drive or an energetic walk takes in the remains of **Skenfrith Castle** (the round tower is an impressive sight), an ancient mill and the Church of St Bridget, dating, like the castle, from the 12th and 13th centuries. And that's just in Skenfrith!

GARWAY
9 miles NW of Monmouth on a minor road

Marvellous views from the wild and remote **Garway Hill** take in the river valley, the Forest of Dean beyond Symonds Yat to the east, and the Black Mountains. The church at Garway was built by the Knights Templar and the influences from the Holy Sepulchre in Jerusalem can clearly be seen. During the

purges of Henry VIII's reign, the Abbot of Monmouth was one of many who sought refuge in the church tower. The most unusual building in Garway is undoubtedly the famous **Dovecote**, the first of several to be mentioned in this book. Built in the 1300s (probably the work of the same good knights) it stands in a farmyard next to the church and has precisely 666 pigeon-holes.

GROSMONT
12 miles NW of Monmouth on the B4347

In the village of Grosmont lies another castle with impressive remains, and another interesting church, this one dedicated to St Nicolas of Myra.

A little way beyond Grosmont is **Kentchurch Court**, a one-time border castle rebuilt by John Nash around 1800 and featuring some splendid wood carvings by Grinling Gibbons. The Court has for many centuries been the home of the Scudamore family, one of whose number married Owen Glendower.

ROSS-ON-WYE

The lovely old market town of Ross-on-Wye is signalled from some way out by the towering spire of St Mary's Church, surrounded up on its sandstone cliffs by a cluster of attractive houses. Opposite the church is a row of Tudor almshouses which have an ancient yet ageless look and which show off the beauty of the rosy-red sandstone to great effect. The town was visited by the Black Death in 1637, and over 300 victims are buried in the churchyard. A simple stone cross commemorates these hapless souls, who were interred in the dead of night in an effort to avoid panicking the populace. Notable features in the church include 15th century stained-glass figures and a tomb chest with effigies of William

Ross-on-Wye from the River Wye

Street Museum is a time capsule of shops and a pub dating from 1885 to 1935, while the **Button Museum** in Kyrle Street is unique in being the first museum devoted entirely to the humble - and sometimes not so humble - button, of which there are more than 8,000 examples on show spanning working clothes and uniforms, leisure pursuits and high fashion. A fascinating little place and a guaranteed hit with visitors - right on the button, in fact.

Rudhall, Attorney General to Henry Vlll and founder of the almshouses, and his wife. Pride of place in the market square goes to the 17th-century **Market House**, with an open ground floor and pillars supporting the upper floor, which is a Heritage Centre. Spot the relief of Charles ll on the east wall. The **Lost**

Ross is full of interesting buildings, and besides those already noted is **Thrushes Nest**, once the home of Sir Frederick Burrows, a railway porter who rose above his station to become the last Governor of Bengal. Opposite Market House stands the half-timbered house

---

THE PHEASANT AT ROSS

52 Edde Cross Street, Ross on Wye, Herefordshire HR9 7BZ
Tel: 01989 565751
e-mail: info@pheasant-at-ross.co.uk
website: www.pheasant-at-ross.co.uk

Small though it is, with only 20 covers, **The Pheasant at Ross** has a huge reputation for outstanding food and wine and has been showered with awards since Eileen Brunnarius opened in 1988. Amongst them Egon Ronays "Country Restaurant of the Year in 1992" and The Good Food Guides "Country Restaurant of the Year 1994". Front of the house Adrian Wells' enthusiasm for intruiging wines has won him The Decanter/Robert

Mondavi "Wine By The Glass Award for the UK 1995" and both the Spanish and German "Wine List of the Year" three times each.So it's not surprising to find that The Pheasant's wine list offers a superb choice of varieties, each with an informative description.

Adrian has also pioneered the "Try Before You Buy" system so that customers can sample a glass of an unfamiliar wine to determine whether it goes with the dishes they have ordered. While Adrian makes sure that the restaurant's reputation for top quality wines is maintained, Eileen is doing the same for The Pheasant's renowned cuisine. A sample dinner menu might include a twice baked Hereford Hop Cheese Souffle among the starters; Baked Sea Bass with a Red Butter sauce as one of the main courses; and figs poached in port and lavender honey for a tasty dessert. Given the restaurant's fame, booking ahead is strongly recommended.

HALCYON DAZE

4 George Place, Gloucester Road,
Ross-on-Wye, Herefordshire HR9 5BS
Tel: 01989 768719
e-mail: jo@halcyon-daze.co.uk
website: www.halcyon-daze.co.uk

Jo Ashman, formerly a manager in the catering industry, changed her career direction when in June 1998 she opened **Halcyon Daze** in Ross-on-Wye's historic market place. Her hobby – and speciality – is artistic craft products and her shop attracts a wide cross-section of local people and tourists, in fact anyone who appreciates well-designed and well-made ornamental pieces. Jo buys work from artists all over the country and their output includes figures in glass, beautiful ceramic fish, steel dragons, medieval knights and wizards of net and steel, dipped in resin and painted. There are also Maasai figures, Lord of the Rings pewter, jewellery, porcelain, crystal and upmarket giftware, all attractively displayed in ingeniously arranged cabinets. Halcyon Daze is housed in what was originally part of an arcade and the pristine premises have allowed the products to be displayed to best advantage. Visitors exploring this historic market town should definitely find time to look at the lovely pieces on offer at Halcyon Daze.

Just 300 metres down the road, a few doors down from Woolworth's, Scentsational is also owned and run by Jo. As the name implies, Scentsational is devoted to "olfactory gratification" derived from a vast range of aromatic sources. Here you'll find scented products in every conceivable shape and size – decorative candleware, "potted" garden scents, herbal scents and many man-made perfumes such as "Chocolate Muffins". Anyone who appreciates fragrances will find Scentsational a joy to visit.

(now shops) of the town's greatest benefactor, John Kyrle. A wealthy barrister who had studied law at the Middle Temple, Kyrle settled in Ross around 1660 and dedicated the rest of his life to philanthropic works: he donated the town's main public garden, **The Prospect**; he repaired St Mary's spire; he provided a constant supply of fresh water; and he paid for food and education for the poor. Alexander Pope was as impressed as anyone by this benefactor, penning these lines some time after the great man died in 1724 at the age of 87:

Rise, honest Muse, and sing the Man of Ross,
Health to the sick and solace to the swain,
Whose causeway parts the vale in shady rows,
Whose seats the weary traveller repose,
Who taught that heav'n directed spire to rise?
'The Man of Ross', each lisping babe replies.

The **Ross International Festival** of music, opera, theatre, comedy and film takes place each August and grows in stature year by year. In and around Ross are several examples of modern public art, including leaping salmon metal sculptures (Edde Cross Street) and a mural celebrating the life of locally-born playwright Dennis Potter. At Ross-on-Wye Candlemakers in Gloucester Road are a shop and workshop showing the manufacture of all types of candles, with evening demonstrations and group visits by appointment.

AROUND ROSS-ON-WYE

WESTON-UNDER-PENYARD

2 miles E of Ross on the A40

Leave the A40 at Weston Cross to Bollitree Castle (a folly), then turn left to Rudhall and you'll come upon Kingstone

SARAH D'ARCY CERAMICS

1B Church Street, Ross-on-Wye, Herefordshire HR9 5HN
Tel: 01989 562484

Just a two-minute walk from the town centre, **Sarah D'Arcy Ceramics** offers a humorous range of ceramic sculptures, all with a wildlife or farm animal theme. Born and bred in Herefordshire, Sarah took up pottery as a hobby which then became a living – she opened her shop here some 21 years ago. On display is a highly imaginative range of animals, not just on their own but in a variety of often humorous situations. There's a Noah's Ark, for example, complete with an elephant

scanning the horizon through a pair of binoculars, a motor-cycling sheep, a hippo playing the piano, another elephant slurping a cup of tea through his trunk. Sarah's ceramic sculptures are all individually made by hand – "They may vary slightly in size" says Sarah, "but I consider this a virtue of original handcrafted work".

You won't find her pieces elsewhere – all her output is sold through this one outlet where you can see her workshop behind the counter. She has never advertised before but built up her notable reputation by word of mouth and received several skilled trade awards for her work. The shop is open from 10am to 5pm, Monday to Saturday, and there's a car parking area nearby.

WOBAGE MAKERS GALLERY

Wobage Farm Pottery, Crow Hill, Upton Bishop, Ross-on-Wye, Herefordshire HR9 7QP
Tel/Fax: 01989 780495

It was back in 1977 that the well-known potters Mick and Sheila Casson began the task of restoring some derelict barns and outbuildings at Wobage Farm. Today, the complex houses the workshops of eight craftspeople, whose striking creations are displayed in the **Wobage Makers Gallery**, a magnificent 18th century threshing barn and haybarn. The community includes five potters, two woodworkers and one jeweller, each producing distinctive hand-made contemporary crafts. In the gallery, which is staffed in turn by the makers themselves, you'll find an extensive range of

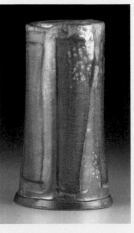

functional and decorative pots, including oven, table and kitchenware, fruit bowls, teapots, a selection of lidded jars, plates, jugs and vases.

One of the woodworkers produces eminently practical furniture, both simple and elegant; the other specialises in making carved fruit troughs, coffee tables, lidded boxes and mirror frames. Jewellery on display includes pieces in silver with traces of gold and semi-precious stones. In addition to the work of the 8 resident makers, the gallery also stocks pots by Andrew and Clare McGarva who became widely known for their blue and white decoration during their time at Wobage from 1978 to 1990. The gallery is open Thursday to Sunday, April to September, from 10am to 5pm; the same hours, weekends only, the rest of the year.

Cottages, whose delightful informal gardens contain the National Collection of old pinks and carnations. Private visits welcome.

South of Weston lies **Hope Mansell Valley**, tucked away between the River Wye and the Forest of Dean, and certainly one of the loveliest and most fertile valleys in the region. It is an area of wooded hills and spectacular views, of farms and small settlements, with the tiny village of **Hope Mansell** itself at the far end. The **Forest of Dean**, over the border in Gloucestershire, is a vast and ancient woodland full of beauty and mystery, with signs of Iron Age settlement. Later a royal hunting ground, and the home of charcoal-burners and shepherds, it became the first National Forest Park.

YATTON

5 miles NE of Ross on the A449

In a remote farmyard setting off the B4224, Yatton Chapel, disused for many years, is a simple little church with a 12th century doorway, a wooden belfry, agricultural floor and largely unplastered walls.

MUCH MARCLE

7 miles NE of Ross on the A449

This is Big Apple Country, with major cider attractions in the shape of **Westons Cider Mill** and **Lyne Down Farm**, where traditional methods of making cider and perry are still employed. The Church of St Bartholomew is notable for some superb tombs and monuments, amongst them an effigy of Much Marcle's "Sleeping Beauty". The well-preserved effigy portrays Blanche Mortimer, daughter of the 1st Earl of March, who died in 1347. As was customary at that time, the effigy depicts her as aged around 30 – the supposed age at which Christ was crucified – suggesting the possibility of marriage to Him in heaven.

The church contains another striking effigy, a rare painted wooden effigy, carved from solid oak, which is thought to be the likeness of a 14th century landowner called Walter de Helyon. Up until the 1970s he was painted a rather sombre stone colour, but was then loaned for an exhibition of Chaucer's London and was repainted in his original colours. The **Great Marcle Yew** is a talking point among all visitors to the village, its massive trunk hollowed out allowing up to eight people to enjoy cosy comfort on the bench inside.

A short distance north of Much Marcle, **Hellens** is an untouched Tudor/Stuart house set in 15 acres of grounds with coppices, lawns and fishponds.

Closer to Ledbury, on the A4172 at Little Marcle, is **Newbridge Farm Park**, where families can enjoy a day out on the farm in the company of a large assortment of friendly farm animals.

LEDBURY

10 miles NE of Ross on the A449

A classic market town filled with timber-framed black-and-white buildings, mentioned in the Domesday Book as Ledeberge and accorded its market status in the 12th century. The centre of the town is dominated by the **Barrett Browning Institute** of 1892, erected in memory of Elizabeth Barrett Browning, whose family lived at nearby Colwall. Alongside it are the almshouses of St Katherine's Hospital, founded in 1232 for wayfarers and the poor. **Church Lane**, much in demand for calendars and film location scenes, is a cobbled medieval street where some of the buildings seem almost to meet across the street. Here are the **Heritage Centre** in a timber-framed former grammar school, **Butcher's Row**

GLAZYDAYZ CERAMIC CAFÉ

Unit 2, Homend Trading Estate, Ledbury,
Herefordshire HR8 1AR Tel/Fax: 01531 636018
e-mail: ledburyceramics@supanet.com
website: www.ledburyceramics.net

What began as a hobby for Jacky Hole has now become a successful operation enabling visitors to the **Glazydayz Ceramic Café** to unleash the artistic well-spring that Jacky believes all of us have. The Glazydayz experience works like this: you choose the item you would like to decorate and are provided with paint, brushes and so on. Tuition is included in the small charge so you don't have to be a Picasso and while you are painting a cup of tea or coffee and a slice of cake are supplied to keep your creative juices flowing.

When you have finished your masterpiece, just leave it to be glazed and fired. Your work – pot, jug, mug, cup, plate, eggcup or whatever – can be collected in a few days or, if you prefer, couriered to you at home. As Jacky says "Apart from the pleasure of knowing you have completed your own ceramic piece, once it is personalised with a message or date of a special occasion it can be presented to become a treasured gift for life". And if you want to continue this satisfying hobby, the Ceramic Café stocks every kind of accessory you need. Another amenity here is an alternative studio which is an ideal place for demonstrations and hands-on experience and can also cater for parties and celebrations for all ages.

FOWLER JONES

13 South End, Ledbury, Herefordshire HR8 2EY
Tel: 01531 634641 website: www.fowlerjones.co.uk

A short walk past the Feathers Hotel and over the crossroads will take you to Fowler Jones in the Southend. The atmosphere of this stunning shop is as relaxed as its mix of decorative French antiques and cool Swedish linens. Well chosen contempory pieces - striking glassware and bespoke oak furniture - nestle amidst Parisian flea-market finds: gilded mirrors, mahogany beds, deep armchairs reupholstered in natural fabrics and armoires in many glorious stages of distress.

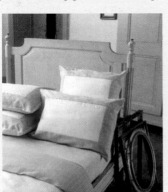

You will also find design led gifts, all as exquisite as they are unusual, as well as modern British jewellery and the cream of coffee table books. Whether you leave with a beautifully gift wrapped cashmere baby blanket or a significant new piece to lift the heart of your home, prices are pleasing. It's no surprise then that Fowler Jones' ever-changing collection, effortlessly mixing old and new, has a growing band of dedicated followers. This gem of a shop has put the quaint town of Ledbury firmly on the design map.

Ledbury Town

Museum, and, upstairs in the old council offices, the **Painted Room**, graced with a series of remarkable 16th century frescoes.

The town's symbol is the **Market House**, dating from about 1650 and attributed to John Abel, the royal carpenter, and another notable landmark is the Norman parish church of **St Michael and All Angels**, with a soaring spire set on a separate tower, some magnificent medieval brasses, fine monuments by Westmacott, Flaxman and Thornycroft, and bullet holes in the door - the scars of the Battle of Ledbury. The town's history has in general been fairly placid, but its peace was broken with a vengeance in April 1645, when Royalist troops under Prince Rupert surprised a Roundhead advance from Gloucester. In the fierce fighting that followed there were many deaths, and 400 men were taken prisoner.

Annual events at Ledbury include a

CAREY (GUNMAKERS) LTD

88 The Homend, Ledbury, Herefordshire HR8 1BX
Tel/Fax: 01531 632838

Established in the town for many years, **Carey (Gunmakers) Ltd** is a family owned business, now in its second generation. They specialise in second hand English game guns of top quality.

Recently, the Carey family have extended their business and now sell a wide range of top quality country clothing – suits, skirts, blouses, sweaters, hats, scarves, footwear and much more. Carey's also sell a range of country accessories such as walking sticks and shooting sticks. The shop is conveniently situated in the town centre with ample car parking available in their own car park. The business is closed on Wednesday afternoons.

THE ORANGERY

15 The Homend, Ledbury,
Herefordshire. HR8 1BN
Tel: 01531 631044
e-mail: office@orangery.biz
website: www.orangery.biz

The Orangery has to be one of the country's best and most versatile gift shops. It's almost worth a trip to Ledbury just to visit this marvellous shop. Located in the town centre, it has two floors stocked with a dazzling variety of items - all of them quality pieces. The shop is owned and run by business partners Sarah Coffey and Mandy Thwaites

who have established The Orangery as a place where you can be sure of finding a suitable present for just about anyone.

The shop focuses on home accessories, women's clothing, fashion accessories, handbags and jewellery, children's toys, Neals Yards and bath products. Last but not least are men's presents. We all know that this is traditionally a contentious area, but The Orangery manages to store everything from clocks and desk accessories to ties, hankies, wallets and unusual 'boy's toys'!

Liz Cox, Brics, Longchamp, Jump and Casani form the backbone of an impressive range of luggage, handbags and smaller leather items. For the summer, the collection is expanded to include bags from Bill Brown and beautifully coloured woven bags from France and Italy.

Younger children are well catered for with a selection of traditional wooden toys and activity puzzles. The children's department also includes the increasingly popular Groovy Girl range from Manhattan Toys, which sits well with the well-known Jellycat soft toys. Older children and teenagers are not overlooked with an ever-changing selection of presents, gadgets and board games.

Everything is attractively presented and, most importantly, Sarah as buyer makes sure that every item is a top quality product. The staff are friendly and always willing to help customers find that special present.

The Orangery is especially good for buying presents for engagements, weddings, christenings and birthday and also offers a wedding list service. The shop is a godsend at Christmas – many shoppers complete their entire present list without leaving The Orangery!

poetry festival in July, a street carnival in August and a hop fair in the autumn. Among the famous sons of the town is one of our most distinguished Poets Laureate, John Masefield. William Langland, who wrote *Piers Plowman,* was from nearby Colwall. The town is a great place for walking, and on the fringes nature-lovers will find plenty to delight in **Dog Hill Wood**, **Frith Wood** and **Conigree Wood**, as well as on **Wellington Heath** and along the **Old Railway Line**.

Eastnor Castle

2½ miles outside Ledbury on the A438 towards Tewkesbury stands **Eastnor Castle**, overlooking the Malvern Hills. This fairytale castle, surrounded by a deer park, arboretum and lake, has the look of a medieval fortress but was actually built between 1812 and 1824 and is a major example of the great Norman and Gothic architectural revival of the time. The first Earl Somers wanted a magnificent baronial castle, and, with the young and inspired architect Robert Smirke in charge, that's exactly what he got; the combination of inherited wealth and a judicious marriage enabled the Earl to build a family home to impress all his

---

THE MALTHOUSE RESTAURANT

Church Lane, Ledbury, Herefordshire HR8 1DW
Tel: 01531 634443 Fax: 01531 634664

After training in London with Rosette chefs and then working abroad as a chef, Adrian Hornsby and his partner Louise Palmer have returned to England to run their own eating place, **The Malthouse Restaurant**. It's tucked away off a cobblestone lane, approached by a garden path. At the front, there's a pleasant little courtyard where customers can dine in good weather. The

restaurant is on two floors, with around 20 covers on each floor, and is elegantly furnished and decorated in pastel shades with prints and pictures around the walls. Adrian's seasonally changing menu offers an eclectic blend of world cuisine – Polenta Crusted Salt Cod Fishcakes with a grilled banana, tomato and mango salsa, for example, amongst the starters.

Main courses include a daily fresh fish special and dishes such as Pan Seared Trelough Duck Breast with balsamic fig and cassis reduction. Specially selected organic ingredients include fresh fish and shellfish, and locally farmed meats and produce. The menu also includes a selection of vegetarian dishes and to accompany your meal, there's a good choice of New World wines. Such is The Malthouse's reputation, booking for dinner is strongly recommended. The restaurant is open from 7pm to 9.30pm, Tuesday to Saturday; for lunch on Friday and Saturday between noon and 2pm; and on the first Sunday of the month from 12pm to 2.30pm for lunch.

GROVE HOUSE

Bromsberrow Heath, nr Ledbury,
Herefordshire HR8 1PE
Tel: 01531 650584

Standing in 13 acres of fields and gardens near the southern end of the Malvern Hills, **Grove House** is a delightful 15th century Grade II listed building with handsome Georgian additions. Ancient beams, wood panelling and open fires are complemented by gleaming antiques and fresh flowers. The 3 elegant and spacious bedrooms (two of them with 4-poster beds) are provided with bowls of fruit, home-made biscuits on the tea trays, books and television.

Grove House is the home of Michael and Ellen Ross both of whom have a passionate interest in food and wine so guests would do well to book the optional evening meal which is based on local food and fresh produce from the house's walled garden. Guests at Grove House have the use of a hard tennis court, a neighbour's swimming pool and there are some wonderful walks in the nearby Malvern Hills. Golf and horse riding are also available within easy reach. Those who prefer self-catering can stay at cottages which are either attached or close to the house – these can also be booked on a B&B basis and are ideal for house parties. And for wedding receptions or private parties, a large converted barn is available.

contemporaries. The interior is excitingly beautiful on a massive scale: a vast 60-feet high hall leads into a series of state rooms including a library in Italian Renaissance style containing a treasure house of paintings and tapestries, and a spectacular Gothic drawing room designed by Pugin. The grounds, part of which are a Site of Special Scientific Interest, are home to a wonderful variety of flora and fauna, and throughout the year the castle is the scene of special events.

How Caple

3 miles N of Ross on the B4224

The Edwardian gardens at **How Caple Court**, set high above the Wye in park and woodland, are magnificent indeed, with formal terraces, yew hedges, statues, pools, a sunken Florentine water garden and woodland walks. How Caple's medieval **Church of St Andrew and St Mary** contains a priceless 16th century German diptych depicting, among other subjects, the martyrdom of St Clare and St Francis, and Mary Magdalene washing the feet of Christ.

BROCKHAMPTON

5 miles N of Ross off the B4224

The **Church of All Saints** is one of only two thatched churches in the country and dates from 1902, designed by William Lethaby, who had close ties with Westminster Abbey, and built by Alice Foster, a wealthy American, as a memorial to her parents. The Norfolk thatch is not the only unusual aspect here, as the church also boasts stained glass made in the Christopher Whall studios and tapestries from the William Morris workshop from Burne-Jones designs.

This is, like so much of the county, great walking country, with the **Marcle**

Ridge, the 500ft **Woolhope Dome** and the Forestry Commission's **Haugh Wood** among the attractions and challenges. The last is best approached from **Mordiford**, once a centre of the mining industry and now free from the baleful man-eating Mordiford Dragon. The story goes that the dragon was found by a local girl while it was still small. She nurtured it lovingly, and although it was at first content to feed on milk, and later chickens and the odd duck, it eventually developed a taste for cows and finally people. The beast terrorised the locals, and indeed one of the paths leading from the woods is still known as Serpents Lane. It was here that he would slink along the river to drink, and it is said that no grass ever grows there. No one was brave enough to face the beast until a man called Garson, who happened to be awaiting execution, decided that he had nothing to lose. He hid in a barrel by the river, and when the creature appeared he shot it through the heart. That was the end of the dragon, and also of poor Garson, who was killed in the fiery breath of the dragon's death throes. Mordiford stands on the River Lugg, just above the point where it joins the Wye, and the River Frome joins the Lugg a little way above the village. **Mordiford Bridge**, with its elegant span of nine arches, was once the source of regular revenue for the kings of this land: apparently every time the king crossed the bridge the local lords had to provide him with a pair of silver spurs as a levy on the manor.

WOOLHOPE

7 miles N of Ross off the B4224

A small village enjoying lovely views of the Black Mountains, Woolhope is named after Wuliva, the sister of Lady Godiva who owned the manor in the 11th century. In the 13th century sandstone **Church of St George** is a modern stained-glass window depicting the siblings. Godiva rides through the streets on her white horse (all in the best possible taste), is seen petting a cat and a dog, while her sister has a dog and some rabbits at her feet.

FOWNHOPE

7 miles NW of Ross on the B4224

A pleasant village set beside the River Wye. Every year on Oak Apple Day, in May or June, the Green Man Inn celebrates the restoration of Charles II with the Heart of Oak Club Walk. The inn's most famous landlord was Tom Spring, a champion bare-knuckle prizefighter who died in 1851. Fownhope's church, known as the "Little Cathedral", has a special treasure in the

---

THE BUTCHER'S ARMS

Woolhope, Herefordshire HR1 4RF
Tel: 01432 860281 Fax: 01432 860821
e-mail: peter@thebutchersarms.org.uk

Hidden away in the Herefordshire countryside, **The Butcher's Arms** is a wonderfully traditional country inn, with black and white half-timbered walls and colourful hanging baskets. Inside, the beamed ceilings, wooden benches and log-burning fires in the two bars all contribute to the welcoming atmosphere. Mine hosts, Peter and Sally Dunscombe, serve real ales along with a wide range of other beverages and also offer an excellent choice of wholesome, home-cooked food. Bed & breakfast accommodation is available in the 2 guest rooms, both with TV and hospitality tray.

form of a Norman tympanum depicting the Virgin and Child with a winged lion and eagle amongst foliage.

HOLME LACY

8 miles NW of Ross on the B4399

Holme Lacy was originally the estate of the de Lacy family in the 14th century, but later passed into the hands of the illustrious Scudamore family. The 1st Viscount Scudamore was the first person to classify the varieties of cider apple, and actually introduced the well-known Red Streak Pippin strain. The fine Palladian mansion dates from 1672 and once sported woodwork by Grinling Gibbons. St Cuthbert's Church, standing away from the village on a bend of the Wye, has a remarkable collection of 16th and 17th century monuments of the Scudamores, and also some fine furnishings and medieval stalls with misericords.

Near the village of Holme Lacy is **Dinedor Court**, a splendid 16th century listed farmhouse with an impressive oak-panelled dining hall. English Heritage is responsible for **Rotherwas Chapel in Dinedor**. This is a Roman Catholic chapel dating from the 14th and 16th centuries and featuring an interesting mid-Victorian side chapel and high altar.

SELLACK

3 miles NW of Ross on minor roads or off the A49

A popular waymarked walk takes in three marvellous churches in three delightful villages. The church in Sellack in uniquely dedicated to St Tysilio, son of a king of Powys, and is Norman in origin.

A short drive north of Sellack, in the churchyard at **King's Caple**, is a plague cross remembering victims of the Black Death of 1348. The church dates mainly from the 13th century and a fascinating little detail is to be found on the

benefactors' board on the west wall. The local charities listed include Cake Money, a gift in perpetuity from a former vicar of King's Caple and Sellack. Pax cakes, signifying peace, are still distributed to the congregations on Palm Sunday.

HOARWITHY

6 miles NW of Ross off the A49

By far the most extraordinary of the three walk-linked churches lies in the unspoilt village of Hoarwithy on the willow-lined banks of the Wye. **St Catherine's Church** is a splendid piece of architecture which owes its origin to the Reverend William Poole, who arrived in 1854, didn't like what he saw – the chapel was, he said, "as bare as the palm of the hand". Poole spent the next 30 years supervising the building of a new church round the chapel. The result is an Italianate building complete with a campanile, arcades, beautiful tiled floors and a white marble altar with lapis lazuli inlay. Worth a look in **Little Birch**, just to the north west, is **Higgin's Well**, named after a local farmer and restored at the time of Queen Victoria's Diamond Jubilee in 1897.

WILTON

1 mile W of Ross on the A40

Wilton, just a short walk from Ross, stands at a crossing point of the River Wye. The bridge was built in 1599, some years after a river disaster which claimed 40 lives. Over the bridge are the ruins of **Wilton Castle**, of which some walls and towers still stand. An 18th century sundial on the bridge bears this numinous inscription:

"Esteem thy precious time,
which pass so swiftly away:
Prepare them for eternity
and do not make delay."

PETERSTOW

2 miles W of Ross on A49

At **Broome Farm**, half a mile off the A49, traditional farmhouse cider has been brewed since the early 1980s, winning many prizes throughout the 90s and featuring apples with evocative names like Fox Whelp or Yarlington Mill. Also at Peterstow is **Kyrle House**, whose country garden contains herbaceous borders, a small grotto, sunken garden and secret garden. Private visits welcome.

HEREFORD

The county town-to-be was founded as a settlement near the unstable Welsh Marches after the Saxons had crossed the Severn in the 7th century. A royal demesne in the 11th century, it had a provincial mint, and was an important centre of the wool trade in the Middle Ages. Fragments of Saxon and medieval walls can still be seen, but the city's crowning glory is the magnificent **'Cathedral of the Marches'**. Largely Norman, it also has examples of Gothic, Early English,

Hereford Cathedral

Decorated, Perpendicular and Modern architecture. The Cathedral demands an extended visit, as it contains, in the impressive New Library building, two of the country's most important historical treasures. *Mappa Mundi* is the renowned medieval world map, the work of Richard of Haldingham. Drawn on vellum, it has

Continued on page 25

JOHN McKELLAR

23 Church Street, Hereford HR1 2LR
Tel: 01432 354460

Since 1984 **John McKellar** has been one of the country's leading galleries showcasing contemporary jewellery. Only two years after he established the business the shop was included in the list of shops and galleries selected for quality by the Crafts Council and has remained in it ever since. Housed in what was formerly the Mayor's Parlour, the shop stocks an extensive range of pieces

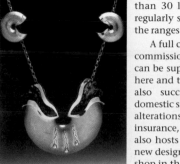

in all materials, precious and non-precious. Work by more than 30 leading designers is regularly shown in addition to the ranges created in John McKellar's own workshop on the premises.

A full custom design service is available for pieces made to special commission – customers' own stones can be mounted or gemstones can be supplied. Wedding and engagement ring sets are a speciality here and the skilled team of qualified designers and craftsmen have also successfully undertaken commissions for ecclesiastical and domestic silverware, and for regalia and presentation trophies. Repairs, alterations and re-stringing are undertaken, as are valuations and insurance, and interest free credit facilities are available. John McKellar also hosts regular exhibitions featuring jewellery from both young new designers and established craftsmen. You'll find John McKellar's shop in the pedestrianised area of the city centre.

WALK 1

King's Caple, Sellack and Hoarwithy

Start	King's Caple Church
Distance	5 miles (8 km)
Approximate time	2½ hours
Parking	Wide verges near King's Caple church
Refreshments	Pub at Hoarwithy
Ordnance Survey maps	Landranger 149 (Hereford and Leominster) and 162 (Gloucester & Forest of Dean), Pathfinder 1064, SO 42/52 (Ross on Wye - West)

There can be few short walks more pleasant than this gentle stroll through one of the loveliest stretches of the Wye Valley, which reveals English riverside scenery at its finest: an intimate patchwork of fields and orchards, rolling hills and woodland, delightful riverside meadows and quiet old villages. The route passes through three of the latter, each with highly distinctive churches, and for most of the way the spire of King's Caple church, the starting point, is in sight.

Start by King's Caple church, the first of three interesting and varied village churches that can be visited on this walk. A handsome building occupying an elevated position above the valley, it is built of the local rich red sandstone. It is a harmonious mixture of styles, ranging mainly from the 12th to the 15th centuries, and is dominated by the 14th century tower and spire, a landmark for miles around. The mound on the opposite side of the road is Caple Tump, site of an early motte-and-bailey castle.

With your back to the church, turn left along the lane through the small village, passing an orchard on the right. Keep ahead at a crossroads and about 50 yds (45m) after passing a school on the left, turn right along a tarmac drive (A) signposted to Seven Acres. After a further 50 yds (45m) bear right onto a track with granite chippings to go through a metal gate and climb a stile beside another metal gate a few yards ahead.

Bear slightly right and head across the field to a fence corner, here veering left to walk along the field edge, by a wire fence on the left, down to a stile. From here there are expansive views ahead over the Wye Valley with the spire of Sellack church prominent. Climb the stile, continue in the same direction along a narrow path, now by the right-hand edge of a field and with a wire fence and hedge on the right. Where the hedge and fence turn to the right, keep straight ahead across a cultivated field, turning left at the bottom end for a few yards to a metal gate and footpath sign. Go through the gate and turn right along a lane to where it bends to the right, here turning left through a metal gate (B). Continue along a hedge-lined path to cross a rather shaky suspension bridge over the River Wye, built in 1895 to replace an earlier ford and ferry – hence the name Sellack Boat on the map.

Walk across the meadow ahead in the direction of Sellack church, crossing a footbridge over a ditch and continuing across this expanse of meadowland to go through a metal gate beside the church **C**. This is another attractive old sandstone building with a fine 14th century spire. The village is tiny and secluded, no more than a few houses and farms.

Immediately turn right through another metal gate and head across meadows, keeping more or less in a straight line and roughly parallel with the wooded cliff of Castlemeadow Wood on the left to reach the riverbank a short distance before a stile. Climb the stile and keep along the riverbank; this is an idyllic part of the walk as the Wye flows serenely through a lush landscape of meadows, fields of green and gold, orchards, farms and villages, with rolling wooded hills beyond and church spires punctuating the skyline. Eventually you follow a path to the left by some cottages; look out for a stile on the right and climb it to a road.

Turn left for a few yards and take the first turning on the right **D**, signposted Kynaston and Hentland, following a road gently uphill for ½ mile (800m) to where it bends sharply to the left. Here turn right at a public footpath sign, along a hedge-lined track **E**, and where the track bends left in front of a pylon keep ahead along a grassy enclosed path, which may be overgrown, to a stile. Climb it and continue along the left-hand edge of a field, by a hedge and wire fence on the left. There are more superb views over the valley, with the spire of King's Caple church the dominant feature. Go over a stile into a long field, still keeping ahead with the hedge to the left. At the bottom left-hand corner of the field there is another stile. Climb it and then cross straight over the track that faces you, passing to the left of a house called Quarry Bank, and continue downhill along a delightful, if in places overgrown, tree-

enclosed path to a road. Follow the road through the village of Hoarwithy, bearing right at a junction in the direction of King's Caple.

To the left is Hoarwithy church, which you reach by climbing some steps. Its Italian design could hardly look more incongruous in this quintessentially English setting. The reason why such an unusual, highly ornate and richly decorated church came to be built here is that the local vicar, William Poole, felt that its predecessor was too plain and therefore used some of his great personal fortune to finance the construction of this lavish replacement in 1885. It took over twenty years to finish and Poole even employed Italian craftsmen to achieve the desired effect. One feature that it has in common with the churches at King's Caple and Sellack, however, is that it is built of the local sandstone.

Continue across the bridge over the Wye and on the other side turn right along a grassy, hedge- and tree-lined track **F**, which shortly meets and keeps by the river for a while, before curving left away from it to reach a lane. Follow the lane for nearly ¾ mile (1.2km) back to King's Caple church. ●

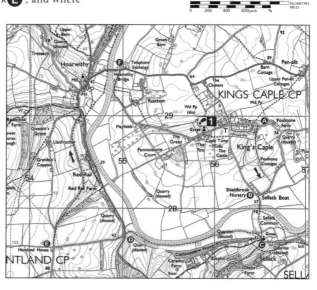

MIKE GELL

7 East Street, Hereford HR1 2LW
Tel: 01432 278226 Fax: 01432 370941
e-mail: mikeygell@hotmail.com website: www.mikegell.co.uk

To walk into Mike's shop is to enter a treasury of quality jewellery by selected makers. The pieces are displayed in glass-fronted cabinets and the variety within each range ensures there is something to suit every aesthetic taste, special occasion and pocket.

Mike's workshop is situated to the back of this friendly shop, where he is often making when not with customers. His signature range of composite rings, set with myriad coloured precious stones are complemented with delicate earrings and elegant necklaces. Unusual gems, colours and shapes feature strongly in Mike's work. You are highly likely to discover original one off pieces amongst the work of over 60 different makers and jewellers, many of whom can work to commissions.

The quality of craftsmanship is reflected in the fact that Mike has been a Freeman of the Worshipful Company of Goldsmiths since 1989, and has been invited to exhibit there and at other renowned galleries around the country. In addition Mike has been an instrumental founder member in the creation of Alloy, a group of 33 jewellers based in the city.

You'll find his shop close to the city centre, near the walkway to the cathedral in the one-way system.

Although small, it is well worth finding!

THE BAY TREE

48 Broad Street, Hereford HR4 9AR
Tel: 01432 277374

Traditional English fare prepared and served with French flair is the attractive combination on offer at **The Bay Tree**, located in the heart of the city. French chef Sebastien Poligne and his English wife Sarah worked together in prestigious hotels and restaurants before opening their own traditional tearoom style restaurant in a charming old house, which is believed to date back to the 1600s. Exposed ancient beams attest to the antiquity of the building and

traditional table linen and fresh flowers add to the charm. The Poligne's pride themselves on their home-made dishes to include soup of the day served with fresh crusty bread and home-made lunchtime main courses of lasagne, shepherd's pie and chicken and mushroom pie.

For smaller appetites there's an extensive choice of freshly filled white or brown baguettes served with salad and home-made crisps, cold or toasted sandwiches and baked potatoes. From 2pm The Bay Tree afternoon teas are served and throughout the day a selection of home-made cakes, patisseries, shortbread, toasted teacakes and scones are all available. The second floor of the building is ideal for functions and can seat up to 28 people. The Bay Tree is open between 10am to 4pm, Monday to Saturday, and 10am to 5pm during the summer months.

Jerusalem as its centre and East at the top, indicating that direction as the source of all things good and religiously significant. Richard was Treasurer of Lincoln Cathedral, which might explain why Lincoln appears rather more prominently on the map than Hereford. The **Chained Library**, the finest in the land, houses 1,500 rare books, including over 200 medieval manuscripts, all chained to their original 17th century book presses. The Cathedral has many other treasures, including the shrine of St Thomas of Hereford in stone and marble, the Norman font, the Bishop's Throne and the John Piper tapestries. There's also a brass-rubbing centre. For details of the Cathedral's opening hours and guided tours call 01432 359880.

Hereford is full of fascinating buildings and museums which visitors should try to include in their tour. **Hereford Museum and Art Gallery** has a changing art gallery programme and hands-on exhibitions. The **Old Hall Museum**, right in the centre of High Town, brings alive the 17th century in a three-storey black-and-white house filled with fascinating exhibits. **Churchill House Museum**, whose grounds include a fragrant garden, displays furniture, costumes and paintings from the 18th and 19th centuries; among its rooms are a costume exhibition gallery and Victorian nursery, parlour, kitchen and butler's pantry. The **Hatton Gallery** shows the

CIDER MUSEUM & KING OFFA DISTILLERY

21 Ryelands Street, Hereford HR4 0LW
Tel: 01432 354207
website: www.cidermuseum.co.uk

In the heart of the apple growing county of Herefordshire, the **Cider Museum** explores the history of traditional cidermaking worldwide. Visit the reconstructed farm ciderhouse, the Champagne Cider cellars, the Vat House, and the Cooper's Workshop. See the Herefordshire 'Pomonas' beautiful books dating from the 19th century which illustrate the varieties of cider apples and perry pears grown from earliest times to the present day. Sample the products made at our own King Offa Distillery Cider Brandy, Apple Aperitif and Cider Liqueur and visit our Gift Shop or enjoy refreshments at the Pomona Tea Room.

A Cider making Festival is held once a year, with various displays, stalls and competitions, including apple pressing for children, Westons Shire Horse and Dray, beekeeping display and the Master Cooper demonstrating the art of making barrels and casks. Under cover with free car and coach parking.

work of local artist Brian Hatton. **St John Medieval Museum** at Coningsby is a 13th century building in an ancient quadrangle of almshouses. Displays include costume models of Nell Gwynne, a famous daughter of Hereford, and the history of the Ancient Order of St John and its wars during the Crusades. Hereford's restored pumping station is home to the **Waterworks Museum**, where Victorian technology is alive and well in the shape of a collection of pumps (some of which can be operated by visitors), a Lancashire Boiler and Britain's largest triple expansion engine. The **Regimental Museum** houses an important collection of uniforms, colours, medals, equipment, documents and photographs - and the flag and pennant of Admiral Doenitz.

Hereford and cider are old friends, and the **Cider Museum** (see panel on page 25) tells the interesting story of cider production down the years. One of the galleries houses the King Offa distillery, the first cider brandy distillery to be granted a licence for more than 200 years. Also on the outskirts of the city are the **Cider Mills** of HP Bulmer, the world's leading cider producer. Look, learn and taste on one of the organised tours.

The original Saxon part of the city includes historic Church Street, full of 17th century listed buildings (most of them modernised in the 19th century). Church Street and Capuchin Yard - the name derives from the hood worn by the Franciscan friars who built a chapel nearby - are renowned for their small specialist shops and craft workshops.

Hereford stages important musical events throughout the year, and every third year hosts the **Three Choirs Festival**, Europe's oldest music festival. The next one will take place in the Cathedral in August 2003.

THE GOLDEN VALLEY

KILPECK

8 miles SW of Hereford off the A465

The parish **Church of St Mary and St David** is one of the most fascinating in the whole county and generally regarded as the most perfect Norman church in England. Built by Hugh de Kilpeck (son of William Fitznorman, who built Kilpeck Castle) round an earlier Saxon church, it has changed little since the 12th century. Much of the church is unique in its rich decoration, but the gem is the portal over the south doorway, with all manner of elaborate carvings. Most of the carvings throughout the church have no apparent religious significance, with some bordering on the bizarre, if not downright bawdy! Very little remains of the castle, it having been largely demolished by Cromwell's men, but on a clear day the castle mound affords very fine views.

EWYAS HAROLD

12 miles SW of Hereford on the B4347

A village at the foot of the lovely Golden Valley, in an area of fine walks. West of the village lay the ancient Welsh kingdom of Ewias; the motte and bailey castle that was part of the border

---

THE OLD RECTORY

Ewyas Harold, Herefordshire HR2 0EY
Tel/Fax: 01981 240498 e-mail: jenny.juckes@btopenworld.com
website: www.golden-valley.co.uk/rectory

The Old Rectory is a charming Georgian country house standing in its own peaceful and secluded grounds, with a lovely garden and views across to the Black Mountains. Chrix and Jenny Juckes welcome bed & breakfast guests to share the relaxed and friendly atmosphere of their home. The rooms which are spacious and elegant, with open fires and ancestral portraits – give a wonderful feel of comfortable antiquity. Awarded 4 Diamonds by the English Tourist Board, the Old Rectory offers a choice of double or twin rooms, operates a no- smoking policy, has ample parking and is open all year round.

defences has disappeared, leaving only the distinctive mound. A Cistercian **Abbey** was founded here in the 12th century and the building, which was substantially restored by John Abel in the 17th century, is still in use as a parish church.

ABBEY DORE

12 miles SW of Hereford on the B4347

Occupying a beautiful setting beside the river are the impressive remains of a 12th century Cistercian **Abbey**, part of which is still in use as the parish church. Most of the building dates from around 1180 but the battlemented tower was added in the 1660s by the Scudamore family, lords of the manor. They also commissioned the noted carpenter John Abel to create the impressive wooden chancel roof and the superb, heavily carved screen.

On the other side of the river, the garden at **Abbey Dore Court** is home to

The Golden Valley

THE TAN HOUSE

Abbey Dore, Herefordshire HR2 0AA
Tel/Fax: 01981 240204
e-mail: jppowell@ereal.net
website: www.golden-valley.co.uk/tanhouse

Located in the heart of the lovely Golden Valley and in the grounds of a traditional working farm, **The Tan House** provides a choice of bed & breakfast or self-catering accommodation in a peaceful setting. The property overlooks Dore Abbey, established in the 12th century; restored in the 1600s and now serving as the parish church. Not quite so old, The Tan House was built of stone some 200 years ago in traditional style. It offers a mixture of double and twin rooms, all fully equipped with TV and hospitality tray.

The accommodation has been awarded a 4 Diamonds rating from Automobile Association and your host, Glenys Powell, is noted for her warm welcome and excellent breakfasts. Families are welcome; smoking is not permitted in the bedrooms. Self-catering guests stay in Tan House Farm Cottage, a detached property with its own garden and lawn. Upstairs there is 1 double bedroom and 1 twin with a modern bathroom, while downstairs there is a sitting room with an open fire, separate dining room, fully equipped kitchen, utility room and WC It also has full Central Heating. Again, families are welcome and a cot can be provided if required.

many unusual shrubs and perennials along with specialist collections of euphorbias, hellebores and peonies. There's also a small nursery, a gift shop and a restaurant.

In **Bacton** itself, a mile along the same B4347, is **Pentwyn Cottage Garden**, where visitors can walk round the peaceful garden before enjoying a cream tea. From the remote, lonely roads that lead west towards Offa's Dyke and the boundary with Wales, motorists should leave their cars, stretch their legs and drink in the wonderful scenery.

The villages of **Longtown** and **Clodock** lie at the foot of the **Olchon Valley**, while further north are the **Olchon Waterfall**, **Black Hill**, the rocky ridge of the **Cat's Back** and the ruins of **Craswall Priory**, which was founded in the 13th century by the rare Grandmontine order and abandoned 200 years later.

PETERCHURCH

10 miles W of Hereford on the B4348

The chief village of the **Golden Valley**, with a very fine parish church. In 786, King Offa brought monks to the village to found the original church. It was a sign of Offa's great power and influence that a bishop from Rome was included in the missionary party established here.

DORSTONE

12 miles W of Hereford off the B4348

A very attractive village with neat sandstone cottages set around the green. St Faith's Church has a connection with Canterbury, as Richard de Brito, one of the knights who murdered Thomas à Becket, established a church here after serving 15 years' penance in the Holy Land for his crime. He returned to build the church and is buried in the churchyard.

South of Dorstone lie the ruins of **Snodhill Castle**, from which the views are spectacular even for this part of the world. To the north, on wild, exposed Merbach Hill, is the much-visited landmark of **Arthur's Stone**, a megalithic tomb of great antiquity which was used for the burial of tribal chieftains. Some say (but few believe it!) that the body of King Arthur himself was buried here.

ALONG THE WYE VALLEY

The A465 out of Hereford soon reaches Belmont Abbey, whose architect, the renowned Pugin, was responsible for part of the House of Commons. One of the stained-glass windows in the church at Clehonger is probably also his work.

SWAINSHILL

3 miles W of Hereford on the A438

The Weir (National Trust) in Swainshill is a charming riverside garden, spectacular in early spring, with 'drifts of flowering bulbs'. The garden enjoys grand views of the Wye and the Welsh Hills. At **Credenhill**, a little way north of Swainshill on the A480, the **National Snail Farming Centre** is a unique attraction showing snail farming and a display of wild British snails both static and alive.

MADLEY

6 miles W of Hereford on the B4352

There's more fine stained glass from the early 1300s in the church at Madley, which also claims to have one of the largest stone fonts in the country. A curiosity here is the **Lulham Pew** in the north aisle. Constructed mostly from a medieval screen it has high sides and curtains, thus allowing the Lulham family to pursue their devotions in privacy. They didn't even emerge to take Communion but received it through a small door in the pew.

According to legend, St Dyfrig, the man who some say crowned King Arthur, was born at Madley.

MOCCAS

10 miles W of Hereford off the B4352

Moccas Court, designed by Adam and built by Keck, stands in seven acres of Capability Brown parkland on the south bank of the Wye. In the grounds stands the beautiful Church of St Michael, built in Norman times using the local stone known as tufa limestone. Dominating the chancel is the impressive effigy of a 14th century knight with a dog lying at his feet – contemporaries would understand this signified that the knight had not died on the battlefield but in his own bed.

HAY-ON-WYE

18 miles W of Hereford on the B4348

And so to the border town of Hay-on-Wye, where bookworms will wriggle with delight as they browse through its 38 secondhand bookshops. Richard Booth, known as the King of Wye, opened the first bookshop here 40 years ago, and is a leading player in the annual **Hay Book Festival**. The famous diarist Francis Kilvert was a local man, and his Diary is just one of millions of books on sale. But books are not the only attraction: Hay also has a large number of antique shops, and the River Wye is never far away, with its shifting moods and ever-changing scenery.

BOWIE & HULBERT

5 Market Street, Hay on Wye,
Herefordshire HR3 5AF
Tel: 01497 821026 Fax: 01497 821801
e-mail: info@hayclay.co.uk
website: www.hayclay.co.uk

Located in the heart of this appealing little town, **Bowie & Hulbert** provides a fascinating showcase for the best of British contemporary crafts – ceramics, jewellery, textiles and more. The gallery specialises in functional ware and works made in Britain. These are attractively displayed throughout the premises and in the traditional

Victorian shop front window. Owner Sara Bowie is also a goldmine of information, especially on potters and other craft artists working in Wales. She opened her shop in 2000 and the following year her enterprise won her a Rural Business Award. The business is a member of the Arts Council of Wales Collectorplan Scheme which provides interest free credit on purchases. Bowie & Hulbert is open daily from 10am; Sundays from 11am.

Sara's husband Simon is a potter himself and some of his pots and ceramics are on display here. Simon and his partner Bill Parkes have their own pottery a short walk away in Brook Street where they produce fine contemporary terracotta pieces. Visitors are welcome.

FORWOOD'S

2 Castle Street, Hay on Wye,
Herefordshire HR3 5DE
Tel: 01497 820539
e-mail: enquiries@forwoodsdirect.com
website: www.forwoodsdirect.com

At **Forwood's,** located in the heart of this
delightful small town, collectors will find
what is probably the most comprehensive
range of antique prints and maps in
middle England.

Sally and Kemeys Forwood have spent
years building up this remarkable treasure
store and now offer more than 10,000 prints and maps, every one of which is a genuine antique - they
do not sell modern reproductions. In the brightly-lit, attractively arranged gallery you might come
across some wonderful Heath Robinson prints, Gillray caricatures, Eighteenth Century botanical prints
or some 17th Century county maps by John Speed.

All the prints and maps are guaranteed to have been published around the date stated and all the
prints (and many of the maps) are in bevel-edged mounts that have acid free cores and backs, ready to
take straight to a framer. The prints and maps make very welcome presents for birthdays, anniversaries,
weddings or corporate gifts – as well as distinctive additions to your own collection.

The gallery is conveniently located next to a car park but if you are unable to visit, all the prints
and maps in the gallery can be viewed on the website, each with its own image, the facility to view the
prices in dollars and secure online ordering.

HAY-ON-WYE BOOKSELLERS

14 High Town, Hay-on-Wye, Herefordshire HR3 5AE
Tel: 01497 820875 Fax: 01497 847129
e-mail: sales@hayonwyebooksellers.com
website: www.booksathay.com

Housed in a charming old black and white building in the town
centre, **Hay-on-Wye Booksellers** is a place to gladden the heart of

any serious book collector. Inside,
the warren of rooms there are
literally thousands of books on every
conceivable subject, from film to
fishing, politics to photography,
social history to science fiction.

Jane and Mike Bullock have built
up this exemplary business over
many years and now preside over
what is undeniably one of the best book shops in this town noted for
its good book shops. In addition to the large general stock of
antiquarian and second hand books, the shop also sells a wide variety
of new books at half price. The Bullocks are always looking for new
stock and pay the best prices in cash for quality antiquarian and
second hand books. They will travel anywhere to examine libraries or
small collections. Hay-on-Wye Booksellers is open every day of the
year except Christmas Day and there's convenient parking nearby.

THE GRANARY

By the Clock Tower, Hay-on-Wye,
Herefordshire   HR3 5DB
Tel: 01497 820790

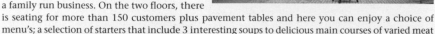

For some 20 years Jeanette Barker and Caroline Pryce-Mason have been providing wholesome and home-cooked appetising fare at **The Granary** opposite the Clock Tower in Hay on Wye. This outstanding licensed café and restaurant is housed in a former granary and is a family run business. On the two floors, there is seating for more than 150 customers plus pavement tables and here you can enjoy a choice of menu's; a selection of starters that include 3 interesting soups to delicious main courses of varied meat

dishes including game and authentic curries. The vegetarian and vegan food on offer is original and very popular. The Granary produces a wide selection of sophisticated salads such as salad paysanne, smoked fish and local goat's cheeses. There is a large selection of home made cakes and puddings all of which are baked at the Granary including patisseries such as apple strudel, meringues and baked cheesecakes.

The Granary is open 7 days a week all year round (excluding 25th and 26th December) from 10am to 5.30pm and opens through to 10pm during the Hay Festival of Literature and the Summer holidays.

WINDUP@HAY

Tredegar House, The Pavement,
Hay-on-Wye, Herefordshire
Tel: 01497 821434
mobile: 07831 609889
e-mail: jo@joltd.co.uk

Windup@Hay offers a striking collection of contemporary giftware, art works, country clothing, pottery and ceramics. Most of the ceramics are the creation of Jo Lord, the vivacious owner of **Windup@Hay** who

trained in the craft and now creates a distinctive range of attractive and collectable pieces. The shop is divided in two: one room devoted to ceramics by Jo and other craftspeople, the other crammed with a fascinating array of items to brighten up one's own décor or to give as memorable gifts. Along with these pieces, the shop also stocks a wide selection of quality cards. **Windup@Hay** is conveniently located in the town centre with car parking nearby.

NORTH OF HEREFORD

Sutton St Nicholas

4 miles NE of Hereford off the A465

Just outside the village is a group of stones known collectively as the **Wergin Stone**. In the hollow base of one of the stones, rents or tithes were laid, to be collected later by the local squire. There is a story that in 1652 the Devil picked up the stone and removed it to a spot a little distance away. It took a team of nine oxen to return the stone to its original place, though why the villagers bothered is not related. South of the village is the Iron Age hill fort of **Sutton Walls**, where King Offa once had a palace. One day in 794, Offa, the King of Mercia, promised the hand of his daughter Alfreda to Ethelbert, King of East Anglia. Ethelbert journeyed to Sutton Walls, but the trip was full of bad omens: the earth shook, there was an eclipse of the sun, and he had a vision that his mother was weeping bloody tears. In spite of all this he pressed on, but after he had reached the palace, and before the wedding ceremony, Offa had him beheaded. There is little now to see at the camp, as a lot of the land has been worked on. Many skeletons have been unearthed, some showing signs of very violent ends.

Just outside Sutton, **Overcourt Garden Nursery** is situated in the grounds of a Grade II listed 16th century house with connections to the Crusader Knights of St John. A wide range of unusual plants is for sale. Private visits welcome.

Bromyard

13 miles NE of Hereford on the A44

Bromyard is an attractive market town on the River Frome with hills and good walking all around. In the town itself the

---

THE OLD COWSHED & THE CALF-COTE

Avenbury, nr Bromyard, Herefordshire HR7 4LA
Tel: 01885 482384 Fax: 01885 482367
e-mail: combes@cowshed.uk.com
website: www.cowshed.uk.com

Deep in the heart of the serene Herefordshire countryside, **The Old Cowshed and The Calf-Cote** offer the choice of bed & breakfast or self-catering accommodation in a peaceful rural setting surrounded by fields, hills and woods. Just step out the door and there are lovely walks through unspoilt areas where sightings of badgers, buzzards, kestrels and other wildlife are not uncommon. The Old Cowshed guesthouse is part Victorian cowshed, part ancient barn, and has been imaginatively renovated and converted. It now provides accommodation of 4-Diamond standard for up to 6 guests in comfortable, centrally heated king size or twin bedded rooms, each tastefully furnished with traditional country antiques and fresh garden flowers.

Breakfast is cooked and served in the beamed and galleried Aga farmhouse kitchen and your hosts, Richard and Helen Combe, are happy to provide a delicious home-cooked dinner by arrangement. For those who prefer self-catering, The Calf-Cote is a comprehensively equipped holiday home sleeping up to 6 guests. Children are welcome with a cot, high chair, stairgate and guest bed available on request. The cottage has its own private walled garden with a spacious lawn area, patio and barbecue, and there are superb views down a quiet country lane. Wonderfully relaxing!

Teddy Bear Museum, housed in a former bakery, is a magical little world of bears, dolls and Disney-related toys. It also has a bear hospital.

Bromyard Heritage Centre tells the stories of the local hop-growing industry, the railway age and life in Bromyard through

Lower Brockhampton

the centuries. Find time to look at the 12th century St Peter's Church with its historic Walker organ. Late June and early July see Bromyard's **Great Hereford Show and Steam Rally**, an event which has built up to major proportions over the years. Later on, in early September, **Bromyard's Folk Festival** brings in the crowds.

EDVIN LOACH

3 miles N of Bromyard off the B4203

Here are the remains of one of Britain's rare Saxon churches. The church at nearby Edwyn Ralph is noted for its unusual monument and medieval effigies under the tower.

LOWER BROCKHAMPTON

2 miles E of Bromyard off the A44

The 1,900 acres of wood and farmland that comprise **Lower Brockhampton Estate** (National Trust) are the essence of Herefordshire. Springtime sees the park at its best when daffodils provide a mass of colour but there are delightful woodland and lakeside nature walks to be enjoyed throughout the year. Within the grounds stands a late-14th century

half-timbered moated manor house with a very unusual detached gatehouse and the ruins of a 12th century chapel.

STANFORD BISHOP

3 miles SE of Bromyard off the B4220

the **Church** at Stanford Bishop once possessed an old oak chair in which it is believed St Augustine sat when he presided over a synod of bishops here in 603. The chair was retrieved by an antiquarian visiting the church during a 19th century restoration, minutes before workmen were about to chop it up for firewood. The chair is now in Canterbury Cathedral.

BISHOP'S FROME

3 miles S of Bromyard on the B4214

Lying close to the Worcestershire border, in hop country, is the **Hop Pocket Craft Centre**, which has working kilns and machinery, a craft shop and a restaurant.

St Mary's Church is notable for its massive font more than 700 years old. Entry to the church is by way of a handsome lychgate, a 19th century porch and a beautiful Norman doorway. Inside,

MIKE ABBOTT

Greenwood Cottage, Bishops Frome, Herefordshire WR6 5AS
Tel: 01531 640005
e-mail: abbott@living-wood.co.uk website: www.living-wood.co.uk

Mike Abbott's interest in working with green wood was sparked off in 1976 when he came across a book on traditional woodland crafts. Green woodworkers aim to harness the inherent suppleness and strength of wood to create products that share the resilience and character of the living tree. In 1985 Mike set up Living Wood Training to teach green wood skills and four years later published his first book, *Green Woodwork*. A year later, together with a small group of enthusiasts, he founded the Association of Pole-lathe Turners which has grown from an original band of six to more than 500 members in 2002.

Mike has also exported his enthusiasm by teaching various organisations not just throughout Britain but also in the USA, Sweden, Denmark and Finland. In 1993 he was joined by his former pupil, Tamsin Allum, who is now his wife. Tamsin is a talented artist, writer and craftsperson who recently provided the illustrations for Mike's latest book, *Living Wood*. They work together making chairs, baby rattles and other products for sale in their purpose-built timber-framed workshop. Between May and September, Mike holds woodland courses of 3, 6 or 9 days which have attracted students from as far away as Scandinavia, the USA, Japan and New Zealand. During the winter months Mike also offers personal tuition for one or two people.

THE VAULD HOUSE FARM

nr Marden, Herefordshire HR1 3HA
Tel: 01568 797347 Fax: 01568 797366

The Vauld is a peaceful hamlet surrounded by unspoilt countryside but only a few miles from Hereford. **The Vauld House Farm** is set within more than an acre of beautiful grounds, with ponds, a moat and wooded gardens. It's the home of Judith Wells whose family runs the adjoining stock farm. Visitors to this rural retreat have the choice of either bed & breakfast or self-catering accommodation. The bed & breakfast tariff includes a full traditional breakfast served in the beamed, period-furnished dining room overlooking the gardens. Evening meals are available by arrangement and comprise a 4-course dinner imaginatively cooked and based on fresh local seasonal produce. Light suppers are available and small dinner parties can also be arranged.

Guests have the use of a comfortable lounge with an open log fire and colour TV. For those who prefer self-catering, there's a choice of two properties. The Cider House, a former cider-making barn, has accommodation on the ground floor and is suitable for a couple or small family. It's also ideal for the elderly or disabled. The Oast House Cottage is an appealing 2-storey converted Victorian hop kiln and retains the characteristic exposed timbers and brickwork. The three bedrooms can sleep up to 5 guests; there's a spacious lounge overlooking the farmyard, meadows and apple orchards, a well-fitted kitchen and dining room.

a battered figure of a knight in armour lies sword in hand and with a lion at his feet.

HOPE UNDER DINMORE

8 miles N of Hereford on the A49

To the south of the village stretch the green spaces of **Queen's Wood Country Park**, a popular place for walking and enjoying the panoramic views. There's also an arboretum with a wonderful variety of specimen trees.

Adjoining the park is **Dinmore Manor and Gardens**, where the Knights Hospitallers had their local headquarters. The gardens are sheltered, but as they rise some 550ft above sea level, they afford marvellous views across to the Malvern Hills. The gardens are a sheer delight, and among the many attractions are a 12th century chapel near the rock garden and pools, a cloister with a roof walk, wonderful stained glass, a yew tree believed to be 1,200 years old, medieval sundials and a grotto. Many varieties of plants, shrubs, alpines and herbs are available for sale in the Plant Centre.

A more recent addition to the county's notable gardens is **Hampton Court** (see panel below). Within the 1,000-acre estate surrounding a fortified medieval manor house are walled gardens, canals, pavilions, a maze with a secret tunnel and a waterfall in a sunken garden. There are river and woodland walks, a restaurant and shop.

LEOMINSTER

The hub of the farming community and the largest town in this part of the county, made wealthy in the Middle Ages through wool, and still prospering today. Leominster (pronounced Lemster) is well

---

HAMPTON COURT ESTATE

Hope under Dinmore, Leominster, Herefordshire HR6 0PN
Tel: 01568 797676 Fax: 01568 797472
e-mail: office@hamptoncourt.org.uk
website: www.hamptoncourt.org.uk

Country Living regarded **Hampton Court Estate** as "possibly the most ambitious private garden of our time". Since 1996 the garden has been undergoing a major transformation with new water canals, pavilions, avenues and borders complementing the old walled gardens with their original Victorian walls. Gardeners and groundsmen work alongside stonemasons, bricklayers and carpenters in a way that was once common practice but is rare today. Dazzling herbaceous borders stretch out from a 150-year-old wisteria tunnel that leads to vast lawns and ancient trees beside the late-medieval castle.

Adjoining the castle is an impressive conservatory designed in 1846 by Joseph Paxton of Crystal Palace fame. It houses the Orangery Restaurant which draws on fruit and vegetables grown organically in the ornamental kitchen garden. The restaurant was voted no.7 in the *Independent*'s "50 best places for afternoon tea". Visitors to Hampton Court can tackle a maze of 1000 yews with a Gothic tower at its centre, climb the tower for a panoramic view of the gardens or descend underground to a tunnel that leads to a waterfall in the sunken garden. Another popular attraction here is the Garden Shop which sells plants from the garden, home-made produce from the castle kitchens and local crafts and gifts.

CROFT CASTLE

Leominster, Herefordshire HR6 9PW
Tel: 01568 780246
e-mail: croft@smtp.ntrust.org.uk
website: www.nationaltrust.org.uk

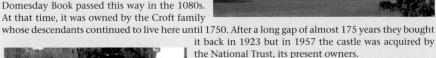

Re-opening in Spring 2003 after extensive structural work, **Croft Castle** is an appealing building of honey-coloured stone the oldest parts of which date back to the 14th or 15th century. It's believed to be the third castle on this beautiful site – certainly, there was some kind of fortress here when the compilers of the Domesday Book passed this way in the 1080s. At that time, it was owned by the Croft family whose descendants continued to live here until 1750. After a long gap of almost 175 years they bought it back in 1923 but in 1957 the castle was acquired by the National Trust, its present owners.

Inside, the impressive Georgian Gothic staircase and ceilings were added in the 1700s. Some of the rooms are lined with panelling brought from other houses and there's an interesting collection of Croft family portraits and heirlooms.

The stone church standing beside the castle has a pretty, tower crowned by a bell turret and cupola added around 1700 but the church itself is considerably older since there are records of it being "enlarged or more beautifully made" in 1515.

Castle and church are surrounded by thickly wooded parkland within which is the famous line of Spanish chestnut trees stretching for half a mile. Some of these trees are about 350 years old. Also within the 1500-acre estate is the Iron Age hill fort of Croft Ambrey – climb to the top on a clear day for a panoramic view.

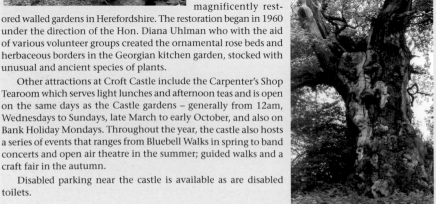

Croft also boasts one of the most magnificently rest-ored walled gardens in Herefordshire. The restoration began in 1960 under the direction of the Hon. Diana Uhlman who with the aid of various volunteer groups created the ornamental rose beds and herbaceous borders in the Georgian kitchen garden, stocked with unusual and ancient species of plants.

Other attractions at Croft Castle include the Carpenter's Shop Tearoom which serves light lunches and afternoon teas and is open on the same days as the Castle gardens – generally from 12am, Wednesdays to Sundays, late March to early October, and also on Bank Holiday Mondays. Throughout the year, the castle also hosts a series of events that ranges from Bluebell Walks in spring to band concerts and open air theatre in the summer; guided walks and a craft fair in the autumn.

Disabled parking near the castle is available as are disabled toilets.

known as one of the most important antiques centres in the region. Some have linked the unusual name with Richard the Lionheart, but there was in fact an earlier king who earned the title. In the 7th century, Merewald, King of Mercia, was renowned for his bravery and ferocity and earned the nickname of 'the Lion'. He is said to have had a dream concerning a message from a Christian missionary, while at the same time a religious hermit had a vision of a lion coming to him and eating from his hand. They later met up at what was to be Leominster almost by accident, and when the King heard of the hermit's strangely coincidental dream, he was persuaded to convert to Christianity. Later, the King requested that a convent and church be built in the town; a stone lintel on the west door of the church depicts the chance meeting of King and hermit. Other, more likely explanations of the name revolve around Welsh and medieval Latin words for 'stream' and 'marsh'.

The magnificent ruins of the Priory **Church of St Peter and St Paul**, originally King Merewald's convent, became a monastery in the 11th century, and the three naves, built in the 12th, 13th and 14th centuries, attest to its importance. A curio here, standing in the north aisle, is the last ducking stool to be used in England. It's recorded that the miscreant was one Jennie Pipes, the year was 1809, but it's not known which of the two crimes that were punished in

View

20 Drapers Lane, Leominster, Herefordshire HR6 ND
Tel: 01568 610810

Appropriately located in Drapers Lane, a pedestrian precinct in the centre of Leominster, **View** offers a copious choice of quality ladies fashions along with a wide range of jewellery and accessories. The shop is owned and run by Rebecca Rumsey, a young and enthusiastic lady with a background in designer clothing.

Amongst the covetable brands stocked here are French Connection, Nougat, East, Great Plains, Inwear and other sought-after labels. The garments are attractively displayed and Rebecca is at hand to give advice if required. In addition to the Leominster shop, View also has outlets in Church Street, Hereford and High Street, Ludlow.

TWENTY TWO

22 Broad Street, Leominster, Herefordshire HR6 8BS
Tel: 01568 620426

Ardent collectors of antiques will find **Twenty Two** irresistible. No. 22 is a charming period house in the town centre and its five rooms offer a wonderful selection of country and painted furniture, mirrors, lighting and textiles. It's great fun exploring the house

with its many nooks and crannies, and there's always the chance of discovering an unusual collectable or an item that would add distinction to one's own décor. Sourced from both the UK and Europe, the regularly changing stock includes a wide range of silks and natural fabric textiles.

The owner, Daphne Sturling, has a lifetime's experience in the business so she is very knowledgeable about the items on sale and is always on hand to offer friendly and honest advice. Whether you are looking for a quality gift or something for your own home, you'll almost find something to suit here. And the very reasonable prices ensure that you'll also get real value for money. There's parking on the street itself or in the nearby spacious car park.

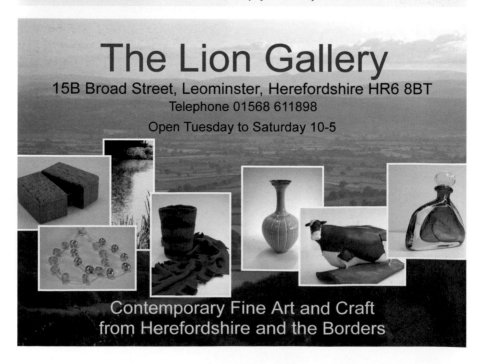

The Lion Gallery

15B Broad Street, Leominster, Herefordshire HR6 8BT
Telephone 01568 611898

Open Tuesday to Saturday 10-5

Contemporary Fine Art and Craft
from Herefordshire and the Borders

ORCHARD, HIVE AND VINE

4 High Street, Leominster, Herefordshire HR6 8LZ
Tel: 01568 611232
website: www.orchard-hive-and-vine.co.uk

Located in a shop which dates back to 1450 on Leominster's historic High Street, **Orchard, Hive and Vine** is a gourmet's paradise. Joint winners of a special award for outstanding excellence in the Flavours of Herefordshire, Geoff and Sue Morris describe their shop as "an off-licence that specialises in locally produced drinks". There is a huge choice of locally produced cider,perry, bottled beers and wines. They sell all that is best from the Marches and beyond. So look out for an eclectic range of wines and Belgian beers. Mail order is available both by telephone and over the web.

THE ROYAL OAK

South Street, Leominster, Herefordshire HR6 8JA
Tel: 01568 612610   e-mail: reservations@theroyaloak.net
Fax: 01568 612710   website: www.theroyaloakhotel.net

Built in the early1700s as an elegant coaching inn, **The Royal Oak** maintains its dignified Georgian façade while providing 21st century comfort. The oak-panelled bar is a great place for a pint of real ale or a hearty bar meal – look out for the deep brick-lined well in which the water level never varies. The hotel's unique pine-floored restaurant, decorated in blues and golds, serves the best of traditional English food with a modern twist. The 18 bedrooms (including one with a 4-poster bed) are all en suite with TV, direct dial telephone, trouser press, and hospitality trays.

THE OLD MERCHANT'S HOUSE

10 Corn Square, Leominster, Herefordshire HR6 8LR
Tel: 01568 616141

Corn Square is a picturesque part of Leominster and **The Old Merchant's House** is the most picturesque building in the square. The black and white half-timbered house is believed to be more than 400 years old and its interior presents a charming picture with

its ancient low beams, antique furnishings and wooden floors. The ground floor is now devoted to a quality tea room where friendly waitresses in period costume serve a wide choice of wholesome and appetising food. Available throughout the day are main courses such as Steak & Kidney Pie, Broccoli & Stilton Quiche or Vegetable Chilli & Rice, salads, baked potatoes and freshly prepared sandwiches, as well as some really enticing desserts.

Outside the lunchtime period (noon until 2pm) snacks like Cheese on Toast, cream teas and other teatime treats are also served. The tea room is licensed and offers a selection of wines, local and continental beers and ciders. Elaine Griffin and her husband, who run this outstanding tearoom, also manage the upstairs antiques centre with its fascinating range of quality antiques of every kind. The warren of rooms is filled with everything from furniture to jewellery and textiles – whatever you're looking for there's a very good chance you'll find it here.

this way she had committed – being a "scold" or selling adulterated goods.

A short walk away, in Priory Park, is **Grange Court**, a fine timbered building which for many years stood in the market place. Built in 1633, it is the work of John Abel, and shows typical Abel flamboyance in its elaborate carvings.

Other buildings to be visited in Leominster are the **Leominster Folk Museum**, the Lion Gallery, featuring the best of local arts and crafts, and **The Forbury**, a 13th century chapel dedicated to Thomas à Becket.

AROUND LEOMINSTER

Kimbolton

3 miles NE of Leominster off the A49

There are two delightful gardens to visit near Kimbolton. At **Stockton Bury** (turn right off the A49 on to the A4112) the sheltered four-acre garden has an extensive variety of plants set among medieval buildings, a kitchen garden, pigeon house, tithe barn, cider press and ruined chapel. At **Grantsfield** (turn right off the A49) are the gardens of an old farmhouse with a wide range of unusual plants and shrubs, old roses, climbers, orchard, kitchen garden - and superb views. Private visits welcome.

Ashton

4 miles N of Leominster on the A49

Four miles north of Leominster on the road to Ludlow stands the National Trust's **Berrington Hall**, an elegant 18th century mansion designed by Henry Holland (later architect to the Prince Regent) in parkland laid out by his father-in-law Capability Brown. Features of the interior include a spectacular

The Buzzards

Kingsland, Leominster, Herefordshire HR6 9QE
Tel: 01568 708941
e-mail: holiday@thebuzzards.co.uk
website: www.thebuzzards.co.uk

Enjoying a beautiful location surrounded by the glorious north Herefordshire countryside, **The Buzzards** offers a choice of both self-catering or bed & breakfast accommodation. The 300-year-old farmhouse has been renovated and furnished to the highest standards to provide cosy and comfortable accommodation. It is set amidst 16 acres of woodland, pastures and ponds which are home to an abundance of wildlife. Bed & breakfast guests stay either in self-contained cottages or in the farmhouse itself. There are plenty of good pubs and restaurants within easy reach but evening meals at the farmhouse are sometimes available by prior arrangement. For those who prefer self-catering, the self-contained cottages are ideal, all of them spacious, comfortable and attractively furnished with

antique and modern furniture. Each is comprehensively equipped – including television with video and an abundance of tourist literature.

Bullfinch Cottage sleeps 4 people in two bedrooms and the ground floor is accessible to wheelchair users. Redstart Cottage has one large bedroom with a double and single bed and, like Bullfinch Cottage, has a garden and patio with garden furniture. Cuckoo's Nest has been designed to provide convenient accommodation for two visitors who may have limited mobility. A charming and spacious conservatory provides an additional dining/sitting area.

staircase hall, gilt tracery, fine furniture and paintings, a nursery, Victorian laundry and tiled Georgian dairy. Most notable of all are perhaps the beautifully decorated ceilings: in the drawing room, the central medallion of Jupiter, Cupid and Venus is a composite scene taken from *The Council* and *The Banquet of the Gods* by Penni and del Colle in the Villa Farnesina in Rome. In the grounds are a walled garden with a collection of old-fashioned local apple trees, a woodland walk and a living willow tunnel in the children's play area.

Wigmore Castle

YARPOLE

4 miles N of Leominster off the B4361

In this delightful village with its jumble of cottages and their colourful gardens stands the Church of St Leonard, which has a detached bell tower, a wooden structure with a stone outer wall. At neighbouring **Eye** are **Eye Manor** and the **Church of St Peter and St Paul**, where Thomas Harley, a Lord Mayor of London, is buried. An unusual feature of this church is the pulpit with carvings of Red Indians.

Near Yarpole, reached from the B4362 between Bircher and Mortimer's Cross, stands **Croft Castle**, an atmospheric property in the care of the National Trust. Behind a defensive exterior that tells of the troubled times of Marcher territory, the state rooms are elegant and comfortable, with rare furniture, fine plasterwork and portraits of the Croft family, who have occupied the place with only one break since it was built in the 14th century. In the park are ancient oaks and an avenue of 350-year-old Spanish chestnut trees. Also looked after by the National Trust, and just a short

walk away, is **Croft Ambrey**, an Iron Age fort which affords stunning views.

ORLETON

6 miles N of Leominster off the B4361

The churchyard at Orleton is thought by some to be the likely setting for the Resurrection at the Day of Judgemnt, and for that reason people from all over the country used to ask to be buried here in the hope that they would be among the first in the queue when life began again. The road north from Orleton leads to **Richard's Castle** on the Shropshire border. This Norman castle, which lies in ruins on the hillside above the church, was, like so many others, built as a defence against the marauding Welsh. The church played a similar role, and in the 14th century it was refurbished for use as a chapel by the Knights Hospitallers.

MORTIMER'S CROSS

7 miles NW of Leominster on the A4110/B4362

The site of one of England's greatest and bloodiest battles. Here, on 3 February 1461, was enacted a decisive episode in the War of the Roses, with the Yorkists defeating the Lancastrians. Hundreds died that day, but 19-year-old Edward Mortimer, the Duke of York's eldest son, survived and was crowned King Edward IV in the following month. Visit the Battle Centre at Watermill.

WIGMORE

11 miles NW of Leominster on the A4110

A few miles on from Mortimer's Cross, Wigmore is noted for its ruined **Castle** and abbey. With its impressive vantage point, the hillside at Wigmore was a natural site for building a castle, which is what William FitzOsbern did in the 11th century. This was one of a chain of fortifications built along the Welsh border. By the time of his death in 1071, FitzOsbern had also built Chepstow, Berkeley, Monmouth, Guenta (perhaps Winchester?) and Clifford, and had rebuilt Ewyas Harold. Wigmore passed into the hands of the Clifford family, then the ambitious Mortimers, and it was

no doubt here that the future Edward IV prepared himself for the battle at Mortimer's Cross. Enough of the ruins remain to show that Wigmore was once a very serious castle, and one which protected the village and its environs for many centuries until the Civil War.

BRAMPTON BRYAN

16 miles NW of Leominster on the A4113

Many of the thatched cottages in the village as well as its castle, had to be rebuilt after a siege during the Civil War in 1643. The chief relic of the castle is the gatehouse, which now stands in the gardens of a charming 18th century house near the Church of St Barnabus. Sir Robert Harley, a relation of Thomas Harley of Berrington Hall, owned the castle and it was due to his allegiance to Cromwell that it was besieged not once but twice by the Royalist army. Following the eventual destruction of the castle by

CREATIVE BREAKS

Tel: 07813 871019
e-mail: enquiries@creativebreaks.co.uk
website: www.creativebreaks.co.uk

Creative Breaks brings you the best of Herefordshire's art and craft holidays. Whether you want a 'taster' day, a weekend course or are looking for a longer break to practise an art or craft, they can help you find what you're looking for. You could try your hand at chair-making in a tranquil woodland workshop, sketch the view from a cosy studio that looks out over breathtaking countryside, learn about natural plant dyes in a magical garden on the banks of the River Wye. There are so many wonderful courses to choose from!

They run courses for children and for adults, for beginners and 'old hands' - and if you're looking for an original present their Gift Vouchers are an excellent idea.

To find out more, visit the website for full course listings, prices etc, or phone for a brochure.

the Royalists, Harley fell out with Cromwell. They remained at loggerheads until the day that Cromwell died, and on that day in September 1658 it is said that a violent storm swept through Brampton Bryan Park, destroying a great number of trees. Harley was convinced that the storm was caused by the Devil dragging Cromwell down to Hell.

SHOBDON

8 miles W of Leominster on the B4362

The **Church of St John the Evangelist**, which stands on the site of a 12th century priory, is the most jaw-dropping in the county. In the 1750s, Lord Bateman demolished the medieval priory, (relocating selected fragments as a hilltop folly a quarter of a mile away), and built a new church which has been described as "a pastiche of the Countess's boudoir in Mozart's opera *The Marriage of Figaro*". The overall effect is of being inside a giant wedding cake, with white and pale blue icing everywhere, and lovely stained glass adding to the dazzling scene. Such is its flamboyance, the *Shell Guide* declared that this church was *"an inconceivable place to hold a funeral"*. It has to be seen to be believed.

Just north of the village are the **'Shobdon Arches'**, a collection of Norman sculptures which have sadly been greatly damaged by centuries of exposure to the elements, but which still demonstrate the high skills of the sculptors of the 12th century.

Country roads signposted from the B4362 lead west from Shobdon to **Lingen**, where the **Nursery and Garden** are a horticultural haven for visitors to this remote area of the Marches. The gardens are home to National Collections of Iris Sibirica and Herbaceous Campanula.

Even nearer the Welsh border, between **Kinsham** and **Stapleton** (signs from the B4362 at Combe) is **Bryan's Ground**, a three-acre Edwardian garden with topiary, parterres, formal herb garden, shrubbery and apple orchard, plus a specialist collection of old roses.

EARDISLAND

8 miles W of Leominster on the B4529

"An uncommonly pretty village", said Pevsner of this renowned spot on the banks of the River Arrow. Certainly glorious Eardisland is one of the most beautiful villages in the county (and the competition is very strong), and with its inns, bowling green, river and charming buildings spanning the centuries, this is essential England. Dominating the scene is the 12th century **Church of St Mary the Virgin**, where each year, from Easter until late autumn, an exhibition of village and parish life is staged. A mile outside the village is **Burton Court**, whose centrepiece is the sumptuous 14th century

River Arrow, Eardisland

Great Hall. Many additions have been made to the building down the years, and the present entrance, dating from 1912, is the work of Sir Clough Williams-Ellis of Portmeirion fame. Highlight of the various attractions is a collection of European and Oriental costumes, but of interest, too, are a model ship collection, a wide range of natural history specimens and a working model fairground.

PEMBRIDGE

10 miles W of Leominster on the A44

The influential Mortimer family were responsible for the medieval prosperity of historic Pembridge, and many handsome buildings bear witness to their patronage and its legacy. The most famous building is the 14th century church, a three-storey structure in stone and timber with a marvellous timber **Belfry**. The bell and the clock mechanism can be viewed from inside the church. Two other buildings which the visitor should not miss are the delightful 16th century **Market Hall** standing on its eight oak pillars and the **Old Chapel Gallery** in a converted Victorian chapel. A little way south of Pembridge is **Dunkerton's Cider Mill**, where cider and perry are produced from organically grown local fruit.

STAUNTON ON ARROW

10 miles W of Leominster on minor roads

A mile north of Pembridge, across the River Arrow, Staunton is a most attractive village that enjoys particularly delightful views.

Tucked away in the village is a real gem – **Horseway Herbs** (free) where the ancient art of cultivating herbs is carried on in grounds absolutely full of herbs and flowers. Visitors can buy all sorts of fresh-cut herbs, herb plants and herbal preparations while enjoying the magical

OLD CHAPEL GALLERY

East Street, Pembridge, Herefordshire HR6 9HB
Tel: 01544 388842
e-mail: yasminstrube@yahoo.com
website: oldchapelgallery.co.uk

Established in 1989 by Yasmin Strube, the **Old Chapel Gallery** in the village of Pembridge has become a popular stop along the black and white tourist trail in the heart of north Herefordshire. As the name suggests, the gallery occupies a fine Victorian chapel which provides plenty of space to showcase the intriguing items on sale. Whether you are a casual browser or a serious collector, you'll find an enticing range of contemporary art and crafts that includes work by both established local and nationally known artists along with innovative works by talented newcomers.

The ever-changing kaleidoscope of crafts ranges from ironwork to wood-turning, quality hand-blown glass to sculpture, ceramics to jewellery and textiles. Yasmin began in the craft world as a knitter and is especially keen on finding and including top knitters in her exhibitions. These are held seasonally four times a year in the upstairs gallery and usually offer a mixed media display. Also on regular display is an eclectic selection of original framed watercolours, gouaches, oils, pastels, etchings and aquatints in the £75 to £500 price range. There's also an interesting collection of unframed prints in browsers and a huge selection of cards. The Gallery is open every day, all year round, from 10am-5.30pm (Monday to Saturday); 11am-5.30pm on Sunday.

surroundings. Bedding plants and hanging baskets are also on sale.

LYONSHALL

14 miles W of Leominster on the A480

Church and castle remains are at some distance from the main body of the village, a fact which is often attributed to the plague causing older settlements to be abandoned. The Church of St Michael and All Angels dates mainly from the 13th century and was restored in 1870 when close to collapse. The ruins of the castle include some walls and part of the moat, making this the most "complete" of all the castle ruins in the area. Among the fine old buildings in the village itself are the Royal George Inn, Ivy House, The Wharf and The Woodlands. There are two 12th century water corn mills in the parish, one of them, **Bullock's Mill**, being documented continuously from 1580 to 1928.

KINGTON

4 miles W of Leominster on the A44

The road up to Kington passes many places of interest, and for two in particular a short pause will be well worth while. The National Trust's **Cwmmau Farmhouse**, which lies 4 miles south of Kington between the A4111 and A438 at **Brilley**, is an imposing timber-framed and stone-tiled farmhouse dating from the early 17th century. Viewing is by guided tour only. Call 01497 831251.

Half a mile off the A44 on the Welsh side of Kington are **Hergest Croft Gardens** (see panel on page 47), four distinct gardens that include rhododendrons up to 30ft tall, spectacular azaleas, an old-fashioned kitchen garden and a marvellous collection of trees and shrubs.

Nearby is the impressive **Hergest Ridge**, rising to around 1,400ft, and, on

THE ROYAL GEORGE INN

Lyonshall, Kington, Herefordshire HR5 3JN
Tel: 01544 340210
e-mail: thrsdrw@aol.com

Back in 1840 the village of Lyonshall boasted no fewer than seven pubs; today only the charming black and white **Royal George Inn** survives. Its origins go back to 1600 when it was a one-storey building named The George Inn – the name was changed in 1782 following the sinking of the flagship the *Royal George* at Spithead with the loss of 900 lives. In the 1930s a cider mill was still operating in what is now the kitchen, the apples gathered from 4 acres of orchards behind the pub. Traditionally furnished and decorated, the Royal George is run by Richard and Teresa Drew, a friendly and welcoming

couple with many years experience in the hospitality business.

A major attraction here is the excellent food on offer. The various menus offer the choice of a full menu in the delightful Country Restaurant; light and tasty morsels or substantial snacks in the lounge bars and garden. Traditional and imaginative dishes are available every lunchtime and evening (with fish & chips a speciality on Fridays), along with real ales, fine wines and a well-stocked cellar. The Royal George also offers comfortable accommodation with full central heating, colour TV – and a breakfast to satisfy the heartiest of appetites!

CHURCH HOUSE

Church Road, Kington, Herefordshire HR5 3AG
Tel: 01544 230534   e-mail: darwin@kc3.co.uk
website: www.churchhousekington.co.uk

Standing in extensive gardens with lovely countryside views,
Church House is an elegant Georgian house with spacious
rooms and a relaxed, welcoming atmosphere. Andrew and
Liz Darwin stress that this is a home, not a guest house so
"you won't find a telly in your bedroom, nor a trouser press,
nylon sheets, bossy notices etc!" What you will find is service
beyond the call of duty – if you've been walking along nearby Offa's Dyke Path you can get your
clothes washed, for example – and an excellent breakfast with the finest local ingredients.

its southern edge, **Hergest Court**, once
owned by the Vaughan family. Two
members of the family who gained
particular notoriety were Thomas
"Black" Vaughan and his wife, who was
known as "Gethen the Terrible". She is
said to have taken revenge on a man
who killed her brother by taking part in
an archery competition disguised as a
man. When her turn came to compete,
she shot him dead at point blank range
and escaped in the ensuing melee.
Thomas died at the Battle of Banbury in
1469, but, being a true Vaughan, that
was not the last of him. He is said to
have haunted the church in the guise of
a bull, and even managed to turn himself
into a horsefly to annoy the local horses.
He was back in taurine form when he
was finally overcome by a band of clerics.
One of the band managed to shrink him

and cram him into a snuff box, which
was quickly consigned to the waters of
Hergest Pool. Later owners of the estate
found and unwittingly opened the box,
letting Black Vaughan loose once more.
The next band of intrepid clerics
confined the spirit under an oak tree, but
he is currently at large again - though
not sighted for many years. These feisty
Vaughans are buried in the Vaughan
Chapel in Kington parish church.

Kington itself lies on the England/
Wales border and, like other towns in the
area known as the Marches, had for
many years to look closely to the west,
whence the wild Welsh would attack.
Kington's castle was destroyed many
centuries ago, but outside the town, on
Wapley Hill, are earthworks of an
ancient hill fort which could be the site
of King Caractacus' last stand.

PENRHOS FARM

Lyonshall, Kington, Herefordshire HR5 3LH
Tel: 01544 231 467 e-mail: penrhosrichard@totalise.co.uk

Located 1 mile from the market town of Kington, **Penrhos Farm**
with ETB 4 diamonds rating offers traditional farmhouse bed &
breakfast with all the comforts of a modern establishment. The
farmhouse of weathered grey stone, built in 1776 is furnished
attractively with antiques and taste, and has its own lounge,
dining room and garden for guests to enjoy. There are two guest
bedrooms, one double and one twin, both en suite, with
hospitality trays and TVs. Guests can start their day with a hearty
breakfast and are in a perfect place to explore the beautiful unspoilt Herefordshire countryside or
cross the border into Wales. Evening meals by prior arrangement.

HERGEST CROFT GARDENS

Kington, Herefordshire HR5 3EG
Tel: 01544 230160 Fax: 01544 232031
e-mail: banks@hergest.kc3ltd.co.uk
website: www.hergest.co.uk

Four gardens for all seasons from spring bulbs to autumn colour include an old-fashioned kitchen garden growing unusual vegetables, with spring and summer borders and roses. Brilliantly coloured rhododendrons and azaleas up to 30ft grow in Park Wood with over 60 champion trees in one of the finest collections in the British Isles.

Most notable by far of all the defences in the region is **Offa's Dyke**, the imposing ditch that extends for almost 180 miles along the border, from the Severn Estuary at Sedbury Cliffs near Chepstow, across the Black Mountain ridge, through the Wye Valley and north to Prestatyn on the North Wales coast. Offa was a Mercian king of great influence, with strong diplomatic links with the Popes and Charlemagne, who ruled the land south of the Humber from 757 to 796. Remnants of wooden stakes unearthed down the years suggest that the Dyke had a definite defensive role, rather than acting merely as a psychological barrier. It was a truly massive construction, in places almost 60ft wide, and although nowadays it disappears in places, much of it can still be walked, particularly in the Wye Valley. A stretch north of Kington is especially well preserved and provides excellent, invigorating walking for the energetic.

The walk crosses, at **Bradnor Hill**, the highest golf course, over 1200ft above sea level. Other major traces of the Dyke remain, notably between Chepstow and Monmouth and by Oswestry, and at many points Offa's Dyke Path, opened by the Countryside Commission in 1971, diverts from the actual Dyke into magnificent scenery.

DILWYN

7 miles SW of Leominster on the A4112

The village lies in a hollow, so its Old English name of 'Secret Place' is an appropriate one. The main body of the parish church was built around 1200, with additions in the following century and a spire put up in the 1700s. The workmen who built the church were also associated with nearby **Wormsley Priory**, and one of the figures in Dilwyn's church is thought to be a member of the Talbot family, founders of the priory. The church registers go back over 400 years, providing a valuable trail of local history.

WEOBLEY

9 miles SW of Leominster on the B4230

The steeple of the parish church of St Peter and St Paul is the second highest in the county, a reminder that this prettiest of places (call it Webbly) was once a thriving market town. One of its more unusual sources of wealth was a successful glove-making industry which flourished in the early 19th century when the Napoleonic Wars cut off the traditional French source of gloves. At certain times in its history Weobley returned two Members of Parliament, but there have been none since 1832. One of the effigies in the church is of Colonel John Birch, who was rewarded for his successes with Cromwell's army with the Governorship of Hereford and who later became a keen Royalist and Weobley's MP. Little but the earthworks remain of

Weobley Castle, which was built before the Norman Conquest and was captured by King Stephen in 1138. One of Weobley's many interesting buildings is called **The Throne**, but it was called The Unicorn when King Charles I took refuge after the Battle of Naseby in 1645.

KINNERSLEY

5 miles SW of Weobley on the A4112

On the main road lie the village and **Kinnersley Castle**, which has the look of a fortified manor house. Famous occupants down the years include the Morgans (the 17th century buccaneer Sir Henry Morgan was one of them) and the Vaughans. Black Vaughan's huge dog is believed to have been the inspiration for Conan Doyle's *Hound of the Baskervilles*.

EARDISLEY

8 miles W of Weobley on the A4111

The greatest treasure of Eardisley's **Church of St Mary Magdalene** is its font, dating from the early 12th century. The figures depicted round the font represent not only familiar religious themes but also two men in armed struggle. It is thought that these are a 12th century lord of the manor, Ralph de Baskerville, and his father-in-law, Lord Drogo, whom he killed in a dispute over land. As a penance, Ralph was ordered by the church authorities to commission this extraordinary font.

Outside this pretty village, the most notable feature, standing majestically by an old chapel, is the **Great Oak**, which is believed to be some 800 years old.

BOLLINGHAM HOUSE

Eardisley, Herefordshire HR5 3LE
Tel: 01544 327326 e-mail: bollhouse@bigfoot.com
Fax: 01544 327880   website: www.bollinghamhouse.com

Commanding one of the finest views in the county, looking across the Wye Valley to the Black Mountains and the Malvern Hills, **Bollingham House** is a Georgian gentleman's residence which has recently been refurbished to a very high standard and now offers elegant bed and breakfast accommodation. The house stands in an impressive 4-acre garden with terraced lawns, ponds, tree-lined walks and a walled garden with a perfumed rose walk, ornamental French parterres and a charming old orchard. Within the grounds there's a Victorian chapel and a 14th century black and white barn which has been restored and decorated and is now available for dinners and other social events.

The house itself has an authentic country house atmosphere with fine family paintings on the

walls and handsome furniture. Stephanie Grant has cleverly combined elegance with strong vibrant colours for the gracious rooms. The 4 comfortable bedrooms (1 spacious double with French country bed; 1 large twin; 1 double with Victorian bedstead; 1 single) enjoy lovely views across the formal gardens and terraced lawns to tranquil fields. A stylish breakfast is included in the tariff and evening meals are available by arrangement. Children are welcome; pets, too, by arrangement. Bollingham House is open all year except for Christmas and New Year.

2 WORCESTERSHIRE

In the southern part of the county lies the spectacular ridge of the Malvern Hills in the west, with marvellous walking and breathtaking views. Moving eastwards we reach the towns of Upton-upon-Severn, Pershore and Evesham, along with many charming villages and ancient sites. The Vale of Evesham is one of the country's most important and prolific horticultural regions, and in springtime the Vale is alive with colour from the blossom of the fruit trees. High-quality fruit and vegetables are distributed from here throughout the land, and motorists will come across numerous roadside stalls selling a wonderful array of

Malvern Hills

produce. At the eastern edge of this part of the county lies Broadway, a quintessential Cotswold village of outstanding beauty, beloved of tourists and not to be missed on any visit to this most delightful county.

Severn Bridge, Upper Arley

Set on either side of the curving River Severn, Worcester is a bustling county capital and cathedral city. Its architecture spans many centuries and there are some marvellous examples from all of them. In the heart of England, this is an area characterised by red earth, apple orchards, hopyards, quiet inns, stone farmhouses and black-and-white timbered dwellings. As a visible legacy of the ancient forest that once surrounded Worcester, the half-timbered buildings lend colour and variety to the villages around this historic city.

Most of Worcestershire's industry was centred in the northern part of the county, and there are numerous examples of industrial archaeology to interest the historian. Salt and scythes, carpets, porcelain and needles all contributed to the local economy, along with ironworks and corn mills, and many fine old buildings survive as monuments to industries which have dwindled or disappeared.

Canals here were once as important as roads, and in this part of the county the Worcester & Birmingham Canal, the Staffordshire & Worcester Canal and the Droitwich Canal were a quicker means of transport than the Severn and more reliable than the roads. They themselves lost a good deal of their practical advantages when the railways arrived. The railway network has shrunk considerably over the last 40 years, so it's back to the roads for most local communications. The Severn Valley Railway, from Kidderminster to Bridgnorth, has survived and flourished, and today people come from far and wide for the chance to ride behind a steam engine through some incredibly beautiful scenery. Enthusiasts have also ensured that much of the canal system has survived, finding a new role as a major leisure and tourist attraction.

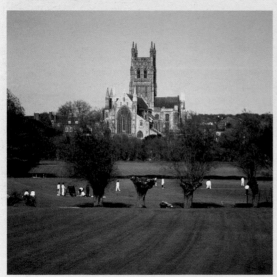

Worcester Cathedral

The route north from Droitwich towards Bromsgrove takes in much that is of interest to the industrial historian, including the Worcester & Birmingham Canal. Opened in 1815 and 30 miles in length, the canal passes Stoke works and Stoke Prior, where John Corbett set up his salt works after leaving Droitwich.

LOCATOR MAP

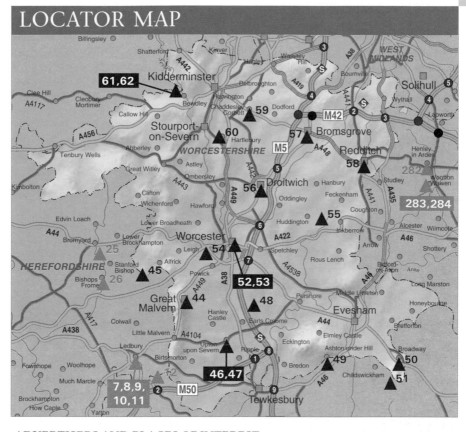

ADVERTISERS AND PLACES OF INTEREST

GREAT MALVERN

Beneath the northeastern slopes of the **Malvern Hills**, Great Malvern is known for its porcelain, its annual music and drama festivals, Malvern water and Morgan cars. Though invaded by tourists for much of the year, Great Malvern has retained its dignity and elegance, with open spaces, leafy avenues and handsome houses. Close to the start of the Malvern walking trail, on a path leading up from the town, is a Regency cottage housing one source of the water – **St Anne's Well** – where one can sample the water and drink in the views. Great Malvern was for many centuries a quiet, little-known place with a priory at its heart, and even when the curative properties of its spring waters were discovered, it took a long time for it to become a fashionable spa resort. Hotels, baths and a pump room were built in the early 19th century, and the arrival of the railway provided easy access from the middle of the century. The station is one of many charming Victorian buildings, and with its cast-iron pillars, stone ornaments and beautifully painted floral designs, is a tourist attraction in its own right.

The Priory **Church of St Mary and St Michael** is a dominant feature in the

Malvern Hills

centre of the town. Its windows, the west a gift from Richard III, the east from Henry VII, contain a wonderful collection of 15th century stained glass, and another unique feature is a collection of more than 1,200 wall tiles on the chancel screens. These also date from the 15th century. Among many

BREDON HOUSE HOTEL

34 Worcester Road, Malvern, Worcestershire WR14 4AA
Tel: 01684 566990   e-mail: suereeves@bredonhousehotel.co.uk
Fax: 01684 575323   website: www.bredonhousehotel.co.uk

"A house that loves company" is how resident proprietor Sue Reeves describes **Bredon House Hotel**, an elegant Grade II listed house built in the 1820s supposedly for the mistress of a local gentleman. Standing high on the hill above Malvern, the house enjoys spectacular views across the peaceful Severn Valley but is within easy walking distance of the town centre. Comfortable and intimate, the hotel has 9 well-appointed rooms, most with superb views and all with en suite facilities, television, radio, telephone and hospitality tray. Easily reached from the M5, Bredon House is just a short drive from the cathedral cities of Worcester, Gloucester and Hereford.

interesting graves in the cemetery is that of Jenny Lind, "The Swedish Nightingale", who was born in Stockholm in 1820 and died at Wynd's Point, Malvern, which she used as a summer retreat, in 1887. In the churchyard at West Malvern Peter Mark Roget (the Thesaurus man) is buried (interred, entombed, coffined, laid to rest, consigned to earth). The 14th century **Abbey Gateway**, whose huge wooden gateposts can be seen in the archway, houses the **Malvern Museum**. Open Easter to October, its displays include the geology of the Malvern Hills, the history of Malvern spring water and the development of Morgan cars. In Tanhouse Lane stands the factory of

Church of St Mary and St Michael, Great Malvern

Boehm of Malvern, where the remarkable American Edward Marshall Boehm (call it 'Beam') founded the centre which has become known worldwide for the quality of its porcelain. Great Malvern has a distinguished tradition of arts and culture, much of it the legacy of Sir

WHITEWELLS FARM COTTAGES

Ridgway Cross, nr Malvern, Worcestershire WR13 5JR
Tel: 01886 880607 Fax: 01886 880360
e-mail: whitewells.farm@btinternet.com
website: www.whitewellsfarm.co.uk

Idyllically set around a duck pond with an ancient cider press featured in the gardens, **Whitewells Farm Cottages** are perfect examples of traditional Herefordshire farmsteads. Built on a south-facing slope and set in 10 acres of unspoilt countryside, the buildings cluster around the former farmyard, now a lawn, and enjoy glorious views across an area of outstanding natural beauty with views of the Malvern Hills. Each of the 7 cottages has its own individual charm whether it be the Old Hop Kiln with its circular kitchen and bathroom or Sparrows Nest Cottage which is set in the original vast doorway of the old barn. Saddlestones and Haywain Cottages are "upside-down cottages" with the living room and kitchen upstairs giving views of the Malvern Hills.

Cider Press Cottage is light and airy and suitable for the disabled with full wheelchair access. The cottages sleep between 2 to 6 people and are all comprehensively equipped and maintained to the highest standard. Amenities include a purpose-built fully equipped laundry room and a former stable which has been converted into a general information room with lots of information of local attractions as well as a small library of light reading matter. Pets and children are welcome and there are some delightful walks locally and, of course, in the Malvern Hills themselves.

Main Street, Great Malvern

Edward Elgar and George Bernard Shaw, and the **Victorian Winter Gardens** are an exciting setting for performances of music and drama. Malvern is the home of the excellent English Symphony Orchestra, formed in 1980 by William Boughton.

Great Malvern is the largest of six settlements that make up the Malverns: to the south are Malvern Wells and Little Malvern, to the north North Malvern and to the northeast Malvern Link. A permanent site on low ground below Great Malvern is the venue for the **Three Counties Show**, one of England's premier agricultural shows.

AROUND GREAT MALVERN

LITTLE MALVERN
4 miles S of Great Malvern on the A449

At Little Malvern stands the **Church of St Wulstan**, where a simple headstone marks the grave of Sir Edward Elgar and his wife Caroline. Their daughter is buried next to them.

Little Malvern Court, off the A4104, enjoys a glorious setting on the lower slopes of the Malvern Hills. It stands next to **Little Malvern Priory**, whose

hall, the only part that survived the Dissolution, is now incorporated into the Court. Of the priory church, only the chancel tower and south transept remain. The Court was once a Catholic safe house, with a chapel reached by a secret staircase. The Court and gardens are open Wednesday and Thursday afternoons from mid-April to mid-July.

Just to the north at **Malvern Wells**, where the first medicinal wells were discovered, stands St Peter's Church, dating from 1836 and notable for some original stained glass and a William Morris window of 1885.

AROUND THE MALVERNS

The whole area is glorious walking country, with endless places to discover and explore. **British Camp**, on Herefordshire Beacon 2 miles west of Little Malvern, is one of the most important Roman settlements in Britain, and a little way south is **Midsummer Hill**, site of another ancient settlement. Six miles south of Great Malvern on the B4208 is the **Malvern Hills Animal and Bird Garden**, whose collection of animals includes snakes, monkeys and wallabies.

COLWALL
2 miles SW of Great Malvern off the B4218

On the west side of the Malverns, Colwall lies just across the border in Herefordshire. Its chief claim to fame is the enormous lump of limestone which stands at its centre. How it got there no one knows, but the Devil and a local giant are among the suspects. Less mysterious are the attractions of the **Picton Garden**, which contains a

National Collection of Michaelmas daisies which flower in September/ October. The 14th century poet William Langland, author of *Piers Plowman*, lived at Colwall.

BIRTSMORTON

7 miles S of Great Malvern off the B4208

In the Church of St Peter and St Paul are monuments to the Nanfan family, owners of the nearby **Birtsmorton Court**. Other notable residents of this magnificent building (not open to the public) include William Huskisson, a former colonial secretary, who in 1830 became the first person to be killed in a railway accident.

HANLEY CASTLE

6 miles SE of Great Malvern on the B4209

The village takes its name from the castle, which was originally a hunting lodge for King John, and which

disappeared, except for its moat, many centuries ago. There's still plenty to see in this attractive little spot, including picturesque cottages, a 15th century inn, (The Three Kings), a 16th century grammar school and the Church of St Mary in stone and brick.

UPTON-ON-SEVERN

7 miles SE of Great Malvern on the A4104

An unspoilt town which gained prominence as one of the few bridging points on the Severn. The first records indicate that it was a Roman station, and it is mentioned in the Domesday Book. It became an important medieval port, and its strategic position led to its playing a role in the Civil War. In 1651, Charles sent a force to Upton to destroy the bridge, but after a long and bloody struggle the King's troops were routed and Cromwell regained the town. A Dutch gabled building used for stabling

CLIVE'S FRUIT FARM

Willingsworth, Upton on Severn, Worcs. WR8 0SA
Tel: 01684 592664 Fax: 01684 594982
e-mail: clivesfruitfarm@ivillage.co.uk
website: www.4avisit.com/rw4

Having won 9 firsts out of 11 classes at the Malvern Show, it's clear that **Clive's Fruit Farm** definitely possesses the knack of producing top quality fruit. Charlie Clive was born on the farm which his family has owned and run for more than a century. Originally, pigs were farmed and the fruit trees were a source of food for them. In the 1960s, Charlie's father, Felix, felt that fruit was a more important crop and converted completely to fruit production. He was one of the first farmers in the country to introduce the Pick Your Own method of retailing.

Today, Charlie and his wife Jane have developed the business further by converting the 100-year-old farm buildings into a highly successful shop. It enjoys a picturesque location, looking across to the attractive town of Upton on Severn with its two church steeples. In addition to a wide variety of fruit, the spacious farm shop also stocks a good selection of local cheeses, meats, preserves and honey. Charlie and Jane also produce their own apple juice, cider and perry which all visitors to the farm are encouraged to taste. Outside, free range chickens wander at will and the Clives have introduced a highly successful Pick Your Own Eggs opportunity, an innovation that was featured in Rick Stein's book *Food Heroes*.

TILTRIDGE FARM & VINEYARD

Upper Hook Road, Upton-upon-Severn,
Worcestershire WR8 0SA
Tel: 01684 592906 e-mail: sandy@tiltridge.com
Fax: 01684 594142   website: www.tiltridge.com

Peter and Sandy Barker run this busy vineyard and
farmhouse B&B just a mile outside the attractive
riverside town of Upton-upon-Severn. Edward
Elgar is closely associated with Worcester and the
Malvern Hills, and for that reason the vineyard has
named some of their wines after him and his music.
The white wines produced, both still and sparkling,
are typical of the English style - fresh, crisp and
fruity. Visitors are welcome to wander round the vineyard and enjoy a free tasting.

Tiltridge has three en-suite bedrooms available - two double and one twin - and has been given a
grading of Four Diamonds with a Silver Award by the English Tourism Council. The original 17th
century cottage has been extended with a Georgian frontage and also by the Victorians. Guests
appreciate its warm relaxed atmosphere and peaceful location. However there is plenty of good walking
and sightseeing nearby as well as many 'eateries'. Importance is placed on using quality, locally produced
food for breakfast, including sausages from Malvern, bread and bacon from Upton, fruit and fruit
juices from the farm next door and home produced jams and preserves as well as eggs from their free
range chickens.

Winner of "The Best Breakfast in Worcestershire 2002" award. B&B available all year except
Christmas to New Year. Vineyard usually open Mon-Sat 11am to 5pm and Sunday 12noon to 5pm,
but phone for details.

during the War still stands. The medieval
church, one of the most distinctive
buildings in the whole county, is
affectionately known as **'The
Pepperpot'**, because of its handsome
tower with its copper-covered cupola,
the work of the 18th century architect
Keek. This former place of worship is
now a heritage centre, telling of the Civil
War battles and the town's history. The
Church of St Peter and St Paul, built in
1879, has an interesting talking point in
a large metal abstract hanging above the
altar. **The Tudor House**, which contains
a museum of Upton past and present, is
open daily on summer afternoons. The
White Lion Hotel, in the High Street,
has a history going back to 1510 and was
the setting for some scenes in Henry
Fielding's *Tom Jones*. The commecial
trade has largely left the Severn, replaced
by a steady stream of summertime
pleasure craft.

RIPPLE

10 miles SE of Great Malvern off the A38

The village square with its stocks and
whipping post is tiny, making the
Church of St Mary seem even larger than
it is. Note the series of 12 misericords
each depicting the seasonal activities of
country life. They are full of detail and
wondrously carved. In the churchyard is
the **Giant's Grave**, the final resting place
of Robert Reeve who was said to be 7ft
4in tall when he died in 1626, aged 56.
On his well-preserved gravestone the
epitaph reads:

*Ye who pass by behold my length
But never glory in your strength*

EARLS CROOME

6 miles SE of Great Malvern on the A4104

There are several attractions in the area
of Earls Croome. **Croome Park** (see

CROOME PARK

High Green, nr Upton upon Severn, Worcestershire
Tel: 01905 371006 Fax: 01905 371090
e-mail: clare.joynes@nationaltrust.org.uk
website: www.nationaltrust.org.uk

"If there be a spot upon the habitable globe to make a death-bed terrible, it is Lord Coventry's (park) at Croome". So wrote a correspondent to the *Gentleman's Magazine* in 1792. **Croome Park** was the home of the Earls of Coventry who lived here up until the 1940s but with their departure the park was allowed to decline. By 1996 nature and modern agriculture had combined to hide the carefully planned lines of the landscape under brambles and arable crops. Now, in its most ambitious garden restoration project to date, the National Trust is returning Croome Park to its former glory. The project is especially significant because the park was the first complete landscape design by the famous Lancelot "Capability" Brown.

Commissioned by the 6th Earl of Coventry in 1751, the park made Brown's reputation. At Croome he established the English Landscape Style, a vision of Ideal Nature which was admired and copied throughout the western world. His great achievement is now being restored, buildings and statues reclaimed, the lake and river cleared of choking weeds and 14 acres of shrubberies are being planted. Visitors to Croome Park have a unique opportunity of travelling back in time to see how England's greatest gardener created this magical landscape from marsh and scrubland some 250 years ago.

panel above), was Capability Brown's first complete landscape. It made his reputation and set a pattern for parkland design that lasted half a century. The buildings have equally distinguished pedigrees, with Robert Adam and James Wyatt as architects. The **Hill Croome Dovecote** is a very rare square building next to the church in **Hill Croome**. **Dunstall Castle** folly at **Dunstall Common** is a folly in the style of a Norman castle, put up in the 18th century and comprising two round towers and one square, connected by arches.

At **Croome d'Abitot**, a little way north of Earls Croome, the 18th century Church of St Mary Magdalene is filled with memorials to the Coventry family – it stood on their estate.

ECKINGTON

10 miles SE of Great Malvern on the B4080

The small village of Eckington can be traced back to 172AD; it was originally a Roman settlement on land belonging to the British tribe of Dobuni. The bridge over the Avon, which dates from the 15th century, has an adjacent car park which is a popular picnic site.

The area south of Pershore towards the boundary with Gloucestershire is dominated by **Bredon Hill**, which is surrounded by charming villages such as Great and Little Comberton and Elmley Castle on the north side, and Bredon, Overbury and Kennerton to the south. Bredon Hill is almost circular, a limestone outcrop of the Cotswolds covering 12 square miles, accessible from many of the villages that ring it, and rising to over 900 feet. On the crest of its northern slope, best accessed from Great Comberton, are the remains – part of the earthworks – of the pre-Roman settlement known as Kennerton Camp. Much more visible on the top is a curious brick tower called Parsons Folly, built by a Mr Parsons in the 18th century.

ELMLEY CASTLE

13 miles SE of Great Malvern on a minor road

Just one of the many enchanting villages around Bredon Hill, no longer boasting a castle but with this memorandum of 1540: *"The late Castle of Elmley standing on high and adjoining the Park, compassed in with wall and ditch is uncovered and in decay."*

The village's main street is very wide and lined with trees, with a little brook flowing to one side. Picturesque cottages with thatched roofs lead up to a well-preserved 15th century cross, then to St Mary's Church with its handsome tower and battlements. Inside are some of the finest monuments to be found anywhere in England, most notably the 17th century alabaster tomb of William Savage, his son Giles and Giles's wife and children.

BREDON

14 miles SE of Great Malvern off the B4080

Plenty to see in this sizeable village, notably the Church of St Giles with its 14th century stained glass and some very elaborate stone monuments; an Elizabethan rectory with stone figures on horseback on the roof; and some fine 18th century stables. **Bredon Barn**, owned by the National Trust, is a huge 14th century barn built of local Cotswold stone. 132ft in length, it has a dramatic aisled interior, marvellous beams and two porches at the wagon entrances. Open April-November.

PERSHORE

9 miles E of Great Malvern on the A4104

A gem of a market town, with fine Georgian architecture and an attractive setting on the banks of the Avon. Its crowning glory is the **Abbey** which combines outstanding examples of Norman and Early English architecture. The Abbey was founded by King Oswald in 689, and in 972 King Edgar granted a charter to the Benedictine monks. Only the choir remains of the original church, but it is still a considerable architectural treasure. The south transept is the oldest part, while among the most impressive features is some superb vaulting in the chancel roof.

Pershore Bridge, a favourite picnic spot, still bears the marks of damage done during the Civil War. A mile east of town on the A44 is Pershore College of Architecture. Originally part of the Wyke Estate, the college has been developed round an early 19th century mansion and is the Royal Horticultural Society's Centre for the West Midlands. The grounds contain many unusual trees and shrubs, and in the glasshouses are tropical, temperate and cool decorative plants.

EVESHAM

A bustling market town at the centre of the Vale of Evesham, an area long known as the Garden of England, with a prolific harvest of soft fruits, apples, plums and salad vegetables. The **Blossom Trail**, which starts in the town, is a popular outing when the fruit trees burst into blossom. The Trail follows a signposted route from the High Street to Greenhill, where the Battle of Evesham took place. The River Avon performs a loop round the town, and the Abbey park is a good place for a riverside stroll; it is also the start point for boat trips. The magnificent bell tower (110ft) is the only major building remaining of the **Abbey**, which was founded around 700 by Egwin, Bishop of Worcester, and was one of the largest and grandest in the whole country. It was knocked down by Henry VIII's men at the time of the Dissolution of the Monasteries. The story of the town is told in vivid detail at the **Almonry Heritage Centre**, which was formerly the home of the Abbey Almoner and was built around

Almonry Heritage Centre

1400. It now houses a unique collection of artifacts as well as exhibitions showing the history of the Abbey, and the defeat of Simon de Montfort at the Battle of Evesham in 1265 (the Leicester Tower stands on the site of the Battle). The Almonry also houses Evesham's Tourist Information Centre.

There are many other interesting buildings in Evesham, including the neighbouring churches of All Saints and St Lawrence. The former is entered through a porch built by Abbot Lichfield in the 16th century, and the Lichfield Chapel, with a lovely fan-vaulted ceiling, contains his tomb. Much of the building, as well as the stone pulpit, dates from

Victorian times, when major restoration work was carried out. The latter, declared redundant in 1978, was also the subject of extensive restoration, in the 1830s and again in the 1990s. In the market place is a free-standing grand old timbered building called the **Round House** – a curious name, because it is actually square. One theory claims that it was so called because "you can walk all *round* it".

AROUND EVESHAM

A little way north of Evesham is **Twyford Country Centre**, where all kinds of plants and garden equipment can be bought, along with craftwork and antiques. There's a farm shop and café on the site, along with a picnic area leading to footpaths by the river. Nearby, in the village of **Offenham**, is a rare sight – a terrace of seven half-timbered medieval cottages from the 1460s which share one long continuous thatched roof. They stand on Main Street at the end of which is another rarity – a permanent Maypole of red, white and blue crowned by a golden cockerel.

Boats on the River, Evesham

RAILS END NURSERY

Back Lane, Ashton under Hill, Worcestershire WR11 7RG
Tel/Fax: 01386 881884 e-mail: salski@btopenworld.com

A family-run business, **Rails End Nursery** is widely known for its
extensive range of plants designed to provide a continuous show
of colour in your garden from early spring to late autumn.
Everything you need is here – spring-flowering violas, summer
bedding plants, late-flowering perennials and winter-flowering
pansies. The nursery specialises in hanging baskets – either ready made or made to order – and their
creations have won prizes as part of the Britain in Bloom competitions. During the spring and summer
months the nursery hosts popular social events known as "Tea on the Lawn", the opportunity for a
leisurely look round, a cup of tea and, sometimes, spontaneous song, music and dance!

ASHTON UNDER HILL

5 miles SW of Evesham off the A46

Ashton under Hill sits at the foot of
Bredon Hill, its main street flanked by
stone half-timbered, black and white
buildings. At the crossroads stands an
unusual survival, an 18th century cross
with a sundial.

BROADWAY

6 miles S of Evesham on the A44

One of the most beautiful villages in
England and a magnet for tourists
throughout the year. The quintessential
Cotswold village, its eponymous broad
main street is lined with houses and
cottages built of golden Cotswold stone.
Broadway was settled as
far back as 1900BC, and
later the Romans came
and occupied the hill
above the village.
Broadway was probably
re-established after the
Battle of Dyrham in
557AD by conquering
Saxons advancing
towards Worcester. The
parish records tell of
hospitality being offered
at a Broadway hostelry as
early as 1532. This was
the time of the advent of
the horse-drawn carriage,

when Broadway became an important
staging post. A journey from London to
Worcester took about 17 hours including
stops and a change of horse, and at one
time Broadway boasted an incredible
33 public houses.

One of the must-sees on any trip to
Broadway is the enchanting **Teddy Bear
Museum**, housed in a picturesque 18th
century shop in the High Street. The
atmosphere within is of an Edwardian
carnival, with music playing, rides
revolving and many other surprises. The
hall of fame tells of celebrity bears,
including Paddington, Pooh and the
three who came upon Goldilocks. Bears
of all ages and sizes are kept in stock,

Broadway Village

and some bears and dolls are made on the premises. Old bears and dolls are lovingly restored at – wait for it – St Beartholomew's Hospital.

In the centre of Broadway is a wide village green from where the main street continues gently upwards for nearly a mile, with the surrounding hills always in view. The gradient increases at Fish Hill then rises to more than 1,000 feet above sea level at **Broadway Beacon**. At the top of the Beacon is **Broadway Tower**, standing in a delightful country park with something to interest all ages, from animal enclosures and adventure playground to nature walks and barbecue sites. The tower was built as a folly by the

Broadway Tower

6th Earl of Coventry at the end of the 18th century as part of the great movement of the time towards picturesque and romantic landscapes. James Wyatt designed the tower, which now contains various displays and exhibitions.

Broadway's St Michael's Church (1839)

Aboriginalia UK

3 Cotswold Court, The Green, Broadway,
Worcestershire WR12 7AA
Tel/Fax: 01386 853770
e-mail: sales@aboriginalia.co.uk
website: www.aboriginalia,co.uk

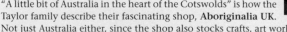

"A little bit of Australia in the heart of the Cotswolds" is how the Taylor family describe their fascinating shop, **Aboriginalia UK**. Not just Australia either, since the shop also stocks crafts, art works, musical instruments and other items from Africa, the Far East and South America. The Taylor family philosophy is to ensure that proceeds from sales reach the people who created these authentic pieces. On display are a range of aboriginal art panels and prints; Jacaru oiled leather and suede bush hats; a wide selection of collectable brushwood animals hand-made in the Philippines; Native Indian dreamcatchers; African soapstone carvings; and soapstone chess and draughts sets.

Aboriginalia UK also stocks a range of musical instruments from around the world, including

African djembes, South African thumb pianos and Peruvian pan pipes. From Australia comes a variety of starter bamboo didgeridoos and naturally termite-hollowed professional eucalyptus didgeridoos, both in bare wood and hand-painted by aboriginal artists. If you would like to learn to play the world's oldest wind instrument, Aboriginalia UK holds regular workshops throughout the year with an expert tutor on hand to help with mastering the circular breathing required. Also from Australia is a colourful range of aboriginal print T-shirts and Emaroo knitwear.

CHARITY FARM COTTAGES

Stanton, nr Broadway, Worcestershire WR12 7NE
Tel: 01386 584339 Fax: 01386 584270
e-mail: kennethryland@ukonline.co.uk
website: www.myrtle-cottage.co.uk/ryland

These charming Cotswold stone cottages are in the picturesque
village of Stanton. Charity cottage nestles in the centre of the
village, just 5 minutes walk from the village Pub and on the
Cotswold Way, providing attractive accommodation for 6 adults.
The Monk's Retreat is adjacent to the farmhouse high above the village with spectacular panoramic
views. Comprehensively equipped this cottage sleeps 2. Their gardens offer 'al fresco' dining, and on
arrival you will find fresh flowers and a crusty loaf awaiting.

boasts an intricate Elizabethan pulpit
which came from the nearby St
Eadburga's Church and was installed in a
thanksgiving service marking the end of
World War I.

CHILDSWICKHAM

4 miles SE of Evesham off the A44

The **Church of St Mary the Virgin**, its
tall, slender spire a prominent landmark,
is a good place to start a walk round the
old part of the village. Close by, on the
Broadway road, is the **Barnfield Cider
Mill Museum**, where visitors can see a
display of cider-making down the years
before sampling cider, perry or one of
the wines produced from local plums
and berries.

BRETFORTON

4 miles E of Evesham on the B4035

A pub in the care of the National Trust is
a rarity indeed, and it's well worth a trip
to Bretforton to visit the **The Fleece Inn**,
a medieval half-timbered building that
was originally a farmhouse. It has
changed very little since being first
licensed in 1848, and an interesting
feature is the Witches' Marks carved in
the hearth to prevent witches coming
down the chimney. The Church of St
Leonard boasts a number of interesting
and intricate carvings, notably a scene

depicting St Margaret emerging
(through a hole she made with her cross)
from the side of the dragon which has
just swallowed her.

HONEYBOURNE

5 miles E of Evesham on minor roads off the B4035

The **Domestic Fowl Trust and
Honeybourne Rare Breeds** is a
conservation centre for pure breeds of
poultry and rare breeds of farm animals.
All are in labelled breeding paddocks,
and visitors are welcome to "stroke the
sheep and say hello to the cows". Books,
gifts and animal equipment and
feedstuffs are available from the shop,
and the centre also has a tea room.

MIDDLE LITTLETON

3 miles NE of Evesham off the B4085

The Littletons – North, Middle and
South – lie close to each other and close
to the River Avon. In Middle Littleton is
a huge and wonderful **Tithe Barn**, built
in the 13th century and once the
property of the Abbots of Evesham. Now
owned by the National Trust, it is still in
use as a farm building, but can be visited.

Nearby, a bridleway leads off the B4510
to **Windmill Hill Nature Reserve**, an
area of fertile limestone which continues
up to Cleeve Prior, where the Church of
St Andrew is well worth a visit.

WORCESTER

The **Cathedral** (see panel opposite), with its 200ft tower, stands majestically beside the Severn. The 11th century crypt is a classic example of Norman architecture and was built by St Wulstan, who is remembered in a stone carving. He was the only English bishop not to be replaced by a Norman after the Conquest. To many of the local people the task of building the Cathedral must have seemed endless; the central tower collapsed in 1175 and a fire destroyed much of the building in 1203. The Cathedral had only just been re-dedicated after these disasters when Bishop Blois began pulling it down again, only to rebuild it in the fashionable Gothic style. The nave was rebuilt in the 14th century under the auspices of Bishop Cobham, but the south side was not completed until much later, and in a far less elaborate style. King John requested that he be buried in the choir, and his tomb stands near the high altar. It is a masterpiece of medieval sculpture, showing the King flanked by the Bishops Oswald and Wulstan. Prince Arthur, elder brother of Henry VIII, is also entombed near the high altar.

There's a great deal more to see than the Cathedral, of course, and in the **City Museum and Art Gallery** are

WORCESTER CATHEDRAL

10a College Green, Worcester WR1 2LH
Tel: 01905 28854/21004 Fax: 01905 611139
e-mail: info@worcestercathedral.org.uk
website: www.cofe worcester.org.uk

Worcester Cathedral is one of England's loveliest cathedrals, with Royal tombs of King John and Prince Arthur, medieval cloisters, an ancient crypt and Chapter House, and magnificent Victorian stained glass. For an unequalled view to the Malvern Hills and south to the Cotswolds, climb the Tower on Saturdays and school holidays in the summer.

Worcester Cathedral was founded in Anglo Saxon times and during the middle ages there was a Benedictine monastery attached to the cathedral. In 1540, the monastery was closed down, but the new Chapter of the Cathedral continued collecting books, giving alms to the poor, and educating local boys.

During the Civil War, King Charles II used the Cathedral tower to survey the battle of Worcester in 1651. In the nineteenth century there was much Victorian Restoration and in the twentieth century the Cathedral's connections include Sir Edward Elgar, featured on the current £20 note.

The Cathedral today welcomes families, groups, and individuals, with a coffee shop, a quality gift shop, and disabled access to all facilities and gardens. Entry is free. There is nearby parking, bus and train stations. Worcester Cathedral is open daily 7.30am 6pm, with Services three times daily.

contemporary art and archaeological displays, a 19th century chemist's shop and the military collections of the Worcestershire Regiment and the Worcestershire Yeomanry Cavalry. Friar Street has many lovely old timber houses. **Greyfriars**, in the care of the National Trust, is a medieval house that has managed to survive right in the heart of the city, and passing through its archway visitors will come across a pretty walled garden. The imposing Guildhall in the High Street is a marvellous example of Queen Anne architecture, designed by a local man,

River Severn, Worcester

Thomas White. **The Commandery Civil War Centre** is a stunning complex of buildings behind a small timber-framed entrance. At the Battle of Worcester in 1651 the Commandery was used as the Royalist headquarters, and today period rooms offer a fascinating glimpse of the architecture and style of Tudor and Stuart times while acting as the country's only museum devoted to the story of the Civil War. The story takes in the trial of Charles I, visits a Royalist encampment on the eve of the battle and enacts the last battle of the war narrated by Charles II and Oliver Cromwell.

The **Royal Worcester Porcelain** Visitor Centre is an absolute must on any sightseer's list. Royal Worcester is Britain's oldest continuous producer of porcelain and is world famous for its exquisite bone china. The factory was founded in 1751 by Dr John Wall with the intention of creating *"a ware of a form so precise as to be easily distinguished from other English porcelain"*. The collection in the museum contains some of the finest treasures of the factory, and visitors can take a guided tour of the factory to observe the many stages of production and the premises include a shop and a restaurant where the food is, naturally, served on Royal Worcester china. In the 1930s the company was acquired by (Charles William) Dyson Perrins, the grandson of William Perrins, founder of the Worcester Sauce company.

The **Museum of Local Life** reflects the history of Worcester and its people, with displays covering the past 700 years. There's a Victorian kitchen scene, a turn-of-the-century schoolroom and a variety of changing exhibitions throughout the year. The site is a 16th century timber-framed building in wonderful Friar Street. Famous sons of Worcester, where the **Three Choirs Festival** was first held in 1717, include Sir Edward Elgar, born at nearby Broadheath; his statue is a notable landmark opposite the Cathedral.

To the east of the city and signposted from the M5 (J6) and from the city centre

---

King Charles Restaurant

29 New Street, Worcester WR1 2DP
Tel: 01905 22449

After his defeat at the Battle of Worcester in 1651, it was through the back door of what is now the **King Charles Restaurant** that Charles II escaped, hotly pursued by Cromwell's troops. Today, this delightful old building with its oak-panelled walls, antique furniture and huge open fire serves as an outstanding restaurant offering superb international cuisine. In the upstairs bar, reputedly the king's bedchamber, customers can enjoy a pre-meal drink before descending to the ground floor dining room with its lace tablecloths, crystal glasses and candlelit tables. Also on the ground floor is a curious Bottle Dungeon where a 17th century judge kept prisoners awaiting trial.

via the A44, **Worcester Woods Country Park**, open daily, has 50 hectares of ancient oak woodland, 10 hectares of traditional wildflower meadow, waymarked trails, a picnic area, children's play area, visitor centre, café and shop.

AROUND WORCESTER

POWICK

2 miles S of Worcester on the A449

Powick Bridge was the scene of the first and last battles in the Civil War; the last, in 1651, ending with Charles hiding in the Boscobel Oak before journeying south to nine year's exile in France. Cromwell's power had been overwhelming, and the long years of strife were at an end. Powick Bridge's skyline is today dominated by Worcester's first power station, built in 1894.

SPETCHLEY

3 miles E of Worcester on the A422

All Saints Church, 14th century with a 16th century chapel, is home to a fine collection of monuments to the Berkeley family, who owned adjoining **Spetchley Park**. The park, which extends over 12 hectares, has lovely formal gardens, wooded areas, lawns and a lake with an ornamental bridge.

HUDDINGTON

6 miles E of Worcester on minor roads

Two buildings of particular note: the simple little Church of St James, with a timber-framed bell turret; and **Huddington Court**. The Court has been described as the most picturesque house in Worcestershire. An excellent example of a 16th century timber-framed building, it was once the home of the Wintours, a

ROOTS AT RUSHWICK

Bransford Road, Rushwick, Worcestershire WR2 5TD
Tel: 01905 421104
e-mail: roots@rushwick.co.uk

Catering for the increasing number of people who want to buy their meat, fruit and vegetables from local sources, **Roots at Rushwick** is a lively enterprise run by Meg and Will Edmonds. After their marriage three years ago they abandoned their corporate careers and returned to Will's family farm in a beautiful part of the Teme

Valley near Worcester. They quickly recognised the need to diversify and so they established Roots at Rushwick as a retail outlet for everything produced on their 300-acre organic farm.

Surrounded by growing crops which are harvested daily, the shop offers an ever-expanding range of home-grown organic meat, eggs, fruit and vegetables and they have discovered a market for much more than their own produce. Roots has become an outlet for an enormous range of the best of Worcestershire's food producers – cheeses, wines, ciders, pickles, preserves and much more. A unique and very successful part of the business was inspired by Meg's love of Sweet Peas. She now has a special reputation for growing some 30 old-fashioned scented varieties of these colourful plants and has found a demand for her cut flowers, bouquets and posies much father afield than she imagined when she chose these special flowers for her own wedding.

staunchly Catholic family who were involved in the Gunpowder Plot. When the plot was exposed and the conspirators finally arrested, both Thomas and Robert Wintour, cousins of Robert Catesby, confessed their guilt and were executed. The Court is a private residence, but you can get a good view of it from the churchyard.

A mile or so north of Huddington lies the village of **Himbleton**, where the Church of St Mary Magdalene has a picturesque bell turret with a memorial clock.

ROUS LENCH

7 miles E of Worcester on a minor road

The Lenches are attractive little villages in an area known for its particularly rich soil. Rous Lench church has a chapel with monuments to the Rous family and an oil painting of Jesus in the house of Simon the Pharisee. The road to the hilltop village of **Church Lench** (a mile

south), with the church at the very top of the hill, passes by **Rous Lench Court**,the seat of the Rous family for many centuries from 1382. The Court is a splendid half-timbered mansion with a tall Italianate tower in the beautiful gardens.

INKBERROW

8 miles E of Worcester off the A42

A very pleasant and pretty spot to pause awhile, with the Church of St Peter (note the alabaster of John Savage, a High Sheriff of Worcester who died in 1631), the inn and other buildings round the village green, some in red brick, others black and white half-timbered. The **Old Bull Inn** has two claims to fame, one that William Shakespeare stayed there in 1582, the other that it is the original of The Bull at Ambridge, home of *The Archers*. Photographs of the cast adorn the walls, and the inn has become a place of pilgrimage for fans of the programme.

CRANESBILL NURSERY

Stock Green, nr Redditch,
Worcestershire B96 6SZ
Tel: 01386 792414
Fax: 01386 792280
e-mail: cranesbilluk@aol.com
website: www.cranesbillnursery.com

It was back in 1981 that Janet and Mel Bates set to work on the green field that is now the excellent **Cranesbill Nursery**. They began by laying out the beautifully maintained lawns and in 1986 developed the Stream Garden and a colourful Wildflower Meadow which looks at its best in springtime. A formal garden and pond was then added, followed by the Rockery and "island" beds. The most recent addition was the Rose Garden.

Cranesbill Nursery specialises in hardy geraniums and now boasts a collection of more than 200 varieties but there's also an extensive choice of herbaceous plants with the varieties growing in the gardens available for sale in the nursery. These are at their most eye-catching in May and June and another good time to visit is in September and October for some glorious autumn colours. There's a small entrance fee for visiting the lovely formal and informal gardens but visitors are welcome to look around the nursery without charge.

The Old Vicarage, a handsome 18th century building in the Tudor style, was host in an earlier guise to King Charles I, who stayed there on his way to Naseby; some maps he left behind are kept in the church.

At nearby **Dormston**, a timber-framed **Dovecote** stands in front of the Moat farmhouse.

One mile south of Inkberrow is the village of **Abbots Morton**, whose dwellings are mainly 17th century yeomen's houses. The village was once the site of the Abbot of Evesham's summer residence, but only some mounds and fishponds now remain.

ODDINGLEY

5 miles NE of Worcester on minor roads

The parish church of Oddingley stands on a hill overlooking the Worcester & Birmingham Canal. Its principal treasure is the mostly 15th century stained glass in the east window which is regarded as some of the finest of that period. Behind the communion rail is a memorial to a rector, George Parker, who was murdered in 1806 because of a dispute over tithes.

DROITWICH

6 miles NE of Worcester on the A38

"Salinae", the place of salt, in Roman times. Salt deposits, a legacy from the time when this area was on the seabed, were mined here for 2,000 years until the end of the 19th century. The natural Droitwich brine contains about 2.5 pounds of salt per gallon - ten times as much as sea water - and is often likened to the waters of the Dead Sea. The brine is pumped up from an underground lake which lies 200ft below the town. Visitors do not drink the waters at Droitwich as they do at most other spas, but enjoy the therapeutic properties floating in the warm brine. The first brine baths were built in the 1830s and were soon renowned for bringing relief to many and effecting seemingly miraculous cures. By 1876, Droitwich had developed as a fashionable spa, mainly through the efforts of John Corbett, known as the "Salt King".

This typical Victorian businessman and philanthropist introduced new methods of extracting the brine and moved the main plant to Stoke Prior. The enterprise was beset with various problems in the 1870s and Corbett turned his attention to developing the town as a spa resort. He was clearly a man of some energy as he also served as an MP after the 1874 General Election. Many of the buildings in present-day Droitwich were owned by Corbett, including the Raven Hotel (a raven was part of his coat of arms) in the centre. His most remarkable legacy is undoubtedly **Chateau Impney**, on the

ST ANDREW'S HOUSE HOTEL

St Andrew's Drive, Droitwich Spa, Worcestershire WR9 8AL
Tel: 01905 779677   Fax: 01905 779752
e-mail: amy.Gregory@st-andrewshotel.com
website: www.st-andrewshotel.com

St Andrew's House Hotel is a delightful, creeper-clad Grade II listed building erected in the 1820s as the home of the Town Clerk of Droitwich Spa. Many of the trees planted then still stand in the grounds of this outstanding hotel which, although only a 5-minute walk from the town centre, enjoys an extremely quiet and secluded location. Over the last few years, all 29 bedrooms have been upgraded and each has en suite facilities, direct dial telephone, colour TV, trouser press and hospitality tray. The hotel is licensed to hold civil wedding ceremonies, has 5 function/ conference rooms and lovely Victorian gardens.

eastern side of town at Dodderhill. It was designed by a Frenchman, Auguste Tronquois, in the style of an ornate French chateau, with soaring turrets, mansard roof and classical French gardens. It was intended as a home for Corbett and his wife Anna, but she apparently didn't like the place; their increasingly stormy marriage ended in 1884, nine years after the completion of the flamboyant chateau, which is now a high-class hotel and conference centre.

The Heritage and Information Centre includes a local history exhibition (Salt Town to Spa) and a historic BBC radio room.

In the centre of the town is St Andrew's Church, part of whose tower was removed because of subsidence, a condition which affected many buildings and which can be seen in some fairly alarming angles. One of the chapels, dating from the 13th century, is dedicated to St Richard de Wyche, the town's patron saint, who became Bishop of Chichester. On the southern outskirts of Droitwich is the **Church of the Sacred Heart**, built in Italianate style in the 1930s and remarkable for its profusion of beautiful mosaics made from Venetian glass. Many of these mosaics also commemorate the life of St Richard.

One of Droitwich's most famous sons is Edward Winslow, born the eldest of eight children in 1595. He was one of the pilgrims who set sail for the New World to seek religious freedom and he later became Governor of the colony. A bronze memorial to Edward Winslow can be seen in St Peter's Church, Droitwich.

Salwarpe on the southwest fringes of Droitwich, is truly a hidden hamlet, approached by a stone bridge over James Brindley's **Droitwich Canal**.

Opened in 1771, the canal linked the town to the River Severn at Hawford. The Church of St Michael, by the edge of the canal, has several monuments to the Talbot family, who owned nearby Salwarpe Court. **Salwarpe Valley Nature Reserve** is one of very few inland sites with salt water, making it ideal for a variety of saltmarsh plants and very well worth a visit.

Hawford
4 miles N of Worcester off the A449

Another amazing dovecote, this one half-timbered, dating from the 16th century and owned by the National Trust.

Ombersley
6 miles N of Worcester off the A449

A truly delightful and very English village with some superb black-and-white timbered dwellings with steeply-sloping roofs. **St Andrew's Church,** rebuilt in 1825, contains memorials to the Sandys family and also their family pew. Large and square, it stands beside the pulpit and is comfortably furnished with cushioned seats, matching blue embroidered kneelers and an ornate open fireplace. For their heating, the congregation had to rely on the

Cricket Match, Ombersley

impressive Howden Heating Stove, set against the north wall. Installed in 1829, it rises some 12ft and is in the shape of a miniature church tower complete with buttresses, arcaded top and a fuel opening just like a church doorway.

The Sandys family lived at nearby **Ombersley Court** (private), a splendid Georgian mansion which can be seen from the churchyard.

WICHENFORD

5 miles NW of Worcester on the B4204

A famous landmark here is the National Trust's **Wichenford Dovecote**, a 17th century timber-framed construction with a lantern on top. With its 557 nesting holes, it is the largest surviving dovecote in England. When it was constructed, only the Lord of the Manor had the right to build one and to kill the birds for winter meat – a source of resentment to the villagers whose crops were pillaged by these voracious birds.

CLIFTON

10 miles NW of Worcester on the B4204

In lovely countryside near the River Teme, the village boasts a number of charming dwellings around the green and the **Church of St Kenelm**. Parts of the church go back to the 12th and 14th centuries. Collectors of unusual tombstones will find two here. Just inside the porch is the grave of "Elizabeth Taylor, Gent." who "Lived and dyed A Virgin"; on the north wall a marble tablet includes an inscription recording that "William" achieved the intriguing feat of being born on August 22nd 1714 and dying on November 23rd 1713.

There are other interesting churches at nearby **Shelsey Beauchamp**, in red sandstone, and **Shelsey Walsh**, with many treasures including the tomb of Sir Francis Walsh. The name of Shelsey Walsh will be familiar to fans of motor sport as the location of a very famous hill climb.

LOWER BROADHEATH

3 miles W of Worcester off the A44

The **Elgar Birthplace Museum** is a redbrick cottage that is crammed with items from the great composer's life. He was born here in 1857 and, despite long periods spent elsewhere, Broadheath remained his spiritual home. The violin was his first instrument, though he eventually succeeded his father as organist at St George's Church in Worcester. He played at the Three Choirs Festival and began conducting locally. He married in 1889 and was soon devoting almost all his time to composing, making his name with *The Enigma Variations* (1899) and *Dream of Gerontius* (1900). He was knighted in 1904 and when in 1931 he was made a baronet by King George V he took the title 1st Baronet of Broadheath. Various Elgar Trails have been established, the one in Worcester city taking in the statue and the *Dream of Gerontius* window in the Cathedral.

LEIGH

5 miles W of Worcester off the A4103

The **Church of St Eadburga** is very fine indeed, with some imposing monuments and a marvellous 15th century rood screen. A curious legend attaches to the church. A man called Edmund Colles is said to have robbed one of his colleagues who was returning from Worcester and known to be carrying a full purse. It was a dark, gloomy night, and as Colles reached out to grab the man's horse, holding on to the bridle, the other struck at him with a sword. When he visited Edmund the next day, the appalling wound testified to the man's guilt;

although forgiven by his intended victim, Colles died shortly after and his ghost once haunted the area. A phantom coach pulled by four fire-breathing steeds would appear and race down the hill to the church by Leigh Court, where they would leap over the tithe barn and disappear beneath the waters of the River Teme. A midnight service attended by 12 clergymen eventually laid the ghost to rest. Leaping over the tithe barn was no mean feat (though easier of course if you're a ghost), as the 14th century barn is truly massive, with great cruck beams and porched wagon doors. Standing in the grounds of Leigh Court, a long gabled mansion, the barn is open for visits on summer weekends.

Leigh Brook is a tributary of the Teme and wends its way through a spectacular valley cared for by Worcestershire Nature Conservation Trust. The countryside here is lovely, and footpaths make the going easier. Up on Old Storridge Common, birch, ash, oak and bracken have taken a firm hold, and there is a weird, rather unearthly feel about the place. Nearby, the hamlet of **Birch Wood** is where Elgar composed his *Dream of Gerontius*.

ALFRICK

7 miles W of Worcester off the A44

Charles Dodgson (Lewis Carroll) once preached at the village Church of St Mary Magdalene, which enjoys a delightful setting above the village green. In the vicinity are two major attractions for nature-lovers. A little way to the northwest is **Ravenshill Woodland Nature Reserve** with waymarked trails through woodland that is home to many breeding birds, while a mile south of Alfrick is the **Knapp and Papermill Nature Reserve**, with 25 hectares of woodland and meadows rich in flora and fauna.

BROMSGROVE

A visit to the **Avoncraft Museum of Historic Buildings**, just south of Bromsgrove, is a walk through seven centuries of English history, with each building providing a snapshot of life in its particular period. The first building, a timber-framed merchant's house from Bromsgrove, was brought to the site in 1967, since when over 20 more have been installed. In addition to the buildings themselves, the Museum has regular demonstrations of such crafts as wood-turning, windmilling, racksawing, brick-making, chain-making and nail-making. There's also a shop, refreshment area, picnic site, a children's area, horse-drawn wagon rides and farm animals wandering around freely. One of the most treasured exhibits is the original 14th century beamed roof of Guesten Hall from Worcester Cathedral, now covering a modern brick building. In an area behind the shop is another unique collection, the **BT National Telephone Kiosk Collection**.

Bromsgrove Museum (see panel opposite), near the town centre, has displays of local crafts and industry, including the Bromsgrove Guild, an organisation of craftsmen founded in 1894. The Guild of highly skilled craftsmen had its finest hour when commissioned to design and make the gates and railings of Buckingham Palace. Another popular exhibit is a street scene of Victorian shops.

Besides the museums, there is plenty to see, including some very handsome timber-framed buildings in the High Street, where stands a statue of AE Housman, the town's most famous son. **Alfred Edward Housman** was born one of seven children at Fockbury, Bromsgrove, in 1859, and spent his

BROMSGROVE MUSEUM

Bromsgrove, Worcestershire
Tel: 01527 831809

Much of the earlier history of Bromsgrove can be seen at **Bromsgrove Museum**, which contains exhibits of the glass, salt and nail industries, and of the Bromsgrove Guild. It also contains an attractive range of shop windows, which feature costumes, toys, cameras and much more. The building is the

former Coach House of Davenal House, built in 1780. On the front of the Museum the wrought iron balcony that originally adorned the stationmasters house at Bromsgrove can be seen. It is said that, in 1848, Stephenson, the great engineer, stood on it. The Museum, (incorporating the Tourist Information Centre) is open Monday to Saturday, 10.30am to 12.30pm and 1.00pm to 4.30pm. Free admittance.

schooldays in the town. After a spell at Oxford University and some time teaching at his old school, he entered the Civil Service in London, where he found time to resume his academic studies. He was appointed Professor of Latin at University College, London, in 1892 and soon afterwards he published his first and best-known collection of poems – *A Shropshire Lad*. His total output was not large, but it includes some of the best-loved poems in the English language. He died in 1936 and is buried in the churchyard of St Lawrence in Ludlow. The forming in 1972 of a Housman Society brought his name to the forefront of public attention and in the region of Bromsgrove walking and driving trails take in the properties and places associated with him.

Bromsgrove has a prestigious annual music festival held during the month of May, when the town plays host to a wide range of musical entertainment from orchestral concerts to jazz, and featuring many well-known artists. Another annual event is the revival of the Court Leet, an ancient form of local administration. A colourful procession moves through the town and there's a lively Elizabethan street market.

The **Church of St John the Baptist** – see his statue over the south porch entrance – contains some superb 19th century stained glass and an impressive collection of monuments, notably to members of the Talbot family. Side by side in the churchyard are tombs of two railwaymen who were killed in 1840 when the boiler of their engine exploded while climbing the notorious **Lickey Incline**.

This stretch of railway, near the village of **Burcot** three miles northeast of Bromsgrove, is, at 1 in 37.7, the steepest gradient on the whole of the British rail network. One specially powerful locomotive, no. 58100 (better known as Big Bertha), spent its days up until the late 1950s helping trains up the bank, a task which was later performed by massive double-boilered locomotives that were the most powerful in the then BR fleet. The steepness of the climb is due to the same geographical feature that necessitated the construction of the unique flight of **Locks** at **Tardebigge**, between Bromsgrove and Redditch. In the space of 2.5 miles the canal is lifted by no fewer than 30 locks. In the actual village of Tardebigge, on the A448, the Church of St Bartholomew enjoys a lovely setting with views across the Severn lowlands.

AROUND BROMSGROVE – SOUTH

HANBURY

3 miles S of Bromsgrove off the B4090

Hanbury Hall is a fine redbrick mansion in William & Mary style, completed by Thomas Vernon in 1701. Internal features include murals by Sir James Thornhill, known particularly for his Painted Hall in the Royal Naval Hospital, Greenwich, and frescoes in the dome of St Paul's. See also a splendid collection of porcelain, the Long Gallery, the Moorish gazebos at each corner of the forecourt and the formal gardens with orangery and 18th century ice house.

In beautiful rural surroundings a mile north of the village of Hanbury stands the award-winning **Jinney Ring Craft Centre**. Richard and Jenny Greatwood created this marvellous place by restoring and converting a collection of old timbered barns next to their 17th century farmhouse home. Craftspeople with many diverse skills can be seen at work in their own craft studios, including two potters, a violin-maker, a jeweller, a picture-framer, a leatherworker, a sign-maker and an antiques restorer. Also on the premises is a craft gallery with changing exhibitions by British craftsmen and artists, and a clothes and knitwear department.

FECKENHAM

7 miles SE of Bromsgrove on the B4090

A pretty village with half-timbered, redbrick and Georgian houses and the fine Church of St John the Baptist. Inside

ARROW VALLEY COUNTRY PARK

Battens Drive, South Moors Moat, Redditch B98 0LJ
Tel/Fax: 01527 464000

A great place for a family day out is the **Arrow Valley Country Park.** Stretching from Forge Mill Needle Museum in the north down to Washford Mill in the south, the 600-acre expanse of the park effectively bonds the new and old parts of the town. One of the major attractions here is the Arrow Valley Lake which offers sailing, canoeing and fishing – the lake holds carp of more than 25lbs as well as bream and roach. A

shoreline path gives full disabled access and there are well-placed picnic sites all around the lake. For the young and active, Redditch Skate Park – one of the best outdoor parks in the country – provides opportunities for BMX, skate boarding and in-line skating.

Walkers can enjoy the woodland pathways or follow the River Arrow upstream to the ruins of Bordesley Abbey, a medieval Cistercian abbey where archaeological finds are on display and a new archaeological activity centre can be booked for special events. Nearby, the **Forge Mill Needle Museum** threads its way through the fascinating history of the Redditch needle-making industry, with the original water-powered machinery and re-created scenes showing vividly how needles were made in the 19th century. A major annual event here is the Charles Henry Foyle Trust-sponsored national needlework competition.

the church a board displays the benefaction which Charles I bestowed upon the village in 1665 - £6. 13 shillings and fourpence, payable out of forest land to the school. The forest in question once surrounded the village, but the trees were all felled for fuelling the saltpans and no trace of the forest now remains.

REDDITCH

6 miles E of Bromsgrove on the A448

A "New Town" from the 60s, but there is plenty of history here, as well as some great walking. The **Arrow Valley Country Park** (see panel opposite), a few minutes walk from the town centre, comprises a vast expanse of parkland with nature trails, picnic areas and lovely walks. Sailing, canoeing, windsurfing and fishing are popular pastimes on the lake.

WYTHALL

10 miles NE of Bromsgrove on the A435

Right on the other side of Redditch, and well on the way to Birmingham, is the **Birmingham and Midland Museum of Transport**. Founded in 1977, the museum's two large halls house a marvellous collection of some 100 buses and coaches, battery vehicles and fire engines, many having seen service in Birmingham and the West Midlands. Open Saturday and Sunday in summer.

WASELEY HILL

5 miles N of Bromsgrove of the B4551

5 miles north of Bromsgrove lies Wasely Hill where open hillside and woodland offers great walking and spectacular views from the top of Windmill Hill. There is also a visitor centre. Just to the east there is more great walking and views in a varied landscape around the **Lickey Hills** which also has a visitor centre.

BELBROUGHTON

6 miles N of Bromsgrove on the B4188

This village was once a centre of the scythe-making industry. Holy Trinity Church occupies a hillside site along with some pleasing Georgian buildings.

A little to the north are the village of **Clent** and the **Clent Hills**, an immensely popular place for walking and drinking in the views. On the top are four large upright stones which could be statement-making modern art but for the fact that they were put there over 200 years ago by Lord Lyttleton of Hagley Hall. Walton Hill is over 1,000 feet above sea level.

HAGLEY

8 miles N of Bromsgrove off the A491

George, 1st Lord Lyttleton, commissioned in 1756 the creation of what was to be the last great Palladian mansion in Britain, **Hagley Hall**. Imposing without, exotic and rococo within; notable are the Barrell Room with panelling from Holbeach Hall, where two of the Gunpowder Plotters – the Wintour brothers – were caught and later put to death in the favourite way of hanging, drawing and quartering. Temples, cascading pools and a ruined castle are some of the reasons for lingering in the park, which has a large herd of deer.

Another attraction at Hagley is the **Falconry Centre** on the A4565, where owls, hawks, falcons and eagles live and fly.

DODFORD

3 miles W of Bromsgrove off the A448

Not far out of Bromsgrove, north of the A448, lies the village of Dodford, whose Church of the Holy Trinity and St Mary is an outstanding example of an Arts and Crafts church, designed in 1908 by the

ROWBERRY'S NURSERY

Lodgeford Hill, Lower Chaddesley Corbett,
Kidderminster, Worcestershire DY10 4QN
Tel: 01562 777017 Fax: 01562 777902

Conveniently located just off the Kidderminster to
Bromsgrove road, **Rowberry's Nursery** was established
over 25 years ago by Chris and Maria Rowberry who
began by selling from home and moved to their present
site in 1989. It was then just a field but has grown
rapidly and the business now employs 15 people. Most
of these are working in the background, pricking out
bedding plants, fuchsias, geraniums and so on, or potting shrubs and herbaceous plants.

The Rowberrys attribute the nursery's success to their policy of selling plants at nearly wholesale
prices. Most of the wide range of plants on sale have been
grown here and there are always special offers – 4 shrubs
for £10 for example. These are not starter shrubs but well-
grown 2-litre plants. The nursery also grows fruits, potatoes
and other vegetables for sale in the farm shop where you'll
also find a wide variety of seeds, potted plants, wild bird
food and care, cards and much, much more. A recent
addition to the staff is a full time florist who prepares
colourful floral displays to brighten up the dullest room.
Gift flowers are also on sale. During the summer months
the nursery offers visitors the chance to "Pick Your Own"
strawberries. Rowberry's is open every day from 9am to 6pm.

Bromsgrove Guild in their interpretation
of the neo-Gothic style.

CHADDESLEY CORBETT

4 miles W of Bromsgrove on the A448

A fairly sizeable village, dominated at its
southern end by the 14th century Church
of St Cassian. It is the only church in
England to be dedicated to this saint,
who was born in Alexandria in the 5th
century and became a bishop in Africa.
He was also a schoolmaster and was
apparently killed by his pupils.

HARVINGTON

5 miles W of Bromsgrove near junction of A448/ A450

Harvington Hall is a moated medieval
and Elizabethan manor house with a
veritable maze of rooms. Mass was
celebrated here during times when it was
a very dangerous thing to do, and that is
perhaps why the Hall has more priest
holes than any other house in the land.

HARTLEBURY

7 miles W of Bromsgrove off the A449

Hartlebury Castle, a historic sandstone
castle of the Bishops of Worcester and a
prison for captured Royalist troops in the
Civil War, now houses the **Worcester
County Museum**. In the former servants'
quarters in the north wing numerous
permanent exhibitions show the past
lives of the county's inhabitants from
Roman times to the 20th century. Visitors
can also admire the grandeur of the
three Castle State Rooms.

On Hartlebury Common, **Leapgate
Country Park** is a nature reserve in
heath and woodland, with the county's
only acid bog.

BELL'S FARM SHOP

Chadwick Bank, Hartlebury, nr Stourport-on-Severn,
Worcestershire DY13 9RQ
Tel/Fax: 01299 251364 website: www.4avisit.com/rwl
e-mail: penny@rcolwill.freeserve.co.uk

Bell's Farm Shop and Pick Your Own, which was runner-up in
the Best Farm Shop competition for the West Midlands in 2001,
was established by the Bells some 50 years ago but is now owned
and run by another local farming family the Colwills. The 40
acres surrounding the Farm Shop are devoted to almost 200 different varieties of fruit and vegetables
for Pick Your Own and to supply the shop with the freshest possible crops. Other produce is sourced
locally and includes eggs, ice cream, milk and cream, cheeses, cakes, bread and free range bacon and
pork products. The Farm Shop is open 7 days a week year round.

KIDDERMINSTER

Known chiefly as a centre of the carpet-
making industry, which began here early
in the 18th century as a cottage industry.
The introduction of the power loom
brought wealth to the area and
instigated the building of carpet mills.
Standing on the River Stour, the town
has a variety of mills, whose enormous
chimneys dominate the skyline and serve
as architectural monuments to
Kidderminster's heritage. St Mary's
Church, on a hill overlooking the town,
is the largest parish church in the county
and contains some superb tomb
monuments. The Whittall Chapel,
designed in 1922 by Sir Charles Gilbert
Scott, was paid for by Matthew Whittall,
a native of Kidderminster who went to
America and made a fortune in carpets.
Three beautiful windows depicting the
Virgin Mary, Joan of Arc and Florence
Nightingale, were given by his widow in
his memory.

Kidderminster's best-known son is
Rowland Hill, who founded the modern
postal system and introduced the penny
post; he was also a teacher,
educationalist and inventor. His statue
stands outside the Town Hall. By the
station on the Severn Valley Railway is
the **Kidderminster Railway Museum**
with a splendid collection of railway
memorabilia. Run by volunteers, it is
housed in an old GWR grain store.

Just outside town, at **Stone**, on the
A448, is Stone House Cottage Garden,
a lovely walled garden with towers.
Unusual wall shrubs, climbers and
herbaceous plants are featured, most
of them for sale in the nursery.

In the Stour Valley just north of
Kidderminster is the village of
Wolverley, with charming cottages and
pretty gardens, the massive Church of St
John the Baptist, and the remains – not
easy to see – of prehistoric cave dwellings
in the red sandstone cliffs.

AROUND KIDDERMINSTER

SHATTERFORD

3 miles NW of Kidderminster on the A442

Shatterford Wildlife Sanctuary is home
to Sika deer, red deer, goats, sheep, wild
boar, pot-bellied pigs and koi carp.

Two miles further north, off the A442,
Kingsford Country Park covers 200
acres of heath and woodland that is
home to a wide variety of birdlife. It
extends into Kinver Edge, across the
border into Staffordshire, and many
waymarked walks start at this point.

BEWDLEY

3 miles W of Kidderminster on the A456

On the western bank of the
Severn, linked to its suburb
Wribbenhall by a fine Thomas
Telford Bridge, Bewdley was once
a flourishing port, but lost some
of its importance when the
Staffordshire & Worcestershire
Canal was built. It's a quiet,
civilised but much visited little
town with some good examples
of Georgian architecture, and
has won fame with another
form of transport, the **Severn
Valley Railway**.

River Severn, Bewdley

Guaranteed to excite young and old
alike, the Severn Valley Railway operates
a full service of timetabled trains hauled
by a variety of steam locomotives. The
service runs from Kidderminster to
Bridgnorth, home of the railway since
1965, and the route takes in such scenic
attractions as the Wyre Forest and the
Severn Valley Country Park and Nature
Reserve. Each of the six stations is an
architectural delight, and there are
buffets at Bridgnorth and Kidderminster,
and a tea room at Bewdley. One of the
most popular offerings is Sunday lunch
on the move, with trains starting from
both Bridgnorth and Kidderminster.
Advance booking for dining is essential:
call 01299 403816. The same number
gets through to the booking service for
the footplate experience courses, where
railway buffs and children (current or
second time round) can realise a dream
by learning to fire and drive a steam
locomotive. Special events take place
throughout the year, and include
Thomas the Tank Engine weekends in
May, a nostalgic 1940s weekend in July,
an autumn steam gala in September, and
a classic vehicle day in mid-October. In
Kidderminster itself additional
attractions include a railway museum
and the King & Castle public house
serving an excellent choice of home-
cooked food and real ales.

Bewdley Museum, which also
incorporates the Tourist Information
Centre, is a great place for all the family,

Severn Valley Railway

WEST MIDLAND SAFARI & LEISURE PARK

Spring Grove, Bewdley, Worcestershire DY12 1 LF
Tel : 01299 402114   Fax : 01299 404519
e-mail : info@wmsp.co.uk website : www.wmsp.co.uk

Go wild on a fantastic day out to **West Midland Safari and Leisure Park**. See a magnificent display of rare and exotic animals in the four mile drive through safari, including the endangered African Wild Dogs; beautiful White Tigers; African Elephants; Lions; Rhino; Giraffe, to name just a few.

There's plenty to explore on foot too; including the Explorers Trail with Sealion Theatre; Seal Aquarium; Reptile House; Friendly Animal & Reptile Encounter, Creepy Crawlies and Seaquarium Exhibit. Furthermore, the Hippo Lakes are home to the largest family group of Hippo in Europe. And, if it's pure adventure you're seeking, then the Leisure Area packed with a variety of family fun rides, is sure to excite.

There are lots of places to picnic; souvenir shops to browse and places to eat. Between March and November the Park is open every day and there is wheelchair access throughout. Dogs are not allowed in the Park but kennels are provided for those visitors who arrive with their pet.

For a small additional charge, guided tours are available by Safari Bus and there is free parking.

with exhibitions themed around the River Severn and the **Wyre Forest**. Crafts depicted include charcoal-burning, coopering and brass-making. Bewdley was the birthplace of Stanley Baldwin, three times Prime Minister between the Wars.

CALLOW HILL

5 miles W of Kidderminster on the A456

The **Wyre Forest Visitor Centre** (see panel on page 80) is set among mature oak woodland with forest walks, picnic area, gift shop and restaurant. Wyre Forest covers a vast area starting

northwest of Bewdley and extending into Shropshire. The woodland, home to abundant flora and fauna, is quite dense in places. It was once inhabited by nomadic people who made their living from what was around them, weaving baskets and brooms, burning charcoal and making the little wooden whisks which were used in the carpet-making process. Just south of Callow Hill, the village of **Rock** has an imposing Norman church in a prominent hillside position with some lovely windows and carving.

STOURPORT-ON-SEVERN

3 miles S of Kidderminster on the A451

At the centre of the Worcestershire waterways is the unique Georgian "canal town" of Stourport, famous for its intricate network of canal basins. There was not much trade, nor even much of a town, before the canals came, but prosperity came quickly once the **Staffordshire & Worcestershire Canal** had been dug. The commercial trade has gone, but the town still prospers, the barges laden with coal, timber, iron and grain having given way to pleasure craft. Many of the old barges have been renovated and adapted to this new role.

ASTLEY

5 miles S of Kidderminster on the A451

Stanley Baldwin (1867-1947) died at Astley Hall, opposite which, by the B4196, stands a memorial stone inscribed

Continued on page 80

WALK 2

Witley Court and Abberley Hill

Start	Great Witley - car park at junction of A443 and B4197
Distance	6½ miles (10.5 km). Shorter version 5 miles (8km)
Approximate time	3½ hours (2½ hours for shorter version)
Parking	Great Witley
Refreshments	Pub at Great Witley, pub at Abberley
Ordnance Survey maps	Landranger 138 (Kidderminster & Wyre Forest) and Pathfinder 973, SO 66/76 (Great Witley)

There is considerable historic and scenic appeal on this walk amidst the well-wooded Abberley Hills, which rise to almost 1000ft (305m) above the fields and orchards that lie between the Severn and Teme valleys. Historic interest is provided by the extensive remains of Witley Court, the flamboyant 18th century church next to it and, in complete contrast, the ruins of the simple Norman church at Abberley. The main scenic attraction is the splendid ridgetop walk along Abberley Hill, which is reached by a fairly steep climb from the starting point at Great Witley. The shorter version of the walk omits an initial detour to visit Witley Court.

If following the shorter version, start with your back to the road and climb a stile on the right-hand side of the car park. Walk along a paved path in front of a building and follow it round to the left to another stile. Climb that and walk diagonally across a field to come out on to a road, turning left to join the longer route just before **B** *below.*

The full walk includes a detour of about 1½ miles (2.4km) to visit Witley Court and church, which is eminently worthwhile. From the car park turn left along the road, take the first turning on the right (signposted 'Witley Court and Church') and then follow a rough broad track for ¾ mile (1.25km) to reach the entrance to Witley Court **A**.

Originally built in the 17th century, Witley Court was rebuilt on a palatial scale by the 1st Earl of Dudley in 1860, but was gutted by fire in 1937. Since then it has stood, a rather melancholic but impressive empty shell, and

the remains of its state rooms, orangery, terraces and the gardens still convey something of the former grandeur of this huge palace. The church that adjoins it looks as if it has been transplanted from Italy or Austria. It was built by the 1st Lord Foley in 1735 in the Rococo style; unusual and very un-English but undeniably beautiful with a most ornate and colourful interior.

Retrace your steps back to the road, keep straight ahead on the road, signposted to Stourport, and follow it to a T-junction **B**. Turn left and, at a public bridleway sign to Shavers End, turn right on to a tarmac track. The track soon becomes a sunken path, initially between trees and embankments on both sides, and later continues uphill between orchards. Pass through a gate to a footpath sign just ahead and, ignoring a bridleway turning to the right, keep straight ahead, climbing steeply through woodland to a T-junction of paths **C**.

WALK 2

Turn left along a clear path that winds between trees, take the left-hand upper path at a fork and continue along the wooded ridge, heading uphill to a Worcestershire Way post. Here follow the direction of the yellow waymark slightly to the right to continue along this fine ridge walk, with spectacular views through the trees on both sides, still winding uphill all the time to reach the triangulation pillar at the top of Abberley Hill, 928ft (283m) high. Follow Worcestershire Way signs past the triangulation pillar, now heading downhill, to climb a stile on to a lane.

Turn right and, at a Worcestershire Way sign **D**, turn left to head steeply downhill once more, making directly for Abberley village in front. Climb one stile, turn left along the edge of a field, climb another and continue, crossing a concrete path to a third stile. Climb that, head downhill across a field to climb a stile in the bottom corner and keep ahead a few yards to a track, turning right into the village. In front of you are the remains of a small 12th century church and to the left you can see the tower and spire of its 19th-century successor, built by the Victorian era the Norman church was considered to be beyond repair, following centuries of neglect. After the construction of the new church, the earlier building continued to deteriorate until restoration began in 1963. Two doorways and the foundations of the west end belong to the original 12th century building; the restored chapel is a 14th century extension.

Turn left along the road to a T-junction **E** and then left again. At a footpath sign to Abberley Common, turn left through a metal kissing-gate and head gently uphill, by a hedge and wire fence on the left, continuing past a now redundant kissing-gate to keep along the right-hand edge of a field. From here there are wide open views, especially to the right looking across to the line of the Clee Hills. On reaching a road **F**

turn left and continue for just over ¼ mile (400m) to a junction, keep ahead for a few yards and, opposite a lane leading off to the left, turn right on to a track, at a Worcestershire Way sign and public bridleway sign to Stanford Road **G**.

The track heads uphill, passing to the right of an ornate Victorian clock-tower, built in 1883 by the owner of Abberley Hall, which is now a school. At a junction of tracks keep ahead, walking to the right of school buildings, and continue along a broad track lined with trees to pass through the lodge gates of Abberley Hall to a road. Turn left along the road for almost ½ mile (800m) and, just before reaching a junction, turn right along a narrow lane **H**. After about ½ mile (800m) before the road starts to bear to the right, turn left over a stile **J**.

Continue along the field edge to a stile. On the left is a fine view of Abberley Hill. Climb this stile and then a second to walk across the next field towards a pool. Go through a metal gate and keep by the edge of the pool to join a track that leads to a road. Turn left for the short distance back to the start.

WYRE FOREST VISITOR CENTRE & DISCOVERY CENTRE

Callow Hill, Bewdley, Worcestershire DY14 9XQ
e-mail: wyre.forest.discovery.centre@forestry.gsi.gov.uk

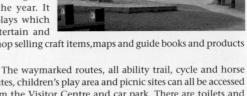

The Forestry Commission's Wyre Forest is one of the largest areas of semi natural oak woodland in Britain. It is managed for visitors, wildlife, timber and education.

The **Wyre Forest Visitor Centre**, in its delightful woodland setting, is open throughout the year. It provides home cooked food, unique displays which change with the seasons, designed to entertain and inform. There is an information point and shop selling craft items, maps and guide books and products for walkers.

The waymarked routes, all ability trail, cycle and horse routes, children's play area and picnic sites can all be accessed from the Visitor Centre and car park. There are toilets and disabled and baby changing facilities. For further information about the Visitor Centre, please phone 01299 266944.

The **Wyre Forest Discovery Centre** is situated close to the Visitor Centre and offers a wide range of educational programmes for schools, as well as holiday activities for families, craft and wildlife courses for adults, talks and guided walks. For further information about the Discovery Centre, please phone 01299 266929.

"Thrice Prime Minister". Astley is also home to **Astley Vineyards**, a working vineyard producing award-winning white wines, with a vineyard trail and a shop. Go by car, by bus - or by boat, as they have mooring facilities.

ABBERLEY

7 miles SW of Kidderminster off the A451

A truly delightful little place, surrounded by hills. The Norman Church of St Michael was saved from complete dilapidation in the 1960s, and the part that survives, the chancel, is certainly well worth a visit, not only for its charming ambience but also for the treasures it holds. On the other side of the hill is Abberley Hall, now a school, with a Big Ben-like bell tower that can be seen for miles around. Old Boys include former Foreign Secretary Geoffrey Howe and the late actor Sir Anthony Quayle.

GREAT WITLEY

8 miles SW of Kidderminster on the A443

There are two great reasons not to miss this place! **Great Witley Church**, almost ordinary from the outside, has an unbelievable interior of Baroque flamboyance that glows with light in a stunning ambience of gold and white. Masters of their crafts contributed to the interior, which was actually removed from the Chapel of Canons in Edgware: Joshua Price stained glass, Bellucci ceiling paintings, Bagutti plasterwork.

Next to the church are the spectacular and hauntingly beautiful remains of **Witley Court**, a palatial mansion funded by the riches of the Dudley family. Destroyed by fire in 1937, it stood a neglected shell for years, until English Heritage took over these most splendid of ruins and started the enormous task of

Witley Court

making them safe and accessible. If you only see one ruin in the whole county, this should be it. Across from the ruins is a magnificent fountain, said to be the largest in Britain. Inspired by Bernini's fountains in Rome, it rises 26ft feet and is crowned by an opulent sculpture that depicts Perseus rescuing Andromeda from a sea-monster. Also within the grounds is the **Jerwood Sculpture Park** which has a permanent collection including work by Elizabeth Frink and Anthony Gormley and also stages temporary exhibitions during the summer months.

TENBURY WELLS
12 miles SW of Kidderminster on the A456

The A443 leads from Great Witley towards Shropshire and the border town of Tenbury Wells in a delightfully rural setting on the River Teme. The "Wells" was added when a source of mineral water was discovered, but its heyday as a spa resort was very brief. **Tenbury Museum** tells the spa story and depicts other aspects of local life, including hop-growing and the railway days. In the market place is a curious oval-shaped building with rather ecclesiastical-looking windows. This is the **Market House** which was built in 1811 and used as a corn and butter market.

Set in sweeping lawns on the banks of the Teme, in the village of **Burford** a mile west of Tenbury (and just in Shropshire) stands **Burford House**, whose four-acre gardens are filled with well over 2,000 varieties of plants. This is the home of the National Collection of Clematis, and in the nursery attached to the garden almost 400 varieties of clematis are for sale, along with many other plants and gifts. The ground floor of the house is open as a gallery of contemporary art. Teas and light meals are served in the Burford Buttery.

3 SHROPSHIRE

Shropshire was recently accorded the title of *"The Most Romantic County in Britain"* and it doesn't take long to succumb to its charm. Its tranquil face belies an often turbulent past that is revealed at scores of sites by the remains of dykes and ramparts and hill forts, and by the castles of the Marcher Lords, who seem to have divided their time between fighting the Welsh and fighting each other. The county boasts some of Britain's most important Roman sites, notably at Wroxeter, which at one time was the fourth largest Roman town in the land. Shropshire beckons

Offa's Dyke

with a landscape of great variety: the little hills and valleys, the lakes and canals of the northwest, the amazing parallel hill ranges towards the south, the rich farming plains around Oswestry, the forests of Clun and Wyre, Ironbridge Gorge, called "the birthplace of the Industrial Revolution". This stretch of the Severn Valley is now a World Heritage Centre, which ranks it alongside the Pyramids, the Grand Canyon and the Taj Mahal, and several interesting museums can be found here. Add to this the historic towns of Shrewsbury, Ludlow and Oswestry, the churches and the stately homes and the glorious gardens and you have a part of the world just waiting to be explored, whether by car, on a bike or on foot. South Shropshire affords a trip through romance and history, including the wonderful town of Ludlow and the spectacular scenery of Wenlock Ridge, Long Mynd and Clun Forest.

ADVERTISERS AND PLACES OF INTEREST

LOCATOR MAP

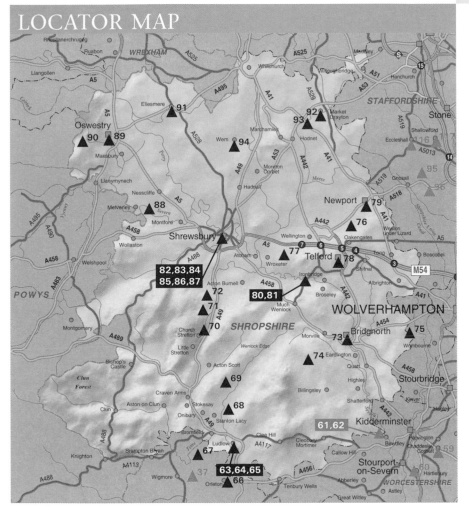

LUDLOW

Often called *"the perfect historic town"*, Ludlow is an enchanting place with more than 500 listed buildings and a medieval street pattern that has been kept virtually intact. There are some lovely walks along the banks of the River Teme with its plentiful wildlife, markets on Mondays, Fridays and Saturdays (plus Wednesdays in summer), a livestock market on Mondays, and regular flea markets on Sundays.

Ludlow Castle was built by the Normans in the 11th century, one of a line of castles along the Marches to keep out the Welsh. Under its protection a large town was planned and built - and prospered, due to the collection and sale of wool and the manufacture of cloth. The Castle has been home to many distinguished families and to Royalty: Edward V, Prince Arthur and other Royal children were brought up in Ludlow, and the Castle became the headquarters of the Council of the Marches, which governed Wales and the border counties until 1689. Nowadays the past combines dramatically with the future in the **Holodeck**, where hologram images create ultra-realistic 3D illusions.

Ludlow Castle

The Giant Kaleidoscope gives the viewer the sensation of standing before a globe of light and an ever-changing surface of colours, and the **Well of Infinity** is an apparently bottomless hole in the

THE CHOCOLATE GOURMET

16 Castle Street, Ludlow, Shropshire SY8 1AT
Tel: 01584 879332
e-mail: sales@chocmail.co.uk website: www.chocmail.co.uk

For chocoholics **The Chocolate Gourmet** must seem like heaven on earth. Janette Rowlatt's town centre shop offers a huge selection of confectionery from around the world, not just chocolate but also hand-beaten fudge, traditional sweets such as butter brazils, mint humbugs, Russian toffees, and the original gourmet "Jelly Belly" jelly beans with authentic flavours in both the centre and shell. Also on sale are high quality truffles, couverture chocolate, organic chocolate, 'grand cru' and single origin chocolate bars. Luxury gift boxes are a speciality, tied with exquisite ribbons. And if you can't get to this chocolate lovers paradise, a mail order service is available.

Broad Street, Ludlow

rebuilding in the 15th century. There are fine misericords and stained glass, and the poet AE Housman, author of *A Shropshire Lad*, is commemorated in the churchyard. Other places which should be seen include **Castle Lodge**, once a prison and later home of the officials of the Council of the Marches, and the fascinating houses that line Broad Street.

ground – on the first floor. The parish **Church of St Laurence** is one of the largest in the county, reflecting the town's affluence at the time of its

Ludlow Museum, in Castle Street has exhibitions of local history centred on, among other things, the Castle, the

Mr Underhill's at Dinham Weir

Dinham, Ludlow, Shropshire SY8 1EH
Tel: 01584 874431 website: www.mr-underhills.co.uk

Mr Underhill's occupies a glorious position below the castle on the banks of the river Teme. Nestled in a conservation area the wooded walks of the Whitcliffe Common and Mortimer trail are just the other side of the river, whilst the market square is only five minutes walk away. Ludlow is a very special little town famed for amongst other things its 500 listed buildings, Shakespeare & Food Festivals and good eating. This stylish Restaurant with rooms was hailed as the winner in its class by the Good Hotel Guide in 2000, an achievement consolidated when Mr Underhill's received a similar award from the *Which Hotel Guide 2002*.

Chris and Judy Bradley moved to Ludlow in 1997 having previously run a restaurant, also called Mr Underhill's, in Stonham, Suffolk. They believe that there is more to a meal than just good food- it should be combined with caring attentive service in relaxed, comfortable surroundings. Chris, whose cooking has won a coveted Michelin star, is totally self taught. The emphasis is on freshly prepared local produce. Your personalised menu might start with a risotto of locally smoked haddock moving on to fillet of Mortimer Forest venison with red wine and pure dark chocolate followed by cheeses or an apple and quince crumble with honey and calvados ice cream. The attention to detail and comfort continues in the newly styled bedrooms, all with large, comfortable, hand-made beds, ultra large fluffy towels and wonderful river views.

BROMLEY COURT

Broadgate Mews, 73/74 Lower Broad Street, Ludlow,
Shropshire SY8 1PH
Tel: 01584 876996 Reservations: 'Local call rate' 0845 0656 192
website: www.ross-b-and-b-ludlow.co.uk
Bromley Court offers much more than just bed & breakfast. Located
within the Ludlow conservation area and originally three Tudor
cottages, each suite has its own sitting room and en suite bathroom,
and each is beautifully decorated and furnished. Each suite has a breakfast bar provided with everything
you need for a Continental breakfast or you can wander across the road to Mews Cottage Breakfast
Room for a full traditional English breakfast. And if you appreciate great food, there are plenty of
Michelin restaurants within walking distance.

town's trade and special features on local
geology and archaeology. At one time in
the last century glove-making was one of
the chief occupations in the town. Nine
master glovers employed some 700
women and children, each required to
produce ten pairs of gloves a week,
mainly for the American market.

The Ludlow Festival, held annually
since 1960 and lasting a fortnight in
June/July, has become one of the major
arts festivals in the country. The
centrepiece of the festival, an open-air
performance of a Shakespeare play in the
Castle's inner bailey, is supported by a
number of events that have included
orchestral concerts, musical recitals,
literary and historical lectures,
exhibitions, readings and workshops.

ORLETON FARM SHOP

Orleton Farm, Orleton, Ludlow, Shropshire SY8 4HZ
Tel/Fax: 01568 780750
website: www.orletonfarmshop.co.uk

The Lewis family have been farming for a number of
generations and in 1990, were one of the first in the
area to set up a farm shop to sell their produce. With
the farm (just a mile from the gourmet renowned town
of Ludlow), currently in organic conversion, the shop
concentrates mainly on sale of their traditionally home
reared Angus Beef, Lamb and Poultry. To compliment
this, the shop offers a range of quality fruit, veg, pies, cakes, preserves and much more. Two years ago,
saw the opening of Jenny's Kitchen, a modern and fully equipped kitchen which produces the cakes,
pies, preserves and jams sold in the shop. As Rosemary Lewis remarked, "Although the kitchen is
modern, satisfying hygiene standards, we have done out
best to stick to Grandma's recipes!"

In 1999 George Lewis introduced his market trailer to
Ludlow's historic market square. Each Friday and Saturday
the family sells a range of items from the shop, including
cakes, pies, jams and a full and extensive meat counter.
The year 2000 saw an extensive re-decoration of the shop
with a whole range of new shelving and the addition of a
cutting room to extend the work capability of the shop.
The family's enterprise was rewarded in 2002 when Orleton
Farm Shop was regional winner of the National Farmers
Union Great British Food Award.

THE BRAKES COUNTRY HOUSE

Downton, Ludlow, Shropshire SY8 2LF
Tel: 01584 856465 Fax: 01584 856764
e-mail: inquiry@the-brakes.co.uk
website: www.the-brakes.co.uk

Set in beautiful rolling Shropshire countryside, just ten minutes from historic Ludlow, **The Brakes Country House** is a charming old converted farmhouse that dates back to the 17th century. It stands in three acres of grounds where guests can relax, play croquet or badminton, or just enjoy the colourful garden with its lawns, rose beds and profusion of plants and flowering shrubs. The Brakes is the home of Tim and Tricia Turner, a welcoming couple who moved here in 1994 and have made their house one of the best guest houses in the area, earning themselves a 4-Diamonds Silver Award from the English Tourism Council.

Tricia is an accomplished cook and supervises all the catering herself – her 3-course dinner with a choice of 2 menus is a culinary treat based on top quality local produce such as Shropshire pork or Herefordshire beef. Their restaurant, The Dining Room at Brakes, has recently been opened to non-residents on Thursday, Friday and Saturday evenings. Accommodation at The Brakes comprises 3 spacious and well-appointed double bedrooms (which can also be arranged as twins), all with en suite facilities, colour television and hospitality tray. There are some delightful walks from the house – one ten-minute stroll leads to the River Teme where in summer you may well see otters at play.

AROUND LUDLOW

CLEOBURY MORTIMER

8 miles E of Ludlow on the A4117

A famous landmark in this pleasing small town just west of the Forest of Wyre is the crooked spire of **St Mary's Church**, whose east window commemorates the 14th century poet, William Langland. His best known work is *Piers Plowman,* an indignant tract against rural poverty in a landscape still recognisable as south Shropshire.

It was in Cleobury Mortimer that Maisie Bloomer, a witch, gained notoriety in the 18th century. Curses and love potions were her speciality, and the villagers were in no doubt that she was in league with the Devil.

Two miles east of Cleobury stands **Mawley Hall**, an 18th century stone house with some very fine internal features.

CLEE HILL

4 miles E of Ludlow on the A4117

The Clee Hills to the north of the village include the highest peaks in the county. The summit of **Brown Clee** is 1750 feet above sea level.

STANTON LACY

2 miles NW of Ludlow off the B4365

This charming little village with its black and white cottages sits on the bank of the River Corve and is notable for its Church of St Peter which has some Saxon features and Victorian stained glass.

BROMFIELD

3 miles NW of Ludlow on the A49

Although the busy A49 runs through the

SUTTON COURT FARM

Little Sutton, Stanton Lacy, Ludlow, Shropshire SY8 2AJ
Tel: 01584 861305 e-mail: suttoncourtfarm@hotmail.com
Fax: 01584 861441 website: www.suttoncourtfarm.co.uk

Set in the beautiful Corve Dale, just 5 miles from Ludlow, **Sutton Court Farm** offers quality self-catering accommodation in imaginatively converted stone barns. The 6 cottages are grouped around an attractive courtyard next to Jane Cronin's lovely 16th century timbered farmhouse and all have "stable doors" to admit fresh air and sunshine in good weather. Each has been individually furnished and comprehensively equipped and accommodates either 2, 4 or 6 guests. Shared amenities include a walled garden, indoor children's play area, tourist information room, paperback lending library and laundry facilities.Sutton Court Farm has been awarded 4 stars by the English Tourist Council.

centre of the village, **St Mary's Church** is beautifully sited close to where the River Teme joins up with the River Onney. Originally a priory, it became a private residence for one George Foxe following the dissolution of the monasteries. What is now the chancel was once the dining room but the extraordinary painted ceiling was created after the building once again became a church in the mid-1600s. The swirling figures with their ribbons bearing biblical texts have been described as "the best example of the worst style of ecclesiastical art". Another striking feature here is the huge mural coat of arms of Charles II on the south wall.

About a mile northeast of Bromfield is **Ludlow Racecourse** where Bronze Age barrows have been brought to light.

ONIBURY

5 miles NW of Ludlow off the A49

"I didn't know chickens could be so beautiful" was the comment of one visitor to **The Wernlas Collection**, a living museum of rare poultry. The setting of this 20-acre smallholding is a joy in itself, and the collection is an internationally acclaimed conservation centre and vital gene pool where over 15,000 chicks are hatched each year, all year round. Besides the 220 breeds of chickens

there are rare breeds of goats, sheep and pigs, and some donkeys. The gift shop is themed on chickens - a chickaholic's paradise, in fact - and eggs and vaccinated and salmonella tested chicks are also on sale.

STOKESAY

7 miles NW of Ludlow off the A49

The de Say family of nearby Clun started **Stokesay Castle** in about 1240, and a Ludlow wool merchant, Lawrence de Ludlow, made considerable additions, including the Great Hall and fortified south tower. It is the oldest fortified

Stokesay Castle

manor house in England and is substantially complete, making it easy to see how a rich medieval merchant would have lived. Entrance to this magnificent building is through a splendid timber-framed gatehouse and the cottage-style gardens are an extra delight. An audio tour guides visitors round the site.

The adjacent parish church of **St John the Baptist** is unusual in having been restored during Cromwell's rule after sustaining severe damage in the Civil War. A remarkable feature in the nave is a series of biblical texts written in giant script on the walls, the 17th century box pews and pulpit are still in use and, outside, the churchyard is managed as "semi-wild", allowing some 88 species of wild flowers to flourish.

CRAVEN ARMS

The village takes its name from the hotel and pub built by the Earl of Craven. The coming of the railways caused the community to be developed, and it was also at the centre of several roads that were once used by sheep-drovers moving their flocks from Wales to the English markets. In its heyday Craven Arms held one of the largest sheep auctions in Britain, with as many as 20,000 sheep being sold in a single day.

Shropshire's landscape has inspired the music of Vaughan Williams, the poems of A.E. Housman and the novels of Mary Webb. At the recently-opened **Secret Hills**, Shropshire Hills Discovery Centre, visitors can discover the heritage, wildlife and traditions of the area in a striking all-weather building with a grass roof made from 1,000 square metres of turf weighing more than 70 tons. Rocks that have travelled 7,000 miles from the equator over the last 560 million years; a mammoth skeleton from Shropshire's last Ice Age 13,000 years ago, and a simulated balloon flight over the hills are just some of the attractions. Outside, visitors can wander through 25 acres of attractive meadows sloping down to the River Onney. The centre has a gift shop, café and information point, and there's a programme of regular events and craft exhibitions throughout the year.

AROUND CRAVEN ARMS

CLUN

8 miles W of Craven Arms on the A488/B4368

A quiet, picturesque little town in the valley of the River Clun, overlooked by the ruins of its **Castle**, which was once the stronghold of the Fitzalan family. The shell of the keep and the earthworks are the main surviving features. The **Church of St George** has a fortress-like tower with small windows and a lovely 17th century tiered pyramidal top. There

Clun Castle

are also some splendid Norman arcades with circular pillars and scalloped capitals. The 14th century north aisle roof and restored nave roof are an impressive sight that will keep necks craning for some time. Some wonderful Jacobean woodwork and a marvellous medieval studded canopy are other sights worth lingering over at this beautiful church, which is a great tribute to GE Street, who was responsible for its restoration in 1876. Geological finds are the main attractions in the little **Local History Museum** in the Town Hall. The real things are to be found on site at **Bury Ditches**, north of Clun on the way to Bishop's Castle. The Ditches are an Iron Age fort on a 7-acre tree-covered site.

Down the valley are other Cluns: **Clunton, Clunbury** and **Clungunford**. This quartet was idyllically described by AE Housman in *A Shropshire Lad:*

> *In valleys of springs and rivers,*
> *By Onny and Teme and Clun,*
> *The country for easy livers,*
> *The quietest under the sun.*

ASTON ON CLUN

3 miles W of Craven Arms off the B4368

Not one of Housman's Cluns, but well worth a mention and a visit. The village's **Arbor Tree Dressing** ceremony has been held every year since 1786. Following the Battle of Worcester in 1651, King Charles spent some time up a tree (see under Boscobel) and to commemorate his escape he proclaimed Arbor Day, a day in May, as a national holiday when tree-dressing took place. The custom generally died out but was revived here in 1786 when a local landowner married. As Aston was part of his estate he revived the tradition of dressing the Black Poplar in the middle of the village, a custom that still survives.

BISHOP'S CASTLE

9 miles NW of Craven Arms off the A488

This small and ancient town lies in an area of great natural beauty in solitary border country. Little remains of the castle, built in the 12th century for the Bishops of Hereford, which gave the place its name, but there is no shortage of fine old buildings for the visitor to see. The **House on Crutches Museum**, sited in one of the oldest and most picturesque of these buildings, recounts the town's history. Its gable end is supported on wooden posts – hence the name. North of Bishop's Castle lie the **Stiperstones**, a rock-strewn quartzite outcrop rising to a height of 1,700ft at the Devil's Chair. A bleak place of brooding solitude, the ridge is part of a 1,000-acre National Nature Reserve and on the lower slopes gaunt chimneys,

CHADSTONE GUEST HOUSE

Aston Munslow, nr Ludlow, Shropshire SY7 9ER
Tel: 01584 841675   e-mail: chadstone.lee@btinternet.com
Fax: 01584 841620   website: www.chadstonebandb.co.uk

Chadstone Guest House enjoys a ravishing location in beautiful Corvedale with panoramic views of the Clee Hills. It stands in two acres of delightful landscaped grounds and is within easy reach of historic Ludlow (just 9 miles away), Much Wenlock and Wenlock Edge. Your hosts, John and Judith Lee, offer a full English breakfast based on local produce and evening meals are available by arrangement. There are 3 guest bedrooms (2 twins, 1 double), all with en suite facilities, remote control TV, clock radio and hospitality tray. Guests also have the use of a spacious lounge well-provided with books, maps and tourist information.

derelict buildings and neglected roads and paths are silent reminders of the lead-mining industry that flourished here from Roman times until the 19th century. To the west, on the other side of the A49 near **Chirbury**, is **Mitchell's Fold** stone circle, a Bronze Age circle of 15 stones. This is Shropshire's oldest monument, its origins and purpose unknown.

ACTON SCOTT

5 miles NE of Craven Arms off the A49

Signposted off the A49 just south of Church Stretton, **Acton Scott Historic Working Farm** offers a fascinating insight into farming and rural life as practised in the South Shropshire hills at the close of the 19th century. Owned by Shropshire County Council, it is a living museum with a commitment to preserving both traditional farming techniques and rural craft skills. Every day visitors can see milking by hand and butter-making in the dairy. There are weekly visits from the wheelwright, farrier and blacksmith, while in the fields the farming year unfolds with ploughing, sowing and harvesting; special attractions include lambing, shearing, cider-making and threshing with steam and flail. The waggoner and his team of heavy horses provide the power to work the land, while the stockman looks after the farm's livestock, among which are many rare breeds of cattle, sheep and pigs.

CHURCH STRETTON

The town has a long history - King John granted a charter in 1214 - and traces of

WILLOWFIELD COUNTRY GUEST HOUSE

Lower Wood, Church Stretton, Shropshire SY6 6LF
Tel/Fax: 01694 751471
website: www.willowfieldguesthouse.co.uk

Occupying a lovely position in the heart of Shropshire, surrounded by spectacular hills and valleys, **Willowfield Country Guest House** offers all the warmth of a traditional country home together with accommodation awarded a 5 Diamonds ratng by both the English Tourism Council and the AA. The house was originally built in 1630 for the widow of the manor of Stretton-en-le-dale and at that time was called "Widowsfield". Extended in the early 1900s, the house has a fascinating blend of Elizabethan and Edwardian architecture, each room full of character. Willowfield is the home of Philip and Jane Secrett who assure all visitors of a warm and friendly welcome – and excellent food.

At breakfast time you'll find an extensive menu to suit all palates, guests can also enjoy a memorable candlelit dinner, including home grown fruit, vegetables and free range eggs, in the Elizabethan dining rooms with individual tables. Willowfield has 6 stylish en-suite bedrooms, each with its own character and each named after local hills. There's a choice of double, twin and king size posture sprung beds and one of the rooms is on the ground floor. Guests have the use of a charming lounge with an open fire or they can relax in the superb garden with its views of Caradoc and Lawley hills and beyond towards The Wrekin and Shrewsbury. The Willowfield Country Guest House is licenced and has a no smoking policy.

JINLYE

Castle Hill, All Stretton,
Church Stretton, Shropshire SY6 6JP
Tel: 01694 723243
Mrs Janet Tory & Miss Kate Tory.
e-mail: info@jynlye.co.uk
website: www.jinlye.co.uk

Standing 1400ft above sea level in 15 acres of private grounds, **Jinlye** occupies a

stunning position commanding some of the most spectacular views in the country. The house immediately adjoins the Long Mynd and 6000 acres of National Trust land which is designated as an area of outstanding natural beauty. It also provides a secure habitat for an enormous amount of wildlife – many rare birds, foxes and badgers, with wild ponies and sheep grazing outside the house.

Originally built as a crofter's cottage some 200 years ago, the house has always been known as Jinlye although throughout the 1800s it was often spelt "Gin-Lye". Owner Kate Tory explains that "lye" means meadow and she presumes that "gin" has something to do with gin traps being laid in the meadows.

It's difficult to credit now but when Kate's parents bought this charming property it had been derelict for nearly 15 years. The family rebuilt and extended the house in the 1970s and they have now been welcoming guests to their award winning B&B for more than 20 years. Fully refurbished in period style, Jinlye has a wealth of old beams, open log fires and leaded light windows, and a wonderfully relaxed atmosphere. Especially in the superb Reading Lounge which was once the barn but now has a large inglenook fireplace surrounded by comfortable deep sofas and easy chairs. Guests also have the use of a cosy television room, a large Victorian conservatory, and a seating area around an impressive stone fireplace in the dining room – a perfect place to catch up with the morning papers. There is also the award winning garden to enjoy and explore - over an acre full of many rare and interesting plants.

The guest bedrooms are all named after the particular hill that can be seen from the window. Each room is spacious, en suite and with its own particular charm. One has a splendidly carved 17th century French wedding bed; another boasts a king-size Gothic bedstead and there's also a 1940s Italian boudoir suite. There are also 2 ground floor rooms, one of which is suitable for the disabled.

If you prefer self-catering, you will enjoy the delightful self-catering cottage recently converted from an old stable block. The accommodation is extremely comfortable with wonderful views and peace and quiet.

Remote and beautiful though it is, Jinlye is only a mile from the village and within easy reach of Ludlow, Welshpool, Shrewsbury and the World Heritage Site of Ironbridge. All in all, an ideal base for exploring Shropshire and a wonderful house to which you will want to return again and again.

the medieval town are to be seen among the 18th and 19th century buildings in the High Street.

Elsewhere in the town, many of the black-and-white timbered buildings are not so old as they look, having been built at the turn of the century when the town had ideas of becoming a health resort. Just behind the High Street stands the **Church of St Laurence**, with Saxon foundations, a Norman nave and a tower dating from about 1200. Over the aisle is a memorial to a tragic event that happened in 1968 when three boys were killed in a fire. The memorial is in the form of a gridiron, with flakes of copper simulating flames. The gridiron is

Church Stretton

the symbol of St Laurence, who was burnt to death on one in AD258. The Victorian novelist Sarah Smith, who wrote under the name of Hesba Stretton, was a frequent visitor to nearby All Stretton, and there is a small memorial window to her in the south transept.

RECTORY FARM

Woolstaston, nr Church Stretton, Shropshire SY6 6NN
Tel: 01694 751306

Reached by quiet country lanes, just off the main A49 Shrewsbury to Hereford road, the tiny village of Woolstaston sits 750ft high on the flanks of the Long Mynd. Here you'll find **Rectory Farm**, a beautiful half-timbered farmhouse which enjoys spectacular views across the plains to Shropshire's best known landmark, The Wrekin. This historic house has a wonderful atmosphere and your host, Allison Rodenhurst, gives the warmest of welcomes – and the heartiest of country breakfasts! It's no surprise to discover that the Worldwide Bed & Breakfast Association voted Rectory Farm the "Best Bed & Breakfast in the Cotswolds and the Welsh Marches".

There are 3 guest bedrooms (1 double; 2 twins), each with colour TV and a well-appointed en suite bathroom. All command panoramic views of the surrounding countryside. Natural spring water, tea and coffee are provided in all rooms. Guests may also relax in the spacious oak-beamed lounge and cosy television room. A full English breakfast is included in the tariff; evening meals are not provided but there are many good pubs and restaurants within easy reach. So too are the beautiful moorlands and valleys of the Long Mynd, historic Shrewsbury and Ludlow, the World Heritage Site of Ironbridge and the Acton Scott Historic Working Farm.

WALK 3

The Long Mynd

Start	Church Stretton
Distance	8 miles (12.9 km)
Approximate time	4 hours
Parking	Church Stretton
Refreshments	Pubs and cafés at Church Stretton, National Trust café at Carding Mill Valley, pub at Little Stretton
Ordnance Survey maps	Landranger 137 (Ludlow and Wenlock Edge) and Pathfinder 910, SO 49/59 (Church Stretton)

The Long Mynd is the prominent whale-backed hill that rises abruptly above the western side of the Onny valley between Church Stretton and Craven Arms, looking out over the Welsh border country. Indeed the word 'mynd' is Welsh for mountain. On its eastern side it is cut into by a number of narrow valleys, locally called 'batches', and the walk begins by ascending one of these, the well-known Carding Mill Valley, to reach the ridge. Then follows a superlative ridgetop walk, with magnificent views on both sides, passing the highest point on the Long Mynd before descending back into the valley and returning to the start. Most of this spectacular and quite energetic walk is on National Trust land.

The pleasant little town of Church Stretton, lying at the foot of the Long Mynd, has all the ingredients that make up an excellent walking centre: cradled by hills and at the hub of a network of footpaths, with good communications by both road and rail, parking facilities and a number of hotels and guest houses, pubs and teashops. It has an agreeably old-fashioned air, as befits a town that became a health resort in the late Victorian era, but its main building is much older – a fine parish church which dates back to the Norman period.

The walk begins in the Square, off the High Street. Head northwards along the High Street and, at a crossroads, turn left along Burway Road, soon bearing right and following signs for the Burway and Long Mynd. The narrow lane heads steadily uphill for nearly ½ mile (800m), crossing a cattle-grid to enter the National Trust property of Long Mynd Ⓐ.

Here bear slightly right on to a track that heads along the side of the beautiful, steep-sided, gorse-, bracken- and heather-covered slopes of the Carding Mill Valley, with a stream below on the right. Ahead are fine views looking towards the head of the valley, which gets its name from the carding process, by which wool was 'carded' or combed prior to spinning. The track descends to the stream and joins a road; follow the road through the valley, passing by buildings that now belong to the National Trust, which include a gift shop and café. Turn right over a footbridge, turn left along a track – now the stream is on your left – soon rejoining the road, and continue along this as it climbs gently to reach a car park.

Bear slightly left to cross a footbridge and continue along a track, with the stream on the right, still climbing gently. Where the valley divides, bear right to cross the stream and continue uphill through the narrow, secluded right-hand valley, across heathery expanses and still with a stream on your right, eventually to reach the top of the broad ridge at a footpath sign and junction of tracks. Keep

WALK 3

ahead for a few yards and then turn left **B** on to the track that runs along the top of the Long Mynd, giving superb views in all directions.

Continue along this main track – there are at this point several parallel tracks – and at a junction of tracks keep straight ahead along a narrower track, passing to the left of a shooting-box to reach a lane **C**. Cross over and continue along the track ahead, crossing another track and heading up through heather to the triangulation pillar and toposcope on Pole Bank, at 1693ft (516m), the highest point on the Long Mynd. As might be expected, the all-round views over the Shropshire hills and Welsh borders are magnificent, and the toposcope shows that, in clear conditions, Cadair Idris and the Brecon Beacons can be seen, as well as closer features, including the Stiperstones, the hills of central Wales, Ragleth Hill, Caer Caradoc, the Clee Hills and Wenlock Edge.

Keep ahead past the triangulation pillar, descending gently to a lane and turn right along it to follow the line of a medieval trackway called the Port Way. Soon you pass a rare group of trees on the right and shortly afterwards, at a footpath sign to Little Stretton, turn left along a broad track **D**.

At a junction bear slightly left along a path through heather which keeps above the side of, and with views to the left over Ashes Hollow, one of the most beautiful of the 'batches' that cut into the flanks of the Long Mynd. The path later broadens into a track, heads downhill into an open grassy area called Barrister's Plain and then climbs again over the hill in front, passing to the left of a small isolated group of trees. Keep along this attractive green track high above Callow

Hollow on the right, continuing over the shoulder of another hill (Callow) above the right-hand side of the valley of Small Batch on the left. Ahead there is a glorious view across the Onny valley, overshadowed by Ragleth Hill, with the village of Little Stretton below and Wenlock Edge beyond.

The track descends gently, joining and keeping by a wire fence on the right. Later it bears slightly left away from the fence and descends more steeply to a stream. Go through a gate and keep ahead, walking along the right-hand side of the stream, and then crossing it to reach a track. Continue past cottages on the left, cross a footbridge and then turn right into Little Stretton, taking the first turning on the left to a T-junction **E**. Opposite is Little Stretton's unusual black-and-white wooden thatched church.

At the T-junction turn left along the road for 1½ miles (2.4km) back to Church Stretton; a pleasant and generally quiet road with a footpath on the right for most of the way. ●

A mile from the town centre are **Carding Mill Valley** and the extensive ridge known as **Long Mynd**. The valley and the moorland into which it runs are National Trust property and very popular for walking and picnicking. This wild area of heath affords marvellous views across Shropshire to the Cheshire Plains and the Black Mountains.

AROUND CHURCH STRETTON

LITTLE STRETTON

2 miles S of Church Stretton on the B4370

The village of Little Stretton nestles in the **Stretton Gap**, with the wooded slopes of Ragleth to the east and Long Mynd to the west. It is a peaceful spot, bypassed by the A49, and is a delightful place for a stroll. The most photographed building is **All Saints Church**, with a black and white timbered frame, a thatched roof and the general look of a cottage rather than a church. When built in 1903 it had an iron roof, but this was soon found to be too noisy and was replaced with thatch (heather initially, then the straw that tops it today). Among many other interesting buildings are **Manor House**, a cruck hall dating from 1500, and **Bircher Cottage**, of a similar vintage.

"Switzerland without the wolves and avalanches" is a description sometimes applied to this beautiful, serene part of the world.

ACTON BURNELL

7m NE of Church Stretton off the A49

This charming small village takes its name from Robert Burnell who was Bishop of Bath and Wells and Lord Chancellor to Edward I. In his latter role he entertained the king here in 1283 and one of the first true Parliaments took place in the castle (more of a fortified residence, really) whose ruins of bright red sandstone stand behind the church. Burnell had built the church of St Mary only a decade before the king's visit. It's an elegantly proportioned Early Gothic building with a simple interior that shows off to advantage the impressive late-16th century alabaster tomb of a later Lord of the Manor, Sir Richard Lee.

BRIDGNORTH

The ancient market town of Bridgnorth, straddling the River Severn, comprises **Low Town**, and, 100 feet up sandstone cliffs, **High Town**. The year 1101 is a key date in its history – the year in which the **Norman Castle** was built by Robert de Belesme from Quatt. All that remains of the castle is part of the keep tower, which leans at an angle of about 17 degrees (more than that of the Leaning Tower of Pisa) as a result of an attempt to demolish it after the Civil War. The castle grounds offer splendid views of the river, and when King Charles l stayed here in 1642 he declared the view from the **Castle Walk** to be the finest in his dominion. The **Bridgnorth Museum** is a good place to start a tour of this interesting town. It occupies rooms over the arches of the **North Gate**, which is the only one of the town's original fortifications to survive - though most of it was rebuilt in the 18th century. The **Costume and Childhood Museum** incorporates a costume gallery, a complete Victorian nursery and a collection of rare minerals. It's a really charming place that appeals to all ages. The Civil War caused great damage in Bridgnorth and the lovely **Town Hall** is one of many timber-framed buildings put up just after the war. The sandstone arched base was completed in 1652 and later covered in brick; Charles II took a great interest in it and when improvements were needed he made funds available from his own purse and from a collection he ordered be made in every parish in England.

St Mary's Street is one of the three streets off High Street which formed the planned new town of the 12th century. Many of the houses, brick faced over timber frames, have side passages leading to gardens which contained workshops and cottages. **Bishop Percy's House** is the oldest house standing in the town, a handsome building dating from 1580 and one of the very few timber-framed houses to survive the fire of 1646. It is named after the Reverend Dr Percy, who was born in the house in 1729 and became Bishop of Dromore.

For many visitors the most irresistible attraction in Bridgnorth is the **Castle Hill Cliff Railway**, funicular railway built in 1892 to link the two parts of the town. The track is 200ft long and rises over 100ft up the cliff. Originally it operated on a water balance system but it was converted in 1943 to electrically driven colliery-type winding gear. John Betjeman likened a ride on this lovely little railway to a journey up to heaven. For all but the very energetic it might feel like heaven compared to the alternative ways of getting from Low to High Town - seven sets of steps or Cartway, a meandering street that's steeped in history.

The bridge across the Severn, rebuilt in 1823 to a Thomas Telford design, has a clock tower with an inscription commemorating the building, in 1808, of the first steam locomotive at John Hazeldine's foundry a short distance upstream.

Talking of steam locomotives, Bridgnorth is the northern terminus of the wonderful **Severn Valley Railway.**

QUILTERS QUEST

7B Whitburn Street, Bridgnorth, Shropshire WV16 4QN
Tel: 01746 766632

The only needlecraft specialist suppliers in the area, **Quilters Quest** is a treasure house containing every conceivable item relating to the art and craft of needlework. This town centre shop is owned and run by Jane Rawlings, an accomplished craftswoman who is thoroughly skilled in all aspects of quilting, needlework and allied skills and always happy to offer help and advice.

A comprehensive range of quilting fabrics and panels is always in stock, including a new range of cotton fabrics, along with DMC and Maderia embroidery supplies, craft supplies, kits, fabrics and haberdashery.

For embroiderers, there's a wide range of DMC threads, silk ribbons and other materials available. Jane has introduced a new line in the form of a "Wedding Favours" service -either made to order, or supplies for clients to make their own. One of her most impressive creations is a specially commissioned tapestry of Bridgnorth's striking medieval Town Hall which is only available from Quilters Quest. Throughout the year Jane runs needlecraft classes and workshops for both adults and children. For full details of the variety of topics covered just send an SAE to Jane at Quilters Quest.

LOBBY STABLES

Lobby Farm, Oldfield, Bridgnorth, Shropshire WV16 6AQ
Tel: 01746 789218
e-mail: lobby_stables@lineone.net
website: www.shropshire-cottage.co.uk

Lobby Stables offers quality self-catering accommodation in a
peaceful rural location surrounded by lovely unspoilt countryside.
This imaginatively converted property has 3 bedrooms 1 double, 1
single, and 1 twin (the twin room and a bathroom are on the ground
floor), all are attractively furnished and decorated. The spacious ground floor lounge has a woodburning stove, storage heaters, TV, video, telephone and dining room. The kitchen is well-equipped,
including automatic washing machine, dishwasher, tumble dryer and microwave. Outside, there's an
enclosed garden with seating and barbecue, and ample parking space.

Guaranteed to excite young and old
alike, the railway operates a full service
of timetabled trains hauled by a variety
of steam locomotives. The service runs
from Kidderminster to Bridgnorth, home
of the railway since 1965, and the route
takes in such scenic attractions as the
Wyre Forest and the Severn Valley
Country Park and Nature Reserve. Each
of the six stations is an architectural
delight, and there are buffets at
Bridgnorth and Kidderminster, and a tea
room at Bewdley. One of the most
popular offerings is Sunday lunch on the
move, with trains starting from both
Bridgnorth and Kidderminster. Advance
booking for dining is essential: call
01299 403816. The same number gets
through to the booking service for the
footplate experience courses, where
railway buffs and children (current or

second time round) can realise a dream
by learning to fire and drive a steam
locomotive. Special events take place
throughout the year and include Thomas
the Tank Engine weekends in May, a
nostalgic 1940s weekend in July, an
autumn steam gala in September and
a classic vehicle day in mid-October

AROUND BRIDGNORTH

QUATT

4 miles SE of Bridgnorth on the A442

Quatt is the location of the National
Trust's **Dudmaston Hall**, a late 17th
century house with fine furniture, Dutch
flower paintings, modern pictures and
sculptures (Hepworth, Moore), botanical
art, watercolours, family and natural
history and colourful gardens with

WHITE COTTAGE COUNTRY CRAFTS

24 Post Office Road, Seisdon, nr Wombourne, Staffordshire WV5 7HA
Tel: 01902 896917

At **White Cottage Country Crafts** in the pretty village of Seisdon 6 miles east
of Bridgnorth enthusiasts will find a huge choice of patchwork and quilting
supplies, along with a wide selection of books and patterns. Owner Jacqueline
Taylor, who established her "cottage industry" in 1988, is one of the UK's leading
experts in her field. She gives talks all over the country and also conducts day
and weekend courses at local hotels. (Booking is essential.) The shop is open
10am to 5pm, Wednesday to Saturday; at other times by appointment, and a
mail-order service is also available.

lakeside walks, a rockery and a wooded valley. The church at Quatt contains some splendid monuments and memorials to the Wolryche family.

Nearby, in the grounds of Stanmore Hall on the Stourbridge road, is the **Midland Motor Museum**, with an outstanding collection of more than 100 vehicles, mostly sports and racing cars. The grounds also include a touring caravan site.

BILLINGSLEY

5 miles S of Bridgnorth on the B4363

In a beautiful wooded valley near the village, **Rays Farm Country Matters** is home to many farm animals including Highland cattle, deer, donkeys, goats and pigs, plus more than 50 owls. The longest bridleway in Shropshire, and one of the longest in the country, starts at the farm. This is the **Jack Mytton Way**, named after a 19th century hard-living squire and sometime MP for Shrewsbury. It runs all the way to Llanfair Waterdine in the Teme Valley, a distance of some 70 miles.

EARDINGTON

2 miles SW of Bridgenorth on the B4555

Eardington is a southern suburb of Bridgnorth, where, a mile out of town on the B4555, stands **Daniel's Mill**, a picturesque working watermill powered by an enormous (38ft) wheel. Family-owned for 200 years, the mill still produces flour.

MORVILLE

2 miles W of Bridgnorth on the A458

Morville Hall, 16th century with 18th century additions, stands at the junction of the A458 and B4368. Within its grounds, the **Dower House Garden** is a 1.5 acre site

designed by Dr Katherine Swift and begun in 1989. Its aim is to tell the history of English gardens in a sequence of separate gardens designed in the style of different historical periods. Particular attention is given to the use of authentic plants and construction techniques. Old roses are a speciality of the garden. Parking is available in the churchyard of the fine Norman Church of St Gregory, which is also well worth a visit.

MUCH WENLOCK

8 miles NW of Bridgnorth on the A458

The narrow streets of Much Wenlock are a delight to explore, and among the mellow buildings are some absolute gems. The **Guildhall** is one of them, dating from 1540 and added to in 1577 with a chamber over the stone medieval prison. The Guildhall was until recently used as a courtroom, and the Town Council still meets here once a month. The **Museum** is housed in the former market hall, which was built in 1878. There are interesting displays on the geology, flora and fauna of **Wenlock Edge** (see below), as well as local history items including Dr William Penny Brookes's Olympian Games. A forerunner of, and inspiration for the modern

Much Wenlock

TELFORD EQUESTRIAN CENTRE

Granville Country Park, Granville
Road, Donnington Wood, nr Telford,
Shropshire TF2 7QG
Tel/Fax: 01952 619825
Mobile: 07977 467455

Telford Equestrian Centre is located
within the Granville Country Park, an
ideal setting since the park provides
many safe hack routes with very little
or no road work. As well as having a
large indoor school, the Centre has a
varied selection of mounts to suit all
riders from absolute beginners to the
very proficient. The Centre was
established in 1992 by Mike and
Caroline Khan who stress the importance of riders being taught by qualified instructors. Mike himself
has a master's degree in Equine Science and they are both British Horse Society authorised instructors.

In addition to qualified instruction and hacking over varied terrain, the Centre also runs stable
management courses suitable for adults and children who wish to learn more about horse care. Outside
instructors are occasionally brought in to teach specialised lessons such as dressage and show jumping
and shows are arranged on a regular basis giving clients and liveries an opportunity for some friendly
competition. Particularly popular are the Centre's "Loan a Pony" weeks which provide a full 4-day
course in riding and pony care and are usually arranged during school holidays. The Centre offers all
types of livery and has its own shop - "Equine Togs".

AVENUE FARM B&B

Avenue Farm, Uppington, Telford, Shropshire TF6 5HW
Tel: 01952 740253 Fax: 01952 740401
e-mail: jones@avenuefarm.fsnet.co.uk
website: www.virtual-shropshire.co.uk/avenue-farm

Although located only 2 miles from junction 7 of the M54, **Avenue
Farm** enjoys a tranquil setting in the peaceful village of Uppington.
This charming 18th century farmhouse set in a large secluded garden
with superb views of the Wrekin is the home of Mig and Simon Jones
whose family have lived here since the early 1900s. Simon continues
the family tradition by farming the 600 acres that extends from the rear
of the house. The house itself looks delightful with its walls of mellow
red brick swathed in Virginia creeper.

Inside, there's a warm family atmosphere with lots of antique
furniture and a traditional country style of furnishings. Guests have

the use of a comfortable residents' sitting room with television
and a hearty breakfast, cooked on the faithful Aga, is served in
the attractive dining room. The accommodation has a 4-
Diamond rating from the AA and comprises 2 double rooms
with en suite facilities and 1 twin room with private bathroom.
The house is non-smoking; children are welcome, so too are
horses and ponies – stabling is available. Avenue Farm provides
an ideal base for exploring unspoilt Shropshire with the World
Heritage Site of Ironbridge, historic Shrewsbury, Weston Park
and the Severn Valley Railway all just a few miles away.

Olympic Games, they are an annual event in the town every year, having started in 1850. The good doctor lived in what is now Lloyds Bank.

Holy Trinity Church, "mother" to ten churches in villages around Much Wenlock, is a dominant presence in the town, though less conspicuous than it was until 1931 when its spire was removed. Its nave and chancel are Norman, the porch 13th century. The Parish Registers date from 1558.

The sight that simply must not be missed on a visit here is the ruined **Priory of St Milburga**. The Priory was originally a nunnery, founded in the 7th century by a Mercian princess and destroyed some 200 years later. Leofric, Earl of Mercia and husband of Lady Godiva, re-established it as a priory in 1050 and the current spectacular ruins belong to the Cluniac Priory rebuilt in the 12th and 13th centuries. The best remaining features are the wall carvings in the cloisters and the Norman interlacing of arches and doorways in the Chapter House. **The Prior's Lodge**, dating from about 1500, is particularly impressive with its steeply pitched roof of sandstone tiles above the rows of mullioned windows. Away from the main site is **St Milburga's Well**, whose waters are reputed to cure eye diseases.

WENLOCK EDGE

4 miles S of Much Wenlock on the B4371

Wenlock Edge is one of the most spectacular and impressive landmarks in the whole county, a limestone escarpment dating back 400 million years and a paradise for naturalists and lovers of the outdoors. It runs for 15 miles all the way down to Craven Arms. For centuries its quarries have produced the stone used in many of the local buildings; it was also a source of lime for agricultural fertiliser and much went into the blast furnaces that fired the Industrial Revolution.

TELFORD

Telford is a sprawling modern development that absorbed several existing towns in the region of the Shropshire coalfield. Wellington, Hadley, Ketley, Oakengates, Madeley and Dawley were among the towns to be incorporated, and the name chosen in the 1960s commemorates Thomas Telford, whose influence can be seen all over the county. Thomas Telford was a Scot, born in Eskdale in 1757, who came to Shrewsbury in 1786. Appointed County Surveyor, he quickly got to work on such enterprises as Shrewsbury jail, Bridgnorth, a host of bridges, an

JEWELLERY WITH MEANING

121a, Ashdown Lane, Telford, Shropshire TF3 4DY
Tel: 01952 299911
e-mail: sales@jewellery-with-meaning.com
website: www.jewellery-with-meaning.com

When you buy a piece of jewellery at Helen Bradley's **Jewellery with Meaning** you'll also be given information on how the item was made and the significance of whichever semi-precious stone has been used. Self-taught, Helen makes most of the items on sale in this colourful town centre shop, including hematite magnetic bracelets. These are reputed to be beneficial for ailments of the hands, wrists and fingers and can also be good for tension headaches and light migraines. Helen's bracelets are comfortable to wear and made of natural materials that will not irritate or leave any mark when worn.

Aqueduct, canals and the Holyhead Road. He designed distinctive milestones for the road, one of which is now at the Blists Hill Museum. Telford's many ambitious developments include the huge (450-acre) Town Park, with nature trails, sports fields, lakes, gardens and play areas. **Wonderland** is an enchanting and enchanted woodland whose fairytale attractions include Snow White's Cottage, the Three Little Pigs and the Wrekin Giant. On the northern outskirts, at Preston-on-the-Weald Moor, is **Hoo Farm Animal Kingdom**, which numbers among its inhabitants ostriches, chipmunks, deer and llamas. Events include lamb feeding, milking and the famous sheep steeplechase.

Telford Steam Railway Trust keeps a number of old locomotives, some of them ex-GWR, in working condition at the old shed and yard at Horsehay.

AROUND TELFORD

OAKENGATES
1 mile NE of Telford on the A5

Oakengates, on the eastern edge of the metropolis of Telford, is the birthplace of Sir Gordon Richards, perhaps the greatest jockey this country has ever produced. His father was a miner and the young Gordon first learned to ride on pit ponies. When he retired from the saddle, he had ridden 4,872 winners and was champion jockey for 20 years. Frankie and Kieren have a long way to go!

NEWPORT
6 miles NE of Telford off the A41

A handsome town which lost many of its buildings in a fire in 1665. Most of the buildings on the broad main street are Georgian or early Victorian. There's

THE ROCKING HORSE WORKS

Newport, Shropshire
Tel: 01952 811266 e-mail: steve@rockinghorseworks.co.uk
Fax: 01952 811266 website: www.rockinghorseworks.co.uk

At **The Rocking Horse Works**, Steve and Alison Smith continue a long tradition of fine craftsmanship producing exquisitely modelled wooden rocking horses. These enduringly popular playthings were originally created as a device to provide a child with basic riding instruction but quickly became beloved nursery companions. Steve and Alison began making them in 1985 when they were travelling the English canals in a 72ft narrowboat. As the business flourished "We abandoned our romantic, nomadic lifestyle" they say, "and gave our rocking horses a secure footing on land".

There's still a canal connection however since their workshop is located on a quiet, rural arm of the

canal network. Here, they and their small team of artist-craftsmen create individual and unique horses, each of which is the work of a single craftsman from start to finish. Real horsehair is used for the mane and tail, and the tack is crafted by a Master Saddler from the famous leatherworking district of Walsall in the Black Country. A brass plate is fitted to each horse, engraved with the company name, an individual registration number and, if desired, your own short message. The workshop also has a number of restored rocking horses for sale and offers a comprehensive restoration service.

plenty to keep the visitor active in the area, including the **Lilleshall National Sports Centre** and the ruins of Lilleshall Abbey, the extensive and evocative remains of an Augustinian abbey.

SHIFNAL

3 miles E of Telford on the A464

Once a staging post on the Holyhead Road, Shifnal has an unexpectedly large church with a Norman chancel arch, a 14th century east window, carved Italian pulpit and an Italian reredos.

On the A41, at **Cosford** near Shifnal, the **RAF Museum** (free) is home to an important collection of aircraft, aero engines and missiles from all over the world. Classic British airliners like the Comet, Britannia, Viscount and VC10 share space with warplanes such as the Spitfire, Mosquito, Lincoln and Liberator. The missile collection, numbering over 40, charts the development of these weapons of war from the 1920s to the present time.

TONG

5 miles E of Telford on the A41

Tong is an attractive village which once had a castle, founded, according to legend, by the wizard Merlin. Where was he when the castle was blown up in 1954? The Vernons and the Durants were the Lords of the Manor in Tong for many years and they are commemorated in 15th century **Church of St Bartholomew**. The Vernons were a particularly distinguished lot: one was a Speaker of the House of Commons and another was Lord High Constable to Henry V. In the Golden Chapel, which has a superb gilded, fan-vaulted ceiling, there is a bust of Arthur Vernon, who was a don at Cambridge University. Venetia Stanley, descended from the Vernons and the Earls of Derby, was a famed beauty who

was lauded by poets and artists. She counted Ben Jonson, Van Dyck and the Earl of Dorset among her lovers, but in 1625 she made the unfortunate move of marrying Sir Kenelm Digby, whose father had been executed for his part in the Gunpowder Plot. She died tragically young, some say at the hands of her jealous husband.

BOSCOBEL

7 miles E of Telford off the A41

After Charles II was defeated by the Roundheads at the Battle of Worcester in 1651, he fled for his life and was advised to seek refuge in a remote hunting lodge called **Boscobel House**, already known as a safe house for royals on the run. By day the King hid in the branches of an old oak tree, while at night he would creep into the house and hide in secret rooms with one of his trusty officers. He eventually escaped, of course, and nine years later was restored to the throne. The house has changed considerably since Charles's time, but it's still full of atmosphere and interest, with an exhibition giving a vivid account of the King's adventures. Every visitor naturally wants to see the famous oak in which he hid, but it is no longer standing, destroyed by souvenir-hunting loyalists. Today there stands a descendant of the original, itself now more than 300 years old.

BROSELEY

5 miles S of Telford on the B4373

Broseley, which stands on the south side of the River Severn opposite Ironbridge, was the headquarters of John Wilkinson, the great ironmaster and head of a giant empire. It was while he was living at **The Lawns** in Broseley that he commissioned the Shrewsbury architect Thomas Pritchard to design the world's first iron bridge. He also launched the first iron boat, *The Trial*, on the Severn in 1787 and even designed his own iron coffin. Broseley was the centre of an ancient local industry in clay products and tobacco pipes, and the **Pipe Museum**, untouched for more than 40 years, is a time-capsule factory where the famous Broseley Churchwarden pipes

View of the Bridge, Ironbridge

were made until 1957. Just north of Broseley, off the B4375, on a plateau above a gorge, stands **Benthall Hall**, a 16th century building in the care of the National Trust, with mullioned windows and a magnificent interior with a carved oak staircase, elaborate plaster ceilings and the Benthall family's collection of furniture, ceramics and paintings. There's a carefully restored plantsman's garden and, in the grounds, an interesting Restoration church.

IRONBRIDGE AND IRONBRIDGE GORGE

4 miles SW of Telford on the B4373

This is it, the town at the centre of Ironbridge Gorge, an area which has been designated a World Heritage Centre by UNESCO, ranking it alongside the likes of the Pyramids, the Grand Canyon and the Taj Mahal. It was the first British site on the list. The **Bridge** itself is a pedestrian right of way with a tollgate at one end, and the series of museums that spread along the banks of the Severn in **Ironbridge**, **Coalbrookdale**, **Coalport** and **Jackfield** pay tribute to the momentous events that took place here 250 years ago. The first iron wheels were made here, and also the first iron rails

and the first steam railway locomotive.

The **IronbridgeVisitor Centre** offers the ideal introduction to the attractions, and plenty of time should be devoted to the individual museums. The **Museum of Iron** in Coalbrookdale in the most historic part of the valley shows the whole story of ironmaking. Next to it is the original furnace used by Abraham Darby when he first smelted iron with coke; a little way north are **Rosehill House**, one of the homes of the Darby family, and **Dale House**, where Abraham Darby's grandson made his plans for the iron bridge.

Also in Coalbrookdale is **Enginuity**, the latest of Ironbridge's ten museums to open. Here, visitors can become apprentice engineers for the day, free to experiment with all the gadgets and acquire the know-how involved in producing everyday items. You can find out whether you can pull a real locomotive; test your speed and accuracy against a robot; control water to generate electricity or work as a team to make the "Crazy Boiler" blow its top!

The Old Police Station, owned by John and Lynn Youngman, is one of Ironbridge's less well known museums, but one that is well worth a visit, and for a variety of reasons. The Victorian station and its cells have been painstakingly restored to provide a fascinating insight into the judicial and prison systems at the turn of the century. After it closed for duty in 1964 it was used for various purposes before becoming home to police memorabilia from handcuffs and truncheons to uniforms and documents. The cells are particularly arresting – Cell 4 was the birching centre for Shropshire, and a birching stool still stands in the middle of the room. In the upper-floor theatre, using the unique backdrop of the former station and courthouse, Courthouse Productions put on a wide variety of corporate and personal events, from plays with a buffet supper to Courtroom trial re-enactments; from Victorian Music Halls to jazz and other musical events. Also on the premises is a tearoom where home baking, traditional afternoon teas and a Victorian buffet are among the offerings. Weddings are catered for at the station, and for an eve-of-wedding night with a difference the groom and best man can spend a night in the cells after the evening's celebrations, then wake up to a healthy breakfast before being delivered in style to the church! Also to be found in the Police Station is the **Left Centre**, which holds a vast stock of knives, scissors, kitchen tools and writing

aids for left-handers, plus anti-clockwise clocks and "the best of ambidextrous".

Also at Coalbrookdale is the **Ironbridge Open Air Museum of Steel Sculpture**, a collection of 60 modern steel sculptures of all shapes and sizes set in 10 acres of beautiful countryside.

The **Jackfield Tile Museum**, on the south bank, stands on the site of a world centre of the tile-making industry. The museum houses a fine collection of wall and floor tiles from Victorian times to the 1950s. Demonstrations of traditional tile-making take place regularly. Back across a footbridge to the **Coalport China Museum**, with its marvellous displays of two centuries of porcelain. Coalport was once one of the country's largest manufacturers of porcelain, starting life here but moving its factory to Stoke in the 1920s. Nearby is the extraordinary **Tar Tunnel** with its gushing spring of natural bitumen. It was a popular attraction for tourists in the 18th century, and it remains one of the most interesting geological phenomena in Britain. The tunnel was started in 1786, under the direction of ironmaster William Reynolds, who intended that it should be used for a canal to reach the shafts to the coal seams ¾ of a mile away on Blists Hill. After they had driven the tunnel about 300 yards the miners struck a spring of natural bitumen. Reynolds immediately recognised the scientific

THE GINGHAM CHICKEN

Maws Craft Centre, Jackfield, Nr Ironbridge,
Shropshire TF8 7LS
Tel: 01952 881138

Located in the Ironbridge Gorge World Heritage Site Helen at the Gingham Chicken specialises in producing a wide variety of useful and original gifts made from carefully selected fabrics from the USA and Europe. She has a keen interest in New England styles and bold colour combinations. From wall-hangings to childrens bags, everything is made on the premises to a high standard. Items can also be made to order.

MAW'S CRAFT CENTRE

Jackfield, nr Ironbridge, Shropshire TF8 7LS
Tel: 01952 883030 Fax: 01952 883285
e-mail: sabine@mawscraftcentre.co.uk
website: www.mawscraftcentre.co.uk

Located within the World Heritage Site of the Ironbridge Gorge, 1.5 miles from the historic bridge, **Maws Craft Centre** is almost a craft village, comprising as it does residential units and more than 20 individual workshops operated by a wide variety of art, craft and design specialists. The huge range includes furniture, pottery, glass, jewellery, fine art, sculptures, floral art, tiles, toys, knitwear,

textiles, baskets, woodturning and picture framing. Many of the craft people specialise in interpreting your own designs, or designing and making items to your specific requirements. Some also offer classes in their own speciality. They are usually open most afternoons and weekends throughout the year but if you are planning to visit a particular workshop it's advisable to call in advance to make sure they are available.

The complex also includes a gift shop and gallery selling a comprehensive range of crafts made at the centre and elsewhere. Also on sale are chocolates, candles, cruelty-free cosmetics, organic paints, oils and woodstains. To round off your visit, sample the home-baked cakes, savouries and light lunches available in the award-winning licensed tea room. There's good wheelchair access to ground floor units and ample free parking.

The Centre is housed in the former factory buildings of Maw and Co. In the late 19th century Maw and Co. was the largest tile manufacturer in the world, producing more than 20 million items a year at the height of the tile boom. The company was formed in 1850 by George Maw and his brother Arthur who quickly gained a high reputation for their encaustic "Mock-Medieval" floor tiles. By the 1880s the company's client list ran to 5 pages and included the Royal Family, Tsar Alexander II,

two maharajas, nine dukes, twelve earls, the railway companies, thirteen cathedrals, thirty-six hospitals, fifty-three public buildings, nineteen schools and colleges, and five warships.

The recession following World War I, building restrictions and the closure of many railway lines in the 1960s proved very detrimental for tile production at this site and eventually the factory closed in 1970. Two thirds of the site was demolished between 1974 and 1977 but in the early 1980s the Telford Development Corporation converted some of the remaining buildings into small business units and flats. When the Corporation was wound up, a group of tenants formed a limited company to buy the site in 1988 and named it Maw's Craft Centre in honour of its former owners.

interest of the discovery and sent samples of the bitumen to eminent scientists, who declared that the properties of the bitumen were superior to those of tar made of coal. The tunnel was almost forgotten over the years, but in 1965 the Shropshire Mining Club persuaded the owner of the village shop in **Coalport** to let them explore the darkness which lay beyond a door opening from his cellar. They rediscovered the Tar Tunnel, but it was another 18 years before visitors were allowed access to a short stretch.

At **Blists Hill Victorian Town** visitors can experience the atmosphere and way of life of a working Victorian community; there's a shop, domestic animals, a squatter's cottage, a schoolhouse and a bank which distributes its own legal tender.

Passport tickets are available to admit holders to all ten Ironbridge Gorge Museums – call 01952 433522 for details.

Two miles west of Ironbridge, on a minor road off the B4378, stands **Buildwas Abbey**, one of the finest ruined abbeys in England. After 850 years the church is virtually complete except for the roof, and the setting, in a meadow by the Severn against a backdrop of wooded grounds, is both peaceful and evocative. The place is full of things of interest, like the lead-glazed tiles depicting animals and birds in the Chapter House.

WELLINGTON

2 miles NW of Telford on the A442

Wellington is part of the new town of Telford but still retains much of its Victorian look. The Church of All Saints is the work of George Steuart, better known for St Chad's in Shrewsbury. A recent addition to the town's attractions is the National Trust's **Sunnycroft**, a late-Victorian gentleman's suburban villa

typical of the kind that were built for wealthy business and professional men. The house and its contents are largely unaltered, and in the grounds are pig sties, a kitchen garden, orchards, a conservatory and a Wellingtonia avenue.

A couple of miles north of Wellington, at **Longdon-on-Tern**, stands the **Aqueduct** built by Thomas Telford as a pilot for other, better-known constructions.

South of here, on the other side of the M54/A5, is one of the best-known landmarks in the whole country. **The Wrekin**, which reaches up over 1,300 feet, is the site of a prehistoric hill fort, visible for many miles around and accessible by a network of public footpaths. The reward for reaching the top is a beautiful panoramic view across the neighbouring counties. In Roman times it was used as a base by the Cornovii tribe before they were moved to Viroconium. Shropshire folklore tells us that it was "put" there by a malicious giant who was carrying a huge load of earth to dam the Severn and flood Shrewsbury, simply because he didn't like the people. The giant met a cobbler, who persuaded him against this evil act, whereupon the giant dropped the load he was carrying – and that's The Wrekin.

WROXETER

7 miles W of Telford on the B4380

In the village of Wroxeter, beside the B4380, is one of the most important Roman sites ever brought to light. **Viroconium** was the first town to be established by the Romans in this part of the country and developed into the 4th largest city in Roman Britain with more than 5000 soldiers and civilians living here. It's an absolutely fascinating place, where the highlights include extensive remains of a 2nd century bathhouse complex. Some of the major excavated items are on display here, many more at Rowley's House Museum in Shrewsbury. Also in the village is Wroxeter Roman Vineyard where there is not only a vineyard producing both red and white wines but additional attractions in the shape of rare-breed animals and a lavender field.

ATCHAM

7 miles W of Telford on the B4380

The village stands at the point where the Severn is crossed by the Roman road. The splendid old seven-arched bridge is now redundant, having been replaced by a new neighbour some time ago, but is still in situ. The old bridge was designed by John Gwynne, who was a founder member of the Royal Academy and the designer of Magdalen Bridge in Oxford.

Attingham Park, run by the National Trust, is perhaps the finest house in Shropshire, a splendid neo-classical mansion set in 250 delightful acres. Designed by George Steuart for the 1st Lord Berwick, it has the grandest of Regency interiors, ambassadorial silver, Italian furniture and Grand Tour paintings hanging in the John Nash gallery. The tea room is lined with paintings of the 5th Lord Berwick's Herefordshire cattle. Humphrey Repton landscaped the park where visitors can enjoy woodland and riverside walks and see the deer.

From the park visitors can take a trailer ride to **Attingham Home Farm**, the original home farm of the grand house. It comprises buildings dating mainly from about 1800 and the yard retains the atmosphere of a traditional Shropshire farm. Many breeds of farm animals are represented: pigs - Oxford, Sandy, Iron Age, Vietnamese pot-bellied; sheep - Jacob, Shetland and Ryeland; cattle - Jerseys, Longhair, Dexter, Red Poll,

British White. The rabbit house is particularly popular with youngsters, and there are usually some orphaned lambs for children to bottle-feed.

SHREWSBURY

"High the vanes of Shrewsbury gleam,
Islanded in Severn stream"

So wrote A.E. Housman in *A Shropshire Lad* and the town is indeed almost an island, caught in a wandering loop of the River Severn. It was on two hills within this protected site that the Saxon town developed. A good introduction to the city's topography is to take one of the river cruises that leave from Victoria Quay daily during the summer months.

The Normans under Roger de Montgomery took over after the conquest, building the castle and the great Benedictine abbey. In the 15th and 16th centuries Shrewsbury prospered through the wool trade, and evidence of its affluence shows in the many "Magpie" black-and-white timbered buildings that still line the streets. In Victorian times steam made Shrewsbury an important railway centre whilst at the same time Charles Darwin, born and educated in the town, was rocking the world with his theories. Everywhere there is a sense of history, and the Museums do a particularly fine job of bringing the past to life, in terms of both human and natural history. **Rowley's House** is a glorious timber-framed building of the late 16th century, with an adjoining brick and stone mansion of 1618. The home of William Rowley, 17th century draper, brewer and leading citizen, now contains an impressive collection of pieces from Viroconium, along with spectacular displays of costumes, natural history and geology. A short walk away is **Clive House**, in the

Georgian area of the town. Clive of India lived here in 1762 while he was Mayor, and one or two mementoes can be seen. The major displays are of Shropshire ceramics and the life of Charles Darwin, whose statue stands opposite the Castle.

The **Castle** (see panel below), dating from 1083, was built by the Norman Earl Roger de Montgomery and last saw action in the Civil War. It was converted by Thomas Telford into a private residence and now houses the **Shropshire Regimental Museum** (see panel on page 110) with the collections of the Kings Shropshire Yeomanry Cavalry and the Shropshire Royal Horse Artillery.

Begun in the same year as the castle, **Shrewsbury Abbey** survived the dissolution of the monasteries in 1540 and still serves as the parish church. The Abbey, like the Castle, was founded by

Rowley's House

Roger de Montgomery on the site of a Saxon wooden church. In 1283 a parliament met in the Chapter House, the first national assembly in which the Commons were involved. The Abbey Church remains a place of worship, and in 1997 a stained glass window depicting St Benedict was dedicated to the memory of Edith Pargeter. This lady, writing under the name of Ellis Peters, created the character of Brother Cadfael, who

SHREWSBURY CASTLE

Castle Street, Shrewsbury, Shropshire
Tel: 01743 358516 Fax: 01743 358411
e-mail: museums@shrewsbury.gov.uk
website: www.shrewsburymuseums.com

Noted for its commanding position and fantastic views, **Shrewsbury Castle** dates back more than 900 years to its founding in 1083. That was when Roger de Montgomery, a kinsman of William the Conqueror, was granted Shrewsbury and much of Shropshire as a reward for his loyalty. The fortress was part of the Normans' attempts to control the lawless border with Wales but by the time of Elizabeth I it had become a virtual ruin with no military significance. Of that Norman structure only the gateway remains along with one side and two corner towers from the 13th century.

During Elizabeth's reign the castle was used as a private residence but it saw action again during the Civil War when a small Parliamentary force captured the castle and town with little bloodshed. Two centuries passed and then the young Thomas Telford remodelled the castle, inside and out, for Sir William Pulteney. In 1924, Shropshire Horticultural Society bought the castle and presented it to the Corporation of Shrewsbury. It is now in the care of their successors, Shrewsbury and Atcham Borough. The castle has returned to a military role, in a peaceful way, by becoming home to the Shropshire Regimental Museum.

lived at the Abbey and became one of the country's best-loved fictional characters when portrayed by Derek Jacobi in the television series.

To the east of the abbey, in front of the Shire Hall, rises the lofty **Lord Hill's Column**. Four magnificent sculpted lions guard the base of this, the largest Grecian Doric column in the world which reaches a total height of 133ft 6in. Inside, there's a spiral staircase which unfortunately is not open to the public because of safety reasons. Completed in 1816, the column celebrates Rowland Hill who was born in Shropshire and achieved distinction as a soldier in the

Shrewsbury Abbey

SHROPSHIRE REGIMENTAL MUSEUM

Castle Street, Shrewsbury, Shropshire
Tel: 01743 358516 Fax: 01743 270023
e-mail: shropsrm@zoom.co.uk
website: www.shropshireregimental.co.uk

Housed in Shrewsbury Castle the **Shropshire Regimental Museum** tells the proud story of the four Shropshire Regiments – King's Shropshire Light Infantry, Shropshire Yeomanry, Shropshire Royal Horse Artillery and 4th Battalion King's Shropshire Light Infantry TA. On display are the colours bearing hard-won battle honours, now beautifully restored and hung around the Great Hall, the splendid regimental silver and china, the exotic uniforms and badges, weapons ranging from sword to machine gun, and medals gained in campaigns around the world, including three Victoria Crosses. Copious exhibits trace the history of the regular regiments as they helped to carve out and then garrison a world-wide empire, and of the territorial regiments at home ready for any crisis that might threaten the nation.

Of particular interest amongst the many treasures on display are the Standard of the Harford Dragoons, seized from the American Army outside Washington in 1814; the Croix de Guerre presented by the French nation to the 4th Territorial Battalion KSLI for their gallantry at the Battle of Bligny in 1918; and the baton of Grand Admiral Doenitz, Hitler's successor, taken in 1945. The last figure visitors see as they leave wears the uniform of the 5th Battalion The Light Infantry – today's volunteers and inheritors of the long tradition of service in Shropshire.

Napoleonic wars, notably at Waterloo. He was created a viscount and later succeeded the Duke of Wellington as commander-in-chief.

Shrewsbury has more than 30 churches and among the finest are St Mary's and St Chad's. **St Mary's**, the town's only complete medieval church, originated in the late Saxon period, but the earliest features of the present building are of the 12th century. The stained glass, monuments and fittings are quite out of the ordinary, and the spire has claims to being the third highest in the land. One of the memorials is to Admiral Benbow, a national hero who died in 1702 who is also remembered in innumerable pub signs. **St Chad's** is the work of Attingham Hall's designer George Steuart, who was commissioned to design a replacement for the original, which fell down in 1788. His church is very unusual in having a circular nave.

The best examples of Shrewsbury's Tudor buildings are to be found in **Bear Steps**, close to the main square. This charming group of Tudor cottages and a timbered hall now houses two floors of paintings and craft exhibits, usually featuring local artists and images.

Guided tours and suggested walks cover all aspects of this marvellous town, including a **Brother Cadfael tour** and walks in the beautiful countryside that is all around. One walk takes in the spot to the north of town now known as **Battlefield**, where in 1403 the armies of Henry IV and the insurgent Harry Percy (Harry Hotspur) met. Fifty thousand men were deployed in all, and in the brief but bloody battle Hotspur was among the many casualties. A church was built near the mass grave, where 1,600 bodies are buried, a monument to the fallen and

TUDOR HOUSE

AA 4 Diamond
2 Fish Street, Shrewsbury, Shropshire SY1 1UR
Tel: 01743 351735
website: www.tudorhouse.co.uk
e-mail:
enquire@www.tudorhouseshrewsbury.co.uk

Shrewsbury boasts some 660 listed buildings but there aren't many offering quality bed & breakfast accommodation. **Tudor House** is an eye-catching black and white building dating back to 1460 and located in a quiet medieval street in the heart of this picturesque and historic town. The town's major attractions – its Norman Abbey, medieval castle and wonderful Victorian railway station – are all within easy walking distance, as are its many and varied shops, cafés, restaurants and pubs. Tudor house is a non-smoking guest house, small and select,and is home to many famous visitors. This unique place to stay is highly popular with tourists and friends from nearby counties.

The house is redolent of history with its ancient oak beams and beautifully restored guest rooms. Hosts Kevin and Sue Jones greet arriving guests with a warm and friendly welcome and will cater for any dietary requirements in their hearty English breakfasts which incorporate fresh organic ingredients wherever possible. The guest bedrooms are all tastefully decorated, and equipped with colour TV and wash basins; some have en suite facilities. In addition to Shrewsbury's many attractions, the World Heritage site of Ironbridge and its famous 9 museums is just a short drive away, as are Attingham Park, a wonderful deer park landscaped by Humphrey Repton, and Wroxeter Roman City – the remains of the fourth largest city in Roman Britain. Tudor House a magical and memorable experience.

ALBRIGHT HUSSEY HOTEL & RESTAURANT

Ellesmere Road, Shrewsbury, Shropshire SY4 3AF
Tel: 01939 290523/290571 Fax: 01939 291143
e-mail: abhhotel@aol.com
website: www.albrighthussey.co.uk

In a county that boasts a great treasury of fine old buildings, the **Albright Hussey Hotel & Restaurant** is undoubtedly one of the most striking. A Grade II listed building dating back to around 1524, the house still has its original moat where black swans glide elegantly by and, inside, a wealth of oak panelling, huge open fireplaces and original moulded beams create a comfortable, welcoming ambience. The house was converted to a restaurant in 1967 and was bought in 1988 by Franco Subbiani, a hotelier and restaurateur with an international reputation. His son Paul ensures that the Albright Hussey continues to be renowned for the excellence of its cuisine.

The hotel's world class chef offers an extensive choice of dishes based on the freshest local ingredients and complemented by a wide selection of fine wines from the spacious cellar. The Albright Hussey is widely regarded as providing the finest accommodation in the Midlands. Guests have the choice of staying in the historic old house or in the recently built extension. All rooms have en suite facilities, several have 4-poster beds and most enjoy lovely views of the moat, lawns and surrounding countryside. The hotel is licensed for civil weddings and its Imperial Suite is ideal for weddings, conferences and parties of up to 250 guests.

ENJOY! LIVING NATURALLY

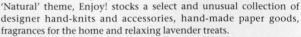

13 Dogpole, Shrewsbury, Shropshire SY1 1EN
Tel: 01743 241533 Fax: 01743 356743
website: www.purescents.co.uk

A shop which is refreshingly wholesome, **Enjoy! Living Naturally** is the place for all things natural. Looking for an unusual gift, or a treat for yourself? Enjoy! stocks a whole host of products which promote a natural lifestyle on all levels of mind, body and spirit. Locally made vegetable soaps, with a botanical theme inspired by the colours and

textures of Mother Nature, are a speciality – all of them packed full of therapeutic essential oils. Alongside these are health and beauty products which are free from unnecessary chemicals. In keeping with the 'Natural' theme, Enjoy! stocks a select and unusual collection of designer hand-knits and accessories, hand-made paper goods, fragrances for the home and relaxing lavender treats.

Underlining the theme of a healthy lifestyle and the "feel-good factor", Enjoy! has a thriving Holistic Health Centre on the premises where a wide range of complementary therapies are available by appointment. These include acupuncture, homoeopathy, reflexology, Reiki, therapeutic and aromatherapy massages – to name but a few. Tired or stressed from your travels and need some pampering? Then call them for a therapeutic or aromatherapy massage – and Enjoy!

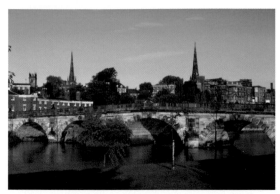

Bridge over the River, Shrewsbury

been held in the picturesque grounds of **Quarry Park** and includes a musical programme and fireworks displays.

Incidentally, if you've been wondering which is the correct pronunciation of the town's name, Shropshire Tourism goes along with the announcer at the railway station: *"'Shrewsbury, this is Shrowsbury" says the clever young lady. And of course she is absolutely right."*

also an oasis of wildlife in the town environment. Special events are being planned for the 600th anniversary of the battle in 2003.

Complementing the town's Museum and Archaeological Services, a Records and Research Service was opened in a new building in 1995. It has 5.5 miles of material relating to Shropshire past and present, including many original records and extensive microfilm records.

A museum with a difference is **Coleham Pumping Station** at **Longden Coleham**, which houses the splendid Renshaw pumping engines that powered Shrewsbury's sewerage system until 1970.

Shrewsbury Flower Show is Britain's best two-day summer show. Each August for more than a century the show has

AROUND SHREWSBURY

HADNALL

5 miles NE of Shrewsbury on the A49

Hadnall is the burial place of Rowland Hill – not the man who conceived the idea of the Penny Post in Victorian times but the distinguished soldier who was Wellington's right hand man during the Peninsula War and covered himself with glory by routing Napoleon's Imperial Guard at the Battle of Waterloo. Hill was created a viscount and after succeeding Wellington as Commander in Chief retired to Hardwicke Grange near Hadnall. That house no longer stands and the viscount himself is buried beneath the church tower.

HOUSE OF NEEDLEWORK

11 Wyle Cop, Shrewsbury, Shropshire SY1 1XB
Tel: 01743 355533

The huge picture window of **The House of Needlework** reveals an amazing range of needlecraft creations and stocks all the materials necessary to produce them, including an impressively wide range of quality designs from artists such as Elizabeth Bradley, Designers Forum and Cleopatra's Needle. Owner Jackie Williams has a lifetime's experience in needlework and allied skills and stresses the fun and satisfaction that needleworking brings. Her two assistants, Sylvia Clarke and Pat Morgan, share this enthusiasm and through their morning help groups endeavour to "spread the word still wider!"

WOLLASTON

8 miles W of Shrewsbury on the A458

The church here has a memorial to Thomas Parr, widely claimed to be the longest-lived Englishman, dying at the ripe old age of 152. He lived through ten reigns, married for the first time at 88, raised a family and married again at 122. He is buried in Westminster Abbey, so someone must have believed his story.

MONTFORD

4 miles W of Shrewsbury off the A5

It's worth pausing at Montford to look at the church where Charles Darwin was buried for a time. His body was subsequently moved to Westminster Abbey, showing that the furore caused by his theories had largely died down soon after his death – but not entirely, as the *The Origin of Species* and *The Descent of Man* can still arouse fierce debate. Just

beyond Montford are the ruins of Shrawardine Castle.

MELVERLEY

10 miles W of Shrewsbury off the B4393

Country lanes lead to the remarkable **Church of St Peter**, which stands serenely, if somewhat precariously, on the banks of the River Vyrnwy. From the outside, flanked by two massive yew trees, the church looks rather like a black-and-white manor house; the interior reveals one of England's few timber-framed churches. It was built in 1406 after its predecessor was destroyed by Owen Glendower. Great open screens of oak divide the interior into three areas and most of the furnishings - pulpit, altar table and chairs - are Jacobean.

NESSCLIFFE

9 miles NW of Shrewsbury on the A5

Near the village of Nesscliffe, which lies

MARCUS MOORE ANTIQUES

Tel/Fax: 01939 200333
e-mail: mmooreantiques@aol.com
website: www.marcusmoore-antiques.com

Marcus Moore Antiques was established by Marcus and Mechelle Moore both of whom have been lifetime lovers of fine art. They stock a wide range of antique furniture of all periods, many hundreds of pieces displayed in a recently completed

showroom at their country house home, which is in a lovelysetting surrounded by many acres of meadows.

A team of skilled craftsmen renovate the furniture, including Oak and Country, and Georgian Mahogany chests of drawers, lowboys, tallboys, side tables, dining tables and chairs, as well as interesting 19th century items. Prospective buyers are welcome by appointment – please telephone first.

halfway between Shrewsbury and Oswestry, is **Nesscliffe Hill Country Park**, where paths lead up through woodland to the summit and fine views over Shropshire. The hill is a sandstone escarpment, popular for walking and rock climbing; cut into the face of an abandoned quarry are caves, one of them reputedly the lair of the 16th century worthy-turned-highwayman Humphrey Kynaston.

A short distance north of Nesscliffe, on the B4397, is the village of **Ruyton-XI-Towns**, which acquired its unusual name in medieval times when 11 communities were united into the borough of Ruyton.

OSWESTRY

Close to the Welsh border, Oswestry is an important market town whose look is mainly Georgian and Victorian, due in part to the fires which regularly ravaged timber-framed buildings. The town grew up around **St Oswald's Well**. Oswald was a Saxon king who was killed in a battle in 642 against a rival Saxon king, Penda of Mercia. Oswald's body was dismembered and hung on the branches of a tree. An eagle swooped and carried off one of his arms and where the limb fell to the ground a spring bubbled up to mark the spot. Thus St Oswald's Well came into being, soon to become a place of pilgrimage renowned for its healing powers.

There are many fine old buildings in Oswestry, none finer than the **Church of St Oswald**. It played an important part in the Civil War, when it was used as an observation point during the siege of the town by the Parliamentarians. The oldest section is the tower, which dates back to around 1200. The interior is beautiful, and among the treasures are a font presented by Colonel Lloyd of Llanforda

MAB & CO.

11 English Walls, Oswestry, Shropshire SY11 2PA
Tel: 01691 661328

After several years experience in the jewellery and silverware retail trade worldwide, including the USA and Australia, Julie Bennion decided in 1998 to open her own shop right in the heart of Oswestry. In its two showrooms – one at the front, one at the back – **Mab & Co.** offers an exciting range of contemporary pieces all enticingly displayed.

In addition to the jewellery and silverware, the shop stocks gold jewellery, precious and semi-precious stones, beautiful glassware of every kind from Leonardo and others, Newgate clocks that are made in Oswestry, covetable handbags from Radley Hidesign, Henra Buller cards, quality soft toys, contemporary giftware and much, much more.

Whether you are looking for an unusual and striking gift, or something to enhance your own décor, you will almost certainly find something appropriate and collectable here. Parking is easy, with car parks nearby and the town's attractions – notably the 15th century Holbache House, the impressive Church of St Oswald and, for steam buffs, the Cambrian Museum of Transport – are all within easy reach.

as a thanksgiving for the restoration of the monarchy, a Gilbert Scott war memorial and a memorial to Hugh Yale, a member of the family that founded Yale University.

Standing in the grounds of the church is the 15th century **Holbache House**. Once a grammar school, this handsome building now houses the Tourist Information Centre and the **Heritage Centre** with displays of local interest and exhibitions of arts and crafts. Ferrequinologists (railway buffs) will make tracks for the **Cambrian Museum of Transport** on Oswald Road Oswestry was the headquarters of the Cambrian Railway Company until it amalgamated with the GWR in 1922, and as late as the 1960s there were over 1,000 railwaymen in the area. Locomotives, carriages and wagons have been built and repaired in Oswestry for over 100 years, and the maintenance of 300 miles of track was

directed from offices in the station building. One of the old engine sheds now houses a small museum with a collection of railway memorabilia and also some old bicycles and motorbikes. One of the locomotives is regularly steamed up by the volunteers of the Cambrian Railway Society. In 1559 a plague killed almost a third of the town's population and the **Croeswylan Stone** commemorates this disaster, marking the spot to which the market was moved during the plague. It is sometimes referred to as the Cross of Weeping.

On the northern edge of town, **Old Oswestry** is an impressive example of an Iron Age fortress, first occupied in about 300BC. It was on the border of the territory held by the Cornovii and is one of several in the region. At the southwest corner of the fort can be seen **Wat's Dyke**, built at the same time and for the same purpose – delineating the border

---

CREATIVE DAYS

The Old Vicarage, Llansilin, Oswestry, Shropshire SY10 7PX
Tel: 01691 791345
e-mail: pam@creativedays.co.uk
website: www.creativedays.co.uk

At the Georgian Old Vicarage in the tiny village of Llansilin, Creative Days offers not just excellent bed & breakfast accommodation but also the opportunity of taking short courses in textiles, art and design, "Inspired Interiors" or traditional country skills.

Topics range from Stained Glass Boxes to Silk Painting, from Willow Weaving for the garden to Dry-stone Walling and Hedge-laying. Many of the courses are suitable for beginners but the experienced tutors have the skills to support more adventurous spirits. A full programme of the courses is available on request.

The guest bedrooms at The Old Vicarage are light, spacious and with either en suite or private facilities, and your host Pam Johnson is famous for her splendid breakfasts!

between Saxon Mercia and the Welsh – as the better-known Offa's Dyke. Who was Wat? We know not, but he could have been one of Offa's officers.

AROUND OSWESTRY

MAESBURY

2 miles S of Oswestry off the A5 or A483

The Mere, Ellesmere

The village was one of the main transit points on the **Montgomery Canal**, and many of the canal buildings at **Maesbury Marsh** are still standing, along with some boatmen's cottages.

Immediately south of Maesbury Marsh is the village of **Woolston**, where **St Winifred's Well** is said to have been a resting place for saints' bones being carried to their final destinations.

LLANYMYNECH

7 miles S of Oswestry on the A483

A small diversion is well worth while to visit Llanymynech, once a town of some standing, with a major canal and a thriving industry based on limestone. It was also a railway junction. The **Llanymynech Hills**, which include a section of **Offa's Dyke**, make for good walking, with the old limestone workings to add interest – you can still see the old bottle lime kilns and an unusual Hoffman rotary kiln. The quarried limestone was taken to the kilns on a tramway and, after processing, to the nearby canalside wharf. Part of the quarry is now a designated nature reserve and supports abundant bird life. On top of the hill are traces of an ancient hill fort. **The Montgomery Canal** was built at the end of the 18th century mainly for the transportation of limestone from the Llanymynech

quarries. Large sections of it are now unnavigable, indeed dry, but a restoration project is under way with the aim of opening 35 miles of waterway from Oswestry through Welshpool to Newtown. Until the boats return there are some delightful walks along the towpath, as well as fishing where it is possible.

ELLESMERE

8 miles NE of Oswestry on the A495

The centre of Shropshire's Lakeland, Ellesmere is a pretty market town where the market is held every Tuesday, just as it has been since 1221. The town has been regional winner of the Britain in Bloom competition in both 2000 and 2001 and along its medieval streets rise Georgian and half-timbered buildings. The **Old Town Hall** and the **Old Railway Station** are two of the most striking buildings, but nothing except the mound remains of the castle. The most impressive of all is the parish church of St Mary the Virgin, built by the Knights of St John. It is particularly beautiful inside, with an exceptional 15th century carved roof in the chapel.

The church overlooks **The Mere**, largest of several lakes that are an equal delight to boating enthusiasts, anglers

STONE'S THROW POTTERY

3 Church Street, Ellesmere,
Shropshire SY12 0HD
Tel/Fax: 01691 623143

As you approach **Stone's Throw Pottery** you may see Anthea Hadley beside the window working at her potter's wheel. Trained as an artist and a qualified teacher, Anthea was, until recently, a Master upholsterer and Portrait Artist.

Thrown pottery is her latest endeavour and she now produces a marvellous range of individually crafted pots. Her shop at the rear displays a huge selection of her work; practical pieces for the oven and table as well as a range of decorative items, such as her exquisite doves and jardinières. Anthea also teaches throwing to small classes of aspiring potters

and birdwatchers. Herons, Canada geese and swans are among the inhabitants of The Mere. For an insight into the creation some 15,000 years ago of the Shropshire meres, a browse around the **Meres Visitor Centre** is recommended. From the centre, there's a pleasant half-mile promenade along the lakeside and through Cremorne Gardens.

Ellesmere forms the hub of a regional canal network with the **Llangollen Canal** linking the Shropshire Union Canal to the Mersey. It was from his offices in Ellesmere that Thomas Telford designed and supervised the building of the entire canal whose most spectacular feature is the aqueduct, 125ft high and 1,000ft long, which spans the Vale of Llangollen. The project was initiated by the Duke of Bridgewater who in just one day raised over a million (18th century) pounds at a hotel in the town to fund the scheme.

A mile or so east of Ellesmere, on the A495, is **Welshampton**, whose church was built by Sir George Gilbert Scott in 1863. One of its memorial windows is dedicated to a Basuto chieftain; he had been a student of theology at Canterbury and part of his studies brought him to Welshampton, where he lodged with the vicar. Unfortunately he fell ill and died in the same year that saw the completion of the church.

MARKET DRAYTON

Market Drayton was mentioned in the Domesday Book as Magna Draitune. It changed its name when Abbot Simon Combermere obtained a Royal Market Charter in 1245:

"Know that we have granted and by this our present charter confirmed to Brother Simon Abbot of Combermere and the monks

serving God there that they and their successors forever shall have a weekly market in their manor of Drayton on Wednesday."

And so they have, every Wednesday since.

The fire of 1651 razed most of the town, so there is now quite a diversity of styles among the buildings, including black and white half-timbered residences and former coaching inns. One of the most interesting structures is the **Buttercross**, built in 1842 to enable farmers' wives to display their wares protected from the weather. The crest it carries is of the Corbet family, Lords of the Manor since 1650.

Market Drayton is often referred to as 'The Home of the Gingerbread'. Gingerbread has been baked here for 200 years and is made in all shapes and sizes, the best known being the Gingerbread Man. Traditionally dunked in port, it's also very good to nibble on the **Discovery Trail** that takes in the sights of the town. Gingerbread dates back far more than 200 years, of course, and Shakespeare had a good word for it:

"An' I had but one penny in the world thou shouldst have it to buy gingerbread."

Just a few hundred yards from the town centre, the **Shropshire Union Canal** gives boaters the chance to moor up and explore the town, while the towpath walk takes in flights of locks, wharfside cottages and the breathtaking 40-steps Aqueduct.

Market Drayton's most famous son (actually born just outside) was Clive of India, whose childhood escapades in the town included climbing the church tower and sitting on one of the gargoyles, and building a dam to flood a shop whose owner was unwilling to pay protection money.

THE BUTTERCROSS TEA ROOM

22 Cheshire Street, Market Drayton,
Shropshire TF9 1PF   Tel: 01630 656768
e-mail: buttercross.tearoom@virgin.net

It seems right and proper that the town where the "gingerbread man" traybake originated should have an outstanding tea room and **The Buttercross Tea Room** is precisely that. As you walk through the door your first impressions are of a warm and friendly

establishment with staff to match. The tea room/restaurant/patisserie is housed in a spacious Edwardian building and the décor reflects the elegance of that era. Crisp white linen tablecloths, top quality porcelain and china and crystal glassware all add to the allure.

The extensive menu starts with a choice of breakfast options, moves on to a selection of lunchtime dishes that includes a home-made soup of the day, omelettes, freshly-made salads, a fresh pâté of the day, a home-made savoury flan and a choice of baked potatoes. Available throughout the day are freshly baked filled baguettes and sandwiches, hot toasted baguette melts and hot toasted ciabattas. Teatime treats include Cream Teas, High Tea, and a choice of cakes, pastries and scones all home-baked on the premises using only the best ingredients. And you certainly shouldn't miss out on the traditional pudding of the day, a good old-fashioned dish home-made daily and served with creamy dairy custard or fresh cream. Scrummy!

JIM SADLER FURNITURE

Tel: 01630 653143/07929 258867
e-mail: jimsadler14@hotmail.com
website: axisartists.org.uk

Jim Sadler began making furniture at the age of 12 and now, some thirty years later, he is one of a group of British crafts people who have been selected to take part in the prestigious *HMS Victory* project. Jim designs and makes one-off pieces of contemporary furniture from native and European hardwoods that he personally selects. At the national Artists website and in many Crafts Council listed Galleries throughout the UK you can see examples of his distinctive contemporary utility pieces. As well as making tables, bedroom furniture and storage units, Jim also makes highly collectable Shropshire green oak Sculptural furniture for the private garden, home and public space, Jim also accepts commissions.

AROUND MARKET DRAYTON

HODNET

4 miles SW of Market Drayton on the A53

The sizeable village of Hodnet is overlooked by the church of St Luke from its hilltop position. The church is Norman, with some unusual features including a christening gate and wedding steps, and it has a very distinctive octagonal tower. There are some ornate carvings around the 17th century font, and a chapel is dedicated to the Heber-Percy family, owners of **Hodnet Hall**. The most illustrious member of the family was Bishop Heber, who wrote, among many other hymns, *From Greenland's Icy Mountains*. Hodnet Hall is an Elizabethan-style mansion built in the 1870s, but the real reason for a visit here is the wonderful gardens, which extend over 60 acres and were carefully planted (Brigadier Heber-Percy masterminded the transformation) to provide a show of colour throughout the seasons.

MARCHAMLEY

4 miles SW of Market Drayton on the A442

The beautiful Georgian mansion **Hawkestone Hall** was the ancestral

home of the Hill family from 1556 until 1906. The Hall is now the seat of a religious order, but the principal rooms, including the splendid Venetian Saloon, are open for a short time in the summer (tel: 01630 685242). **The Pleasure Gardens** comprise terraces, lily pond, herbaceous borders and extensive woodland.

MORETON CORBET

6 miles N of Shrewsbury on the B5063

Take the A53 to Shawbury and turn left on to the B5063 and you'll soon come across the splendid ruins of **Moreton Corbet Castle**, seat of the local bigwig family. Its stark greystone walls are an entrancing and moving sight, and not at all like a castle. In fact, what remains is the shell of a grand Italian-influenced mansion which was never completed (Corbet funds ran out) and was severely damaged in the Civil War.

WEM

11 miles N of Shrewsbury on the B5476

A peaceful enough place now, but Wem has seen its share of strife, being virtually destroyed in the Wars of the Roses and attacked in the Civil War. On the latter occasion, in 1643, Lord Capel at the head of 5,000 Royalist troops got a pretty

SOULTON HALL

near Wem, Shrewsbury, Shropshire SY4 5RS
Tel: 01939 232786 Fax: 01939 234097
e-mail: j.a.ashton@farmline.com

Built of mellow Tudor brick, **Soulton Hall** is a striking country house with a long and interesting history. The "Manor of Suleton" is recorded in the Domesday Book of 1086 and the site of the original moated castle or fortified manor house can still be seen near by. The present house was built shortly before Elizabeth I became queen and was bought in 1556 by Rowland Hill, the first Protestant Lord Mayor of London. It was his descendant, Thomas Hill, a High Sheriff of Shropshire, who in 1668 placed his impressive marital coat of arms above the front door. The hall looks very much as it did in his day and is lovingly cared for by his descendant, the present owner, Ann Ashton and her family.

Guests have the use of a spacious lounge hall with

comfortable armchairs and an open fire. They can enjoy a quiet drink in the friendly and well-stocked bar, a unique room with mullioned windows and original oak beams. The elegant dining room provides an attractive setting for a leisurely 5-course dinner offering cuisine that is both traditional and imaginative. The emphasis is on fresh and home-grown produce and is complemented by a choice of wines.

Soulton Hall offers the options of either fully catered or self-catering accommodation. Accommodation in the main house comprises 4 well-appointed double rooms, three of which have en suite bathrooms; all have colour television, radio and tea-making facilities. Each room has its own character with many architectural features dating back to the 16th century. Further accommodation is available in the converted coach house across the lawn which offers 2 spacious

ground floor double rooms with en suite spa bathrooms, one with an adjoining sitting room.

For those who prefer self-catering, there are 3 charming cottages within the extensive grounds. Keeper's Cottage, formerly the home of the Hill Estate gamekeepers, provides accommodation for 6, with a ground floor double room and 2 twin-bedded rooms upstairs. Shooter's Lodge is a 1970s bungalow in a wonderful open country setting which has 2 double rooms and 2 twin-bedded rooms providing accommodation for up to 8 people. Ploughman's Cottage has a large garden with fruit trees, lawn and flower beds and can sleep up to 5 people. All the cottages are comprehensively equipped and enjoy attractive views across the unspoilt north Shropshire countryside.

hostile reception, and his defeat by a much smaller band, including some townswomen, gave rise to this mocking couplet:

*"The women of Wem and a few volunteers
Beat the Lord Capel and all his Cavaliers."*

It was another woman – actually a 14-year-old girl called Jane Churm – who nearly did what Capel proved incapable of doing. In setting alight the thatch on the roof of her home she started a fire that destroyed 140 properties in one hour. Some notable buildings survived, including **Astley House**, home of the painter John Astley. This and many of the town's most impressive houses are in **Noble Street**. Famous people associated with Wem include Judge Jeffreys of Bloody Assize fame, who became Baron Wem in 1685, with his official residence at Lowe Hall. Wem is the home of the modern sweet pea, developed by the 19th century nurseryman Henry Eckford. **The Sweet Pea Show** and the carnival are great occasions in the Wem calendar.

WHITCHURCH

17 miles N of Shrewsbury on the A49

First developed by the Romans as Mediolanum, Whitchurch is the most important town in the northern part of the county. Its main street is dominated by the tall sandstone tower of **St Alkmund's Church**, in whose chapel lies the body of Sir John Talbot, 1st Earl of Shrewsbury, who was killed at the Battle of Castillon, near Bordeaux, in 1453.

The Shropshire Way passes nearby, so too the **Llangollen Canal**, and nature-lovers can explore the local wetland habitats – **Brown Moss** is 2 miles to the south off the A41. Whitchurch is the home of **Joyce Clocks**, the oldest tower clockmakers in the world, and is also, somewhat oddly, where Cheshire cheese was created.

Hidden away in the heart of the town are the **Old Town Hall Vaults**, where the composer Edward German (*Merrie England*, *Tom Jones*) was born in 1862.

4 STAFFORDSHIRE

The southwest of Staffordshire encompasses many changing landscapes, from the busy, industrial towns of Stafford and Burton upon Trent to the peace and quiet of Cannock Chase. Along with the Hednesford Hills, the Chase provides a wonderful open area of woodland and moorland that is one of the county's great recreational centres. Well-supported by an interesting and informative visitors' centre, the Chase is a must for anyone visiting this part of Staffordshire. The southeast of Staffordshire, although lying close to the Black Country – the depressing product of the heavy industrialisation of the 18th and 19th centuries

Ancient Cave Dwellings, Kinver Edge

– has managed to escape in the main. One legacy of the era and a feature throughout the whole of Staffordshire, however, is the canal network. Built to link Birmingham with the Trent & Mersey Canal, the less well known Coventry Canal and the Birmingham & Fazeley Canal pass through tiny villages and hamlets and the towpaths provide the opportunity to walk in some unexpectedly scenic countryside.

Thors Cave, Manifold Valley

Extending along the southern edge of the Peak District, the Staffordshire Moorlands certainly rival their neighbour in terms of scenic attraction. The undulating pastures of the moorlands, along with the fresh air and ancient weather-worn crags, make this the ideal place to walk, cycle or trek. It is also an area full of character, with charming scattered villages, historic market towns and a wealth of history. The Industrial Revolution also left its mark on the landscape, though the two great reservoirs of Rudyard and Tittesworth, built to provide a water supply to the growing industry and population of the Midlands, now offer peaceful havens for a wide variety of plants, animals and birds as well as recreational facilities such as fishing and boating.

The area around Stoke-on-Trent is famous the world over for its pottery industry. Originally centred on the five towns of Stoke, Tunstall, Burslem, Hanley and Longton, The Potteries were at the heart of the Industrial Revolution. Both coal and clay were found locally which gave rise to the start of the industry, though imported clay from Cornwall was later used - but it was the foresight and ingenuity of men such as Wedgwood and Minton that really turned the cottage industry into production on a much larger scale. To support the industry in and around the centre, a network of canals and, later, railways was begun. The Trent & Mersey Canal, built by James Brindley with the support of Wedgwood and his friend the Duke of

Stoke-on-Trent pottery

Bridgewater, was finally completed in 1777 and made possible navigation from coast to coast, between the busy ports of Liverpool and Hull. Together, the Trent & Mersey Canal, the Staffordshire & Worcester Canal, begun in the same year, the Shropshire Union Canal to the west and the Middlewich branch of the Llangollen Canal, form a wonderful four counties ring that can be undertaken wholly or partly by boat. These canals, with their accessible towpaths, run through the very heart of the towns as well as through the often delightful countryside.

ADVERTISERS AND PLACES OF INTEREST

LOCATOR MAP

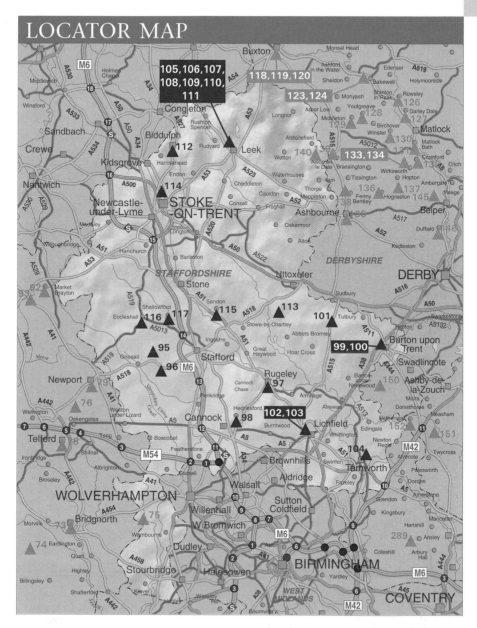

STAFFORD

The Saxon origins of the county town of Staffordshire are still visible in the extensive earthworks close to the Castle and the foundations of a tiny chapel in the grounds of St Mary's Church. **Stafford Castle** is the impressive site of a Norman fortress where visitors can follow the castle trail, wander around the medieval herb garden and explore the visitor centre built in the style of a Norman Guardhouse. The Castle grounds are often used for historical re-enactments by such groups as the Napoleonic Society and are the site for Sealed Knot battles as well as other outdoor entertainment. Stafford originally had a medieval town wall and evidence of it can still be seen today in the names of the town's main streets. However, only the **East Gate** remains of the structure. Stafford lies on the banks of the River Sow, and **Green Bridge** marks the site of the ancient ford across the river. There has been a bridge on this spot since the late 1200s but the gate in the town's medieval walls that was also at this point was demolished in 1777. Just to the east of the Bridge is **Victoria Park**, opened in 1908 and later extended to incorporate land reclaimed from the River Sow. There are many pleasant walks through the Park, which includes a mill pond and a weir, in particular to the **Windmill at Broad Eye**. Built in 1796 by John Wright, the mill moved over to steam power in 1847 and continue to be used until 1880. Like many towns today, Stafford has its busy shopping streets and also an impressive shopping centre. However, many picturesque cobbled lanes still remain and provide the visitor with a quiet and relaxing contrast to the hurly burly of the 21st century. Of particular note are **Church Lane**, with its timbered buildings, and Mill Street

with a varied array of shops, restaurants and pubs.

A place well worth visiting during any stay in Stafford is **The Ancient High House**, a beautiful Elizabethan house built in 1595 and now the largest surviving timber-framed town house in England. Through painstaking efforts over several years, Stafford Borough Council have restored this breathtaking piece of architecture to its former glory. Today the building houses the Museum of the Staffordshire Yeomanry and the Tourist Information Centre. The Ancient High House's varied history can be followed through the permanent displays in the period room settings taking the visitor through the 17th, 18th and 19th centuries and telling the stories of people who came to know this House so intimately. Not surprisingly, the house has royal connections: both King Charles I and Prince Rupert having stayed here in 1642. The House also has a small heritage shop selling a variety of interesting and locally crafted gifts. The **Shire Hall Gallery** (1798) on the market square was the town courthouse and still retains the original panelled courtrooms. It is now a venue for contemporary exhibitions and children's workshops, and has a teashop and a workshop.

Close to the High House is the **Collegiate Church of St Mary**, an unusual building which dates in part from the late 1100s, but has received additions in the early English, Gothic and Victorian styles. The huge tower arches in the nave seem to divide the building into two, which is, in fact, exactly what they were intended to do, as St Mary's is two churches under one roof. The nave was the parish church of Stafford with its own altar while the chancel beyond was used by the Deans of the College of St Mary whose duty it was to pray for deceased members of the

Royal family. Although the College was abolished in 1548, the screens which divided the Church remained until 1841 and today the Church is still referred to as the Collegiate. Sir Izaak Walton was baptised here on 21st September 1593 and his bust can be seen on the north wall of the nave. Each year, at a civic service, a wreath is placed around the bust to commemorate his probable birthday (9th August). Those interested in ecclesiastical architecture should also find time to visit the little Norman and medieval Church of St Chad.

Best known today for his work *The Compleat Angler*, **Sir Izaak Walton** was famous throughout his lifetime as a writer of biographies. However, the story of his own life is somewhat obscure, though it is certain that he was born in Stafford in 1593. From humble origins, Walton became accepted in the intellectual and ecclesiastical circles of

the day and, during the Civil War, he remained a staunch Royalist and stayed in the Stafford area.

St Mary's Mews dates back to the mid-19th century and is a Grade II listed building. The architect was the renowned Gilbert Scott, the famous church restorer of the 1850s. Other notable buildings include The Infirmary, designed by Benjamin Wyatt and completed in 1772; the Noell Almshouses dating back to 1680, and Chetwynd House, the 17th century town house of the Chetwynd family and now used as the town's main Post Office.

AROUND STAFFORD

GNOSALL
6 miles W of Stafford on A518

Some beautiful ash and sycamore trees form a delightful shaded arch over the

THE YEW TREE INN

Long Compton, nr Ranton, Stafford ST18 9JJ
Tel: 01785 282278
e-mail: info@theyewtreeatranton.co.uk
website: www.theyewtreeatranton.co.uk

In the 14 years he has been at **The Yew Tree Inn,** John Rushbrook has made this charming old country inn one of the most popular eating places in west Staffordshire. The inn itself dates back to 1624 when it was built as a farmhouse, a role in which it continued right up until the 1970s. Massive ceiling beams attest

to the inn's antiquity. The award-winning Jonathon's Pantry offers a very extensive menu with "the finest foods from around the world" – Haggis-stuffed Mushrooms or Mussels Côte d'Azur amongst the starters; espetadas, Caribbean, Mexican, Cajun, Italian and Chinese dishes for main courses.

Vegetarian options include a creamy Asparagus, Lemon & Thyme Risotto and there's also a good choice of steaks, fish, seafood and pasta dishes. At lunchtimes, Monday to Saturday, traditional pub dishes, hot open sandwiches, sizzlers and char-grilled dishes are all on offer. Although only a few miles from junction 14 of the M1, the Yew Tree enjoys a peaceful rural location – an ideal base for exploring the area. If you are planning to stay, the Yew Tree has 3 quality guest rooms, all with a 4 Diamonds rating and all with en suite facilities.

road through this village (the name is pronounced 'Nawzell') and it also has its very own ghost! On the night of January 21st 1879 a man was attacked at Gnosall canal bridge by an alarming black monster with enormous white eyes. The police were quite sure it was the ghost of a man–monkey who had haunted the bridge for years after a man was drowned in the canal. It is worth staying a while in the village, ghost permitting, to have a look around the fine collegiate Church of St Lawrence. As well as containing some of the best Norman work to be seen in the county, the church, most of which dates from the 13th and 15th centuries, has a particularly ornate west crossing arch.

Despite its name, a large portion of the **Shropshire Union Canal**, some 23 miles, lies within the county of Staffordshire. Indeed, much of this southern section passes through wonderful countryside. Extending from Ellesmere Port, Cheshire, on the Manchester Ship Canal to Autherley junction near Wolverhampton, the Shroppie, as it is affectionately known, has a long history.

Built by three separate companies, at three different times, the Canal was begun as early as 1772 but not finished until 1835, a few months after the death of Thomas Telford, who had worked on its construction. In order to compete with the new railways, the canal had to

be built as simply and economically as possible and so, unlike many canals before it, the Shropshire Union's route was short and straight, cutting deeply through hills and crossing lower ground on embankments rather than talking the longer route on level ground.

The Canal's **Cowley Tunnel**, near the village, was originally intended to be longer than its actual 81 yards but, as it was being constructed, the rock towards the southern end, being softer, gave way. The dramatic fault, where the more solid sandstone of the northern end meets the soft marlstones, can still be seen by taking the towpath through the tunnel and cutting.

WESTON-UNDER-LIZARD

11 miles SW of Stafford on the A5

Situated on the site of a medieval manor house, **Weston Park** has been the home of the Earls of Bradford for 300 years. Disraeli was a frequent visitor here and on one visit presented the house with a grotesque stuffed parrot. The parrot became famous when the present Earl, after leaving Cambridge, published a book entitled *My Private Parts and the Stuffed Parrot*. The stuffed parrot still enjoys the hospitality of Weston Park. The parkland at Weston has matured over several hundred years into a masterpiece of unspoilt landscape. Many have left their mark, yet each successive

RED LION FARM ICE CREAM PARLOUR

Church Eaton Road, Haughton, nr Stafford ST18 9EY
Tel: 01785 780587 Fax: 01785 780644
e-mail: info@red-lion-farm.co.uk   website: www.red-lion-farm.co.uk

The major attraction at the **Red Lion Farm Ice Cream Parlour** is the delicious range of ice creams made with the milk from Graham and Janis Hollinshead's own herd of Jersey cows. The 27 varieties, including honeycomb, ginger & lime, cappuccino and passion fruit, are made in the traditional way to a family Italian recipe are scrumptious. In addition to ice cream, the farm shop also sells home-made fruit pies, cakes and steak & kidney puddings; visitors can watch the cows being milked. Ample parking.

generation has taken note of its predecessors. Disraeli loved the Park. In one of his letters to Selina, 3rd Countess of Bradford, he refers to the 'stately woods of Weston'. There are some wonderful architectural features in the Park, including the Roman Bridge and the Temple of Diana, both designed and built by James Paine for Sir Henry Bridgeman in about 1760. Fallow deer and rare breeds of sheep roam the vast parklands and there are plenty of other interesting attractions for visitors of all ages including nature trails, a miniature railway and a Museum of Country Bygones.

FEATHERSTONE
12 miles S of Stafford off the A449

Just to the south of the village is **Moseley Old Hall**, which visitors can be forgiven for thinking belongs to the 19th century. In fact, it dates from the first Elizabethan Age and, inside, much of the original panelling and timber framing is still visible. The Hall once sheltered King Charles II for a short time following his defeat at the Battle of Worcester in 1651 and it is for this that the house is best remembered. Under cover of darkness the defeated King, disguised as a woodcutter, was escorted into the house by Thomas Whitgreave, the owner, and his chaplain, John Huddlestone. He rested here for two days and even evaded capture when Parliamentarians visited the house in search of the monarch before leaving, again in disguise, and fleeing to France. In 1940, the house was acquired by the Wiggin family and, in 1962, it became the property of the National Trust. At that time it had no garden to speak of, but fairly soon two experts recreated the garden in the style of the century. The outstanding feature is the knot garden with its box hedges and gravel beds. There is interest everywhere

in this wonderful garden, which is full of rare 17th century plants and herbs. In the barn is an exhibition showing the escape of King Charles.

GREAT HAYWOOD
5 miles E of Stafford on the A51

This ancient village is famous for having the longest packhorse bridge in England. Built in the 16th century, the Essex Bridge (named after the famous Elizabethan Earl who used nearby Shugborough Hall when hunting in the area) still has 14 of its original 40 arches spanning the River Trent. Here, too, is the interesting Roman Catholic Church of St John the Baptist. Built in 1828, in 1845 the whole church was moved from its original site at Tixall to Great Haywood by the local Roman Catholic community. With an ornate west front and Perpendicular windows, it is the richness of the west gallery that is the highlight of the building.

Most visitors to the village however, pass swiftly through it on their way to one of the most impressive attractions in the county, **Shugborough Hall**, the 17th century seat of the Earls of Lichfield. This magnificent 900-acre estate includes Shugborough Park Farm, a Georgian farmstead built in 1805 for Thomas, Viscount Anson, and now home to rare breed animals and to demonstrations of traditional farming methods such as hand milking, butter and cheese making and shire horses at work. The former servants' quarters have been restored to the days of the 19th century and offer an insight into life below stairs. The mansion itself is a splendid piece of architecture, altered several times over its 300 years, but always retaining its distinct grandeur. Outside, in the beautiful parkland, can be found an outstanding collection of neoclassical monuments dotted around and the Lady

Walk leads along the banks of the River Sow to the delightful terraced lawns and rose garden.

INGESTRE

4 miles E of Stafford off the A51

The beautiful **Church of St Mary the Virgin**, in this small estate village, is something of a surprise. Standing close to the Jacobean Ingestre Hall, the sophisticated church was built in 1676 and has been attributed to Sir Christopher Wren. One of the few churches that Wren designed outside London, it has an elegant interior with a rich stucco nave ceiling and some of the earliest electrical installations in any church. The chancel, which is barrel vaulted, is home to a delightful garlanded reredos and there are many monuments to the Chetwynds and Talbots, who were Earls of Shrewsbury from 1856 and had their seat in the village.

STOWE-BY-CHARTLEY

5 miles E of Stafford on the A518

On the A518 Stafford-Uttoxeter road, a mile east of Weston, **Amerton Farm** has something for everyone, with a garden centre, craft centre, farmyard and trail, animal rescue centre and a steam railway, a shop selling doll's houses, puppet-making, a bakery and tea rooms.

RUGELEY

7 miles SE of Stafford on the A51

On first arriving in the town, visitors can be mistaken for thinking that Rugeley is all modern but, at its heart, there are some fine 17th and 18th century buildings that have survived the years of industrialisation. Between 1860 and 1967, the cattle market was held behind the inn and a market bell was rung from the steps of the hostelry to summon the farmers back from their lunch.

Rugeley's original parish church, the **Old Chancel**, was founded in the 1100s though it is only the tower, chancel and north chapel that remain from those early days; the rest of the building dates back to the 13th and 14th centuries. The nave was demolished in 1823 to help pay for the building of the imposing new church which, too, is well worth a visit.

Next to the Old Chancel is **Church Croft**, a fine Georgian house and the birthplace of William Palmer. Later in life, as Dr William Palmer, he brought unhappy notoriety to the town in Victorian times as he poisoned his hapless victims after insuring them. Eventually he was caught, put on trial, found guilty of murder and publicly hanged in Stafford in 1856. The Tudor house rented by the evil Dr Palmer still stands.

ROSS ART & CRAFT

6 Bow Street, Rugeley, Staffordshire WS15 2BT
Tel/Fax: 01889 579598 website: docrafts.co.uk
e-mail: rossartandcraft@btopenworld

A former art teacher, Ross Slater established **Ross Art & Craft** in 1999 to provide a comprehensive range of art materials – paints, brushes, paper – along with a wide selection of books on art. She also offers an excellent framing service with an extensive choice of frames available. In the adjacent Ross Art Studio, there are art classes every day of the week except Sunday: beginner or intermediate watercolour; oils or acrylics; craft classes; life drawing (once a month); art and design. On Saturday mornings there's a children's art club and on Tuesday evenings an art class for ages 14 to 18.

Ridware Arts Centre, just outside the town, is within the Tudor walls of the ancient manorial site of Hamstall Hall and is home to a fascinating group of shops, studios and a restaurant. Also nearby is **Wolseley Garden Park**, which has a whole variety of themed gardens within its 45 acres.

CANNOCK CHASE

5 miles SE of Stafford on the A34

Though close to areas of dense population, Cannock Chase is a surprisingly wild place of heath and woodland that has been designated an Area of Outstanding Natural Beauty. Covering some 20,000 acres, the Chase was once the hunting

Cannock Chase

THE MUSEUM OF CANNOCK CHASE

Valley Road, Hednesford, Staffordshire WS12 5TD
Tel: 01543 877666   Fax: 01543 428272
e-mail: museum@cannockchaedc.gov.uk

This museum illustrates the rich social and industrial heritage of the area, from medieval hunting forest to coal field community, reflecting the social and domestic life of times past. The new Toys Gallery has a collection of toys from the Victorian era right up to present day, including lots to do for 'kids' of 'all ages'. Enter the Coal Face gallery to discover the harsh working conditions of a coal miner.

Temporary exhibitions and a full events diary ensure that there is always something new to see or do. Admission free. Open Easter to end September - daily 11am-5pm; October to Easter - Monday to Friday 11am-4pm.

ground of Norman kings and, later, the Bishops of Lichfield. Deer are still plentiful. Conifers now dominate but it is still possible to find the remains of the ancient oak forest and, in the less well-walked marshy grounds, many rare species survive. A popular place for leisurely strolls, the Chase is also ideal for more strenuous walking and other outdoor recreational activities. Excellent view points can be found at **Coppice Hill** and **Brereton Spurs**, while **Castle Ring**, an impressive Iron Age hill fort, is well worth the effort to find.

Amid all this natural beauty, there are also reminders of the 20th century and, in particular, the unique military cemeteries near **Broadhurst Green**, where some 5,000 German soldiers from the First World War lie buried. Cannock Chase was used as a training ground during that war and was the last billet for many thousands of soldiers before they left for France. The

Continued on page 134

WALK 4

Marquis Drive and Castle Ring

Start	Brereton Spurs car park and picnic area
Distance	5 miles (8 km)
Approximate time	2½ hours
Parking	Brereton Spurs
Refreshments	None
Ordnance Survey maps	Landranger 168 (Derby and Burton upon Trent) and explorer 6 (Cannock Chase)

Two commanding viewpoints are the chief focal points of this hilly walk on easy and well-defined tracks amidst the woodland and heathland of Cannock Chase. One of these, Castle Ring, has the distinction of being the highest point in the Chase, at 801ft (244m), and occupies the site of an extensive prehistoric fort.

Brereton Spurs car park and picnic area occupy an open and elevated position from which there are fine views over both the Trent valley and Cannock Chase.

Turn left out of the car park and walk along the road, descending gently to reach a junction. A few yards before the junction turn sharply to the right along a broad downhill track **A**; this is the Marquis Drive, named after a 19th century Marquis of Anglesey who had it constructed as a carriage drive. The track undulates through an area of conifer forest edged with broadleaved trees, with fine wooded views, curving to the left and then to the right, and passing to the right of a pool to continue downhill, by a stream on the right, to a road.

Just before reaching the road, turn sharp left (passing beside a forestry barrier) along an uphill track **B**. Bear right at a fork and at a junction of four tracks a few yards ahead, keep straight ahead along an uphill track between conifers. This track later levels out to arrive at a crossroads of tracks on the edge of a golf course. Continue across the course, taking care to avoid low-flying golf balls, to another crossroads of tracks and keep ahead again, descending to a road. Turn left and, opposite the entrance to the golf club car park **C**, turn right, passing beside a forestry barrier, along a track that continues between more tall conifers. This area was once part of Beaudesert Old Park but the hall, home of the Pagets (marquises of

Anglesey) who owned a great deal of Cannock Chase, was demolished in 1932.

After a while the track bears left and then continues in more or less a straight line, later passing to the left of a pool beyond which is the partially landscaped tip of a former colliery – a reminder of the chase's industrial history. (Coal mines became established around its southern fringes in the 19th century.) Continue gently uphill to a crossroads, here bearing left along an uphill path to cross a track and, a few yards ahead, reach a second and broader track **D** .

A short detour ahead brings you to Castle Ring, a large Iron Age fort whose well-preserved ramparts and ditches offer extensive views of the Trent valley.

The route continues by turning left (or right if you have made the detour) along this broad track, which heads downhill. Keep ahead at a junction and, where the track later forks, take the left-hand track, cross a small stream, keep ahead to cross another and continue uphill

in a straight line to reach a road. Just before the road turn right, at a Heart of England Way sign, along a track. At the next such sign, turn left and pass beside a barrier on to the road. Turn right for a few yards to a junction **A** , where you rejoin the outward route, bearing left along Stile Cop Road to retrace your steps to the starting point.   ●

remnants of the training area can still be seen, as can the prisoner of war camp. The use of the Chase as a training ground was not a new idea: in 1873, there were extensive manoeuvres here with one army base at Etching Hill and the other at Hednesford Hills.

The **Museum of Cannock Chase** (see panel on page 131) at the Valley Heritage Centre is only one of the many wonderful parts of Cannock Chase. Opened in May 1989, the Centre is set in the corn store of a former colliery where the pit ponies' feed was kept. Its galleries provide a variety of exhibitions, with rooms dedicated to the natural history of the Hednesford Hills and Castle Ring hill fort. Subjects covered in these galleries change every six months to deal with as many aspects of the area's history as possible. The colliery was a training pit where thousands of trainee miners worked in simulated underground conditions before beginning work in a real mine.

HEDNESFORD
8 miles S of Stafford on the A460

This former mining town lies on the edge of Cannock Chase and its oldest building, The Cross Keys Inn, was built around 1746. The Anglesey Hotel, built in 1831 by Edmund Peel of Fazeley, was originally designed as a form of summerhouse in a Tudor style with stepped gables and this too lies on the heart of Hednesford.

Nearby, the **Hazel Slade Reserve** shows the adaptability of nature with an old-fashioned countryside of small fields, hedges, streams, marshes and woodland. In the 1960s the old broadleaf wood was felled for timber; hedges were planted and cattle grazed the cleared fields. However, a small area of the wood managed to recover and grew from the stumps and seeds that remained in the

ground. Then, five years later, a pool and marsh started to form as the land began to subside as a result of the local mining activity. The Reserve is a popular place for fishermen as well as those interested in natural history.

Rising over 700 feet above sea level, the **Hednesford Hills** are a prominent local landmark, which bring the countryside of Cannock Chase into the heart of Hednesford. Originally covered in oak and birch, these 300 acres of heathland have been the scene of varied activities over the years. They have been quarried for sand and gravel, mined for coal and used for military training. The land is now a registered common and the hills are a tract of wild landscape with a plethora of heathland plants, abundant wildlife and the opportunity for recreation for the people who live nearby.

The hills have other sporting connections, too. Cockfighting once took place at **Cockpit Hill** though the exact location of the old cockpit is unknown. In the 1900s, prize fighters prepared themselves at the nearby Cross Keys Inn for boxing bouts on the hills and racehorses were trained on the land. Race meetings were held here regularly until 1840 when the racetrack at Etchinghill, near Rugeley, became more popular. In particular, three Grand National winners were stabled and trained on the Hednesford Hills: Jealousy won the race in 1861, Eremon in 1907 and Jenkinstown in 1910.

CANNOCK
9 miles S of Stafford on the A34

Lying on the southern edge of Cannock Chase, this colliery town goes back to the time of the Norman Conquest and appears as 'Chenet' in the Domesday Book. It was an important market town for centuries (Henry III granted the charter in 1259), and the attractive market place still holds busy market days on Tuesdays, Fridays and Saturdays.

On the far side of the market place is the Parish Church of St Luke which, according to the records, had a chantry and a grammar school linked to it as early as 1143. The battlemented church tower dates from the 1300s and, together with the west end of the nave, is the oldest surviving part of the building. The arms of Humphrey de Stafford, who was killed at the Battle of Northampton in 1460, are on display.

The ancient bowling green has been there since time immemorial and, overlooking the green, is an imposing Georgian house that was once home to the Council. Nearby is the former conduit head building of Cannock Conduit Trust. Founded in 1736 to bring a water supply to the town, the Trust building, known as the **Tank House**, supplied water to the area until 1942.

BURTON UPON TRENT

The 'capital' of East Staffordshire, Burton upon Trent is famous for its brewing industry. It began many centuries ago, and even the monks of the Benedictine Abbey, founded here in 1100, were not

the first to realise that the Burton well water was specially suited to brewing. William Bass began brewing in Burton in 1777, and by 1863 the brewery had grown to produce half a million barrels of beer each year on a 750-acre site. In 1998 Bass acquired the Burton premises of Carlsberg-Tetley, creating the biggest brewery site in the UK – 830 acres, brewing 5.5 million barrels yearly. The brewery is open for tours, and the entry fee includes a tour of the **Bass Museum of Brewing** in Horninglow Street, and up to three pints of beer or lager. As well as being offered the opportunity of seeing, sniffing and sampling the traditionally brewed beer, visitors can tour the machinery, inspect the fleet of old vehicles (including the famous Daimler Worthington White Shield Bottle Car) and admire the famous Bass shire horses. During your visit, you will find out about bottom fermentation, dry hopping, kilning, mashing, pitching and sparging – but if you've downed all your three pints you might have forgotten some of it by the end.

A Benedictine Abbey, founded by a Saxon earl called Wulfric Spot, was established on the banks of the River Trent, where the **Market Place** now stands. The focus of Burton, it was from

JANNEL CRUISERS

Shobnall Marina, Shobnall Road, Burton upon Trent, Staffordshire DE14 2AU
Tel: 01283 542718 Fax: 01283 545369
e-mail: boats@jannel.co.uk
website: www.jannel.co.uk

With more than 30 years of experience in boat building and cruising, **Jannel Cruisers** maintain a fleet of purpose-designed luxury narrowboats built in-house by the owners. This family-run business keeps its fleet of vessels small – just 5 in all – to provide customers with personal service. The comprehensively equipped boats vary in size from a 40-footer for 2 or 3 people, up to a 65-footer for up to 8 persons. Don't worry if you have never navigated a narrowboat before – staff will show you how to handle the boat and work the locks. There is a well stocked chandlery and gift shop for that unusual gift.

JUSTIN PINEWOOD LTD

The Maltings, Wharf Road, Burton upon Trent, Staffordshire DE14 1P2
Tel: 01283 5105800 Fax: 01283 510865
e-mail: zac@strippedpinedoors.co.uk
website: strippedpinedoors.co.uk

Housed in a former maltings in this brewing town, **Justin Pinewood Ltd** is an Aladdin's Cave of architectural antiques and reproductions of every kind, anything from unusual and beautiful fire surrounds to kitchen and bathroom fittings, from stained glass to statuary, from mirrors to magnificent items of furniture. There are more than 1000 different doors in stock making it simple to find that special door for a period home, cottage or barn conversion.

This family-run business, established more than 20 years ago, also offers bespoke stained glass panels to fit any door or window and can restore existing doors, stained glass and fittings to their original condition. A second major operation at Justin Pinewood is carried out by son Zac who specialises in creating bespoke kitchens, cabinets, period doors and much more. He also provides a stripping service to remove paint from doors, cast iron pieces, in fact, almost everything that has once been painted.

Most items can be stripped in a large vat which ensures fast and efficient removal of paint and varnish. The stripped article is then rinsed off using high pressure water to remove any remaining debris. The company's 25 years of experience in paint removal means that customers can be confident that their doors or furniture will be stripped sympathetically and without damage.

here that the town grew. In the 12th century, the monks constructed a large stone bridge of some 36 arches across the River Trent – today's bridge replaced the medieval structure in 1864. The area along the banks of the Trent, between Burton Bridge and the later structure of Ferry Bridge, which opened in 1889, is known as the **Washlands**. Rich in native wildlife, the Washlands is a haven for all manner of birds, small mammals, trees and plants. This ancient area, now a wonderful, traditionally managed recreational centre for the town, has a history dating back beyond that of Burton itself. It was at Washlands, in the 7th century, that St Modwen is said to have built her chapel and settlement on Andresey Island. No evidence of the constructions remain and they are thought to have been destroyed in a Danish raid in 874. The site of the chapel is marked by a cherry orchard and some yew trees.

AROUND BURTON UPON TRENT

TUTBURY
4 miles N of Burton upon Trent on the A50

The historic village of Tutbury is dominated by the imposing remains of the Castle, which has stood on a naturally defensive outcrop of rock for many centuries. From 1086 to 1265, **Tutbury Castle** belonged to the Ferrers family, who had connections here and in Derbyshire, and for a time it belonged to the Duchy of Lancaster. Today, the Castle is in ruins but it remains an attraction particularly for those interested in Mary, Queen of Scots, who was imprisoned

---

GRANARY COURT

Stubby Lane, Draycott in the Clay, Ashbourne, Derbyshire DE6 5BU
Tel: 01283 820917
e-mail: webmaster@granarycourt.demon.co.uk
website: www.granarycourt.demon.co.uk

Located on the edge of Needwood Forest and situated on the **Staffordshire** and **Derbyshire** borders, **Granary Court** offers superb 4 star ETC rated self-catering accommodation in a beautifully converted 18th century grain store and barn. This accommodation is equally well placed for many attractions

in Staffordshire and Derbyshire. **Sudbury Hall** and **The National Museum of Childhood** is one of the most individual of late 17th Century houses by George Vernon and only 5 minutes by car. Whilst **Calke Abbey** a baroque mansion-"the house that time forgot" is only 20 minutes drive. The only medieval cathedral with three spires can be found in the heart of the historic city of **Lichfield** and is a short trip down the A515.

The internationally famous brewing town of **Burton on Trent** is nearby. A dramatic 11th Century castle can be found at **Tutbury**. Tutbury is also famous for the glass factories which are well worth a visit. For **Family Fun** try the innovative and interactive centre **Conkers** and the **National Forest Centre** at Moira. Not forgetting **Alton Towers**(20 mins) and **Drayton Manor Park** (30 mins) for thrill seeking rides. Other activities within a short distance of Granary Court include **Golf, Skiing, Cycling and Sailing**. So if you are looking for accommodation which is an excellent base for exploring the delights of Derbyshire and the splendours of Staffordshire do not hesitate to call Lynne. Granary Court can also accommodate **groups** of up to 20 people.

here for a while. During the Civil War, Tutbury Castle remained loyal to the Crown while the town was under the control of Parliament. After a three week siege, the Castle surrendered and in the following year, 1647, Parliament ordered its destruction. In the shadow of the castle stands the Priory Church of St Mary the Virgin, one of the finest of all Norman churches. The town itself is both charming and full of character with many Georgian-fronted shops and a wide variety of antiques showrooms in the Tutbury Mill Mews, which was originally an ironmongery and wheelwright.

HOAR CROSS

7 miles W of Burton upon Trent off the B5234

The magnificent Roman Catholic **Church of the Holy Angels** is by the Victorian architect GF Bodley and it so impressed Sir John Betjeman that he called it Bodley's masterpiece. It was

commissioned by the widow of Hugo Francis Meynell Ingram, in his memory, and much of its beauty it due to this remarkable lady.

ABBOTS BROMLEY

10 miles W of Burton upon Trent on the B5234

This delightful 13th century village in the Vale of Trent has some notable timber-framed buildings, among which are the Goat's Head Inn and the village school. The butter cross in the centre of the village is where the local farmers used to sell their produce. Abbots Bromley is known chiefly for its annual **Horn Dance**, and the ancient reindeer horns used in the ceremony are kept in the **Hurst Chapel** of the Church of St Nicholas. The origins of this dance are lost in the mists of time, but it is thought that it was first performed at the three-day Bartelmy Fair, granted to the Abbots of Burton by Henry III in 1226 to

THE STAFFS BOOKSHOP

4 and 6 Dam Street, Lichfield, Staffordshire WS13 6AA
Tel: 01543 264093
e-mail: steph@staffsbookshop.co.uk
website: www.staffsbookshop.co.uk

With some 25,000 books displayed on 2 floors **The Staffs Bookshop** is a bookworm's paradise. Just down the road from the Cathedral and housed in a Grade II listed building, this has been a bookshop for 65 years. The shop is owned by Stephanie Hawkins, an English graduate with a real love for books. She takes pleasure in the thought that the young Samuel Johnson would have walked to his lessons past the cottages that are now the shop, to be taught at Dame Oliver's school two doors down. Dam Street today has several teashops, as well as the bookshop.

Naturally, the shop has a good selection of books about Lichfield and its famous sons such as Dr Johnson, his friend the actor David Garrick, and Erasmus Darwin, grandfather of the more famous Charles Darwin. But amongst those 9 rooms of books you'll find a comprehensive range of topics covered – topography and travel, music and military subjects, as well as a wide range of classic and modern fiction, not to mention children's books. Also on sale are ephemera, postcards and prints. The Staffs Bookshop is open from 9.30am to 5.30pm, Monday to Saturday, and from 1pm to 4pm on Sunday. Our website is open 24 hours a day at staffsbookshop.co.uk.

celebrate St Bartholomew's Day. In early September each year six male dancers carry the horns around the village with six others and a fool, a hobby horse, a bowman and Maid Marian, the last being a man dressed up as a woman. There's dancing and even mock battles with deer heads and reindeer antlers. The procession starts at about 8am and passes by some local farms before arriving at Blithfield Hall around midday. After lunch, the procession wends its way back to the village, where the horns are returned to the church.

Lichfield Cathedral

LICHFIELD

Despite its 18th century prominence Lichfield lagged behind other towns in extensive rebuilding programmes and

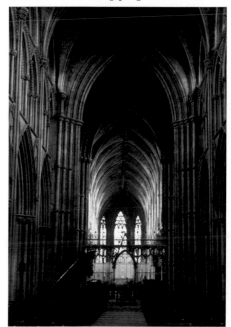

Interior of Lichfield Cathedral

consequently it still retains its medieval grid pattern streets with elegant Georgian houses and, mixed in among them, black and white Tudor cottages. First settled by the Celts and also close to the crossroads of the two great Roman roadways, Ryknild Street (now the A38) and Watling Street (now the A5), Lichfield was one of the most important towns of ancient days; the King of Mercia offered St Chad the seat of Lichfield and, on his death, the town became a place of pilgrimage and an important ecclesiastical centre.

The first cathedral was built here in 669 but no traces of this building, or the later Norman structure, remain. The **Lichfield Cathedral** seen today dates from the 12th century and is particularly famous for the three magnificent spires which dominate the City skyline. Inside there are many treasures, including the beautiful 8th century illuminated manuscript *The Lichfield Gospels* and Sir Francis Chantrey's famous sculpture *The Sleeping Children*.

The surrounding Cathedral Close is regarded by many as the most original and unspoilt in the country. Since it is separated from the rest of the city by **Stowe and Minster Pools**, it is also a peaceful haven of calm. These two wonderful pools, Stowe and Minster, are used for fishing and sailing as well as being the site of the Festival fireworks display each July. The Minster Pool is particularly beautiful – it was landscaped in the late 1700s by Anna Seward and is now a haven for wildfowl.

At the very heart of Lichfield is the **Lichfield Heritage Centre**, part of St Mary's Centre in the Market Place. A church has stood on this site since the 12th century and the present building, the third, dates from 1868. As with many ecclesiastical buildings, the decline in the church-going population made St Mary's redundant and, to save it from being demolished altogether, the Centre was formed. A stroll round here is a fascinating experience and for the energetic, there are spectacular views across the city from the viewing platform on the spire. There are exhibitions on the history and everyday life of the city as seen through the eyes of its inhabitants over the centuries and it also includes the story of the siege of Lichfield Cathedral during the Civil War and displays of the city's silver, ancient charter and archives.

The City has been a place of pilgrims and travellers for centuries and, in 1135, **St John's Hospital** was founded to offer shelter to those passing through Lichfield. One of the finest Tudor brick buildings in the country, the Hospital is now a home for the elderly. The **Hospital Chapel**, with its magnificent stained glass window by the designer of the celebrated east window at Coventry Cathedral, John Piper, is open daily.

The Guildhall, the meeting place of the city governors for over 600 years, has, at various times been a courthouse, police station and prison. Behind its Victorian façade, lie the remains of the city jail, complete with stocks and cells and the City Dungeons can be visited on Saturdays throughout the summer.

Lichfield's most famous son is Dr Samuel Johnson, the poet, novelist and author of the first comprehensive English dictionary. The son of a bookseller, Johnson was born in 1709 in Breadmarket Street, and the house is now home to the **Samuel Johnson Birthplace Museum**. Open every day except Sundays, the Museum, as well as exhibiting artefacts relating to his life and works, also has a series of tableaux showing how the house looked in the early 1700s. Dr Johnson was justly proud of his city:

'I lately took my friend Boswell (a Londoner) and showed him genuine civilised life in an English provincial town. I turned him loose in Lichfield, that he might see for once real civility.'

Here are a few more Johnson gems:

The Plant Plot

Stafford Road (A51), Lichfield, Staffordshire WS13 8JA
Tel: 01543 262805
e-mail: info@theplantplot.com website: www.theplantplot.com

At **The Plant Plot** Dave and Diana Muir have dedicated themselves to "making gardens beautiful". To help pamper your plot they have gathered together an astonishing variety of bedding plants, pot plants, herbs, seeds and seedlings, conservatory plants, alpines, shrubs, trees, and aquatics. They also stock hanging baskets, landscaping material, pots, water features, growing media and other garden supplies. Settle down after your purchases in the relaxing coffee shop serving home made cakes, pastries, scones, soups and light meals. The Plant Plot is open daily from 9.30am to 5.30pm.

'A tavern chair is the throne of human felicity';

'Depend on it sir, when a man knows he is to be hanged in a fortnight, it concentrates the mind wonderfully'

'When two Englishman meet their first talk is of the weather.'

Memorials to Dr Johnson's stepdaughter Lucy Porter can be seen in the medieval St Chad's Church, which has a Norman tower. In the churchyard is a well in the place where St Chad used to baptise people in the 7th century. The ancient practice of well-dressing was revived at St Chad's in 1995 to celebrate the 50th anniversary of Christian Aid and is now an annual event.

Apart from the historic pleasure that Lichfield gives there is also plenty of parkland to enjoy and, in particular, the Beacon Park and Museum Gardens. The 75-acre Park encloses playing fields and a small boating lake and, in the Museum Gardens, can be found a statue of Commander John Smith, captain of the ill-fated *Titanic*, sculpted by Lady Katherine Scott, widow of Scott of the Antarctic.

Anna Seward, the landscaper of Minster Pool, is another of Lichfield's famous sons and daughters. She lived in the Bishop's Palace and was a poet and letter writer as well as being at the centre of a Lichfield-based literary circle in the late 1700s. Erasmus Darwin, the doctor, philosopher, inventor, botanist and poet, and the closest friend of Josiah Wedgwood, lived in a house in Beacon Street on the corner of The Close. The **Erasmus Darwin Centre**, just three minutes from the Cathedral, is a fascinating place to visit, with touch-screen computers to access Darwin's writings and inventions, and a garden where herbs and shrubs that would have

Erasmus Darwin Centre

been familiar to the doctor are grown. Erasmus was the grandfather of Charles Darwin, and had his own theories about evolution. David Garrick, probably the greatest actor-manager of the 18th century theatre, had a home which stands opposite the west gate of the Cathedral.

Lichfield is a festival city, the premier event being the **Lichfield International Arts Festival** held in July.

AROUND LICHFIELD

BURNTWOOD

4 miles W of Lichfield on the A5190

The 700 acres of land and water known as **Chasewater Heaths** are an unexpected find in this otherwise urban setting. On the fringes of the village, Chasewater offers a true wilderness experience with a combination of heath and woodland environments. Criss-crossed by paths and bridleways, the collection of plants and animals found here is so rare that a large area has been designated a Site of Special Scientific Interest. The volunteer-run **Chasewater Railway**, a former colliery railway, operates passenger services behind tank engines between Brownhills West and Norton Lakeside stations. The two-mile trip takes about 25 minutes and trains run every 45 minutes on Sundays and Bank Holiday Mondays from March to October. Old buildings from the industrial days of coal mining can still be seen as can reminders of the time when this was an inland waterside resort.

ARMITAGE
5 miles NW of Lichfield on the A513

Situated on the banks of the **Trent and Mersey Canal**, the village is synonymous with sanitary ware – the manufacturer Armitage Shanks is still located on the canalside. Less well known is the splendid Norman font in the church. Close to the village is the only tunnel along the Trent and Mersey Canal with a towpath. Cut through red sandstone rock, it withstood the test of time and the vibrations of the traffic crossing over it, until, finally the heavy lorries of the late 20th century took their toll. The tunnel was opened out completely but the tunnel effect remains as the widened road still crosses the cutting.

ALREWAS
5 miles NE of Lichfield on the A38

The main street of this enchanting village is lined with delightful black and white thatched cottages, some of which date back to the 1400s. The village Church of All Saints is equally beautiful.

Its doorways are all that remain of the original Norman church; the chancel was built in the 13th century.

The National Memorial Arboretum, on the A513 Alrewas-Tamworth road, is the first large arboretum and wildlife reserve to be created in Britain for 200 years. A substantial grant from the Millennium Commission has transformed a 150-acre former gravel quarry into a sylvan temple whose theme is remembrance and reconciliation. The central feature is the Millennium Avenue, created from cuttings from a 2,000 year old lime tree.

EDINGALE
5 miles E of Lichfield off the A513

A new regional forest, **National Forest**, is reshaping the landscape between this village and Alrewas to the west. The project, which stretches over the three counties, blends the new plantations with ancient woodland and includes farmland, villages and open country.

WHITTINGTON
3 miles SE of Lichfield off the A51

Whittington is home to the **Museum of the Staffordshire Regiment** (The Prince of Wales's), housed in the Victorian Whittington Barracks. The regiment incorporates the former South and North Staffordshire Regiments which were amalgamated in 1959. The Regiment's origins go back to 1705 when the 38th Foot, (later the 1st Battalion of the South Staffordshire Regiment), was raised at Lichfield. The Museum exhibits a good range of uniforms, shako and helmet plates, belt plates and clasps, badges and buttons, and weapons from pistols to machine guns. There are relics from the Sikh Wars, the Crimean, Indian Mutiny, Zulu War, Egypt, Sudan, South Africa and both World Wars. The bravery of the Regiment is in no doubt as among the medals on display there are no fewer than 13 Victoria Crosses. Regimental archives are available for research by prior appointment.

TAMWORTH

8 miles SE of Lichfield off the A5

A modern, busy town, Tamworth is actually much older than it first appears. Straddling the famous Roman Watling Street (now the A5), it has a fascinating and turbulent past. The first reference to the town dates back to the 8th century when it was the capital of the Kingdom of Mercia. King Offa built a palace here. Raiding Danes managed to destroy the town twice and it was later invaded by other Scandinavians who left evidence of their visit in some of the street names such as Gungate.

Alfred's daughter, Ethelfleda, was busy here, too, and excavations in the town centre have revealed Saxon fortifications.

Dominating Tamworth today is the fine Norman motte and bailey **Castle** set in the Pleasure Grounds, which have truly magnificent floral terraces. The sandstone castle, with its superb herringbone wall, dates originally from the 1180s, having replaced a wooden tower on the present artificial mound constructed shortly after the Norman Conquest. A Saxon nun, Editha, is said to haunt Tamworth Castle. The story goes that when de Marmion took possession of his lands he expelled the nuns from a nearby convent. The order had been founded by Editha in the 9th century so the expelled nuns summoned her from her grave. Editha attacked de Marmion in his bedroom and, as a result of her severe beating, he restored the nuns to their home. The Parish Church of St Editha, founded in 963, is vast and was rebuilt after the Norman Conquest; then, again, after the Great Fire of Tamworth

TAMWORTH CASTLE

Tamworth, Staffordshire
Tel: 01827 709626
e-mail: heritage@tamworth.gov.uk

Follow in the footsteps of English kings from William the Conqueror to James 1st and explore over 900 years of history in this magnificent motte and bailey castle which once belonged to the Royal Champion of England. Behind the ancient fortress walls, tudor and jacobean buildings tower over the medieval timber framed Great Hall. Inside, delightfully restored period rooms give a glimpse into upstairs and below stairs life in Tamworth Castle over the centuries and into the life and times of past occupants.

See for yourself the changes made to turn a forbidding fortress into a delightful and intimate family home. Venture into the dungeon and imagine life as a prisoner chained to the damp walls, or into the 12th century undercroft, where you will be greeted by Baron Marmion, Champion to Henry 1st and Henry2nd, in person. And explore our haunted bedroom, where the ghost of St. Editha materialised in 1139, and from where you can hear the ghostly moans and cries of our famous White Lady.

Tamworth Castle in situated in the Town Centre of the historic market town of Tamworth, adjacent to the main shopping precinct and surrounded by pleasant park land, formal gardens and attractive riverside walks. Open 12.00noon to 5.15pm Tuesday to Sunday from Easter to September. Adult admission £4.50, all concessions £2.50. An extensive series of guided tours and costumed events takes place throughout the year . Please phone for further details and for special group rates.

in 1345. The splendid 15th century tower at the west end contains a most remarkable double staircase. The mixture of Victorian and modern stained glass found inside is surprisingly harmonious.

The **Town Hall**, built in 1701, is charming with open arches and Tuscan columns below. The building was paid for by Thomas Guy, the local Member of Parliament, who is probably more famous as the founder of the London hospital that bears his name. Thomas Guy also gave the town its 14 almshouses in **Lower Gungate**, which were rebuilt in 1913.

FAZELEY

9 mile SE of Lichfield on the A4091

Although **Drayton Manor Family Theme Park** cannot really describe itself as a hidden place with over one million visitors a year, the Park has a lot more to offer than just white knuckle rides. As well as the zoo, farm and garden centre there are two museums, one of which is particularly interesting as it charts the history of the Peel family, former owners of Drayton Manor.

The **Birmingham & Fazeley Canal**, which joins up with the Trent & Mersey Canal to the west of Alrewas, made this small town one of the key centres of the English canal system for over 200 years and in the 18th century it had one of the most complete cotton mill complexes in the country. Not only did the Peel family set up their cotton factory here to take full advantage of the canal network but other cotton manufacturers also saw the potential for business at Fazeley. The old factory buildings and mills are being restored to their former glory and a wander along the towpath provides interesting glimpses into the industrial history of the area.

SWINFEN

3 miles S of Lichfield on the A38

On the A38 between Swinfen Island and Weeford Island stands the **Heart of the Country Village**, a country centre set around attractive courtyards in converted farm buildings with a range of shopping outlets and two restaurants.

LEEK

Known as the 'Capital of the Moorlands', Leek is an attractive textile centre on the banks of the River Churnet, noted for its range and variety of antiques shops. It was here that French Huguenots settled, after fleeing from religious oppression, and established the silk industry that thrived due to the abundance of soft water coming off the nearby moorland. Until the 19th century, this was a domestic industry with the workshops

---

ODEON ANTIQUES AND LIGHTING

76-78 St Edward Street, Leek, Staffordshire ST13 5DL
Tel: 01538 387188 Fax: 01538 384235

Odeon Antiques and Lighting occupies a splendid half-timbered building near the town centre, its three floors and 140,000 square feet of display room filled with a huge selection of antique furniture, vintage lighting fitments, garden furniture and interesting collectables. Steve Ford has been trading from this prime location since 1990 and in addition to the antiques also offers a comprehensive restoration service, returning damaged items to their original prime condition. He will also create bespoke kitchens on commission. Deliveries can be arranged to all parts of the United Kingdom and the USA.

on the top storeys of the houses; many examples of these 'top shops' have survived to this day. Leek also became an important dyeing town, particularly after the death of Prince Albert, when 'Raven Black' was popularised by Queen Victoria, who remained in mourning for her beloved husband for many years.

William Morris, founder of the Arts and Crafts movement, lived and worked in Leek for many months between 1875 and 1878. Much of his time here was spent investigating new techniques of dyeing but he also revived the use of traditional dyes. His influence cannot only be seen in the art here but also in the architecture. **Leek Art Gallery** is the place to go to find out more about the wonderful and intricate work of the famous Leek School of Embroidery that was founded by Lady Wardle in the 1870s.

Leek is by no means a recent town that grew up in the shadow of the Industrial Revolution. An ancient borough, granted its charter in 1214, Leek was a thriving market centre rivalling Macclesfield and Congleton. **The Butter Cross**, which now stands in the Market Place, was originally erected near the junction of Sheep Market and Stanley Street by the Joliffe family in 1671. Every road coming into the town seems to converge on the old cobbled Market Place and the road to the west leads down to the Parish Church. Dedicated to Edward the Confessor (the full name is St Edward's and All Saints' Church), the original Church was burnt down in 1297 and rebuilt some 20 years later though the building is now largely 17th century. The timber roof of the nave is well worth a second look and is the Church's pride and joy – it is said that each of the cross beams was hewn from a separate oak

Simpsons Antiques

39 St Edward Street, Leek, Staffordshire ST13 5DN
Tel/Fax: 01538 371515

Simpsons specialise in original painted furniture, potted artifical flowers, lighting and decorative items for the home and garden, all housed on three floors, with French background music, for a taste of France.

Mark sources the elegant furniture from various European countries, including original and restored French mirrors with

painted and guilded finishes, dressers and armoires in rustic, shabby chic and formal finishes.Other pieces are restored and hand painted using decorations from original french designs of flowers and toile by Simpsons at their workshops in Leek. They will also source specific items or

reproduce bespoke designs to customers requirements.

The flowers, oriental orchids, cottage garden flowers, foxgloves, bluebells (too many to mention them all) are potted by Justine, at Simpsons, in old terracotta pots and containers, it's hard to believe they're not real. Decorative items include lamps, shades, hurricane lamps, candlesticks, french throws and cushions, along side a wide selection with elegant garden accents.

COTTAGE DELIGHT AT NO. 64

64 St Edward Street, Leek, Staffordshire ST13 5DL
Tel: 01538 381900 Fax: 01538 370918
e-mail: enquiries@number64.com
website: www.number64.com

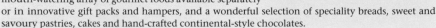

Occupying a beautiful listed Georgian building, **Cottage Delight at No. 64** is a unique speciality food emporium with an award-winning restaurant, a cellar wine bar, an elegant private dining room and stylish bed & breakfast accommodation. In the speciality food shop and patisserie (open 10am to 5pm, Tuesday to Saturday) you'll find a mouth-watering array of gourmet foods available separately or in innovative gift packs and hampers, and a wonderful selection of speciality breads, sweet and savoury pastries, cakes and hand-crafted continental-style chocolates.

The spacious restaurant serves morning coffee, lunch (from 12.00pm), afternoon tea, and dinner (from 7pm) Tuesday - Saturday, Sunday lunch is also available. In good weather, customers can take advantage of the delightful terrace garden. In the Cellar Bar a selection of fine wines, champagnes, British speciality beers and ciders are served and light meals are available at lunchtime. The bar itself is open Tuesday to Friday from 12 noon until 2.30pm, and from 5pm to 11.00pm; on Saturdays from noon until 11.00pm. And if you are planning to stay in this scenic part of the county, Cottage Delight has 3 attractively furnished and decorated double rooms, one with a 4-poster bed and en suite bath; two with en suite showers.

JOHN MOLLAND ANTIQUE MIRRORS

2 Duke Street, Leek, Staffordshire ST13 5LG
Tel: 01538 372553
e-mail: sales@mollandmirrors.co.uk

John Molland is well-known in the fraternity of antiques dealers as a "master of mirrors" and "the best mirror man in the UK". At **John Molland Antique Mirrors** you can understand why he has achieved this glowing reputation during his 21 years experience in the trade. Selling antique mirrors is a very specialised area of the antiques business and John, who has also had outlets in London and Bristol, is only one of 3 such dealers in the UK. His key words are, he says, "knowledge, experience and tradition".

On display in his Duke Street shop is a wonderful range of mirrors in every shape and size, and ranging from ones with simple surrounds to masterpieces of ornate design. John sources many of them from France. As well as selling and restoring these lovely pieces, the company will also make any style of mirror to the same standard and with the same attention to detail lavished on the originals. The most complex mirrors can take up to 300 hours to complete but the company accepts commissions with prices starting as low as £200.

tree. In the west part of the nave, an enormous 18th century gallery rises up, tier on tier, giving the impression of a theatre's dress circle!

Although much has been altered inside the Church, most notably in 1865 when GE Street rebuilt the chancel, reredos, sanctuary, pulpit and stalls, there still remains a rather unusual wooden chair. Traditionally this is believed to have been a ducking stool for scolds that was used in the nearby River Churnet. Outside, in the churchyard, can be found a rather curious inscription on a gravestone: "James Robinson interred February the 28th 1788 Aged 438"! To the north side of the Church is an area still known locally as 'Petty France'; it holds the graves of many Napoleonic prisoners of war who lived nearby.

Another building worthy of a second glance is the imposing **Nicholson Institute**, with its copper dome. Completed in 1884 and funded by the local industrialist Joshua Nicholson, the Institute offered the people of Leek an opportunity to learn and also expand their cultural horizons. Many of the great Victorian literary giants, including George Bernard Shaw and Mark Twain, came here to admire the building. The town's **War Memorial**, built in Portland stone and with a clock tower, has a dedication to the youngest Nicholson son, who was killed in the First World War. Leek was the home of James Brindley, the 18th century engineer who built much of the early canal network. A water-powered corn mill built by him in 1752 in Mill Street has been restored and now houses the **Brindley Water Museum**, which is devoted to his life and work. Visitors can see corn being ground and see displays of millwrighting skills.

PERIOD FEATURES

60b St Edward Street, Leek, Staffordshire ST13 5DL
Tel: 01538 372202
e-mail: enquiries@periodfeatures.net
website: www.periodfeatures.net

Leek is well known for its many antiques shops and **Period Features** complements them perfectly! This very special shop is an excellent source of products for period homes. Lucie Storrs opened her shop in 2001 and it now stocks a vast range of fittings and accessories for the home, both antique and high-quality reproduction. You'll find an excellent

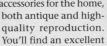

selection of door knobs, letter boxes, bell pulls and pushes, servant's bells, old-fashioned light switches, shelf brackets, toilet roll holders, light pulls, door knockers, cupboard knobs and much more. Lucie and her staff also supply old-fashioned candles, wax furniture polishes and many different products for period gardens.

Period Features is proud to stock a wide range of traditional paints by Farrow and Ball, including sample pots in all 150 colours. The Farrow & Ball wallpaper books are also available for browsing. Period Features is open from 10am to 5pm, Monday to Saturday. Although the actual shop is reminiscent of a Victorian hardware store, Lucie also has an e-commerce site which is open for business 24 hours a day. Visit www.periodfeatures.net to view and purchase many of the products.

Leek has a traditional outdoor market every Wednesday, a craft and antiques market on Saturday and an indoor 'butter market' on Wednesday, Friday and Saturday.

The **River Churnet**, though little known outside Staffordshire, has a wealth of scenery and industrial archaeology and, being easily accessible to the walker, its valley deserves better recognition. The river rises to the west of Leek in rugged gritstone country but for most of its length it flows through softer red sandstone countryside in a valley that was carved out during the Ice Age. Though there are few footpaths directly adjacent to the riverbank, most of the valley can be walked close to the river using a combination of canal towpaths and former railway tracks.

Four miles to the north of Leek on the A53 rise the dark, jagged gritstone

THE GREEN MAN GUEST HOUSE

38, Compton, Leek, Staffordshire ST13 5NH
Tel: 01538 388084   e-mail: diane@greenman.fsworld.co.uk
website: www.greenman-guesthouse.co.uk

Conveniently located in the centre of Leek, **The Green Man** is a former public house that now provides motel-style and guest house accommodation. There are two guest rooms within the main building with a further four in the adjoining annexe. The great attraction is that guests have their own doors and the freedom to come and go as they please. All rooms are en suite with remote control TV and hospitality tray. Accommodation is on a bed & breakfast basis with evening meals available

LEEK GALLERY

17a Broad Street, Leek,
Staffordshire ST13 5NR
Tel: 01538 372961

Opened in 1999, **Leek Gallery** showcases an excellent selection of original watercolours of the Peak District villages and landscapes by artists including Ivan Taylor, Anita Hill, Leslie Gilbert and Tom Mountford. Also on display in the spacious gallery upstairs are works by some of the best local sculptors including beautiful and

unusual ceramic mirrors by Phil Hardaker, modern sculptures by Steve Lovatt and elegant stoneware goblets by Gill Macmillan If you like wood turnery there are some excellent bowls in fine and unusual woods by Micheal Pritchard The Gallery holds several exhibitions a year, work varying from contemporary to traditional. They also stock a wide range of paints and art materials and offer an in-house framing service by skilled picture framers.

outcrops of **The Roaches,
Ramshaw Rocks** and **Hen
Cloud**. Roaches is a corruption of
the French word 'roches' or rocks
and was reputedly given by
Napoleonic prisoners: 'cloud' is
a local word used for high hills.
Just below The Roaches there is
another delightful stretch of
water, **Tittesworth Reservoir**,
which is extremely popular with
trout fishermen. It has some
super trails, a visitor centre with
an interactive exhibition, a
restaurant and a gift shop.

Hen Cloud, The Roaches

AROUND LEEK

RUDYARD
2 miles NW of Leek off the A523

In fond memory of the place where they
first met in 1863, Mr and Mrs Kipling
named their famous son, born in 1865,
after this village. The nearby two mile long
Rudyard Lake was built in 1831 by John
Rennie to feed the Caldon Canal. With
steeply wooded banks the lake is now a
leisure centre where there are facilities for
picnicking, walking, fishing and sailing.
On summer weekends and Bank Holidays,
visitors can enjoy a magical 3-mile return
trip alongside the lake behind the vintage
locomotives of the Rudyard Lake Steam
Railway. The west shore of the Reservoir is
also a section of the Staffordshire Way, the
long distance footpath which runs from
Mow Cop to **Kinver Edge**, near
Stourbridge. This is a sandstone ridge
covered in woodland and heath, and with
several famous rock houses which were
inhabited until the 1950s.

Back in Victorian days, Rudyard was a
popular lakeside resort – in 1877 more
than 20,000 people came here to see
Captain Webb, the first man to swim the
English Channel, swim in the Reservoir.

RUSHTON SPENCER
5 miles NW of Leek on the A523

Well known for its lonely church, the
'Chapel in the Wilderness', this is a
pleasant, moorland village nestling
under the Cloud. Originally built of
wood in the 14th century, the church,
which served both Rushton Spencer and
neighbouring Rushton James, has been
almost rebuilt in stone.

BIDDULPH
6 miles W of Leek on the A527

John Wesley was a frequent visitor to this
isolated moorland town but the history
of Biddulph goes back to long before the
days of Methodism. After the Norman
Conquest the manor of Biddulph was
granted by William the Conqueror to
Robert the Forester, an overlord of what
was then the extensively forested area of
Lyme. The Biddulphs, a staunchly
Catholic family, took control of the area.
John Biddulph fought under the Royal
flag during the Civil War and was killed

BIDDULPH GRANGE GARDEN

Grange Road, Biddulph, Stoke on Trent ST87SD
Tel: 01782 517999

Biddulph Grange Garden, near Stoke on Trent, is a series of picturesque gardens, each with its own character and set of growing conditions. It is one of the most exciting survivals of the great age of Victorian Gardening.

A visit will take you on a journey of discovery around the world, through tunnels and winding pathways. Search for the beauty and tranquillity of China, the magnificence of an Egyptian court and the cool splendour of a Scottish Glen. Unusual and rare plants, mythical beasts and eccentric follies ensure surprises around every corner.

The National Trust owned property is open on Wednesday, Saturday, Sunday and Bank Holiday Monday from April to October and Saturdays and Sundays only during November and December (phone for up to date details and prices). The tearoom offers a wonderful Victorian themed menu with hot and cold lunches, afternoon teas and homemade cakes and biscuits and the shop is full of excellent range of gardening books,gifts and plants.

at the Battle of Hopton Heath. His son entrusted the defence of Biddulph Hall to Lord Brereton who withstood a determined siege until 1644 when he was finally subjected to heavy artillery. The Hall was then demolished to prevent its being re-garrisoned.

Biddulph Grange (National Trust - see panel above) belonged to the Cistercian monks of the Abbey at Hulton until the Dissolution and its garden is one of the most unusual and remarkable in the whole country. It was created by James Bateman in the mid-1800s as a series of connected parts to show specimens from his extensive collection which he had harvested from all parts of the globe.

Highlights include the Egyptian Court and the Great Wall of China.

HARRISEAHEAD

6 miles W of Leek off the A527

Close to the village and perched on top of a hill is **Mow Cop Castle**, which lies exactly on the boundary of Staffordshire and Cheshire. However, the Castle is not all that it appears. The ruined medieval fortress and remains of the round tower are, in fact, what is left of an elaborate summerhouse built by Randle Wilbraham, of nearby Rode Hall, in 1754.

The history of the site goes back much further and the remains of a prehistoric camp have been found here. In 1807, this ancient site gave birth to Primitive Methodism when Hugh Bourne, a Stoke-on-Trent man, and William Clowes, a champion dancer from Burslem, called a meeting on the hill which lasted almost 14 hours. When Mow Cop Castle was given to the National Trust in 1937, 10,000 Methodists marked the occasion with a meeting at the summit.

A small museum of Primitive Methodism can be visited in the school room of **Englesea Brook Chapel** just north of **Balterley**. The chapel is one of the oldest Primitive Methodist chapels to survive.

ENDON

4 miles SW of Leek on the A53

This small village is unusual in that it is the only place in Staffordshire which continues the ancient custom of well-dressing that is so common in neighbouring Derbyshire. Probably based on an ancient pagan ritual, the present ceremony, which was revived in 1845, takes place during the Spring Bank Holiday and includes the coronation of a **Well-Dressing Queen**.

On the Bank Holiday Monday a village fete and fair is held, where there are traditional Morris dancers and the rural competition of 'Tossing the Sheaf' also takes place. In the days before combine harvesters, a heavy sheaf of corn was heaved by pitchfork over a bar which was gradually raised. Today, the game is similar except a 15lb sack of straw is used.

CHEDDLETON

3 miles S of Leek on the A520

The restored **Cheddleton Flint Mill**, in the rural surroundings of the Churnet valley, makes an interesting visit. The water-powered machinery was used to crush flint that had been brought in by canal and then transported, again by water to Stoke where it was used in the hardening of pottery. The small museum includes a rare 18th century 'haystack' boiler and a Robey steam engine. There are also collections of exhibits relating to the preparation of raw materials for the pottery industry. Trips by narrow boats along the Caldon Canal can be taken from the mill.

The village station is home to the **Churnet Valley Railway and Museum**, which will give great delight to all railway enthusiasts. The Museum has a nostalgic collection of beautifully preserved locomotives and other railway memorabilia, and there are steam train rides to Leekbrook Junction and the lovely hamlet of Consall Forge. At present Cheddleton is the only point of vehicular access, but there are plans to extend the line beyond Consall to Froghall, where the main station and visitor facilities will be located. Call 01538 360522 for timetable and other details.

To the west of Cheddleton is **Deep Hayes Country Park**, which lies in a secluded valley by the Caldon Canal and Staffordshire Way. From the ridge there are breathtaking views but, for the less energetic, there is a very pleasant walk around two pools which has many offshoots into lovely countryside.

CONSALL

4 miles S of Leek off the A520

This is a beautiful spot hidden in a particularly deep section of the Churnet Valley downstream from Cheddleton. The little cottages keep close company with the small bridges over the Caldon Canal. Originally known as Consall Forge, the hamlet took its name from an old iron forge that existed here in the first Elizabethan Age. As iron making became uneconomic here, the forge altered its operation and became one of the major lime making centres after the completion of the Caldon Canal.

Reached through Consall village is **Consall Nature Park**, an RSPB reserve that is a quiet and peaceful haven with much to delight the avid birdwatcher. It is accessible only on foot or by canal. The village itself is very popular with walkers and boaters and has a pub to provide the necessary refreshment. Consall Forge Pottery produces hand-thrown stoneware ceramics – teapots are a speciality.

FROGHALL

7 miles S of Leek on the A52

Froghall Wharf was built along the banks of the **Caldon Canal** to act as a trans-shipment area for limestone as it came down a railway incline from the quarries to the south of Waterhouses. Here the limestone was tipped into narrow boats and, from the mid-1800s into railway wagons, to be carried to Stoke-on-Trent. The once-busy Wharf

Caldon Canal

declined after 1920 following the construction of the **Manifold Valley Light Railway**, which directly linked the quarries with Leek and the national railway network. From then on the Canal and Wharf fell into a state of disrepair and it was only due to the efforts of the Caldon Canal Society that the navigation has survived. The Canal, once again open to traffic, is now the sole preserve of pleasure craft and, at the leisurely pace of literally one horse power, narrow boats take visitors along to Consall Forge and back.

CAULDON

8 miles SE of Leek off the A52

This was the site of the quarry from which wagons travelled, down a railway track, to Froghall Wharf. In a former school building in the village can be found the **Staffordshire Peak Arts Centre** which, along with having a craft shop and a restaurant, holds regular exhibitions.

OAKAMOOR

9 miles S of Leek on the B5417

This village was once the home of the Thomas Bolton & Sons copper works that produced some 20,000 miles of copper wire for the first transatlantic cable in 1856. Little now remains of the works, which were demolished in the 1960s, but the site of the mill has been turned into an attractive picnic site complete with the very large mill pond. Nearby **Hawksmoor Nature Reserve** and bird sanctuary covers some 300 acres of the Churnet Valley and is managed by a local committee. The trail through the Reserve includes glorious landscapes, abundant natural history and industrial architecture.

ALTON

11 miles SE of Leek off the B5032

The world-famous **Alton Towers** leisure
park is the main attraction here, but
even this spot has its quieter, lesser
known corners. Originally the home of
the Earls of Shrewsbury, who also owned
much of the surrounding area, the 19th
century mansion by Pugin is now just a
gutted shell. The surrounding gardens
and parkland (which contain most of the
attractions) are older and were laid out
by Capability Brown. Hundreds of
workmen were employed to convert a
whole valley into what is still a
magnificent mix of formal gardens and
parkland. As well as many fountains and
pools there are also numerous paths
which lead to charming follies such as a
Swiss Chalet and a Gothic temple. The
village of Alton has plenty to offer the
visitor. The view up from the valley
bottom to the **Castle**, perched on a

sandstone rock above the River Churnet,
has given this area of Staffordshire the
nickname of 'Rhineland', and the steep
climb up to **Toot Hill Rock** is rewarded
by magnificent views. The Castle, in its
present form, was built mainly by Pugin,
who also built the now restored
Italianate railway station. Note, too, the
old lock-up and water mill.

UTTOXETER

16 miles SE of Leek on the A518

Today, the town is perhaps best known
for its racecourse, a popular National
Hunt track which lies to the southeast of
town. Highlight of the course's 20 days
of racing is the stamina-sapping
Midlands Grand National held in the
spring. Uttoxeter is a traditional, rural
market town, with a busy livestock and
street market on Wednesdays. There are
several pleasant, old, timbered buildings
in Uttoxeter but fires in 1596 and 1672

THE BLYTHE INN

Kingstone, nr Uttoxeter, Staffordshire ST18 0LT
Tel: 01889 500487

Standing in spacious grounds close to the River Blythe,
The Blythe Inn is a handsome old hostelry which
has been restored and extended over the years to
provide a very comfortable and enjoyable place for
lunch, dinner or just a pint of real ale. Barry and Lynda
Edwards arrived here in 1995 and they have
introduced an excellent menu featuring a variety of
traditional favourites alongside more innovative dishes – with the emphasis always on freshness.
There's always a Fresh Fish of the Day option, vegetarian choices, superb steaks, chef's home-made
dishes, a children's menu and some tempting hot or cold desserts.

On Friday and Saturday evenings and at Sunday
lunchtime, a very popular value-for-money Carvery is
available – booking is strongly recommended. To
accompany your meal, there's a choice of 4 or 5 real ales,
house wines and a selection of fine wines. In good
weather, refreshments can be enjoyed on the large patio
and garden. The Blythe Inn is also able to cater for
functions such as wedding breakfasts, private parties or
company presentations and also has its own Caravan
Club Certified Location Site accommodating 5 vans
adjoining the grounds.

destroyed most of the town's architectural heritage. As well as a visit to the Heritage Centre, housed in some old timber-framed cottages in Carter Street, **St Mary's Church** should also appear on a sightseer's itinerary; it has a typical 'preaching box' dating from 1828.

STOKE-ON-TRENT

The city was established as late as 1910 when Fenton joined the five towns (Tunstall, Burslem, Hanley, Longton and Stoke) immortalised by the novels of Arnold Bennett. Once fiercely independent, the towns became progressively involved with each other as improvements in roads, water supplies and other amenities forced them towards amalgamation. The new city's crest, of an ancient Egyptian potter at his wheel in one quarter, sums up the fortune on which the wealth of the area was created. Each of the old towns is also represented in the crest and the joint motto translates to "Strength is stronger for unity".

It was the presence of the essential raw materials for the manufacture and decoration of ceramics, in particular marl clay, coal and water, that led to the concentration of pottery manufacture in this area. Though production started in the 1600s it was the entrepreneurial skills of Josiah Wedgwood and Thomas Minton, who brought the individual potters together in factory-style workplaces, that caused the massive leap forward in production that took place in the 18th century. Their factories were large but there were also hundreds of small establishments producing a whole range of more utilitarian chinaware; production in the Potteries reached its height towards the end of the 19th century. For those interested in pottery and industrial architecture, Stoke-on-Trent is a wonderful place to visit, with many museums and factories open to the public to tell the story of the city. The **Spode Museum & Visitor Centre** in Church Street is one of several famous establishments open to visitors.

Hanley, one of the five towns of The Potteries, and part of the Stoke-on-Trent conurbation, was the birthplace of Arnold Bennett, Sir Stanley Matthews and John Smith (the captain of the ill-fated *Titanic*). **The Potteries Museum & Art Gallery** houses the world's finest collection of Staffordshire ceramics and offers many more attractions, including a natural history gallery and a lively programme of exhibitions, talks, tours and workshops. The Potteries shopping centre, situated in the heart of Hanley, is every shopper's dream with a fantastic range of famous shops all brought together in a beautiful environment. Natural daylight cascades through the centre's many glazed roofs and plants, trees and water features create an outdoor feel.

Burslem, in the northern suburbs, is the home of **Burleigh Earthenware Pottery** (see panel opposite), founded in 1851 and famous for its elegant blue and white patterns. Also in Burslem is the **Royal Doulton Visitor Centre**, which contains the world's largest display of Royal Doulton figures and many other treasures from the company's rich heritage. there are factory tours, demonstrations, a video-theatre, gallery, restaurant and shop. Another Burslem attraction is Ceramica, located in the Old Town Hall, with a huge kiln and an Arnold Bennett study area.

Etruria, to the west of the city centre, was created by Josiah Wedgwood in 1769 as a village for the workers at the pottery factory he built in this once rural valley. Though the factory has gone (it moved to Barlaston in the 1940s), Etruria Hall,

Wedgwood's home, is still standing in what is now the National Garden Festival site. The pottery industry dominated the village and the **Etruria Industrial Museum** displays a steam-powered potters' mill as well as other exhibits connected with the industry.

AROUND STOKE-ON-TRENT

KIDSGROVE
5 miles N of Stoke-on-Trent on the A50

Now chiefly a residential town, Kidsgrove is well worth a visit for anyone interested in canals. The two **Harecastle Tunnels** were major engineering feats of their time and they carry the Trent and Mersey Canal from Cheshire into The Potteries. It was Josiah Wedgwood who first dreamt of building a canal to link the area with the major Trent and Mersey navigation and thus create a

waterway link right across the country from Liverpool to Hull. He fought long and hard to get the necessary Bill passed through Parliament, undaunted by the fact that a 3,000 yard long tunnel would be needed to go through Harecastle Hill. The Bill was passed and, though many scoffed at his plans, Wedgwood's canal and required tunnel, both built by James Brindley, were constructed over an 11 year period.

Those who had their doubts about Wedgwood's grand plan nearly had the last laugh when, some years later, there was almost a catastrophe as Harecastle started to subside. Fortunately, Thomas Telford was on hand to come to the rescue and another tunnel was built alongside the first thus averting disaster. The two tunnels can still be seen today and make a very impressive sight: although Josiah's original tunnel is not in use, the Telford tunnel has been restored.

BURLEIGH EARTHENWARE POTTERY

Port Street, Burslem, Staffordshire ST6 3PE
Tel: 01782 577866 Fax: 01782 575529
e-mail: sales@burleigh.co.uk

Founded in 1851 by William Leigh, **Burleigh Earthenware Pottery** has been a family business ever since. It is the oldest working Victorian pottery left in England and is producing fine earthenware in a multitude of shapes and designs.

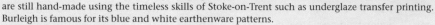

The pottery's products are still hand-made using the timeless skills of Stoke-on-Trent such as underglaze transfer printing. Burleigh is famous for its blue and white earthenware patterns.

Amongst them are the deep cobalt blue pattern of Calico representing the season of Spring with fallen prunus blossom on cracked ice; the romantic gentle blue pattern of Asiatic Pheasants (the most popular pattern in Victorian times); and Chequers, a fun pale blue checked pattern designed in the 1960s by Burleigh's designer David Copeland. The range of products is comprehensive – every possible kind of tableware from soup tureen to roulade tray; jugs starting with a tiny Cream Tot and extending to a 9-litre Dutch Flower Jug; kitchenware that includes a bread crock with a wooden lid, a Stilton Cheese Dome, and a Teabag Holder. There are also planters, crockery sets for babies –and even special plates for your cat! This extraordinary range is displayed in the factory shop (open every day) along with a selection of seconds and many bargains from discontinued and current lines.

LONGTON

2 miles SE of Stoke-on-Trent on the A50

The **Gladstone Working Pottery Museum** on Uttoxeter Road is a fascinating museum of the British pottery industry housed in a Victorian building. It tells visitors the story of how 19th century potters worked, with the display of traditional skills, the original workshops, the cobbled yard and the huge bottle kilns creating a unique atmospheric time-warp. As the brochure proclaims: 'throwing, jiggering, fettling, saggar making, glazing, dipping, firing, painting, sponging, moulding, casting – it's all at Gladstone'. Aynsley China, John Tams and Staffordshire Enamels have their factory shops in Longton.

BARLASTON

5 miles S of Stoke-on-Trent off the A34

A visit to The Potteries would not be complete without a visit to the **Wedgwood Visitor Centre and Museum**, set in a beautiful 500-acre country estate just outside Barlaston. The Museum traces the history of Wedgwood

from the founding of the factory in 1759 to the present day through the displays of Queen's Ware, Jasper, Black Basalt and fine bone china. In rooms designed to recapture the style of specific periods there are hundreds of Wedgwood pieces from those eras. George Stubbs and Joshua Reynolds both painted portraits of the Wedgwood family, these hang in the centre's art gallery. In the craft centre, potters and decorators can be watched as they use traditional skills to create today's Wedgwood products. The centre is open every day.

HANCHURCH

5 miles S of Stoke-on-Trent on the A5182

This tiny hamlet itself is unlikely to ring any bells with visitors as they pass by but the nearby gardens are world famous.

Trentham Gardens were landscaped by Capability Brown and given a more formal style by Sir Charles Barry, whose work can be observed in the lovely Italian gardens. Although the Hall was demolished in 1911, this style can still be recognised in such buildings as the orangery and sculpture gallery which remain today and form a framework for the outstanding conference, exhibition and banqueting centre that is Trentham. There is, normally, unrestricted access to 800 acres of woodland, lake and gardens, with opportunities for woodland walks, boating and jet skiing.

WILLOUGHBRIDGE

9 miles SW of Stoke-on-Trent on the A51

This remote hamlet, on the slopes of the Maer Hills, was once a fashionable spa after warm springs were discovered by Lady Gerard. Those days have long since gone but a trip to the **Dorothy Clive Garden** in the

Gladstone Pottery Museum

rolling countryside by the Shropshire border is well worth making.

NEWCASTLE-UNDER-LYME
2 miles W of Stoke-on-Trent on the A53

This ancient borough, which received its first charter from Henry II in 1173, was, for several centuries, the largest town in north Staffordshire. Today, the town maintains its individuality from its close neighbour, Stoke-on-Trent, and its centre is designated a conservation area. One of the best ways of exploring the delights of Newcastle-under-Lyme is to follow either, or both, of the town trails which take in many of the town's most notable buildings. Both begin in Nelson Place and the first takes in not only the early 19th century Church of St George and Mayer House, the former home of a famous veterinary family, but also some fine Georgian houses and, in Marsh Parade, the vast 19th century building which once housed the town's first silk mill.

The second of the two trails takes in the particularly eye-catching **Merrial Street** before moving on to St Giles's Church, where the base of the tower dates from the 13th century. The original medieval Church was replaced by a brick building in 1720 and, in 1870, it was again rebuilt, this time by George Gilbert Scott, who managed to capture much of the beauty of medieval times.

One of Newcastle-under-Lyme's oldest buildings also features on the route; **The Guildhall**, built in 1713 to replace an earlier timber building, stands beside the base of a medieval cross. The **Borough Museum & Art Gallery**, set in eight acres of parkland, houses a wonderful collection of assorted items from clocks to teapots, paintings to clay pipes, a reconstruction of a Victorian street and exhibitions of local and national artists. A mile from the town centre, the **New Victoria Theatre** was Europe's first purpose-built 'theatre-in-the-round'.

MADELEY
7 miles W of Stoke-on-Trent on the A525

Situated on an ancient packhorse route from Newcastle-under-Lyme, this village's name comes from the Anglo-Saxon 'maden lieg', which means 'clearing in the woods'. The focal point of this enchanting place, which has been designated a conservation area, is **The Pool**, formed by damming the River Lea to provide water power for the corn mill that still stands at its northern end. The pool is a haven for a variety of bird life. Madeley's grandest building is the **Old Hall**, an excellent example of a 15th century squire's timber-framed residence. The village's large sandstone church can be seen through the trees from the mill pond. Standing in a raised churchyard, with ancient yew trees, All Saints Parish Church was originally Norman but was extensively enlarged in the 1400s; the chapel was rebuilt in 1872.

STONE

Augustinian monks founded a priory here in the 12th century, of which only one arch and some cloisters now remain, and in 1251 Henry II granted the monks a charter to hold a market. In its heyday as a trading town, some 38 coaches pulled up daily at the bow-windowed Crown Hotel, still one of the most attractive buildings along the High Street. Built during this period of prosperity, the early Gothic Revival Parish Church of St Michael contains several interesting monuments including a bust of Admiral John Jervis, Earl St Vincent, the hero of the great naval victory off Cape St Vincent in 1797. The Trent & Mersey Canal played a large part in Stone's early economic development and today it still brings work to the town through the building of holiday canal cruisers and a growing tourist trade. The Canal was begun in 1766 and, by 1771, it had reached Stone. The celebrations which accompanied its opening here were so boisterous that one of the four locks in the town and a bridge collapsed under the weight of people! Stone is a true canal town, the dry docks and workshops are still busy today, as they have been for well over 200 years.

AROUND STONE

SANDON
4 miles SE of Stone on the B5066

Near the village stands the ancestral home of the Earl of Harrowby, **Sandon Hall**. Rebuilt in 1850 after the earlier house had been damaged by fire, the Hall

is surrounded by 400 acres of parkland, which include a notable arboretum. The Hall is steeped in history and, along with the impressive interior, makes an interesting and informative visit. The family, too, has led a fascinating life with no less than seven generations in parliament and three successive members of the family holding office in the Cabinet. The museum tells of their lives and also includes costumes, toys and the duelling pistols of William Pitt the Younger. Open throughout the year, with many special events such as antiques fairs, craft shows and vintage car rallies, the Hall is also available for private events and functions.

ECCLESHALL
5 miles SW of Stone on the A519

For over a thousand years **Eccleshall Castle** was the palace of the bishops of Lichfield but, at the beginning of the 19th

---

THE SEVEN STARS COUNTRY INN & RESTAURANT

Sandon Bank, nr Stafford ST18 9TB
Tel: 01889 508316 Fax: 01889 508173
e-mail: thesevenstars@aol.com

Originally built as a coaching inn some 300 years ago, **The Seven Stars Country Inn & Restaurant** still exudes the ambience of a more relaxed age with spacious rooms, real log fires and a welcoming atmosphere. David Stubbs and Steven Sayer are the proprietors of the Seven Stars - David is a qualified chef with 20 years experience in the hospitality industry and Steven has 10 years experience in the service industry. The inn offers not just one but three separate restaurant areas. "The Galley" is a small intimate area, usually chosen for parties of around 20 to 25 guests who prefer a more private evening. The second is "the middle restaurant" which seats approximately 30 diners and is a strictly non-smoking area. Finally, there's

the main restaurant seating up to 60 which is also used as a function room with a late bar and disco facilities.

Options range from an extensive à la carte menu through traditional Sunday lunch to basket meals. Dishes are prepared using local produce wherever possible and are served at tables draped with white linen cloths, napkins and polished king's cutlery by experienced and friendly waitresses. Children are welcome and have their own menu and a play area monitored by closed circuit television. Outside, there's a heated patio area, ideal for private barbecue parties, and ample parking space.

JOHNSON HALL NURSERIES

Newport Road, Eccleshall, Staffordshire ST21 6JA
Tel/Fax: 01785 850400 website: plants4life.co.uk

Just a 10-minute drive from junction 14 of the M6, on the A519, **Johnson Hall Nurseries** occupies the walled garden of an old manor house, complete with Victorian wooden greenhouses. The Edwards family have owned and run the nurseries for some 50 years and offer a huge range of plants and shrubs with camellias a speciality. They also stock teak garden furniture; terracotta, stone and ceramic pots; and hanging baskets - it was the nursery's hanging baskets that earned Eccleshall an outstanding merit award when it won the Britain in Bloom competition, Small Town category, in 2001.

century, it became a family home when the Carter family moved here from Yorkshire. The present simple sandstone house is typical of the best architecture of the William & Mary period and incorporates part of the earlier 14th century Castle. The interior of the house has been augmented by successive members of the family, one of whom added a magnificent Victorian staircase and dome. Perhaps to remind them of the county from which they came, the Carters have collected a very interesting number of 19th century paintings by Yorkshire artists. The gardens have been created around the ruins of the old castle and have a great deal of romantic appeal.

A little way north of Eccleshall, on the A519 at Cotes Heath, is **Mill Meece Pumping Station**, where two magnificent steam engines that once pumped more than three million gallons of water each day are kept in pristine condition.

SHALLOWFORD

4 miles SW of Stone off the B5026

Set in beautiful grounds in this tiny hamlet near Norton Bridge, **Izaak Walton's Cottage** (see panel opposite) is a pretty 17th century half-timbered cottage which was once owned by Izaak Walton, famous biographer and author of *The Compleat Angler*. Fishing collections are on show, and there's a

small souvenir shop.

Within the grounds are an authentic 17th century herb garden, a lovely picnic area and orchard. The Cottage is open daily Tuesday to Sunday and Bank Holidays from April to October.

IZAAK WALTON'S COTTAGE

Worston Lane, Shallowford, Near Stone, Stafford ST15 0PA Tel: 01785 760278 (Apr - Oct) or 01785 619619 (Nov - Mar)
e-mail: izaakwaltonscottage@staffordbc.gov.uk

Stafford's rural heritage is embodied in **Izaak Walton's Cottage**, the charming 17th century home of the celebrated author of 'The Compleat Angler.' The thatched, half-timbered cottage is set in the heart of the Sow Valley at Shallowford, amid the rolling Staffordshire countryside. Izaak Walton's Cottage gives a fascinating insight into the history of angling and the life of a writer whose work remains 'a unique celebration of the English countryside.' Izaak Walton, the son of a Stafford alehouse keeper, purchased the property in 1654, which today is a registered museum and fully restored to reflect its famous heritage.

5 DERBYSHIRE

Traditionally, Derbyshire marks the start of the north of England and the county was also at the forefront of modern thinking at the beginning of the Industrial Revolution. The chief inheritor of this legacy is Derby, the home of Rolls-Royce and Royal Crown Derby porcelain, and it remains a busy industrial centre today. An early landmark of this new age is Richard Arkwright's mill and associated village at Cromford. In the south of the county there is the time capsule of Calke Abbey and the charm of ancient Repton.

Black Tor & Loose Hill, High Peak

However, the county is dominated by the Peak District National Park that covers much of its area. The first of the ten National Parks, it is often divided into White and Dark peak as the landscape changes from deep limestone valleys to bleak, isolate moorland.

Along with numerous attractive villages and small towns, ancient monuments and caves and cavers, the park is home to two of the finest stately homes not just in Derbyshire but also in the country – Haddon Hall and Chatsworth.

Continued on page 162

ADVERTISERS AND PLACES OF INTEREST

LOCATOR MAP

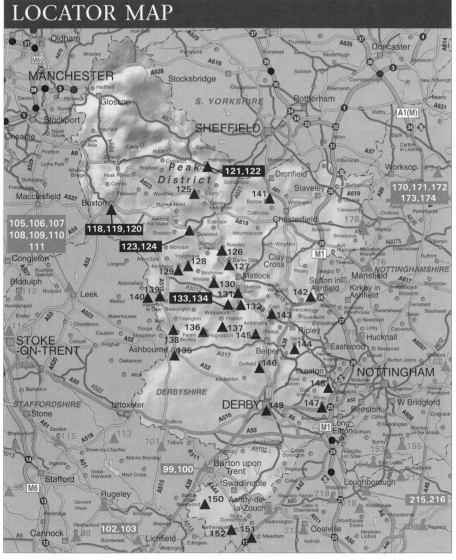

The southern section of the Peak District is probably best known for beautiful Dovedale. The large car park near Thorpe which gives general access to the Dale is often crowded, but there is plenty of room for everyone and the wonderful valley, just a few hundred yards from the car park, is well worth experiencing. It is also the place to have a go at crossing a river on

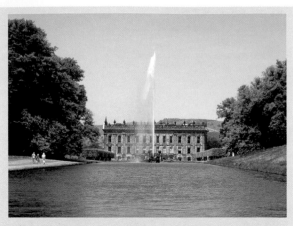

Chatsworth House

stepping stones, something that has delighted children for many, many years. The River Dove is also a Mecca for keen fishermen. It was a favourite spot for Izaak Walton who wrote his famous book, *The Compleat Angler,* in the area.

Monsal Dale Viaduct

The ancient custom of well-dressing is almost exclusively confined to the limestone areas of the county. The porous rock, through which rainfall seeped leaving the surface completely dry just a few hours after heavy rainfall, meant that, for the people of these close-knit communities, the well or spring was of utmost importance. If this dried up, the lives of the whole community were at risk.

The area of northeast Derbyshire and the District of Bolsover centres around Chesterfield. This was the heart of the county's coal-mining area and many of the towns and villages reflect the prosperity the mines brought in Victorian times. Sadly, the vast majority of the collieries are now closed; there was for a while a period of decline, but visitors today will be surprised at the wealth of history and fine architecture to be seen throughout the region.

THE PEAK DISTRICT

The Peak District National Park was the first of Britain's National Parks to be established, in 1951, and ever since then its 555 square miles of glorious scenery has been protected from 'inappropriate development'. Of all the world's national parks, it is the second most popular – only Mount Fuji in Japan attracts more visitors each year.

Referred to as the Dark Peak as well as the High Peak, the northern area of the Peak District National Park is not as foreboding as its name might suggest. These high moors are ripe for exploring on foot, and a walk from the Kinder Reservoir will lead to the western edge of Kinder Scout. This whole area is really a series of plateaux, rather than mountains and valleys, with the highest point on Kinder Scout some 2,088 feet above sea level. In this remote and wild area the walker can feel a real sense of freedom - however, it is worth remembering that the moors, with their treacherous peat bogs and unpredictable mists which can rise quickly even in summer, should not be dismissed as places for a casual ramble.

To the eastern side of this region are the three reservoirs created by flooding of the upper valley of the River Derwent. Howden, Derwent, and Ladybower provide water for the East Midlands but their remote location, along with the many recreational activities found there, make them popular places to visit. The Derwent dam is particularly famous as the site of practice exercises for the Dambusters of the Second World War.

BUXTON

With a population of barely 20,000, the elegant Georgian town of Buxton is

HAREFIELD

15 Marlborough Road, Buxton,
Derbyshire SK17 6RD
Tel/Fax: 01298 24029
e-mail: hardie@harefield1.freeserve.co.uk
website: www.harefield1.freeserve.co.uk

Just a few minutes walk from the town centre, **Harefield** is an elegant Victorian property set in its own grounds and enjoying fine views over Buxton and beyond. Harefield

is the home of George and Ruth Hardie who offer their guests a choice of either bed & breakfast or self-catering accommodation. Bed & breakfast guests stay in the main house which has a comfortable lounge area where you'll find local tourist information, maps of the area and books to browse through. There's a choice of double, twin or single rooms, all of which have en suite shower rooms . A master bathroom is also available.

Each room has a drinks-making facility, colour TV and easy chairs to relax in. A hearty breakfast is included in the tariff, with a choice of cereals, fruit juices and cooked breakfasts, and the Hardies normally offer a 3-course evening meal with a choice of meat or vegetarian main dish. Packed lunches are also available if required. Guests are welcome to enjoy the garden where they can also take part in a game of croquet. For self-catering guests, the 3-bedroomed Garden Flat at Harefield and a 2 bedroomed cottage at Tideswell are available to let on a weekly or short break basis. Please note, Harefield has a no smoking policy.

nevertheless the largest settlement within the boundaries of the Peak District National Park. (The second largest town, Bakewell, has fewer than 5,000 inhabitants). Buxton's gracious architecture can be attributed mainly to the efforts of the 5th Duke of Devonshire who hoped to establish a northern spa town that would rival, possibly surpass, the attractions of Bath in the southwest. In both locations it was the Romans who first exploited the healing waters of apparently inexhaustible hot

Buxton Opera House

springs as a commercial enterprise. The Romans' name for Buxton was *Aquae Arnemetiae* – the Spa of the Goddess of the Grove. The waters still bubble up at Buxton, always maintaining an incredibly constant temperature of 82 degrees Fahrenheit (28 degrees Centigrade). Go on, drink a glass -

Buxton water is reputed to be particularly pure and especially effective in mitigating the symptoms of rheumatism. Countless sufferers from rheumatism are on record attesting that the balmy Buxton water helped to soothe their painful symptoms: Mary, Queen of Scots, a political prisoner detained at nearby Chatsworth but allowed out on day release to Buxton, was one of them.

In the 18th century, the 5th Duke of Devonshire commissioned the building of **The Crescent** to ensure that visitors would flock here. Designed by John Carr of York, the building is similar to the architecture found in Bath and, after suffering from neglect, underwent a huge restoration programme. As with many places, the coming of the railway to Buxton in 1863 marked the height of popularity of the town. Nothing, however, could be done to alter the harsh climate, and the incessant rainfall meant

BUXTON MUSEUM AND ART GALLERY

Terrace Road, Buxton, Derbyshire SK17 6DA
Tel: 01298 24658 Fax: 01298 79394
e-mail: buxton.museum derbyshire. gov.uk
website: www.derbyshire.gov.uk/libraries

Explore the Wonders of the Peak through seven time zones. Discover when sharks swam in warm 'Derbyshire' seas; when lions and sabre tooth cats terrorised mastodons. Meet the Roman legionaries, and the scientists unravelling the history of Earth. In 2003 you will be able to enjoy an audio visit of the gallery.

For art lovers, enjoy intricate Ashford Black Marble inlay and blue john ornaments, and a regular programme of exhibitions, featuring work by national and local artists, photographers and craftworkers. 2003 highlights include the Derbyshire Open

Exhibition and works by Peter Knight. Programmes of activities for all the family accompany the exhibitions. The museum welcomes visits from school parties. Other facilities include access for the disabled, local parking (pay & display), shop, toilets and nearby tearooms.

that the Duke's dream of making Buxton the 'Bath of the North', was never truly realised.

Among the other notable architectural features of the town are **The Colonnade** and the **Devonshire Royal Hospital**. They were originally built as stables for hotel patrons of The Crescent and, after their conversion by the 6th Duke in 1858, the largest unsupported dome in the world was built to enclose the courtyard in 1880.

Originally built in 1905, the attractive **Opera House** was restored in 1979 to its grand Edwardian style. After being used as a cinema for many years, it is once again the host of live performances and, as well as offering a comprehensive and popular programme throughout the year, also has one of the largest stages in England.

The attractive **Pavilion Gardens** have a conservatory and octagon within the grounds – antique markets and arts shows are often held here, and it is a very pleasant place to walk around any time of year. Laid out in 1871 by Edward Milner, with money donated by the Dukes of Devonshire, the 23 acres include formal gardens, serpentine walks and decorative iron bridges across the River Wye. The conservatory was reopened in 1982 following extensive renovation; there is also a swimming pool filled with warm spa water.

St John the Baptist church was built in Italian style in 1811 by Sir Jeffrey Wyatville. That same year Wyatville laid out The Slopes, the area below the Market Place in Upper Buxton. The grand **Town Hall** was built between 1887 and 1889 and dominates the Market Place. Further down Terrace Road is the **Buxton Museum** (see panel opposite), which reveals the long and varied history of the town and its surrounding area. As well as housing an important

---

Buxton's Victorian Guest House

3a Broad Walk, Buxton, Derbyshire SK17 6JE
Tel: 01298 78759 Fax: 01298 74732
e-mail: buxvic@tiscali.co.uk
website: www.buxtonvictorian.co.uk

Overlooking the superb Pavilion Gardens and just a 2-minute stroll from Buxton's imposing Opera House, **Buxton's Victorian Guest House** offers high quality bed & breakfast accommodation in a delightfully refurbished Victorian Grade II listed property. It was built in 1860 by the Duke of Devonshire who is commemorated in the Devonshire Drawing Room, a charming room with a small library of books of local and historical interest. Breakfast is served in the Oriental Dining Room and is based on local produce wherever possible including free range eggs from one of the highest farms in England!

There's a good choice of guest bedrooms, ranging from the Premier Room with its elegant antique furniture, 4-poster bed and double aspect views over the Pavilion Gardens. The Superior Rooms are tastefully furnished with Victorian and Edwardian antiques and some interesting artefacts while the comfortable and well-appointed Standard Rooms all have interesting themes such as the Egyptian Room, the Victorian Craftsman's Room and the Imperial Room. All rooms are en suite with colour TV and hospitality tray. Centrally located, the guest house has its own car park and is surrounded by a score or more of restaurants, pubs and bars catering for all tastes.

local archaeology collection, the Museum also has a fine collection of Ashford Marble, Blue John ornaments, paintings, prints, pottery and glassware.

St Anne's Church, built in 1625, reflects the building work performed here before Buxton's 18th century heyday when limestone was the most common construction material rather than the mellow sandstone that dominates today.

Buxton is surrounded by some of the most glorious of the Peak District countryside. These moorlands also provide one of the town's specialities – heather honey. Several varieties of heather grow on the moors: there is *ling*, or common heather which turns the land purple in late summer; there is bell-heather which grows on dry rocky slopes; and there is cross-leaved heather which can be found on wet, boggy ground.

AROUND BUXTON

To the west of the town lies **Axe Edge**, the highest point of which rises to 1,807 feet above sea level. From this spot on a clear day (and the weather here is notoriously changeable) the panoramic views of Derbyshire are overwhelming. Just beyond, at 1,690 feet above sea level, the **Cat and Fiddle Inn** is the second highest pub in England. **Axe Edge Moor**, which receives an average annual rainfall of over 4 feet, is strictly for hardened walkers. It should come as no surprise that this Moor is the source of several rivers which play important roles in the life of the Peak District. The **River Dove** and the **River Manifold**, which join at Ilam, rise not far from one another; the **River Wye** rises above Buxton to join the Derwent further south; the **River Goyt**, a major source of the Mersey, rises to the west of Axe Edge. The entire length of the River Goyt can be walked, from its source to its confluence with the River Etherow

to the north and just outside the boundaries of the National Park.

Those who venture to **Errwood Reservoir** will be surprised to see rhododendrons growing near the banks of a man-made lake. They once stood in the grounds of Errwood Hall, which was built in the 1830s for the Grimshawe family. The house was demolished before the Reservoir was flooded, but the gardens were left to grow wild. Not far away can be seen the strange-looking Spanish Shrine. Built by the Grimshawes in memory of their Spanish governess, it is a small stone building with an unusual beehive roof.

Also to the west of town, **Poole's Cavern** on Green Lane is a natural limestone cave which was used by tribes from the Neolithic period onwards. It was visited by Mary, Queen of Scots and the 'chair' she used is pointed out during the regular tours of the cave on offer. Above the cavern and about 20 minutes' walk away is **Grin Low Country Park** and the prominent folly and scenic viewpoint, built in 1896, known as **Solomon's Temple**.

Poole's Cavern

Combs

3 miles N of Buxton off the A6

Combs Reservoir southwest of Chapel-en-le-Frith is crossed at one end by Dickie's Bridge. 'Dickie' is said to have resided at a farm in Tunstead where he was known as Ned Dixon. Apparently murdered by his cousin, he nevertheless continued his 'working life' as a sort of guard-skull, alerting the household whenever strangers drew near. Various strange occurrences are said to have ensued when attempts were made to move the skull.

On Castleton Road just a few miles northeast of the town, the **Chestnut Centre** is a fascinating wildlife conservation centre, popular with children and adults alike. It is famed for its otters, with award-winning otter and owl enclosures set along an extensive circular nature trail which meanders through some historic wooded parkland.

Chapel-en-le-Frith

4 miles N of Buxton off the A6

This charming town is often overlooked by travellers on the bypass between Buxton and Stockport, but it repays a closer look. In 1225 the guardians of the High Peak's Royal Forest purchased land from the Crown and built a chapel here, dedicating it to **St Thomas à Becket** of Canterbury. A century later the chapel was replaced with a more substantial building; further modernisation took place in the early 1700s. The building of the original chapel led to the foundation of the town and also its name, which is Norman French for 'chapel in the forest'. A curious legacy has been passed down allowing owners of freehold land in the district the right to choose their vicar. The interior of the church boasts 19th century box pews and a monument to 'the Apostle of the Peak', William Bagshawe of nearby Ford Hall, a

Nonconformist minister of the late 17th century. In 1648 the church was used as a gaol for 1,500 Scottish prisoners and the dreadful conditions arising from such close confinement caused unimaginable suffering. Their ordeal lasted for 16 days; a total of 44 men died.

Whaley Bridge

6 miles N of Buxton off the A5004

This small industrial town at the gateway to the Goyt Valley grew up around the coal-mining and textile industries. Both have now gone, but the **Peak Forest Canal** flowing through the town remains very much the centre of activity. The 'bridge' of the village's name crosses the River Goyt, on the site of what may once have been a Roman crossing.

Many of the old warehouses in Whaley Bridge have been restored and converted to meet the needs of the 21st century and, where once narrow boats transported goods and raw materials to and from the town, boats can now be hired. The **Toddbrook Reservoir** was built in 1831 to be a feeder for the Peak Forest Canal. The wharf here is dotted with picturesque narrowboats.

Lyme Park

8 miles NW of Buxton off the A6

Lyme Park (National Trust) is an ancient estate originally granted to Sir Thomas Danyers in 1346 by a grateful King Edward III after a battle at Caen. Danyers then passed the estate to his son-in-law, Sir Piers Legh, in 1388. It remained in the family until 1946, when it was given to the Trust. Not much remains of the original Elizabethan manor house; today's visitors are instead treated to the sight of a fantastic Palladian mansion, the work of Venetian architect Giacomo Leoni. Not daunted by the bleak landscape and climate of the surrounding Peak District, Leoni built a corner of Italy here in this much harsher countryside. Inside the mansion there is a mixture of styles: the elegant Leoni-designed rooms with rich rococo ceilings, the panelled Tudor drawing room, and two surviving Elizabethan rooms. Much of the three-dimensional internal carving is attributed to Grinling Gibbons, though a lot of the work was also undertaken by local craftsmen. As well as the fantastic splendour of the mansion, the estate includes a late 19th century formal garden and a medieval deer park.

HAYFIELD
9 miles N of Buxton off the A624

This small town below the exposed moorland of **Kinder Scout** is a popular centre for exploring the area and offers many amenities for hillwalkers. Like its neighbour New Mills, Hayfield grew up around the textile industry, in this case wool weaving and calico printing. Many of the houses seen today were originally weavers' cottages.

Three miles northeast of the town is **Kinder Downfall**, the highest waterfall in the county, found where the River Kinder flows off the edge of Kinder Scout. In low temperatures the fall freezes solid – a sight to be seen. It is also renowned for its blow-back effect: when the wind blows, the fall's water is forced back against the rock and the water appears to run uphill! There are not many natural waterfalls in Derbyshire, so Kinder Downfall appears on most visitors' itineraries.

GLOSSOP
13 miles N of Buxton off the A624

At the foot of the Snake Pass, Glossop is an interesting mix of styles: the industrial town of the 19th century with its towering Victorian mills and the 17th century village with its charming old cottages and cobbled streets.

From Glossop, the A57 East is an exhilarating stretch of road with hair-pin bends, known as the **Snake Pass**. The road is frequently made impassable by landslides, heavy mist and massive snowfalls in winter but, weather permitting, it is an experience not to be missed. For much of the length of the turnpike road that Thomas Telford built across Snake Pass in 1821, the route follows the line of an ancient Roman road, known as **Doctor's Gate**, which ran between Glossop and a fort at Brough. The route was so named after it was rediscovered, in the 16th century, by Dr Talbot, a vicar from Glossop.

HADFIELD
14 miles N of Buxton off the A624

The small village of Hadfield is the terminus of the **Longdendale Trail**, a route following the line of a former railway line and part of the Trans-Pennine Trail. **Old Hall** in The Square is the oldest building in the village, built in 1646. The Roman Catholic **Church of St Charles** was built in 1868 by Baron Howard of Glossop; members of the Howard family are buried here.

The Longdendale Trail continues eastward from here. Longdendale itself is the valley of the River Etherow, and is a favourite place for day-trippers. Along the footpath through this wild and desolate valley there are many reminders of the past, including **Woodhead Chapel**, the graveyard of which has numerous memorials to the navvies, and their families, who died in an outbreak of cholera in 1849 while working on the Sheffield to Manchester railway line.

EDALE
8 miles NE of Buxton off the A625

In the valley of the River Noe, Edale marks the start of the **Pennine Way**.

Opened in 1965, this long-distance footpath follows the line of the backbone of Britain for some 270 miles from here to Kirk Yetholm, just over the Scottish border. Though the footpath begins in the lush meadows of this secluded valley, it is not long before walkers find themselves crossing wild and bleak moorland before heading further north to Bleaklow. Many travellers have spoken of Derbyshire as a county of contrasts, and nowhere is this more apparent than at Edale. Not only does the landscape change dramatically within a short distance from the heart of the village, but the weather can alter from brilliant sunshine to snowstorms in the space of a couple of hours.

Tourism first came to Edale with the completion of the Manchester to Sheffield railway in 1894, though at that time there was little in the way of hospitality for visitors. Today there are several hotels, camping sites, a large Youth Hostel and adventure and walking centres.

CASTLETON
8 miles NE of Buxton off the A625

Situated at the head of the Hope Valley, Castleton is sheltered by the Norman ruin of **Peveril Castle** with its spectacular views over Castleton and the surrounding countryside. The Castle, originally called Castle of the Peak, was built as a wooden stockade in 1080 by William Peveril, illegitimate son of William the Conqueror. Later rebuilt in stone, the keep was added by Henry II. It remains the only surviving example of a Norman castle in Derbyshire, and is among the best preserved and most complete ruin in Britain. Approaching Castleton from the west along the A625, the road runs through the **Winnats Pass**, a narrow

limestone gorge. Thought to have been formed under the sea, from currents eroding the seabed, the gorge has been used as a road for centuries and is still the only direct route to the village from the west.

Originally laid out as a planned town below its castle, the shape of the village has changed little over the years and it has become a popular tourist centre. The mainly 17th century Church of St Edmund was heavily restored in 1837, but retains its box pews and a fine Norman arch, as well as a Breeches Bible dated 1611.

The hills to the west of Castleton are famous for their caves. The **Blue John Mine and Caverns**, which have been in the hands of the Ollerenshaw family for many years, are probably one of Derbyshire's most popular attractions. Amazing trips down into the caves themselves can be made. Above ground, in the gift shops various items can be bought made with the distinctive Blue John fluorspar with its attractive purplish veining. The village's **Ollerenshaw Collection** of huge vases

Blue John Mine and Caverns

Castleton Village

and urns made with the same unique stone is open to the public. Once prized by the Romans, it is said that Petronius paid the equivalent of around £40,000 for a wonderfully ornate vase carved from the stone. It is said that in a fit of petty-mindedness he preferred to smash the vase rather than relinquish it to the Emperor Nero.

At the bottom of Winnats Pass lies **Speedwell Cavern**, a former lead mine which used boats on an underground canal to ferry the miners and iron ore to and from the rockface. Visitors can follow the same boat journey underground in the company of a guide. The mine had a short life: it started up in 1771 and, despite an investment of £14,000, closed in 1790 after only £3,000 worth of iron ore had been extracted.

Peak Cavern, reached by a delightful riverside walk, has the widest opening of any cave in Europe. Up until the 17th century, little cottages used to stand within the entrance. The rope-makers who lived in these tiny dwellings used the cave entrance, dry in all weathers, for making rope: the ropewalk, which dates back some 400 years, can still be seen.

Guides re-enact the process of making rope, and one rope-maker's cottage is still extant. Recently the cave was used by the BBC who filmed an episode of *The Chronicles of Narnia* series here. Over the years successive Kings and Queens would entertain deep within the belly of the cave, which would be festooned with candles and other open flames – visitors can see the ledge on which the Royal musicians would perch. Peak Cavern was originally known as The Devil's Arse, but the fastidious Victorians felt this was 'inappropriate' and changed it to the name it carries today.

No description of Castleton would be complete without a mention of **Mam Tor**. The name means 'Mother Hill', and locally the tor is referred to as Shivering Mountain, because the immense cliff face near the summit is constantly on the move owing to water seepage. A climb to the top of the ridge is well worth while, as the views are splendid – in particular of the two diverse rock formations which separate the White (limestone) Peak from the northern Dark (gritstone) Peak.

HOPE

9 miles NE of Buxton off the A625

Hope gets its first mention in 926 as the site of a battle won by King Athelstan. By the time of the Domesday survey of 1086, the parish of Hope had extended to embrace much of the High Peak area and included places such as Buxton, Chapel-en-le-Frith and Tideswell. It remained one of the largest parishes in the country until the 19th century, though a market charter was not granted it until 1715. Hope lies at the point where the River Noe meets Peakshole Water; the stream rises in **Peak's Hole** (better known as Peak Cavern), hence its name.

The parish **Church of St Peter** was built at the beginning of the 1200s; the only part remaining from the original church is the Norman font. The Latin inscription on a chair in the north aisle reads (in translation) 'You cannot make a scholar out of a block of wood' and is said to have been carved for Thomas Bocking, the vicar and schoolmaster here during the 17th century. His name also appears on the fine pulpit; his Breeches Bible is displayed nearby. The **Hope Agricultural Show** is held every year on August Bank Holiday Monday.

BAMFORD
11 miles NE of Buxton off the A6013

This charming village situated between the Hope Valley and Ladybower Reservoir, stands at the heart of the Dark Peak below Bamford Edge and close to the Upper Derwent Valley Dams. When the Derwent and Howden Dams were built in the early years of the 20th century, the valley of the Upper Derwent was flooded, submerging many farms under the rising waters. The 1000 or so navvies and their families were housed at Birchinlee, a temporary village which came to be known locally as 'Tin Town' because of its plethora of corrugated iron shacks. During the Second World War the third and largest reservoir, the **Ladybower**, was built. This involved the inundating of two more villages – Derwent and Ashopton. The dead from Derwent's church were re-interred in the churchyard of St John the Baptist in Bamford. The living were rehoused in Yorkshire Bridge, a purpose-built hamlet located below the embankment of the Ladybower Dam. There is a Visitor Centre at **Fairholmes** (in the Upper Derwent Valley) which tells the story of these 'drowned villages'.

The **Derwent Dam**, built in 1935, was the practice site for the Dambusters,

who tested dropping their bouncing bombs here.

Bamford's **Church of St John the Baptist** is unlike any other in Derbyshire. Designed in 1861 by the famous church architect William Butterfield, it has a slender tower and an extra-sharp spire. Also worthy of note, particularly to lovers of industrial architecture, is **Bamford Mill**, just across the road by the river. This cotton mill was built in 1820; it retains its huge waterwheel and also has a 1907 tandem-compound steam engine.

The village lies in the heart of hill-farming country, and each Spring Bank Holiday Bamford plays host to one of the most famous of the Peak District Sheepdog Trials.

Along the A57 towards Sheffield, the road dips and crosses the gory-sounding **Cutthroat Bridge**. The present bridge dates back to 1830, but its name comes from the late 1500s when the body of a man with his throat cut was discovered under the bridge which then stood here.

HATHERSAGE
12 miles NE of Buxton off the A625

Once a centre for needle-making, it is difficult to know whether to classify Hathersage as a large village or a small town. In either event, it is a pleasant place with interesting literary connections. Charlotte Bronte stayed at Hathersage vicarage, and the village itself appears as 'Morton' in her novel *Jane Eyre*. The name Eyre was probably gleaned from the monuments to the prominent local landowners with this surname, as can be seen in the village Church of St Michael and its churchyard. The 15th century head of the family, Robert Eyre, lived at Highlow Hall. Within sight of this Hall he built seven houses, one for each of his seven sons.

GREENS HOUSE STUDIO

Outseat, Hathersage, Hope Valley S32 1BQ
Tel: 01433 650737

Trained in embroidery and textile design, Lyn Littlewood taught at Loughborough College of Art before moving to her present idyllic country retreat with unparalleled views of the Peak District hills. Lyn was inspired by the breathtaking vistas to take up painting and now displays her work in a 500-year-old barn in her grounds – visitors are welcome by appointment only. Lyn also conducts day courses in landscape and flower painting – the fee includes a tasty lunch. There are some delightful walks from her house, one of them leading to North Lees Hall, a lovely Elizabethan tower house where Charlotte Bronte stayed on holiday.

THE RIVERSIDE HERB CENTRE

Main Road, Hathersage, Hope Valley, Derbyshire S32 1EG
Tel/Fax: 01433 651435
e-mail: herbtable@freeuk.com website: www.herbexpress.net

Fresh herbs make all the difference for discerning cooks and just about every conceivable kind of herb can be found at **The Riverside Herb Centre**, set beside the River Derwent. As well as herbs the Centre also stocks a wide range of herbal foods, spices, herb hampers, seeds, wildflowers and traditional plants. There's also a herb hot-house containing seasonal herbs, topiary, structural and tender plants. Another attraction is the picnic area beside the river. The Centre is open all year, Monday to Friday, weekends in season, and its products are also available by mail order.

North Lees was one, and the grounds of this Elizabethan tower house are open to the public. Another was **Moorseats**, where Charlotte Bronte stayed on holiday and used as the inspiration for Moor House in *Jane Eyre*.

In Hathersage churchyard lie the reputed remains of Little John, Robin Hood's renowned companion. Whether or not the legend is to be believed, it is worth mentioning that when the grave was opened in the 1780s, a 32-inch thighbone was discovered. This would certainly indicate that the owner was well over seven feet tall.

BAKEWELL AND THE WHITE PEAK

This region of the Derbyshire Dales, sometimes also known as the Central Peaks and occupying the central area of the Peak District National Park, is less

wild and isolated than the remote High Peak area. The two main rivers, the Wye and the Derwent, which both have their source further north, are, in this region, at a more gentle stage of their course. Over the centuries, the fast-flowing waters were harnessed to provide power to drive the mills situated on the riverbanks; any walk taken along these riverbanks will not only give the opportunity to discover a wide range of plant and animal life, but also provide the opportunity to see the remains of buildings that once played an important part in the economy of north Derbyshire.

BAKEWELL

The only true town in the Peak District National Park, Bakewell attracts many day-trippers, walkers and campers as well as locals who come to take advantage of its many amenities. The beautiful medieval five-arched bridge spanning the River Wye is still in use today as the main crossing point for traffic. A stone-built town set along the banks of the River Wye, Bakewell enjoys a picturesque setting among well-wooded hills. With only 4,000 inhabitants it is nevertheless generally acknowledged as the capital of the Peak District National Park.

However, for most people it is a dessert that has made the name of Bakewell so famous, but please remember it is referred to locally as a *pudding* and most definitely not as a tart! Its invention is said to have been an accident when what was supposed to have been a strawberry tart turned into something altogether different. The cooking mishap took place in the kitchens of the Rutland Arms Hotel which was built in 1804 on the site of a coaching inn.

One of the hotel's more famous guests was the novelist Jane Austen, who stayed there in 1811. The Rutland Arms featured in her book *Pride and Prejudice*, while Bakewell itself appears as the town of Lambton.

Bakewell is the market town for this whole central area of the Peak District – markets were held here well before the granting of a charter in 1330. In fact, its importance during the 11th century was such that, as recorded in the Domesday Book of 1086, Bakewell had two priests. Monday is now Bakewell's market day and the cattle market, one of the largest in Derbyshire, is an important part of the area's farming life. The annual Bakewell Show started in 1819 and has gone on to become one of the foremost agricultural shows in the country. Across the River Wye stands the enormous, new Agricultural and Business Centre, where the livestock market takes place.

PATCHWORK DIRECT

The Square, Bakewell, Derbyshire DE45 1BT
Tel/Fax: 01629 815873
website: www.patchworkdirect.com

Housed in what was formerly part of the adjoining Rutland Arms Hotel, **Patchwork Direct** offers patchwork and quilting enthusiasts a treasure trove of materials, including some 2000 bolts of fabric, a huge range of threads and a variety of coloured fleeces. Patchwork Direct's owner, Ann

Esders says that her grandmother taught her all she knows. "She attended the Royal School of Needlework for 3 years and was a very talented needlewoman."

Ann was born in New Zealand and came to England when she was 16 years old. After marrying she and family lived in North and South America for several years but returned to the UK when the Falklands war broke out. Because they had lived in a hot climate for so long they owned few warm clothes. "So I went out and bought a knitting machine and began to produce clothes for the family." Ann also made children's clothes and christening robes and eventually rented a small unit in a craft centre to sell patchwork fabrics. From this modest beginning the business has grown rapidly and now Ann also offers classes in patchwork and embroidery. All the classes are day classes and take place on different days of the week with a maximum of 7 students in each class.

CHAPPELLS

King Street, Bakewell, Derbyshire DE45 1DZ
Tel: 01629 812496   e-mail: ask@chappellsantiquescentre.com
Fax: 01629 814531   website: chappellsantiquescentre.com

Housed in two adjoining Georgian buildings, **Chappells** antiques
centre offers an amazing array of quality antiques and collectables.
More than 30 professional dealers have their own individual
displays including English and Continental furniture in various
woods, glassware, silver and Old Sheffield plate, books, maps and prints, watercolours and oil paintings,
clocks, barometers, pottery, porcelain, brassware, pewter and copper, needlework, tapestries and much
more. Visitors can also enjoy home cooking in the licensed Tea & Coffee House.

The large parish **Church of All Saints**
was founded in Saxon times, as revealed
by the ancient preaching crosses and
stonework. Its graceful spire, with an
octagonal tower, can be seen for miles
around. One of the few places in
Derbyshire in the Domesday book to
record two priests and a church, the
churchyard and church itself contain a
wonderful variety of headstones and
coffin slabs and, near the porch, a most
unusual cross. Over 1,200 years old, it
stands an impressive 8 feet high. On one
side it depicts the Crucifixion, on the
other are the Norse gods Odin
and Loki. The Vernon Chapel in
the south aisle contains
impressive monuments to 'The
King of the Peak', Sir George
Vernon of Haddon Hall, who
died in 1567, and also to Sir
John Manners, who died in
1584, and his wife Dorothy
Vernon – these latter two feature
in one of the great romantic
legends of the Peak District as
we'll see later.

Behind the church is the
lovely **Old House Museum**,
housed in a building on
Cunningham Place which dates
back to 1534. It is thought to be
the oldest house in Bakewell.
This beautiful building narrowly
escaped demolition but has been

lovingly restored by the Bakewell
Historical Society and now displays its
original wattle and daub interior walls.
Now established as a folk museum, it
houses a fascinating collection of
rural bygones.

The town is full of delightful, mellow
stone buildings, many of which date
from the early 1600s and are still in use
today. The **Old Town Hall** is now the
Tourist Information Centre of the Peak
District. Few buildings remain from the
days when Bakewell was a minor spa
town, but the **Bath House**, on Bath

River Wye, Bakewell

Haddon Hall

Street, is one such building. Built in 1697 for the Duke of Rutland, it contained a large bath which was filled with the spa water and kept at a constant temperature of 59 degrees Fahrenheit.

Only a mile to the south of Bakewell down the Matlock Road, on a bluff overlooking the Wye, the romantic **Haddon Hall** stands hidden from the road by a beech hedge. The home of the Dukes of Rutland for over 800 years, the Hall has enjoyed a fairly peaceful existence, in part no doubt because it stood empty and neglected for nearly 300 years after 1640, when the family chose Belvoir Castle in Leicestershire as their main home. Examples of work from every century from the 12th to the 17th are evident in this architectural treasure trove.

Little construction work has been carried out on the Hall since the days of Henry VIII and it remains one of the best examples of a medieval and Tudor manor house. The 16th century terraced gardens are one of the chief delights of the Hall and are thought by many to be the most romantic in England. The Hall's splendour and charm have led it to be used as a backdrop to television and film

productions including *Jane Eyre, Moll Flanders* and *The Prince and the Pauper.* Nikolaus Pevsner described the Hall as "The English castle par excellence, not the forbidding fortress on an unassailable crag, but the large, rambling, safe, grey, loveable house of knights and their ladies, the unreasonable dream-castle of those who think of the Middle Ages as a time of chivalry and valour and noble feelings. None other in England is so complete and convincing".

The Hall's chapel is adorned with medieval wall paintings; the kitchens are the oldest extant part of the house, and feature time-worn oak tables and dole cupboards. The oak-panelled Long Gallery features boars' heads (to represent Vernon) and peacocks (Manners) in the panelling.

AROUND BAKEWELL

EDENSOR
2 miles E of Bakewell off the B6012

This model village (the name is pronouced Ensor) was built by the 6th Duke of Devonshire between 1838 and 1842 after the original village had been demolished because it spoilt the view from Chatsworth House. The village church was built by Sir George Gilbert Scott; in the churchyard is buried the late President Kennedy's sister Kathleen, who had married into the Cavendish family. Both she and her husband, the eldest son of the 10th Duke, were killed during the Second World War.

The home of the Dukes of Devonshire, **Chatsworth House**, known as the "Palace of the Peak", is without doubt one of the finest of the great houses in

Britain. The origins of the House as a great showpiece must be attributable to the redoubtable Bess of Hardwick, whose marriage into the Cavendish family helped to secure the future of the palace.

Bess' husband, Sir William Cavendish, bought the estate for £600 in 1549. It was Bess who completed the new House after his death. Over the years, the Cavendish fortune continued to pour into Chatsworth, making it an almost unparalleled showcase for art treasures. Every aspect of the fine arts is here, ranging from old masterpieces, furniture, tapestries, porcelain and some magnificent alabaster carvings.

The gardens of this stately home also have some marvellous features, including the Emperor Fountain, which dominates the Canal Pond and reaches a height of 290 feet. There is a maze and a Laburnum Tunnel and, behind the house, the famous Cascades. The overall appearance of the park as it is seen today is chiefly due to the talents of "Capability' Brown, who was first consulted in 1761.

STONEY MIDDLETON
4 miles N of Bakewell off the A623

This village, known simply as Stoney locally, is certainly well named as,

particularly in this part of **Middleton Dale**, great walls of limestone rise up from the valley floor. Further up the Dale there are also many disused limestone quarries as well as the remains of some lead mines. Not all industry has vanished from the area, as this is the home of nearly three-quarters of the country's fluorspar industry. Another relic from the past also survives, a shoe- and boot-making company operates from the village and is housed in a former corn mill.

The unusual octagonal village church was built by Joan Padley in thanksgiving for the safe return of her husband from the Battle of Agincourt in the 15th century. The lantern storey was added to the Perpendicular tower in 1759.

Higher up the dale from the village is the dramatically named **Lover's Leap**. In 1762, a jilted girl, Hannah Badderley, tried to jump to her death by leaping from a high rock. Her voluminous skirts, however, were caught on some brambles and she hung from the ledge before gently rolling down into a sawpit and escaping serious injury.

EYAM
5 miles N of Bakewell off the B6521

Pronounced 'Eem', this village will forever be known as the **Plague Village**. In 1666, a local tailor received a bundle of plague-infected clothing from London. Within a short time the infection had spread and the terrified inhabitants prepared to flee the village. However, the local rector, William Mompesson, persuaded the villagers to stay put and, thanks to his intervention, most neighbouring villages escaped the disease. Eyam was quarantined for over a year,

Maypole Dancing, Stoney Middleton

EYAM HALL

Eyam, Hope Valley, Derbyshire S32 5QW
Tel: 01433 631976 Fax: 01433 631603
e-mail: Nicola@eyamhall.com website: www.eyamhall.com

A handsome 17th century manor house, **Eyam Hall** has been the home of the Wright family for more than 300 years and contains a wealth of furniture, paintings and tapestries. Rooms open to the public include a library with an 18th century love poem inscribed on a window pane; a nursery with Victorian dolls' houses and toys; a Victorian dining room, kitchen and wash house. The Buttery serves tasty home-made lunches and teas and Saddleback's Gift & Craft Shop is open all year round. The Hall itself is open for Easter, from June until August, and at Christmas for pre-booked parties.

relying on outside help for supplies of food which were left on the village boundary. Out of a total of 350 inhabitants, only 83 survived.

The home of the Wright family for over 300 years, **Eyam Hall** is a wonderful, unspoilt 17th century manor house that is now open to the public. As well as touring the house and seeing the impressive stone-flagged hall, tapestry room and the magnificent tester bed, there is also a cafe and gift shop. The Eyam Hall Crafts Centre, housed in the farm building, contains several individual units, which specialise in a variety of unusual and skilfully-fashioned crafts.

GRINDLEFORD

6 miles N of Bakewell off the B6521/B6001

This is one of the smallest Peak District villages and from here, each year in July, there is a pilgrimage to **Padley Chapel** to commemorate two Catholic martyrs of 1588. The ruins of ancient Padley Manor House, found alongside the track bed of the old railway line, are all that remain of the home of two devout Roman Catholic families. It was from the manor house that two priests, Robert Ludlam and Nicholas Garlick, were taken to Derby and sentenced to death by hanging, drawing and quartering. The then owner of the house, Thomas

Fitzherbert, died in the Tower of London three years later whilst his brother died at Fleet Prison in 1598. In 1933, the charming chapel seen today was converted from the still standing farm buildings.

To the northwest of the village is the **Longshaw Country Park**, some 1,500 acres of open moorland, woodland, and the impressive Padley Gorge. Originally the Longshaw estate of the Dukes of Rutland, the land was acquired by the National Trust in the 1970s.

BRADWELL

9 miles NE of Buxton off the B6049

Usually abbreviated in the unique Peak District way to 'Bradder', Bradwell is a charming little limestone village sheltered by Bradwell Edge. At one time this former lead-mining community was famous as the place where miners' hardhats – hard, black, brimmed hats in which candles were stuck to light the way underground – were made; thus these hardhats came to be known as Bradder Beavers.

A key attraction here is the massive **Bagshawe Cavern**, a cave reached by a descending flight of 98 steps through an old lead mine. Along the half-mile walk to the main show cave there are wonderful rock formations and other interesting sights. For the more adventurous there are caving trips available.

ASHFORD IN THE WATER
1 mile NW of Bakewell off the A6

Not exactly in the water, but certainly on the River Wye, Ashford is another candidate for Derbyshire's prettiest village. It developed around a ford across the river and was once an important crossing place on the ancient Portway. The medieval **Sheepwash Bridge** crosses the Wye, with overhanging willows framing its low arches. It is one of three bridges in the village, and a favourite with artists. There is a small enclosure to one side that provides a clue to its name, as this is still occasionally used for its original purpose – crowds gather to witness sheep being washed in the river to clean their fleece before they are shorn. Mill Bridge dates back to 1664.

The great limestone parish **Church of the Holy Trinity**, largely rebuilt in 1871 but retaining the base of a 13th century tower, has a fine Ashford marble table on show as well as a tablet to the memory of Henry Watson, the founder of the marble works who was also an authority on the geology of the area. Several of the pillars within the church are made of the rare Duke's Red marble, which is only found in the mine at Lathkill Dale owned by the Duke of Devonshire. Hanging from the roof of Ashford's church are the remains of four 'virgin's crants' – paper garlands carried at the funerals of unmarried village girls.

Ashford is perhaps most famous for its six beautifully executed well-dressings, which are held annually in early June. The village also has a pleasant range of mainly 18th century cottages, and a former tithe barn which now serves as an art gallery.

MONSAL HEAD
3 miles NW of Bakewell off the B6465

Monsal Head is a renowned, and deservedly so, beauty spot from which there are tremendous views, particularly over **Monsal Dale** through which the River Wye flows.

WARDLOW
6 miles NW of Bakewell off the B6465

At a crossroads near Wardlow the highwayman Anthony Lingard was hanged in 1812 for the murder of a local widow. He was the last felon to hang in the county, and his execution drew an enormous crowd – so much so that the local lay-preacher at Tideswell found himself preaching to virtually empty pews. Determined not to waste this opportunity to speak to so large a congregation, he relocated to the gallows in order to deliver his sermon.

TIDESWELL
8 miles NW of Bakewell off the B6049

One of the largest villages in the area, Tideswell takes its name from a nearby ebbing

Sheepwash Bridge, Ashford in the Water

and flowing well. Over 900 feet above sea level, the surrounding countryside offers many opportunities to wander, stroll, or take a leisurely (or energetic) hike through some varied and impressive scenery.

Known as the 'Cathedral of the Peak', the magnificent 14th century **Church of St John the Baptist** has a wealth of splendid features. The tower is impressive, the windows are beautiful, there is a fine collection of brasses inside and the 'Minstrel of the Peak', William Newton, is buried in the churchyard.

Today the village is home to a number of craftspeople working in buildings converted from other uses. The excellence of their work is apparent not only in the items they display but also in the splendid well-dressing they help to enact annually on the Saturday nearest St John the Baptist's Day (24th June).

PEAK FOREST
11 miles NW of Bakewell off the A623

High on the White Peak plateau, Peak Forest takes its name from the fact that it once stood at the centre of the Royal Forest of the Peak. The parish **Church of King Charles the Martyr** speaks of the fierce independence of the village inhabitants. It was built in 1657 by the wife of the 2nd Earl of Devonshire, during a time when there was a ban on building churches. The church that stands today on the site of the former chapel was built in 1878.

A quirk of ecclesiastical law ensured – up until early in the 19th century – that the village was outside the jurisdiction of the bishop. Thus it was not subject to the laws regarding posting the banns before marriage; hence it became known as 'the Gretna Green of the Peak'. If one or other of the couple had lived in the village for 15 days prior to the ceremony, to this day they can still be married in the church without banns being read.

Within walking distance of Peak Forest is the 'bottomless' pit of **Eldon Hole**. Once thought to be the Devil's own entrance to Hell, stories abound in which various people were lowered down on increasingly longer pieces of rope. They all returned, in differing states of mental anguish, but none ever reached the bottom! However, seasoned pot-holers, who view the hole as no more than a practice run, maintain that it is, in fact, 'only' 180 feet deep.

SHELDON
3 miles W of Bakewell off the A6

Magpie Mine, to the south of the village, produced lead for over 300 years. This important site of industrial archaeology has been preserved, from the Cornish-style chimney stack, engine house and dynamite cabin right down to the more recent corrugated-iron-roofed buildings. It is now owned by the Peak District Mines Historical Society which conducts guided tours of the site.

MONYASH
5 miles W of Bakewell off the B5055

Monyash was once at the centre of the Peak District's lead mining industry and had its own weekly market (the charter being granted in 1340); the old market cross still stands on the village green.

Today, Monyash, which is situated at the head of **Lathkill Dale**, is busy during the season with walkers keen to explore the valley of the River Lathkill, a road-free beauty spot with ash and elm woods that was designated a National Nature Reserve in 1972. The River Lathkill, like others in the limestone area of the Peak District, disappears underground for parts of its course. In this case the river rises in winter from a large cave above

Monyash Village

Monyash, known as Lathkill Head Cave. In summer, the river emerges further downstream at Over Haddon

LONGNOR
8 miles E of Bakewell off the B5053

Over the county line into Staffordshire yet in the heart of the Peak District, on a gentle slope between the River Manifold and the River Dove, Longnor was once the meeting-point of several packhorse routes. Its **Market Hall** was built in 1873 – outside the hall there is a posting of the market charges of the time. The town's prosperity declined with the onset of the agricultural depression, and there was an accompanying fall in the population. However, this decline has in recent years been reversed. Longnor is now a conservation area and has attracted a good many craftspeople.

Main showroom for the work of local craftspeople and artisans, **Longnor Craft Centre** occupies the beautifully restored Market Hall in the centre of Longnor village. The village also has some fascinating narrow flagged passages which seem to go nowhere but suddenly emerge into the most beautiful scenery.

Though the late 18th century **Church of St Bartholomew** is rather plain, the churchyard has a most interesting gravestone. The epitaph tells the tale of the life of William Billinge, born in 1679, died in 1791 – which made him 112 years old at the time of his death! As a soldier Billinge served under Rooke at Gibraltar and Marlborough at Ramillies; after being sent home wounded, he recovered to take part in defending the King in the Jacobite rebellions of 1715 and 1745.

ROWSLEY
4 miles SE of Bakewell off the A6

This small village, at the confluence of the Rivers Wye and Derwent, is home to the impressive Peacock Hotel. Built originally as a private house, it is aptly named since the carved peacock over the porch is actually part of the family crest of the Manners family, whose

DEREK TOPP GALLERY

Chatsworth Road, Rowsley, Matlock, Derbyshire DE4 2EH
Tel: 01629 735580   e-mail: info@derektoppgallery.com
website: www.derektoppgallery.com

In the pleasant village of Rowsley, the **Derek Topp Gallery** sells an exciting range of contemporary applied art and craft. It was established in 1995 with the criteria that everything on show is hand made in Britain and of the highest quality and artistic integrity. Many of the artists featured are listed on the Craft Council's Index of Selected Makers, or are receiving a Setting-up Grant. Drawn from across the country, all have been selected for their flair, skill and imagination. The Gallery is open from 10am to 5pm, Tuesday to Sunday (closed Christmas week).

descendants still live at nearby Haddon Hall.

On the banks of the River Wye lies **Caudwell's Mill**, a unique Grade II listed historic flour mill. A mill has stood on this site for at least 400 years; the present mill was built in 1874, powered by water from the River Wye, and was run as a family business for over a century up until 1978. Since then the Mill has undergone extensive restoration by a group of dedicated volunteers and, using machinery

Park & Gardens, Matlock

that was installed at the beginning of this century, the Mill is once again producing wholemeal flour. Other mill buildings on the site have been converted to house a variety of craft workshops, shops and a restaurant.

On Chatsworth Road near the terminus of the Peak Rail line, **Peak Village** is an extensive factory outlet shopping centre offering a range of ladies' and men's fashion, sports and outdoor wear, home furnishings, jewellery, toys and books, and eateries. Also on-site is the charming **Wind in the Willows** attraction, created by an award-winning team of craftsmen and designers to bring the adventures of Ratty, Mole, Badger and Mr Toad to life.

MATLOCK

As the northern, gritstone landscape of the Peak District is often referred to as the Dark Peak, the southern, limestone plateaux have gained the equally obvious name of White Peak. Though the hilltops are often windswept and bleak, the numerous dales, cut deep into the limestone, provide a lush and green haven for all manner of wild and plant life. Several of the rivers are famous for

their trout, particularly the Lathkill, which was greatly favoured by the keen angler and writer Izaak Walton.

Matlock is a bustling town nestling in the lower valley of the River Derwent, and is the administrative centre of Derbyshire as well as being a busy tourist centre bordering the Peak District National Park. There are actually eight Matlocks making up the town, along with several other hamlets. Most have simply been engulfed and have lost their identity as the town grew, but **Matlock Bath**, the site of the spa, still maintains its individuality.

Matlock itself, at one time, had the steepest-gradient (a 1-in-5½) tramway in the world; it was also the only tram system in the Peak District. Opened in 1893, the tramcars ran until 1927 and the Depot can still be seen at the top of Bank Street. The old Ticket Office and Waiting Room at Matlock station have been taken over by the Peak Rail Society and here can be found not only their shop, but also exhibitions explaining the history and aims of the society. **Peak Rail** has its southernmost terminus just a few minutes' walk from the mainline station; from here the railway runs through the charming rural station of Darley Dale to the terminus at Rowsley

South. In future it is hoped that the line can be extended to Bakewell. Run entirely by volunteers, this lovely old steam train operates on different days throughout the year. A restaurant car is fitted for every journey. The full journey (one way) takes just 20 minutes, and passengers can alight to enjoy the picnic area at the entrance to Rowsley South Station, or the exhibition coach at Darley Dale platform to learn about the history of the re-opening of the line. Special events are held throughout the year, and engine-driving courses can be taken – the perfect gift for the steam enthusiast!

Inside Matlock's **Church of St Giles** can be seen the faded and preserved funeral garlands or 'virgin crants' that were once common all over Derbyshire. Bell-shaped, decorated with rosettes and ribbons and usually containing a personal item, the garlands were made in memory of a deceased young girl of the parish. At her funeral the garlands were carried by the dead girl's friends and, after the service, would be suspended from the church rafters above the pew she had normally occupied.

High up on the hill behind the town is the brooding ruin of **Riber Castle**. The castle was built between 1862 and 1868 by John Smedley, a local hosiery manufacturer who became interested in the hydropathic qualities of Matlock. He drew up the designs for the building himself and spent lavishly on its interior décor. Smedley constructed his own gas-producing plant to provide lighting for the Castle and it even had its own well.

Following the death of first Smedley and then his wife, the castle was sold and for a number of years it was boys' school. During the Second World War the castle was used as a food store before it was left to become a ruined shell. Today the building and surrounding grounds are home to a sanctuary for rare breeds and endangered species; the **Wildlife Park** has been particular successful at breeding lynx, and boasts the world's largest collection of these magnificent animals.

AROUND MATLOCK

DARLEY DALE
2 miles NW of Matlock off the A6

The charming name for this straggling village along the main road north from Matlock dates only from the 19th century, and was either devised by the commercially-minded railway company at work in the area or by the romantically-inclined vicar of the parish. Darley Dale makes up one of three stops on the Matlock-to-Rowsley South Peak Rail line.

FIRCLIFFE HALL

Whitworth Road, Darley Dale, Derbyshire DE4 2HJ
Tel: 01629 732910

Fircliffe Hall is a fine old Georgian house built in 1760 and later extended by Sir Joseph Whitworth, the celebrated engineer and inventor. Now providing luxurious bed and breakfast accommodation, the house retains many interesting features – it has been used for filming by BBC-TV – and has been attractively furnished and decorated by its owner Penny Snaith, a former antiques dealer. The house has an attractive informal garden and is conveniently located just 3 miles from Chatsworth and with easy access to the M1. Enchanting Haddon Hall and the spa town of Buxton, noted for its Opera Festival in July, are also within easy reach.

One of the most unassuming heroines of this part of Derbyshire must be Lady Mary Louisa Whitworth, the second wife of Sir Joseph Whitworth, the famous Victorian engineer. Following his death in 1887, Lady Mary undertook to bring sweeping changes to the lifestyle of the local poor and needy. The **Whitworth Institute** was opened in 1890, bringing to the community a wide range of facilities including a swimming pool, an assembly hall, a natural history museum and a library. Lady Whitworth died in France in 1896, and is buried next to her husband at the parish Church of St Helen, in the hamlet of Churchtown. The churchyard is also home to the **Darley Yew**, one of the oldest living trees in Britain which has a girth of some 33 feet. The yew predates the Norman origins of the Church and may even be older than the Saxon fragments found here in the mid-1900s.

Darley Dale has an extensive park which is very pretty in all seasons. Another of this small village's attractions is **Red House Stables**, a working carriage museum featuring some fine examples of traditional horse-drawn vehicles and equipment. One of the finest collections in the country, it consists of nearly 40 carriages, including one of the very few surviving Hansom cabs, a stage coach, Royal Mail coach, Park Drag and many other private and commercial vehicles.

Carriage rides are available, making regular trips through the countryside to places such as Chatsworth and Haddon Hall, and the carriages and horses can be hired for special occasions.

STANTON IN PEAK
5 miles NW of Matlock off the B5056

The gritstone landscape of **Stanton Moor**, which rises to some 1096 feet and overlooks the village, is encircled by footpaths and is a popular walking area. There are also several interesting features on the moorland. The folly, **Earl Grey's Tower**, was built in 1832 to commemorate the reform of Parliament. There is also an ancient stone circle, dating from the Bronze Age, with over 70 burial mounds. Known as the **Nine Ladies**, the stone circle has a solitary boulder nearby called the King's Stone. Legend has it that one Sunday nine women and a fiddler came up onto the moor to dance and, for their act of sacrilege, they were turned to stone.

The nearby **Rowtor Rocks** contain caves which were carved out at some stage in the 1600s. Not only was the living space made from the rock but tables, chairs and alcoves were also made to create a cosy retreat for the local vicar, Rev Thomas Eyre. Prior to these home improvements, the caves were reputedly used by the Druids, who did not believe in such creature comforts.

ROSE COTTAGES

Copper Pot, Conksbury Lane, Youlgrave, nr Bakewell,
Derbyshire DE45 1WR
Tel: 01629 636487
e-mail: enquiries@rosecottages.co.uk
website: www.rosecottages.co.uk

Ideally located for exploring the Peak District National Park and with some lovely local walks, **Rose Cottages** provide the perfect base for a rural holiday. These three luxury 4-star stone cottages are full of character, enjoy wonderful views and have ample off-road parking. They stand in the friendly village of Youlgrave and within easy walking distance of 3 child-friendly pubs with extensive menus of quality meals. Sorry, no pets.

YOULGREAVE

6 miles NW of Matlock off the B5056

This straggling village, known locally as Pommey, lies in Bradford Dale. The village **Church of All Saints** contains some parts of the original Saxon building though its ancient font is, unfortunately, upturned and used as a sundial. Inside, the working font is Norman and still retains its stoop for holding the Holy Water. It is well worth taking the time to have a look at, since it is the only such font in England. The Church also contains a small tomb with an equally small alabaster effigy; dated 1488, it is a memorial to Thomas Cockayne, who was killed in a brawl when only in his teens.

Further up the village's main street is **Thimble Hall**, the smallest market hall in the Peak District and still used for selling goods today. Typical of the White Peak area of Derbyshire, the Hall dates from 1656 and there are also some rather grand Georgian houses to be found in the village.

Lathkill Dale, which can really only be experienced by walking along the path by the banks of the quiet river, is noted for its solitude and, consequently, there is an abundance of wildlife in and around the riverbank meadows. The upper valley is a National Nature Reserve; those who are lucky enough may even spot a kingfisher or two here. One of the country's purest rivers, the Lathkill is famed for the range of aquatic life that it supports as well as being a popular trout river. Renowned for many centuries, it was Izaak Walton who said of the Lathkill, back in 1676;

Well Dressing, Youlgreave

> *"the purest and most transparent stream that I ever yet saw, either at home or abroad; and breeds, 'tis said, the reddest and best Trouts in England."*

MIDDLETON BY YOULGREAVE

7 miles NW of Matlock off the A5012

Just outside this leafy village is **Lomberdale Hall**, once the home of Thomas Bateman, the 19th century archeologist who was responsible for the excavation of some 500 barrows in the Peak District over a 20 year period - it is

---

HOLLY HOMESTEAD

The Square, Middleton-by-Youlgreave, Derbyshire DE45 1LS
Tel: 01773 550754 website: www.holly-homestead.co.uk
e-mail: daveedge@turnditch82.freeserve.co.uk

Holly Homestead was originally two stone cottages, some 250 years old and now with a Grade II listed building status. This charming property stands in the middle of the village and within easy reach of the market town of Bakewell - in the heart of The Peak National Park. It has been sensitively modernised and renovated and has a 4 Star rating from the English Tourist Council. The accommodation comprises a main bedroom with a king size bed and en suite facilities, and two twin-bedded rooms with another bathroom. The lounge has a woodburning stove and leads to a dinning room and a well-fitted kitchen. There's a pretty cottage garden at the front and a secluded garden to the rear.

said that he managed to reveal four in one single day! Many of the artefacts he unearthed can be seen in Sheffield Museum. The village lies in the valley of the River Bradford, at the point where it becomes Middleton Dale, and is unusual among villages in this area of the Peak District in that it has a large number of trees.

BIRCHOVER

4 miles W of Matlock off the B5056

The strange **Rocks of Rowtor**, behind The Druid Inn, are said to have been used for Druidical rites. The Revd Thomas Eyre, who died in 1717, was fascinated by these rocks and built the strange collection of steps, rooms and seats which have been carved out of the gritstone rocks on the summit of the outcrop. It is said that the Reverend

would take his friends there to admire the view across the valley below – a view which nowadays is obscured by trees.

The equally strange outcrops of **Robin Hood's Stride** and **Cratcliff Tor** can be found nearby. A medieval hermit's cave, complete with crucifix, can be seen at the foot of Cratcliff Tor hidden behind an ancient yew tree.

WINSTER

4 miles W of Matlock off the B5056

This attractive gritstone village was once a lead-mining centre and market town. Today, it is a pleasant place with antique shops in the high street and some fine late-18th century houses. Less splendid than the surrounding houses, but no less interesting, are the ginnels – little alleyways – that run off the main street. The most impressive building here,

---

THE DOWER HOUSE

Main Street, Winster, Derbyshire DE4 2DH
Tel: 01629 650931 Fax: 01629 650932
e-mail: fosterbig@aol.com
website: www.SmoothHound.co.uk/Hotels/Dowerhou

An imposing 16th century manor house, **The Dower House** is a Grade II listed building of historic and architectural interest, located in the conservation village of Winster in the Peak National Park, within easy reach of Chatsworth House and Haddon Hall. The Dower House has associations with the Curzon family of Kedleston Hall who owned the property from 1737 to 1861 and is now the home of Marsha and John Biggin. Marsha loves interior design and the house reflects her style in contemporary and traditional furnishings and her love of antique collecting. She is also an accomplished cook, serving speciality English breakfasts with home-cured local produce, catering also to the needs of special diets. John enjoys meeting guests and has an endless supply of walks from the house and places of interest to visit.

The Dower House has 3 spacious guest bedrooms – 1 double en suite; one 4-poster bedroom with private bathroom; 1 twin bedded room with private bathroom. All beautifully furnished and equipped with washbasin, colour TV, hair dryer, bathrobes and speciality teas and fresh coffee tray. Guests have the use of a beamed sitting room, with wood burning fire, and a dining room with pretty 17th century wallpaper, oak tables and antique furniture. There's also a licensed bar. Deservedly, the Dower House has been awarded a Heart of England Tourist Board 5-Diamonds rating, plus a gold award for the standard of facilities and welcome.

however, must be the **Market House**, owned by the National Trust and found at the top of the main street. The Trust's first purchase in Derbyshire, the rugged, two-storey Market House dates from the late-17th and early-18th centuries and is a reminder of Winster's past importance as a market town. Built from an attractive combination of brickwork and stone, the House is open to the public and acts as an information centre and shop for the Trust.

The annual Shrove Tuesday Pancake Race, from the Crown Inn to the Market House is a much-anticipated event that is taken seriously in the village. Small frying pans are issued to the men, women and children, it is an open event, and the pancakes are specially made with an emphasis on durability rather than taste.

Finally, although Morris dancing is traditionally associated with the Cotswold area, two of the best known and most often played tunes, The Winster Gallop and Blue-eyed Stranger, originate from the village. Collected many years ago by Cecil Sharpe, a legend in the world of Morris dancing, they were rediscovered in the 1960s. The Winster Morris men traditionally dance through the village at the beginning of Wakes Week in June, finishing, as all good Morris dances, do at one of the local pubs.

MATLOCK BATH
1 mile S of Matlock off the A6

As with many other spa towns up and down the country, it was not until the Regency period that Matlock Bath reached its peak. As well as offering cures for many of the ills of the day, Matlock Bath and the surrounding area had much to offer the visitor. The spa town was compared to Switzerland by Byron and it has also been much admired by Ruskin, who stayed at the New Bath Hotel in

1829. Many famous people have visited the town, including the young Victoria before she succeeded to the throne.

One of the great attractions of the town is **The Aquarium**, which occupies what was once the old **Matlock Bath Hydro** that was established in 1833. The original splendour of the Bath Hydro can still be seen in the fine stone staircase and also in the thermal large pool which is now without its roof. The pool, maintained at a constant temperature of 68 degrees Fahrenheit, was where the rheumatic patients came to immerse themselves in the waters and relieve their symptoms. Today, the pool is home to a large collection of Large Mirror, Common and Koi Carp whilst the upstairs consulting rooms now house tanks full of native, tropical and marine fish. Down by the riverbank and housed in the old Pavilion can be found the **Peak District Mining Museum and Temple Mine**, the only one of its kind in the world. Opened in 1978 and run by the Peak District Mines Historical Society, the Museum tells the story of lead mining in the surrounding area from as far back as Roman times to the 20th century. The Museum also houses a huge engine, dating from 1819, which was recovered from a mine near Winster.

For many, model railways are an interesting and absorbing hobby that friends and family find hard to understand but **The Model Railway** on show in Temple Road is more a work of art than just another model railway. It is a reconstruction of the Midland Railway Company's track through some of the most scenic areas of the Peak District. Combining magnificent dioramas with locomotives and carriages based on the designs of 1906, the trains, slowed down to a speed in scale with the models, travel the realistic route.

Found in the Victorian Railway Station buildings is the **Whistlestop Countryside Centre**, which aims to inform and educate the public on the wildlife of the county as well as manage wildlife conservation. Set up by the Derbyshire Wildlife Trust and run by volunteers, the Centre has an interesting and informative exhibition and a gift shop and the staff are qualified to lead a range of environmental activities.

For spectacular views of Matlock Bath, nothing beats a walk on **High Tor Grounds**. There are 60 acres of nature trails to wander around, while some 400 feet below the River Derwent appears like a silver thread through the gorge. A popular viewing point for Victorian visitors to the town, today rock climbers practise their skills climbing the precipitous crags of the Tor.

On the opposite side of the valley are the beautiful wooded slopes of Masson Hill, the southern face of which has become known as the **Heights of Abraham** (see panel below). This particular name was chosen after General Wolfe's victory in Quebec – this part of the Derwent valley being seen to resemble the gorge of the St Lawrence River and the original Heights of Abraham lying a mile north of Quebec. Today it is a well-known viewing point, reached on foot or, more easily, by cable car.

In 1812, the **Great Rutland Show Cavern**, on the slope, was opened to the public, a new experience for tourists of the time, and it was visited by many including the Grand Duke Michael of Russia and Princess Victoria. Following this success, in 1844, the **Great Masson Cavern** was opened and construction of the Victoria Prospect Tower was begun. Built by redundant lead miners, the Tower became a new landmark for the

THE HEIGHTS OF ABRAHAM

Heights of Abraham (Matlock Bath) Limited, Matlock Bath, Derbyshire DE4 3PD
Tel: 01629 582365   Fax: 01629 580279
e-mail: office@h-of-a.co.uk
website: www.heights-of-abraham.co.uk

Featuring steep rocky gorges, vast caverns, fast running rivers, wide panoramic views and a cable car, it is easy to understand why the Victorians called Matlock Bath "Little Switzerland"; however, the **Heights of Abraham Country Park and Caverns** overlooks the famous spa town, and provides a unique aspect to a day out or holiday in the Derbyshire Dales and Peak District.

The journey to the summit of the country park is easily made by taking the cable car adjacent to Matlock Bath railway station and car park. The cable car ticket includes all the attractions in the grounds, as well as the two spectacular underground caverns. Tours throughout the day allow you to experience the exciting underground world within the hillside, with the "miner's tale" in the Great Rutland Cavern Nestus Mine, and the multivision presentation of the "story in the rock" at the Masson Cavern Pavilion.

The sixty acre country park also features woodland walks, the Owl Maze, the Explorers Challenge, play and picnic areas, Victoria Prospect Tower, plus the High Falls Rocks & Fossils Shop featuring Ichthyosaur remains. When you have worked up an appetite, why not relax with a drink on the terrace and take in the views, or enjoy a snack in the Coffee Shop or a meal in the Woodlanders Restaurant. So next time you are planning a trip to the mountains, remember The Heights of Abraham at Matlock Bath "Little Switzerland" is nearer than you think.

area and today still provides a bird's eye view over Derbyshire.

To the south of the town centre is a model village with a difference; **Gulliver's Kingdom** theme park makes a great day out for all the family. Set on the side of a wooded hill, each terrace is individually themed with styles including Fantasy Land, the Old Wild West and the Royal Mine ride. There are plenty of fun rides, a monorail, water slides and other diversions, as well as a cafe and restaurant.

CROMFORD

2 miles S of Matlock off the A5012

Cromford is a model village known the world over. It was developed by Richard Arkwright into one of the first industrial towns. In addition to housing, he also provided his workers with a market place and a village Lock-Up. Born in Lancashire in 1732, Arkwright was the inventor of the waterframe, a machine for spinning cotton that was powered by water. He built his first mill at Cromford in 1771, the project taking a further 20 years to complete. It was the world's first successful water-powered cotton spinning mill. The area he had chosen proved to be perfect: the River Derwent, described by Daniel Defoe as "a fury of a river", provided an ample power supply; there was an unorganised but very willing workforce, as the lead-mining

industry was experiencing a decline and, probably most importantly, Cromford was away from the prying eyes of Arkwright's competitors. In 1792, Arkwright commissioned the building of the village church, where he now lies. The Mill proved to be a great success and became the model for others both in Britain and abroad, earning Arkwright the accolade 'Father of the Factory System'. His pioneering work and contributions to the great Industrial Age resulted in a knighthood in 1786, and one year later he became High Sheriff of Derbyshire. **Cromford Mill** and the associated buildings are now an International World Heritage site. Tours of the mill and Cromford village are available throughout the year.

Cromford has a rather odd 15th century bridge, which has rounded arches on one side and pointed arches on the other. It was from this bridge, in 1697, so local folklore has it, that a horse and rider took a flying leap from the parapet, plunged into the river 20 feet below and lived to tell the tale.

For lovers of waterways, there is an opportunity at **Cromford Canal** to potter along the five-mile stretch of towpath to Ambergate, or better still, to take a peaceful canal boat ride. The Cromford Canal Society, which organises the boat trips along the canal, also maintains the **Cromford Wharf Steam**

MALCOLM DAVID SMITH

29 Market Place, Cromford, nr Matlock, Derbyshire DE4 3RE
Tel: 01629 826620 website: www.malcolmdavidsmith.co.uk
e-mail: enquiries@malcolmdavidsmith.co.uk

"Furniture that just might be alive" is the description **Malcolm David Smith** applies to his strikingly original handmade furniture. Using native oak or ash, each piece is individually made in Malcolm's studio and is inspired by natural forms. The designs are constantly evolving and are based on animals and insects. All of them are practical, interesting, visually exciting. Malcolm's Studio and Attic Gallery is usually open from 10am to 5pm daily, except Tuesdays and Wednesdays.

Museum. Its exhibits include the 1902 Robey horizontal engine donated by Friden Brickworks from nearby Hartington. The Museum is open by arrangement for private steamings and working demonstrations. The old **Leawood Pumping Station**, which transferred water from the River Derwent to the Cromford Canal, has been fully restored. Inside the engine house is a preserved Cornish-type beam engine which is occasionally steamed up. Close by the Pump House is the **Wigwell Aqueduct**, which carries the Canal high over the River Derwent.

Leawood Pumping Station, Cromford Canal

The **High Peak Trail**, which stretches some 17 miles up to Dowlow near Buxton, starts at Cromford and follows the trackbed of the Cromford and High Peak Railway. First opened in 1880, the railway was built to connect the Cromford Canal with the Peak Forest Canal and is somewhat reminiscent of a canal as it has long level sections interspersed with sharp inclines (instead of locks) and many of the stations are known as wharfs. After walking the trail it is not surprising to learn that its chief engineer was really a canal builder! The railway was finally closed in 1967; the old stations are now car parks and picnic areas; there is an information office in the former Hartington station signal box. Surfaced with clinker rather than limestone, the trail is suitable for walkers, cyclists and horses.

WIRKSWORTH
4 miles S of Matlock off the B5023

Nestling in the lush green foothills of the Peak District where north meets south, Wirksworth is home to a distinctive **Heritage Centre** (see panel on page 190) which takes visitors through time from the Romans in Wirksworth to the present

---

ART DESIGN & CRAFT CENTRE AND MAYS CELEBRATION CAKES & SAVOURIES

11 Coldwell Street, Wirksworth, Derbyshire DE44 4FB
Tel: 01629 826766

A family-run business established some ten years ago, **Art Design & Craft Centre** incorporating **May's Cakes** provides a showcase for the work of local artists, sells a good range of home -made cakes and savouries and also has a small tea room serving delicious home-made food. Prints, paintings, cards, calendars and a selection of organic, vegetarian, diabetic produce and local honey are also on sale. Healthy lunch boxes are available to order. Outside catering can be arranged.

WIRKSWORTH HERITAGE CENTRE

Crown Yard, Wirksworth, Derbyshire DE4 4ET
Tel: 01629 825225

A visit to **Wirksworth Heritage Centre** takes you from the Romans in Wirksworth to the present day. Houses in a former silk mill, the mysteries of the town's ancient lead mining industry are unveiled. Pit your wits against the computer and rescue the injured Lead Miner! Enter the Dream Cave and imagine how it felt to discover the remains of the prehistoric Woolly Rhino! Discover the local customs of Clypping the Church and Well Dressing. Learn about the regeneration of this historic market town and its George Eliot connections and enjoy some of the best views of Wirksworth in town!

day. Quarrying, lead-mining and local customs such as clypping the church (a ceremony in which the parish church is encircled by the congregation holding hands around it) and well-dressing are explored with interactive and fascinating exhibits. One of the town's most interesting sights is the jumble of cottages linked by a maze of jitties on the hillside between The Dale and Greenhill, in particular the area known locally as 'The Puzzle Gardens'.

Babington House dates back to Jacobean Wirksworth. Another former lead-merchant's house, **Hopkinsons House**, was restored in 1980 as part of a number of restoration schemes initiated by the Civic Trust's Wirksworth Project. The ancient **parish church of St Mary's** is a fine building standing in a tranquil close and bounded by Elizabethan 'Gell Almshouses' and the former (Georgian) grammar school. The church holds one of the oldest stone carvings in the country: known as the Wirksworth Stone, it is a coffin lid dating from the 8th century.

The **National Stone Centre** tells "the story of stone", with a wealth of exhibits, activities such as gem-panning and fossil-casting, and outdoor trails tailored to introduce topics such as the geology, ecology and history of the dramatic Peak District landscape. Nearby, the **Steeple Grange Light Railway Society** runs along a short line over the High Peak Trail between Steeplehouse Station and Dark Lane Quarry. Power is provided by a battery-electric locomotive; passengers are carried in a manrider salvaged from Bevercotes Colliery in Nottinghamshire. Visitors to **North End Mills** are able to witness hosiery being made as it has been for over half a century; a special viewing area offers an insight into some of the items on sale in the Factory Shop.

ASHBOURNE

Ashbourne is one of Derbyshire's finest old towns, with a wealth of wonderful Georgian architecture as well as some older buildings, notably the Gingerbread Shop which is timber framed and probably dates from the 1400s. The triangular cobbled **Market Square** was part of the new development begun in the 1200s that shifted the town to the east, away from the church. Weekly markets have been held in the square since 1296, and still take place every Saturday. It was in this market place, once lined with ale houses, that Bonnie Prince Charlie proclaimed his father as King James III, and so started the Jacobite

WATSON WATSON

29 Church Street, Ashbourne, Derbyshire DE6 1AE
Tel: 01335 345796 e-mail: info@watsonwatson.co.uk
Fax: 01335 345628 website: www.furrythrows.com/

After working in London for several years as an interior designer, Lucie-Clare Watson moved to Ashbourne and established her own design company and shop, **Watson Watson.** Occupying a handsome Georgian house, her shop has a warm, friendly atmosphere and Lucie-Clare offers a highly individualised service. The shop is stocked with a wide range of 18th and 19th century French furniture, quality lighting, design accessories, gift ware and much, much more. Look out for Lucie-Clare's striking faux fur throws and accessories which have been featured in the national press and are also available from Watson Watson by mail order.

Rebellion. Traditional Ashbourne gingerbread is said to be made from a recipe that was acquired from French prisoners of war who were kept in the town during the Napoleonic Wars.

Also worthy of a second glance is the **Green Man and Black's Head Royal Hotel**. The inn sign stretches over the St John's Street and was put up when the Blackamoor Inn joined with the Green Man in 1825. Though the Blackamoor is no more, the sign remains and it claims to be the longest hotel name in the country. Of Georgian origin, the amalgamated hotel has played host to James Boswell, Dr Johnson and the young Princess Victoria. Ashbourne was, in fact, one of Dr Johnson's favourite places; he came to the town on several occasions between 1737 and 1784. He also visited the hotel so often that he had his own chair with his name on it! The chair can still be seen at the Green Man.

A stroll down Church Street, described by Pevsner as one of the finest streets in Derbyshire, takes the walker past many interesting Georgian houses – including the Grey House which stands next to the **Grammar School**. Founded by Sir Thomas Cockayne on behalf of Elizabeth I in 1585, the school was visited on its 400th anniversary by the present Queen. Almost opposite the Grey House is **The**

Mansion, the late-17th century home of the Reverend Dr John Taylor, oldest friend of Dr Johnson. In 1764, a domed, octagonal drawing room was added to the house, and a new brick facade built facing the street. Next to The Mansion are two of the many almshouses established in Ashbourne during the 17th and 18th centuries. Ashbourne also retains many of its narrow alleyways and, in particular, there is Lovatt's Yard where the town lock-up can be seen.

In **St Oswald's Parish Church** Ashbourne has one of the most impressive and elegant churches in the country, described by George Eliot as "the finest mere parish church in England". James Boswell said that the church was "one of the largest and most luminous that I have seen in any town of the same size". St Oswald's stands on the site of a minster church mentioned in the Domesday Book, though most of what stands today dates from rebuilding work in the 13th century.

The alabaster tombs and monuments to the Bradbourne and Cockane families in the north transept chapel are justly famous. Perhaps the best-known monument is that to Penelope Boothby, who died in 1791 at the tender age of five. Thomas Banks' white Carrara marble figure of the sleeping child is so lifelike that she still appears to be only sleeping. The moving epitaph reads: "She was in form and intellect most exquisite; The unfortunate parents ventured their all on this frail bark, and the wreck was total". It is said that Penelope's parents separated at the child's grave and never spoke to each other again.

Ashbourne is home to the famous Shrovetide football game played on Shrove Tuesday and Ash Wednesday. The two teams, the 'Up'ards' (those born north of the Henmore Brook) and the 'Down'ards' (those born south of it) begin their match at 2pm behind the Green Man Hotel. The game continues until well into the evening. The two goals are situated three miles apart, along the Brook, on the site of the old mills at Clifton and Sturston. It is rare for more than one goal to be scored in this slow-moving game.

AROUND ASHBOURNE

HOGNASTON
4 miles NE of Ashbourne off the B5035

This hillside village, with its extraordinary Norman carvings over the church doorway, lies close to **Carsington Water**, Britain's newest reservoir, owned by Severn Trent Water. There is plenty to do here besides the more usual water sports such as canoeing, sailing and fishing. Opened by the Queen in 1992, the reservoir has already blended well with the local countryside. Unlike many of the Peak District reservoirs, which draw their water from the acid moorland, Carsington is able to support a whole host of wildlife. One controversial resident is the American ruddy duck. Once unknown outside wildlife reserves, the duck escaped and in little over 50 years the breed has become widespread throughout Europe.

TURLOW BANK

Hognaston, Ashbourne, Derbyshire DE6 1PW
Tel: 01335 370299
e-mail: turlowbank@btinternet.com website: www.turlowbank.co.uk

Close to Carsington Water with its water sports, birdwatching and cycling facilities, **Turlow Bank** offers top quality bed & breakfast accommodation with an AA 5-Diamond rating. Set in 6 acres and surrounded by glorious views, this early 19th century farmhouse has recently been renovated to a very high standard. Guests have the use of a spacious, traditionally furnished lounge and provided with a video and local books. There are 2 guest bedrooms (1 double; 1 twin/double), one en suite, the other with a private bathroom. In good weather, guests can enjoy the delightful patio or the peaceful landscaped garden.

BARLEY MOW INN

Kirk Ireton, Ashbourne, Derbyshire DE6 3JP
Tel: 01335 370306

For more than 20 years the Short family have owned and run the **Barley Mow Inn** in the pretty village of Kirk Ireton and have established a reputation for warm hospitality and for serving excellent real ales and ciders. The striking 3-storey building is over 300 years old and still retains its 17th century character with features such as the mullioned windows, old beams and welcoming open fire. The Barley Mow is a delightful place to stay, offering home-from-home accommodation and a hearty English breakfast. Evening meals are available by arrangement and snacks are available in the bar at other times.

HOPTON

8 miles NE of Ashbourne off the B5035

This village, now by-passed by the main road, is dominated by the Carsington Water Reservoir. The land rises to the north of Hopton and here can be found the **Hopton Incline**, once the steepest railway incline in the British Isles. Lying on the **High Peak Railway** line, carriages on their journey from Cromford to Whaley Bridge were hauled up using fixed engines. It is now part of the High Peak Trail.

BRASSINGTON

7 miles NE of Ashbourne off the B5056

Protected from the wind by the limestone plateau that soars some 1,000 feet above sea level, the village sits by strange shaped rocks, the result of weather erosion, with names like **Rainster Rocks** and **Harborough Rocks**.

Stone Age man found snugs amongst these formations and there is evidence that animals like the sabre-toothed tiger, brown bear, wolf and hyena also found comfort here in the caves. As late as the 18th century families were still living in the caves.

FENNY BENTLEY

2 miles N of Ashbourne off the A515

Inside **St Edmund's Church** can be found the tomb of Thomas Beresford, the local lord of the manor who fought, alongside eight of his 16 sons, at Agincourt. The effigies of Beresford and his wife are surrounded by those of their 21 children – each covered by a shroud because by the time the tombs were built nobody could remember what they had looked like! During the Civil War, much of the Church and its rectory were destroyed. On returning to his parish after the restoration of Charles II in

BENTLEY BROOK INN

Fenny Bentley, Ashbourne, Derbyshire DE6 1LF
Tel: 01335 350278 Fax: 01335 350422
e-mail: all@bentleybrookinn.co.uk
website: www.bentleybrookinn.co.uk

Owned and operated by the Allingham family since 1977 **Bentley Brook Inn** is an outstanding hostelry with an excellent restaurant, its own craft brewery, an all day bar with pub food, and value for money

accommodation. Since they took over in 1977, David and Jeanne Allingham with the help of their family and staff, some of who have worked at the inn for many years, have restored the fabric of the buildings and established a reputation for superb food, real ales and true hospitality. Located in the heart of the Peak District, England's premier National Park, the inn also offers a large child-friendly garden, a meadow, woodland and trout fishing.

At the front of the inn there is a formal terrace and sweeping lawns, while to the rear are a large car park, the brewery yard with skittle alleys and a boules court, and the poultry pen housing the hens that lay eggs for your breakfast. The Allingham's second son, Edward, runs the bar, looks after the beers and sells Leatherbritches beers to real Ale pubs around the country. He also organizes the annual Beer Festival during the Bank Holiday at the end of May and other occasional special events. Bill is the third and youngest son. He created the Inn's on-site craft brewery, Leatherbritches.

1661, the rector resolved to rebuild the rectory, which was all but rubble, and restore the Church to its former glory. Both of these he managed. The 15th century square tower of the fortified manor house, now incorporated into Cherry Orchard Farm which belonged to the Beresford family and was once the home of Charles Cotton, is a local landmark that can be seen from the main road.

TISSINGTON
4 miles N of Ashbourne off the A515

Sitting at the foothills of the Pennines, Tissington is, perhaps, most famous for its ancient festival of well-dressing, a ceremony which dates back to at least 1350. Today this takes place in the middle of May and draws many crowds who come to see the spectacular folk art created by the local people.

There are plenty of theories as to why well dressing began or was revived at Tissington. One centres on the purity of the Tissington wells during the Black Death which swept through the country in the mid-1300s. During this time some 77 of the 100 clergy in Derbyshire died and the surviving villagers simply returned to the pagan custom of well dressing. Another plausible theory dates back only as far as the great drought of 1615, when the Tissington wells kept flowing though water everywhere was in very short supply. Whichever theory is true, one thing is certain, that in the last 50 years or so many villages who had not dressed a well for centuries, if ever, are now joining in the colourful tradition.

A total of six wells are dressed at Tissington: the Hall, the Town, the Yew Tree, the Hands, the Coffin and the Children's Wells. Each depicts a separate scene, usually one from the Bible. Visitors should follow the signs in the village or ask at the Old Coach House.

Home of the FitzHerbert family for 500 years, **Tissington Hall** is a distinguished and impressive stately home which was built by Francis FitzHerbert in 1609. The estate consists of 2,400 acres comprising 13 farms, 40 cottages and assorted lettings. The Hall boasts a wealth of original pieces, artwork, furnishings and architectural features tracing the times and tastes of the FitzHerbert family (now headed by Sir Richard FitzHerbert) over the centuries. Tissington Hall and Gardens are open to the public on 28 afternoons throughout the summer.

Following the old Ashbourne to Parsley Hay railway line, the **Tissington Trail** is a popular walk which can be combined with other old railway trails in the area or country lanes to make an enjoyable circular country walk. The Tissington Trail passes through some lovely countryside and, with a reasonable surface, is also popular with cyclists. Along the route can also be found many of the old railway line buildings and junction boxes and, in particular, the old Hartington station, which is now a picnic site with an information centre in the old signal box.

ALSOP-EN-LE-DALE
5 miles N of Ashbourne off the A515

The old station on the Ashbourne-Buxton line which once served this tiny hamlet is today a car park on the Tissington Trail. The tranquil hamlet itself is on a narrow lane east of the main road towards Parwich, just a mile from Dovedale. Alsop-en-le-Dale's parish church of St Michael is Norman, though it was rebuilt substantially during Victorian times. The nave retains Norman features, with impressive double zigzag mouldings in the arches, but the west tower is only imitation Norman, and dates from 1883. One unusual feature which dominates this small

CHURCH FARM COTTAGES

Alsop en le Dale, Ashbourne, Derbyshire DE6 1QP
Tel: 01335 390216 e-mail: churchfarmcottages.alsop@virgin.net
website: www.cressbrook.co.uk/ashborn/churchfarm

Nestling at the head of one of the most beautiful but undiscovered dales in the Peak District National Park, **Church Farm Cottages** provide high quality self catering accommodation in a lovely setting. The owner, Christine Duffell, created these two charming cottages from an old stone barn that stands in the cobbled yard of the farm which specialises in rare breeds. Pinster Cottage sleeps 4; Winnets sleeps 5: both have central heating, are fully carpeted, have a comprehensively equipped kitchen and colour television. A cot is available, so too is a baby sitting service. No smoking.

church is its extraordinary 19th century, square mock-Gothic pulpit.

The renowned **Viator's Bridge** at Milldale is only a mile away to the west. It was immortalised in Izaak Walton's *The Compleat Angler* by the character Viator who complains to another about the size of the tiny, two-arched packhorse bridge, deeming it "not two fingers broad".

ARBOR LOW

13 miles N of Ashbourne off the A515

This remote **Stone Circle** is often referred to as the "Stonehenge of the Peaks", and although many of the stones now lie on the ground it is still an impressive sight. There are several stone circles in the Peak District but none offer the same atmosphere as Arbor Low, nor

Arbor Low Stone Circle

the same splendid views. Built around 4,000 years ago by the early Bronze Age people, there are a total of 40 stones each weighing no less than 8 tonnes. Probably used as an observatory and also a festival site, it is likely that the stones, which have been placed in pairs, never actually stood up.

MAPPLETON

2 miles NW of Ashbourne off the A515

Mappleton is a secluded and charming village of the Dove Valley, with attractive views and a wealth of exciting natural beauty. The 18th century Church of St Mary's is unusual in that it has a dome rather than a tower or steeple.

The village's main claim to fame is its annual New Year's Day charity bridge jump when 10 teams of 3 people each paddle down half a mile of the River Dove and then jump off a bridge. The Dove is not easily navigable, the bridge is 30ft high and after the jump there is a 500 yard sprint to the pub. It is grand spectator sport and hundreds of people come to watch.

THORPE

3 miles NW of Ashbourne off the A515

Thorpe lies at the confluence of the Rivers Manifold and Dove, and is dominated by the conical hill of **Thorpe Cloud** which guards the entrance to **Dovedale**. Although the Dale becomes over-crowded at times, there is always plenty of open space to explore on the hill as well as excellent walking. For much of its 45-mile course from Axe Edge to its confluence with the River Trent, the **River Dove** is a walker's river as it is mostly inaccessible by car. The steep sides to its valley, the fast-flowing water and the magnificent white rock formations all give Dovedale a special charm. Dovedale, however, is only a short section of the valley. Above Viator Bridge it becomes **Mill Dale** and further upstream again are **Wolfscote Dale** and **Beresford Dale**.

ILAM

4 miles NW of Ashbourne off the A52

Now a model village of great charm, Ilam was originally an important settlement belonging to Burton Abbey. Following the Reformation in the 16th century, the estate was broken up and Ilam came into the hands of the Port family. In the early 1800s the family sold the property to Jesse Watts Russell, a weathly industrialist. As well as building a fine mansion, **Ilam Hall**, for himself, Russell also spent a great deal of money refurbishing the attractive cottages. Obviously devoted to his wife, he had the Hall built in a romantic Gothic style and, in the centre of the village, he had the Eleanor Cross erected in her memory. Ilam Hall is now a Youth Hostel.

Many places in the Peak District have provided the inspiration for writers over the years and Ilam is no exception. The peace and quiet found here helped William Congreve create his bawdy play *The Old Bachelor*, whilst Dr Johnson wrote *Rasselas* whilst staying at the Hall. Ilam lies in the valley of the River Manifold and is a popular starting point for walks along this beautiful stretch of

river. In summer the Manifold disappears underground north of the village to reappear below Ilam Hall. The village is also the place where the Rivers Manifold and Dove merge. The two rivers rise close together, on Axe Edge, and for much of their course follow a parallel path, so it is fitting that they should also come together. Though Dovedale is regarded, and probably deservedly so, as the most scenic of the Peak District valleys, the Manifold Valley is very similar and whilst being marginally less beautiful it is often much less crowded.

WATERHOUSES

6 miles NW of Ashbourne off the A523

Between here and Hulme End, the Leek and Manifold Valley Light Railway, a picturesque narrow-gauge line, used to follow the valleys of the Manifold and the Hamps, crisscrossing the latter on little bridges. Sadly trains no longer run but its track bed has been made into the **Hamps-Manifold Track**, a marvellous walk which is ideal for small children and people in wheelchairs, since its surface is level and tarred throughout its eight miles. The Track can be reached from car parks at Hulme End, Waterhouses, Weags Bridge near Grindon, and Wetton.

WETTON

7 miles NW of Ashbourne off the B5053

Wetton Mill has been sympathetically converted by the National Trust into a café, a very welcome sight for those walking the **Manifold Valley Trail**. There is also a car park here for the less energetic and a picnic area for those who would rather cater for themselves. Much of the hillside either side of the track also belongs to the National Trust and is a splendid place for walks.

Below the Mill can be found the ominous-sounding **Thor's Cave**, situated some 250 feet above the River Manifold. Though the Cave is not deep, the entrance is huge, some 60 feet high, and the stiff climb up is well worth the effort for the spectacular views, all framed by the great natural stone arch. The acoustics too are interesting – conversations can easily be carried out with people far below. The openings at the bottom of the crag on which the Cave sits are known as **Radcliffe Stables** and are said to have been used by a Jacobite as a hiding place after Bonnie Prince Charlie had retreated from Derby.

ALSTONEFIELD

7 miles NW of Ashbourne off the A515

This ancient village, situated between the Manifold and the Dove valleys, lies at the crossroads of several old packhorse routes and had its own market charter granted in 1308. The market ceased in 1500 but the annual cattle sales

continued right up until the beginning of the 20th century.

Its geographical location has helped to maintain the charm of this unspoilt village. There has been no invasion by the canal or railway builders (it lies at 900 feet above sea level) and it is still two miles from the nearest classified road. Around 150 years ago Alstonefield was at the centre of a huge parish which covered all the land between the two rivers. There has been a church here since at least 892AD but the earliest known parts of the present Church are the Norman doorway and chancel arch of 1100. There is also plenty of 17th century woodwork and a double-decker pulpit dated 1637. Izaak Walton's friend, Charles Cotton, and his family lived at nearby Beresford Hall, now unfortunately no more, but the family's elaborate greenish pew is still in the church, and the fishing temple built by

CHURCH FARM

Stanshope, nr Alstonefield, Dovedale, Ashbourne, Derbyshire DE6 2AD   Tel/Fax: 01335 310243
e-mail: sue@fowler89.fsnet.co.uk
website: www.dovedalecottages.co.uk

Enjoying an idyllic location on the brow of a hill between Dovedale and the Manifold Valley, **Church Farm** offers a choice of two superb self-catering cottages. They stand on Sue and Steve Fowler's 80-acre farm which they farm organically "as our forefathers

did before us, using no fertilisers or pesticides". In summer, the meadows are speckled with wild flowers and herbs, and there are some wonderful rambles, starting from the farmhouse door, around Dovedale, Ilam Rock and the Manifold Valley.

Church Farm Cottage is a lovingly restored and beautifully decorated cottage which originally formed part of the main farmhouse which dates back to the 16th century and is Grade II listed. It is full of character and charm, with beamed ceilings, flagstone and quarry tiled floors, antique furniture, and open black range fire. There's a sunny sitting room with TV and open fire, a pretty kitchen/dining room, two bedrooms and two bathrooms, (4 star rated). Up to 6 guests can be accommodated in the 3 en suite bedrooms of the Ancestral Barn which is also Grade II listed and some 200 years old. Beautifully furnished with antiques, the lounge has a glorious open range fireplace and all the bedrooms feature glorious canopy beds,(5 star rated).

Cotton survives in Beresford Dale.

The village also retains its ancient **Tithe Barn**, found behind the late-16th century rectory. The internal exposed wattle and daub wall and the spiral stone staircase may, however, have been part of an earlier building.

CHESTERFIELD

This friendly, bustling town on the edge of the **Peak District National Park** grew up around its open-air market which was established over 800 years ago and claims to be England's largest. As the town lies at the crossroads of England, the hub of trade routes from all points of the compass, the town's claim seems easily justified. It was earning Royal revenue in 1165, as the Sheriff of Derbyshire recorded in the Pipe Rolls and, in that year, the market earned the princely sum of £1 2s 7d for the Crown. The Pipe Roll of 1182 also mentions a fair in Chesterfield. Such fairs were large markets, usually lasting for several days and drawing traders and buyers from a much wider area. Chesterfield's formal charter, however, was not granted until 1204, but this charter made the town one of the first eight free boroughs in the country. Escaping the prospect of redevelopment in the 1970s, the markets are as popular as ever and are held every Monday, Friday and Saturday, with a flea market each Thursday.

The town centre has been conserved for future generations by a far-sighted council, and many buildings have been saved, including the Victorian **Market Hall** built in 1857. The traditional cobbled paving was restored in the Market Place, and New Square was given a complete facelift. There are several Tudor buildings in the heart of Chesterfield, most notably the former Peacock Inn which is now home to the

St Mary & All Saints' Church

Peacock Heritage Centre and the tourist information office. It was built in 1500 for the wealthy Revell family, who later moved to Carnfield Hall near Alfreton. The black-and-white timbering in Knifesmithgate, however, was built only in the 1930s, to resemble the famous rows in Chester.

Visitors to the town are drawn to a peculiarly graceful spire reaching high into the skyline; twisting and leaning, it is totally confusing to the eye. The **Crooked Spire** of St Mary & All Saints' Church has dominated the skyline for so long that local folk have ceased to notice its unusual shape. Superstition surrounds it, and sadly the real story to its unusual appearance has been lost over the years. The truth probably lies in the wake of the Black Death during the 14th century when the people of Chesterfield were building their beautiful new church and awe-inspiring steeple. Many must have fallen to the plague, amongst them skilled craftsmen who knew how to season wood. The survivors built the spire out of green timber which over the years has distorted under the heavy lead covering. However, some stories say it was the Devil, who, pausing for a rest during one of his flights, clung to the spire for a moment or two. Incense from the Church drifted upwards and the Devil sneezed, causing the spire to twist out of shape.

This magnificent spire rises to 228 feet and leans 9 feet 4 inches from its true centre-point. It is eight-sided, but the herringbone pattern of the lead slates trick the eye into seeing 16 sides from the ground. The Crooked Spire is open most Bank Holidays and at advertised times; the church is open all year, Monday to Saturday 9am to 5pm (9am to 3pm, January and February), and Sundays at service times only.

AROUND CHESTERFIELD

WHITTINGTON
3 miles NE of Chesterfield off the B6052/A61

During the 17th century, **Revolution House** was part of an alehouse called the Cock and Pynot (*pynot* being the local dialect word for magpie). It was here that three local noblemen – the Earl of Devonshire, the Earl of Danby and John D'Arcy – met to begin planning their part in the events which eventually led to the overthrow of James II in favour of his daughter Mary and her husband, William of Orange. The Glorious Revolution took place later in the same year, November 1688, and it was in the year of its 250th anniversary that this modest house was turned into a museum.

Revolution House, a tiny cottage with thatched roof, flower border and charming garden gate which belies its rather incendiary name, is now open to the public and features period furnishings and a changing programme of exhibitions on local themes. A video relates the story of the Revolution and the role which the house played in those fraught and dangerous days.

BARLBOROUGH
7 miles NE of Chesterfield off the A619

Lying close to the county borders with both Nottinghamshire and Yorkshire, this village still retains its manor house. Lying just north of the village centre, **Barlborough Hall** (private) was built in 1584 by Lord Justice Francis Rodes to plans drawn up by the designer of Hardwick Hall, Robert Smythson. Those who visit both houses will notice the strong resemblance. As well as building houses, Rodes was also one of the judges at the trial of Mary, Queen of Scots. The Hall is supposed to be haunted by a grey lady, said to be the ghost of a bride who received the news of her groom's death as she was on her way to the 12th century village church. Barlborough Hall should not be confused with **Barlborough Old Hall**: this is an easy mistake to make as Barlborough Old Hall is actually the younger of the two! Built in 1618, as the date stone over the front door states, the Old Hall is of a large H-plan design and has mullioned windows.

CRESWELL
9 miles E of Chesterfield off the A616

Lying close to the Derbyshire-Nottinghamshire border, the limestone gorge known as **Creswell Crags** is well worth seeing. Formed thousands of years ago by the erosion of a river which cut through the limestone, this rock, which is porous and subject to erosion underground as well as on the surface, contributes by its very nature to the forming of natural chambers. The subterranean movement of water created a vast network of caves, which were subsequently exposed and used by Neanderthal man as shelters while out hunting. Tours can be taken from the visitor centre where there is also a display of artefacts found in the area. Testimony to the artistry of the later inhabitants of these caves was the discovery of a bone carved with the head of a horse. The carving is about 13,000 years old and can now be seen in the British Museum. The largest cavern, Church Hole Cave, extends some 170 feet into the side of the gorge; it was here that hand tools were found.

BOLSOVER

7 miles E of Chesterfield off the A632

The approach to Bolsover from the north and east is dominated by the splendid, sandstone structure of **Bolsover Castle** (English Heritage), which sits high on a limestone ridge. A castle has stood here since the 12th century, though the present building is a fairytale 'folly' built for Sir Charles Cavendish during the early 1600s on the site of a ruined castle. By the mid-1700s much of the building had been reduced to the ruins seen today, though thankfully the splendid keep has withstood the test of time.

Pevsner remarked that not many large houses in England occupy such an impressive position as Bolsover Castle, as it stands on the brow of a hill overlooking the valley of the River Rother and Doe Lea. The first castle at Bolsover was built by William Peverel, illegitimate son of William the Conqueror, as part of his vast Derbyshire estates. Nothing remains of that Norman building. Visitors can

explore the Little Castle, or Keep, which is decorated in an elaborate Jacobean style with wonderful fireplaces, panelling and wall paintings. The whole building later descended to the Dukes of Portland, and it remains a strangely impressive place, though even now it is threatened by its industrial surroundings and the legacy of centuries of coal-mining beneath its walls: subsidence.

AULT HUCKNALL

6 miles SE of Chesterfield off the A617

The strange name of this village probably means 'Hucca's high nook of land', and this pleasant place, standing on a ridge close to the Nottinghamshire border, is home to the magnificent Tudor house, **Hardwick Hall** (National Trust). "More glass than wall", it is one of Derbyshire's Big Three stately homes alongside Chatsworth and Haddon, all three glorious monuments to the great landowning families who played so great a role in shaping the history of the county. The letters E S can be seen carved in stone on the outside of the house: E S, or Elizabeth of Shrewsbury, was perhaps better known as Bess of Hardwick. This larger-than-life figure had attachments

Hardwick Hall

with many places in Derbyshire, and the story of her life makes for fascinating reading.

She was born in the manor house at Hardwick in 1520. The house stood only a little distance from the present-day Hall and was then not much more than a farmhouse. The young Bess married her neighbour's son, Robert Barlow, when she was only 12. When her young husband, himself only 14, died a few months later she naturally inherited a great deal of property. Some 15 years later she married Sir William Cavendish and, when he died in 1557, she was bequeathed his entire fortune. By this time she was the richest woman in England, save for one, Elizabeth, the Queen.

Bess began the building of Hardwick House in 1590, towards the end of her life and after her fourth lucrative marriage to George Talbot, 6th Earl of Shrewsbury. It stands as a monument to her wealth and good taste, and is justly famous for its magnificent needlework and tapestries, carved fireplaces and friezes, which are considered as among the finest in Britain.

Though Bess is the first person that springs to mind with regard to Hardwick Hall, it was the 6th Duke of Devonshire who was responsible for the Hall's antiquarian atmosphere. He inherited the property in 1811 and, as well as promoting the legend that Mary, Queen of Scots stayed here, he filled the house with furniture, paintings and tapestries from his other houses and from Chatsworth in particular.

PILSLEY
5 miles S of Chesterfield off the B6039

The Herb Garden in Pilsley is one of the foremost gardens in the country. It consists of four display gardens, the largest of which is the Mixed Herb Garden, boasting an impressive

established parterre. The remaining three gardens are the Physic, the Lavender and the Pot Pourri, each with its own special theme and housing many rare and unusual species. Areas of native flowers and wild spring bulbs can be enjoyed from March to September.

HOLYMOORSIDE
3 miles W of Chesterfield off the A632

Surrounded by attractive moorland and lying in the picturesque valley of the River Hipper, this scattered village has grown into a popular residential area for the nearby towns. The custom of well-dressing in the village was revived in 1979 after a gap of about 80 years. Two wells are dressed, a large one and a smaller one for children, on the Wednesday before the late summer Bank Holiday in August.

The dressers follow the tradition of Barlow, where only flowers and leaves are used and not wool, seed and shells, though they do not stick to biblical themes. In 1990 the well-dressing depicted a scene commemorating the 50th anniversary of the Battle of Britain, one of their most spectacular dressings to date, and won the dressers pictures in the national press.

CUTTHORPE
4 miles W of Chesterfield off the B6050

Before the Second World War the well-dressings in this village, which take place on the third Friday in July, had no religious links. After the war the custom died out, but was revived again by three people from nearby Barlow in 1978. The three dressed wells are blessed during a service of thanksgiving for the pure water.

Near the village are the three **Linacre Reservoirs**, set in the attractive wooded Linacre Valley. Built between 1855 and 1904, until recently they supplied water to Chesterfield. Today the area is home

HACKNEY HOUSE ANTIQUES

Hackney House, Hackney Lane, Barlow, Dronfield,
Derbyshire S18 7TD
Tel: 0114 289 0248   e-mail: hacnee@aol.com

Centrally located in the village of Barlow, **Hackney House
Antiques** occupies a fine old stone building once owned
by the Duke of Rutland. Janet and Edward Gorman opened
their antiques shop here in 1984 and in the following year
added the tea room serving wholesome home cooked food, including vegetarian dishes, and teatime
treats. The antiques area offers a good selection of longcase and other clocks, quality silver, pictures,
furniture and other items. Both shop and tearoom are open Tuesday to Sunday throughout the year.

to many species of fish, waterfowl,
mammals and plant life, and is
considered one of the most important
ecological sites in the area. There are
very pleasant walks, nature trails and
fishing, and a scenic picnic area.

BARLOW

3 miles NW of Chesterfield off the B6051

Barlow is mentioned in the Domesday
Book, and was the home of Robert
Barlow, the first of Bess of Hardwick's
four husbands. Although situated outside
the limestone area, Barlow has been
dressing its main well for longer than
most. It is not known for certain when
the custom began in the village, though
it *is* known that, like Tissington, the well
here provided water throughout the
drought of 1615; this may have marked
the start of this colourful practice. The
wells are dressed during the second week
of August every year. West of the village,
Barlow Woodseats are not as
uncomfortable as they sound for this is
the name of an irregular gabled 16th
century house, also called Woodseats
Hall (private), which has a cruck barn in
its grounds. It was home to the Mower
family, one of whom, Arthur Mower, was
the agent to the Barlow family in the 16th
century, and kept a truly remarkable
diary from 1555 to 1610. All 52 volumes
are now kept in the British Museum. He
records the death of Bess of Hardwick in

1608, recalling her as "a great purchaser
and getter together of much goods" and
notes that she "builded Chattesworth,
Hardwick and Owlcotes".

ALFRETON

This historic town dates back to Saxon
times and, despite local legends to the
contrary, Alfred the Great was not
immortalised in the naming of the place.
This attractive former coal-mining town
stands on a hill close to the
Nottinghamshire border. Along the
charming High Street can be found the
George Hotel, a fine Georgian building
that looks down the length of the High
Street. There are also a number of other
18th century stone built houses, the most
impressive of which is **Alfreton Hall**
(private), the centrepiece of an attractive
public park. In soft mellow stone, the
Hall was built around 1730, with 19th
century additions. The home until fairly
recently of the Palmer Morewood family,
owners of the local coal mines, it is now
used as an Arts and Adult Education
Centre. The park is quite extensive,
boasting its own cricket ground and a
horse-riding track around its perimeter.
In **King Street** there is a house of
confinement, or Lock-up, which was
built to house lawbreakers and catered
mainly for the local drunkards. The close
confines of the prison with its two cells,

THE BOUNDARY

Lea Vale, Broadmeadows, South Normanton, Alfreton,
Derbyshire DE55 3NA
Tel: 01773 819066 Fax: 01773 819006 website: www.theboundary.co.uk

Just five minutes drive from Junction 28 of the M1 Motorway at South
Normanton, 'The Boundary' boasts 'something for everyone' Our main Bar/
Restaurant offers a superb menu and delicious Sunday Carvery. There are
FREE indoor and outdoor Play Areas for children and FREE weekend
entertainment. For Weddings, Conferences and Banquets, we can cater for
up to 250 people in our magnificent 'Meridian Suite', whilst The Ashton and Eden Suites are suitable
for smaller groups. On site is 'The Boundary Lodge' boasting 14 luxuriously appointed bedrooms,
including Bridal, Executive and Family Suites. Ground floor rooms are available. ETB four diamond
Silver Award AA four diamond. *(Prices based on Room only. Special weekend Rates available).*

minute windows and thick outer walls must have been a very effective deterrent.

AROUND ALFRETON

SOUTH WINGFIELD

2 miles NW of Alfreton off the A6

Above the village, on the rise of a hill, stand the graceful ruins of the 15th century **Wingfield Manor**. Built by Ralph Lord Cromwell, the manor house was used as Mary Queen of Scots' prison on two separate occasions in 1569 and 1584 when she was held under the care of the Earl of Shrewsbury. The local squire, Anthony Babington, attempted to rescue the Queen and lead her to safety but the plot failed and, instead, lead to them both being beheaded. One of the less well-known of Derbyshire's many manor houses and mansions, the history and architectural interest provided by the ruins make it one of the more fascinating homes in the area. A wander around the remains reveals the large banqueting hall with its unusual oriel window and a crypt which was probably used to store food and wine. Whatever its use, it is a particularly fine example and rivals a similar structure at Fountains Abbey.

CRICH

4 miles SW of Alfreton off the A6

This large village, with its hilltop church and market cross, is probably most

CRICH TRAMWAY VILLAGE

Crich Tramway Village, Crich, Matlock, Derbyshire DE45DP
Tel: 0870 75 TRAMS (87267) Fax: 01773 852326

Crich Tramway Village offers a family day out in the relaxing atmosphere of a bygone era. Explore the recreated period street with its genuine buildings and features, fascinating exhibitions and most importantly, its trams. Unlimited tram rides are free with your entry fee, giving you the opportunity to fully appreciate the Village and surrounding countryside.

Journey on one of the many beautifully restored vintage trams, as they rumble along the cobbled street past a traditional police telephone known as the 'TARDIS', the Red Lion Pub & Restaurant, exhibition hall, workshops, children's play and picnic area, before passing beneath the magnificent Bowes Lyon Bridge. Next it's past the bandstand, through the woods, and then on to Glory Mine taking in spectacular views of the Derwent Valley.

famous as the home of the **National Tramway Museum** (see panel on page 203). Referring to itself intriguingly as "the museum that's a mile long", it offers a wonderful opportunity to enjoy a tram ride along a Victorian Street scene.

Back in the centre of the village is the tower of **Crich Stand**, a local landmark that looks rather like a lighthouse. In fact this is the Regimental Memorial for the Sherwood Foresters and, erected in 1923, stands almost 1,000 feet above sea level. From its viewing gallery, on a clear day, it is said that seven counties can be seen: a climb to the top certainly offers some fantastic views. This large, straggling village, which retains its medieval market cross, was also a flourishing knitting centre at one time; the telltale 18th century cottages with their long upper windows can still be seen. The part-Norman parish Church of St Michael has a built-in stone lectern which, though common in Derbyshire, is rare elsewhere in the country.

AMBERGATE
6 miles SW of Alfreton off the A6

Where the River Amber joins the mighty Derwent, Ambergate is one of the main gateways to the Peak District for travellers going north on the A6. A marvellous bridge crosses the Derwent. The village itself is surrounded by deciduous woodland, including the fine **Shining Cliff Woods**, an important refuge for wildlife. The railway, road and canal here are all squeezed into the tight river valley, and the railway station, standing 100 feet above the road, was one of the few triangular stations in Britain. Built in the late 19th century, the church of St Anne was a gift to the village from the Johnson family of the Ambergate Wire Works, now known as the business concern Richard Johnson and Nephew.

RIDDINGS
2 miles S of Alfreton off the A38/A610

Riddings, now a tranquil village, has twice been the scene of important discoveries. In the mid-1700s, 800 precious Roman coins were uncovered here. A century later, James Oakes, a colliery proprietor and ironmaster, discovered a mysterious liquid flowing on his property. He called in the assistance of his brother-in-law, Lyon Playfair, one of the most brilliant practical scientists of his day. Playfair found the liquid to be petroleum – then an unknown product commercially, although it had been known (as naphtha, 'salt of the earth'), from Biblical times.

Playfair summoned the help of his friend James Young, who soon after he came to Riddings approached Playfair in dismay to show him that the oil was in a turbid condition. Playfair recognised at once the presence of paraffin, and instructed Young to extract enough paraffin to make two candles – the first paraffin-wax candles ever produced. With one candle in his left hand and the other in his right, Playfair illuminated a lecture he gave at the Royal Institution. From these small beginnings date the enormous petroleum industry and the rich trade in paraffin and its wide range of by-products.

RIPLEY

Once a typical small market town, Ripley expanded dramatically during the Industrial Revolution when great use was made of the iron, clay and coal deposits found nearby. The town's Butterley ironworks, founded in 1792 by a group of men which included renowned engineer Benjamin Outram, created the roof for London's St Pancras station. Outram's even more famous son, Sir

James, enjoyed an illustrious career that saw him appointed Bayard of India, and earned him a resting place in Westminster Abbey.

AROUND RIPLEY

HEAGE
1 miles W of Ripley off the B6013

This village is home to a famous tower **Windmill**, the only one in Derbyshire to retain all its six sails, fan tail and machinery. The Grade II listed building, situated to the west of the village, is built of local sandstone. Now more than 200 years old, the mill has been restored to full working order and is open to the public at weekends and bank holidays.

DENBY
2 miles S of Ripley off the A38/B6179

Denby Pottery (see panel below) is one of the biggest visitor attractions in Derbyshire. It was established in 1809 and nearly 200 years later, classic ranges such as Imperial Blue and Regency Green are still best sellers. Its Visitor Centre now welcomes nearly 300,000 visitors a year and on site attractions include a Factory Shop, a Cookery Emporium offering cookery demonstrations and a stock of more than 3,000 kitchen gadgets, supplies and equipment; workshop tours and a restaurant.

HEANOR
3 miles SE of Ripley off the A608

The hub of this busy town centres on the market place, where the annual fair is held, as well as the twice-weekly market (Fridays and Saturdays). Away from the bustle of the market are the **Memorial Gardens**. This peaceful setting always promises a magnificent spread of floral arrangements, herbaceous borders and shrubberies.

To the south of Heanor is the **Shipley Country Park**, on the estate of the now demolished Shipley Hall. In addition to its magnificent lake, the Country Park boasts over 600 acres of beautiful countryside which should keep even the most enthusiastic walker busy. Well known as both an educational and holiday centre, there are facilities for horse riding, cycling and fishing. Restoration over the years has transformed former railways into wooded paths, reservoirs into peaceful lakes, and has re-established the once-flowering meadows and rolling hills which had been destroyed by colliery pits.

BELPER

Famous for its cotton mills, the town is situated alongside the **River Derwent** on the floor of the valley. In 1776, Jedediah Strutt, the wheelwright son of a South

DENBY VISITOR CENTRE

Derby Road, Denby, Derbyshire DE5 8NX
Tel: 01773 740799 Fax: 01773 740749
website: www.denby.co.uk

A warm welcome awaits you at **Denby Visitor Centre**. Set around an attractive cobbled courtyard with shops and restaurant next to the working factory, the centre is open all year round apart from Christmas Eve and Christmas Day. Activities include free cookery demonstrations, glass-blowing

studio, pottery tours and bargain hunting in the extensive Factory Shop. Pottery tours are fully guided and include painting a plate in glaze and making a souvenir to take home. School holiday activities, special events and factory shop offers are listed on www.denbyvisitorcentre.co.uk

Normanton farmer, set up one of the earliest water-powered cotton mills here to harness the natural powers of the river to run his mills. With the river providing the power, and fuel coming from the nearby South Derbyshire coalfield, the valley has a good claim to be one of the cradles of the Industrial Revolution. Earlier, in 1771, Strutt had gone into profitable partnership with Richard Arkwright to establish the world's first water-powered cotton mill at Cromford. Great benefactors to Belper for 150 years, the Strutt family provided housing, work, education and even food from the model farms they established in the surrounding countryside.

The mills are still standing and, along with them, are some unique mill-workers' cottages. To discover more about the cotton industry, a visit to the **Derwent Valley Visitor Centre** is a must. It records the influence of the

Strutt family on the town and of Samuel Slater, Strutt's apprentice who emigrated to America in 1789, built a mill there and went on to become "the Father of American manufacturers".

The oldest mill still surviving is the two-storey **North Mill** at Bridgefoot, near the magnificent crescent-shaped weir in the Derwent and the town's main bridge. Built in 1876, the mill has cast-iron columns and beams, and hollow tile floors which provided a warm-air central heating system. It is now the visitor centre. The massive, neighbouring redbrick **East Mill** was constructed in 1912, but now is largely empty. A Jubilee Tower in terracotta was erected on the mill site in 1897 to mark Queen Victoria's sixty years on the throne.

Train travellers through Belper are among those treated to a glimpse of George Stephenson's mile-long cutting, walled in gritstone throughout and

DANNAH FARM

Bowman's Lane, Shottle, Derbyshire DE56 2DR
Tel: 01773 550273 Fax: 01773 550590
e-mail: reservations@dannah.demon.co.uk

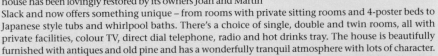

A delightful 18th century farmhouse, **Dannah Farm** nestles just below Alport Height with its panoramic views across six counties. Recent winners of the Best of Tourism award, the house has been lovingly restored by its owners Joan and Martin Slack and now offers something unique – from rooms with private sitting rooms and 4-poster beds to Japanese style tubs and whirlpool baths. There's a choice of single, double and twin rooms, all with private facilities, colour TV, direct dial telephone, radio and hot drinks tray. The house is beautifully furnished with antiques and old pine and has a wonderfully tranquil atmosphere with lots of character.

There are two comfortable sitting rooms and a superb award-winning fully licensed dining room. Included in the tariff is a freshly cooked English farmhouse breakfast, a special treat with free range

eggs, the farm's own organic sausages and home made bread. Dinner is served by prior arrangement and vegetarians and those on special diets are happily catered for. The farm itself is a working farm with 128 acres dedicated to arable crops and naturally reared beef. "Additional" livestock includes a naughty nanny goat, some very spoilt farm cats, Meadowsweet hens and a brace of adorable Kune Kune pigs. Joan and Martin have recently completed a raised Koi pond and replanted the old orchard. No wonder their enterprise was shortlisted as Alternative Farmer of the Year!

spanned by no fewer than 10 bridges. When completed in 1840 it was considered the engineering wonder of its day. In addition to all its industrial history the town goes back to well before the Industrial Revolution. Not only was it mentioned in the Domesday Book (as *Beau Repaire* - the beautiful retreat), but in 1964 the remains of a Roman kiln were found here.

The River Gardens were established in 1905 and today they are a pleasant place for a stroll among the beautifully tended gardens. Rowing boats can be hired for a trip along the Derwent. The Gardens are a favourite with the film industry, having been used in Ken Russell's *Women in Love*, as well as television's *Sounding Brass* and *In the Shadow of the Noose*.

AROUND BELPER

DUFFIELD
2 miles S of Belper off the A6

This ancient parish is a charming place, with Georgian houses and cottages lining the banks of the River Ecclesbourne. For such a cosy place, it seems odd that the Parish Church is situated in isolation down by the river. Inside the Church there is an impressive monument dedicated to Anthony Bradshaw whose great-nephew went on to officiate over the court which called for the execution of Charles I. Also in

the village is a large mound, all that remains of **Duffield Castle** (National Trust) which was ransacked and burnt to the ground in 1266.

ILKESTON

The third largest town in Derbyshire, Ilkeston received its royal charter for a market and fair in 1252; both have continued to the present day. The history of the town, however, goes back to the days when it was an Anglo-Saxon hilltop settlement known as Tilchestune. Once a mining and lace-making centre, its history is told in the **Erewash Museum**, housed in a fine Georgian house on the High Street. Other fine examples of elegant 18th century houses can be found in East Street whilst in Wharncliffe Road there are period houses with art nouveau features.

Ilkeston commands fine wide views from the hillside above the valley of the **Erewash**, which here bounds the county. The town's church-crowned hilltop is a landmark that can be seen from far afield.

AROUND ILKESTON

WEST HALLAM
2 miles W of Ilkeston off the A609

West Hallam stands on a hilltop; its church, set between the great expanse of **West Hallam Hall** and the rectory, is

WAYSIDE ANTIQUES

62 Town Street, Duffield, Derbyshire DE56 4GG
Tel: 01332 840346

Brian and Jeanette Harding have owned and run **Wayside Antiques** for over 25 years and have established an excellent reputation for quality antiques. Housed in a building dating back to 1730, formerly part of an old malthouse, Wayside Antiques offers a wide choice of 19th century furniture, silverware, porcelain, prints, clocks and other decorative pieces. Everything is attractively displayed, arranged as though in authentic period rooms. The Hardings live on the premises and are happy to meet customers by appointment outside normal opening hours. Duffield itself lies in the Derwent Valley, now designated an International Heritage Area.

approached via a lovely avenue of limes. The rector's garden has a glorious lime tree, and looks out over the valley to a great windmill with its arms still working as they have done since Georgian times.

One of the premier attractions in the area, **The Bottle Kiln** is a handsome and impressive brickbuilt former working pottery, now home to contemporary art and craft. Visitors can take a leisurely look at exhibitions (changing throughout the year) of both British studio ceramics and contemporary painting in the European tradition. From figurative and descriptive to abstract, many styles and media are displayed here. In addition there is a selection of imaginative contemporary British jewellery and craftware on display in and around the old kiln. Two shops filled with jewellery, cards, gifts, objets-d'art, soft furnishings and housewares with an accent on style, design and originality can also be found at this superb site.

DALE ABBEY
3 miles SW of Ilkeston off the A6096

The village takes its name from the now ruined abbey that was founded here by Augustinian monks in the 13th century. Beginning life in a very humble manner, local legend has it that a Derbyshire baker came to the area in 1130, carved

himself a niche in the sandstone and devoted himself to the way of the hermit. The owner of the land, Ralph FitzGeremunde, discovered the baker and was so impressed by the man's devotion that he bestowed on him the land and tithe rights to his mill in Borrowash. The sandstone cave and the romantic ruined 40 feet high window archway are popular attractions locally and a walk around the village is both an interesting and pleasurable experience. Nearby **Hermit's Wood** is an ancient area of woodland with beech, ash, oak and lime trees. It is wonderful at any time of year, but particularly in the spring when the woodland floor is covered with a mist of bluebells.

To the north of the village stands the **Cat and Fiddle Windmill**, built in the 1700s and a fine example of the oldest type of mill. The stone roundhouse is capped with a box-like wooden structure which houses the machinery and which is fitted onto an upright post round which it can rotate to catch the wind.

RISLEY
4 miles S of Ilkeston off the B5010

This small village has once again become a quiet backwater now that the main Derby to Nottingham road bypasses it to the south. Apart from ribbon building

ℛISLEY ℋALL
Derby Road, Risley, Derbyshire DE72 3SS
Tel: 0115 939 9000 e-mail: enquiries@risleyhallhotel.co.uk
Fax: 0115 939 7766   website: risleyhallhotel.co.uk

Risley Hall is one of Derbyshire's best kept secrets, just two minutes from junction 25 of the M1. It is an independently owned Grade ll listed building situated in rural surroundings, within 17 acres of beautifully landscaped gardens, surrounded by some of England's most beautiful countryside. The accommodation is luxurious; each of the 20 Executive Luxury Suites and the 16 individually appointed double bedrooms have en suite facilities with television and radio and 24-hour room service adds to the pampered feeling. There's an excellent restaurant, which is also open to non-residents; a choice of 5 conference rooms; the Aqua Health Spa, and the lovely setting makes Risley Hall a popular venue for wedding receptions.

along the former main road, Risley consists of no more than a small group of old buildings, but they are unique and well worth a visit. In 1593, Michael Willoughby started to rebuild the village church. Although small, even by the standards of the day, it is charming and essentially Gothic in style. In the same year his wife founded a school and, although none of the original schoolhouses exist, those seen today date from the early 1700s and were constructed by a trust founded by the family. The central school building is a perfect example of the Queen Anne style and acted as both the school and schoolhouse, with the boarders sleeping in the garrets. The trustees still maintain this wonderful building, along with the Latin School of 1724, the English School of 1753 and another School House built in 1771.

BREASTON

5 miles S of Ilkeston off the A6005

On the southern borders of the county, close to Nottinghamshire and Leicestershire, Breaston occupies the flat countryside near the point where the River Derwent joins the River Trent before continuing on its long journey to the North Sea. The mainly 13th century **Church of St Michael** boasts the 'Boy of Breaston' – a small, chubby-faced child immortalised in the 13th century by the mason of the nave arches. He has smiled down on worshippers and visitors for the past seven centuries. The story has it that this boy would come in and watch the masons at work while the church was being built. The master mason decided to make the child part of the church, so that he could always have a good view of it!

Coffins had to be carried to

THE GLORY HOLE

14-16 Station Road, Sandiacre, Notts NG10 5BG
Tel: 0115 939 4081 Fax: 0115 939 4085

Moving into a new house, restoring a traditional property? The place to make for is **The Glory Hole** where you'll find an interesting selection of old and new furniture and accessories.Owned and run by Colin and Debbie Reid who share a love of quality and traditional interiors. Colin is responsible for the design, manufacture and installation of the kitchens and fireplaces made at his factory in Sawley Notts. They are proud of the fact that their staff are all highly

trained and talented when it comes to producing bespoke, all timber furniture, kitchens and fire surrounds (no chipboard whatsoever!) freestanding or fitted. Installation includes all necessary gas, electrical, plumbing and carpentry work by The Glory Hole Staff.If you are looking for inspiration

there are 8 rooms of occasional furniture, lamps, mirrors, tables and chairs, radiator covers, bookcases, wardrobes ect plus a wide range of cabinet and door fittings. Colin & Debbie started the business in 1984 gradually changing from just dealing in antique furniture to restoring and then producing quality bespoke items to order. Now this side has completely taken over, customers can have their own ideas and designs created and installed, no two kitchens are the same! The Shop is situated close to The Erewash Canal and in the shadow of Springfield Mill. The area is currently being developed, to coincide with this Colin and Debbie are converting the old Barn at the rear of the Glory Hole into a licensed restaurant serving traditional food.

neighbouring **Church Wilne** for burial up until the early 1800s, as there was no burial ground at Breaston until that time. For this reason the footpath over the fields of Wilne continues to be known by villagers as the 'Coffin Walk'.

ELVASTON

8 miles SW of Ilkeston off the B5010

Elvaston is gathered around the edge of the **Elvaston Castle** estate, home of the Earls of Harrington. The magnificent Gothic castle seen today replaced a 17th century brick and gabled manor house; part of the original structure can be seen on the end of the south front. Designed by James Wyatt, the castle was finished in the early 1800s but, unfortunately, the 3rd Earl died in 1829 and had little time to enjoy his new home.

It is, perhaps, the grounds which make Elvaston Castle famous today. They were originally laid out and designed for the 4th Earl by William Barron. Barron, who was born in Berwickshire in 1805, started work in 1830 on what at first appeared to be an impossible task. The 4th Earl wanted a garden 'second to none', but the land available, which had never been landscaped, was flat, water-logged and uninspiring with just two avenues of trees and a walled kitchen garden (but no greenhouses or hot houses). First draining the land, Barron then planted trees to offer shelter to more tender plants. From there the project grew. In order to stock the gardens, Barron began a programme of propagation of rarer tree species and, along with the tree-planting methods he developed specially to deal with Elvaston's problems, his fame spread. The gardens became a showcase of rare and interesting trees, many to be found nowhere else in Britain. Now owned by Derby County Council, the gardens, after years of neglect, have been completely restored and the delights of the formal gardens, with their fine topiary, the avenues and the kitchen garden can be enjoyed by all visitors to the grounds, which are now a Country Park.

No visit to Elvaston would be complete without a walk down to the **Golden Gates**. Erected in 1819 at the southern end of the formal gardens, the gates were brought from the Palace of Versailles by the 3rd Earl of Harrington. Little is known of the Gates' history, but they remain a fine monument and are the symbol of Elvaston.

DERBY

Essentially a commercial and industrial city, Derby's position, historically and geographically, has ensured that is has remained one of the most important and interesting cities in the area. Consequently there is much for the visitor to see, whether from an architectural or historical point of view. There are, however, two things almost everyone, whether they have been to the city before or not, associate with Derby: Rolls-Royce engines and Royal Crown Derby porcelain. When in 1906 Sir Henry Royce and the Hon C.S. Rolls joined forces and built the first Rolls-Royce (a Silver Ghost) at Derby, they built much more than just a motor car. Considered by many to be the best cars in the world, it is often said that the noisiest moving part in any Rolls-Royce is the dashboard clock! The home of **Royal Crown Derby**, any visit to the city would not be complete without a trip to the factory and its museum and shop. The guided tours offer an intriguing insight into the high level of skill required to create the delicate flower petals, hand gild the plates and to hand paint the Derby Dwarves.

The city's **Cathedral of All Saints** possesses a fine 16th century tower, the

JOAN GILBERT, CANE & RUSH SEATING SPECIALIST

50 Ashbourne Road, Derby DE22 3AD
Tel: 01332 244303

Joan Gilbert has been replacing cane and rush in chairs, settees and bedheads for many years and the results are exquisite as can be seen at her workshop in Ashbourne Road, Derby. She began some 40 years ago, practising her skill on some chairs at home. "Then my aunt saw some old chairs that needed re-caning at Locko Park, a big house in Derbyshire". That led to more work at Chatsworth House and then Joan was discovered by London antique furniture restorers.

She is expert in all the complex cane patterns including sunbursts, hanging medallions and double-sided caning on chairs, bergère sofas and bedheads. Only the best materials are used – split cane imported from Indonesia in six widths and English rush from the Fen country and the River Thames. She is a specialist in fine rush ie drop-in seats. Joan points out that it is not normally possible to repair cane or rush seats: once there is a break it is a sure sign that the material is brittle and must be completely replaced. "In any case" Joan adds, "new cane or rush does not match the old in colour". Her work in progress is always available for inspection and she is prepared to estimate costs for any repair work.

second highest perpendicular tower in England. The airy building was actually built in the 1720s by James Gibbs. Inside is a beautiful wrought-iron screen by Robert Bakewell and, among the splendid monuments, lies the tomb of Bess of Hardwick Hall. Originally Derby's Parish Church, it was given cathedral status in 1927.

One of Derby's most interesting museums is **Pickford House**, situated on the city's finest Georgian street at number 41. It is a Grade I listed building, erected in 1770 by the architect Joseph Pickford as a combined family home and place of work. Pickford House differs from the majority of grand stately homes; unlike most it does not have a wealth of priceless furniture and works or art. Instead, visitors are able to gain an insight into everyday middle-class life during the 1830s.

Just a short walk from Pickford House

is the **Industrial Museum**. What better place to house a museum devoted to the preservation of Derby's industrial heritage than the beautiful old **Silk Mill**, a building which stands on one of the most interesting sites in the country and which preceded Richard Arkwright's first cotton mill by over 50 years.

The **City Museum and Art Gallery** is also well worth visiting. Opened in 1879, it is the oldest of Derby's museums and the displays include natural history, archaeology and social history exhibits. One section of the museum is devoted to a Military Gallery and relates to Derby's local historical regiments. The walk-in First World War trench scene attempts to capture the experience of a night at the front. A ground floor gallery houses the city's superb collection of fine porcelain, manufactured in Derby from the mid-18th century. The **Derby Heritage Centre** has local history displays, tea room and

ROSLISTON FORESTRY CENTRE

Burton Road, Rosliston, Swadlincote,
Derbyshire DE12 8JX
Tel: Weekdays- 01283 515524 Weekends-01283 563483
Fax: 01283 500585
e-mail: rosliston@south-derbys.gov.uk
website: www.south-derbys.gov.uk

Part of the National Forest, **Rosliston Forestry Centre**
provides a very satisfying day out for the whole family.
Within its 154 acres some 120,000 trees were planted
between 1994 and 1996, creating a young woodland. Visitors

can follow one of the waymarked walks looking out for the varied
wildlife that includes kestrels, owls, kingfishers, skylarks, lapwings
and buntings. You can watch them feeding from the purpose-built
wildlife hide and, if you're lucky, spot a vole or rabbit. Children
will enjoy the well-equipped Adventure Play Area or the indoor
soft play area; adults will appreciate the peaceful Sensory Gardens.
There's a 9-hole Crazy Golf Course or you can bring your own
basketball and try out your skill on the pitch. Other activities
include fishing in the Rolls-Royce Greenheart Lake; cycle hire;
carriage rides (some weekends); archery lessons and guided walks.

Within the Visitor Centre are a number of craft shops. **Country
Cousins** offer a wide range of individual hand made bears, and
also is the midlands main retailer of quality collectors dolls, selling
top names such as Gotz, Himstedt, Sigikid and many more, along
with dolls beds, chairs and giftware. A beautiful selection of Bears
made by Midlands Artists are always available. Bear making classes
run throughout the year. We also stock bear making
supplies. For information telephone 01283 569886.

Acorn Impressions is a craft shop specialising in the
sale of rubber stamps and card accessories, stencils, beads
and jewellery findings. Demonstrations and Workshops
are always available. In the Workshops you can learn about
the craft of rubber stamping, this will be using embossing
inks, powders, background papers, card, special scissors
and punches, to make cards, pictures and other decorative
pieces. Workshops on other crafts are also available. Please
phone to enquire: 01283 511550.

A well established Dolls House Shop here also, is **ABC
Crafts**, a large selection of 1/12th houses, both built and in kit form, plus accessories galore. Have a
Break, Build a House, workshops and holidays can also be arranged. Here also the Sewing Box, offering
quilting materials, kits and sewing accessories, for both the miniaturist and full size. Our own designs
will be available later this year, for all details phone Beryl or
Chris at 01283 500585 or e-mail sales@abccrafts.co.uk.

Ready for some refreshment? The **Falcon Restaurant** is
open daily for breakfast, lunches and afternoon teas with
delicious home-made cakes and scones. The regular menu
offers a good choice or light meals, sandwiches, house baps
and loaded jackets, supplemented by daily specials listed
on the blackboard. The restaurant also has a Sunday Carvery
and will cater for children's parties, buffets, barbecues and
business lunches. Resuarant fully licensed.

souvenir shop housed in one of the city's oldest buildings. Another of the city's treats is the **Derbyshire Constabulary Memorabilia Museum** (free), which has a display of uniforms and weapons dating from the mid-1600s to the present day.

AROUND DERBY

KEDLESTON
4 miles NW of Derby off the A52

Kedleston Hall has been the family seat of the Curzon family since the 12th century and, until it was taken over the by National Trust, it had the longest continuous male line in Derbyshire and one of the longest in the country. The present elegant mansion was built between 1759 and 1765 by Robert Adam and it remains one of the finest examples of his work. Since taking over the property, the National Trust have embarked on a major restoration programme. The three-mile Long Walk was created in 1776. Along with the house itself, there is the park with its lakes, boat house and fishing pavilion to explore.

SUDBURY
12 miles W of Derby off the A50

Sudbury is the estate village to **Sudbury Hall**, the late-17th century mansion and home of a branch of the Vernon family who lived at Haddon Hall. The house is intriguing, the garden restful. Gifted to the National Trust in 1967, the Hall is an unexpected mixture of architectural styles. A splendid example of a house of Charles II's time, the interior of Sudbury Hall contains elaborate plasterwork and murals throughout, wood carvings by Grinling Gibbons, and some fine examples of mythological paintings by Laguerre. Of particular interest is the **Museum of Childhood**, which is situated in the servants' wing and provides a fascinating insight into the lives of children down the ages. Fascinating displays range from a wealthy family's nursery and an Edwardian schoolroom to a 'chimney climb' and coal tunnel for the adventurous. The formal gardens and meadows lead to the tree-fringed lake. Wildlife abounds, including kestrels, grey herons, grass snakes, dragonflies, newts, frogs, toads, Little and Tawny Owls and woodpeckers. Special events are held throughout the year.

SWADLINCOTE

Here at the extreme edge of Derbyshire, well south of the River Trent, Swadlincote shares many characteristics with Staffordshire. Among the town's thriving industries, based on the clay and coal on which it stands, are large

ELMS FARM B&B

Appleby Magna, Swadlincote, Derbyshire DE12 7AP
Tel: 01530 270450 Fax: 01530 272718
e-mail: geofffrisby@hotmail.com

Although only 5 minutes from Junction 11 of the M42, **Elms Farm B&B** occupies a delightful rural situation bordering Leicestershire and Warwickshire and with many pleasant walks within easy reach. Guests receive a warm welcome from Liz and Geoff Frisby at this attractive farmhouse on a working farm. The atmosphere here is very much "home from home" and the spacious, tastefully furnished guest bedrooms (1 double; 1 twin; 1 single) are either en suite or with private facilities. The non-smoking house is open throughout the year, apart from Christmas, and is conveniently placed for local attractions.

potteries founded in 1795 as well as brickworks.

AROUND SWADLINCOTE

NETHERSEAL
6 miles S of Swadlincote off the A444

Netherseal is a picturesque village on the banks of the River Mease. 'Seal' means forested and Netherseal was recorded in the Domesday Book as a wooded area on the edge of Ashby Woulds. It was once a mining community with a two-shaft colliery and several related industries. The mining activity has long ceased and the centre of the village is now a conservation area with many listed buildings including some charming 17th century almshouses.

CALKE
5 miles NE of Swadlincote off the B587

In 1985 the National Trust bought **Calke Abbey**, a large Baroque-style mansion built in 1701 on the site of an Augustinian priory founded in 1133. However, it was not until 1989 that the Trust were able to open the house to the public, for this was no ordinary house at all. Dubbed "the house that time forgot" since the death of the owner, Sir Vauncy Harpur-Crewe in 1924 nothing had been altered in the mansion! In fact, the seclusion of the house and also the rather bizarre lifestyle of its inhabitants had left many rooms and objects untouched for over 100 years. There was even a spectacular 18th century Chinese silk state bed that had never been unpacked.

GRANGEFIELDS PINE LODGE

Clifton Road, Netherseal, Swadlincote,
Derbyshire DE12 8BT
Tel: 01827 373253 or 01283 761445

Enjoying a lovely rural situation with panoramic views across the Mease Valley, **Grangefields Pine Lodge** offers superb self-catering accommodation in an elegant Scandinavian-style pine lodge. There are polished floors and well-chosen furnishings in all rooms. The spacious living area has a comfortable sofa bed, armchairs, television and video.

The oak-fitted kitchen is comprehensively equipped, including locally made Wedgwood china. There are 2 bedrooms (1 double; 1 twin), with hypo-allergenic bed linen, duvets and pillows, while the bathroom has a large bath and separate shower. Outside, there's a spacious, safe garden and a well-stocked shop is just a mile away by car, at Netherseal.

Calke Abbey

Today, the Trust has repaired the house and returned all 13,000 items to their original positions so that the Abbey now looks just as it did when it was bought in 1981. The attention to detail has been so great that none of the rooms has been redecorated. Visitors can enjoy the silver display and trace the route of 18th century servants along the brewhouse tunnel to the house cellars. Calke Abbey stands in its own large park with gardens, a chapel and stables that are also open to the public. There are three walled gardens with their glasshouses, a restored orangery, vegetable garden, pheasant aviaries and the summer flower display within the unusual "auricular" theatre.

MELBOURNE

6 miles NE of Swadlincote off the B587

This small town, which lent its name to the rather better-known city in Australia, is a successful market garden centre. A famous son of Melbourne, who started his working life in one of the market gardens, was Thomas Cook, who was born here in 1808. He went on to pioneer personally conducted tours and established the famous worldwide travel company.

Full of Georgian charm, Melbourne has many fine buildings which include one of the noblest Norman churches in the country, the **Church of St Michael and St Mary**. This seems rather a grand church for this modest place and indeed, it is no ordinary parish church. In the 12th century, when the Bishopric of Carlisle was formed, there needed to be a place of safety for the clergy when Carlisle was being raided by the Scots. So this church was built at Melbourne and, while Carlisle was subjected to raids and violence, the Bishop retired to Melbourne and continued to carry out his duties. The church was built between 1133 and 1229 and, in 1299, the then Bishop built a palace on land that is now home to Melbourne Hall.

The birthplace of the 19th century statesman Lord Melbourne, and also the home of Lady Caroline Lamb, **Melbourne Hall** is another fine building in this area of Derbyshire. A modest building, the Hall is surrounded by beautiful gardens, the most notable feature of which is a beautiful wrought-iron birdcage pergola built in the early 1700s by Robert Bakewell, a local blacksmith from Derby. The house is only open to the public in August, but the formal gardens are open throughout the summer season.

SWARKESTONE

9 miles NE of Swadlincote off the A5132

It was at **Swarkestone Bridge** in 1745 that Bonnie Prince Charlie's hopes of seizing the English crown were finally dashed. To everyone's surprise, his advance guard had successfully penetrated so far south and victory seemed within his grasp. But when the Jacobite soldiers reached the bridge with its seven arches and three-quarter-mile long causeway crossing the River Trent they were confronted by a strong force of King George's troops. If Prince Charles's soldiers had managed to force their way across the river at this point, they would have faced no other natural barriers along the 120-mile march to London. As it transpired, the Scottish army retreated and fled north. Bonnie Prince Charlie himself managed to escape but the Jacobite Rebellion was all over bar the shouting.

Legend has it that the original bridge at Swarkestone was built by two daughters of the Harpur family in the early 13th century. The girls were celebrating their joint betrothals when their fiancés were summoned to a barons' meeting across the river. While they were away torrential rain fell, flooding the river, and the two young men drowned as they attempted to ford the raging torrent on their return. The girls built the bridge as a memorial to their lovers. Both girls later died impoverished and unmarried.

REPTON

5 miles N of Swadlincote off the B5008

This village, by the tranquil waters of the River Trent, is steeped in history. The first recorded mention of Repton was in the 7th century when it was established as the capital of the Saxon kingdom of Mercia. A monastery, housing both monks and nuns, was founded here sometime after 653 but the building was sacked by the Danes in 874. A battleaxe, now on display in the school museum, was excavated a little distance from the church. It had apparently lain undisturbed for well over 1,000 years.

The parish **Church of St Wystan** is famous for its Anglo-Saxon chancel and crypt, but it also contains many of the major styles of medieval architecture. When the chancel and part of the nave were enlarged in 1854, the original Anglo-Saxon columns were moved to the 14th century porch. The crypt is believed to be one of the oldest intact Anglo-Saxon buildings in England. The burial place of the Kings of Mercia, including St Wystan in 850, the crypt was rediscovered by chance in 1779 by a workman who was digging a hole for a grave in the chancel floor.

The ancient **Cross**, still at the central crossroads in the village, has been the focal point of life here for centuries and it has also stood at the heart of the Wednesday market. Right up until the late 1800s a Statutes Fair, for the hiring of farm labourers and domestics, was held here at Michaelmas.

Parts of an Augustinian priory, founded in 1170, are incorporated in the buildings of **Repton College**, itself founded in 1557. Sir John Port had specifically intended the college to be a grammar school for the local poor children of Etwall, Repton and Burnaston. These intentions have somewhat deviated over the passing years and now Repton stands as one of the foremost public schools in the country. Interestingly, two of its headmasters, Dr Temple and Dr Fisher, went on to become Archbishops of Canterbury. A third archbishop, Dr Ramsey, was a pupil at the school under Dr Fisher's guiding light. Film buffs will recognise the 14th century gatehouse and causeway, as they featured in both film versions of the popular story *Goodbye, Mr Chips*.

6 NOTTINGHAMSHIRE

The county of Nottinghamshire, in the north Midlands, lies mainly on the low ground basin of the River Trent between the peaks of Derbyshire and South Yorkshire and the lowlands of Lincolnshire. It is a county of contrasts: Nottinghamshire has plenty of industry but it has also retained much of its rural heritage as well as the remains of the famous Forest of Sherwood.

As any local lad will be happy to tell you, Nottingham used to be called 'Snotingham' after the unfortunately named Snot, chief of a 6th century Anglo-Saxon tribe. But there was a settlement here long before then. In Celtic times it was known as Tigguocobauc, 'the house of caves', an appropriate name since this ancient people lived in the caves that occur naturally in the

soft local sandstone. When the Vikings arrived in England in 878, they recognised Nottingham's importance by making it one of the five boroughs of the 'Danelaw' - the area of Middle England they controlled. There was more significant development in Norman times when the famous Castle that features so prominently in the Robin Hood legends was built.

Trent Bridge, Nottingham

The glory of the central part of the county is Southwell Minster, a uniquely graceful building which is perhaps the least well-known cathedral in the country. Southwell itself is small, with a population of less than 7,000, but is a delightful town with many fine buildings and a picturesque old coaching inn where Charles I spent his last night of freedom. Surrounding this appealing little town is a maze of country lanes and ancient villages.

With an historic castle, magnificent parish church and a host of fine buildings, Newark is an immensely likeable place. In medieval times, the town thrived as a centre for the wool trade, benefiting from its position on the Great North Road and beside the River Trent. The Civil War brought great suffering but, apart from the Castle, surprisingly little damage to the town's buildings. South of Newark lies the Vale of Belvoir, an unspoilt pastoral landscape dotted with the spires of village churches and overlooked by the mighty towers and turrets of Belvoir Castle, just across the border in Lincolnshire.

Sherwood Forest is known to old and young alike, all over the world, thanks to the tales of Robin Hood and the various stories, films, and television series made about this legendary hero of the people. Sherwood, the shire wood of Nottinghamshire, was once part of a great mass of forest land which covered much of central England. Now officially designated as "Robin Hood Country", the tract of land running north from Nottingham is an attractive mix of woodland and rolling hills.

Sherwood Forest, Birklands

To the north of the forest is the area known as The Dukeries, which is scenically one of the most attractive parts of the county. Here in the 18th century, no fewer than four different Dukes acquired huge estates: Rufford, Welbeck, Clumber, and Thoresby. All their great houses are now put to different uses but the glorious parks they created, especially at Clumber, make this a delightful area to visit.

The area around Mansfield was once the industrial heart of Nottinghamshire, its landscape dominated by pit-head wheels and chimneys, and the serried ranks of miners' terraced houses. This is "Pilgrim Fathers' Country"since it was here that the unorthodox worship of Richard Clyfton inspired such men as William Brewster of Scrooby, and William Bradford of Austerfield, later Governor of New England. The best introduction to their story is to follow the "Mayflower Trail", devised by Bassetlaw District Council, which follows a circular route starting from Worksop. Also in Worksop is the unusual National Trust property, Mr Straw's House, a time-capsule from the 1920s where nothing has altered in the subsequent 80 years. Retford and Blyth are both attractive old market towns: the former with some fine Georgian building; the latter boasting one of the most monumental Norman churches in the country.

ADVERTISERS AND PLACES OF INTEREST

LOCATOR MAP

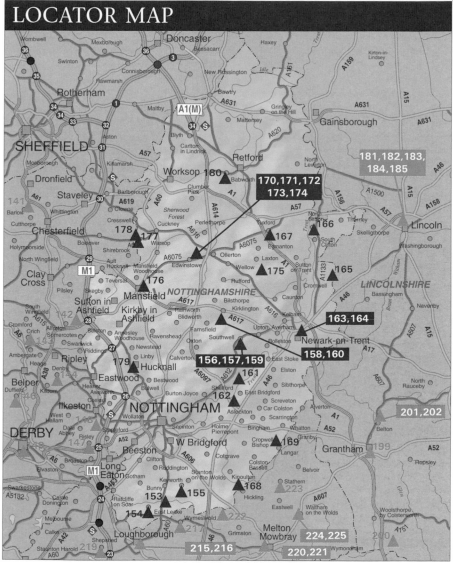

NOTTINGHAM

A lively city of some 300,000 inhabitants, Nottingham offers a vast choice of shops, restaurants (more than 200 of them), cinemas, art galleries, two theatres, a world-class concert hall, and a host of other visitor attractions. The city also boasts a leading University, a major medical centre and a legendary football team, Nottingham Forest. The self-proclaimed "Queen of the Midlands", Nottingham is known worldwide because of the legendary Robin Hood and his persecutor, the villainous Sheriff of Nottingham. Others associate the city with Boots the Chemist, Players cigarettes (whose packets carry a picture of Nottingham Castle), Raleigh cycles and motor-cycles, and with the ice skaters Torvill and Dean - their world-beating performances led directly to the siting in Nottingham the National Ice Centre.

A good place to begin exploring the city is in the Old Market Square, known to locals as "Slab Square" and believed to be largest market square in the country. Although no market has been held here since the 1920s, the vast expanse of the square still lies at the centre of Nottingham life. At its eastern end stands the dignified **Council House** with its porticoed frontage and a dome that is a replica of St Paul's in London. Part of the stately ground floor with its lofty ceilings and neo-classical architecture now houses some prestigious shops.

Until the Council House was built, the Market Square was the setting for the famous Nottingham **Goose Fair** which began in medieval times and gained its name from the large flocks of geese that were sold here around Michaelmas. Mentioned in a charter dated 1284, the Goose Fair still takes place in early October but has grown so much it is now held at Forest Fields on the edge of the city.

A short walk from the Market Square, in the appropriately named Maid Marian Way, **The Tales of Robin Hood** tells the story of the celebrated outlaw through a series of historically accurate displays depicting scenes such as Robin's imprisonment by the Sheriff of Nottingham to feasting in Sherwood Forest. After a tour by chair, ride visitors can then explore the history of the legend and also learn about the detective work undertaken in the 1930s in an attempt to authenticate the legend.

A further couple of minutes walk brings you to the entrance to **Nottingham Castle**, which commands an imposing position on a rocky outcrop high above the city centre. However, those looking for the famous castle which features so frequently in the tales of Robin Hood will be sorely disappointed as the present buildings

Tales of Robin Hood

Robin Hood Statue, Nottingham Castle

the castle which gradually fell into disrepair until Charles I came to Nottingham in 1642 and raised his standard, marking the beginning of the Civil War. Unfortunately, the king found little support for his cause in the city (only 30 citizens joined his troops) so he moved on to Shrewsbury, leaving Nottingham and its castle in the hands of the Parliamentarians. During the course of the war, the Royalists made several attempts to recapture the castle but Cromwell's supporters held out. After the fighting was over the castle building was rendered uninhabitable and was finally demolished in 1674 by the Duke of Newcastle who then built his own palace on the site.

date from after the English Civil War and precious little remains of the original medieval fortification.

The original castle was built soon after the Battle of Hastings by William Peveril as part of William I's general fortification of many strategically important sites. Its elevated position, overlooking the city and the River Trent, made Nottingham Castle one of the foremost castles in Norman England and it played host to many important visitors. Of a typical Norman motte and bailey design, the stone walls are thought to have been added in the early 12th century and it was further fortified by Henry II. Nottingham Castle's heyday came in the 14th and 15th centuries however, when not only was King David II of Scotland held prisoner here for a while around 1346 but, in the mid-1400s, Edward IV proclaimed himself king from Nottingham Castle. Later his brother, Richard III, rode out from here to the Battle of Bosworth field and his death.

For some reason, the Tudors shunned

Today, that palace is home to the **Castle Museum and Art Gallery** (free on weekdays). Some remains of the original castle still stand, most notably the 13th century gatehouse, though much restored, and parts of the moat and outer bailey are visible. The museum, when it was opened by the Prince of Wales in 1878, was the first municipal art gallery in the country outside London. Today, the collection is particularly noted for its fine selection of Victorian paintings. The museum also has an outstanding collection of silverware and ceramics.

Alongside the Castle Museum is the **Sherwood Foresters Regimental Museum**, which continues the castle's connections with the military. The regiment was first raised in 1741 and among the many displays there is an area dedicated to the Nottingham flying ace of World War I, Captain Albert Ball, VC. He died in 1917, at the age of 20, having shot down 43 enemy aircraft. A statue erected to his memory stands in the castle grounds.

At the base of Castle Rock lies the famous **Trip to Jerusalem Inn** where crusaders are said to have stopped for a pint before setting off on their long journey to the Holy Land. Dating back to around 1189, it claims to be the oldest pub in England, a claim hotly contested by other hostelries it must

Trip to Jerusalem Inn

be said. Set back into the sandstone rock, the building was once the brewhouse for the castle and from here travellers to the Holy Land bought their ale. In the pub's cellars is **Mortimer's Hole**, a cave hewn out of the sandstone rock which leads to the castle. It is through this passageway that some two dozen conspirators crept to capture Roger de Mortimer, the lover of Queen Isabella. When her husband, Edward II was murdered, Isabella had allowed Mortimer to effectively rule in place of her 18-year-old son, Edward III. De Mortimer's presumption was later punished by death. Edward III was in the castle at the time of Mortimer's capture and is believed to have known about, and encouraged, the plot.

Also at the base of Castle Rock and housed in a terrace of four 17th century cottages is the **Brewhouse Yard Museum**. Depicting the life of the people of the city up to the 1990s, the museum has accurately furnished rooms as well as a series of reconstructions that includes a Victorian kitchen and shop window displays of the 1920s.

Just around the corner, the **Museum of Costume and Textiles** (free) in Castle Gate contains a fine collection of costumes from 1790 to the mid-20th century, all displayed in period rooms. There are also many other exhibits on show including tapestries; knitted, woven, and printed textiles; and fashion accessories through the ages. The museum is housed in a terrace of brick houses that was constructed in 1788 by Cornelius Launder, a former High Sheriff. Castle Gate is an interesting street in itself and well worth a second look. The entrance to the museum has one of the finest examples of an 18th century doorcase and fanlight to be seen in the area.

Further down Castle Gate is **Newdigate House**, built in a refined fashion in 1680 and distinguished by a wrought iron screen and gates dating from the early 1700s. The house now forms part of the United Services Club but between 1705 and 1711 it was the home of Marshal Tallard, commander of the defeated French army at the Battle of Blenheim in 1704.

Nearby, in Castle Road, is a charming medieval building that is home to the

Lace Centre (free). As well as holding lace-making demonstrations, the Centre stocks a vast selection of high quality lace available for purchase. A remarkably well-preserved example of a timber framed house of around 1450, the building was moved from its original site on Middle Pavement in 1968. Continuing the textiles theme, not far away and set in the heart of Nottingham's historic and recently revitalized Lace Market, is the Lace Market Centre, occupying a restored chapel in High Pavement. Here the story of Nottingham's famous industry is told, from the days when it was a cottage craft through to

Council House, Old Market

mechanisation and the days of the great textile factories. Visitors can see some of the giant machines that produced the delicate material and also various types of lace being made.

Across the road from the Museum, in the impressive Shire Hall, the **Galleries of Justice** provides an unusual and interesting insight into justice 19th century style. "Condemned", a major crime and punishment experience, allows visitors to put themselves in the place of an accused in the harsh days around 1833. Real trials are re-enacted in the imposing Courtroom where the hapless criminal faced the possibility of capital punishment or transportation to the New World. Their discomfort is made very real by the restored period settings.

Also in High Pavement is Nottingham's largest parish church, St Mary's, which is also probably the city's oldest as it appears to have been founded in Saxon times. However, today's church dates from the 15th century though there are some 19th and early 20th century additions which include windows by a series of renowned stained glass makers. Also inside is a Bishop's Throne carved in 1890 when it was thought that the church would become the cathedral for the diocese of Southwell.

Another short walk brings you to the **Caves of Nottingham**, a popular attraction which lies beneath the Broadmarsh Centre, one of the city's major shopping precincts. The city is built on sandstone and throughout Nottingham's history the rock has been tunnelled to provide first shelter and then hiding places. More than 400 man-made caves run beneath the city streets. Now, thanks to local voluntary groups, these caves have been saved for future generations. The most spectacular cave in the system, the Pillar Cave, was carved out back in 1250 and contains remnants of the country's only underground tannery. The caves were commonly used as pub cellars: the constant temperature being ideal for the storage of beer and wine. More recently, they served as air raid shelters during the blitz of World War II and one of the caves has been left as a memorial to those desperate times.

AROUND NOTTINGHAM

WOLLATON

2 miles W of Nottingham on the A609

Built in creamy white Ancaster stone, **Wollaton Hall** (free on weekdays) is one of the most attractive and elaborate Elizabethan mansions in the Midlands. Set in a spacious park, the house was built in the 1580s to the designs of Robert Smythson, who also designed Hardwick Hall in Derbyshire. His client was Francis Willoughby whose family had made a fortune from the local coal mines. The Elizabethan passion for symmetry is extravagantly displayed on the magnificent front façade with its matching classical columns, busts of philosophers and mythological characters, and flamboyant gables.

The building is also home to the **Natural History Museum** which is based on the collection of Francis Willoughby, a noted naturalist of the mid-1600s, while some of the Hall's outbuildings have been transformed into the Nottingham Industrial Museum where the city's major industries are all represented. The park surrounding the Hall is one of the city's great amenities. The 525 acres are contained within a 7-mile long wall, providing security for the herds of deer that roam here as they have for more than 400 years.

BULWELL

3 miles N of Nottingham on the B682

Originally the whole area surrounding

the village was covered by forest and it is probable that the settlement took its name from a spring in the old woodland. However, a local legend tells the story of the naming of the village rather differently. Apparently, an enraged bull gored a rock here and released a stream of sparkling spring water.

BESTWOOD

6 miles N of Nottingham off the A60

Bestwood was a favourite hunting ground of Charles II who often stayed here with Nell Gwynne. One local story tells of a wager the king struck with Nell, saying she could have all the land she could ride around before breakfast. Nell, not known for being an early riser, made an exception on this occasion. The next morning, she rose at dawn and rode around the countryside dropping handkerchiefs along the way. Arriving back before breakfast, Nell claimed her winnings and Charles kept his side of the bargain. Whether or not the story is true, the king certainly gave Nell substantial landholdings in the area.

Part of the old royal hunting park is now **Bestwood Country Park** whose 450 acres offer many differing landscapes. Here you'll also find the Bestwood Pumping Station, erected in the early 1870s. The Duke only gave his permission for it to be built after the architect solemnly promised that it would look nothing like a pumping station. With its 150ft tower, cooling pond disguised as an ornamental lake, and surrounded by beautifully maintained gardens, the station certainly lives up to the architect's promise.

SNEINTON

1 mile E of Nottingham on the A612

Sneinton's main claim to fame is as the birthplace, in 1829, of William Booth, the founder of the Salvation Army. The small terraced house where he and his family lived until 1831 is still standing in Notintone Place, fronted now by a statue of the great man. The family home has become the **William Booth Birthplace Museum**: entry to the house is free but by appointment only.

After his father's early death, Booth's mother was forced to move to Goosegate, Nottingham where she ran a shop selling toys and sewing materials and it was whilst living in this deprived area that Booth first became aware of the appalling conditions in which the urban working classes lived. He was only 16 when he gave his first sermon in a house in Kid.

In 1849, Booth left Nottingham for London where he became a Methodist minister. But, finding the church structures too constraining, he established in 1865 the Christian Missions which, in 1878, was renamed the Salvation Army. During the next 10 years, the movement spread to all corners of the world, including America, Australia, and South Africa. The Army is still mobilised, with more than 1,000 local corps in the UK involved in both social and evangelistic work. Its missing persons bureau traces anything up to 5,000 people each year.

Holme Pierrepont
3 miles E of Nottingham off the A52

Although Holme has been in the hands of the Pierrepont family since 1284, the present **Holme Pierrepont Hall** dates from the early 1500s and is regarded as one of the best examples of a brick built house in the county. Opening times are restricted but the hall is well worth a visit. Some of the ground floor rooms been restored to their original state and furnished in the style of the early 17th century, and the Upper Lodging still has superb ceiling timbers dating from the 1400s. There are two Victorian bedrooms

with 4-poster beds, one with its original William Morris fabrics. Refreshments are available in the Long Gallery with its walnut furniture and family portraits gazing down from the walls. Outside, the Charles II Grand Staircase leads down to a formal Courtyard Garden with an elaborate parterre, created around 1875, and in the park Jacob sheep graze peacefully.

These days, Holme Pierrepont is more widely known as the home of the **National Water Sports Centre** (free, except during special events). Built to Olympic standards, the Centre boasts a full size rowing course and a wild water slalom course, all man-made from the pasture and quarries which once dominated the area.

Beeston
3 miles SW of Nottingham off the A52

Lying on the southwest outskirts of Nottingham, Beeston is famous as the home of **Boots the Chemist**. Jesse Boot was born in 1850 and left school at the age of 13 to work in his mother's herbalist shop in the centre of Nottingham. She had started the business to supplement her husband's meagre income as a farm labourer. Following his death, when Jesse was only 10 years old, the shop became the mainstay of the family. Jesse quickly learnt the trade and in 1888 he set up the Boots Pure Drug Company.

In a business where quacks and charlatans abounded, Boot's emphasis on the purity of his drugs and medicines (and his competitive prices), attracted customers everywhere and by 1896 the company had a chain of over 60 shops. It was at his wife's suggestion that Jesse expanded the lines in the shops to include jewellery, stationery, books and art. In 1920 the business was sold to an American company only to be bought back by Jesse's son during the depression in 1933. A great benefactor to the city and surrounding area, Jesse was knighted in 1903, created a baronet in 1917, and finally raised to the peerage as Lord Trent in 1929, two years before his death.

CLIFTON

2 miles SE of Beeston on the A453

At first sight this village near the River Trent seems swamped by modern development but the character of the old village can be found in and around the green. The manor of Clifton was held by the family of that name from the 13th century up until 1953 when they gave up the hall to what is now Nottingham Trent University.

Along the banks of the River Trent is **Clifton Grove**, a wooded cliff above the riverbank, where visitors can stroll in the footsteps of Paul Morel and Clare Dawes, characters in D.H. Lawrence's *Sons and Lovers*. This stretch of the River Trent was also the setting for a tragic love story. In 1471, a young squire called Henry Bateman went to the Crusades with his master. When he returned, he discovered that his sweetheart Margaret had fallen for another man and married him. The heartbroken lover threw himself into the Trent from Clifton Grove. Some time later, Margaret herself took the same way out, presumably in remorse for her

STAPLEFORD

2 miles W of Beeston off the A52

In Stapleford churchyard can be found the best preserved Saxon carving in the county in the form of a 10ft high cross shaft. Dating from the late 11th century, the intricate carving depicts an eagle standing on a serpent - said to be the symbol of St Luke, the physician. The church, which dates mainly from the 13th and 14th centuries, has many war memorials to lost heroes. The village was

once a thriving centre for framework knitting and terraced cottages built specifically for the workers can still be seen in Nottingham Road.

One other feature of Stapleford worthy of a look is the **Hemlockstone**, a massive redstone boulder standing 30 feet high and weighing around 200 tons situated opposite Bramcote Park. Geologists believe the rock was probably deposited here by glacial action, whilst wind erosion has contributed to its brooding appearance. Its geological make up consists of sandstone, cemented by the mineral barite which is found in large quantities throughout the Stapleford and Bramcote Hills.

The village school was renamed the Arthur Mee Centre in memory of the writer who grew up in the town and was educated at the school. Born in 1875, Mee left school at 14 to work for the Nottingham Evening Post before moving to London and finding his niche writing for children. His works include the Children's Bible, the Children's Encyclopaedia, and the Children's Shakespeare but it is probably for The King's England, a series of guide books that ran to some 80 volumes, that Mee is best remembered.

RUDDINGTON

4 miles S of Nottingham off the A60

This historic village, whose name is derived from the Saxon word Rudda - meaning headman - was once the home of many hosiery workers and several of their cottages still remain. In 1829, a factory and frameworkers cottages were built around a courtyard in Chapel Street. Later, a school was built and this is now occupied by the **Ruddington Framework Knitters' Museum** which depicts community life through several reconstructed shops and an Edwardian schoolroom. Of the 25 hand frames seen here today, most are fully operational and there is an opportunity to buy samples made at the museum.

The industry reached its height in 1880, with the staggering number of 20,000 frames operating in Nottingham, Derbyshire, and Lincolnshire. As well as the knitting frames on show, the museum also has other machinery of specific importance to the village and to the hosiery industry. Regular demonstrations are given using the working exhibits. Visitors can try out their own weaving skills on one of the collection of circular sock machines.

Not far away is the **Ruddington Village Museum**, housed in the old village school building of 1852. Concentrating on the everyday life of the villagers, the museum has reconstructions of several shops and craftsmen's workshops including an Edwardian fish and chip shop. As well as having one of the school rooms restored to look as it once did, there is also a room devoted to a collection of farming implements.

GOTHAM
3 miles SW of Ruddington off the A453

The name is actually pronounced 'Goat'm' and the village should not be confused with the home of the caped crusader, Batman. However, the village is remembered as the home of the Wise Men. King John had decreed that he wished to build a hunting lodge here in the village. Naturally displeased at having to give up their land to the king's whims, the villagers devised a plan. They decided that the best way to dissuade the royal presence was to feign madness. When the king's messengers entered the village, the inhabitants reacted in such a peculiar way that the men returned to His Majesty with the suggestion that the

SIX ACRE NURSERIES

Loughborough Road, Costock, Loughborough,
Leicestershire LE12 6XB
Tel: 01509 856079 Fax: 01509 856845

When John and Jo Morris opened **Six Acre Nurseries** in 1985 they named it because it did indeed extend over 6 acres. Today it stands at 13 acres, although alot of this is for the growing and wholesale side of the buisness. The retail site offers a wide range of plants, shrubs and trees which provide gardeners with an excellent choice of robust, healthy specimens. John's father was a highly respected horticulturalist and John himself studied horticulture. He is happy to provide expert advice on choosing plants and guidance on all aspects of gardening both wholesale and retail.

The nursery specialises in trees, offering a wide range of deciduous, ornamental and fruit trees eg- acer, betula, malus, prunus, sorbus, apple, cherry, and pears; many of them sourced from around the country. You'll also find an extensive range of shrubs, herbaceous, alpines and climbers. Six Acre Nurseries also stocks house plants and a good selection of garden sundries including pots in all shapes and sizes. Conveniently located on the A60 between Loughborough and Nottingham, the nursery is open 7 days a week, 52 weeks a year, with the exception of Christmas Day, Boxing Day and New Years Day.

mad men of Gotham should be left well alone. Such were the odd tales of their bizarre acts that Dr Andrew Borde published the *Merrie Tales of the Mad Men of Gotham* in the 16th century. There are many bizarre stories but one of the finest is kept alive in the name of the village pub - The Cuckoo Bush. A group of villagers, captivated by the song of a cuckoo, decided to capture the bird by encircling the bush in which it was sitting by a fence. Unfortunately, the men did not think to build a roof so the cuckoo simply flew away.

RATCLIFFE ON SOAR
6 miles SW of Ruddington off the A453

The tiny village of Ratcliffe on Soar has a pretty little church, with an eye-catching blackened spire, and a handsome manor farmhouse set picturesquely on the meadow banks of the River Soar. Although a massive power station looms over everything and the railway clatters by, this charming village is still definitely worth a visit.

MANOR FARM ANIMAL CENTRE & DONKEY SANCTUARY

Castle Hill, East Leake, nr Loughborough, Nottinghamshire LE12 6LU
Tel: 01509 852525

Manor Farm Animal Centre & Donkey Sanctuary is a fun day out for all the family, with an amazing variety of activities on offer. As well as the assortment of animals to see, there is a nature trail, pond dipping, a wild flower meadow and a living willow village to stroll around. Young children are very well catered for with an adventure playground, straw maze and an art & craft activity centre

and for those a little older, donkey and pony rides as well as quad bikes, are available. The facilities here make it easy to stay all day with a cafe, gift shop, picnic area, toilets, free parking and disabled facilities.

EAST LEAKE
4 miles S of Ruddington off the A60

Like its neighbour, West Leake, the village name is derived from the Anglo-Saxon word Leche, meaning water meadow, and both villages lie on the banks of a tributary of the River Soar. The village church, which was mentioned in the Domesday Survey of 1086, was extensively restored in the 19th century but has retained its prize possession, a Vamp Horn or shawm. This extraordinary instrument is some 8 feet long and only five others are known to exist. Invented in 1670 by Samuel Morland, the horn was used by the bass singer to lead the choir from the gallery.

STANTON ON THE WOLDS
4 miles SE of Ruddington off the A606

This rural village, which was until the 1960s home to seven dairy farms, has few really old buildings though the village dates back to Norman times. In the late 18th century, Stanton was hit by a freak storm in which giant hailstones rained down on the cottages and smashed their roofs. The ancient village Church of All Saints did, however, survive and it can be found standing alone in a field and reached by a footpath. Dating from the 11th century, the church, one of the smallest in south Nottinghamshire, is built mostly of boulders some of which, undoubtedly, were purloined from the nearby Fosse Way.

BUNNY
2 miles S of Ruddington on the A60

This pretty village has a wealth of lovely architecture and owes much of its charm to the eccentricities of its one-time squire, Sir Thomas Parkyns (1663-1741). A man obsessed with the sport of wrestling, Sir Thomas employed two full time professionals to spar with him at Bunny Hall. He also organised an annual tournament in the village to promote local wrestling talent and this event continued for nearly 70 years after his death. In St Mary's Church, which was designed by Sir Thomas, his memorial graphically illustrates his commitment to the sport. It depicts the squire standing victorious over his defeated opponent on a wrestling mat, while Old Father Time stands by, perhaps as referee.

Another of Sir Thomas' hobbies was collecting stone coffins which he provided free to those of his tenants in need of one. During his long lifetime he rebuilt much of the village to his own designs, provided a school, gave his tenants free medical and legal advice,

and also found time to write a Latin Grammar and a book on wrestling, *Cornish Hugg Wrestling*.

KEYWORTH
3 miles E of Ruddington off the A606

In the heart of south Nottinghamshire's farming country this, until very recently, small village prides itself on having produced no fewer than 30 professional cricketers, one of whom went on to be capped for England. The village too has had its share of scandals and one local legend tells of a tenant farmer who was visited by the rector who had a complaint to discuss. The farmer was not very agreeable to the criticism and soundly horse-whipped the clergyman before sending him on his way. This whip is still in existence though the nature of the complaint the rector was making is unknown.

THE GEOLOGY SHOP

The British Geological Survey, Keyworth, Notts. NG12 5GG
Main tel: 0115 936 3100 Shop tel: 0115 936 3581
website: www.bgs.ac.uk
Online Shop: www.geologyshop.com

The Geology Shop is part of the British Geological Survey, which was founded in 1835 and is presently located in the village of Keyworth. The Geology Shop deals with the oldest materials in Britain-the rocks that shape and give character to the country's varied landscapes. An incredibly wide range of objects can be crafted from rocks and minerals, and in the Geology Shop you'll find some stunning gift ideas-onyx, agate and soapstone ornaments, bookends, candle-holders, paperweights, bowls and vases.Jewellery of course makes brilliant use of precious stones, so the display includes classic jewellery featuring amethyst, topaz, opal, amber and jade, and there is designer jewellery from Hot Diamonds, Silver Willow, Java and Goldmajor.

The shop also features fascinating fossils such as ammonites, trilobites and prehistoric fish along with fabulous natural minerals and crystals – amazing amethyst and citrine cathedrals and exotic natural minerals for collectors as well as fun packs for kids. Geologists and students will find a wide range of specialist geological maps, books and reports and the shop also stocks a comprehensive range of Ordnance Survey maps, guides, compasses, pedometers, map measurers, map cases and much more. The Geology Shop is open Monday to Friday (excluding national holidays) from 8.30am to 5pm.

SOUTHWELL

Southwell is undoubtedly one of England's most beguiling towns, miraculously preserved from developers and with scarcely an ugly building to be seen. From whichever direction you approach, it is the twin towers of **Southwell Minster** that first catch the eye. With their pyramidal "Rhenish Caps", these towers are unique in this country although they would look perfectly in place anywhere in the Rhineland.

James VI of Scotland was mightily impressed by Southwell when he passed through the town in 1603 en route to his coronation as James I: "By my blude" he is said to have exclaimed, "this kirk shall justle with York or Durham or any other kirk in Chistendom".

Perhaps the least well-known of English cathedrals, Southwell's history goes back to 956 when Oskytel, Archbishop of York, established a church here. The present building was erected in three phases. The nave, transept and western towers are the oldest part, completed around 1150; the east end was built around 1240, and the superb Chapter House around 1290.

Octagonal in design, the Chapter House has been hailed as the pinnacle of the Decorated period of architecture - "among chapter houses as the rose amongst flowers". The architectural historian, Nikolaus Pevsner devoted a whole book, The Leaves of Southwell, to the incredible wealth of stone carvings of foliage decorating the arcades above the Canons' seats.

The word most often applied to the cathedral is *"serene"* and, as one visitor put it, *"Other churches may be older, a few may be larger, but none are more beautiful"*.

There is no space here to detail all the cathedral's other treasures but the striking eagle lectern in the choir has an interesting story attached to it. The lectern was originally installed at Newstead Abbey. However, during the widespread looting at the time of the Dissolution of the Monasteries, the monks threw the lectern into the lake, intending to retrieve it later. "Later" turned out to be 200 years later, in 1750 in fact. Half a century after that the 5th Lord Byron presented the lectern to the Minster.

The Minster stands in a delightful precinct, surrounded by attractive buildings. To the south stand the ruins of the palace of the archbishops of York built in the 14th and 15th centuries. Parts of the old palace, closest to the minster's south doorway, have been incorporated into the present Bishop's Palace.

At the east end of the minster is **Vicar's Court**, a charming group of five Queen Anne houses built for the Vicars

THE DELI

85a King Street, Southwell, Notts NG25 0EH
Tel: 01636 815523

Occupying a listed building close to the centre of town, **The Deli** was opened in 1996 by Gail Dandy and her daughter Claire and now offers their customers an excellent delicatessen along with a bright and cheerful restaurant. The menu includes a good choice of breakfast options (toasted focaccia topped with fried egg and bacon, for example), appetising lunches such as Stuffed Peppers with salad and crusty bread, baguettes, quiche and jacket potatoes. There's also a takeaway menu of baguettes and, the speciality of the house, hot grilled paninis. The Deli is open 7 days a week and the Sunday breakfast is especially popular!

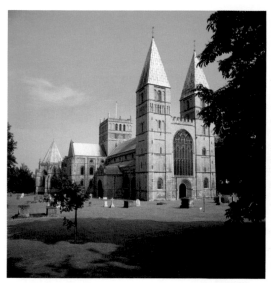

Southwell Minster

1803 and 1807 whilst on holiday from Harrow and Cambridge. He joined the local theatrical group and it was his friends in the town who encouraged him to publish his first set of poems. Under the title *Hours of Idleness*, the book was published by Ridges of Newark and brought great acclaim to the young poet.

Southwell can also be credited as the birthplace of the Bramley apple. The story goes that in the early 19th century, two ladies planted some apple pips in their cottage garden in the nearby village of Easthorpe. Nature took its course and one of the seedlings grew into a tree. By this time, Matthew Bramley owned the cottage and the quality of the tree's fruit began to excite public interest.

Choral around 1702. Just across the road from the Minster is a picturesque old coaching inn, the 16th century Saracen's Head. Charles I spent his last hours of freedom before his final surrender in this delightful half-timbered building. At that time the inn was known as the King's Head: the name was changed after Charles was beheaded.

Just to the north of the Saracen's Head is Burgage Manor (private), a handsome Georgian pile where the young Lord Byron stayed with his mother between

Mr Henry Merryweather, a local nurseryman, persuaded Bramley to let him take a cutting, which he consequently propagated with enormous success. Permission had been granted on the condition that the apples took Mr Bramley's name and not the two ladies'! The **Bramley Apple Exhibition** (free) in Halam Road explains the full history and development of this famous fruit. Whilst in the town visitors should also look out for a Southwell Galette, a scrumptious

THE HEN HOUSE

1 Bull Yard, off King Street, Southwell, Notts NG25 0EH
Tel/Fax: 01636 812855 website: www.henhouseinteriors.co.uk

If you are looking for distinctive items to brighten up your home, a good place to look is **The Hen House** in Southwell. Established in 2001 by Louise Chambers & Jo Hetherington, it is a showcase for their favourite interior accessories, fabrics and antiques. They stock Cath Kidston fabrics and products such as ironing board covers and wash bags, also Vanessa Arbuthnott's fabric collections including Cockerel & Spot, plus a comprehensive range of Farrow & Ball paints and wallpapers. Durance en Provence's range of linen care products and a variety of gifts such as candles, soaps and pictures are gorgeous too. Opening times are Mon-Fri 10am-5pm and Saturdays 9.30-5pm.

HILLS FARM SHOP

Ashcroft, Edingley Hill, Edingley, nr Newark,
Notts NG22 8BU
Tel: 01623 882664 Fax: 01623 883299

The Hills family has been growing fruit and
vegetables for more than 100 years, with a stall
at Mansfield market that enjoys an excellent
reputation. In 1989 John and Margaret Hill
developed the business further by opening **Hills
Farm Shop** just across the yard from their farmhouse. It offers a huge choice of fresh fruit and vegetables,
most of it home grown on their 213-acre farm, as well as bedding plants, hanging baskets, cut flowers
and, at Christmas time, festive trees and holly wreaths.

In 2002, the Hills expanded the business yet again when they took over a farm shop at Farnsfield,
about 3 miles to the east. Conveniently located on the A614, **Combs Farm Shop** offers a very different

product mix being based on meats from the
Lincolnshire Red beef cattle on the
surrounding 360-acre farm and other local
suppliers. Bacon is dry-cured on the premises
and the shop's hand-raised pork pies are
especially popular. The meats and pies are also
sold at the Hills Farm Shop. John also
established a 2.5 acre Pick Your Own plot at
Combs Farm, the only one in the area, and
planted with strawberries, raspberries and
carrots.

THE OLD FORGE

Burgage Lane, Southwell, Notts NG25 0ER
Tel: 01636 812809 Fax: 01636 816302
website: www.southwell.online.co.uk/localpages/
theoldforge.htm

Low-beamed ceilings, antique dressers, patchwork quilts
and pretty touches of Victoriana – the old-world
ambiance of **The Old Forge** is full of character and
charm. This cottage-style guesthouse is the home of
Hilary Marston, a friendly and welcoming hostess who
does everything she can to make her guests feel at home. There are 4 guest bedrooms, all with firm and
comfortable beds, en suite facilities, hospitality tray, colour TV and telephone.

Guests have the use of a residents' lounge and an attractive conservatory while outside there's a
small but beautiful garden from which the towers of Southwell Minster can be seen. In good weather,

some guests prefer to take breakfast here on the patio
beside the fish pond and waterfall. The Old Forge enjoys
a quiet location but it's only a short walk to the centre of
this delightful old town and its glorious 12th century
Minster which is renowned for some superb examples of
stone carving. There's a choice of several eating places of
varying prices and style of cuisine, and some fine old
coaching inns. Newstead Abbey, once the home of Lord
Byron; Belvoir Castle, home of the Dukes of Rutland; and
Lincoln, with its cobbled streets and majestic cathedral,
are all within easy reach.

pastry confection of hazelnuts, sultanas, and, of course, Bramley apples.

The disused railway line from Southwell to Mansfield, opened in 1871, is now an attractive footpath known as the **Farnsfield to Southwell Trail**. As well as the varied plant and wildlife that can be found along the 4½ mile walk, there is also plenty of industrial archaeological interest including the **Farnsfield Waterworks** of 1910, a late 18th century cotton mill, and **Greet Lily Mill**, a corn mill on the banks of the River Greet.

Norwood Park (by appointment only) is the only one of the four original parks around Southwell that remains today. The property of the Archbishops of York, the park remained in the possession of the Church until 1778. A house was built here in Cromwell's day but the present building dates from 1763. Open to visitors during the summer months, the house has a very lived-in feel. The surrounding parkland was laid out in the 18th century at the same time as the ice house and temple were built, and the lime avenue planted.

AROUND SOUTHWELL

KIRKLINGTON
3 miles NW of Southwell on the A617

Kirklington's church is partly Norman and anyone venturing inside will see that the pulpit has some small holes in its side that have been plugged with more recent wood. The explanation for this odd feature is that in the early 1800s, Kirklington's sporting rector would use the pulpit as a portable screen when he went duck shooting. He would fire at the ducks through the holes in the pulpit's sides.

CAUNTON
7 miles NE of Southwell off the A616

The village Church of St Andrew was rebuilt by the Normans at the beginning of the 13th century but by the 1800s the building had fallen into such a state of disrepair that the altar, a wooden box, was only used as a resting place for the hat and gloves of visiting curates. Restored in 1869, the church contains many monuments to the Hole family, Lords of the Manor here since Elizabethan times.

The best known member of the Hole family was Samuel Reynolds Hole who became known as the Rose King - a title bestowed on him by Tennyson. Before becoming Dean of Rochester, Hole lived at Caunton Manor as the squire and vicar and it was here that he began his extensive study of roses. By 1851, Samuel recorded that he possessed over 1,000 rose trees in more than 400 varieties, a collection which was to make him the most famous amateur rose grower of all.

ASHDENE

Halam, nr Southwell, Notts NG22 8AH
Tel: 01636 812335 e-mail: david@herbert.newsurf.net

Ashdene is a wonderfully picturesque old house dating back to 1540. It's been the home of David and Glenys Herbert for the past 25 years and since 2000 they have been welcoming bed & breakfast guests. Awarded a 4 Diamonds rating by the English Tourist Council, Ashdene has 2 guest bedrooms – a double with en suite shower, and a twin with 4-poster bed and private bathroom, both attractively furnished and decorated. The house stands in a lovely 2½ acre garden which is open to guests at all times and to the public four times a year.

UPTON

2 miles E of Southwell on the A612

Upton boasts a couple of very good pubs and its nine-pinnacled church is worthy of a visit too. A famous son of the village was James Tenant, the man who cut the world-renowned Koh-I-Noor diamond. But perhaps the most impressive building here is Upton Hall, a stylish Grecian villa with a central dome and elegant colonnade, built in the early 1800s. The hall is now the headquarters of the British Horological Institute and, inside, visitors can see the **National Exhibition of Time** - a fascinating display of clocks, watches, and other horological pieces.

ROLLESTON

3 miles E of Southwell off the A617

Holy Trinity Church is certainly one of the county's finest churches and is also the source of a great treasure: a portion of the original paper register covering the years 1584 to 1615. An interesting and historic document completed by the vicar of the time, Robert Leband, it gives the local gossip as well as the price of corn and notes of local events. A curiosity in the church is a fragment of a Saxon cross, built into the wall and scratched with the words Radulfus me fe, (Radulfus made me). It is one of very few surviving Saxon works in England to bear its author's signature.

EAST BRIDGFORD

7 miles S of Southwell off the A6097

The village is situated on a ridge overlooking a crossing of the River Trent and the edge of Sherwood Forest beyond. The village Church of St Peter is believed to stand on one of the earliest Christian sites in Nottinghamshire. There was already a church here in the 9th century since it is known to have been plundered

OLDE MILL POTTERY

Main Street, Caythorpe, Nottingham NG14 7ED
Tel: 0115 966 5205/3851
e-mail: geoff.firmin@btopenworld.com

Olde Mill Pottery enjoys a picturesque location and occupies an old water mill, built in 1745, which was grinding corn for local farmers until the 1950s. The Dover Beck flows straight through the property and the splendid original water wheel is still in place in a corner of the studio. The mill is now home to Nottingham-born Judy Firmin who studied agriculture, in which she

has a degree – pottery was a hobby that developed into a career. Her small studio and gallery enjoys views of the beck and provides a showcase for her wide range of individually made stoneware pottery that is glazed and fired on the premises.

The pieces are often bought as local gifts as well as for personal use and include a wide variety of domestic ware, decorative pieces, unusual Nottingham lace and volcanic designs, plus a charming range of children's pottery. Judy also accepts personal commissions – anything from named mugs through to specially designed anniversary plates and house plaques. Visitors are welcome to view the display, watch Judy at work or discuss individual ideas or requirements. Easily found – it's on the main street opposite the Black Horse pub – the pottery is open 11am to 5pm, including weekends.

NEWTON CROSS COUNTRY COURSE

Newton House Farm, Newton, Nottingham NG13 8HN
Tel/Fax: 01949 20235
e-mail: carole@newtoncrosscountry.co.uk
website: www.newtoncrosscountry.co.uk

Noted horsewoman Lucinda Green has nothing but praise for the **Newton Cross Country Course** near Nottingham: "It's an excellent facility. It is well-maintained and caters for all standards of riders. I have used it for my clinics and wouldn't hesitate to recommend it". Each year, Lucinda holds an annual cross country clinic at Newton and accommodation for riders and stabling for horses can be arranged. The course was established in 1984 by Carole Fisher, who has been riding since she was 8 years old, and her husband James.

Approximately one mile long, the course runs over old grassland and includes 2 water complexes, a 40m by 30m manège, show jumps and more than 60 fences. The course caters for all levels of experience from novices to professionals and can be hired by individuals, groups and clubs. A pony club triathlon competition is held once a year and there's a special weekend for children with their own ponies when they receive riding instruction, take part in a cross country ride and receive advice on various equestrian topics – ending with a course on various beauty treatments.

by the Danes when they came up the river to Nottingham.

SHELFORD

8 miles S of Southwell off the A6097

The name Shelford means the place of the shallow ford so, presumably, there was once a ford here across the River Trent which flows in a horseshoe bend around the village. Though now a quiet and tranquil place, in the winter of 1644 Shelford was the site of a particularly fierce battle. Royalist soldiers, taking shelter in the church tower, were smoked out by the Parliamentarian army who set fire to straw at the tower's base. During the same weekend, some 140 men were slaughtered by Cromwell's men at the manor house which was subsequently burnt to the ground.

The Royalist troops were commanded by Shelford's Lord of the Manor, Philip Stanhope, a member of the illustrious family who later became Earls of Chesterfield. There are some fine memorials to the Stanhopes in the village church, including one by Nollekens.

OXTON

4 miles SW of Southwell on the B6386

A charming village near the edge of Sherwood Forest and surrounded by parkland, Oxton has a goodly number of 17th and 18th century houses and cottages. The Sherbrooke family have been the lords of the manor here since the 16th century and Oxton still retains the feel of an estate village even though the hall was demolished in 1957. An oddity is to be found in a yard opposite the Green Dragon Inn. Here stands the tomb of Robert Sherbrooke who died in 1710. The unusual location is explained by the fact that Sherbrooke was a Quaker and this was the site of their meeting house.

The uncovering of **Oldox Camp**, one of the largest and best preserved Iron Age hill forts in Nottinghamshire, to the north of the village suggests that this was the original site of Oxton. Extending over some 3 acres, the fort is surrounded by a single ditch and bank, except at the entrance to the fort where the defences are doubled.

CALVERTON
6 miles SW of Southwell off the B6386

The charming cottages in this industrial village date back to the early 19th century and were once the homes of framework knitters. Carefully restored by the Nottinghamshire Building Preservation Trust, the cottages originally formed three sides of a rectangle, though one side is now missing. Unusually, the large windows which provided the light for the knitters are found on the ground floor instead of the more usual upper storey.

It was a curate of Calverton, William Lee, who invented the stocking knitting frame in 1589. According to an old story, his invention was the result of an unsuccessful love affair. Whenever William visited the girl he wanted to marry she "always took care to be busily employed in knitting...He vowed to devote his further leisure to devising an invention that should effectually supersede her favourite employment of knitting". Lee succeeded in creating an immensely complicated machine that could produce top quality work between 10 and 15 times as quickly as the fastest hand knitters. To develop it further he sought the patronage of Elizabeth I but the queen refused to encourage something that would mean great job losses for her loyal subjects.

After being refused a patent by Elizabeth I, Lee travelled to France and gained the promise of support from Henry of Navarre. Unfortunately, Henry was assassinated before any promises were made good and it is believed that Lee died in Paris in 1610. Lee's brother, James, brought the frame back to London where the hosiery industry first developed before it settled in the Midlands later in the 17th century.

Also at Calverton is **Patchings**, formerly known as Painters' Paradise, a series of gardens that have been designed with the artist in mind. Here, amongst the rolling hills of north Nottinghamshire, is a perfect reconstruction of Claude Monet's garden at Giverney, complete with the elegant little bridge and the pool of water lilies that he painted so often. Attractive gazebo studios are dotted around the 50 acres of grounds, each designed to provide a picturesque view. An impressive building of Norwegian spruce – one of the largest wooden structures in England – offers further facilities for artists and visitors: studios, workshop and dark room as well as a licensed restaurant.

NEWARK-ON-TRENT

John Wesley considered Newark one of the most elegant towns in England; more recently the Council for British Archaeology included it in their list of the best 50 towns in the country; and in 1968 Newark town centre was designated as one of the first Conservation Areas. Its medieval street plan remains intact, complete with a fine market square which is still busy every day of the week, except Tuesdays, with a market of one kind or another - plus a Farmer's Market once a month.

The square is lined with handsome houses and inns. The most remarkable of them is the 14th century former **White**

Hart Inn (now a bank), which has a magnificent frontage adorned with 24 plaster figures of angels and saints. Close by are the Saracen's Head where Sir Walter Scott often stayed, and the Clinton Arms, the preferred lodging of W.E. Gladstone during his 14 years as Newark's Member of Parliament.

Dominating one side of the square is the noble Georgian **Town Hall**, built in 1777 and recently fully restored. It now houses the town's civic plate and regalia, and an art gallery displaying works by Stanley Spencer, William Nicholson and notable local artists.

The grandest building of all though is the **Church of St Mary Magdalene**, by common consent the finest parish church in the county. Its slender, elegant spire soars above the town and serves as a landmark for miles along the Trent Valley. The church dates back to the early 12th century though all that

survives of that structure is the crypt which now houses the treasury. Much of the building seen today dates from the 14th, 15th, and 16th centuries and its exterior is a fascinating blend of carvings and tracery. The interior is spacious and airy, and the treasures on display include a huge brass commemorating Alan Fleming, a Newark merchant who died in 1373; a dazzling Comper reredos of 1937; a splendid east window depicting Mary Magdalene; a Victorian mosaic reproducing Van Eyck's Adoration of the Lamb; and fragments of a painted "Dance of Death" from around 1500.

Newark's recorded history goes back to Roman times when the legionaries established a base here to guard the first upstream crossing of the River Trent. One of their major arterial roads, Fosse Way, passes close by on its way to Lincoln. Saxons and Danes continued the settlement, the latter leaving a legacy

PEARMAN ANTIQUES & INTERIORS

9 Castle Gate, Newark, Notts. NG24 1AZ
Tel: 01636 679158
e-mail: pearman@onetel.net.uk

Occupying a handsome Georgian house looking across to Newark Castle, **Pearman Antiques & Interiors** offers three floors of quality antiques and interior decoration materials. It's a family-run business owned and operated by Jan and Stan, their daughter Samantha and partner Sally Moulds. At Castle Gate they stock a varied range of 18th and 19th century furniture in oak, mahogany or

walnut, oil and watercolour paintings, prints and engravings, antique lighting fitments, as well as paints and fabrics from Morris & Co. Most of the antiques are displayed in themed rooms – dining room, bedroom and even an Oriental room.

The Pearmans also offer a soft furnishing and fabrics bespoke service and stock an interesting range of locally-made cushions and throws. The family also own another shop with the same name at Long Acre Studios in Bingham, about 12 miles down the A46. Here they specialise in antique English and French beds, works by contemporary artists and craftsmen in glass, woodturning and ceramics. There's a workshop here where Stan and Sally carry out furniture restoration and make beds to their own designs, while Jan is an expert in upholstering antique furniture.

of street names ending in "gate", from *gata*, the Danish word for street.

When the Normans arrived, they replaced the wooden **Castle** with one of stone. The present building is mostly 12th century and for some 300 years it was owned by the powerful Bishops of Lincoln. Then in 1483, ownership of the castle was transferred to the Crown and leased out to a succession of noblemen.

The castle's most glorious days occurred during the Civil War. The people of Newark were fiercely loyal to Charles I and endured 3 separate sieges before finally surrendering to Cromwell's troops. Parliament ordered the "slighting" of the castle, rendering it militarily useless, but left the demolition work to the townspeople. Understandably, they showed little enthusiasm for the task of demolishing the 8ft thick walls. As a result, the ruins are quite substantial, especially the mighty gateway that Pevsner called "the biggest and most elaborate of its period (1170-75) in England". It was here that King John, devastated by the loss of his treasure while crossing the Wash, came to die in 1216. The castle crypt and an intimidating beehive dungeon have also survived. Guided tours of the castle (and the town) are available and its history is colourfully interpreted at the **Gilstrap Centre**. This lies within the Castle Grounds which, with its gardens and

Victorian bandstand, is a popular venue for special events as well as a pleasant spot for a picnic.

Newark possesses several other reminders of the Civil War. As a defensive measure two small forts were built to guard this strategic crossing over the River Trent. The King's Sconce, to the northeast, has since disappeared but its twin, the **Queen's Sconce**, still lies to the southeast. Named after Queen Henrietta Maria, who brought supplies into the town after the first siege in 1643, this square earthwork has a bastion in each corner and a hollow in the middle.

In the town centre, on Kirk Gate, are **Henrietta Maria's Lodgings**, where according to tradition the queen stayed in 1643. Travelling from Bridlington to the king's headquarters at Oxford, the queen was bringing with her men and arms from the continent. She had paid for them by selling off some of the Crown Jewels.

Nearby is the **Governor's House** where the governors of Newark lived during the Civil War and also the place where Charles I quarrelled with Prince Rupert after the prince had lost Bristol to Parliament. This wonderful timber framed building was restored in the late 19th century and during the work a medieval wall and some beam paintings were revealed along with graffiti dating from 1757. With such a wealth of history

IL CASTELLO RISTORANTE ITALIANO

46-48 Castle Gate, Newark, Notts NG24 1BB
Tel: 01636 674000 Fax: 01636 674211

Opened in October 2000 and housed in a listed building, **Il Castello Ristorante Italiano** has quickly established a reputation for serving authentic Italian cuisine in a friendly, lively atmosphere. As they say in Italy, the food "jumps into the mouth" – appetising starters such as fried wild mushrooms served with coriander and garlic mayonnaise and a wide choice of pasta, fish, meat and poultry main dishes to follow. The wine list, naturally, highlights Italian wines. In good weather, diners can enjoy their meals in the courtyard at the rear. Il Castello is open for lunch, Thursday to Saturday, from noon until 2.30pm; for dinner, Monday to Saturday, from 6.30pm to 10.30pm.

inside its boundaries, Newark naturally has its fair share of museums. **Newark Museum** (free) is housed in a former school which dates back to 1529 and the history of the area is traced from the Stone Age to the 19th century. A large Anglo-Saxon cemetery, discovered in Millgate, is also on display.

Occupying a former riverside warehouse, the **Millgate Folk Museum** (free) concentrates on everyday life in the 19th and 20th centuries. The exhibits include an interesting array of shops and shop fronts, and there is also a reconstruction of an early 20th century terraced house. The Mezzanine Gallery within the museum hosts temporary exhibitions featuring the work of local artists, designers and photographers.

On the outskirts of the town, at **Beacon Hill**, one of the greatest victories over the Roundheads took place, in 1644, when Prince Rupert arrived to lift the second of Newark's sieges. Under Sir John Meldrum, the Parliamentarians lost more arms and equipment than during any other engagement of the Civil War.

Just east of the town, close to the A1, lies the **Newark Air Museum**, one of the largest privately managed collections in the country. Opened in the 1960s, the museum has more than 50 aircraft and cockpit sections on display. Visitors can see jet fighters, bombers, and helicopters which span the history of aviation as well as a great deal of aviation memorabilia, relics, and uniforms on display in the Exhibition Hall.

AROUND NEWARK-ON-TRENT

CROMWELL
5 miles N of Newark off the A1

The large 17th century rectory in the village is now home to the **Vina Cooke**

CHURCH FARM SHOP

Main Street, South Scarle, Newark, Notts NG23 7JH
Tel: 01636 892003 Fax: 01636 893556

Located right next to St Helena's church in the village of South Scarle, **Church Farm Shop** offers a huge array of farm produce, food treats, gifts and much, much more. The shop is housed in an 18th century former barn which was used to stable shire horses but is now stacked with wonderfully fresh fruit and vegetables, all of it locally grown wherever possible. Anita and Steve Clements began their enterprise in 1988 – selling daffodils from a bucket at the end of the road with an honesty box for the money.

The following year they acquired a portacabin to display their wares and the present shop was opened in 1992. A local market garden supplies tomatoes and salads; potatoes come from another local farm and the delicious cakes and pies are made by Anita and her mother-in-law in the kitchen at the back of the premises. These last are available either fresh or frozen. Also on sale are some good English cheeses; meats;fresh eggs from free range hens; apple juice and organic cordials; Thaymar real dairy ice cream – and wild bird food. As if that weren't enough the shop also serves as the village Post Office and is the only Autogas supplier for miles around. Church Farm Shop is open all year round from Tuesday to Saturday, 9am until 5pm.

PURE LAND RELAXATION MEDITATION CENTRE & JAPANESE GARDEN

North Clifton, nr. Newark, Notts NG23 7AT
Tel/Fax: 01777 228567

Pure Land Relaxation Meditation Centre & Japanese Garden tries to provide everyone who visits with an experience of relaxation, peace and Higher Self-awareness by means of the simple and pure approach that Buddha Maitreya has been teaching for more than 30 years. Maitreya was born and brought up in Handa, near Nagoya in Japan. During his teenage years he began a desperate search for truth which at first led him to Christianity. One summer, during a meditation course for lay people at a monastery, he had the experience of Enlightenment that was to lay down the foundations for his life as a meditation teacher.

Maitreya went on to university to complete an MA degree in Buddhist Theology and lived as a Zen monk for a time. But he felt the monastic life was too harsh, rigid and out of date. He left to spend a year in Thailand, then travelled through India and Nepal where he began teaching meditation. An invitation from a friend brought him to England where he lectured in various universities. It was while he was staying in Teversal near Nottingham that he discovered a property for sale in North Clifton which became a base from which to teach meditation. Pure Land was born in 1973.

Maitreya offers individual tuition and consultation for 1 person or a couple; group relaxation and meditation meetings and he has also recorded a "Pure Relaxation and Meditation" tape, and "Poems for Peace".

An attractive feature of the Centre is its Japanese Garden which Buddha Maitreya began to create in 1980 with the main aim of providing a peaceful, beautiful area which guests and visitors to the Centre could enjoy. The 2-acre site was flat and Maitreya missed the hilly and mountainous scenery of Japan so he began to create his own in miniature. The earth dug out by the JCB in order to create the pond was heaped roughly into "hills" that were later shaped by hand. Little by little, other features were added from the Japanese repertoire of traditional garden elements – water, carp, bridges, moss, bamboo, evergreens, maples, stone lanterns. These are blended with a dash of English plants and elements. A small pagoda, a Zen garden and a Japanese Tea house for tea ceremony use have also been added. The garden is open from April 1st to October 31st, Tuesday to Friday from 10.30am to 5.30pm; weekends and Bank Holidays, 10am to 5.30pm, but closed on Mondays. Light refreshments served. In summer (August & September) "Lantern lit evening garden" is held every weekend. The centre is sign posted and can be found half way between Newark and Gainsborough off the A1133 twelve miles from Newark.

Museum of Dolls and Bygone Childhood. Appealing to adults and children alike, there are all manner of children's toys on display but perhaps the most fascinating are the handmade dolls depicting royalty, stars of stage and screen, and famous historical characters. Vina Cooke, a well-known doll artist, exhibits her own hand-made dolls here.

SUTTON ON TRENT
7 miles N of Newark off the B1164

One of the largest Trentside villages, Sutton was once famous for basket-making, fishermen's baskets in particular. It has a fine church, first established in Saxon times and noted for its Mering Chapel. Dating from the early 1500s, the chapel was brought here from the village of Mering on the other side of the Trent. Mering has since vanished completely into the watery lowlands surrounding the Trent. The superb **Mering Chapel**, however, contains a distinguished memorial in Purbeck marble to Sir William Mering. The tomb is separated from the aisle by a very rare oak screen crafted around 1510. Sir William's family, like his village, is extinct.

SOUTH CLIFTON
9 miles N of Newark off the A1133

This pleasant village along the banks of the River Trent still has the remains of an old wharf where the coal from Derbyshire and Yorkshire was unloaded before being distributed throughout the surrounding area. The river here is still much used though the local fishermen now have to contend with water-skiers travelling up and down. On the village green stands a young oak tree, planted in 1981, along with a plaque commemorating the achievements of a local farmer, Dusty Hare, who has lived in the parish all his life, scored the highest number (7,000) of points in Rugby Union Football and was honoured with an MBE in 1989.

NORTH CLIFTON
10 miles N of Newark off the A1133

The village, like its neighbour South Clifton, also lies on the east side of the Trent, close to the border with Lincolnshire. The two villages are, however, quite separate, but they share the same church, dedicated to St George the Martyr, which lies between them and has an imposing 15th century tower.

An unusual attraction here is the **Pureland Meditation Centre and Japanese Garden** (see panel opposite) which offers a haven of peace for all ages who wish to come and experience the benefits of relaxation and meditation. Buddha Maitreya, a former Zen monk from Japan, has devoted the last 20 years to creating the delightful Japanese with its large central pond, bridges, and a small pagoda where visitors can relax and meditate amidst an abundance of flourishing plants and trees. The garden is open every afternoon, except Mondays, between April and October.

THORNEY
11 miles N of Newark off the A57

In 1805, this once peaceful little village was the site of a dreadful murder. A local labourer, Thomas Temporell, also known locally as Tom Otter, was forced to marry a local girl whom, it was claimed, he had made pregnant. Tom was so upset by the accusations and the enforced marriage that, in a frenzy, he murdered his bride on their wedding night. The story goes that he then took her body and left it on the steps of a public house in Saxilby, Lincolnshire. Caught and tried, Tom was sentenced to death with the extra penalty of gibbeting (the practice of hanging the offender's body in chains at the scene of their crime).

Small though it is, Thorney possesses a huge and magnificent church, built in 1849 by the Nevile family of nearby Thorney Hall (now demolished). Constructed in the Norman style, the church contains a wealth of superb stone carvings, both inside and out. Amongst them are no fewer than 17 fearsome dragons' heads.

TUXFORD

12 miles NW of Newark off the A1

This pleasant little town used to have its own market and, because of its position on the Great North Road, prospered greatly during the days of stage coach travel. A devastating fire in 1702 destroyed most of the town but the rebuilding produced some attractive Georgian buildings. Amongst the buildings that did survive are the pleasing little Grammar School with its hipped roof and dormer windows, founded in

1669, and the medieval Church of St Nicholas. The church contains some interesting memorials to the White family and a striking font of 1673 standing beneath a magnificent hanging canopy.

KELHAM

3 miles W of Newark on the A617

Originally an estate village serving Kelham Hall, the village farms were amongst the first to grow sugar beet when it was introduced to England during World War I. A lane still leads from the village to the huge sugar beet factory a mile or so to the west. **Kelham Hall**, now council offices, is the third manor house to be built on the site. The first was the "Kelum Hall" where Charles I was briefly imprisoned. That building was destroyed by fire in 1690. Another mansion was built for the Sutton family, Lords of the Manor of Kelham. That too went up in flames, in 1857. The present

THE MUSSEL & CRAB

Sibthorpe Hall, Tuxford, Notts. NG22 0PJ
Tel: 01777 870491 Fax: 01777 871096
e-mail: musselandcrab1@hotmail.com
website: www.musselandcrab.co.uk

Located just moments from the A1, **The Mussel & Crab** is an outstanding restaurant specialising in fish dishes but also offering a varied choice that includes Pork Wellington, Roast Gressingham Duck or tender steaks. The Mussel & Crab is owned by Bruce and Alison Elliott-Bateman who have extensive experience in the hospitality business and are devoted to making sure their customers enjoy a dining experience they will want to tell their friends about! Cordon Bleu chef Philip Wright heads a team of 5 chefs who take pride in producing individual dishes to the highest standards.

Most of the seafood is purchased direct from South West ports and arrives at the restaurant as fresh as when it was trawled from the ocean. Bruce also buys fish from other parts of the world so, on the 20-odd blackboards that adorn almost every wall, you might find Kingfish and Halibut from the Red Sea, or Parrot Fish or Coral Trout from the Western Australian Reef. Also listed on the boards is a fascinating selection of the latest wines to arrive from some of the finest vineyards throughout the world. Not surprisingly, tables at the Mussel & Crab are always in great demand – booking ahead is almost always essential.

building was designed by George Gilbert Scott and opinions are sharply divided over the merits of its red-brick towers, pinnacles, gables and Gothic windows.

Like the Hall, Kelham's bridge over the Trent also suffered misfortune: during the frightful winter of 1881 ice packs floating down the river demolished the old wooden structure.

AVERHAM
4 miles W of Newark on the A617

Pronounced locally as "Airam", this pleasant village is somewhat overshadowed by the nearby power station at Staythorpe. But there's a picturesque corner off the main road where the Norman church and Georgian rectory form an appealing little group on the edge of the Trent. In the rectory grounds stands the remarkable **Robin Hood Theatre**, established by a former Rector and built by a local carpenter. The Rev. Cyril Walker opened it in 1913 as a private theatre for opera lovers. It had a fully equipped stage and orchestra pit, and boasted the rare amenity of being lit by electricity. The late, great Sir Donald Wolfit, a local man born at nearby Balderton, gave his first performances here. The theatre went through a rocky period in the 1960s and closed for several years but it is now operating successfully again, offering a variety of shows and plays throughout the year.

EAST STOKE
4 miles SW of Newark on the A46

The village is the site of the last great conflict of the War of the Roses: the **Battle of Stoke Fields** that took place here on 16th June 1487. The battle saw the army of Henry VII defeat the Yorkists and the pretender Lambert Simnel in a bloody conflict that lasted for three hours and left a toll of 7,000 deaths. The defeated army fled across the meadows

to the river which is known locally to this day as the Red Gutter. Many of those who died in battle lie in Deadman's Field nearby, and local farmers have occasionally uncovered swords and other relics from the battle when ploughing their fields.

ELSTON
7 miles SW of Newark off the A46

This rural village was once well-known for the local trade of skep-making, or basket-making, using specially grown willows, but the craft has all but died out. A curious building on the outskirts of the village is the deserted **Elston Chapel**, a quaint little building with a Norman doorway and many other Norman and medieval features. Its origins have been shrouded in mystery but recent research has suggested that the building was the chapel to the hospital of St Leonard that once existed in this locality.

SIBTHORPE
5 miles S of Newark off the A46

All that remains above ground of a priests' college, founded here in the 14th century, is the parish church and a **Dovecote** (NT). Standing in the middle of a field and some 60 feet high, this circular stone building has a conical tiled roof and provided nesting places for more than 1200 birds.

SCREVETON
7 miles S of Newark off the A46

The ancient village, whose name means farm belonging to the sheriff, has a delightful, small 13th century church which lies in a secluded position some way from the village. Reached by a footpath, the **Church of St Wilfrid** is home to a fine alabaster tomb of Richard Whalley who is depicted with his three wives and 25 children at his feet.

CAR COLSTON

8 miles S of Newark off the A46

Now a conservation area, this village is fortunate in that it has remained unspoiled by modern development. Of particular interest here are the village's two greens which both date from the reign of Elizabeth I. At that time individual strips of land were cultivated by the villagers and the typical ridge and furrow appearance can still be made out. In 1598, the parish was enclosed, the land being turned into the fenced fields that became the norm, but the land in the middle of the village was left open so that the villagers could graze their cattle. The Large Green, at 16.5 acres, is the largest in the county and, at the other end of the village lies Little Green (a mere 5.5 acres).

There are several interesting houses in the village but **Old Hall Farm**, which dates from 1812, is probably the one that receives most attention. The interest is generated, not so much by the building itself but because it was the home of Robert Thoroton, who in 1677 published his Antiquities of Nottinghamshire. The first major history of the county, the work was updated in the late 18th century by John Throsby and remains today one of the prime sources for local historians.

SCARRINGTON

8 miles S of Newark-on-Trent off the A52

The main attraction of this small village is not a grand house or a splendid village church but a remarkable man-made edifice. A pile of around 50,000 horseshoes towers 17 feet high and was built by the former blacksmith, Mr Flinders. Over the years, souvenir hunters have taken the odd shoe here and there, with the result that the monument is bending over very slightly at the top.

However, the obelisk which Mr Flinders began in 1945, stands rock solid though all he used to bond the shoes was his skill and a great deal of luck! At one time it was coveted by an American visitor who wished to buy it and transport it to the United States.

ALVERTON

7 miles S of Newark-on-Trent off the A52

A small hamlet of just a handful of houses, Alverton's tiny population is occasionally augmented by two resident ghosts. The first has been seen in the old Church of England schoolhouse, which is now a private residence, and is believed to be the ghost of a teacher who was murdered at the school.

Alverton's second ghost, an elderly lady dressed in Victorian clothes, has been sighted at one of the hamlet's larger houses. The lady is believed to be Mary Brown, a sewing maid to Queen Victoria, who gave up her job after the death of her sister-in-law. Mary moved back to her brother's house to act as housekeeper to him and his four children and, by all accounts, she proved to be a formidable woman. She ruled the house with a rod of iron. In later years, when noises were heard on the upper floors, it was said that "Aunt Polly was on the warpath again!"

BINGHAM

The unofficial "capital" of the Vale of Belvoir, Bingham is an ancient medieval market town which grew up around the church. After passing through a period of depression in the 20th century, the town is once again thriving. The area around the market square has been smartened up and the octagonal Butter Cross with its Victorian tiles and inscriptions provides an attractive focus here. Most of the buildings around the market place are also Victorian but All Saints' Church is medieval, dating from the 13th century though, again, there are many Victorian additions and decorations.

Bingham was the third Nottinghamshire town to provide an Archbishop of Canterbury. George Abbot's tenure of office was almost as unremarkable as that of Thomas Secker of Sibthorpe except for one unfortunate accident in 1621. Abbot was out shooting deer with a crossbow when he missed and killed a gamekeeper instead.

AROUND BINGHAM

COTGRAVE
4 miles SW of Bingham off the A46

The discovery of an Anglo-Saxon burial ground on **Mill Hill**, Cotgrave's highest point, confirms that there has been a settlement here for many centuries. The excavation team uncovered the skeletons of nearly 100 people including some 13 children and the remains have been dated to around the mid to late 6th century.

Close to the burial ground stood the village's old post mill, itself the site of an unsolved mystery. One of the millers disappeared without trace after having been accused of pilfering corn. Rumours in the 19th century suggested that a body had been discovered in the mill foundations and, despite believing that this could be the remains of the missing miller, the villagers kept quiet and the rumour was never investigated. During an excavation of the post mill site in the 1970s the skeleton of a male was uncovered which showed injuries that suggested that the unfortunate man was killed by a blow to the head. Whether or not this was all that remained of the missing miller has never been established.

Cotgrave is probably most well known as the home of Cotgrave Colliery which opened in 1964 and was a showplace mine for a number of years. The promise of work here for the next 100 years brought many miners from other coalfields to the village and also generated a huge expansion and building programme. Unfortunately, major geological faults made it impossible to mine the huge reserves and the colliery is now closed.

KINOULTON
6 miles S of Bingham off the A46

The village, on the edge of the wolds, stands on high ground and from this vantage point there are views over the Vale of Belvoir to Belvoir Castle. Today, Kinoulton is a large commuter village but it has a long and interesting past. In the 12th century, there was a castle here, its commanding position being ideal since it was also close to the Fosse Way. Archbishop Cranmer had a palace nearby and, to the west of the village, lies the spring which brought the village to prominence in Georgian times as a spa with curative properties. Later, the arrival of the Grantham Canal ushered in a period of mild prosperity. (The canal still passes through the village and provides some pleasant walking).

Standing beside the canal, Kinoulton's **Church of St Luke** was a gift of the squire, the Earl of Gainsborough, in the 1760s. The earl felt the old church was too near what was then a major thoroughfare, the Fosse Way. The slate headstones in the old churchyard have some fine inscriptions but not all of the stones have survived. Some were "borrowed" by the local baker to line his oven, a piece of recycling that was exposed when a customer noticed that his loaf was imprinted with the words "In loving memory".

CLEEVE HOUSE

Melton Road, Hickling Pastures, Melton Mowbray,
Leicestershire LE14 3Q
Tel: 01949 81828 Fax: 01949 81829

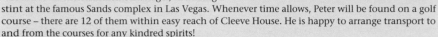

Enjoying pastoral views across the Vale of Belvoir,
Cleeve House is a stylish modern house set back from
the A606 Melton Mowbray to Nottingham road and
close to the junction with the A46 Leicester to
Newark route. It's the home of Peter and Theresa
Boyle who have travelled the world because Peter
worked as an entertainments manager, including a
stint at the famous Sands complex in Las Vegas. Whenever time allows, Peter will be found on a golf
course – there are 12 of them within easy reach of Cleeve House. He is happy to arrange transport to
and from the courses for any kindred spirits!

The Boyles began offering bed and breakfast accommodation in November 2000 after buying and
completely refurbishing the spacious house. It has 4 guest
bed rooms (3 doubles; 1 twin), all of them en suite and
with full facilities. A full English breakfast is included in
the tariff and vegetarians and other dietary requirements
can be catered. Fresh local produce is used wherever possible.
Guests have the use of a comfortable residents lounge with
a welcoming open fire. The pleasant market towns of Melton
Mowbray, Oakham and Stamford are just down the road;
other attractions in the neighbourhood include Belvoir
Castle, Burghley House and Rutland Water.

HICKLING

7 miles S of Bingham off the A606

Lying on the western edge of the Vale of
Belvoir, this agricultural village was the
site of a busy basin on the Grantham
Canal. Building work on the basin
finished in 1797 and the canal, which
carried coal, building materials, and
agricultural goods, was in constant use
until the 1930s when it began to fall into
disrepair. Recently cleared, Hickling
Basin is once again attracting people,
this time visitors who come to see the
resident flocks of wildfowl.

COLSTON BASSETT

4 miles S of Bingham off the A46

For centuries this small village was the
property of the Bassett family and later
the Hackers and the Goldings. Between
them they planted the many trees that
shade the winding lanes, built a noble
manor house, landscaped the gracious

park, and in 1892 added a striking if
rather over-elaborate church. The
cumulative effect is to make Colston
Bassett one of the most picturesque
villages in the Vale of Belvoir.

At one time the village was large
enough to sustain its own weekly market
and the partly medieval Market Cross
can still be seen. Since 1933, the **Cross**
has been owned by the National Trust -
the first property it acquired in
Nottinghamshire. The Cross stands near
the old post office, itself a picture
postcard building that used to feature in
GPO advertisements during the 1960s.

On the outskirts of the village stand the
forlorn ruins of the former village church
which has been abandoned since 1892.

CROPWELL BISHOP

3 miles S of Bingham off the A46

Much of the furniture from Colston
Bassett's old church was moved to

Cropwell Bishop and installed in **St Giles' Church**. St Giles is the oldest building in this sizeable village and dates back to around 1215.

The village lies close to the old Roman road, the Fosse Way, now the A46. The coaching inns of Cropwell Bishop are said to have given shelter to highwayman Dick Turpin whilst he was plundering the coaches using the busy thoroughfare.

In modern times, the village has prospered from gypsum works. Two of the works' bottle kilns still stand alongside the Grantham Canal.

LANGAR

3 miles SE of Bingham off the A52

"Really, the English do not deserve great men", declared George Bernard Shaw. "They allowed Butler to die practically unknown". He was referring to Samuel Butler, author of *The Way of All Flesh*, who was born in the elegant Georgian rectory at Langar on December 4, 1834. A trenchant satirist, Butler mocked the pomposity and exposed the hypocrisy of the Victorian middle classes. No wonder they didn't much care for him. Langar itself appears in his major work as Battersby-on-the-Hill and the portraits of its residents are far from flattering. The year 2002, the centenary of Butler's death, provided an opportunity to commemorate one of the village's most famous residents in some way but no-one bothered.

'One of the village's most famous residents', because this small rural village in the heart of the Vale was also the home of Admiral Richard, Earl Howe (1726-99), "Black Dick of Lanagar". Richard achieved national fame on the Glorious 1st of June, 1794, at the Battle of Ushant where his victory included the capture of seven French ships of the line.

LANGAR HALL

Langar, Nottingham, NG13 9HG
Tel: 01949 860559 Fax: 01949 861045
e-mail: langarhall-hotel@ndirect.co.uk
website: www.langarhall.com

Set in the unspoilt Vale of Belvoir, **Langar Hall** is a charming country house hotel and restaurant which enjoys a reputation for exceptional hospitality, friendly and efficient service, comfortable bedrooms, good food and an interesting wine list. Built in 1836, the Hall stands on the site of an earlier mansion which was the home of Admiral Lord Howe. It overlooks gardens and parkland with a network of medieval moats stocked with carp. Inside, the atmosphere is that of a private home, much loved and cared for by Imogen Skirving and her family. The public rooms feature fine furnishings and most rooms afford beautiful pastoral views.

The elegant pillared restaurant seats 30 at individual candlelit tables or up to 50 at long narrow tables for formal dinners. There are 12 beautifully appointed guest bedrooms, each named after people who have figured in the Hall's history. They vary in size and character but all contain excellent facilities, including a good size desk, remote control television, direct dial telephone, trouser press and hospitality tray. Guests have the use of the tranquil White Sitting Room which faces south overlooking the garden, and west overlooking the park. This delightful hotel was the first venue in Nottinghamshire to be licensed for civil marriages and specialists in ceremonies and receptions for up to 50 guests.

The Admiral himself merits only a modest plaque in **St Andrew's Church**, but other generations of the Howe family; their predecessors, the Scropes, as well as the Chaworths from nearby Wiverton Hall, are all celebrated by an extraordinary gathering of monuments. The most splendid is a four-poster free-standing alabaster monument to Thomas, Lord Scrope, who died in 1609, and his wife: according to Pevsner "the figures are good enough to be in Westminster Abbey".

To the south of Langar, the former airfield is surrounded by an unsightly industrial estate which nevertheless contains the **Wild Flower Farm Visitors Centre**, part of a commercial nursery, where visitors are able to explore the wild flower meadows and see a wide variety of species in their natural habitat.

GRANBY
4 miles SE of Bingham off the A52

This small, once self-sufficient village is still proud that its name was adopted by the Dukes of Rutland, of nearby Belvoir Castle, as the courtesy title of their eldest son. It was John, son of the 3rd Duke, who brought most lustre to the name as Commander in Chief of the British forces in Germany in the mid-1700s. The Marquis was immensely popular with his troops, many of whom followed an old tradition on leaving the Army and became publicans. Which explains why so many hostelries up and down the country are named The Marquis of Granby – including naturally the inn at Granby itself.

WHATTON
3 miles E of Bingham off the A52

The Norman St John's Church was restored in the 1860s under the direction of Thomas Butler, rector of Langar, and the stained glass windows, including some crafted by William Morris to the designs of Burne-Jones, were added later that century. The font, which is dated 1662, replaced one that had been damaged during the Commonwealth. This church was used by Thomas Cranmer and his family until he left the area to take up his studies at Cambridge. A memorial to his father, Thomas Cranmer senior, who died in 1502, can be found inside.

ASLOCKTON
2 miles E of Bingham off the A52

This village is now separated from its neighbour, Whatton, by the main Nottingham to Grantham railway line, though the footpaths linking the two can still be walked today. This was the village in which Thomas Cranmer was born and spent his early years. Born in 1489, he attended the parish church at Whatton and also a local grammar school, possibly at Southwell, before leaving at the age of 14 to continue his education at Cambridge. It was in 1533 that Henry VIII proposed this obscure theologian and academic as Archbishop of Canterbury, an appointment which had to be approved by the Pope – the last time Rome had any say over who should be Primate of All England.

One of Cranmer's first duties on gaining his appointment was to pronounce the marriage between Henry VIII and Catherine of Aragon null and void. During the course of his 23 years in office, Cranmer also pronounced invalid Henry's marriage to Anne Boleyn and granted him a divorce from Anne of Cleves. Loyal to his monarch throughout, Cranmer aided Henry in effecting the independence of the Church in England from Rome. He was also responsible for drafting much of the Common Prayer book that was used right up until the 1970s when it was replaced by a modern language version. Following the death of Henry VIII, Cranmer was convicted of treason under Mary I and burnt at the stake in 1556.

Though not built until the late 19th century, Aslockton Church is appropriately dedicated to Thomas whilst the village school also bears the name of its most famous resident. Cranmer's Mound, to the east of the church, is a high Norman motte some 15 feet high which is clearly visible from the footpath to Orston. Further along this same footpath can be seen the site of the manor house where Cranmer was born.

SHERWOOD FOREST

It seems likely that it was William the Conqueror who designated Sherwood as a Royal Forest, an administrative term for the private hunting ground of the king. The land was not only thickly wooded but also included areas of rough heathland as well as arable land, meadow land, small towns, and villages. The Norman kings were passionate about

their hunting and, to guard their royal forests, there were a set of rigidly upheld laws, to conserve the game (known as the venison) and vegetation (known as the vert). No one, even those with a private estate within the royal forest, was allowed to kill or hunt protected animals, graze domestic animals in the forest, fell trees, or make clearings within the boundaries without the express permission of the king or one of his chief foresters. It is little wonder then, with such strict rules imposed upon them, that the people turned to the likes of Robin Hood and others who defied the laws and lived off the kin

EDWINSTOWE

Lying at the heart of Sherwood Forest, the life of the village is still dominated by the forest, as it has been since the 7th century. Edwin, King of Northumbria, who gave the village its name, died in the Battle of Hatfield in 632. The village developed around the church built on the spot where he was slain. In 1912 a cross was erected by the Duke of Portland to mark the king's grave. From then on until the time of the Domesday Survey, Edwinstowe remained small. Following the Norman Conquest, the village found itself within the boundaries of the royal hunting forest of Sherwood and it became subject to the stringent laws of the verderers. Dating from the 12th century, the **Church of St Mary** was the first stone building in Edwinstowe and according to legend it was here that the marriage took place between Robin Hood and Maid Marian. Buried in the graveyard is Dr Cobham Brewer whose *Dictionary of Phrase & Fable*, first published in 1870 and still in print, is possibly

Sherwood Forest

FIREFLY GLASS

17 Sherwood Forest Craft Centre, Forest Corner, Edwinstowe,
Nottinghamshire NG21 9RN
Tel/Fax: 01623 824003
e-mail: dan@fireflyglass.co.uk
website: www.fireflyglass.co.uk

Dan Aston first became interested in glassware and ceramics as he helped
his father, the potter Chris Aston, in his studio. He went on to study art
and design at Mansfield College of Art and then spent 3 years studying
three-dimensional glass and ceramics at the University of Sunderland.
He now has his own hot glass studio, **Firefly Glass**, at the Sherwood Forest Craft Centre in Edwinstowe
where visitors can watch the process of glassmaking in progress. At the heart of the studio is the
furnace containing a huge pot of molten glass held permanently at a temperature of 1120^0 C.

The methods and tools Dan uses for making his glass are exactly the same as those which have
been used by glass makers for thousands of years. But Dan's
pieces are very distinctive and contemporary – exquisitely
engraved lizards, frogs and dragonflies adorn colourful
vases, bowls, paperweights and other colourful items. Dan
says "I like to use deep translucent colours, often combined
with gold and silver leaf to produce completely unique and
individual work with both colour and texture". The
completed pieces are displayed in the gallery shop area of
the studio where there's a wide and changing variety of
glass for sale – ideal as gifts or to add distinction to your
own décor.

HARBOUR LIGHTS

Sherwood Forest Craft Centre, Forest Corner,
Edwinstowe, Nottinghamshire NG21 9RN
Tel/Fax: 01623 822250
e-mail: dougledger@hotmail.com

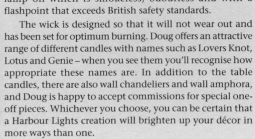

Doug Ledger trained as a scientific glass engineer in
London and now combines that experience with artistic
inspiration to create the eye-catching glass oil candles
on display at **Harbour Lights** in the Sherwood Forest
Craft Centre. Doug's unique and elegant designs are all
blown by hand – you can actually watch him at work in
his studio here – and he is brilliantly imaginative in his use of colour. The candle wicks are made of
glass fibre, fully encased in the same durable glass as the lamp itself, and are submerged in ultra pure
lamp oil which is smokeless, odourless and with a
flashpoint that exceeds British safety standards.

The wick is designed so that it will not wear out and
has been set for optimum burning. Doug offers an attractive
range of different candles with names such as Lovers Knot,
Lotus and Genie – when you see them you'll recognise how
appropriate these names are. In addition to the table
candles, there are also wall chandeliers and wall amphora,
and Doug is happy to accept commissions for special one-
off pieces. Whichever you choose, you can be certain that
a Harbour Lights creation will brighten up your décor in
more ways than one.

the most readable reference book ever compiled.

A little way up the road leading northwards out of Edwinstowe is the **Sherwood Forest Visitor Centre**. Sherwood, the 'Shire Wood', was once a great woodland mass stretching from Nottingham to Worksop. Although only relatively small pockets of the original forest remain today, it is still possible to become lost amongst the trees. Whether or not Robin and his Merry Men ever did frolic in the greenshawe is, however, debatable. Arguments still rage as to which particular historical figure gave rise to the legend of the famous outlaw. Records from the 12th century suggest a number of possible candidates, including the Earl of Huntingdon.

During the 15th century, several references to the outlaw can be found in the writings of two Scottish historians. In 1521 a third Scotsman, John Major, wrote *"About the time of King Richard I, according to my estimate, the famous English robbers Robert Hood and Little John were lurking in their woods, preying on the goods of the wealthy."* However, none of the historians gave any clues as to the sources of their writings. By the 16th century, there were two conflicting stories emerging as to the birthplace of Robin, one suggesting Kirklees whilst the other suggested Locksley.

Tracing the stories of Robin Hood is a difficult task as the tales, which have been told for over 600 years, were spoken rather than written since few local people could read and write. One of the earliest known stories of the outlaw's exploits can be found on a piece of parchment which dates from the mid-15th century but it was not until William Caxton set up his printing press in London in 1477 that cheaper books could be produced. From then on, the story of Robin Hood, his merry band of men, Guy of Gisborne, and the evil Sheriff of Nottingham has inspired countless books and at least a dozen major films. Amongst others, the medieval outlaw has been portrayed by Douglas Fairbanks, Kevin Costner and Sean Connery.

Undeterred by the vague foundations upon which the legend is built, visitors still flock to see the great hollow tree which the outlaws purportedly used as a meeting place and as a cache for their supplies. The **Major Oak** is located about 10 minutes walk along the main track in the heart of the forest and presents a rather forlorn appearance. Its 30ft girth and branches 260ft in circumference are now supported by massive wooden crutches and iron corsets. There is no denying that the tree is at least 500 years old, and some sources claim its age to be

Continued on page 254

STONE TREASURES

Unit 4, Sherwood Forest Craft Centre, Forest Corner, Edwinstowe, Notts. NG21 9RN
Tel/Fax: 01623 824976   website: www.stonetreasures.com

What started as a hobby for Richard Hawkes some 30 years ago developed into a business when, together with his son Mark, he established **Stone Treasures** in 1989. Here, he and Mark offer a wide range of fine fossils, gemstones and jewellery, much of which is made on site using Blue John, amber, Whitby jet and other semi-precious stones. They also stock mineral specimens from all over the UK along with amethysts from South America. Impressively, the Hawkes even have an ammonite named after them following their discovery of a hitherto unknown type at Lyme Regis in February 2001.

WALK 5

Edwinstowe, Birklands and the Major Oak

Start	Sherwood Forest Country Park, ½ mile (800m) north of Edwinstowe
Distance	7 miles (11.3 km), Shorter version 6 miles (9.7km)
Approximate time	3½ hours, 3 hours for shorter walk
Parking	Sherwood Forest Country Park
Refreshments	Café at visitor centre, pubs and cafés at Edwinstowe, pub at Clipstone
Ordnance Survey maps	Landranger 120 (Mansfield and Worksop, Sherwood Forest), Pathfinder 780, SK66/76 (Ollerton)

This is the classic Sherwood Forest walk that reveals the now largely-vanished landscape of the traditional English greenwood at its finest and most varied. The walk includes a pleasant stroll beside the River Maun and a detour to view the scanty remains of King John's Palace at Clipstone, then continues through the glorious oak and birch woodlands of Birklands (which claims to be the largest area of ancient oak forest in Western Europe) and across the open heathland of Budby South Forest. Near the end you pass by the mighty Major Oak, the most visited spot in Sherwood and a fitting finale to the walk. The shorter version omits the detour to Clipstone.

At the entrance to the visitor centre, take the path signposted 'Edwinstowe Village'. At a crossroads of paths turn left to emerge from the trees and skirt the left side of a cricket field to reach a road **A**. Continue along the road through the village, passing to the left of Edwinstowe's fine 13th century church, the legendary setting for the marriage between Robin Hood and Maid Marian.

At a crossroads keep ahead down High Street, and after crossing the River Maun, turn right along Mill Lane. Just before reaching a railway bridge, turn right **B**, at a public bridleway sign, on to a path beside the tree-lined banks of the Maun. Turn right to cross a footbridge over the river, keep ahead across another one and turn left at the footpath sign in front. Walk initially along the right edge of

a field, then along the right inside edge of woodland above the river, and finally alongside the Maun to a T-junction of tracks by a brick bridge **C**.

*The shorter walk turns right here on to a track, picking up the route where **C** next appears in the text.*

For the detour to Clipstone, turn left over the brick bridge and keep ahead towards a railway bridge. Go under the first of two bridges, turn right between two railway embankments and bear left to pass under another bridge. Continue along a broad track into Clipstone **D** for a view of King John's Palace, a medieval royal hunting lodge built not by John but by his father Henry II in the 12th century. It is hard to believe that these

WALK 5

now scanty and forlorn-looking ruins were used frequently by medieval kings while hunting in Sherwood, and that even meetings of Parliament were held here.

Retrace your steps to the bridge over the River Maun **C** and keep ahead along the track, heading up to pass to the left of Archway House, built by the 4th Duke of Portland in 1842 as a replica of the gatehouse of Worksop Priory, except that the statues are of Sherwood outlaws rather than saints! Continue through trees to a road, turn right and after 200 yds (183m) turn left **E**, at a public bridleway sign, along a narrow, winding path that later becomes a straight track. Keep ahead at the first bridleway sign and continue to a crossroads of tracks by the Centre Tree **F**, a tall oak that is supposed to mark the centre of the forest. Turn right, pass beside a metal barrier and after 100 yds (91m) you come to a three-way fork.

Take the left-hand path and continue through the oaks and silver birches of Birklands, the best-preserved part of the old forest. This is a superb section of the walk as you wander past giant oaks – some of them dead or dying, with often grotesquely twisted shapes that look positively menacing. Here, too, are masses of slender silver birches and glades of grass and bracken, all amidst a landscape that can have changed little since the days of Robin Hood and the Sheriff of Nottingham.

Keep ahead at all path junctions, eventually entering the Dukeries Training Area and emerging into the open heathland of Budby South Forest. While in this training area it is most important that you do not stray off the waymarked rights of way. Keep in a straight line, following a series of yellow waymarks, to reach a broad track on the corner of woodland **G**. Here turn sharp right to head back along a sandy track across the heathland, following the regular yellow-topped posts, to re-enter Birklands. After passing beside a wooden barrier you leave the Dukeries Training Area and keep ahead through more ancient oak and birch woodland to a crossroads of tracks **H**.

Turn right along a well-constructed, broad track, signposted Major Oak, and keep by a fence on the left, curving left to arrive at the veteran giant, an awe-inspiring sight. The tree gets its name from Major Rooke who first identified and described it in 1799. Estimates of its age vary from around 500–600 years, well past the normal age of an oak, and it has to receive much attention to prolong its life, including being supported by iron chains and wooden props to prevent its massive branches from breaking off.

From the Major Oak continue along the track, following signs to the visitor centre and passing more ancient oaks, to return to the start. ●

nearer to 1,000 years. Despite its decayed appearance the tree is still alive thanks to careful preservation. Recent tests have established that some parts of the tree have successfully taken to grafting and there are hopes that at some stage a whole colony of minor oaks may be produced.

The Major Oak, Sherwood Forest

The visitor centre also houses a display of characters from the Robin Hood stories, with appropriate scenes of merry making. This theme has also been successfully translated to the city of Nottingham in the Tales of Robin Hood exhibition.

Another impressive attraction in Edwinstowe is the **Sherwood Forest Fun Park**, which can be found to the north of the A6075 Mansfield to Ollerton road. This family-run funfair contains a variety of popular fairground rides including dodgems, a ghost train, and a giant

---

STAG PINE

Unit 9, Sherwood Forest Craft Centre, Forest Corner, Edwinstowe, Notts NG21 9RN
Tel: 01636 700142 Mobile: 07703 524977

Born in Scotland and trained as a carpenter/joiner, John Adamson has since 1998 had his own workshop, **Stag Pine**, within the Sherwood Forest Craft Centre. Here he produces a comprehensive range of furniture of every kind – bookshelves, chests of drawers, tables, chairs, stools, sideboards, dressers, radiator covers, mirrors, picture frames and much, much more. John specialises in fitted bedrooms, kitchens and bathrooms, all made to measure in quality pine, as well as

barrel-back dome corner units and glass fronted display cabinets.

All the pieces are available in a variety of different finishes – hand-waxed, modern lacquered finish or farmhouse painted finish – and John can supply an extensive range of accessories such as knobs, hinges and handles. He is also happy to give advice on repairs to any of your own pieces that may be in a distressed condition. Stag Pine also offers a delivery service "Anywhere in the U.K. London – Paris – Newark!" Prices are very reasonable and John's quality furniture will certainly add a touch of class to any decorative scheme.

Astroglide. The park is open daily, 10.00 to dusk between mid-March and mid-October, and admission is free, pay as you go on the rides.

Not far from Edwinstowe, off the A6075, is the **Sherwood Pines Forest Farm Park**, a naturalist and animal lover's delight. Enjoying a peaceful setting in a secluded valley on the edge of Sherwood Forest, the Farm Park boasts no fewer than 30 rare and threatened species of farm animal and is beautifully laid out, with ornamental ponds and three wildfowl lakes. A peaceful spot to relax can be found by visitors even on the busiest of days. The pets' corner and the aviary of exotic birds is always a delight. There is so much to see and do here that it is every bit as much a fun day out for the adults as for the younger family members. Youngsters will appreciate the adventure playground and everyone can enjoy playing spot the baby wallabies in their mums' pouches while wandering round the scenic farmland.

A couple of miles south-east of Edwinstowe is **Vicar Water Country Park.** Open daily throughout the year, from dawn to dusk, the Park covers 80 hectares of attractive countryside, complete with a large lake, and provides excellent walking, fishing, cycling and horse-riding. Footpaths and bridleways link the Park to the Sherwood Pines

Forest Farm Park; the Timberland Trail; the Maun Valley Way and the Robin Hood Way. The Visitor Centre has ample information about the area and also a café.

AROUND EDWINSTOWE

CUCKNEY
5 miles NW of Edwinstowe on the A60

Five main roads converge on this sizeable village which in medieval times was a marshy island. A large mound in the churchyard is all that is left of Thomas de Cuckney's 12th century castle. Because the nearby church was built on the marshes it was necessary in the 1950s to shore it up by building a concrete platform underneath. In the course of this work the remains of hundreds of skeletons were uncovered. At first it was thought the bones were the grisly relics of some 12th century battle. More recent research has revealed that the remains are much older. They have now been linked to the 7th century Battle of Heathfield between Edwin of Northumbria and Penda of Mercia.

An estate village to the country seat of the Dukes of Portland, Welbeck Abbey, Cuckney is made up of farm workers cottages. Along with Clumber House, Thoresby Hall, and Rufford Abbey, **Welbeck Abbey** makes up the four large

ROBIN'S DEN

17 High Street, Edwinstowe, nr Mansfield, Notts. NG21 9QP
Tel: 01623 824117

Set in the heart of Robin Hood Country, Edwinstowe is known as the "Robin Hood Village" so it's appropriate that **Robin's Den** should be devoted to souvenirs and gifts connected in some way with the legendary man in Lincoln green. Established in 1987 by Winona Turvill, a former Chairman of the Chamber of Trade, this High Street shop is stocked with a tremendous selection of Robin Hood souvenirs, Nottingham Lace items, quality cards and other gift ideas. Kids love the Robin Hood outfits and "Tatty" bears while grown-ups will find plenty of choice amongst the glassware, candle sets and other crafts on sale.

estates in this area of Nottinghamshire, all owned by Dukes. Naturally, the area become known as The Dukeries. It was the 5th Duke of Portland who began, in 1854, an extensive building programme that turned Welbeck into what is seen today. The most impressive of his additions was the riding school, the second largest in the world, complete with a peat floor and gas jet lighting. The building is now owned by the Ministry of Defence and is used as an Army training college, though the abbey and the grounds have been maintained in perfect condition.

CLUMBER PARK

4 miles N of Edwinstowe off the A614

Clumber Park (NT) was created in 1707 when the 3rd Duke of Newcastle was granted permission by Queen Anne to enclose part of the Forest of Sherwood as a hunting ground. The building of Clumber House began in 1760 though it was much altered in the early 19th century. After a devastating fire in 1879, the house was rebuilt in an Italianate style but, due to the vast expense of its upkeep, Clumber House was demolished in 1938. All that remains today are the foundations.

However, any sense of disappointment is quickly dispelled by the charm of the buildings that remain in this lovely setting. The estate houses with their high pitched gables and massive chimneys are most picturesque. The red-brick stables are particularly fine as they are surmounted by a clocktower crowned by a domed cupola. The inset clock in the tower dates back to 1763 and the stables now house the café and visitor centre.

By far the most striking building on the estate, however, is the **Chapel of St Mary the Virgin**, built by G.F. Bodley in the 1880s. It was commissioned by the 7th Duke of Newcastle to commemorate his

coming of age. A fervent Anglo-Catholic, he spent the then-colossal sum of £30,000 on its construction. The church has many elaborate features including some wonderful stone and woodwork.

The 4000-acre Clumber Park is owned by the National Trust and attracts more than a million visitors each year. The man-made lake is particularly lovely and is crossed by a fine classical bridge. Five different roads enter the park and each entrance is marked by an impressive gateway. Most imposing of them all is the Apleyhead Gate, off the A614, which leads into the glorious Duke's Drive. Stretching for a distance of two miles, the drive is the longest double avenue of limes in Europe and contains some 1296 trees.

PERLETHORPE

4 miles NE of Edwinstowe off the A614

Situated in the valley of the River Meden, Perlethorpe lies within the estate of **Thoresby Hall**, at the eastern end of Thoresby Lake. The first hall was built in the late 17th century for the Earl of Kingston but this was destroyed in 1745 and replaced by a Palladian-style mansion. The hall seen today is a Victorian mansion built by Anthony Salvin in 1864 for the Pierrepont family and is surrounded by the largest park in the county. The Hall itself is now a hotel.

The village church, which was completed in 1876, was built by Salvin at the same time as he was working on the hall. At the beginning of the 20th century Lady Manvers of the great hall took a keen interest in the welfare of the village children and was always informed of any who did not attend Sunday school. She would then visit them and scold those who had failed in their duty. But if a child had been absent because of sickness, she would ensure that hot soup was delivered until the child was well again.

Old Ollerton

2 miles E of Edwinstowe off the A614/A6075

Not to be confused with the more workaday town of New Ollerton, Old Ollerton is a delightfully preserved cluster of old houses, a charming Georgian coaching inn covered in creeper, and a church set beside the River Maun. Straddling the river is **Ollerton Water Mill**, more than 300 years old. Visitors are welcome to wander around the ancient building with its huge water wheel, browse in the Exhibition Area, watch a short video illustrating the age-old milling process, or sample the refreshments in the tea room.

The name of the village was originally Alreton, or Allerton, meaning farm among the alders, and the alders still grow here along the banks of the River Maun. The village lay on the road from London to York (though now it is bypassed) and also on the roads from Newark to Worksop and Lincoln to Mansfield. As a consequence, Ollerton developed as a meeting place for Sherwood Forest officials and the inns became staging posts during the coaching era.

Wellow

2 miles SE of Ollerton on the A616

This pretty conservation village is located on the site of an early settlement and was once fortified by an earthwork and, on the western side, by Gorge Dyke. The remains of the earthwork can still be seen and villagers have retained the right to graze their cattle on enclosed land. On the village green stands the tallest permanent **Maypole** in England - 60ft high, colourfully striped like a barber's pole, and with a cockerel perched on the top. Because earlier wooden poles rotted away, were stolen or got knocked down, this one is made of steel and firmly fixed

in place. It was erected to commemorate Elizabeth II's Silver Jubilee in 1976 and forms the focus for the May Day festivities held on the Spring Bank Holiday Monday. The jollities include dancing around the Maypole and the crowning of a May Queen.

Other notable features of this surprising village include a **Ducking-stool**; part of the old stocks; and a 17th century case clock in the 12th century parish **Church of St Swithin**. The clock face was made locally to commemorate the coronation of Elizabeth II in 1953. Each year on 19th September, the three church bells, which are between 300 and 400 years old, are rung in memory of a certain Lady Walden. Some 200 years ago she was paying a visit to Wellow and became lost in a local wood. Following the sound of the church bells, Lady Walden eventually found her way to the village and, such was her relief, that she left money for the bells to be rung each year on that day.

Laxton

4 miles E of Ollerton off the A6075

Laxton is unique since it is one of a handful of places in the country that have managed to retain their open field farming system. Devised in the Middle Ages, this system was generally abandoned in the 18th and 19th centuries when the enclosure of agricultural land took place. The fields have been strip farmed here for about 1,200 years and the system ensured that farmers had an equal share of both good and poor land. A farmer could hold as many as 100 strips, representing about 30 acres. In the 1600s the strips were, on average, about half an acre in size but, with the advent of more efficient means of ploughing, this increased to three-quarters of an acre. The familiar three year crop rotation also ensured productive use of the land.

Another unique feature of this fascinating village is the magnificent **Dovecote Inn**, which is owned (but not run) by the Queen. Here, a form of manorial government that has survived from medieval times still continues. Each winter, villagers gather at the inn each winter to appoint a jury which is then responsible for inspecting the fallow fields in the next cycle. The jurors tour the fields left fallow for the past year then adjourn for lunch back at the Dovecote. During the afternoon they then discuss any offences committed by farmers. A week later comes the Court meeting. The 18th century was a great time of rebuilding in Laxton and many of the houses display the patterned brickwork that was typical of this period. The still visible stonework around the bottom of some buildings suggests that the foundations were of much older timber framed constructions.

Just north of the village, along a lane close to the church, is another fascinating aspect of Laxton's medieval history. This is the Norman motte, or **Castle Mound**, which lies almost hidden beneath the trees. At the beginning of the 12th century, the stewardship of Sherwood Forest moved to Laxton and the village became the administrative centre for the forest. As a consequence, the motte and bailey castle was one of the biggest in this part of the country. Although no ruined keep or crumbling walls exist today, the castle earthworks are still the largest and best preserved in the county.

EGMANTON

5 miles E of Ollerton off the A1

Reached by quiet winding lanes, Egmanton is little visited these days but during the Middle Ages a local woman claimed to have had a vision of the

---

BRECKS COTTAGE

Green Lane, Moorhouse, Newark, Notts. NG23 6LZ
Tel: 01636 822445 Fax: 01636 821384
e-mail: bandb@breckscottage.co.uk
website: www.breckscottage.co.uk

Located in the tiny hamlet of Moorhouse, just 4.5 miles from the A1, **Brecks Cottage** is a friendly, family-run guest house offering excellent bed & breakfast accommodation. Built of warm red brick and dating from the 1600s, it combines all the charm of a traditional beamed farm cottage with the convenience of first class modern facilities. Your hosts, Sue and John Thomas, make sure their guests start the day well with a superb breakfast freshly prepared from local produce. Special diets can be catered for by arrangement. The 3 guest bedrooms (2 doubles; 1 twin) are attractively furnished and decorated, and have colour TV, bathrobes and beverage facilities.

Guests have the use of a comfortable lounge; internet, e-mail and video facilities are available on request, as are guest safes. Children are welcome, so too are pets, and stabling is also available. There's ample off-road parking and some good quality restaurants and pubs are within easy reach. Brecks Cottage is in the heart of Sherwood Forest – "Robin Hood Country" – and conveniently located for visiting glorious Southwell Minster and Lincoln Cathedral as well as the market towns of Retford and Newark on Trent. Newark is an antique collector's paradise, staging world famous Antiques Fairs several times a year.

Virgin Mary. The **Shrine of Our Lady of Egmanton** became a major place of pilgrimage right up until the Reformation.

The cult was revived in 1896 by the 7th Duke of Newcastle who commissioned Sir Ninian Comper to completely restore and redecorate the church. The result is an exuberant recreation of a medieval church with all its colour and graven images. The exterior is really quite modest but the interior is resplendent and inspiriting, with the light from many tapers and candles helping to create a mesmerising atmosphere.

Rufford
2 miles S of Ollerton off the A614

Rufford Abbey was founded in 1148 by Gilbert de Gant as a daughter house to Rievaulx Abbey. During the Dissolution it suffered the fate of many religious houses and came into the hands of the 6th Earl of Shrewsbury, fourth husband of the redoubtable Bess of Hardwick. The Earl pulled down most of the abbey and built a grand Elizabethan mansion. All that remains of the abbey is a vaulted crypt, said to be haunted by the ghost of a giant monk with a skull-like face. According to the parish register for Edwinstowe, a man died of fright after catching sight of this unholy visitor!

The abbey's stable block now houses an impressive craft centre while the restored 18th century Orangery hosts modern sculpture exhibitions.

The grounds of the abbey, now the **Rufford Country Park**, are well worth a visit. In addition to the nine formal gardens near the house, there are also some hides where birdwatchers can overlook a portion of the lake which has been designated a bird sanctuary. In the grounds too stands an 18th century corn mill, now home to a display of Nottinghamshire history, and two

icehouses dating from the mid-1800s. As well as the majestic Lime Avenue, there is also the Broad Ride, at the southern end of which are several animal graves. Most were pets belonging to the family at the house but one grave is that of the racehorse Cremorne, the 1872 Derby winner.

Bilsthorpe
4 miles S of Ollerton off the A614

The hall where, during the Civil War, Charles I is reputed to have hidden in a cupboard still exists but is now incorporated into a farm that stands opposite the village church.

Bilsthorpe remained a quiet farming community, as it had been for many centuries, right up until 1922 when a coal mine was sunk in the village by Stanton Ironworks. An explosion at the mine with a subsequent loss of life brought the vicar and the mine manager into a dispute over compensation. The manager, unwilling to pay out, built a wooden church away from the main part of the village and near the temporary accommodation provided for the mine workers.

Farnsfield
7 miles S of Ollerton off the A614

Close to the crossroads of the A614/A617 near Farnsfield are two popular family attractions. **White Post Modern Farm Centre** is a working farm with more than 4,000 animals, amongst them llamas, deer, owls, piglets, chicks and even mice. Designed for younger children, **Wonderland Pleasure Park & Garden Centre** offers a large tropical house with exotic butterflies and reptiles; a large indoor soft play area; pets' centre; miniature railway; junior rollercoaster and much more. Both attractions are open daily all year round.

In Farnsfield village itself traces of a

PORTLAND HALL HOTEL

Carr Bank Park, Windmill Lane, Mansfield, Notts. NG18 2AL
Tel: 01623 452525 Fax: 01623 452550
e-mail: enquiries@portlandhallhotel.co.uk
website: www.portlandhallhotel.com

Portland Hall Hotel is a gracious Georgian mansion built in 1805 and once owned by the Duke of Portland. A Grade II listed building, it stands in 15 acres of the most beautiful parkland and within the Carr Bank Park conservation area but still almost in the centre of Mansfield, close to the M1, A1 and East Midlands Airport. It is ideally placed for Nottingham, Sheffield, Derby, Lincoln and Leicester as well as the Peak District National Park and Sherwood Forest. A number of first class golf courses are within easy reach.

Popular amenities include the relaxing Lounge Bar and the elegant Restaurant, both of which are in the front of the building on the ground floor overlooking the beautifully maintained park. The Restaurant serves an extensive range of high quality traditional English cuisine, served from a highly recommended Carvery, and is an ideal venue for a private business lunch, a friendly meal with family or friends, or just a quiet dinner for two. Daily vegetarian options are available.

The hotel has ten guest bedrooms, all with en suite facilities, direct line telephones, television, video, hospitality tray and all the usual executive facilities in each room. Several rooms have 4-poster beds.

On selected weekends the hotel offers live entertainment by way of a disco, jazz group or musical cabaret to accompany your evening meal – an ideal combination for anniversaries, birthday parties or other special occasions. For the most special occasion of all, Portland Hall can provide a complete wedding package. It is licensed to hold Civil Wedding ceremonies; the lovely grounds present a perfect backdrop for wedding photographs; guests can enjoy a sumptuous wedding breakfast and the happy couple can disco the night away with family and friends before retiring to the magnificent bridal suite with its 4-poster bed.

Equally, the hotel can provide a complete range of business facilities for conferences, meetings or training in the Conference Suite.

Roman camp can be found and the ghost of a Roman soldier is reputed to haunt one of village's pubs. More recently, the village was the birthplace of the explorer, Augustus Charles Gregory. After emigrating to Australia, Gregory became the first person to explore the country's interior. The Royal Geographical Society commissioned an expedition led by him in 1855, a journey during which 5,000 miles of the country was mapped. Gregory's respect for the native culture earned him the unofficial title of 'Protector of the Aborigines'.

RAINWORTH

7 miles SW of Ollerton off the A617

Pronounced 'Renoth' locally, this is a mining village and its development is solely due to the now closed pits. There are, however, two very different places of interest within the village. **Rainworth Water**, a series of lakes and streams, which attracts walkers, naturalists, and fishermen, is also the site of a bird sanctuary founded by the naturalist Joseph Whitaker.

Rainworth's other claim to fame is its fish and chip shop which found itself on the front pages of the national newspapers in the early 1980s as the place where the Black Panther was caught. A local shopkeeper had noticed a man loitering in the area and had contacted the police who kept a watch for the suspicious man on the main street of the village. Suddenly realising that he was being followed, the suspect began shooting at the police, injuring one, but the customers in the chip shop, seeing what was going on, apprehended the man. Though at the time the police did not know the identity of the gunman he later turned out to be the notorious Black Panther who was later convicted of murder.

RAVENSHEAD

9 miles SW of Ollerton on the A60

Although the name Ravenshead appears in the Domesday Book, the village of Ravenshead is relatively new and dates from 1966 when the three hamlets of Fishpool, Larch Farm, and Kighill merged. Situated by the side of the main road is the Bessie Shepherd Stone which marks the spot where, in 1817, Bessie was murdered as she walked from Mansfield to Papplewick.

Longdale Lane Rural Craft Centre was established in the 1970s and it is the oldest such centre in the country. It's a re-creation of a 19th century village, complete with flagstones and Victorian street lamps. Behind the decorative, period shop fronts a whole host of professional artists can be seen making both traditional and modern objects.

MANSFIELD

The second largest town in the county, Mansfield stands at the heart of what were once the great North Nottinghamshire coalfields. That industry has now vanished but Mansfield still has the atmosphere of an industrial town although its economy is now based on a broader spread of varying business.

The most distinctive structure in Mansfield is undoubtedly the great railway viaduct that sweeps through and above the town, carried by 15 huge arches of rough-hewn stone. Built in 1875, it is one of the largest viaducts to be found in an English town and gives some dignity to a community which suffered badly from thoughtless development in the 1960s.

The old market place still hosts markets on Mondays, Thursdays, Fridays, and Saturdays with colourful stalls gathered around the impressive Gothic

Bentinck Monument. This was erected in 1848 in memory of Lord George Bentinck, the younger son of the Duke of Portland. Bentinck was a long serving Member of Parliament for the town and a great friend of Disraeli. The memorial was raised by public subscription but unfortunately funds ran out before the finishing touch, a statue of Bentinck himself, could be placed in the central space.

Standing just to the northwest of the market place, **Mansfield Museum** (free) concentrates its collections largely on local interest and includes a model of a Roman villa that once stood at nearby Mansfield Woodhouse. The collection spans the centuries from that early occupation right up to more recent times, with pictures and artefacts relating to the industry of the town and surrounding villages. The adjoining art gallery also carries a local theme and features works by artists of the area including the water-colourist A.S. Buxton, who is well known for his paintings of Mansfield.

AROUND MANSFIELD

MANSFIELD WOODHOUSE
2 miles N of Mansfield on the A60

Originally a settlement within Sherwood Forest, Mansfield Woodhouse is now virtually a suburb of Mansfield but the core of the village remains remarkably intact and several interesting buildings have survived.

Opposite **The Cross**, in the heart of the town, stands one of these fine houses, the Georgian Burnaby House. Still retaining many of its original, elegant features the house was obviously built for a prosperous family and, during the mid-1800s, it was occupied by the Duke of Portland's land agent. On the other side of the road stands a stump which is all that remains of the Market Cross, erected here after a great fire in 1304. The village stocks also stood close by and they were once used to detain George Fox, the Quaker Movement founder, after he had preached the gospel to the villagers.

At the bottom of the street stands the oldest building in Mansfield Woodhouse, **St Edmund's Church**. Most of the original church was lost, along with the parish records, when fire swept through the village in the early 14th century. The present church was built on the same site though it underwent some severe restoration in the 19th century. Standing not far from the church is a manor house known as **Woodhouse Castle** because of the battlements which were added to the building in the early 1800s. Dating from

BLUE BARN FARM

Langwith, Mansfield, Notts NG20 9JD
Tel/Fax: 01623 742248
e-mail: bluebarnfarm@supanet.com

Blue Barn Farm stands at the heart of a 450-acre family-run working farm on the lovely Welbeck Estate bordering the edge of Sherwood Forest. The Ibbotson family offer a choice of bed & breakfast or self-catering accommodation. B&B guests stay in the spacious Victorian farmhouse which has 3 guest bedrooms (1 twin en suite; 1 double room; 1 family room) all with wash basins and TV. Guests have the use of a comfortable lounge with colour TV and a peaceful garden. For self catering, Blue Barn Cottage has 4 bedrooms, lounge, dining room; fully fitted kitchen and utility room.

the 1600s, this was the home of the Digby family and, in particular, of General Sir John Digby, Sheriff of Nottingham, who distinguished himself during the Civil War.

Another building of note is the essentially 18th century **Wolfhunt House** found just off the High Street. The unusual name is derived from a local tale which suggests that the land on which the house is built once belonged to a man who was employed to frighten away the wolves in Sherwood Forest by blowing a hunting horn.

SKEGBY

2 miles W of Mansfield off the A6075

Skegby's church had to be rebuilt in the 1870s because of mining subsidence but some interesting features were salvaged from the old church: some monuments to the Lindley family; a fine east window; and two delightful effigies from

the early 1300s showing a Sherwood Forester and his wife. She is dressed in a wimple and long gown; he carries a hunting horn.

The village is lucky in having a particularly fine example of a 14th century cruck cottage though this was not discovered until restoration work was taking place on the building in the 1950s. The village's pinfold, the place where stray animals were held until their owner claimed them, has also been restored and can be found on the Mansfield road.

TEVERSAL

3 miles W of Mansfield off the B6014

A rural oasis in the heart of this former mining district, Teversal stands on a hill looking across to the lovely Elizabethan Hardwick Hall which is actually just over the border in Derbyshire. Teversal village is the fictional home of Lady Chatterley

GOFF'S RESTAURANT

Langwith Mill House, Nether Langwith, nr Mansfield, Notts. NG20 9JF
Tel: 01623 744538 Fax: 01623 747953
e-mail: goodfood@goffs.60freeserve.co.uk
website: www.goffsrestaurant.co.uk

Generally regarded as one of North Nottinghamshire's premier eating places, **Goff's Restaurant** occupies a stone-built former cotton mill in a delightful rural setting. Wildfowl swim by on the old mill pool, there's a flower-filled terrace where patrons can enjoy a pre-meal drink, while inside candlelit tables, trimly pinafored young waitresses and an eclectic décor all add to the charm. Before moving here in 1989 the restaurant was located over Graham Goff's butcher's shop in Warsop.

Graham's skills as a master butcher continue to provide the talented

young chefs with top quality ingredients for their imaginative dishes – Gamekeeper's Roast, for example, succulent boned duck stuffed with game. Goff's Restaurant's various rooms include one that is ideal for private dinner parties of up to twelve people and the rural location with its backdrop of the historic old mill provides an ideal setting for special celebrations. During the summer months there's also the option of holding parties in the garden when up to 100 additional guests can be catered for in a marquee in the grounds. Recently, Graham has opened a new butcher's shop in Queen's Street, Southwell which caters for the needs of the restaurant as well as the good people of Southwell.

and the woodlands of the Hardwick Hall estate were the meeting place for her and gamekeeper Mellors in D.H. Lawrence's *Lady Chatterley's Lover.*

The village also boasts, according to Pevsner, *"one of the most rewarding village churches in the county"*. It has a Norman door, 12th century arcades and a 15th century tower but eclipsing all these are the wonderful 17th century fittings, all marvellously intact. A wealth of colourful hatchments, ornate monuments to the Molyneux and Carnavon families, Lords of the Manor, and original box pews all add to the interest. The Carnavons own family pew has embroidered cushions and is set apart from the lowlier seating by four spiral columns which give it the appearance of a four-poster bed.

SUTTON IN ASHFIELD
2 miles SW of Mansfield on the A38

This once small village expanded over the years as a result of local coal mining and modern development has not been kind. However, a few of the original 17th and 18th century cottages can be seen near the Church of St Mary Magdalene. The church contains some Norman work on the west wall, 13th century arcades and a 14th century spire. A tombstone lying beside the path leading to the porch commemorates a certain Ann Burton who achieved the remarkable feat of dying on the 30th February 1836.

ANNESLEY WOODHOUSE
5 miles SW of Mansfield on the A608

All that remains of old Annesley is the roofless ruin of what D.H. Lawrence described as a *"mouldering church standing high on a bank by the roadside...black and melancholy above the shrinking head of the traveller"*. Another great writer also knew the village well. Annesley Hall was the home of Mary Chaworth, a lady for whom Lord Byron formed an early affection. The poet and the beautiful heiress would often walk up to the breezy summit of Diadem Hill, 578ft high and visible for miles around. The liaison was a little odd since Mary had inherited her great fortune from William Chaworth: William had been killed in a duel by Byron's great uncle, the 5th Lord Byron. Perhaps because of this unfortunate event, Mary did not succumb to the poet's charms. Instead she married John Musters, the sporting squire of Colwick Hall near Nottingham. She died there in 1832 as the result of an attack on the Hall by Reform Bill rioters.

NEWSTEAD
5 miles S of Mansfield off the A608

A magnificent 13th century ruin attached to a Victorian reworking of a Tudor mansion provides one of the county's most historic houses. **Newstead Abbey** was founded by Henry II around 1170 as part of his atonement for the murder of Thomas à Becket, and sold at the Dissolution of the Monasteries to Sir John Byron who destroyed much of the Abbey and converted other buildings into a mansion. The Newstead estate remained in the Byron family for almost 300 years, its last owner being the celebrated (and notorious) poet, George Lord Byron.

He inherited the property from his great uncle, the 5th Lord Byron, better known as 'Devil Byron'. As mentioned earlier, the 5th Lord had killed an old family friend in a duel and although he was only convicted of manslaughter, he was obliged to pay huge punitive costs. Ostracised by London society, he retreated to Newstead in malevolent mood. To pay his debts he virtually denuded the estate of its great

Newstead Abbey Wood

Col. Wildman spared no expense in refurbishing and extending the dilapidated house, an undertaking that took 12 years to complete. The house and grounds that visitors see today is essentially the creation of Thomas Wildman, but the presiding spirit of the house is undeniably that of the wayward poet.

Over the years, many Byron manuscripts, letters, books, pictures and personal relics have found their way back to the Abbey, and both the house and grounds are beautifully maintained by the present owners, the City of Nottingham, to whom the estate was bequeathed in 1931. The house is open every afternoon from April to September, and the grounds all year round. These include a secret garden; a beautifully carved fountain decorated with fantastic animals; the famous and elaborate memorial to Byron's dog Boatswain, and a large lake where the 5th lord used to re-enact naval battles.

Byron died from a fever while travelling in Greece supporting the patriot's war of independence against the Turks. His body was returned to England but his scandalous reputation for womanizing made a proposed burial in Westminster Abbey unthinkable. Instead, he was interred at Hucknall, a couple of miles south of Newstead Abbey.

plantations of oaks. And just to spite his son and expected heir he ordered the slaughter of the deer herd that had grazed the parkland for generations. As it happened his son died before him and the estate passed to that "brat from Aberdeen" as he referred to his impoverished great nephew who was living there in poverty with his mother.

When the poet arrived at Newstead in 1798, he found that the only room in this huge mansion without a leaking roof was the scullery. The estate was burdened with debts, and so was Byron. He managed to let the estate out for some years but when he finally took up residence in 1808 he was still hard put to make the house even reasonably habitable. In 1817 he gave up the struggle, sold the estate to an old Harrow schoolmate, Col. Thomas Wildman, for £94,000, removed himself to Italy and never saw Newstead again.

LINBY

6 miles S of Mansfield on the B6011

"One of the prettiest villages on the north side of Nottingham" was Pevsner's rather

cautious praise of this small village where a stream runs along the main street with broad grass verges, and enough stone built houses to face down the unfortunate sprawl of 1930s red brick houses near the church.

The village is situated on the banks of the River Leen which, during the late 18th century, was a busy, bustling place with six cotton mills being powered by the water. The mills were strictly functional but George Robinson, their owner, did not want to be out done by his near neighbours at Newstead Abbey so he added battlements and other ornate features and thus gave **Castle Mill** its name. Young apprentices were brought in from as far away as London to work in Castle Mill. Housed in small lodges near the mill, the children worked long hours weaving cotton cloth in terrible conditions with minimal food and clothing provided. Brought to work

in the mills from a young age (some were no more than 10 years old) many died early. In Linby churchyard the graves of 42 apprentice children bear witness to Robinson's callous pursuit of profit.

When the 5th Lord Byron dammed the River Leen upstream from Linby, in order to create a lake on his estate, he also played havoc with the water supply to the mills. With a reduction in power, Robinson had to find another reliable power source and in 1786 his sons were the first to apply steam power to a cotton mill when they installed a Boulton and Watt engine.

HUCKNALL

7 miles S of Mansfield off the A611

An undistinguished little industrial town, Hucknall nevertheless attracts a constant stream of visitors. They come to **St Mary Magdalen Church**, not so much for its 14th century font or for the

IVORY GATE ANTIQUES

Curiosity Corner, 86 Watnall Road, Hucknall,
Nottinghamshire NG15 7JW
Tel: 0115 963 0789
e-mail: ivorygateantique@aol.com

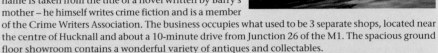

A former head teacher, Barry Orridge spent 38 years in the profession before retiring and setting up **Ivory Gate Antiques** with business partner Hannah Clayton. The name is taken from the title of a novel written by Barry's mother – he himself writes crime fiction and is a member of the Crime Writers Association. The business occupies what used to be 3 separate shops, located near the centre of Hucknall and about a 10-minute drive from Junction 26 of the M1. The spacious ground floor showroom contains a wonderful variety of antiques and collectables.

There's superb Georgian, Victorian and Edwardian furniture – davenports, bureaux, chests of drawers, dressers, tables and chairs – along with porcelain (including mining plates), Crown Derby dinner and teaware, antique boxes and silverware. You'll also find a good choice of collectables (such as antique dolls and toys) and works of art, including ethnic wooden carvings and oriental enamels. Ivory Gate also stocks a range of cut glass items and specialises in decanters. Free parking is available at the front and to the rear of the shop

27 attractive stained glass windows by Kempe, but to gaze at a simple marble slab set in the floor of the chancel. It bears the inscription: *BYRON, Born January 22nd, 1788, Died April 19th, 1824.*

The inscription is surmounted by a laurel wreath, in classical times the only award to winners in the original Olympic Games. The memorial was presented to the church in 1881 by the King of the Hellenes in appreciation of Byron's support for the Greeks against their imperial masters, the Turks.

Byron died in Greece where his body was embalmed and transported to England. For several days the body was exhibited at an inn in Nottingham before being buried in the Byron family crypt at Hucknall. Many years later, in 1938, the vicar of Hucknall entered the now closed crypt to challenge a tradition that the poet's body had been removed. He found the lid of the coffin loose and its lead lining cut open. *"Very reverently, I raised the lid, and before my eyes lay the embalmed body of Byron in as perfect condition as when it was placed in the coffin 114 years ago...The serene, almost happy expression on his face made a profound impression on me. The feet and ankles were uncovered, and I was able to establish the fact that his lameness had been that of his right foot".*

Hucknall boasts another famous son. Eric Coates, the son of a local doctor, was born here on 27th August 1886. He displayed musical talent at an early age, (he demanded and got his first violin at the age of 6), and became the most celebrated viola player of his generation. But Coates became even more famous as a composer of light music – his *Sleepy Lagoon* is immediately recognisable to millions as the signature music of BBC Radio's long-running programme *Desert Island Discs.*

SOMERCOTES SELSTON
9 miles SW of Mansfield on the B600

Mentioned in the Domesday Book as a place with a church and three acres of meadows, like many other village communities in this western area of Nottinghamshire, Somercotes Selston was at that time very much a farming community. But beneath the fertile agricultural land lay coal and leases for coal mining were granted as early as 1206. For centuries the coal mining operation remained small scale but by the 1850s Somercotes Selston had taken on many of the aspects of a modern colliery village. The last coal pit in Somercotes Selston closed in 1956 but almost half a century later the village still has a lacklustre air to it.

From the chuchyard of the partly-Norman Church of St Helen there are some splendid views across the neighbouring Derbyshire hills. The graveyard is the last resting place of Dan Boswell, king of the gypsies. For many years newborn gypsy babies were brought to Boswell's gravestone to be baptised and many gypsies made special journeys to the church to pay their respects.

EASTWOOD

"I have always hated it" wrote D.H. Lawrence of the mining town where he was born in 1885. Reviling the *"ugliness of my native village"*, he wished it could be pulled down, *"to the last brick"*. Local people reciprocated his dislike: *"He were nowt but a big soft gel"* said one of his contemporaries many years later when the gawky lad whose mum insisted he should never go down the pit had become a writer and painter of international repute.

The Lawrence family home, a two up, two down, terrace house at 8a Victoria

Street is now the **D.H. Lawrence Birthplace Museum.** It has been furnished in a late 19th century style with which the Lawrence family would have been familiar. There are also some household items on display which belonged to the family and anyone visiting the museum will see that the house's front window is larger than others in the same street. This is where Mrs Lawrence displayed children's clothes and other linen items which she made and sold to supplement the fluctuating wages brought home by her miner husband.

In 1887, the Lawrence family moved to a larger, end of terrace house in Eastwood which today is known as the Sons and Lovers Cottage since it featured as the Morels' house, The Bottoms, in Lawrence's novel. This house too is open to the public, though by appointment only, and is also laid out with furnishings and artefacts which are appropriate to the time. Lawrence's father was a miner at the nearby Brinsley Pit and though the family moved house in Eastwood several times, the Lawrences remained short of money. Young Lawrence attended the local school and was the first Eastwood boy to gain a scholarship to Nottingham High School where he was a pupil until 1901. Lawrence started his working life as a clerk before undertaking a teacher training course and moving to teach in a school in Croydon.

Though Lawrence had already begun writing, his major novels were not written until after 1912, the year he eloped with his former professor's wife and left England. Drawing heavily on the influences of his upbringing in Eastwood, *Sons and Lovers,* first published in 1913, not only describes the countryside around Eastwood but also portrays many local personalities. The

D H Lawrence Birthplace, Eastwood

unflattering descriptions of, amongst others, Lawrence senior, caused a great deal of local resentment, a resentment that astonishingly persists to this day in the village. Lawrence and his wife, Frieda Weekley, returned to England during World War I but they were unable to settle and at one point were detained as suspected German spies. They were soon on their travels once again.

In the early 1920s, Lawrence published *Women in Love* and, a few years later, was diagnosed with tuberculosis, the disease from which he died in 1930. It was whilst he was in Florence, trying unsuccessfully to find a cure for his crippling condition, that Lawrence wrote his most famous novel, *Lady Chatterley's Lover.* First published in 1928, the full text of the controversial story was not printed until 1960 and, even then, it was the subject of a court case that is almost as famous as the book.

A place of pilgrimage for devotees of Lawrence, Eastwood also attracts those with an interest in railway history. It was at the Sun Inn in the Market Place that a group of "Iron Masters and Coal Owners" gathered on 16th August 1832 to discuss the construction of a railway that would eventually become the mighty Midland Railway. A plaque on the wall of the inn commemorates the seminal meeting.

The railway was formed to compete with the **Erewash Canal**, completed in 1779 and effectively put out of business by the 1870s. Almost a century later, following years of neglect, the canal was cleared and made suitable for use by pleasure craft. The towpath was resurfaced and now provides a pleasant and interesting walk.

AROUND EASTWOOD

AWSWORTH
1 mile S of Eastwood on the A6096

In order to lay the tracks for the Great Northern Railway line from Derby to Nottingham, a viaduct was need to carry the railway over the Erewash Canal, the River Erewash, and the Nottingham Canal which all lie close to Awsworth. The resulting construction, built in 1876-7, is still an impressive sight though the line is now disused. One of only two viaducts in England to be made of wrought iron lattice girders, the **Bennerley Viaduct** has 16 spans, which are set on pillars 56 feet high.

COSSALL
3 miles S of Eastwood off the A6096

Now a conservation area, this village draped across a low hill boasts some attractive buildings, notably the picturesque 17th century Willoughby

almshouses and a farmhouse which includes part of the original home of the Willoughby family. They were a branch of the Willoughbys of Wollaton, a dynasty that was founded by a wealthy 13th century wool merchant from Nottingham named Ralph Bugge. This rather unfortunate name (which means hobgoblin) was understandably changed by his descendants to the more acceptable Willoughby; a name taken from the village of Willoughby-on-the-Wolds, on the border with Leicestershire, where Ralph owned a fair acreage of land.

Cossall was another of D.H. Lawrence's haunts and it featured in his novel *The Rainbow* as the village of 'Cossethay', home of the Brangwen family. The fictional character, William Brangwen, is said to have been based on Alfred Burrows, to whose daughter, Louise, Lawrence was engaged for some time. She duly appears as Ursula Brangwen. The Burrows family lived in a cottage, now marked by a plaque, near the charming village church which contains a fine marble tomb of the Willoughbys.

RETFORD

Retford is actually two communities, East and West Retford, set either side of the River Idle. West Retford is the elder settlement; its twin grew up during the 1100s as a place where tolls could be collected from travellers making the river crossing. Retford has been a market town since 1246 and markets are still held here every Thursday and Saturday.

Retford received a major economic boost in 1766 when the Great North Road was diverted through the town. That was when the Market Square was re-developed and some of the elegant Georgian buildings here, and in Grove Street, still survive from that time. The grand and rather chateau-like Town Hall, however, dates from 1868 and replaced the Georgian hall. Outside the Town Hall can be found the Broad Stone, which is probably the base of an old parish boundary cross. Tradition has it that during the times of the plague in Retford, in the mid-16th and mid-17th centuries, coins were placed in a pool of vinegar in the hollow in the top of the stone to prevent the disease from spreading whilst trading was taking place at the market.

In the northwestern corner of the square is an archway that leads down to the River Idle. Bearing the inscription "JP Esquire 1841", the archway once led to the gardens of John Parker who lived in a nearby house, now business premises. A close inspection of the garden wall will reveal that it has a hollow curve. This was in order to funnel hot air along the wall to warm the fruit trees grown in its shelter.

Cannon Square is home to one of Retford's more unusual attractions: a Russian cannon. Dating from 1855 and weighing over 2 tons, the cannon was captured by British soldiers at Sebastopol and brought to Retford at the end of the Crimean War. The townsfolk paid for its transportation and, in 1859, after arguments raged about its siting, the cannon was finally placed in the square and named the Earl of Aberdeen after the incumbent Prime Minister. During World War II the cannon was threatened with being melted down to help the war effort and was only saved after a Retford gentleman bought it and hid it until the war was over.

Not far from Cannon Square is, reputedly, the oldest chemist's shop in the country still on its original site. Opened in 1779, Norths Chemists first belonged to a local vet, Francis Clater, whose books on animal medicine and

treatment were bestsellers for over 100 years.

One of Retford's most infamous visitors was the highwayman Dick Turpin and several historic inns still stand as a reminder of the romantic days of stage coach travel. Another man who stood and delivered here, though in a more respectable fashion, was John Wesley, who conducted many open air meetings in East Retford.

Whilst in Retford, it is well worth visiting the **Bassetlaw Museum** (free) in Amcott House, Grove Street. This imposing late 18th century town house was once the home of the Whartons, the woollen drapers; Sir Wharton Amcotts, MP for the Borough of East Retford; and the Peglers, local industrialists. It was extensively restored and opened as a museum for the District of Bassetlaw in 1986. The house is noted for its finely executed internal plasterwork and elegant wrought iron staircase which the restoration has returned to their full Georgian splendour. The museum has a distinct local emphasis, with displays of local archaeology, civic, social and industrial history, and fine and applied art. Occupying the former service wing of the house, the **Percy Laws Memorial Gallery** has a permanent display of historic Retford civic plate and also hosts short term exhibitions.

AROUND RETFORD

MATTERSEY
6 miles N of Retford off the B6045

From the eastern end of the village, a rubbly lane leads down to the sparse ruins of the romantically sited **Mattersey Priory**, founded in 1185 for the Gilbertine Order, the only monastic order to be established by an Englishman, Roger de Mattersey. When the Priory was founded, it had only six canons. Though the number of priests fluctuated over the years, Mattersey was never a wealthy institution: at the time of the Dissolution of the Monasteries only five canons had to be turned out onto the streets. The original priory buildings at Mattersey were destroyed by fire in 1279 so the remains seen today are of the 14th century dormitory, refectory, and the walls of the Chapel of St Helen. The site is rarely visited by tourists but, with the River Idle flowing nearby, it is a peaceful and picturesque hidden place, well worth seeking out.

Gringley on the Hill

GRINGLEY ON THE HILL
7 miles NE of Retford on the A631

Gringley commands some astonishingly wide views over Yorkshire, Lincolnshire, and Nottinghamshire. The best vantage point is Beacon Hill (235ft), on the east side of the village. As the name suggests, Beacon Hill was used as the site for beacon fires designed to warn of impending invasion.

The village Church of St Peter and St Paul dates from the 12th century and one of the church bells is, rather unusually, dated to the time of the Commonwealth. During that period, bells and other decorative items were considered frivolous and were generally dispensed with but, as the parish records show, the people of Gringley did not subscribe to such kill-joy ideas: they also celebrated Christmas in defiance of Puritan edicts forbidding the festival.

NORTH LEVERTON
5 miles E of Retford off the A620

The correct name for this attractive village is 'North Leverton with Habblesthorpe', a mouthful which has been hailed in the *Guinness Book of Records* as the longest multiple place name in England.

The 12th century village Church of St Martin is reached via a bridge over a stream and with its 18th century Dutch gables looks rather like an import from Holland. So too does the splendid **North Leverton Windmill**, the only one in Nottinghamshire still grinding corn. When the mill was built in 1813, it was known as the 'North Leverton Subscription Mill' in acknowledgement of the farmers from four surrounding parishes who subscribed to the cost. Three storeys high, the elegant structure has four sails, one of which was struck by lightning in 1958. Thanks to the efforts of local people, assisted by financial support from the County Council, the mill is now fully operational and visitors can follow the whole milling process in action. If they wish, they can also purchase some of the freshly ground flour.

About 3 miles south of the village, **Sundown Kiddies Adventureland** is a unique theme park designed especially for the under 10s. There's a pet shop where the animals join in and sing a musical chorus; a Witches' Kitchen where the kids are in charge of the gruesome cuisine; rides; an adventure play area; café and much more.

BABWORTH
1 mile W of Retford on the A620

Babworth has a fine Georgian Hall, a church with Pilgrim Father associations and a spacious park laid out by Humphrey Repton – but virtually no village. Its inhabitants were moved to the village of Ranby, two miles to the west, when the park was "improved". The old Great North Road used to pass through Babworth and it was here, in 1503, that Margaret Tudor was entertained by the Alderman of Retford at a cost of £12.11s. (£12.55p). She was on her way to marry James IV of Scotland.

Inside the porch of the small Church of All Saints, with its battlements and pinnacles, a plaque records that the Pilgrim Fathers William Brewster and

William Bradford worshipped here before sailing in the *Mayflower*.

WORKSOP

Despite the unattractive modern houses lining the roads leading into Worksop, there are some fine Georgian buildings to be found in Bridge Street. One of the major attractions of Worksop is the **Priory Gatehouse**, which is best approached from Potter Street where the full glory of the 14th century building can be seen. Its great niches house large and beautifully carved statues and the immense entrance is rather reminiscent of a cave opening. Originally the portal to a large Augustinian monastery, the gatehouse together with the Church of St Mary and St Cuthbert is all that remains. There is also a wayside shrine, which makes it a unique ecclesiastical attraction. Today, the upper floor of the

---

THE BARNS COUNTRY GUESTHOUSE

Morton Farm, Babworth, Retford,
Nottinghamshire DN22 8HA
Tel: 01777 706336 Fax: 01777 709773
e-mail: peter@thebarns.co.uk
website: www.thebarns.co.uk

Located just a couple of miles off the A1 and close to the busy market town of Retford, **The Barns Country Guesthouse** offers quality bed & breakfast accommodation in a peaceful rural setting. Peter and Lynda Morton are your welcoming and helpful hosts at this beautiful 18th century property where original beams and country furniture all add to the charm. Breakfast is really something special here – help yourself to cereal and muesli then savour the award-winning local bacon and sausage, cooked in the AGA and accompanied by toasted farmhouse bread served with freshly made coffee and tea. The Mortons are also happy to cater for vegetarians and special dietary needs.

A non-smoking house throughout, The Barns has 6 guest bedrooms, all en suite and with full facilities including remote control TV and hospitality tray. They are tastefully decorated in cottage-style soft furnishings with waxed pine furniture. Pure cotton bed linen and towels are used throughout and one of the bedrooms has a 4-poster bed for that special romantic occasion. Children are welcome and pets can be accommodated by arrangement. There's ample car parking and guests are welcome to relax in the front garden. For evening meals, there are many excellent inns and restaurants in the locality and sightseeing attractions include Clumber Park, Sherwood Forest and the magnificent cathedrals of Lincoln and York.

gatehouse houses an art gallery and exhibitions are put on here regularly.

The first canal to be built in Nottinghamshire was the **Chesterfield Canal**, which runs from Chesterfield in Derbyshire to the River Trent. Some 46 miles long, work on the canal was begun in 1771 and it took 6 years to complete under the supervision of John Varley, the deputy of the great canal engineer, James Brindley. In the mid-1800s, the canal was taken over by the Sheffield and Lincoln Junction Railway, which in 1863 decided to cease maintaining the waterway and allowed it to run down. The collapse of one of the canal's two tunnels, at Norwood in 1908, hastened its decline by effectively cutting off Chesterfield from the rest of the waterway.

During the canal's heyday, in the early 1800s, it was indeed a busy waterway and many buildings lined its route, particularly through Worksop. Pickford's Depository, spanning the canal in the centre of the town, was typical of this time. The trap doors in the stone archway over the canal were used for the loading and unloading of the 'cuckoos', as the narrowboats on the Chesterfield Canal were called.

A recent acquisition by the National Trust, **Mr Straw's House** at 7 Blyth Grove, is quite unique and well worth visiting. The house, together with an endowment of one million pounds, was left to the Trust by William Straw in his will. The Trust's surveyors were surprised to find upon inspection of the Edwardian semi-detached house that they were actually stepping back in time. Inside, everything had remained untouched since the death in 1932 of William Straw senior, a grocer and seed merchant in Worksop. His wife, who died seven years later, neither altered nor added anything. Nor did her two sons, William and Walter, who lived a

bachelor existence at the house. Walter, who took on the family business, died in 1976; his brother, William, in 1990.

In all those years, virtually nothing had changed in the house. The parents' bedroom had been closed up and everything left as it was. A 1932 calendar was still hanging on the wall; William Senior's hats were still perched in the hall; his pipes and tobacco pouch lay ready by the fireside.

Worksop Museum, found in Memorial Avenue, is housed in a large purpose-built gallery within the library and museum provided by the Carnegie United Kingdom Trust. It was opened in 1938. Within the museum are small exhibitions relating to the history of Worksop and the neighbouring area of landed estates known as the Dukeries, together with a larger display on the Pilgrim Fathers whose roots lay in north Nottinghamshire. Presiding over the Pilgrim Fathers Exhibition is a life-size model of the Pilgrim Elder William Brewster, one of the leaders of the movement.

The Museum is also the start of the **Mayflower Trail** which guides visitors around the local sites connected with the Pilgrim Fathers, including William Brewster's Manor House at Scooby and Gainsborough Old Hall, just across the Trent in Lincolnshire.

AROUND WORKSOP

CARLTON-IN-LINDRICK
3 miles N of Worksop on the A616

This village's name has a delightful meaning – the "freedmen's enclosure in the lime wood". In fact it is not one, but two villages, North Carlton and South Carlton, the latter of which is the more ancient. Believed to have been a Saxon settlement, South Carlton, or Carlton

Barron as it was also called, is home to the village church. With its massive Saxon tower, the church is quite awe-inspiring as it soars above the village. In Church Lane is the **Old Mill Museum**, housed in a converted 18th century water mill. On display are some unusual linen pictures, used by the Victorians as educational material, as well as farming implements and mill machinery.

BLYTH
5 miles NE of Worksop on the A634

A village on the old Great North Road, Blyth is distinguished by a fine church and, until the 1970s, also boasted a stately home, Blyth Hall. The latter was demolished and the site is now covered by "executive homes". But the magnificent **Church of St Mary and St Martin** still stands, its great tower surmounted by eight lofty pinnacles soaring high above the village.

The original church was built around 1100 and much of that Norman building has survived in all its sturdy strength. Pevsner thought that there was *"nothing like Blyth to get a feeling for early Norman grimness"*. Opinions differ on that, since the now bare and rough-hewn walls were originally brightly painted. However, most agree that the medieval Gothic additions to the church were eminently successful. The most treasured possession here is a 15th century wall painting of the Last Judgment, one of the largest and most complete medieval murals in England. Restored in 1987, the mural has been described as 'unsophisticated', "probably done by a travelling artist", but it is still mightily impressive.

There are many other buildings of note in the village, including a handsome stable block and the former rectory, surmounted by a cupola. Among the redbrick Georgian houses there are also a number of coaching inns providing a reminder that Blyth was once an important staging post on the Great North Road.

Just to the southwest of the village lies Hodsock Priory (private) and its beautiful Gardens surrounded by parkland and meadows. Although this would seem to be the perfect setting for a medieval monastery, no priory ever stood here. The present house was built in 1829 in the Tudor style to complement the marvellous 16th century gatehouse. The gatehouse is approached across an ancient rectangular moat and, within this area, the gardens have been laid out. The southern arm of the moat was made into a small lake around 1880. **The Snowdrop Garden and Snowdrop Woodland Walk** are open to visitors for four weeks from early February.

Between Blyth and the nearby village of Styrrup, to the north, lies the Tournament Field. Dating back to the Middle Ages, the field was one of only five in the country to be granted a royal licence by Richard I.

CRESSWELL
3 miles SW of Worksop on the A616

Cresswell village is actually in Derbyshire but its most famous feature lies just inside the Nottinghamshire border. **Cresswell Crags** form a dramatic limestone gorge pitted with deep, dark and mysterious caves. Here the bones of prehistoric bison, bears, wolves, woolly rhinos and lions twice the size of their modern descendants have been found. Around 45,000BC, humans took over the caves. One of them was a gifted artist as a bone fragment engraved with a fine carving of a horse bears witness. The Visitors' Centre contains some fascinating archaeological finds and there are some pleasant walks past the lakes to the crags.

7 LINCOLNSHIRE

Known to the Romans as "Lindum Colonia", Lincoln stood at the junction of two major Imperial thoroughfares, Fosse Way and Ermine Street. By the time of the Domesday Book, it had grown into a settlement of around 1,000 households. William the Conqueror won few friends here by peremptorily ordering 166 of these houses to be destroyed to make way for an imposing castle. Around the same time, he authorised the building of a cathedral and made Lincoln the ecclesiastical centre of a vast bishopric that extended from the Humber to the Thames.

The city reached its peak of prosperity during the Middle Ages but when Henry VIII visited in 1541 the town fathers were reduced to begging relief from taxation or *"they would be compelled in short time to forsake the city, to its utter desolation"*. Henry rejected their plea. When Daniel Defoe passed through Lincoln in the 1770s he found *"an ancient, ragged, decayed and still decaying city"*. Half a century later, another traveller dismissed the historic city as *"an overgrown village"*.

Happily, improvements in roads and canals, and the arrival of the railway in the 1840s, returned the city to prosperity and Lincoln became a major centre for heavy engineering, - steam engines, agricultural machinery, excavators, motor cars and other heavy duty items. But you only have to climb the hill to the old town to enter the serenity of the cathedral

Babbling Brook, South Lincolnshire

close, a tranquil enclave lying in the shadow of the noblest and most majestic of all English cathedrals.

The south bank of the River Humber is indeed Lincolnshire's most industrial area but that is only part of the story. Rural north Lincolnshire is as peaceful and unspoilt as anywhere in the county, with scenery that ranges from the northern tip of the Wolds in the east, to the level plains of the Isle of Axholme in the west. The area also includes the largest town in the county, Grimsby (pop. 92,000), once one of the busiest fishing ports in the world and now an important centre of the food processing industry. A striking reminder of Grimsby's days of glory is the magnificent Dock Tower rising high above the town. A few miles up-river and even more imposing is the colossal Humber Bridge, the largest single span suspension bridge in Europe.

Stretching from Wainfleet and Skegness in the south to Cleethorpes and the mouth of the Humber to the north, the Lindsey Coastal Plain runs for about 40 miles, north to south, and extends between five and ten miles wide, east to west. The Plain offers a good range of animal sanctuaries and nature reserves, and there are some interesting connections with the Poet Laureate Tennyson and with

Captain John Smith, founder of the State of Virginia, whose name is inextricably linked with that of the Indian princess Pocahontas.

Nettleton, North Wolds

The area's other main attraction, the splendid sandy beaches running virtually the whole length of the coast, didn't come into their own until the railways arrived in the mid-1800s. The coastal villages of Skegness, Mablethorpe and Cleethorpes have grown steadily to become popular resorts for East Midlanders, each one offering a wide range of family entertainment.

The Elizabethan writer Michael Drayton must have deterred many of his contemporaries from visiting southeast Lincolnshire by his vivid word picture of the "foggy fens". It was, he wrote, *"a land of foul, woosy marsh...with a vast queachy soil and hosts of wallowing waves"*. It can't have been quite that bad - the Romans farmed extensively here, for example. Since Drayton's day, various drainage schemes, from the 16th century onwards, have reclaimed many thousands of waterlogged acres. Spalding is known around the world for its annual Tulip and Spring Flower Festival when a procession of floats, adorned with millions of tulip heads, progresses through the town.

The landscape of this southwestern corner of the county divides into two distinct areas. Grantham and Stamford lie in the gently rolling hills that form the continuation of the Leicestershire Wolds; while to the east, Bourne and the Deepings stand on the edge of the Fens. Historically, this has always been one of the more prosperous parts of the county, a wealth reflected in the outstanding churches at Stamford, Grantham and Corby Glen.

The Great North Road, now the A1, brought Grantham and Stamford a constant stream of travellers and trade, a traffic whose legacy includes some fine old coaching inns. One visitor during the early 1800s regarded this as *"the only gentrified region"* of Lincolnshire. Belton House, Belvoir Castle, Grimsthorpe Castle and the breathtaking Elizabethan splendour of Burghley House are four of the grandest stately homes in England, while the Victorian extravaganza of Harlaxton Manor is almost unique in its unrestrained mock-medieval exuberance.

ADVERTISERS AND PLACES OF INTEREST

LOCATOR MAP

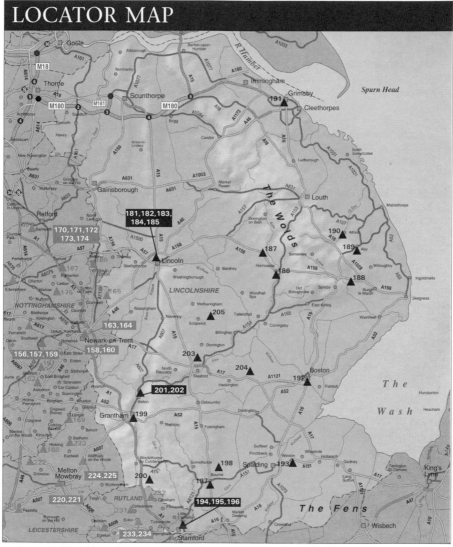

LINCOLN

Apart from Durham, **Lincoln Cathedral** is the only one in England to occupy a magnificent hilltop location, its towers soaring high above the Lincolnshire lowlands and visible for miles around. William the Conqueror ordered the first cathedral to be built here but that was almost entirely destroyed by an earthquake on April 15th 1185. The rebuilding that followed, under the energetic direction of Bishop Hugh of Avalon, resulted in the creation of one the country's most inspiring churches. Among its many superb features are the magnificent open nave, stained-glass windows incorporating the 14th century Bishop's Eye and Dean's Eye, and the glorious Angel Choir, whose carvings include the Lincoln Imp, the unofficial symbol of the city.

Lincoln Cathedral

The imposing ruins of the **Bishops Old Palace** (English Heritage) in the shadow of the Cathedral, reveal the sumptuous lifestyle of the wealthy medieval bishops

---

THE CHEESE SOCIETY

1 St Martin's Lane, Lincoln LN2 1HY
Tel: 01522 511003 Fax: 01522 512114
e-mail: cheese@thecheesesociety.co.uk
website: www.thecheesesociety.co.uk

Located in the heart of Lincoln's Cathedral Quarter, **The Cheese Society** is a unique combination of café, bistro and a delicatessen offering a wonderful range of English and Continental cheeses. Owner Kate O'Meara began a cheese by mail order in 1997, opened her shop in 2000 and the café/bistro in February 2002. The menu, naturally, majors on cheeses in various forms – baguettes, ciabatta, croque monsieur, ploughman's, double baked cheese soufflé, salads and a superb Melted Raclette, a delicious pungent cheese grilled over hot new potatoes and served with a salad garnish. For dessert, what else but cheesecakes of various flavours. The bistro is fully licensed and also offers a good choice of teas and coffees.

Kate's mail order business also continues to flourish. Her brochure lists more than 60 different cheeses from the UK alone, each with detailed notes. Isle of Mull, for example, is "A hard pressed full flavoured, powerful and spicy Cheddar style cheese made by Jeff Reade from the milk of Friesian cows. The texture is lightly granular and the flavour long and lingering. It is rumoured that the cattle are fed on the draught left over from the local whisky distillery". The brochure also offers wines that are particularly good with cheese, and various cheese accessories. All orders are delivered via overnight mail.

whose authority stretched from the Humber to the Thames. Visitors can wander through splendid apartments, banqueting halls and offices, explore the dramatic undercroft, gaze at the views from inside the Roman city walls, relax in the peaceful Contemporary Heritage Garden and see one of Europe's most northerly vineyards.

A good way to explore the city is to follow the Lincoln Heritage Trail which takes in the city's "Magnificent Seven" tourist attractions. The cathedral, naturally, takes pride of place but close by is **Lincoln Castle** which dates from 1068. Visitors can climb to the ramparts, which include Observatory Tower, to savour some fine views of the city. Interesting features abound, notably the keep, known as Lucy Tower, Cobb Hall, where the public gallows were located, and the Victorian prison whose chapel has separate pews like upright coffins.

The building also houses an original version of Magna Carta.

There are some fine Norman buildings on a lesser scale in Steep Hill and the Strait. **Jews House**, which dates from about 1170, is thought to be the oldest domestic building in England to survive intact. Its neighbour is Jews Court, a reminder of the time when there was a thriving Jewish community in Lincoln. Medieval splendour lives on in the black and white half-timbered houses on High Bridge, and in the old city Gateways, while the residences in the Cathedral Close and Castle Square are models of Georgian elegance.

The most impressive survival of the old town walls is **The Stonebow** which spans the High Street pedestrianised shopping mall. The 3-storey building houses the city's Guildhall, its Civic Insignia, royal Charters and other historic artefacts. The Mote Bell on the

OTTANTA TRE

83 Bailgate, Lincoln LN1 3AR
Tel/Fax: 01522 575 1167
e-mail: ottanta.tre@btinternet.com

Just a couple of minutes walk from the Cathedral, in the popular shopping area of Bailgate, **Ottanta Tre** offers an outstanding range of quality giftware with an emphasis on the unusual. Keith and Liz Orme's shop occupies an 18th century house stocked with a wide range of distinctive gifts. Ottanta Tre is one of just two outlets in Lincolnshire selling Alessi products, a high quality brand that ranges from elegant but functional everyday items to modern fun designs. Also on sale are custom jewellery items by Angela Hale, modern glassware from Ritzen Hoff and hand-made designer soaps.

OLIVER'S COFFEE SHOP & BISTRO

7 The Strait, Lincoln LN2 1JD
Tel: 01522 533111

Occupying a Grade II listed building in the heart of the city, **Oliver's Coffee Shop & Bistro** offers a choice of wholesome and appetising food served in 3 different eating areas. Downstairs is the original cellar of the 17th century house, an atmospheric room with old beams, tile and brick floor, and white painted brick walls. "The Front" overlooks the cobbled street while just 7 steps up is "The Loft" with its wooden floor, solid pine furniture and hand-painted mural. Throughout this friendly establishment, run by the McIntosh family, customers can enjoy a good choice of hot meals, lite bites, baguettes, and hot or cold sandwiches. There's a children's menu and Oliver's is licensed.

roof, dated 1371, is still rung to summon the City Fathers to council meetings.

Another place of interest is the **Greyfriars Exhibition Centre** (free), housed in a beautiful 13th century building. The Centre hosts themed exhibitions focused on the collections of the City and County Museum which range from pre-historic times to 1750.

Steep Hill, Lincoln

The Lawn (free), originally built in 1820 as a lunatic asylum and set in eight acres of beautiful grounds and gardens, is an elegant porticoed building whose attractions include an archaeology centre, a tropical conservatory with a display dedicated to the botanist Sir Joseph Banks, an aquarium, a specialist shopping mall and a fully licensed pub and restaurant.

Lincolnshire's largest social history museum is the **Museum of Lincolnshire Life** which occupies an extensive barracks built for the Royal North Lincoln Militia in 1857. It is now a listed building and houses a fascinating series of displays depicting the many aspects of Lincolnshire life. The Domestic Gallery turns the clock back to the beginning of the 20th century, showing what life was like in a middle-class home; settings include a nursery, bedroom, kitchen, parlour and wash house. The Transport Gallery shows the skills of the wheelwright and coachbuilder in such items as a carrier's cart and a horse-drawn charabier (hearse). It also contains a fully restored 1925 Bullnose Morris and a Lincoln Elk motorcycle. In the Agricultural and Industrial Gallery notable exhibits include a First World War tank built by William Foster of Lincoln; a 20-ton steam ploughing engine; a steam traction engine and a number of tractors. Commercial Row features a builder's yard, a printing press, a village post office and several shops. All the above represent just part of the scope of this marvellous museum, where visitors can also pause for refreshment and perhaps a slice of the local speciality plumbread in the Hungry Yellowbelly café. (That peculiar name is applied to anyone born in Lincolnshire!)

GADSBY'S

260 High Street, Lincoln LN2 1HW
Tel: 01522 527485 Fax: 01522 512921

Gadsby's was established in 1898 and is still a family business with two grand-daughters and three great grand children of the founder still active in the company which now has 7 shops scattered across the Midlands. Their High Street, Lincoln, shop spreads over two floors: the upper floor devoted to a picture gallery of original oils and watercolours; the ground floor stocked with a wonderful range of quality giftware. Here you'll find Moorcroft and Poole pottery; Hummel porcelain; Swarowski crystal and elegant jewellery. Attentive, helpful staff add to the pleasure of shopping here and the wide range on offer ensures that you'll almost certainly find something to delight you.

MIDAS

31 Steep Hill, Lincoln LN2 1LU
Tel: 01522 532299 Fax: 01522 827945
website: www.midasarts.co.uk

Located close to the cathedral and castle, **Midas** provides a superb showcase for contemporary applied arts. In Dee Barnes' fascinating gallery you'll find the work of more than 25 jewellers, most working in sterling silver and mixed metals, exquisite hand-blown perfume bottles and decorated kiln-formed glass tiles, and functional kitchenware and decorative ceramic pieces. Dee works with some of the country's leading designers and can commission jewellery such as engagement and wedding rings to your own requirements. Midas can also help you create a wedding list of works that are destined to become collectable.

Set in beautiful landscaped gardens, **The Usher Gallery** was built in 1927 with funds bequeathed by a Lincoln jeweller, James Ward Usher. It is a major centre for the arts, with collections of porcelain, glass, clocks and coins, and a display of memorabilia connected with the Lincolnshire-born Poet Laureate, Alfred Lord Tennyson. The gallery also houses an important collection of works by Peter de Wint and paintings by Turner, Lowry, Piper, Sickert and Ruskin Spear.

Ellis Mill is the last survivor of a line of windmills that once ran along the Lincoln Edge, a limestone ridge stretching some 70 miles from Winteringham by the Humber to Stamford on the county's southern border. This tower mill dates back to 1798 and is in full working order. For those interested in Lincoln's commercial past the Lincoln Engineering Society has produced a leaflet detailing an Industrial Heritage Trail that guides visitors to a score of the city's manufacturing companies, past and present.

Lincoln stages several major annual events, including a flower festival in the Cathedral, the Lincolnshire Show at the Showground just north of the city, and the Jolly Water Carnival on Brayford Pool in the centre of the city. Raising money for charity is the purpose behind this aquatic event, which includes rowing and sailing races and a procession through the streets.

AROUND LINCOLN

Just southeast of the city are the popular open spaces of **Hartsholme Country Park** and **Swanholme Lakes Local Nature Reserve**, 200 acres of woodland, lakes and meadows to explore. A little way further south is **Whisby Nature Park**, set on either side of the Lincoln-Newark railway line and home to great crested grebes, teal and tufted duck. Also on the southern outskirts of the city is the **Lincolnshire Road Transport Museum** where 40 vintage cars, commercial vehicles and buses span more than 70 years of road transport history. Also on display is a wide variety of old road signs, ticket machines and early bus timetables.

About 5 miles west of Lincoln, **Doddington Hall** is a very grand Elizabethan mansion completed in 1600 by the architect Robert Smythson, and standing now exactly as then, with wonderful formal gardens, a gatehouse and a family church. The interior contains a fascinating collection of pictures, textiles, porcelain and furniture that reflect four centuries of unbroken family occupation.

BARDNEY
10 miles E of Lincoln on the B1190/B1202

The dominating feature of this little town beside the River Witham is the British Sugar Corporation's towering beet processing factory. In medieval times, a more elegant structure distinguished the town, and was just as important to its prosperity. **Bardney Abbey** was famous then because it housed the holy remains of St Oswald, an 8th century King of Northumbria. Pilgrims flocked here in their thousands. The original Saxon abbey was demolished by Viking raiders in 870 and its Norman successor fared little better at the Dissolution of the Monasteries. Only the ground plan is now distinguishable. Some fragments from the abbey were incorporated into Bardney's Church of St Lawrence which is otherwise mostly 15th century. Features of interest here include a tomb slab of Abbot Richard Horncastle, who died in 1508, and two unusual Charity Boards dated 1603 and 1639. These list benefactors of the parish, complete with colour portraits of these generous souls.

Connoisseurs of unusual churches will be well rewarded by a short detour to **Southrey**, a remote hamlet set beside the River Witham. Built of timber by the parishioners themselves in 1898, St John the Divine is painted brilliant white outside and sky blue within. Resembling some Mission station in the Australian outback, this quaint little church stands on a plinth incorporating gravestones from Bardney Abbey.

BASSINGHAM
7 miles SW of Lincoln off the A46

A pleasant little village with houses mostly of local warm red brick; an Elizabethan manor house (private) and, on one of the many little greens, an oak seat carved in the shape of a bull. This striking feature is part of an admirable enterprise masterminded by North Kesteven Arts to enhance both the natural and built-up areas of the District with all kinds of sculpture and art work. These imaginative pieces, many of them serving as public benches, range from the Dorrington Demons, based on a local legend, to the Scopwick Woman whose seat, in the lap of her skirt, has become a kind of letterbox with local people leaving tokens, messages or gifts for others to pick up. A booklet titled *In View*, which gives full details of these fascinating works, is available from TICs.

A couple of miles north of Bassingham, **Aubourn** is a charming Elizabethan and Jacobean manor house set in attractive gardens and notable for a finely carved oak staircase. Nearby, the tower of Aubourn's Victorian church stands alone, all that was left after the church was demolished in 1973 and parishioners reverted to worshipping in the chancel of the old church amidst the clutter of memorials to the Meres and Nevile families.

Wood Carving in Field, Bassingham

GAINSBOROUGH

15 miles NW of Lincoln on the A156

Britain's most inland port, Gainsborough is located at the highest navigable point on the River Trent for seagoing vessels. During the 17th and 18th centuries, particularly, the town prospered greatly and although many of the lofty warehouses lining the river bank have been demolished, enough remain to give some idea of its flourishing past.

The town's most famous building is the enchanting **Gainsborough Old Hall**, one of the most striking architectural gems in the county. The Hall was built in the 1470s by Sir Thomas Burgh, a Yorkist supporter in the Wars of the Roses. Sir Thomas later entertained Richard III in the Great Hall with its vast arched roof. The kitchens also remain virtually unchanged since those days. A century or so later, around 1597, a London merchant, William Hickman, extended the building in Elizabethan style. The Hall is generally considered one of the best preserved medieval manor houses in the country. Today, it is run jointly by Lincolnshire County Council and English Heritage, and is open most days throughout the year.

Gainsborough also boasts an outstanding church. Beautifully set in its own grounds in the centre of the town, **All Saints** is a magnificent example of a Georgian classical "city" church. The interior, with its massive columns, box pews and gallery, is richly decorated in gold and turquoise. It is open during daylight hours, tours are available and there's even a cafeteria and gift shop.

Another notable building is **Marshall's Britannia Works** in Beaumont Street, a proud reminder of Gainsborough's once thriving engineering industry. Built around 1850, the quarter-of-a-mile long frontage bears an impressive figure of Britannia herself.

Gainsborough is believed to have provided material for George Eliot's *The Mill on the Floss*. The now-demolished Ashcroft Mill on the River Trent was the model for Tulliver's mill and the *eagre*, or **tidal bore**, that precipitates the tragic climax of the novel is clearly based on the surge that happens at Gainsborough. This usually takes place about 50 minutes after high tide at Grimsby and the bore can be anything between 8ft and 13ft high.

SCUNTHORPE

Up until the 1850s the main activity around Scunthorpe was the maintaining of rabbit warrens - the local breed with their silvery coats being much in demand with furriers. Then a local landowner, Rowland Winn, discovered that the poor local soil lightly covered vast deposits of ironstone. Scunthorpe's rapid rise to becoming a major steel town was under way. Today, the Corus plant produces more than 4 million tonnes of liquid steel, from a 690 hectare site which contains 90 miles of railways.

On selected summer weekends, the **Appleby Frodingham Railway Preservation Society** runs 2 hour railtours around the plant. Pulled by a restored steam locomotive, the fully guided tour takes in all aspects of iron and steel making and includes a glimpse of red hot steel being rolled in the mills.

More of Scunthorpe's industrial and social heritage is on display at the **North Lincolnshire Museum & Art Gallery**, with exhibits that include an ironmonger's cottage. The town has also created a Heritage Trail which takes visitors through three of the parks created by Victorian benefactors - Scunthorpe is proud of its parks and gardens and has claimed the title of "The Industrial Garden Town of rural North Lincolnshire".

AROUND SCUNTHORPE

NORMANBY
4 miles N of Scunthorpe off the B1430

Normanby Hall was built in 1825 for the Sheffield family and extended in 1906. The interior is decorated in Regency style, and displays include eight rooms that reflect the changes made down the years, as well as two costume galleries. The 300-acre Park has plenty to see and enjoy, including a deer park, duck ponds, an ice house in the middle of the miniature railway circuit, a Victorian laundry and a walled garden. The **Normanby Hall Farming Museum** majors on rural life in the age of the heavy horse, and among the exhibits illuminating the workings of a 19th century country estate are traditional agricultural equipment and transport, and country crafts. Near the park gates, some picturesque estate cottages bear witness to the Sheffield family's reputation as good landlords. Rents were low and job security was good, so perhaps the only drawback was that the Sheffield family restricted the number of public houses they would allow on their lands.

A mile or so northwest of the Hall, St Andrew's Church in the agreeable village of Burton-on-Stather contains an impressive range of memorials to the Sheffield family, the oldest of which dates back to the 1300s.

ALKBOROUGH
11 miles N of Scunthorpe off the A1077

A scenic walk leads from Burton to Alkborough, where the medieval maze known as **Julian's Bower** is a perplexing talking point. Not a maze made of hedges, but a pattern cut in the turf, it occupies a beautiful location on a clifftop overlooking the River Trent. The design of the maze is reproduced in the porch of the 11th century village church, and again in a window high above the altar.

BARTON-UPON-HUMBER
10 miles NE of Scunthorpe off the A15

Today, Barton is dominated by the colossal south tower of the **Humber Bridge**, connecting Lincolnshire with East Yorkshire. This has been a major crossing point for more than a thousand years. The Domesday Book recorded a ferry here and the community was then the largest town in north Lincolnshire. In the 1770s, Daniel Defoe gave a vivid description of his passage across the Humber *"in an open boat in which we had about fifteen horses, and ten or twelve cows, mingled with about seventeen or eighteen passengers, we were about four hours tossing about on the Humber before we could get*

Humber Bridge

into the harbour at Hull". (The river at this point is only about 2½ miles wide).

The heart of the town still has some pleasant streets - Fleetgate, Bargate, Beck Hill and Priestgate, all distinguished by mainly Georgian and early Victorian buildings. **Baysgarth House**, now a museum, is an 18th century mansion with a collection of 18th and 19th century English and Oriental pottery, a section on country crafts and an industrial museum in the stable block. The surrounding park has a picnic area, play area and various recreational facilities.

Just to the north of Barton, on the banks of the Humber, is an observation area for viewing the mighty Humber Bridge. Opened in 1981, this is Europe's longest single-span suspension bridge with an overall length of 2,428yds (2,220m). This means that for more than a third of a mile only four concrete pillars, two on each bank, are preserving you from a watery death. From these huge pylons, 510ft (155m) high, gossamer cables of thin-wired steel support a gently curving roadway. Both sets of pylons rise vertically, but because of the curvature of the earth they actually lean away from each other by several inches. The bridge is particularly striking at night when the vast structure is floodlit.

Around the bridge are important nature reserves. **Barton Clay Pits** cover a five-mile area along the river bank and offer a haven for wildlife and recreation for sporty humans. **Far Ings**, with hides and waymarked trails, is home to more than 230 species of wild flowers, 50 nesting bird species and hundreds of different sorts of moths.

BRIGG

7 miles E of Scunthorpe on the A10

King John was not universally liked but one of his more popular deeds was the granting of a charter (in 1205) which permitted this modest little town to hold an annual festivity on the 5th day of August. **Brigg Fair**, along with Widdecombe and Scarborough, has joined the trio of "Best Known Fairs in England", its celebrity enhanced by a traditional song (twice recorded by Percy Grainger), and the haunting tone poem, *Brigg Fair*, composed by Frederick Delius in 1907. Almost 800 years later, the fair still attracts horse traders from around the country, along with all the usual fun of the fair.

King John's son, Henry III, also showed favour to the town. He granted the loyal burghers of Brigg the right to hold a weekly market on Thursdays, a right they still exercise to the full. Each week, the market place is crammed with around 100 stalls. During the summer months, a farmers' market is also held on the 4th Saturday of each month. A pedestrianised town centre, combined with ample parking nearby, has made Brigg's markets some of the busiest in north Lincolnshire.

Many visitors to Brigg, including the architecture guru Nikolaus Pevsner, have commented that some of the town's most interesting buildings are its pubs. Pevsner picked out for special mention the Lord Nelson, with its broad Regency bow window, the Dying Gladiator, remarkable for the *"gory realism"* of its pub sign, and the Black Bull which boasts *"a vigorous Edwardian pub front"*.

HAXEY

18 miles SW of Scunthorpe on the A161

Haxey is the site of a nature reserve, but is best known for the **Haxey Hood Game**, launched around 2.30 on the afternoon of Twelfth Night in front of the parish church. Three hundred men divided into four teams compete to push a leather 'hood' into the pub of their team's choice. The game apparently started in the 12th or 13th century when a lady lost her hood and a number of village men scrambled to retrieve it. The strongest man caught the hood but was too shy to hand it back, and was labelled a fool by the lady, while the man who eventually handed it over was declared a lord. The lady suggested that the scene should be re-enacted each year, and gave a plot of land for the purpose. The "sway" of men struggle across the fields working the hood towards the appropriate pubs and always staying within the sway - no open running. When the sway reaches the winning pub, the landlord touches the hood to declare the game over, and free drinks paid for by a collection end the day in time-honoured style. Rather an elaborate build-up to a drinking session, but just one of the quaint traditions that make English country life so colourful.

EPWORTH
12 miles SW of Scunthorpe on the A161

This small town, the southern "capital" of the Isle of Axholme, is a hallowed place for Methodists from all over the world. From 1696 until his death in 1735 the Revd Samuel Wesley was Rector here. John Wesley was born at the **Old Rectory** on June 17th, 1703: his brother Charles on December 18th, 1707. Two years later, inflamed by one of the Rector's outspoken sermons, local people set fire to the Rectory. The house was rebuilt incorporating ribs and keels from ships broken up in the nearby River Trent. The house still stands today, a charming Queen Anne building. Several of its rooms have been refurnished in period style and some of the brothers' possessions are on display. There are also collections of portraits and prints, and you can even stay for bed and breakfast.

St Andrew's Church, where Samuel

Wesley was minister, is a short walk from the town centre. His table tomb stands near the southeast door and it was from this vantage point that John would address his followers after he had been refused access to the church. Inside, the 12th century font in which both John and Charles were baptized can still be seen.

The best way to follow the footsteps of the Wesleys is to join the Wesley Trail which has information boards placed at various locations connected with the family. A pamphlet giving full details is available from the Old Rectory.

SANDTOFT
10 miles W of Scunthorpe off the A161 or Exit 2 of M180

On a wartime airfield on the Isle of Axholme, **Sandtoft Trolleybus Museum** is home to Britain's largest single collection of trolleybuses and motorbuses. Started in 1969 by a small and enthusiastic group of volunteers, the collection includes vehicles dating from 1927 to 1985, including magnificent 6-wheeled double-decker trolleybuses and a fascinating one-and-a-half decker from Aachen in Germany.

SKEGNESS

In the early 1800s, when the Tennyson family used to visit Skegness with the future Poet Laureate, Alfred, in tow, it was still a tiny fishing village but already famous for its miles of firm sandy beaches and its "oh-so-bracing" sea air. As late as 1871, the resident population of Skegness was only 239 but two years later the railway arrived and three years after that the local landowner, the Earl of Scarborough, built a new town to the north of the railway station.

A huge pier, 1,843ft long, was erected. This survived for almost one hundred years before a gale on the night of January 11th, 1978 left it sadly truncated. Other amenities provided by the Earl of Scarborough for visitors included the Lumley Hotel, St Matthew's Church and a grand promenade. The Jubilee Clock Tower on the seafront was added in 1899, and in 1908 the town fathers amazed even themselves by a stroke of advertising genius – their adoption of the Jolly Fisherman as the town's mascot.

The Jolly Fisherman has an interesting story behind him. In 1908 the Great Northern Railway purchased an oil painting of the plump and prancing fisherman for £12. After adding the famous slogan "Skegness is so Bracing", they used the painting as a poster to advertise trips from London to Skegness (fare 3/-, 15p). Almost a century later the same Jolly Fisherman is still busy promoting Skegness as a holiday resort. There are two statues of him in town, one at the railway station, another in Compass Gardens, and during the summer months he can also be seen strolling around the town.

Naturally, the town is well-provided with funfairs – Bottons, Fantasy Island, and Butlin's, the latter two of which are actually in the contiguous town of Ingoldmells. It was in 1936 that Billy Butlin opened his very first holiday camp with the slogan "A Week's Holiday for a Week's Wage" – about £2.50 in those days. The price included accommodation, meals and entertainment and the holidays were understandably popular with workers – a new law had just guaranteed them a statutory week's leave with pay. Just three years later, World War II erupted and the holiday market imploded. But Billy Butlin still prospered. The government bought his camps to use as army barracks, appointed him Director-General of Hostels, and at the end of the

war sold the camps back to him at a knock-down price. The camp is still operating, now named the Butlin's Family Entertainment Resort, and day visit tickets are available.

Alongside the obvious attractions of the beach and all the traditional seaside entertainment, Skegness and Ingoldmells have other places of special interest. **Church Farm Museum**, a former farmhouse, is home to a collection of old farm implements and machinery, re-created village workshops, a paddock of Lincoln Longwool sheep and a fine example of a Lincolnshire "mud and stud" thatched cottage brought here from the nearby village of Withern. Craft demonstrations can be viewed on most Sunday afternoons and a programme of special events - sheep shearing, steam threshing and so on, continues throughout the season.

Natureland Seal Sanctuary on North Parade provides interest and fun for all the family with its seals and baby seal rescue centre; aquarium; tropical house with crocodiles, snakes and tarantulas; a pets corner and Floral Palace; a large greenhouse teeming with plant, insect and bird life, including butterflies and flamingoes.

Serious birdwatchers should head south along the coast to **Gibraltar Point National Nature Reserve**, a field station among the salt marshes and dunes with hides, waymarked routes and guided tours.

AROUND SKEGNESS

WAINFLEET
5 miles SW of Skegness on the A52

Formerly a thriving port, Wainfleet now finds itself several miles from the sea. Narrow roads lead off the market place with its medieval stone cross, making this a place you really have to explore on foot. The most striking building in the town is the former **Magdalen College School**, built in dark red brick in 1484 for William of Wayneflete, Bishop of Winchester and Lord Chancellor to Henry VI. William first founded Magdalen College, Oxford and later established the college school in the town of his birth. It continued as a school until 1933 but now houses the public library, a small museum, a tea room and a walled tea garden.

This attractive little town has a Friday market, held in the unspoilt Market Place with its **Buttercross** and **Clock Tower**, and amongst the variety of family-run shops here is one which offers an unusual culinary treat: - traditional fish and chips cooked on a coal range.

A curious feature lies about a mile south of the town, on the western side of the A52. Rows and rows of small, rounded mounds are all that remain of an important industry that flourished here from the Iron Age to the 1600s - the extraction of salt from sea water. Throughout these long centuries, salt was an expensive, but absolutely vital, commodity, both as a preservative and a condiment. During the Roman occupation of Britain, part of an Imperial soldier's remuneration was a pouch of salt, his *salarium* or salary. When the mounds at Wainfleet were excavated in the 1950s they were found to contain *salterns* - low hearths surrounded by brick in which fires were lit to evaporate pans of sea water and leave behind the precious salt.

BURGH LE MARSH
4 miles W of Skegness on the A158

Pronounced *"Borough"*, this small town was once the terminus of a Roman road from Lincoln. Although Burgh is now several miles inland, it was from here,

centuries ago, that travellers boarded a ferry to cross The Wash and join the **Peddars Way** in Norfolk.

About 3 miles northwest of Burgh, **Gunby Hall** (National Trust) is reputed to be the setting Tennyson had in mind when he wrote of:

*"an English home – gray twilight pour'd
On dewy pastures, dewy trees
Softer than sleep – all things in order stored,
A haunt of ancient peace".*

Built in 1700 and extended in the 1870s, Gunby Hall is a delightful William & Mary house of plum-coloured brick surrounded by sweeping lawns and flower gardens. The Hall has long been associated with the Massingberd family whose portraits, including several by Reynolds, are on display along with some very fine English furniture. The walled garden is particularly charming and beyond it the Church of St Peter contains some life-size brasses of early Massingberds.

WILLOUGHBY
11 miles NW of Skegness on the B1196

Willoughby is best known as the birthplace of Captain John Smith, founder of what is now the State of Virginia in the USA. A farmer's son, Smith was born in the village in 1580 and educated in nearby Louth. He left England as a young man and, after a spell as a mercenary in Europe, set sail with other optimistic colonists for Chesapeake Bay in 1607. A forceful character, Smith was elected Governor of the new settlement but his diplomatic skills proved unequal to the task of pacifying the local Red Indians. They took him captive and were intent on killing him until one of the chieftain's daughters, Pocahontas, interceded and saved his life. Pocahontas later married one of Smith's fellow colonists, John

Rolfe, and returned with him to England. Beautiful and intelligent, the dark-skinned Pocahontas was welcomed as an exotic celebrity. King James I graciously allowed her to be presented at his Court but within a few months the lovely Indian princess died "of a fever". Four hundred years later, the romantic tale continues to furnish the material for songs, stories, plays and musicals.

Willoughby village celebrates its most famous son with a fine memorial window in the church (a gift from American citizens), and in the Willoughby Arms pub where a portrait painted on an outside wall and, inside, accounts of his adventures may be seen.

HORNCASTLE

"Few towns of Horncastle's size can have so many Regency bow-windows", noted Nikolaus Pevsner. These attractive features, and the houses that went with them, were a direct result of the town's increased prosperity and the building boom that followed the opening of the Horncastle Navigation Canal in 1802. The town also has an unusual number of hotels for its population, currently about 4,500. The hostelries were built to accommodate visitors to the annual Horse Fair which started some time in the 1200s and continued until 1948. Its modern successor is the Horncastle Town & Country Fayre, a popular event that takes place each June.

St Mary's Church has some interesting features. Outside the north porch is the ground level tombstone of a 19th century local doctor. This is an unconsecrated quarter of the churchyard but the doctor insisted on being buried here. It was his personal gesture of solidarity with suicides to whom, at that time and until very recently, the Church of England

ALAN READ

60-62 West Street, Horncastle, Lincolnshire LN9 5AD
Tel: 01507 524324 Fax: 01507 525548 Mobile: 07778 873838

Connoisseurs of period furniture will appreciate the quality of the original and fine copies on display in the 5 ground floor and 3 1st floor showrooms of **Alan Read**. At any one time the rooms may contain a Jacobean oak chest of drawers, an antique Dutch colonial cupboard, or a Regency period mahogany bedside commode. For more than 25 years Alan has specialised in original antique pieces of furniture together with the finest copies made by British craftsmen, some of whom are fellow liverymen in the Worshipful Company of Furniture Makers.

Alan's family had its roots in agriculture but he left to pursue his passion for antique furniture. He joined Liberty's of Regent Street,

London in the early 70s and not only expanded his knowledge of quality 17th and 18th century furniture but also became associated with the leading makers of fine replicas, craftsmen like Arthur Brett of Norwich. They are still personal friends and suppliers of fine copies. As well as selling period furniture, Alan also gives advice on furnishing and decorating late 17th century and Georgian houses and also undertakes valuations. His shop is open from 10am to 4.30pm, Tuesday, Thursday, Friday and Saturday; at other times by appointment.

refused interment in hallowed ground. Inside the church there's a brass portrait of Lionel Dymoke, dated 1519. The Dymokes were the hereditary King's Champions who, at the coronation feast of medieval monarchs, challenged anyone who disputed the validity of the king's succession to mortal combat. Above an arch in the south aisle hang 13 scythe blades. These agricultural tools were the only arms available to the local people who took part in the Pilgrimage of Grace of 1536. This was a mostly northern protest against Henry VIII's policy of closing down every monastery in the country. Their rebellion failed. The king graciously pardoned those who had taken part and the rebels returned peacefully to their homes. Once the crisis had been defused, Henry ordered the summary execution of the most prominent leaders and supporters of the uprising.

SOMERSBY
7 miles NE of Horncastle off the A158

For pilgrims on the Tennyson trail, a visit to Somersby is essential. The poet's father, Dr George Clayton Tennyson, was Rector of the village and the adjoining parish of Bag Enderby. Alfred was born here in 1809 and for most of the first thirty years of his life Somersby Rectory was his home. Many of his poems reflect his delight in the surrounding scenery of the Wolds, Fens and coast. When the family left Somersby in 1837, following the death of Dr Tennyson, Alfred wrote:

We leave the well-beloved place
Where first we gazed upon the sky;
The roofs, that heard our earliest cry,
Will shelter one of stranger race.

The Rectory, now Somersby House (private), still stands, complete with the many additions Dr Tennyson made to

BAUMBER PARK

Baumber, nr Horncastle, Lincolnshire LN9 5NE
Tel: 01507 578235 Mobile: 07977 722776 Fax: 01507 578417
e-mail: baumberpark@amserve.com
website: http://uk.geocities.com/baumberpark/thehouse

A spacious and elegant farmhouse of character, **Baumber Park** was originally built around 1680 and much enlarged in the 1800s. It is surrounded by parkland in which cows and calves graze all summer and there's also a small flock of pedigree Lincoln Longwool sheep which lamb in April. Other traditional farm animals at home here are horses, cats and dogs, chickens to lay eggs for breakfast – and bees for breakfast honey! Your hosts at Baumber Park are Clare Harrison, who looks after her bed & breakfast guests, and husband Michael who runs the adjoining farm.

Clare is also an accomplished horticulturalist who will happily propagate from the plants in her garden for guests. The accommodation, which enjoys a 4-Diamond rating from the English Tourist Board, comprises two principal guest bedrooms – a double en suite and a twin-bedded room with private bathroom. These spacious rooms have bay windows giving excellent views over the garden and farmland. There's also a small (non-inspected) single room with shared facilities. All rooms have a portable TV, radio and hospitality tray. Downstairs is a large guest lounge with open log fire, piano and television, and a dining room with a big mahogany table and a collection of Lincolnshire books. Guests also have the use of a grass tennis court.

Tennyson memorabilia, St Margaret's Church

The nearby village of **Bag Enderby** is associated with another celebrated figure, John Wesley. He preached here on the village green beneath a noble elm tree. The hollow trunk still stands. The church also has a special treasure: a beautifully carved 15th century font *"worth crossing Lincolnshire to see"*. The carvings include a tender Pietà, a hart licking the leaves of a tree growing from its back, and a seated figure playing what appears to be a lute.

SPILSBY

10 miles E of Horncastle on the A16

A pleasant little market town with a population of about 2000, Spilsby sits near the southern edge of the Wolds. Market day is Monday, (with an open air auction as part of the fun), and there's an annual May Day Carnival with dancing round the may pole in the market square. The **Church of St James** has many interesting features, most notably the incredible array of tombs and memorials of the Willoughby family from the 1300s to the early 1600s. Perhaps the most striking of them, a 1580s memorial to the Duchess of Suffolk and Richard Bertie, fills the whole of the original chancel arch. Another monument honours Spilsby's most famous son, the navigator and explorer Captain Sir John Franklin, who

accommodate his family of 10 children. He is buried in the graveyard of the small church where he had been minister for more than 20 years and which now contains a fine bust of his famous son. Also in the graveyard, where a simple tombstone marks the Doctor's burial place, stands a remarkably well-preserved medieval cross.

CANDLESBY CACTUS NURSERY

Candlesby House, Candlesby, nr Spilsby, Lincolnshire PE23 5RU
Tel: 01754 890256 Fax: 01754 890594
e-mail: plantlovers.cacti@amserve.net

Established in 1947, **Candlesby Cactus Nursery** is the oldest nursery in the UK specialising in cacti and succulents. Owner Tim Wilson's aim is to produce a wide range of these plants at reasonable prices - "We do not set out to deal with the rare and expensive varieties" he says. An extensive range of sempervivum is also available. Tim is a regular exhibitor at some 38 shows throughout the year and holds numerous Gold and Large Gold Awards including awards from Chelsea, Hampton Court and Gardener's World Live. The Nursery is almost always open, except when Tim is at a show – a phone call in advance is advisable.

lost his life while in charge of the expedition that discovered the North West Passage. A handsome bronze of the great man stands in the square facing the market hall of 1764.

Vikingway Path, The Wolds

About 2 miles east of Spilsby, on the B1195, the **Northcote Heavy Horses Centre** offers a unique "hands-on" experience with these gentle giants. Visitors have the options of participating in morning or all day sessions during which they have close contact with the horses, including grooming them if you wish. The afternoon programme is for those who simply want to walk around on their own, explore the museum/vehicle workshop, watch the video display of the Centre's activities, enjoy a half-hour horse dray ride through country lanes, or settle down for tea and scones in the Hen's Nest Tea Room.

Old Bolingbroke
8 miles SE of Horncastle off the A155 or B1195

Old Bolingbroke is the site of **Bolingbroke Castle** (free), now in the care of English Heritage. Originally built in the reign of William I it later became the property of John of Gaunt whose son, afterwards Henry IV, was born at the castle in 1367. During the Civil War, Bolingbroke Castle was besieged by Parliamentary forces in 1643, fell into disuse soon after and very little now remains.

East Kirkby
8 miles SE of Horncastle on the A155

The airfield beside the A155 is the setting for the **Lincolnshire Aviation Heritage Centre,** based in the old control tower. Displays include an Avro Lancaster

bomber, a Shackleton, cockpits from Canberras, military vehicles and a wartime blast shelter.

LOUTH

One of the county's most appealing towns, Louth is set beside the River Lud on the eastern edge of the Wolds in an Area of Outstanding Natural Beauty. Louth can make the unusual boast that it stands in both the eastern and western hemispheres since the Greenwich Meridian line passes through the centre of the town.

There was a settlement here long before the Romans arrived. By the time of the Domesday Book, in 1086, Louth was recorded as a prosperous market town. It still is. There's a cattle market on Fridays; a general market on Wednesdays (with an open air auction), Fridays and Saturdays; and a Farmers' Market on the last Wednesday of each month.

The town is a pleasure to wander around, its narrow winding streets and alleys crammed with attractive architecture and bearing intriguing names such as Pawnshop Passage. Westgate in particular is distinguished by its Georgian houses and a 16th century inn. A plaque in nearby Westgate Place marks the house where Tennyson lodged with his grandmother while attending the King Edward VI School. Founded in the 1200s, the school is still operating and amongst its other famous old boys are Sir John Franklin and Captain John Smith of Pocahontas fame. Broadbank, which now houses the **Louth Museum,** is an attractive little building with some interesting artifacts including some amazing locally-woven carpets that were displayed at the 1867 Paris Exhibition. And Tennyson fans will surely want to visit the shop in the market square that published *Poems by Two Brothers* and is still selling books.

But the town's pre-eminent architectural glory is the vast **Church of St James**, which boasts the tallest spire of any parish church in England. Nearly 300 feet high and built in gleaming Ancaster stone, this masterly example of the mason's art was constructed between 1501 and 1515. The interior is noted for its glorious starburst tower vault, beautifully restored Georgian pine roof, a wonderful collection of Decorated sedilia, and a fascinating array of old chests. On summer afternoons, visitors can climb to the base of the spire for a panoramic view that stretches from the Wolds to the North Sea.

An interesting recent addition to the town's attractions is the **Louth Art Trail** linking commissioned works of art, each of which will have some significant connection with the town's history. Already in place are sculptures outside St James's Church, Louth Library and around the Louth Navigation Canal and the River Lud. Both waterways have made important contributions to the town's prosperity although the Lud has also brought disaster. In 1920 a flash flood destroyed hundreds of homes and killed 23 people. A plaque on the side of

the town watermill shows how high the river rose during that disastrous inundation. Another Art Trail commission is based on the theme of the Greenwich Meridian, and there's a further sculpture located in **Hubbards Hills**, a picturesque public park lying in a 125ft-deep glacial valley to the west of the town.

AROUND LOUTH

LUDBOROUGH
6 miles N of Louth on the A16

The only standard gauge steam railway in the county, the **Lincolnshire Wolds Railway** is a noble volunteer enterprise with the ambitious aim of extending its present half-mile track to a full 10 miles. The line is part of the original Great Northern Railway which opened in 1848 and closed in 1980. The old Ludborough station has been restored, visitors can watch ongoing restoration in the engine shed and, on steaming days, travel along the line. The former ticket office now houses a collection of railway memorabilia; there's a gift shop and a buffet car serving home-made light refreshments. Entrance to the site is free.

MABLETHORPE
13 miles E of Louth on the A52 & A1104

Mablethorpe is the northernmost and most "senior" of the three Lincolnshire holiday resorts that almost form a chain along this stretch of fragile coast which has frequently been threatened by the waves, and whose contours have changed visibly over the years. Much of the original village of Mablethorpe has disappeared into the sea, including the medieval Church of St Peter. In the great North Sea flood of January 31st, 1953, seven Mablethorpe residents were drowned.

Long popular with day trippers and holidaymakers, Mablethorpe offers all that could be asked of a traditional seaside town, and a little more. One of the most popular attractions is the **Animal Gardens, Nature Centre & Seal Trust** at North End. This complex houses creatures of all kinds, with special wildcat and barn owl features, and includes a seal and seabird hospital, as well as a nature centre with many fascinating displays. The lynx caves are particularly interesting, displaying 3-dimensional scenes of Mablethorpe as it was 9,000 and 20,000 years ago, along with prehistoric tools and fossils.

A unique collection is on view at **Ye Olde Curiosity Museum** where Graham and Sue Allen have amassed an astonishing collection of more than 18,000 curios. One of the oddest is an 1890 "fat remover", which looks like a rolling pin with suction pads and was used in massage parlours. Almost everything in the museum is on sale - apart from Graham's beloved Morris Minor!

ABY
10 miles SE of Louth on minor roads

Claythorpe Watermill & Wildfowl Gardens (see panel) are a major draw for visitors of all ages to this small village on the edge of the Wolds. A beautiful 18th century watermill

provides the central feature, surrounded by attractive woodlands inhabited by hundreds of waterfowl and other animals. Built in 1721, the mill is no longer working but it provides a handsome setting for a restaurant, gift shop and Country Fayre shop. Open daily between March and October, the gardens also have a Bygone Exhibit Area.

ALFORD
12 miles SE of Louth on the A1114

Often described as Lincolnshire's Craft Centre, Alford is a flourishing little town with markets that were first established

CLAYTHORPE WATER MILL AND WILDFOWL GARDENS

Aby, nr Alford, Lincolnshire. LN13 0DU
Tel: 01507 450687 Fax: 01507 450687

Nestling at the tip of the Lincolnshire Wolds in idyllic picture postcard setting sits **Claythorpe Watermill and Wildfowl Gardens** which is home to over five hundred birds from exotic waterfowl, Ducks, Geese and Swans, to Crowned Cranes, Storks and Ibis. There are Peacocks and Pheasants, cheeky Cockerels, Wallabies, Goats even a Miniature Shetland Pony. In the beautiful waters of the Mill Ponds, Trout to die for swim by and leisurely feed almost from your hands.

There is a Bygone Exhibit Area, Ye Olde Bakery Shop Tableaux a Enchanted Fairy Tale Woods, and little Country Fare and Gift Shops in which to browse Several catering areas, which offer mouth watering delicacies to tempt the palette.

The Mill is open daily from March till the end of October. This is a little flavour of yesteryear where you can sit and watch the world go by

and feel you are in another world far from the hustle and bustle of today's lifestyle.

Groups are catered for and excellent discounts apply. For all further information please contact Sandra Cross.

in 1238 still taking place on Tuesdays and Fridays. These are supplemented by a regular Craft Market every Friday throughout the summer.

Small though it is, Alford boasts some outstanding buildings. **Alford Manor House**, built around 1660, claims the distinction of being the largest thatched manor house in England. It's an attractive building with brick gabling and a beautifully maintained thatched roof. It serves now as a folk museum where visitors are invited to step back into the past and take a look at local life through time-warp shops, an old-fashioned veterinary surgery and a Victorian schoolroom. Reaching even further back into the past, the History Room contains a collection of interesting Roman finds and also displays from the salt works that once prospered in this part of the county. Another exhibit explores the still-flourishing connections between Alford and the USA.

An even more tangible link with the past is provided by **The Five Sailed Windmill** (see panel above) on the eastern side of the town. It was built by a local millwright, Sam Oxley, in 1813. Standing a majestic six floors high, it has five sails and four sets of grinding stones. This sturdy old mill came perilously close to total destruction in 1955. Thanks to the efforts of local enthusiasts it is now back in full commercial operation, complete with a vintage oven producing bakery items with the full flavour that

---

THE FIVE SAILED WINDMILL

Alford, Lincolnshire LN13 9EQ
Tel: 01507 462136
e-mail: enquiries@fivesailed.co.uk

The Five Sailed Windmill, one of England's finest working windmills, is situated on the edge of Alford enjoying views of the town and of the Lincolnshire Wolds. It is a handsome, six storey brick tower mill, c1837, and has four sets of working millstones. It is in commercial use as a flour mill and is open to the public all year round.

The 160 year old mill is full of atmosphere and a tour involves all the senses sight, sound, movement and a characteristic fresh floury smell. A range of organic flours of high nutritional value and flavour is produced and sold in the ground floor shop along with popular cereals and cakes. The local baker, Messrs Gray and Goodliffe (opposite Alford Manor House) offers bread baked with organic wholemeal flour from the Mill.

A converted Sail Shed now houses a stylish Tea Room and Edwardian and Victorian antiques are to be found in the old Engine House. All areas including the ground floor of the Mill are wheelchair accessible and the Windmill and Tea Room are open from 10.00am weekdays and 11.00am Sundays as follows: April, May, June & Oct: Tues, Fri, Sat, Sun; July to Sept: Daily; Nov to March Tues, Sat & Sun.

---

only the old-fashioned methods seem able to produce. Other attractions here include a wholefood shop, tea room and garden.

Alford's handsome medieval **Church of St Wilfrid** dates from the 14th century and amongst its treasures are a curiously carved Jacobean pulpit, the marble tomb of the former Manor House residents, (the Christopher family), and an amazing collection of tapestry kneelers. With so many parish churches nowadays locked for most of the time, it's good to know that St Wilfrid's is open daily from 9am to 4pm. In August, St Wilfrid's hosts a Flower Festival, part of the **Alford Festival**, which began in 1974 and over the years has attracted a growing variety of craftspeople, joined nowadays by dancers, singers, poets and actors.

DONINGTON-ON-BAIN
10 miles SW of Louth via A153/A157

Country roads lead westward into wonderful walking country at Donington-on-Bain, a peaceful Wolds village on the **Viking Way**. This well-trodden route, which was established in 1976 by Lincolnshire County Council, runs 147 miles from the Humber Bridge to Oakham in Rutland and is waymarked by Viking helmet symbols. While in Donington, have a look at the grand old water mill and the 13th century church. There is a story that it was usual at weddings for old ladies to throw hassocks at the bride as she walked up the aisle. This boisterous custom was ended in 1780 by the rector after he was hit by a badly aimed hassock!

To the east of Donington and south of Goulceby is the celebrated **Red Hill Nature Reserve**. The hill itself is an

The Viking Way

outcrop bearing a vein of spectacular red chalk that is rich in fossil finds. The small reserve is home to several species of butterflies and moths, the meadow pipit, common lizard and grass snake. From the clifftop there are some wonderful views across the Wolds. The hill also provides the setting for a Good Friday procession when the vicar of Asterby and three parishioners carrying crosses climb the steep lane. The three crosses are

erected above a chalk pit and a short service takes place with music provided by the Horncastle Brass band.

GRIMSBY

According to tradition it was a Dane called Grim who founded Grimsby. He had been ordered to drown the young Prince Havelock after the boy's father had been killed in battle. Grim could not bring himself to murder the child so he set sail for England. After a tempestuous crossing of the North Sea, Grim and the boy arrived at the Humber estuary where he used the timbers of their boat to build a house on the shore. They lived by selling fish and salt, thus establishing the foundations of an industry for which Grimsby would become known the world over.

But until 1848, Grimsby didn't even rank among Lincolnshire's ten largest towns. That was the year the railway arrived, making it possible for fish to be swiftly transported to major centres of population inland. Only four years later, the town's most famous landmark, the elegant, Italianate **Dock Tower**, was built, soaring more than 300ft above the busy docks. The Tower now enjoys Grade I listed building status, ranking it alongside such national treasures as Buckingham Palace and Chatsworth House. The tower's original function was purely utilitarian, the storage of 33,000 gallons of water to operate the hydraulic system that worked the lock gates. But shortly after it was built in 1852 it was discovered that water in a pressurized tube worked just as well so the tower became redundant. On open days, visitors can undertake the gruelling climb up the inside of the tower to enjoy the breathtaking views from the top.

The Tower stands beside Alexandra Dock, which enjoyed its heyday during

NATIONAL FISHING HERITAGE CENTRE

Alexandra Dock, Great Grimsby, North East
Lincolnshire DN31 1UZ
Tel: 01472 323345 Fax: 01472 323555
website: www.nelincs.gov.uk

In the 1950s Grimsby was the world's largest
fishing port so it's an appropriate location for the
National Fishing Heritage Centre which tells
vividly the story of the men who endured
appalling conditions at sea in order to "bring
home the catch". On arrival, visitors sign on as a
crew member and then travel from the back streets of Grimsby to the Arctic fishing grounds. Convincing

character models are used to demonstrate all aspects of
life on board, often adding their own humorous
dimensions to the scenes. An ingenious arrangement
simulates the pitch and roll of the ship; another creates
the icy blast of the North Atlantic wind. You can follow
the drama of the catch and experience the cramped living
conditions and the sweltering heat of the engine room.
You can try out the communications system in the radio
room; join the captain on the bridge and take over the
wheel; study the maps and charts and plot a course; and
visit the crew's cramped living quarters.

As well as recreating the deep sea fishing industry in
its heyday, the Centre also explores the social setting of
that period, complete with Bill Haley and the Comets,
Brylcreem and Cod Liver Oil! There are reconstructions of
the twisting back streets and alleys of 1950s Grimsby where
you can peek into the living rooms; join the fisherman in
the Freeman's Arms; visit the dockside shops; and queue
at the Settling Office to receive your pay.

The Centre has a genuine trawler, the *Ross Tiger*, around
which you are guided by a former trawlerman with many
tales to tell of the dangers, hardship and bravery that
characterised the life of a deep sea fisherman. To round
off your visit, call in at the Gift Shop for souvenirs and the Café for drinks and snacks.

The Centre is open from late March
to the end of October, Monday to
Friday, 10am to 4pm; weekends and
Bank Holidays, 10.30am to 5.30pm.
The Centre is fully accessible to people
using wheelchairs, prams or buggies;
there are ground floor disabled toilets
and lifts to all floors. However, the steep
steps on the Ross Tiger make access
difficult for visitors who require
assistance walking, and children under
5 years. The Centre is located just a 2-
minute walk from Grimsby town centre
and is clearly signposted from all major
routes. Car and coach parking is
plentiful – and free!

the 1950s when Grimsby was the world's largest fishing port. The story of those boom days is told in vivid detail in the **National Fishing Heritage Centre** (see panel on page 297) in Alexandra Dock, where visitors are challenged to navigate the icy waters of the Arctic, experience freezing winds, black ice, and lashing rain as the trawler decks, literally, heave and moan beneath your feet. A popular all-in arrangement is **The Fishy Tour**. This begins with an early morning visit to the fish auction, (white coats and wellies provided), followed by a traditional haddock and poached egg breakfast. Then on to the fish filleting and smoking houses, after which there's a guided tour of the Heritage Centre and an exploration of the *Ross Tiger*, a classic fishing trawler from the 1950s. A fish and chip lunch rounds off the trip.

The Time Trap (free), housed deep in old prison cells of the Town Hall, recreates the seamier side of life on dry land, and has proved a very popular annexe to the Heritage Centre. Visitors pass through dark, twisting corridors, explore mysterious nooks and crannies, discovering en route some unexpected facets of the town. The **Town Hall** itself, built in 1863, is a dignified building whose frontage has a series of busts depicting Queen Victoria, Prince Albert, local man John Whitgift, later Archbishop of Canterbury, Edward III (who granted the land around here to the Freemen of Grimsby), the Earl of Yarborough, (local landowner and High Steward of the borough at that time), and the historian Gervase Holles who was Mayor of Grimsby in 1640.

Many Victorian buildings were destroyed during World War II but a surviving legacy from that era is the **People's Park** where the facilities include a heart-shaped lake, children's play area, bowling greens, croquet lawn,

ornamental gardens and plenty of open space. There's also a Floral Hall (free) that is vibrant with colour all year round and houses both tropical and temperate species, and a large variety of house and garden plants, shrubs and conifers are on sale. Away from the centre, by the banks of the River Freshney, is **Freshney Park Way**, 300 acres of open space that attracts walkers, cyclists, anglers and birdwatchers as well as picnickers.

A final note for football fans. Be prepared for the question: Why does Grimsby Town Football Club play all its games away? Answer: Because the Mariners' ground is actually in Cleethorpes, a resort which has spread northwards to meet up with Grimsby itself.

AROUND GRIMSBY

IMMINGHAM
7 miles NW of Grimsby off the A180

A small village until the early 1900s, Immingham's breakthrough came when a new port on the south bank of the Humber was proposed. Grimsby naturally thought that the honour should be hers but consultants favoured Immingham because the deep water channel of the river runs close to the shore here. The new Docks were opened by King George V in 1912 and rapidly grew in importance, especially when the Great Central Railway switched its passenger liner service from Grimsby. The Docks expanded yet further when the Humber was dredged in the late 1960s to accommodate the new generation of giant tankers and a huge refinery now stands to the west of the town. Not promising country for tourists but the heart of the old village has survived with St Andrew's Church at its centre.

The **Immingham Museum** traces the links between the Docks and the railways and there's also an exhibit about the group of Puritans who, in 1607, set sail from Immingham to the Netherlands. A memorial to this event, the **Pilgrim Father Monument**, was erected by the Anglo-American Society in 1925. It originally stood near the point of embarkation but is now located near the church. Most of the 20ft-high column is made from local granite but near the top is a block of hewn from Plymouth Rock in New England where these religious refugees first landed.

CLEETHORPES
1 mile S of Grimsby on the A180

One of Cleethorpes' claims to fame is that it stands on zero longitude, i.e. on the Greenwich Meridian line. A signpost on the coastal path marks the Meridian line and points the way to London, the North Pole and other prominent places, an essential snap for the family album.

Just south of Grimsby and almost merged with it, Cleethorpes developed from a little village into a holiday resort when the railway line was built in the 1860s. The Manchester, Sheffield & Lincolnshire Railway Company developed much of the town and also built the splendid promenade, a mile long and 65ft wide, below the cliff. Above the promenade they built the sham ruin known as **Ross Castle**, named after the railway's general secretary, Edward Ross. Swathed in ivy, the folly marked the highest point of the cliffs which the promenade now protects from erosion.

The railway company also funded the construction of a pier. This was opened on August Bank Holiday Monday 1873, when nearly 3,000 people paid the then princely sum of sixpence (2½p) for admission. The toll was reduced the next day to a much more reasonable penny (½p), and it is recorded that in the first five weeks 37,000 people visited. The pier, like many others, was breached during the Second World War as a defence measure to discourage enemy landings, and it was never restored to its full length. The pier now measures 355ft compared to its original 1,200ft but the Edwardian pavilion of 1906 is still in place and is currently the largest nightclub in the area.

The town also boasts the last surviving seaside steam railway, the **Cleethorpes Coast Light Railway.** This narrow-gauge steam railway runs along the foreshore and lakeside every day from Easter to September, and on weekends throughout the year. A recent addition to the town's attractions is the **Cleethorpes Humber Estuary Discovery Centre.** Here visitors can become time travellers, discover extinct creatures and submerged forests, and work off their aggression by participating in a Viking raid. The Lincolnshire clockmaker, John Harrison, who solved the problem of finding longitude is celebrated in one of the many exhibits and the complex also offers refreshments in the Boaters Tea Room.

NORTH SOMERCOTES
12 miles SE of Grimsby off the A1031

Olney's Shrove Tuesday pancake races may be better known but those at North Somercotes are equally popular. Contestants run the length of this straggling village tossing their pancakes as they go. There are separate contests for adults and children.

To the east of the village is the **Donna Nook Nature Reserve** which stretches 6 miles south along the coast to Saltfleet. In summer it's a favoured nesting site for many species of birds, amongst them dunnock, little grebe and meadow pipits.

Large colonies of brent geese, dunlin and other waders are attracted to the mudflats while common and grey seals pup on the sandflats. As well as marram grass and sea buckthorn, the dunes also provide a support for the much rarer pyramidal orchids.

CAISTOR
10 miles SW of Grimsby on the A46

Caistor's market place stands on the plain, looking across corn fields to the distant towers of Lincoln Cathedral; but its narrow streets wind their way up the western slopes of the Wolds. Caistor's name makes it clear that this agreeable little market town did indeed start life as a small Roman camp. Just a few hard-to-find fragments of the once massive walls remain. However, it's known that the camp measured just 300 yards by 100 yards and that the present **Church of St Peter & St Paul** stands at the exact centre of the Roman enclosure. The church, whose oldest part is the Anglo-Saxon tower, contains a curiosity kept in a glass case. This is the famous Gad Whip, which until 1847 was *"cracked over the head of the vicar on Palm Sunday by a man from Broughton in payment for certain parcels of land"*. Another version of the tradition claims that the whip, which had a purse containing 2 shillings tied to it, was simply waved over the head of the clergyman while the latter read the second lesson. Either way, Victorian opinion regarded the performance as not consistent with ecclesiastical decorum and it was suppressed.

A mile or so north of the town, **Pelham's Pillar** commemorates the planting of the surrounding woods by Charles Pelham, Earl of Yarborough. Between 1787 and 1828, the earl had planted 12,552,700 trees – at least that is what the inscription claims. The lofty tower cost a staggering £2,395 to build

and when it was completed in 1849 no less a personage than Prince Albert came to view it. The tower is locked but if you want to climb up inside, a key can be obtained within reasonable hours from the Keeper's Cottage, Pillar Lodge.

The 147-mile long Viking Way passes through Caistor and about 5 miles south of the town climbs to **Normanby-on-the-Wold**, the highest village in Lincolnshire. The path continues through **Walesby** where All Saints Church is known as the Ramblers' Church because of its stained glass window depicting Christ with ramblers and cyclists, and on to the delightful village of Tealby.

MARKET RASEN
18 miles SW of Grimsby off the A46

This pleasing little market town stands between the great plain that spreads north of Lincoln and the sheltering Wolds to the east. Now happily bypassed, the town still has a market on Tuesdays and throughout the year there are regular meetings at the **Market Rasen Racecourse.**

Taking its name from the little River Rase, Market Rasen was once described by Charles Dickens as being *"the sleepiest town in England"*. Much of the central part is a conservation area.

BOSTON

An important inland port on the River Witham, Boston's fortunes reached their peak during the Middle Ages when the town was second only to London in the amount of taxes it paid. Today, it's a prosperous market town of around 37,000 inhabitants and the administrative centre for the region. The market, more than 450 years old now and the largest open air market in

Lincolnshire, takes place every Wednesday and Saturday.

The town's most famous landmark is St Botolph's Church, much better known as the **Boston Stump**. "Stump" is a real misnomer since the tower soars 272ft into the sky and is visible for thirty miles or more from land and sea. Building of the tower began around 1425 and was not completed for a hundred years. The body of the church is older still - it dates back to 1309 and is built mainly in the graceful Decorated style of architecture. St Botolph's is the largest parish church in England (20,070 square feet in all) and its spacious interior is wonderfully light and airy. The church is noted for its abundance of often bizarre medieval carvings in wood and stone - a bear playing an organ, a man lassooing a lion, a fox in a bishop's cope taking a jug of water from a baboon.

One of Boston's most striking secular buildings is the 15th century **Guildhall**, which for 300 years served as the Town Hall and now houses the town museum. The most popular attraction here is connected with the Pilgrim Fathers. In 1607 this famous band of brothers tried to escape to the religious tolerance of the Netherlands but were betrayed by the captain of their ship, arrested and thrown into the Guildhall cells. The bleak cells in which they were detained can still be seen, along with the old town

Boston Guildhall Museum

stocks. Other exhibits range from archaeological finds to a portrait of the botanist Sir Joseph Banks, a local man who sailed with Captain Cook and later introduced sheep to Australia. A recent addition to the museum's attractions is a virtual reality simulation which permits visitors to "walk" through Boston as it was in the 16th century. You can chat with a variety of local characters ranging

HAROLD WAKEFIELD

20 Rochford Tower Lane, Boston, Lincolnshire PE21 9RQ
Tel/Fax: 01205 362785

Harold Wakefield has spent a major part of his life studying horses to which the magnificent sculptures and rocking horses he creates are a testimony. At his workshop he produces what many consider to be the most realistic sculptures of rocking and free standing horses available in this or any other country. "I strive" he says "to create a piece of sculpture which I hope will give the recipient many years of pleasure". Harold accepts commissions for carvings of various animals from 6 inches high to life size after fully discussing the customer's requirements, ensuring that at the end of the day they acquire a unique sculpture to be proud of.

from the Elizabethan composer John Taverner to Lord Hussey, Lord of the Manor and friend of Henry VIII.

Another impressive building is the **Maud Foster Windmill** (1819), the tallest working windmill in Britain and unusual in having 5 sails, or "sweeps". Visitors can climb to the top of the mill, see the machinery and millstones in action, and enjoy some fine views from the outside balcony. There's a tea room and a Mill Shop that sells the mill's own stone-ground organic flour as well as local books and souvenirs.

If you enjoy seeking out architectural curiosities, then there's a splendid one in a quiet back street of the town. The frontage of the **Freemason's Hall** represents a miniature Egyptian temple, complete with columns crowned by papyrus fronds. Half a century earlier, following Napoleon's Egyptian campaign there had been a spate of such monumental buildings, but Boston's temple, built in the 1860s, presents a very late flowering of the style.

AROUND BOSTON

FISHTOFT
3 miles SE of Boston off the A52

This tiny village has just one claim to fame. It was from an obscure creek near the village that the Pilgrim Fathers made their first attempt to escape England's oppressive religious laws. A simple monument is inscribed with the words: *Near this place in September 1607 those later known as the Pilgrim Fathers set sail on their first attempt to find religious freedom across the seas.*

DONINGTON
10 miles SW of Boston on the A52

A small market town, Donington boasts some elegant Georgian buildings,

amongst them the former Grammar School, and a huge church which was bountifully re-endowed in the 14th century when Donington was flourishing as the centre of trade in flax and hemp. Like Deeping St James the church has its own rather elegant *hude*, or movable hut. If inclement weather co-incided with a burial, the hut would be moved to the graveside. Standing inside the shelter (complete with its own coat hook) the parson could smugly observe the mourners being drenched. Inside the church there are a number of memorials to the Flinders family. Their most famous son, Matthew, was born at Donington in 1774 and later became celebrated for his exploration of the Australian coastline. Returning from Australia to England via the Indian Ocean in a decrepit ship, Flinders put in at Mauritius for repairs. At that time, Mauritius was governed by the French who had watched British expansion in Australasia with alarm. They arrested Flinders as a spy and it was seven long years before they allowed him to continue his journey back to England and his home town of Donington.

SPALDING

This small market town is known around the world for its annual **Flower Parade** which attracts half a million visitors each year. Established in 1959, the Festival is held in early May when marching bands lead a succession of colourful floats, each adorned with thousands of tulip heads and spring flowers, through the town. The floats are then displayed at **Springfield Gardens** whose 30 landscaped acres include marvellous show gardens, a carp lake and a sub-tropical palm house.

The two weeks around the Flower Parade co-incide with the South Holland Arts Festival featuring open air concerts, workshops, exhibitions and a host of other activities and performances. The festival is based on the South Holland Centre, a stylish venue which is active throughout the year and also has a café-bar on the first floor overlooking the Market Place.

Spalding itself is an interesting place to stroll around, with Georgian terraces lining the River Welland and with many of the buildings revealing Dutch architectural influences. Before the days of mass car ownership, most visitors to the Tulip Festival arrived by excursion trains and a great mesh of sidings stretch to the north of the town. To cross them, the longest iron footbridge in Lincolnshire was built. Two, actually, because another equally impressive construction stands south of the station, spanning the main line and a now defunct branch line.

Tulip Fields, Spalding

The jewel in Spalding's crown is undoubtedly **Ayscoughfee Hall Museum and Gardens**, a well-preserved medieval mansion standing in attractive gardens by the river and with some venerable Yew tree walks. Pronounced "Asscuffy", the Hall was built around 1429 for Sir Richard Aldwyn. It later became the home of Maurice Johnson (1688-1755), a member of the Royal Society and a leading figure in the intellectual life of his day. In 1710, he founded the Gentlemen's Society of Spalding, which still flourishes from its headquarters and small museum in Broad Street. Part of the Gentlemen's extensive collection of stuffed birds, dating back to 1800, is on display in Ayscoughfee Hall, which also has a prominent exhibit honouring the explorer and oceanographer Capt. Matthew Flinders who has been

mentioned earlier under his birthplace in Donington. Other galleries record Spalding's social and economic history.

Located in the lovely grounds of Ayscoughfee Hall is Spalding's War Memorial which stands at one end of an ornamental pool which in winters past would freeze over. Blocks of ice were hewn from it and stored in the icehouse which still survives, tucked away in a corner of the garden walls.

Connoisseurs of odd buildings should make their way down a lane off Cowbit Road to a red brick building that belongs to no recognisable school of architecture. Known as the **Tower House**, it was built in Victorian times but no one has any idea who built it, why or exactly when. It's a bizarre medley of medieval towers and crenellations, a random obelisk, Georgian-style windows and other bits and pieces. One writer described it as being " *like a giant Lego construction*". It is now a private house but the exterior can be enjoyed from the lane.

BAYTREE NURSERIES

Weston, Lincolnshire PE12 6JU
Tel: 01406 370242   Fax: 01406 372829
e-mail: info@baytree-gardencentre.com
website: www.baytree-gardencentre.com

Winner of the Garden Centre of Excellence Award, **Baytree Nurseries** is much more than just a garden centre. Within its 30-acre site gardeners will find every conceivable item they could need to enhance their gardens as well as a whole range of other attractions.

Reinhard and Yvonne Biehler bought what was then a smallholding in 1970 and year by year have steadily expanded the business. "Many of our customers come regularly just to see what has altered and what is new" says Reinhard. Naturally, the heart of the complex is the outdoor plant area, one of the largest in the country and offering a huge range of well-known and unusual plants. At the information centre on the edge of the plant area visitors can consult with knowledgeable and vastly experienced staff.

Around the plant area are other outlets dedicated to gardening accessories – a Compost Canopy with every kind of planting media imaginable; a Mowers Centre with a huge selection of mowers and other garden machinery; garden furniture, statuary and barbecues; garden tools; fencing; greenhouses, summerhouses, sheds, garages and conservatories; and garden clothing. In the main shop you'll find a staggering choice of chemicals and fertilizers to feed and weed every part of your garden.

Gardening books in abundance are on sale in the book shop along with general interest books, CDs, toys for all ages, giftware and collectables such as Steiff and Corgi. Nearby, a florist's shop is stocked with fragrant fresh flowers in bouquets or arrangements as well as potted plants and flower stems that never need watering – they're artificial but look completely realistic. Another huge shop is devoted to pets and aquatics where visitors can marvel at the colossal Koi in the display ponds and choose from an extensive range of tropical and cold water fish. To keep the kids amused, there's a secure play area with climbing frames and slides, plenty of picnic benches and open grass. They will also enjoy the Owl Centre with its 80-odd birds of prey, some of which can be handled under the guidance of the resident falconer. Flying displays are held most days.

Ready for some refreshment? The Hop-in Restaurant has been recently extended, now seating 250, and has a licensed bar and easy access to the play area and display gardens.

In the run-up to Christmas Baytree Nurseries really excels itself with its Winter Wonderland complete with Santa in his grotto – a grotto which, according to a Channel 4 report, is the best in the country!

A couple of miles south of Spalding, the **Gordon Boswell Romany Museum** has a colourful collection of Romany Vardos (caravans), carts and harnesses along with an extensive display of Romany photographs and sketches covering the last 150 years. A slide show and conducted tour are available and there's also a fortune telling tent. Gordon Boswell and his wife Margaret also arrange Romany Days Out in a horse-drawn Vardo, a trip which includes a meal cooked over a traditional Romany stick fire. The museum is open from March to October but closed on Mondays (except Bank Holidays) and Tuesdays.

AROUND SPALDING

PINCHBECK
2 miles N of Spalding on the B1356

For an interesting insight into how the South Holland Fen has been transformed by man, a visit to the **Pinchbeck Engine and Land Drainage Museum** is strongly recommended. The star exhibit here is the Pinchbeck Engine, a sturdy monster which was built way back in 1833. Each year for almost 120 years, up until 1952, the 20hp engine lifted an average of 3 million tons of water from the soggy fens at a rate of 7,500 gallons per minute.

In 1988 the Drainage Board and South Holland Council restored this superb piece of machinery and it now operates regularly, and is the centrepiece of the museum, which is open daily from April to October.

Also in Pinchbeck is the **Spalding Bulb Museum** which follows the growth of the bulb-growing industry down the years with the aid of tableaux and artefacts, as well as audio-visual and seasonal working demonstrations. A third attraction is **Spalding Tropical**

Spalding Tropical Forest

Forest, actually a water garden centre but promising *"a tropical paradise full of plants, waterfalls, fountains and streams"*.

SURFLEET
4 miles N of Spalding off the A16

The River Glen provides an attractive feature in this popular village with its yachts on the water and holiday homes on the banks. Surfleet church has a tower that leans at an alarming angle, more than 6ft out of true, the result of subsidence in the boggy ground. The north door is pockmarked with musket shot, a permanent reminder of an unwelcome visit from Cromwell's soldiers during the Civil War.

WESTON
3 miles NE of Spalding on the A151

This small village surrounded by tulip fields boasts a fine church, **St Mary's**, which is notable for having one of the most complete Early Gothic interiors in the country. The superb arcades have been compared to those in Lincoln Cathedral and there's a wealth of the carving known as Lincolnshire stiff-leaf. The 13th century font is carved with huge flowers decorating each panel of the bowl and the Victorian pulpit has openwork panels somewhat Islamic in style. An eye-catching feature in the rather dimly-lit interior is the display of colourful kneelers placed on the shelves of the pews.

WHAPLODE ST CATHERINE
5 miles E of Spalding on the B1165

A great find here is the **Museum of Entertainment**, a fascinating collection of mechanical musical instruments, and gramophone and phonograph records. One of the stars of the show is a theatre organ brought here from the Gaumont Cinema in Coventry.

HOLBEACH
10 miles E of Spalding on the A151/B1168

Located deep in the heart of the Fens, Holbeach stands at the centre of one of the largest parishes in the country. It extends some 15 miles from end to end and covers 21,000 acres. Holbeach is a pleasing little town with a market on both Thursday and Saturday and also boasts an impressive church with a lofty spire visible for miles across the flat fields. The curious entrance porch, with its two round towers, is believed to have been "borrowed" from the now vanished Moulton Castle, a few miles to the west.

When William Cobbett passed through Holbeach on his *Rural Rides* in the 1840s he was delighted with the *"neat little town, a most beautiful church, fruit trees in abundance and the land dark in colour and*

Museum of Entertainment

as fine in substance as flour". Surprisingly little has changed since William visited.

GEDNEY
13 miles E of Spalding off the A17

Of all the fine churches in this corner of the county, **St Mary's** at Gedney is perhaps the most spectacular. It is supernaturally light inside, an effect produced by its magnificent clerestory in which the medieval masons reduced the stonework to near-invisibility. The 24 three-light windows drench the interior with light, brilliantly illuminating the carvings and bosses of the roof, and the interesting collection of monuments. The best known of these is a brass in the south aisle which depicts a lady who died around 1400 with a belled puppy crouching in the folds of her gown.

LONG SUTTON
15 miles E of Spalding on B1359

Long Sutton is a very appropriate name for this straggling village. St Mary's Church has an unusual 2-storeyed porch, the upper floor of which was once used as a school, and a rare, lead-covered spire 160ft high.

The surrounding area borders The Wash and is a favourite place with walkers and naturalists, especially bird-watchers. One of the most popular routes is the **Peter Scott Walk** – during the 1930s the celebrated naturalist lived in one of the two lighthouses on the River Nene nearby. Another route, **King John's Lost Jewels Trail**, covers 23 miles of quiet country roads and is suitable for cyclists and motorists. It starts at Long Sutton market place and passes Sutton Bridge where the unfortunate king is believed to have lost all his treasure in the marsh. Sutton Bridge itself is notable for the swing bridge over the River Nene. Built in 1897 for the Midland and Great Northern Railway, it is one of very few examples still surviving of a working swing bridge.

CROWLAND
10 miles S of Spalding on the A1073

It was in 699AD that a young Mercian nobleman named Guthlac became disillusioned with the world and took to a small boat. He rowed off into the fens until he came to a remote muddy island, (which is what the name Crowland means). Here he built himself a hut and a small chapel. Guthlac's reputation as a wise and holy man attracted a host of visitors in search of spiritual guidance He died in 714 and shortly afterwards his kinsman, King Ethelbald of Mercia, founded the monastery that became known as **Crowland Abbey.**

The abbey buildings have suffered an unusually troubled history. Nothing but

Crowland Abbey

some oak foundations remain of the first abbey - the rest was destroyed by Danish invaders. The monastery was rebuilt in Saxon style in about 950 when the community began to live according to the rule of St Benedict. That abbey was also destroyed, on this occasion by a great fire in 1091. An earthquake in 1117 interrupted the rebuilding. Some 50 years later, the third abbey was completed, in the Norman style. Parts of this splendid building can still be seen, notably in the dog-tooth west arch of the central tower. Another fire caused massive damage in 1143 and the restoration that followed provides most of the substantial ruins that remain. They present an impressive sight as they loom forbiddingly over this small fenland village. Happily, the abbey's former north aisle survived and now serves as the parish church.

Crowland is also noted for its extraordinary "Bridge without a River", also known locally as the "Three Ways to Nowhere Bridge". When it was built in the 1300s, **Trinity Bridge** provided a dry crossing over the confluence of three small streams. Hence its unique triangular shape. But the streams dried up and the bridge now serves no purpose apart from being extremely decorative. At one end, there's a large seated figure, possibly of Christ and almost certainly pilfered from the West Front of the abbey where a surprising number of these 15th century statues are still in place.

STAMFORD

Proclaimed as *"the finest stone town in England"*, Stamford was declared the country's first Conservation Area in 1967. Later, *"England's most attractive town"* (John Betjeman's words), became familiar to millions of TV viewers when its wonderfully unspoilt Georgian streets and squares provided an authentic backdrop for the BBC's dramatisation of George Eliot's *Middlemarch*. Stamford is a thriving little town with a wide variety of small shops (including a goodly number of antiques shops), and a bustling street market on Fridays.

A dubious local legend asserts that Stamford was founded in the 8th century BC by the Trojan king of Britain, Bladud, and continued as a seat of learning until the 14th century AD when it was supplanted by the upstart universities of Oxford and Cambridge. Whatever its past, what gives the present town its enchanting character is the handsome Georgian architecture, evidenced everywhere in private houses and elegant public buildings such as the Town Hall, the Assembly Rooms, the theatre and the well-known George Hotel whose gallows sign spans the main street.

Stamford's most ancient ecclesiastical building is **St Leonard's Priory**, founded by the Benedictines in the 11th century and a fine example of Norman architecture with an ornate west front and north side arcade.

Secular buildings of note include Browne's Hospital in Broad Street which was founded in 1494 by the same Browne brothers mentioned above. It now houses the **Museum of Almshouse Life** - the ground floor presenting

aspects of almshouse life; the upper hosting various exhibitions.

The town is well-provided with museums. The **Stamford Museum** (free) includes an exhibit celebrating one of the town's most famous visitors. Daniel Lambert earned a precarious living by exhibiting himself as the world's heaviest man. As an additional source of income he would challenge people to race along a course of his choosing. Daniel would then set off along the corridors of the inn, filling them wall to wall and preventing any challenger from passing. When he died at Stamford in 1809 his body was found to weigh almost 59 stones. He had been staying at the Waggon & Horses Inn and the wall of his bedroom had to be demolished in order to remove the body.

Railway buffs will want to pay a visit to the **Stamford East Railway Station**. The station was built in 1855-6 for the branch line of the Great North Railway. Because the land was owned by the Marquess of Exeter, of nearby Burghley House, the architect William Hurst was obliged to build in the classical style using the local honey-coloured stone. The result is surely one of the most elegant small stations in the country.

A rather more specialised museum is the **Stamford Steam Brewery Museum** which has a collection of original 19th

TRUFFLES OF STAMFORD

16 St Mary's Hill, Stamford, Lincolnshire PE9 2DP
Tel: 01780 757282

In the heart of historic Stamford, looking across to St Mary's Church, you'll find a little gem called **Truffles of Stamford**. Built in 1781, it has been, since 1992, a chocolate shop, tea room and coffee shop rolled into one, owned and run by Sarah Harrington. It's an intimate and very welcoming place with seats for 15, linen tablecloths and watercolours by local artists. Soft, relaxing music plays in the background. Besides the Belgian hand-made truffles, the major temptations are the hand-made cakes in constantly changing varieties. Also on offer are baguettes with a choice of mouth-watering fillings.

century brewing equipment. The museum is housed in the malt house and brewery, which was established by William Burn in 1825 and continued brewing right up until 1974. It is now open to the public by prior arrangement.

Two more of Stamford's famous residents should be mentioned. Buried in the town cemetery is Sir Malcolm Sargent, the "pin-up" conductor of the Henry Wood Promenade Concerts in the 1960s and '70s. The cross on his grave is inscribed with the Promenaders' Prayer. And in St Martin's Church is the splendid tomb of William Cecil, 1st Lord Burghley, who was Elizabeth I's Chief Secretary of State from her accession until his death in 1598. Cecil's magnificent residence, Burghley House, lies a mile south of the town.

"The largest and grandest house of the Elizabethan Age", **Burghley House** (see panel on page 310) presents a dazzling

spectacle with its domed towers, walls of cream coloured stone, and acres of windows. Clear glass was still ruinously expensive in the 1560s so Elizabethan grandees like Cecil flaunted their wealth by having windows that stretched almost from floor to ceiling. Burghley House also displays the Elizabethan obsession with symmetry - every tower, dome, pilaster and pinnacle has a corresponding partner.

Contemporaries called Burghley a "prodigy house", a title shared at that time with only one other stately home in England – Longleat in Wiltshire. Both houses were indeed prodigious in size and in cost. At Burghley, Cecil commissioned the most celebrated interior decorator of the age, Antonio Verrio, to create rooms of unparalleled splendour. In his "Heaven Room", Verrio excelled even himself, populating the lofty walls and ceiling with a dynamic

CHEZ SOI

26/27 High Street, Stamford, Lincolnshire PE9 2AY
Tel: 01780 482845

6 Bailgate, Lincoln, Lincolnshire LN1 3AR
Tel: 01522 544666

Chez Soi is a dream come true for *Country Living* readers with both of their shops offering full ranges from favourites such as Emma Bridgewater, Farrow & Ball, Cath Kidston, Crabtree & Evelyn and Mulberry.

In addition the Stamford shop houses an array of original pieces for the home and garden; scrubbed pine tables, period lighting, furniture painted in Farrow & Ball colours, garden furniture and wirework planters.

BURGHLEY HOUSE

Stamford, Lincolnshire PE9 3JY
Tel: 01780 752451 e-mail: burghley@burghley.co.uk
Fax: 01780 480125 website: www.burghley.co.uk

With stunning architecture, an exquisite collection of ceramics, 17th century Italian paintings, as well as beautifully maintained 'Capability' Brown landscaped grounds, Burghley House is the largest and grandest house of the first Elizabethan Age. Built and mostly designed by William Cecil, Lord High Treasurer of England, between 1565 and 1587, the House is a family home to his descendants to this day.

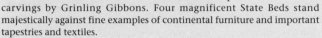

The State Rooms, many decorated by Antonio Verrio, house the earliest inventoried collection of Japanese ceramics in the West, rare examples of European porcelain and wood carvings by Grinling Gibbons. Four magnificent State Beds stand majestically against fine examples of continental furniture and important tapestries and textiles.

An exciting new development at Burghley is the recently opened sculpture park in a reclaimed part of the gardens. This Sculpure Garden provides visitors with a tranquil setting from which to appreciate the meandering line of mature trees and the 26 acre 'Capability' Brown Lake. Children in particular will enjoy the carved 'Teddy Bear's Picnic' sculpture. Within the extensive grounds of the estate is a 160 acre Deer Park. Visitors are able to walk through the deer park, and see the original herd that was established there in the 16th century.

A visit to Burghley offers a wonderful opportunity to experience a living, breathing example of England's Elizabethan history, lavish taste and style.

been reclaimed and planted with specimen trees and shrubs and now provide a sylvan setting for a number of dramatic artworks by contemporary sculptors.

Throughout the summer season, Burghley hosts a series of events of which the best known, the Burghley Horse Trials, takes place at the end of August.

AROUND STAMFORD

THE DEEPINGS
8 miles E of Stamford off the A16

There are four Deepings in all and they lie alongside the River Welland which here forms

gallery of mythological figures.

In the 18th century, Cecil's descendants commissioned the ubiquitous "Capability" Brown to landscape the 160 acres of parkland surrounding the house. These enchanting grounds are open to visitors and are also home to a large herd of fallow deer which was first established in Cecil's time. Brown also designed the elegant Orangery which is now a licensed restaurant overlooking rose beds and gardens.

A more recent addition to Burghley's attractions is the Sculpture Garden. Twelve acres of scrub woodland have

the county boundary with Cambridgeshire. The largest is Market Deeping which was once an important stop on the London to Lincoln coaching route. The triangular town centre has some imposing Georgian buildings, a large antique and craft centre, and a church dating back to 1240.

Today, Deeping St James merges imperceptibly with its larger neighbour. The old village sits on the banks of the Welland which at this point is controlled by two locks. The **Priory Church of St James** is an impressively large structure and was originally built as a satellite cell of Thorney Abbey. Amongst its possessions is a *hude* - a small shelter rather like a sentry box which was designed to keep the Vicar dry when conducting burial services in the rain. Another interesting curiosity is the small square building in the centre of the village. It was originally the Market Cross but was converted into a lock-up in 1819 to contain village drunks and other troublemakers. Three semi-circular stone seats with chains can still be seen through bars in the doors. Incongruously, the rather elegant little building is topped by a graceless modern street lamp.

BOURNE

10 miles N of Stamford on the A6121

A small attractive town, Bourne has a fine church, an impressive Town Hall of 1821 with an unusual staircase entry, delightful Memorial Gardens, and a variety of family shops, craft and antiques emporia, as well as modern shopping precincts. A colourful market takes place every Thursday and Saturday.

It was the springs of clear water that enticed the Romans to settle here. Today, the springs flow into St Peter's Pool from which a small stream known as the Bourne Eau runs into the town and Memorial Gardens. Here, willow trees border the crystal clear water, home to fish, wildfowl and small roosting houses. En route, the Bourne Eau passes Baldocks Mill which functioned between 1800 and the 1920s, and now houses the **Bourne Heritage Centre**.

A mile west of the town, beside the A151, stands **Bourne Wood**, 400 acres of long-established woodland with an abundant and varied plant and animal life. Once part of the great Forest of Brunswald, it's a great place for walking or cycling, and has some interesting

CAWTHORPE HALL

Bourne, Lincolnshire PE10 0AB
Tel: 01778 423830 Fax: 01778 426620
e-mail: cawthorpe@rosewater.co.uk
website: www.rosewater.co.uk

Cawthorpe is a tiny village in open countryside north of Bourne. John Armstrong, born in East Africa, retired to this area with his wife Chantal after a career in civil engineering and started the production of rose water and rose oil at **Cawthorpe Hall**. The hall is a sturdy building with an ashlar stone frontage and a slate roof. In the yard is a small stable block now used for the distillation of roses, the roses being cultivated in a 3.5 acre garden. Varieties used in the process include Galica, Bourbon, Damask, Portland and the short-flowering Kazanlik.

The finished product has uses as a toilet water, in skin care and therapy, as a medicinal treatment and a flavour-enhancer in cooking. The hall is also a marvellous country retreat with 3 large, peaceful and very comfortable en suite double bedrooms and 1 single. An excellent English or Continental breakfast is served in winter in the farmhouse kitchen and at other times in a magnificent studio hung with pictures painted by John and Chantal's daughter, Dominique. Chantal was born in Madeira and is fluent in French and Portuguese. A warm welcome is extended by the owners and also by the two affectionate resident dogs, Ali and Fupi. Cawthorpe Hall is also available for charity functions, weddings and parties.

modern sculpture in wood and stone. The waters around Bourne and the Deepings are credited with curative properties and the Blind Well, on the edge of the wood, is reputed to be particularly efficacious in healing eye complaints.

About 4 miles south of Bourne, near the village of Witham on the Hill, stands the **Bowthorpe Oak**, which is believed to be the largest in terms of its girth than any other tree in Britain. When last measured, the oak was just over 39ft around. The tree is hollow and it's claimed that on one occasion 39 people stood inside it.

GRIMSTHORPE

5 miles NW of Bourne on the A151

Grimsthorpe Castle is definitely two-faced. Seen from the north, it's a stately 18th century demi-palace. Viewed from the south, it's a homely Tudor dwelling.

The Tudor part of the house was built at incredible speed in order to provide a convenient lodging place in Lincolnshire for Henry VIII on his way north to meet James V of Scotland in York. The royal visit to Grimsthorpe Castle duly took place in 1541 but the honour of the royal presence was tarnished by the adultery that allegedly took place here between Henry's fourth wife, Katherine Howard, and an attractive young courtier, Thomas Culpepper. In Tudor times, royal misbehaviour of this nature constituted an act of high treason. The errant Queen and her ardent courtier paid a fatal price for their nights of passion at Grimsthorpe Castle. Both were condemned to the executioner's axe.

The imposing Georgian part of Grimsthorpe Castle was built in the early 1700s. The 16th Baron Grimsthorpe had just been elevated by George I to the topmost rank of the peerage as Duke of

MILL GALLERY

Mill House, 19 Main Road, Dyke, Bourne, Lincolnshire PE10 0AF
Tel/Fax: 01778 393244
e-mail: rwinkworth@aol.com

The Grade II listed building that houses the **Mill Gallery** originally stood several miles to the south but was moved to its present position in the small village of Dyke in the 1990s. The former flour mill now provides a showcase for works of art gathered from all around the world, but especially from Italy, by Richard Winkworth, a former manager of 5 art galleries in and around London. A mix of originals and limited editions, oils and watercolours, and sculptures, the works are displayed throughout the 4-storeyed building which, incidentally, commands grand panoramic views of the south Lincolnshire countryside.

Richard's partner in the gallery, Christine Beardwood, is an

accomplished sculptor and artist whose work was exhibited at the Royal Academy in 1993 and 1999. Self-taught from the age of 16, Christine works in bronze and her commissions vary from life-size statues of people to figures of family pets. In painting, her preferred medium is oils but in both media she aspires to create fluid movement and expression. The Mill Gallery also offers a quality framing service and also produces custom-made stencilling for interior decorating and commercial usage.

Grimsthorpe Castle Gardens

hills, complete with an artificial lake and a sham bridge.

Seventeen generations of the Willoughby family have been Lords of the Manor of Grimsthorpe since they first arrived here in 1516. During that time they have borne a bewildering variety of other titles. All have held the Barony but at different times have also been Earls of Lindsey, Dukes of Ancaster and, later, Earls of Ancaster. The Willoughby genealogy is further complicated by the fact that the Barony is one of the very few peerages in Britain that can descend through the female line. A marriage in 1533 between the 49-year-old Duke of Suffolk and the 14-year-old Margaret Willoughby added yet another title, Duchess of Suffolk, to the Barony's pedigree.

Ancaster. It was only natural that the new Duke should wish to improve his rather modest ancestral home. He commissioned Sir John Vanbrugh, the celebrated architect of Blenheim Palace and Castle Howard, to completely redesign the building. As it happened, only the north front and the courtyard were completed to Vanbrugh's designs which is why the castle presents two such different faces.

There's no such confusion about the grounds of Grimsthorpe Castle. These could only be 18th century and were landscaped by whom else than "Capability" Brown. His fee was £105, about £100,000 in our money. In return for this substantial "consideration" Brown miraculously transformed the flat fields of south Lincolnshire into an Arcadian landscape of gently rolling

GRANTHAM

In a radio poll during the 1980s, Grantham was voted *"the most boring town in England"*. It seems a rather unfair judgement on this lively market town set beside the River Witham. Turn a blind eye to the charmless environs that surround the town from whichever direction you approach. Make your way to its centre which boasts a pleasing core

Westgate Wools & Crafts

14a Westgate, Grantham, Lincolnshire NG31 6LT
Tel: 01476 578644

Occupying a Grade II listed building in the centre of town, **Westgate Wools & Crafts** stocks a huge range of materials for knitting and embroidery enthusiasts. Enthusiasts like June Kirton who used to shop here until the owners retired and she, together with her husband John, took over in April 2002. Along with a vast choice of coloured wools and silks you'll find every kind of knitting accessory, sewing boxes and lamps, rug making kits, cake decoration items, wedding favours, dolls' house accessories and much more. Westgate Wools also stocks Anchor, Venus, Sirdar and Wendy Wools.

of old buildings. These cluster around the town's famous church, **St Wulfram's**, whose soaring spire, 282ft (86 metres) high, has been described as *"the finest steeple in England"*. When completed in 1300 it was the loftiest in England and is still the sixth highest. St Wulfram's interior is not quite so inspirational, dominated as it is by uncharacteristically drab Victorian stained glass, but the rare 16th century chained library of 150 volumes is occasionally open to the public and well worth seeing.

Just across from the church, **Grantham House** in Castlegate is a charming National Trust property, parts of which date back to around 1380. Additions were made in the 16th and 18th centuries. The house stands in 25 acres of garden and grounds sloping down to the River Witham and although the house itself is not open to the public there is a right of way through the meadows on the opposite bank of the river. Also in Castlegate, look out for the only living pub sign in the country. In a lime tree outside the **Beehive Inn** is a genuine bee hive whose bees produce some 30lbs of honey each year. This unique advertisement for the pub has been in place since at least 1830.

After St Wulfram's Church, Grantham's most venerable building is that of the **Angel and Royal Hotel** in High Street. The attractive 15th century façade still bears the weather-beaten sculptured heads of Edward III and Queen Philippa over its central archway. King John held his court here and it was in one of the inn's rooms that Richard III signed the death warrant of the 2nd Duke of Buckingham in 1483.

A hundred yards or so from the inn stands an unusual Grantham landmark. The **Conduit** is a miniature tower built by the Corporation in 1597 as the

---

BLACK BULL INN

Lobthorpe, nr Grantham, Lincolnshire NG33 5LL
Tel: 01476 860086 Fax: 01476 860796

A charming former coaching inn, **The Black Bull Inn** dates back to the 1730s and during its long history has provided hospitality for some interesting guests. Queen Victoria stopped over here on her way to Scotland while a less honourable guest was Dick Turpin who is alleged to have spent time in hiding here. According to local legend, his escape tunnel has still to be discovered. Just minutes from the A1, 2 miles south of the Colsterworth roundabout, the Black Bull is surrounded by quiet gardens and set in the gentle Lincolnshire countryside. Owner Carol Tripp guarantees a friendly, unpretentious atmosphere with delicious home-cooked meals and special menus available.

The 10 spacious guest bedrooms are all elegantly furnished and decorated; children and pets are all welcome. There's plenty to do in the neighbourhood: excellent sporting facilities just 2 miles away; Rutland Water, Europe's largest artificial lake, with fishing and sailing; and one of the country's finest Georgian towns, Stamford, is just a few minutes drive away. Two splendid castles, Belvoir and Grimsthorpe, are within easy reach, as is Burghley House; historic Nottingham is a mere 30 miles away and the inn is also conveniently located for the East of England Show grounds, host to many major show-jumping competitions.

Sir Isaac Newton

receiving point for the fresh water supply that flowed from springs in the nearby village of Barrowby. At the southern end of the High Street stands a monument to Sir Isaac Newton who was born nearby and educated at the town's King's School. It's an impressive memorial, cast in bronze from a Russian cannon captured during the Crimean War. Behind the statue is the ornate Victorian Guildhall (1869), which now houses the **Guildhall Arts Centre.** Originally, the building incorporated the town's prison cells but these now serve as a box office for the Arts Centre.

Just around the corner, the **Grantham Museum** (free) provides a fascinating in-depth look at local history - social, agricultural, industrial, and has special exhibits devoted to Sir Isaac Newton, and to Lady Thatcher, the town's most famous daughter. When elevated to the

peerage she adopted the title Baroness Thatcher of Kesteven - the local authority area in which Grantham is located. She still retains close links with the town and once declared *"From this town I learned so much and am proud to be one of its citizens".*

There is another connection with the former Prime Minister in **Finkin Street Methodist Church,** just off the High Street. Inside this imposing building with its pillared entrance and spacious balcony is a lectern dedicated to Alderman Alfred Roberts, a Methodist preacher, grocer, and father of Margaret Thatcher who worshipped here as a child.

The Thatcher family lived over Alderman Roberts' grocery shop in Broad Street. For a while this became The Premier Restaurant but is currently unoccupied. Margaret Thatcher was Britain's first woman Prime Minister, but Grantham can also boast another distinguished lady who was the first in her profession. Just after World War I, Edith Smith was sworn in as the country's first woman police officer. Edith was reputed to be a no-nonsense lady who made the lives of the town's malefactors a misery.

Before leaving the town, do try to track down the local delicacy, Grantham Gingerbread. It was created in 1740 by a local baker who mistakenly added the wrong ingredient to his gingerbread mix. The unusual result was a white crumbly biscuit, completely unlike the regular dark brown gingerbread. Traditionally, the sweetmeat was baked in walnut-size balls and until the 1990s was always available at Catlin's Bakery and Restaurant whose baker possessed the secret recipe. Sadly, Catlin's is now closed and Grantham Gingerbread is no longer easy to find.

BELTON GARDEN CENTRE

Belton, nr Grantham, Lincolnshire NG32 2LN
Tel: 01476 563700 Fax: 01476 591946

A designated Conservation Area, the pleasant little village of Belton clusters around the grounds of Belton House, a noble late-17th century mansion that was home to the Brownlow family for almost 300 years. The property was given to the National Trust in 1983 and what used to be its walled garden is now home to the **Belton Garden Centre**, a family-run business owned and run by partners Peter and Wendy Coaten, sister-in-law Ann Jackson and Wendy's daughter Jo. Established by Peter and Wendy more than 30 years, the centre stocks a wonderful selection of house and garden plants, stoneware, furniture and aquatics, and specialises in ornamental trees and shrubs.

Sheltered by the garden's 16ft high wall, the plants are healthy and flourishing, and attractively presented. Friendly and experienced staff are always available for advice on all your gardening needs. A separate area is devoted to a range of conservatories, garages, sheds, greenhouses, cane furniture, summerhouses and playhouses. Don't worry about bringing your children to the centre – there's a children's play area for the under 7s, and an excellent woodland adventure play area for older children. Other attractions include an aviary and there are peacocks and chickens wandering freely around.

The centre also has a very good coffee shop selling home made fare – light lunches, afternoon teas and home made cakes. In good weather, customers can enjoy their refreshments on the outside lawn and patio. Like the centre, the coffee shop is open 7 days a week from 9am to 6pm; Sundays, 10.30am to 4.30pm. Also on site, housed in converted stables, is Red the Cat *(see separate entry)* which is owned and run by Peter and Wendy's other daughter Alison and offers a wide range of contemporary crafts.

Close to the Garden Centre is the church of St Peter and St Paul which is crammed with monuments to the Brownlow family and their ancestors, the Custs. There's a particularly fine memorial to Sophia, Lady Brownlow, by Canova. Belton House itself is open during the summer months and is notable for its wood carvings of the Grinling Gibbons school, elaborate plasterwork ceilings, fine paintings, furniture, porcelain and tapestries. The landscaped park contains Dutch and Italian gardens and a pleasant lakeside walk.

BELTON
3 miles N of Grantham on the A607/A153

"An English country-house at its proudest and most serene", **Belton House** stands in 1,000 acres of parkland surrounded by a boundary wall 5 miles long. Built in 1685 of honey-coloured Ancaster stone and in the then fashionable Anglo-Dutch style, Belton was the home of the Brownlow family for just under 300 years before being given to the National Trust in 1983. The Trust also acquired the important collections of pictures, porcelain, books and furniture accumulated by 12 generations of Brownlows. With its Dutch and Italian gardens, orangery, deer park, woodland adventure playground and indoor activity room, Belton provides a satisfying day out for the whole family.

Anyone interested in follies should make a short detour from Belton to the village of Londonthorpe. The original purpose of the *"heavily rusticated stone arch with a horse on the top"* has long since been forgotten but it now serves as a bus shelter.

OSBOURNBY
8 miles E of Grantham on the A15

Set in rolling hill country, *"Ozemby"* is an attractive village with a pleasing mix of architectural styles from the 16th to the 19th centuries. The large church, unusually for Lincolnshire, has a tower rather than a spire and is also notable for its fine collection of medieval bench ends. Hanging on the wall of the nave are paintings of Moses and Aaron of which Pevsner enquires: *"Are they the worst paintings in the county? Anyway, one cannot help liking them"*.

ROPSLEY
6 miles E of Grantham off the A52

Described in Elizabethan times *as "a*

RED THE CAT

Belton Garden Centre, Belton, nr Grantham,
Lincolnshire NG32 2LN
Tel: 01476 590260 Fax: 01476 591946
e-mail: enquiries@redthecat.co.uk
website: www.redthecat.co.uk

Red the Cat is situated in the converted stables on Belton Garden Centre and takes its unusual name from the red tabby cat, currently some 10 yeaars old, who can usually be found in the display window of this independent contemporary craft gallery.

Established in 1995, the gallery is owned and run by Alison Coaten and Stephen Faulkner who display their own ceramics and automata, along with an inspiring collection of selected pieces created by some of the country's leading contemporary makers in ceramics, glass, woodwork, jewellery and clocks.

Both Alison and Stephen graduated with 1st class degrees in Fine Art Sculpture. After leaving collage Alison began working with clay, enjoying the immediacy and flexibilty of the medium. Her striking pieces are mainly animal based and often with humerous touches. Stephen specializes in automata, an interest that derives from a fascination of all things mechanical. He works predominately in wood and metal, but has recently produced joint pieces incorporating ceramics. Their work is made in small editions, although one-off pieces and commissions are also available. Please telephone for opening times.

considerable village remarkably situated as it were in a bason with hills all around", Ropsley was famous then as the birthplace of Richard Fox (1448-1528), a trusted advisor of Henry VII. Fox was appointed to a succession of bishoprics, two of which, Exeter and Wells, he never visited. But he did spend the last 12 years of his life in Winchester as its bishop. Fox founded Corpus Christi College at Oxford, and also established the King's School in Grantham where Sir Isaac Newton was later educated. The house in which Fox was born still stands on Ropsley High Street.

FOLKINGHAM
8 miles E of Grantham on the A15

Once a market town and an important coaching stop, Folkingham was also the venue until 1828 of the Kesteven Quarter Sessions, which were held in the former Greyhound Inn facing the Market Square (the inn is now an Antiques and Craft Centre, open daily and with more than 50 stalls). Convicted prisoners were confined in the nearby **House of Correction** of which only the forbidding gatehouse-cum-governor's house survives. This surprisingly roomy edifice is now available to rent as a holiday "cottage" through the Landmark Trust. Also recalling the penal provisions of the past are Folkingham's village stocks which are preserved in St Andrew's Church.

WOOLSTHORPE BY COLSTERWORTH
7 miles S of Grantham off the A1 at Colsterworth

Recently voted "Man of the Last Millennium", Isaac Newton was born in 1642 in the modest Jacobean farmhouse, **Woolsthorpe Manor**, which has scarcely changed since he lived

here. It was at Woolsthorpe that the "Father of Modern Science" later made some of his greatest inventions and discoveries. The Manor is now owned by the National Trust which has furnished the rooms to reflect life of the period and has converted a 17th century barn into a Science Discovery Centre, which helps explain the achievements of one of the country's most famous men. Almost as famous is the legendary apple tree which helped clear Newton's thinking about the laws of gravity: the apple tree in the garden here is said to have been grafted from the original tree beneath which Newton was sitting when the apple fell on to his head.

A rather strange memento of the young Newton is preserved in the church at nearby Colsterworth. It's a sundial crafted by Newton when he was 9 years old. It seems odd to place a sundial *inside* a church and even odder to install it upside down.

BELVOIR
8 miles SW of Grantham off A607

In Victorian times, the Dukes of Rutland could stand on the battlements of **Belvoir Castle** comfortable in the knowledge that, in whichever direction they looked along the pastoral Vale of

Jousting, Belvoir Castle

Belvoir, everything in sight formed part of their estate, some 30,000 acres in all, (plus large holdings in other parts of the country). William the Conqueror granted this spectacular site to his standard-bearer at the Battle of Hastings, Robert de Todeni and, more than 900 years later, his descendants, now the Dukes of Rutland, still live here. Perched on the hilltop, the present castle looks convincingly medieval with its great tower, turrets and castellations, but it was in fact built in the early 1800s and is the fourth to occupy the site. The opulent interior contains some excellent paintings, including works by Gainsborough, Reynolds and Poussin, and the familiar portrait of Henry VIII by Holbein. In the 130ft long Regent's Gallery are some remarkable Gobelin tapestries, while other magnificent rooms display elegant Regency furniture, a dazzling ceiling copied from the Church of Santa Maria Maggiore in Rome, a dramatic array of 18th century weaponry and a monumental silver collection which includes a wine cooler weighing more than 112lbs. The castle also houses the Museum of the Queen's Royal Lancers. The grounds provide a marvellous setting for special events, amongst which the medieval jousting tournaments are undoubtedly the most colourful.

(Incidentally, Belvoir Castle lies just across the county boundary, in Leicestershire, but has always been regarded as a Lincolnshire attraction.)

SLEAFORD

The history of this busy market town stretches back to the Iron Age. In Roman times there was a massive mint here (730 coins were discovered in one dig), and when a railway was being constructed in

RUSKINGTON GARDEN CENTRE

Newton Lane, Ruskington, Sleaford,
Lincolnshire NG34 9EB
Tel: 01526 833022 Fax: 01526 832005
e-mail: rgc@eliteuk.net

Ruskington Garden Centre is a family run business with Graham and Stephen Elkington and their wives Karen and Clare making sure that the centre lives up to its slogan "Everything you need for the garden of your choice". Established in 1984 and gradually extended over the years, the centre is completing a

major refurbishment as we go to press, to provide an even better service to gardeners. The centre stocks a huge number of flourishing plants, shrubs and trees, and the horticulturally trained staff are always at hand to give advice and recommendations.

A full range of fertilisers, chemicals, garden tools and accessories is available, along with hanging baskets and a wide variety of pots. A newly installed gift department offers gifts and cards for all occassions. A huge selection of pet and animal feeds are also stocked. Also on site, housed in a 17th century stone barn, is a coffee shop serving light lunches and snacks, home made teatime treats and quality tea and coffee. A visit to the centre can be comfortably combined with a short excursion to Tattershall, a few miles to the northeast. Here stands the mighty Keep of Tattershall Castle, built in 1400 with 6 storeys rising to 110ft.

Victorian times a vast Anglo-Roman cemetery was uncovered. Later, the Normans built a sizeable castle of which only a small portion of a wall remains, but much of their other major contribution to the town, the **Church of St Denys**, still survives. Its tower, 144ft high and dating from around 1200, stands separate from the main body of the church, and is among the oldest stone-built towers in England. The interior is notable for the superb 14th century tracery in the north window, two magnificent monuments to the local Carre family, some stained glass by William Morris, and a striking rood loft restored by Ninian Comper in 1918.

Collectors of old inn signs will be interested in the **Bull and Dog** pub in Southgate. Set in the wall above its ground floor is a stone bearing the date 1689 and depicting a bull being baited by dogs. The scene is thought to be unique in the country and the stone itself the oldest surviving pub sign in England.

Sleaford also boasts one of the most unusual locations for a Tourist Information Centre. It is housed in **Money's Mill**, a 70ft high, 8-storeyed building erected in 1796 when the Slea Navigation canal allowed large quantities of corn to be brought by barge and offloaded right outside the door. On the eastern edge of the town, **Cogglesford Mill** (free) has been restored to working order and is open to the public. Probably built around 1750, the Mill contains an exhibition detailing its history.

Other features of interest in Sleaford include the 15th century Vicarage near the church, the landmark Handley Monument, a memorial erected to the town's MP in 1846 and reminiscent of an Eleanor Cross, and the Old Playhouse, purpose-built as a theatre in 1824 and now home to the local theatre company.

AROUND SLEAFORD

NAVENBY
10 miles NW of Sleaford on the A607

One of the county's most unexpected attractions is **Mrs Smith's Cottage**, just off the High Street of this village where Hilda Mary Craven was born on October 28th, 1892. After spending her childhood in Navenby, Hilda moved out of the county but returned in the 1920s to live in a tiny cottage in East Road. At the age of 64 she married, becoming Mrs Smith, but her husband Joseph died less than 4 years later. Hilda stayed on in the cottage, resisting any change she thought unnecessary, until she was 103. During her 80 years of living here, she created a spellbinding time warp. The original ladder access to the first floor is still in place; Hilda's rocking chair and shawl still remain in her favourite place by the range; the original outside privy and washhouse can still be viewed. Opening times are restricted: for more details call 01529 414294.

NORTH RAUCEBY
5 miles W of Sleaford off the A17

Generations of RAF personnel have trained at the Royal Air Force College, Cranwell. When it opened on February 5th, 1920, it was the first Military Air Academy in the world and it later chalked up another first when a jet plane designed by Frank Whittle, a Cranwell graduate, took off from the runway here in 1941. In the nearby village of North Rauceby the **Cranwell Aviation Heritage Centre** (free) tells the Cranwell story and that of the other numerous RAF bases in the region, with the help of photographs, exhibits and film. The museum is open Wednesday, Thursday and Sunday afternoons during the season.

HECKINGTON
5 miles E of Sleaford off the A17

There's plenty of variety and interest here, in particular the tall Church of St Andrew, the Victorian almshouses and the magnificent eight-sailed **Heckington Windmill** by the railway station. When built in 1830 the mill's sails numbered a modest five, but after storms damaged the mill in 1890, eight sails were removed from another mill nearby and installed here. The only surviving eight-sailed mill in Britain rises to five floors and was in use up until 1942. It is now owned by Lincolnshire County Council and can be visited on weekend afternoons, Thursday and Friday afternoons in the season, and at other times by appointment. A few steps away, the **Pearoom** is a contemporary craft centre housed in an old mill building four storeys high.

Heckington's other major attraction is its early-14th century **Church of St Andrew**, which is famous for the wealth of stone carvings on its tower. Inside, there's an outstanding Easter Sepulchre on which medieval master masons depicted the events of Christ's Crucifixion and Resurrection. The same masons were also responsible for the nearby sedilia (stone seats), beautifully carved with scenes from village life and figures of saints.

BILLINGHAY
8 miles NE of Sleaford on the A153

This substantial village on the edge of the Fens was once well-known for its springs which were reputed to have healing properties. Today, the main attraction is **Billinghay Cottage and Craft Workshop**, housed in an attractive limewashed and thatched 17th century cottage, and with a blacksmith's workshop next door.

ABBEY PARKS FARM SHOP

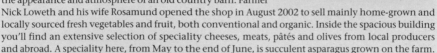

Parks Farm, East Heckington, Boston, Lincolnshire PE20 3QG
Tel: 01205 821610
e-mail: loweth@abbeyparks.freeserve.co.uk
website: www.abbeyparksasparagus.co.uk

Conveniently located on the A17 between Boston and Sleaford, **Abbey Parks Farm Shop** is an attractive wooden building with the appearance and atmosphere of an old country barn. Farmer Nick Loweth and his wife Rosamund opened the shop in August 2002 to sell mainly home-grown and locally sourced fresh vegetables and fruit, both conventional and organic. Inside the spacious building you'll find an extensive selection of speciality cheeses, meats, pâtés and olives from local producers and abroad. A speciality here, from May to the end of June, is succulent asparagus grown on the farm.

All year round the delicatessen stocks a tempting range that includes real dairy ice cream, frozen

and ready-made meals to take home. There's also a huge choice of jams, chutneys, sauces and biscuits, freshly baked bread and delicious cakes and scones – all home cooked daily on the premises. Freshly made baguettes and sandwiches to take away are also available. An additional attraction is the coffee shop which serves excellent tea and coffee, delicious home-made cakes, hot and cold lunches and a superb Sunday lunch with a choice of 2 or 3 roasts. The shop is open daily from 8.30am to 6pm (Sundays, 9.30am to 6pm) and there's ample parking space.

DORRINGTON
5 miles N of Sleaford on the B1188

Run entirely by volunteers, **North Ings Farm Museum** is a fascinating place where vintage tractors, stationary engines, a narrow-gauge railway and a small foundry are among the attractions. The museum is open Sundays during the summer and steam train rides are operational on the first Sunday of each month.

SCOPWICK
8 miles N of Sleaford on the B1188/B1191

Stone cottages line the main street of this small village and a stream splashes alongside the road. In 1838, the Revd George Oliver noted in his booklet, *Scopwickiana,* that the stream invariably overflowed in wet weather making progress along the street possible only by means of stepping stones. This inconvenience continued until fairly recent times. The Revd. Oliver also recorded that the village's only ale house was kept in good order by a formidable landlady who permitted her customers no more than a couple of pints before sending them home to their wives.

Just south of Scopwick is RAF Digby, which was the first Lincolnshire airfield to be attacked by the Luftwaffe in World War II. In the RAF Digby Operations Room Museum the wartime setting has been recreated, complete with plotting table, maps and personnel, and the airfield's story is told with the help of many exhibits, photographs and documents. Guided tours take place on summer Sundays: further details on 01526 327503.

THE STABLES STUDIO
ACCOMODATION-SHOP-GALLERY
ETC RATING 4 DIAMONDS

The Old Brewhouse, 94 High Street, Martin,
Lincolnshire LN4 3QT Tel/Fax: 01526 378528
e-mail: kenjo@stablesstudio.fsnet.co.uk
website: www.stables-studio.co.uk

Located in the small village of Martin, deep in the heart of Lincolnshire fenland, **The Stables Studio** occupies what was formerly a Victorian stable block. It has been sympathetically restored by its present owners, Jo and Ken Slone, and is now a small craft shop and gallery showcasing the work of artists from all around the country. A wide choice of gifts and cards is also on sale. In May and November each year the gallery hosts exhibitions combining paintings, sculpture and craft ware. Outside, Jo and Ken have created a fascinating small sculpture garden which is open from April to October.

The pieces are displayed in a deliberately uncultivated area but the borders away from the sculptures are carefully maintained and full of plants of all kinds. Plants are also available for sale. Entrance to the garden is free and, weather permitting, teas and home made fare are available on the patio area. Jo and Ken also offer bed and breakfast. Stylish en-suite accommodation is available in the renovated farm buildings adjoining the gallery. Come and stay in the 'Tack Room', 'Cart Shed' or 'Pig Swill'. The Old Brewhouse itself is thought to be one of the oldest buildings in the village. Built in 1740 its original use was that of an 'Alehouse'-and its former drinking room now serves as a delightful breakfast room for guests.

METHERINGHAM
9 miles N of Sleaford on B1188

Just outside this large, straggling village is the Metheringham **Airfield Visitor Centre**, one of many Lincolnshire airfields established by the RAF during World War II. A leaflet available from local TICs gives details of the North Kesteven Airfield Trail which includes Metheringham. Here, the Centre's exhibits, photographs and documents tell the story of the airfield and of 106 Squadron, Bomber Command, whose base it was.

WOODHALL SPA

Woodhall Spa is something of an anomaly – a chunk of the Home Counties transplanted to the heart of Lincolnshire. Surrounded by pine and birch woods, spacious Victorian and Edwardian villas are set back from tree-lined avenues and it's said that not a single house in the town is older than the 1830s. Woodhall became a spa town by accident when a shaft sunk in search of coal found not coal but mineral-rich water. In 1838 a pump room and baths were built, to be joined later by hydro hotels. Here, real or imagined invalids soaked themselves in "hypertonic saline waters" heated to 40ºC (103º F). The arrival of the railway in 1855 accelerated Woodhall's popularity, but by the early 1900s the spa had fallen out of favour and the associated buildings disappeared one by one. But this beautifully maintained village has retained its decorous spa atmosphere, pleasantly relaxed and peaceful, and also boasting a Championship golf course.

One interesting survivor of the good old days is a former tennis pavilion, now the **Kinema in the Woods**. When it was converted to a cinema during World War II, it inevitably became known as the "Flicks in the Sticks". It's one of very few back projection cinemas in the country and the entertainment on offer includes performances on an original Compton Organ. The **Cottage Museum** on Iddsleigh Road, also the Tourist Information Centre, tells the story of the establishment of the town as a spa resort.

Woodhall Spa had close connections with 617 Squadron, the "Dambusters", during World War II. The Petwood House Hotel was used as the officers' mess. Memorabilia of those days are displayed in the hotel's Squadron Bar, and in Royal Square a memorial to those intrepid airmen takes the form of a 20ft long model of a breached dam.

There are several sites of interest outside the town. To the north stand the ruins of a 15th century hunting lodge called the Tower on the Moor, built for Ralph, Lord Cromwell of Tattershall Castle. And, standing all alone on Thimbleby Moor in the hamlet of Reeds Beck, is a 36ft high memorial to the Duke of Wellington, erected in 1844 and topped by a bust of the Iron Duke. The column celebrates the successful cultivation of Waterloo Woods, an oak forest planted just after the battle in 1815.

At Kirkstead, off the B1191, stands a towering piece of brickwork, the only visible remains of a 12th century Cistercian Abbey. Close by is the fine 13th century Church of St Leonard, *"a gem of Early Gothic...with an interior like a cathedral aisle"*, according to Simon Jenkins. Originally built as a *"chapel outside the gates"* for visitors to the abbey, St Leonard's was closed in 1877, but restored in 1914 by the Society for the Protection of Ancient Buildings. Miraculously, its beautifully carved chancel screen has survived intact. Dating back to the 13th century, it is believed to be the second oldest such screen in England.

AROUND WOODHALL SPA

CONINGSBY
4 miles S of Woodhall Spa on the A153

The centre of this large village, which started life as a Danish settlement, is dominated by the church tower of St Michael, notable for its enormous single-handed clock; at over 16ft in diameter, this 17th century clock claims to be the largest working example of its kind. South of the village is RAF Coningsby, a major Tornado base and also home to the Battle of Britain Memorial Flight. Created in memory of the gallant airmen who flew in that crucial battle, the Flight operates a Lancaster (one of only two in the world still flying), five Spitfires, two Hurricanes and a Dakota. These historic World War II aircraft are not just museum pieces - they are all still flying and can be seen at a variety of air shows during the summer months. Visiting them on their "home territory" however provides an added dimension and knowledgeable guides provide informative tours. The Centre is open throughout the year, Monday to Friday, and at weekends for special events. More details on 01526 344041.

TATTERSHALL
4 miles S of Woodhall Spa on the A153

Tattershall lies on the opposite bank of the River Bain from Coningsby and is known all over the world for the astonishing keep of **Tattershall Castle**. Its 6 storeys rise 110ft, a huge

rectangular slab built in local red brick. In the 1400s it must have appeared even more formidable than it does now. Construction began around 1445 on the orders of the Lord Chancellor, Ralph Cromwell, and it was clearly designed more as a statement of his power and wealth rather than for defence. Military fashion had moved on from such huge Keeps and in any case the peaceful heart of 15th century Lincolnshire had no need for fortifications on this scale. Originally, the Keep was surrounded by a large complex of other buildings but these have almost entirely disappeared and the tower stands menacingly alone. Despite its magnificence, Tattershall had fallen into near ruin by the early 1900s. There was a very real possibility that it would be dismantled brick by brick, transported to the United States and re-erected there. Happily, the tower was rescued by Lord Curzon who bequeathed it to the National Trust on his death in 1925.

In the shadow of the castle is Tattershall Country Park, set in 365 acres of woods, parks and lakes and offering all sorts of sporting facilities.

As well as this superb castle, Tattershall boasts one of the county's finest churches. **Holy Trinity** was also commissioned by Ralph Lord Cromwell. That was in 1440: the church was finally completed in 1480, long after Ralph's death. Constructed of Ancaster stone, this "glasshouse church" is dazzlingly light and airy inside, but because of its scale and the absence of all but a few adornments, more imposing than likeable. Amongst the items of note is a striking brass of Ralph himself, but sadly his image is headless.

8 LEICESTERSHIRE AND RUTLAND

Leicestershire is generally dismissed by those who have merely driven through it as flat and pretty well covered with red brick towns and villages. Its most attractive features are shy and quiet and have to be sought out but they amply reward the explorer. The county is divided into two almost equal parts by the River Soar, which flows northward into the Trent. It separates the east and west by a broad valley, flowing like a silver ribbon through historic Leicester in the very heart of the county. This capital town was thriving in Roman days and is one of the oldest towns in England. It has managed to retain outstanding monuments of almost every age of English history. Red Leicester cheese was made in the southern part of the county in the 1700s, but now the only genuine product is made at Melton Mowbray, which also makes Stilton and, of course, the superlative pork pies. And every schoolchild knows the name of Bosworth Field, one of the momentous battles which changed the course of English history.

Poppy Fields, Leicestershire

Leicestershire is a pleasant county of fields and woods, ancient earthworks, picturesque villages and some marvellous churches. The towns of Ashby, Coalville, Loughborough, Hinckley, Market Harborough and Melton Mowbray all have great history and character, and the county capital Leicester offers the best of several worlds, with a rich industrial and architectural heritage, a wealth of history, an abundance of open spaces, a firm commitment to environmental issues and an eye to the future with the opening of The National Space Centre.

Just 20 miles across and covering a mere 150 square miles, Rutland delights in its status as England's smallest county. Its 37,800 inhabitants were incensed when the Local Government changes of 1974 stripped the county of its identity and merged it with neighbouring Leicestershire. It took more than 20 years of ceaseless campaigning before bureaucracy relented and Rutland was re-instated as a county in its own right once again. Rutland has villages of thatch and ironstone, clustered around their churches and the countryside is rich in pasture where once deer were hunted. Its central feature is Rutland Water, its 3,100 acres making it one of the largest man-made lakes in northern Europe. Started in 1971 to supply water to the East Midlands towns, it was created by damming the valley near Empingham. Among the lovely villages are the larger towns such as Uppingham and Oakham, offering their own diversions, sights and sounds for the visitor.

Belvoir Castle

LOCATOR MAP

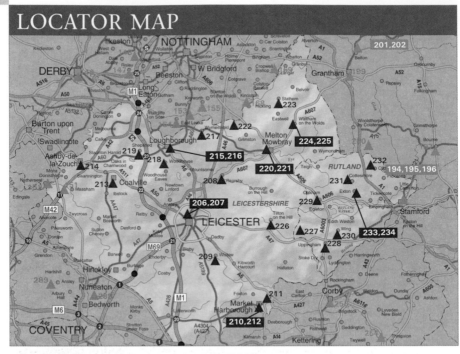

ADVERTISERS AND PLACES OF INTEREST

LEICESTER

Designated Britain's first "environment city" in recognition of its commitment to green issues and the environment, Leicester has numerous parks and open spaces, is one of the country's top ten shopping destinations, has a buzzing nightlife and also boasts a rich architectural heritage with no fewer than 350 listed buildings.

Town Hall Gardens, Leicester

When the Romans built a town here in the 1st century AD they called it Ratae Corielauvorum, and when they left 300 years later it survived in some form. It was the seat of a Christian bishop in the 7th century, and in the 9th century was conquered and settled by the Vikings along with Lincoln, Nottingham, Derby and Stamford. The city flourished in the Middle Ages when the cloth and wool trades became important, and the coming of the canals and the railways brought further prosperity. The development of road transport changed the face of the city, and modern Leicester is a thriving industrial and commercial city with superb shopping and recreational facilities and a mixture of cultures and communities as rich and diverse as any in the land.

At the heart of Leicester's heritage is **Castle Park**, the old town, an area of gardens, churches, museums and other fine buildings. Here are concentrated many of the city's main visitor attractions. **Castle Gardens** was just an area of marshland by the River Soar until it was drained and opened as gardens to the public in 1926. In the gardens is a statue of Richard III who on a sunny August day in 1485 rode out from the city to his death at the Battle of Bosworth Field. Castle Motte is a man-made mound built around 1070 by Leicester's first Norman lord; like the gardens, it is open to the public during daylight hours; interpretation boards explain its history. Adjacent to the gardens is the **Church of St Mary de Castro**, founded in 1107 and still in use. The chancel, stained glass, carvings and tombstones are all well worth taking time to examine. Geoffrey Chaucer was married here and Henry VI was knighted in the church in 1426. Next to the church is the Great Hall of Leicester Castle. The Hall was built in the 12th century by Robert le Bossu and used by successive Earls of Leicester as their administrative headquarters; it is open to the public on special event days. Also in the same space is **Newarke Houses Museum**, a museum of social and domestic history contained in two 16th century houses. Displays include clocks, toys, furniture, a 1940s village grocer's shop and a reconstructed Victorian street scene. Leicester's diverse cultural heritage is represented by the **Jain Centre**, the only one of its kind in the Western world, housed in a converted 19th century Congregational chapel surmounted by a wondrously ornate facade; and the **Guru Nanak Gurdwara**, a Sikh temple and museum. Across the

LEICESTERSHIRE HERITAGE SERVICES

Tel: 0116 264 5800 Fax: 0116 264 5819
e-mail: museums@leics.gov.uk
website: www.leics.gov.uk/museums

Leicestershire Heritage Services has in its care
two interesting museums, at Melton Mowbray
and Market Harborough, and a fascinating old
manor house, Donington le Heath Manor House. Dating back to the late 1200s, this small stone
manor house has been restored in the style of the Tudor and Stuart periods and is set in recently

developed period flower and herb gardens. Its most prized exhibit
is King Richard's Bed, the bed in which the king is said to have
slept (how well, one wonders?) the night before the fateful Battle
of Bosworth.

The huge oak bed had been brought from Nottingham Castle
and installed in the upper front room of the Blue Boar Inn in
Leicester. Almost 150 years later, when the bed was being moved, a
gold coin fell from it. A close examination revealed a secret drawer
containing the then-colossal sum of £300 in gold. The Manor House
is open April to September, 11.30am to 5pm; October to March
from 11.30am to 3pm daily, except December, January and February
when it is open at weekends only. There's a tea room in the old
barn.and a small shop. Entrance and car parking are free. Tel:
(01530) 831259.

Harborough Museum is located in the centre of Market
Harborough, a traditional market town that still retains an old
world look and feel. It occupies the former Symington Corset
Factory building (which also houses the District Council Offices
and the Tourist Information Centre. The museum's displays include
the Symington Collection of Corsetry, a reconstruction of a local
shoemaker's
workshop and
permanent and temporary exhibitions on all aspects
of local history. The museum is open 10am to
4.30pm, Monday to Saturday; 2pm to 5pm on
Sunday. Tel: (01858) 821085.

Recently re-opened after major refurbishment,
the Melton Carnegie Museum in Melton Mowbray
boasts some dynamic displays devoted to the
history of Stilton cheese, Pork Pie manufacturing,
and the development of fox hunting in the area.
Other exhibits include some fine paintings by local
artist John Ferneley (1783-1860) and some beautiful
Stilton tableware. Visitors can also discover the
origin of the phrase "painting the town red".

It goes back to an occasion in 1837 when the
Marquis of Waterford and his pals decided to
decorate the town with red paint after a night's
drinking. Chief victims were Swan Porch (an inn
on the market place) and the keeper of the tollgate.
The museum is open 10am to 4.30pm daily.
Admission to all three sites is free. Tel: (01664)
569946.

road from the Jain Centre is the **Jewry Wall and Museum.** The Wall is not only the oldest surviving Roman civil building in Britain but its wall is also the highest in the country.and was part of the public baths, whose foundations are still visible. The museum chronicles the history and archaeology of the city and the county from Roman times to 1485. The adjacent St Nicholas Church dates back to Anglo-Saxon times and, despite later alterations, Saxon work and re-used Roman bricks can be seen in the walls and tower. The Church of St Martin, which was in existence before 1086, was extended in the 14th and 15th centuries, restored in the 19th century and hallowed as the Cathedral of Leicester in 1927. Stained glass and carvings are impressive, and the memorial to Richard III is a highlight.

Leicester Guildhall

One of the very finest buildings in Leicester is the **Guildhall**, built around 1390 for the Guild of Corpus Christi and used as the Town Hall from the late 15th century to 1876. Concerts and theatrical performances are held regularly in the Great Hall. Across the road from the Cathedral is **Wygston's House**, a part-timber-framed building, one of the oldest in the city, which now houses displays of fashion, textiles and crafts from around the world, along with a reconstruction of a 1920s draper's shop. This museum section also has an activity area where children are encouraged to dress up in replica historical costumes.

Leicester City Museums also include The **New Walk Museum and Art Gallery**, with displays including natural history, geology, ancient Egyptian mummies, a dinosaur skeleton more than 175 million years old, and a

THE CITY GALLERY

90 Granby Street
Leicester LE1 1DJ
Tel: 0116 254 0595
(minicom available)

The City Gallery promotes the best in contemporary arts and crafts through a dynamic and accessible programme of continually changing exhibitions in 3 gallery spaces. The gallery has an innovative and popular education programme, providing a wide range of interpretive events for schools, colleges and community groups of all ages. The City Gallery also runs events for the general public throughout the year, designed for all ages. Please telephone for the current events programme.

The City Gallery is located in the city centre, near to the main train station (few minutes' walk). There is disabled badge parking nearby and level access from the street to the Main and Craft Galleries. A chairlift is available to the Upstairs Gallery. A wheelchair accessible toilet with baby changing facilities is also available. An induction loop system is in the foyer as well as the Main Gallery Minicom on 0116 254 0595.

Opening times: Tuesday to Friday 11am - 6pm, Saturday 10am - 5pm. Sunday and Monday closed, admission free.

fine German Expressionist collection; Belgrave Hall and Gardens, a Queen Anne house whose rooms reflect Edwardian elegance and Victorian cosiness; and the Abbey Pumping Station, an 1891 station with massive beam engines and several exhibitions.

Kirby Muxloe Castle

The city's most recent major attraction is the **National Space Centre**, opened in 2001 as part of the new millennium celebrations. This multi-million pound project offers real rockets and satellites, interactive challenges and the most advanced space theatre in the world, transporting the audience on an awe-inspiring journey through the universe and beyond.

In Western Park, **Ecohouse** is an environment-friendly show home featuring energy efficiency, sustainable living and an organic garden.

AROUND LEICESTER

KIRBY MUXLOE
2 miles W of Leicester off the B5380

Kirby Muxloe Castle is a picturesque ruined fortified manor house dating from 1480. Built of brick rather than the more usual stone, it was started by William, Lord Hastings, but not completed by him – he was executed by Richard III. Only the great gatehouse and one of the four angle towers remain intact.

DESFORD
4 miles W of Leicester off the A47

Tropical Birdland, which opened its doors to the public in 1987, is a breeding centre for rare and endangered species: Birds of the Rainforest, 85 species, walk-through aviaries, chick room, woodland walk, koi ponds, picnic gardens, bird shop, free parking – all this adds up to one of the county's most popular attractions. Open Easter to end October.

NEWTOWN LINFORD
5 miles NW of Leicester off the A50

A picturesque village of thatched dwellings and timbered style buildings, Newtown Linford lies alongside the River Lin, which flows through the village and into **Bradgate Country Park**. This is the largest and most popular park in the county with well over a million visitors every year exploring its 850 acres. The park was created from Charnwood Forest 700 years ago as a hunting and deer park, and the scene is probably little changed since, a mixture of heath, bracken, grassy slopes, rocky outcrops and woodland – and the deer are still there. Man-made features of the park include a well-known folly called **Old John Tower**. Built in 1784 by the 5th Earl of Stamford in memory of a former member of his household, it stands nearly 700 feet above sea level and affords fine views.

Also here are the ruins of **Bradgate House**, built of brick at the beginning of the 16th century. This was the home of the Grey family and it was here that Lady Jane Grey was born in 1537. Her father was the scheming and ambitious Duke of Suffolk who forced her at the age of 16 to marry the son of the Duke of Northumberland, Regent to Edward VI. With his own eye on power, Northumberland prevailed on the dying Edward to name Jane as heir to the throne. On hearing the news, Jane fell fainting to the ground. Public opinion recognized Mary Tudor as the rightful heir and within days both Jane's father and father-in-law had deserted her. Jane spent nine days as reluctant queen and a further seven months as a prisoner in the Tower of London – before a swift death on the executioner's block on 12 February 1554. Today the lovely rose-red ruins of Bradgate House where Jane passed much of her brief life look too benign and inviting ever to have been involved in such a murderous tale of 16th century politics.

The story is that the foresters at Bradgate cut off the heads of the oaks in the park as a mark of respect to Lady Jane; pollarded oaks can still be seen here.

ANSTEY

3 miles NW of Leicester off the A46

The 16th century **Packhorse Bridge** that crosses Rothley Brook at Anstey is a particularly fine specimen: 5ft wide to give space for the horse's bulging panniers, 54 ft long and supported by five low arches. In the late 18th century when the bridge was the only way to get to Leicester, some 4 miles distant, it would have been crossed many times by Ned Ludd who gave his name to the Luddites. They saw that the new mechanical stocking-frames were reducing the home-knitters to penury and their response was to set fire to the new textile mills. The government's response was to swoop on 6 of the leaders and hang them all at Nottingham.

REARSBY

5 miles NE of Leicester on the A607

According to meticulous accounts that have survived, the lovely old bridge in Rearsby was built by 6 men in just 9 days during the summer of 1714. The village constable's accounts showed the total cost as £11 2s 2d (£11.11p) – with the largest expense £2 12s 6d being for 21 quarters of lime, the smallest a payment

KAYES GARDEN NURSERY

1700 Melton Road, Rearsby, nr Melton Mowbray,
Leicestershire LE7 4YR
Tel: 01664 424578
e-mail: hazelkaye.kgn@nascr.net

Established over twenty years ago, **Kayes Garden Nursery** offers a wide range of interesting plants including herbaceous, aquatic and climbers. All of the plants for sale are home grown and a few, notably campanulas, violas and primulas have been hybridised on site. A national collection of hardy Tradescantias is housed in owner Hazel Kaye's extensive and beautiful garden, which is also open to visitors. Open March to October and Bank Holiday Mondays 10-5pm, Tuesday to Saturday; 10am -12 noon on Sundays.

WISTOW RURAL CENTRE

Wistow, Great Glen, Leicestershire LE8 0QF

Tiny though it is the little hamlet of Wistow boasts an interesting Georgian church, a fine old Hall – and **Wistow Rural Centre**, a group of small enterprises providing a wide selection of goods and services.

You will find an enticing mix of decorative furniture and accessories for your home and garden at **Powder Blue**.(tel: 0116 2593031. Period armoires and beds, Louis style chairs, mirrors and chandeliers from France, Italy and Denmark. An extensive range of romantic linens, quilts and cushions. Glass and table wares, linen waters and soaps, exclusive jewellery, gifts and cards. Also available at Loseby Lane Leicester. (tel: 0116 2517719 www.powder-blue.co.uk).

Lovers of by-gones, curios and collectables will be in their element in **The Attic** which Laureen Philipson has filled with a wondrous agglomeration of interesting and unusual items. One of her specialities is militaria with examples from both world wars. Chairs and small pieces of furniture, mirrors, glassware, Alchemy pewter, silver jewellery, tea sets and trinket boxes all make The Attic a browsers delight. Tel: 07802 66 990 66 or fax: 0116 2402000.

Gardeners are well-provided for at **Ken Bailey at Wistow** (tel: 0116 259 2009), a home and garden plant centre set in a walled garden with an undercover area for rainy days. Ken is well known in Leicestershire as an experienced plantsman offering a healthy and vigorous range of shrubs, hardy perennials and house plants. The centre also stocks an excellent selections of pots and other garden accessories. An additional attraction is the interesting model village.

At **The Finishing Touch & Bear Society** (tel: 01162 590041) Val Kelham offers an astonishing range of quality crafts, gifts, cards – and one

of the largest collection of Teddy Bears to be found in Leicestershire, including the Gillies range of collectable teddies. Amongst the multifarious items on display are hand-made quilts, cushions, tea cosies, aprons and oven gloves, cross-stitch kits, haberdashery materials, the Island range of porcelain ducks and birds, picture frames, and much, much more.

To round off your visit, a sampling of the wholesome fare on offer in Tina Bale's **Tearooms at Wistow** (tel/fax: 01162 593756) is strongly recommended. This licensed tearoom offers a wide choice that ranges from 'light bites' to 4-course dinners served either in the restaurant with its bright décor and waitress service, in the conservatory at the front or in the spacious courtyard outside. A speciality of the house is its Cream Tea with home made scones and cakes.

of 5d (2p) "to George Skillington for Nailes". The bridge was paid for by a levy of ratepayers of 8d in the pound but according to constable Richard Harrison he ended up '£1 11s 0 ½ d out of Pockett'. A small consolation must have the inscription on the sixth arch of his initials, RH, alongside the date 1714.

OADBY
3 miles SE of Leicester off the A6/A47

Effectively a suburb of Leicester, Oadby nevertheless has three venues of interest to those who care for the environment. There's a treat for horticulturalists in the form of the University of Leicester's **Botanical Gardens** which include an arboretum, herbaceous borders, water garden and glass houses that shelter tropical and temperate plants, alpines and succulents.

In Gartree Road is the entrance to Farmworld at **Stoughton Farm Park**, Britain's biggest and brightest working farm park. A great family day out is provided by shire horses, cart rides, rare farm animals, lakeside and woodland walks, a working dairy farm, toy tractor park, chicken hatchery, milking parlour, children's farmyard and playgrounds. There's also a café and pub.

In Washbrook Lane, **Brocks Hill Country Park & Environment Centre** is a remarkable building, completely self-sufficient and needing no electricity, gas or water supplies – not even a sewer. It was built to demonstrate wind and solar power, photovoltaics, rainwater re-cycling and sewage composting. The centre stands in 67 acres of newly planted Country Park with woodland, meadowland, community orchard and arboretum. There's an Exhibition Area, café, and classroom facilities.

In Oadby graveyard is the tombstone of **James Hawker**, one of the most engaging rogues of all time. In his entertaining autobiography, *James Hawker's Journal*, he reveals that he found his vocation when he was 18 years old and poached his first bird. That was in 1844 and from then until his death in 1921 he honoured his declaration that "I will poach until I die". He was only caught once and on that charge, he indignantly claims, he was innocent – *"They knew me and seized the occasion to punish my earlier misdemeanours"*. In later life James combined a respectable daytime career as a parish councillor and member of the school board with a nocturnal pastine of depleting his aristocratic neighbour's lands of their edible game. For 60 years his grave remained unmarked until EMMA Theatre Company, which had performed a play about his life, erected a simple monument bearing as epitaph his defiant, and true, claim:

"I will poach till I die".

WISTOW
6 miles SE of Leicester off the A6

Only two churches in the country are dedicated to St Wistan, a Christian prince of Mercia who was murdered by his wicked uncle Brifardus near this tiny hamlet in 849AD. Wistow's Church of St Wistan was largely remodelled in 1746 so its interior has mainly Georgian fittings including box pews and ironwork communion rails. There are striking memorials to members of the Halford family of nearby Wistow Hall (private) where they lived continuously from 1603 to 1896. Their most distinguished visitor, albeit in some distress, was Charles I who stopped here briefly to change horses on his flight from the Battle of Naseby. In their haste, the king and his party left their battle horses with their saddles and other gear still in place. Charles even left his sword behind; many years later it was given to George IV by Sir Henry Halford,

THE FURNITURE BARN

Rockingham Road, Market Harborough,
Leicestershire LE16 7QE
Tel: 01858 433444 Fax: 01858 461301

Richard Kimbell has been active in the furniture business for some 36 years and for the past two years has been established at **The Furniture Barn**, a custom built showroom and warehouse which has a massive 20,000 square feet of sales area and a further 55,000 square feet of warehouse space. The two floors

of sales area are crammed with quality designer furniture of all kinds – sofas of every shape and size, chairs and tables, beds, wardrobe and much, much more.

There are cabinets in oak, pine, mahogany or cherry and a wide range of lamps, mirrors and accessories. The wide range of soft furnishing fabrics has something for every taste and there are huge discounts on end of line fabrics.

THE FRANK HAYNES GALLERY

50 Station Road, Great Bowden, Market Harborough,
Leicestershire LE16 7HN
Tel: 01858 464862
website: www.marketharborough.com/gallery

From its opening in 1987 **The Frank Haynes Gallery** has showcased some of the best original **paintings**, drawings and studio **ceramics** produced in the area. Frank Haynes is himself a potter producing domestic ware in his workshop on site. The Picture Gallery mounts regular monthly exhibitions of paintings and drawings in a wide variety of styles, subjects and media, as well as a few local prints. In the Pottery Shop are studio ceramics by professional members of the Craft Potters association and other talented Midlands' potters, together with Frank's own pieces, he also stocks and sells colourful ceramics from France.

One of his aims is to provide quality pictures and ceramics at prices well below similar items in town centre or city galleries. Each April the Gallery hosts a special exhibition with the theme of "The Human Figure in Art" as depicted in photography, ceramics and sculpture. The Gallery also mounts occasional shows when the Gallery is hired for one person or group shows. There's no obligation to buy at this pleasant little gallery; helpful advice is always available as well as a reasonably priced framing service. The Gallery is open Thursday to Sunday, from 10am to 5pm. Bed & breakfast accommodation is available in 2 twin bed rooms with no single occupancy supplement.

physician to George III, George IV and William IV. The saddles and other equipment are now held by the New Walk Museum in Leicester.

KIBWORTH HARCOURT

8 miles SE of Leicester on the A6

The earliest type of windmill used in the county was the post mill, where the whole wooden body complete with the machinery was positioned on a post and could be turned so that the sails faced the wind. The only surviving one – dating from the early 18th century – is here.

Old Grammar School , Market Harborough

MARKET HARBOROUGH

Halfway between Leicester and Northampton at a crossing point of the River Welland, Market Harborough was created as a planned market town in the mid-12th century. The booths that filled its market place were gradually replaced by permanent buildings, and many of these, along with the courts that led off the High Street, still stand. In 1645 Charles I made Market Harborough his headquarters and held a council of war here before the Battle of Naseby. The development of turnpike roads - the motorways of their day – led to prosperity and the establishment of coaching inns in the town, many of them still in business. The canals and the railways transformed communications and manufacturing industry became established, the most notable company being RW & H Symington, creators of the Liberty Bodice.

The town trail takes in the major buildings, including the 14th century parish **Church of St Dionysius** with its superb limestone broach. The church has no graveyard because it was, until the early 1900s, a daughter church of St Mary in Arden with the status of a chapel. The **Old Grammar School** is a timber-framed building with an open ground floor; built in 1614 to serve the weekly butter market and "to keepe the market people drye in time of fowle weather", it later became a school, a role which it sustained until 1892. The factory of the Symington Company, which grew from a cottage industry of staymakers to a considerable economic force in the town, now houses the Council offices, the library, the information centre and the **Harborough Museum**, which incorporates the Symington Collection of Corsetry.

Among the town's distinguished past residents are William Bragg, whose nephew and son shared the Nobel Prize for Physics in 1915; Jack Gardner, who was British Empire and European Heavyweight boxing champion between 1950 and 1952; and Thomas Cook, who

THE FORBIDDEN APPLE

27 Adam and Eve Street, Market Harborough,
Leicestershire LE16 7LT
Tel: 01858 461200

Its name inspired by the street address, **The Forbidden Apple** is
an extremely stylish gallery selling unique home accessories,
furniture with an individual character and designer-led gifts. The
covetable commodities Heidi James has gathered here include
attractive leather sofas from Italy; a range of good-looking
polished pewter coffee sets from Sheffield; ceramic ware from Stoke-on-Trent; house fragrances from
Ashleigh & Burwood; distinctive local hand-made greeting cards and wrappng paper; mirrors; paintings
and much, much more. Like Adam and Eve, you won't be able to resist the temptation!

spent ten years of his life here and was
married in the town. While travelling
one day by road to Leicester he
conceived the idea of an outing using
the then newly opened railway. He
organised the excursion from Leicester to
Loughborough on July 7 1841; the fare
of a shilling (5p) included afternoon tea.
Cook later moved to Leicester, where he
is buried at Welford Road cemetery.

AROUND MARKET HARBOROUGH

HALLATON
6 miles NE of Market Harborough off the B664

On the village green of this picturesque
village in the rich grazing lands of the
Welland Valley stands an unusual
conical **Buttercross**. Every Easter
Monday the cross is the setting for the
crowning ceremony of the **Hare-Pie
Scrambling & Bottle-Kicking** contest.
The captain of the winning team is lifted
to the top of the conical monument and
there he broaches a bottle of ale. The
contest is a free-for-all struggle between
the neighbouring villages of Hallaton
and Medbourne to get two out of three
bottles of ale across the village boundary
by whatever means possible. (The
"bottles" are actually small oak casks). As
many as 400 players may be milling
around in the scrum and the battle has

been known to continue for eight or
nine hours). The day's events begin with
a procession to Hare Pie Bank where
pieces of a huge hare pie are thrown to
the crowd. The antiquarian Charles
Bilson believed the custom was a relic of
a time when the hare was worshipped as
a divine animal, but he has no
explanation for the origins of the bottle-
kicking contest. A display of this curious
event is on show in the **Hallaton Village
Museum**, along with relics from the
motte and bailey castle and some
unusual agricultural items.

FOXTON
2 miless NW of Market Harborough off the A6

The most famous site on the county's
canals is the **Flight of Ten Locks** on the
Grand Union Canal, one of the great
engineer Thomas Telford's most
impressive constructions. In the **Canal
Museum**, the remains of a steam-
powered boat lift of 1900 have been
restored, and there are several other
buildings and bridges of interest
(including a swing-bridge) in this
pretty village.

LUTTERWORTH
12 miles W of Market Harborough on the A4304

John Wycliffe was rector here under the
tutelage of John of Gaunt. His
instigation of an English translation of

Foxton Locks

the Bible into English caused huge dissent. He died in 1384 and was buried in the church here, but when he was excommunicated in 1428 his body was exhumed and burned and his ashes scattered in the River Swift. Close to the church, **Lutterworth Museum and Historical Society** contains a wealth of local history from Roman times to World War II.

About 3 miles southeast of Lutterworth and set in meadows beside the River Avon, **Stanford Hall** has been the home of the Cave family since 1430. The present house – pleasantly-proportioned, dignified and serene was built by the celebrated architect William Smith of Warwick in the 1690s. A superb staircase was added in around 1730, one of very few structural alterations to the house in its 300-year-old history. One other was the Ballroom which contains paintings

that once belonged to Bonnie Prince Charlie's younger brother, Henry Stuart. They include the last major portrait of the middle-aged Bonnie Prince Charlie, two of James III – the Old Pretender – and a particularly fine portrait of Charles II by Sir Peter Lely. The Cave family became Barons and it was the 6th Baron, Adrian, whose fascination with motor-cars is perpetuated in Stanford's collection of cycle-cars and motor cycles. Adrian was also closely associated with the pioneer aviator, Percy Pilcher, who in 1895 had accomplished the first controlled flight in Britain. Pilcher made several experimental flights in Stanford Park but a flight in his glider, *The Hawk*, on September 30th 1899 ended in disaster when a bamboo strut in the tail fractured, the machine turned on its back and crashed. In the stable Block at Standord there's a fascinating full-size replica of *The Hawk* "with its innumerable wires like the ribs of an umbrella".

HINCKLEY

Many of the old timbered houses still stand in the town of Hinckley, whose Fair is mentioned in Shakespeare's *Henry IV*. A thriving industrial town nowadays, Hinckley was already well-established in Saxon times. When the Domesday Book was compiled, Hinckley had 60 families – four times as many as in contemporary Birmingham. The turning point in its fortunes came in 1640 when William Illife set up the first stocking frame in Hinckley and so initiated the hosiery and knitwear industry that has made the town known internationally. A surviving example of framework knitters' cottages still stand in Lower Bond Street. This terrace of restored 17th century thatched cottages is home to **Hinckley & District Museum** whose displays depict aspects of the history of Hinckley and district and include amongst the hosiery exhibits a stocking frame of 1740.

It was around 1740 that gossip across the county told of a tombstone in Hinckley churchyard that dripped blood. It was a memorial to a young man of 20 killed in a public house by a recruiting sergeant he had offended by some "trifling joke". The violence of the young man's death lent credence to the notion of a bleeding tombstone but, sadly, a more mundane explanation was provided by a local historian: "The tombstone used to abut the east end of the church and it was frequently noticed to be spattered with red spots. The superstitious took this for blood but in fact it came from the ironstone in the church wall above". The stone was moved away from the wall and the "bleeding" has been staunched.

AROUND HINCKLEY

BURBAGE
1 mile E of Hinckley on the B4668

The village was originally called Burbach, a name that came from the burr thistles that grew in profusion in the fields. The 9th Earl of Kent was an early incumbent, being rector here for 50 years at the Church of St Catherine, whose spire is a landmark for miles around. **Burbage Woods** are nationally important because of the spectacular ground flora, and Burbage Common is one of the largest areas of natural grassland in the locality. For the visitor there's a network of footpaths, bird observation hide, picnic tables and a visitor centre.

SUTTON CHENEY
4 miles N of Hinckley off the A447

Bosworth Battlefield is the historic site of the Battle of Bosworth in 1485, where

King Richard III was defeated by the future King Henry VII. The Visitor Centre gives a detailed insight into medieval times with the aid of models, replicas and a film theatre, and also on site are a picnic area, a country park and a battle trail, a self-guided trail of 1¾ miles which takes the visitor round the field of battle, passing the command posts of Richard and Henry. Huge flags are frequently flown from these sites, adding colour and poignancy to the scene. Visitors can see the well where Richard drank during the battle, and pause at the memorial stone on the spot where Richard died. A fascinating addition to the site is a display of weapons from the Tudor period, found on the *Mary Rose,* one of Henry VIII's warships, which sank in Portsmouth Harbour in 1545.

The Battlefield is on the route of the **Ashley Canal**, whose towpath offers delightful walks through beautiful countryside. It connects Hinckley, Bosworth Battlefield, Market Bosworth, Battlefield Railway, Measham Museum and Moira Furnace.

MARKET BOSWORTH
5 miles N of Hinckley off the A447

Market Bosworth has been a Britain in Bloom winner for the years 1995-1998. This market town is of course most famous as the battle site for the turning point in the Wars of the Roses – Richard III (Duke of York, the "White Rose" county) was routed here by "Red Rose" forces (Henry Bolingbroke, later Henry IV, of Lancaster) and killed in 1485. This was the battle immortalised in Shakespeare's play *Richard III*, where the desperate king is heard to cry *"My kingdom for a horse"*. Richard's defeat led to the accession of the Tudor dynasty, Shakespeare's patrons and perhaps, therefore, the impetus behind his less-than-complimentary portrayal of

LEICESTERSHIRE AND RUTLAND

Richard which is disputed by historians to this day.

Market Bosworth Country Park is one of many beautiful open spaces in the area. Another is **Bosworth Water Trust's Leisure and Water Park** on the B585 west of town. This is a 50-acre leisure park with 20 acres of lakes for dinghy sailing, boardsailing and fishing. At nearby Cadeby is the unusual combination that is the **Cadeby Light Railway & Brass Rubbing Centre**, comprising a narrow-gauge steam railway, model and miniature railways, a steam road engine and a brass rubbing centre in the church. More railway nostalgia awaits at Shackerstone, 3 miles northwest of Market Bosworth, where the **Battlefield Railway** offers a steam-hauled nine-mile round trip from Shackerstone to Shenton through the delightful scenery of southwest Leicestershire. At Shackerstone is an impressive museum of railway memorabilia, locomotives and rolling stock. On summer weekends there's a steam and diesel service; this also runs on Wednesdays in July and August. Call 01827 880754 for timetable details.

TWYCROSS
7 miles NW of Hinckley off the A444

Five miles northwest of Market Bosworth, on the A444 Burton-Nuneaton road, **Twycross Zoo** is an ideal family attraction, home to a wide variety of animals including gorillas, chimps, orang-utans, gibbons, elephants, lions and giraffes. Pets corner, adventure playground, penguin pool, and in summer donkey rides and train rides. Open daily throughout the year.

On a side road parallel to the A444 three miles north of Market Bosworth a village with the wonderful name of **Barton-in-the-Beans**. The county was apparently once known as 'bean-belly'

Leicestershire, on account of the large reliance on the bean crops that formed part of the staple diet in needy times. The beans were said to have been sweeter and tenderer than anywhere else in the country.

COALVILLE

Originally called Long Lane, the town sprang up on a bleak common when Whitwick Colliery was opened in 1824. The big name in the early days was George Stephenson, who not only established the railway here (in 1832) but also built the churches.

SNIBSTON DISCOVERY PARK

Ashby Road, Coalville,
Leicestershire LE67 3LN
Tel: 01530 278444 Fax: 01530 813301
e-mail: snibston@leics.gov.uk

One of the largest and most dynamic museums in the Midlands, **Snibston** is Leicestershire's all-weather science and industry museum. Visitors can get their 'hands-on' loads of fun in the popular Science Alive! Gallery or explore the County's rich heritage in the Transport, Extractives, Engineering and Textiles and Fashion Galleries. Other attractions include guided colliery tours, outdoor science and water playgrounds, sculptures and Nature Reserve. Open daily 10am - 5pm

THE ROYAL HOTEL

Ashby-de-la-Zouch, Leicestershire LE65 2GD
Tel: 01530 412833 Fax: 01530 564548
e-mail: theroyalhotel@email.com
website: www.royalhotelashby.com

The magnificent **Royal Hotel** was built in 1826 when the town was prospering from a tourist influx inspired by Sir Walter Scott's best-selling novel *Ivanhoe* in which the "stately ruins of Ashby Castle" featured prominently along with the Tournament Field where Ivanhoe jousted successfully in defence of his lady love. The Royal was built on a grand scale in the Regency style and stands in 4 acres of its own grounds less than 5 minutes walk from the town centre. A Grade II listed building, the hotel has recently been refurbished to maintain its original character and the sumptuous surroundings go hand in hand with a warm and friendly atmosphere.

The excellent Castle Room Restaurant overlooks beautifully landscaped gardens and offers

traditional English and Continental cuisine of the highest standard and quality. To complement your meal there's a well-chosen list of wines from around the world. The Castle Room is the perfect setting for relaxed lunches or dinners; for more formal occasions – boardroom meetings, seminars, receptions or banquets – the Hastings Room, Lys Room and Boardroom offer the very best facilities. All have been decorated to the highest standard of comfort and style and dedicated and experienced staff are on hand to ensure the smooth running of each event.

The Royal is licensed for civil marriage ceremonies and offers a comprehensive wedding package that takes care of every detail. For dinner dances the Castle Room Restaurant is available to accommodate up to 80 seated, or 150 for a more informal occasion.

Naturally, the accommodation at The Royal maintains the same high standards evident throughout the hotel. The 34 guest bedrooms are all en suite and are provided with the latest in hotel facilities, including colour television, direct dial telephone, trouser press, hairdryer, hospitality tray and computer points. Family rooms and 4-poster rooms are available.

Ashby itself is a pleasant market town – the historic Castle is definitely worth a visit – and places of interest within easy reach include Twycross Zoo, Drayton Manor Park, Tamworth Snow Dome, Snibston Discovery Park and Kingsbury Water Park. There's golf at Willesley Park Golf Club and excellent motorway connections to the National Exhibition Centre and the East Midlands Airport.

At Ashby Road, Coalville, **Snibston Discovery Park** (see panel on page 339) is built on the 100-acre site of the former Snibston Colliery. Visitors can explore a unique mixture of nature, history, science and technology: topics covered include the industrial heritage of Leicestershire, and former miners conduct a lively surface tour of the colliery. There are rides behind a diesel locomotive on the newly restored colliery line and the Science Alive Gallery allows visitors to play with lightning, walk through a tornado or cycle with a skeleton. You can test your strength against a pulley system in the Engineering Gallery; see the clothes of days gone by in the Textile and Fashion Gallery; or relax in the Grange Nature Reserve and Victorian arboretum.

AROUND COALVILLE

OAKS IN CHARNWOOD
2 miles NE of Coalville off the B587

In a beautiful elevated position in Charnwood Forest, **Mount St Bernard Abbey** was the first Catholic abbey to be founded in England after the Reformation. It is a Cistercian Monastery of white monks founded in 1835 as a continuation of Garendon Abbey (1133-1538).

SWANNINGTON
1 mile NW of Coalville on the A511

One of the first railway lines in Britain to use steam engines was the Leicester & Swannington Railway, which was opened in 1833 to bring coal to the city. The incline at Swannington is now part of one of the many heritage trails in the county. Traces of some of the many shallow "bell pits" once common in this mining area can be seen in scrubland near the windmill on Swannington Common.

IBSTOCK
3 miles S of Coalville off the A447

Sense Valley Forest Park, at Heather near Ibstock, is a 150-acre site that has been transformed from an opencast mine into a woodland and wildlife haven. The site includes several large lakes and areas of conservation grassland, and the number of species of birds recorded grows each year.

Also a little way south of Coalville is **Donington Le Heath Manor House**, an attractive stone manor that is one of the few of its period (1280) to remain intact. It is now a museum.

ASHBY-DE-LA-ZOUCH

A historic market town whose name comes from the Saxon Aesc (ash) and Byr (habitation); the ending de la Zouch was added in 1160 when a Norman nobleman Alain de Parrhoet la Zouch became lord of the manor by marriage. In the 15th century Edward IV granted Ashby Manor to his favourite counsellor, Lord Hastings, who converted the manor house into a castle and rebuilt the nearby St Helen's Church. During the Civil War **Ashby Castle** was besieged for over a year by the Parliamentarian Army until the Royalists surrendered in 1646. After the war the castle was partly destroyed to prevent its further use as a centre of resistance and almost wholly forgotten until the publication of Sir Walter Scott's *Ivanhoe* in 1820. He used the castle as the setting for the archery competition which Robin Hood won by splitting the shaft of his opponent's arrow in the bull's eye. The most striking feature of the imposing ruins is the Hastings Tower of 1464, which visitors can still climb to enjoy the view. The earliest parts predate the conversion and include parts of the hall, buttery and pantry of the 12th century manor house.

Hard by the castle ruins stands **St Helen's Church**, built by Lord Hastings in the 1400s on the site of an 11th century church. Restored and enlarged in 1880, it contains much of interest, including some exceptionally fine stained glass depicting the life of Christ. There are several monuments to the Hastings family and an unusual relic in the shape of a finger pillory used to punish parishioners misbehaving in church. Ashby de la Zouch Museum contains a permanent display of Ashby history, the highlight being a model of the castle during the Civil War siege.

Ashby was for a while in the 19th century promoted as a spa town; the **Ivanhoe baths** were designed in 1822 by Robert Chaplin in Grecian style and had a 150ft colonnaded front with 32 Doric columns. Nearby Georgian terraces, also by Chaplin, stand as testimony to the seriousness of the spa project, but a period of decline set in and the baths closed in the 1880s; the buildings were demolished in 1962. Yet another Chaplin building, the grand railway station, ceased to function as a station when the Leicester-Burton line was axed in the 1960s but was restored in the 1980s for use as offices.

AROUND ASHBY DE LA ZOUCH

MEASHAM
5 miles S of Ashby off the A42

Measham was a place of brick-making and coal-mining, with the Ashby Canal flowing past and the River Mease nearby. It was in his warehouse near the canal at Measham that Joseph Wilkes produced his double-size bricks, known as *gobs* or *jumbies*, to try to avoid the brick tax of 1784. Those bricks can still be seen in some of the buildings in the village. In the High Street, opposite St Lawrence's Church, **Measham Museum** is a small village museum with an interesting collection of artefacts, documents and illustrations preserved by a former village doctor and his father. They provide a unique personal history of a community over a period of almost 100 years. Look out for the collection of colourful Measham Teapots which were once very popular on canal boats. Many prehistoric artefacts have been found preserved in peat in the area, including stone hammerheads, solid wooden wheels and flint wedges bound in hazel.

MOIRA
2 miles SW of Ashby on the B586

Contrasting attractions here. The **National Forest** is a truly accessible, multipurpose forest for the nation that is transforming 200 square miles in the Heart of England. Spanning parts of Derbyshire and Staffordshire as well as Leicestershire, the forest is providing a full range of environmental, recreational and social benefits for current and future generations. **Conkers**, the visitor centre for the

Ashby Castle

forest located off the B5003 Ashby-Overseal road, features interactive displays, 120 acres of themed trails, demonstrations, two licensed lakeside restaurant, shop, garden and plants centre, amphitheatre and a number of craft workshops. The site adjoins **Sarah's Wood**, a 25-acre farmland site transformed into a woodland and wildlife haven, with trails and paths suitable for wheelchairs and a children's play area.

Near Donisthope, 2 miles south of Ashby, **Willesley Wood** was one of the first National Forest planting sites and is now an attractive 100-acre area of mature woodland, a lake and meadows. One of the walks leads to Saltersford Valley, which features woodland sculptures, a lake and a picnic area.

The industrial heritage of the region is remembered in the **Moira Furnace**, an impressive, perfectly preserved blast furnace built in 1804 by the Earl of Moira. The site includes lime kilns, a casting shed and engine house, and a range of craft workshops, woodland walks, nature and industrial trails, country park and children's playground.

STAUNTON HAROLD
4 miles N of Ashby off the B587

Another craft centre here, with 16 craft workshops within a magnificent Georgian courtyard. Crafts at **The Ferrers Centre** include contemporary furniture, ceramics, copper-smithing and forge, picture framing and sign studio, designer clothing and textiles, automata, stained glass, china restoration, stone carving and silver jewellery. Gift shop, gallery and tea room on site. Staunton Harold Hall and Holy Trinity Church are surrounded by the beautiful parkland and lakes of the Staunton Estate. The Palladian-style hall is not open to the public, but the church is open for afternoon visits April to September daily except Thursday and Friday. In the care of the National Trust, the church is one of the few to have been built during the Commonwealth period in 1653 and retains the original pews, cushions and hangings, together with fine panelling and a painted ceiling.

Staunton Harold Reservoir, covering over 200 acres, has two nature reserves, fishing, sailing and a visitor centre with exhibitions and 3-D models. Footpaths and nature walks provide a link with the nearby 750-acre Calke Abbey park at Ticknall, near Melbourne. The National Trust's **Calke Abbey** is a baroque mansion built in 1701-3 which has remained virtually unchanged since the death of the last baronet, Sir Vauncey Harpur-Crewe, in 1924.

LOUGHBOROUGH

In Loughborough's Market Place is a statue of a seated man admiring his sock. Titled **The Sock**, this whimsical piece by sculptor Shona Kinlock celebrates the town's premier industry in times past, beginning with wool, then woollen stockings and progressing to knitwear and hosiery machinery and engineering.

Another major industry since mid-Victorian times is represented by the lofty **Carillon** in Queen's Park which was built as an imaginative War Memorial to the dead of the First World War. The 151ft high carillon tower, the first to be built in Britain, contains a unique carillon of 47 bells, covering four chromatic octaves, under the care of the borough carilloner. Carillon recitals are given on Thursday and Sunday afternoons during the summer months. Visitors who climb the 138 steps to the viewing gallery are rewarded with magnificent views of the Charnwood scenery. The **Museum of Armed Forces** in

LOWE OF LOUGHBOROUGH

37/40 Churchgate, Loughborough, Leicestershire LE11 1UE
Tel: 01509 217876

Located opposite Loughborough's 15th century parish church, **Lowe of Loughborough** also has a long history. The company was founded more than 150 years ago and the present owner, Richard Lowe, is the fourth generation of his family to sell and restore antiques and produce stunning replicas in English oak created on site by talented craftsmen. There are 16 showrooms on two floors – these are open Monday to Friday only.

Queen's Park has displays relating to the Great War and is open seven days a week.

Loughborough's connection with bells began in 1858 when the bell foundry of John Taylor moved here from Oxford. It is still producing and restoring bells for customers all over the world. Situated alongside the working factory, the **John Taylor Bell Foundry Museum** covers all aspects of bell-founding from early times and show the craft techniques of moulding, casting, tuning and fitting up of bells. The museum is open all year, including some weekends, and tours of the foundry itself can be arranged with notice.

The recently opened **Charnwood Museum** (free) displays the natural and local history of Charnwood, the district around Loughborough that includes the majestic Charnwood Forest.

For many visitors to Loughborough, the most irresistible attraction is the **Great Central Railway**, Britain's only main line steam railway. Its headquarters are at Loughborough Central Station, where there is a museum, a working signal box and a collection of historic steam locomotives. The station, with its ornate canopy over the island platform, is worth a visit in its own right, and is in regular demand from film companies. It was used a few years ago for the filming of *Shadowlands* – other stars who have been filmed here include Nicole Kidman, Anthony Hopkins and Kate Winslet. The line runs eight miles to Quorn and Birstall, crossing the Swithland Reservoir viaduct, and the service operates every weekend and Bank Holiday throughout the year, and weekdays from June to September. A meal on the move makes the trip even more memorable: traditional lunch on the Silver Jubilee every Saturday and Sunday; dinner on the Charnwood Forester and Master

PAPERWEIGHT

14 Devonshire Square, Loughborough,
Leicestershire LE11 3DW
Tel/Fax: 01509 217575

Still with its original Victorian shop front – one of very few in the town – **Paperweight** offers two floors of distinctive and elegant gifts. Owner Karen Cunnington, who took a degree in Russian Language and Literature at Birmingham, opened her shop in 1983 after a period in the gift retail trade. Her stock comprises a vast range of gifts with something for everyone but especially for men – executive toys, for example, and designer cuff-links. Also on offer are Crabtree & Evelyn toiletries; Bridgewater pottery; designer jewellery from Dover & Hall, Kenzo and YSL; traditional teddy bears, hand-painted wooden children's toys, and much more.

Cutler Saturday and Sunday evenings.

In the **Phantom & Firkin**, Loughborough's only brew pub, visitors can see how traditional cask ales are made. Call 01509 262051 for details of free brewery tours.

Loughborough Market is one of the finest street markets in the country. Full of tradition and atmosphere, it is held in the market place and adjacent streets every Thursday and Saturday. November sees the annual Loughborough Fair, with stalls, shows, rides and other attractions.

AROUND LOUGHBOROUGH

CASTLE DONINGTON
7 miles NW of Loughborough off the A6

Originally just Donington – the "Castle" was added when the Norman castle was built to defend the River Trent crossing.

It was demolished by King John to punish the owner for supporting Magna Carta and was rebuilt in 1278.

The **Donington Grand Prix Collection**, in Donington Park, is the world's largest collection of single-seater racing cars. The five halls contain over 130 exhibits of motor racing.

WYMESWOLD
5 miles NE of Loughborough on the A6006

A large conservation village whose Georgian houses give it the air of an 18th century market town – more than 30 of them are Grade II listed. The 14th century parish church was restored by Pugin in 1844.

MOUNTSORREL
5 miles SE of Loughborough off the A6

Peaceful since the A6 bypass was opened, Mountsorrel lies on the west bank of the

WYMESWOLD COUNTRY FURNITURE

17 Far Street, Wymeswold, Leicestershire LE12 6TZ
Tel/Fax: 01509 880309

Occupying two floors in converted Georgian stables, **Wymeswold Country Furniture** was founded in 1983 and has become one of the most respected and successful dealers in genuine old pine furniture. The glowing mellowness of old pine enhances any room, blends happily with all colour schemes, gives years of pleasure and also appreciates in value. Owned and run by Bill and Jenny McBean, the business carries extensive stocks of furniture for all rooms of the house – beds, chests of drawers, wardrobes, blanket boxes for the bedroom; a good selection of desks and useful cupboards for the home office; tables, chairs, dressers, plate racks, base units, wine racks and much more for the kitchen.

To complement the furniture there's an extensive choice of home accessories, ornaments and

giftware including mirrors, clocks, prints, ceramics, glassware, a varied range of both electric and candle lighting, cushions, crystals and many other unusual and decorative items. Like the Italian Terramundi – Etruscan money pots whose hand-thrown design has remained unchanged for more than 2000 years. The work of local craftspeople is also on display, original work that includes watercolours, pottery, ironwork, needlework and greetings cards. If you are looking for a distinctive gift then you'll almost certainly find one at Wymeswold Country Furniture!

Soar. Its elegant **Butter Market**, or Dome, lends distinction to an otherwise unremarkable little town. The Dome was built in 1793 by the eccentric Lord of the Manor, Sir John Danvers, and the town was surprised that he didn't have it painted red – almost everything else in Mountsorrel that could be painted was covered in brilliant red, a colour for which Sir John had an insatiable pattern. His clothes were predominantly red, set off by discreet touches of black: "being a broad-set man his appearance was like that of the Knave of Spades".

A great attraction in the village for the whole family is **Stonehurst Family Farm & Motor Museum**, winner of the "Best Leicestershire Visitor Attraction 2000/ 2001". Highlights range from baby rabbits and guinea pigs in "Cuddle Corner" to all the familiar farm animals, free tractor rides, a working smithy and an impressive collection of vintage cars, motorcycles and memorabilia. Restaurant, tea shop, farm shop are all open daily all year.

OLD WOODHOUSE
3 miles S of Loughborough on minor roads

The most impressive stained glass window in Leicestershire is to be found not in any of the county's churches but at **Beaumanor Hall**, the seat of the Herrick family from 1595 to the 1930s. The present Tudor-style mansion was built in 1848 and it was then that the extraordinary window, 15ft high and 25ft wide, was installed by William Perry Herrick. All his life William was obsessed with his family pedigree so each of the 21 panels in the great window features the brilliantly coloured coat-of-arms of one of his ancestors. It's a breathtaking riot of heraldry. Sadly, for a man who took such pride in his ancestry, William died without a direct heir to succeed

LANE END COTTAGE

School Lane, Old Woodhouse, Loughborough, Leicestershire LE12 8UJ
Tel: 01509 890706 Fax: 01509 890246
e-mail: mary.hudson@talk21.com

Enjoying a village location within Charnwood Forest, **Lane End Cottage** is a charming 17th century cottage standing within delightful secluded gardens. It's the home of Mary and Rod Hudson who have been welcoming bed & breakfast guests here since 1996. The house has an interesting history. It was built of local stone and slate in 1691 as a school for poor children, funded by Thomas Rawlins and named after him. The school closed in 1865 and the house is now a Grade II listed building. School Lane itself has been designated a Conservation Area, and there are many interesting walks in the vicinity.

The accommodation at Lane End Cottage enjoys a 4-Diamond Silver Award rating from the English Tourism Council, one of its highest classifications. There are 2 guest bedrooms: 1 double, 1 twin, both en suite and attractively furnished and decorated in cottage style. Guests have the use of an elegant conservatory lounge overlooking the meticulously tended garden which they are also welcome to enjoy (along with the wildlife). Breakfast at Lane End Cottage is definitely something to look forward to, served in the dining room it's based on local produce and includes delicious home-made bread. For an evening meal, the neighbourhood offers a wide range of excellent inns and restaurants.

him. Beaumanor Hall is now a Leicestershire County County training centre but the window may be viewed by prior arrangement by calling 01509 890119.

WOODHOUSE EAVES
3 miles S of Loughborough on minor roads

The oldest house in this attractive village is Long Close, which is thought to have once been a royal hunting lodge. Secluded behind a high wall, the 5 acres of **Long Close Gardens** have become known as the Secret Garden. They've also been described as "A Cornish Garden in Leicestershire" because of the rare and interesting plants that flourish here. The gardens are open from March to July and group visits can be arranged at other times by appointment.

Woodhouse Eaves takes its name from being on the edges, or eaves, of Charnwood Forest. The views are superb,

especially from the summit of **Beacon Hill Country Park**, one of the highest points in Leicestershire at 818ft.

SHEPSHED
4 miles W of Loughborough on the A512

The hosiery industry was once the principal activity here with some 900 stocking frames clattering away at the peak of the town's prosperity. Shepshed still offers factory outlet shopping for knitwear and clothing as well as traditional and farmers' markets. Around the medieval marketplace are some thatched cottages once used by framework knitters in the 1800s.

MELTON MOWBRAY

The very name of this bustling market town makes the mouth water, being home to the pork pie, one of the most traditional of English delicacies. The

---

THE GRANGE COURTYARD

Forest Street, Shepshed, Leicestershire LE12 9DA
Tel: 01509 600189 Fax: 01509 603834
e-mail: linda.Lawrence@thegrangecourtyard.co.uk
website: www.thegrangecourtyard.co.uk

Although only a mile from Junction 23 of the M1, **The Grange Courtyard**, recently commended for the Best Visitor Award in Leicestershire, stands in its own beautifully tended grounds which positively radiate peace and tranquillity. It's believed that part of this lovely Grade II listed building dates back to the 11th century. The house was extended in Tudor and Georgian times and amongst the distinguished men and women renowned to have stayed here is no less a personage than Queen Elizabeth I. Recently, the owner of the Grange, Linda Lawrence, has lovingly restored the house to provide luxury accommodation, all rooms have en suite bathrooms, with both bath and a shower, and are provided with luxury bathrobes, hair dryer and organic toiletries especially created for the Grange.

The rooms all have direct dial telephones and internet access, along with a television, video cassette player and clock radio alarms.The comfortable residents' lounge overlooks the garden and there's a fully licensed bar on the balcony above the lounge, in one of the cottages which have been imaginatively created from former agricultural buildings attached to the Grange and provide luxury accommodation in 12 individually designed ececutive suites. These have their own dining room, kitchen and cooker. The Grange has secure private parking with electronic gates, CCTV and staff on call 24 hours a day.

Melton Hunt Cake, a rich fruit cake spiced with Jamaican rum, is another local speciality, and Stilton, "king of English cheeses", is also made here. The cheese has the longest history, dating back possibly as far as the 14th century. It is only manufactured in Leicestershire, Nottinghamshire and Derbyshire. Of the six producers, four are in the Vale of Belvoir and one in Melton itself. The noble cheese became nationally popular in the 1740s when Frances Pawlett of Wymondham came to an arrangement with the landlord of The Bell Inn at Stilton to market the cheese. The inn was a coaching stop on the Great North Road and travellers who sampled the noble cheese soon spread its fame. Later, Melton Mowbray became the market centre for Stilton and from 1883 to 1914 three specialist fairs were held each year – 12,672 cheeses were sold at the first! A 16lb Stilton takes 17 gallons of milk to produce and a minimum of two months to mature.

Hand-raised pork pies have been made here since 1831 and since 1851 in the oldest surviving bakery, **Ye Olde Pork Pie Shoppe**, where visitors can watch the traditional hand-raising techniques and taste the pies and the Hunt Cake. Markets have long been a feature of life in Melton Mowbray, and the Domesday Book of 1086 records the town's market as the only one in Leicestershire. Large street markets are held on Tuesdays and Saturdays in the Market Place, and butter and corn crosses still stand at two of the town's former market points. The town also has regular livestock auctions and a farmer's market

St Mary's Church, considered the largest and stateliest parish church in the whole county, dates from 1170. It has a particularly imposing tower and impressive stained glass windows.

SYSONBY KNOLL HOTEL

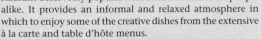

Asfordby Road, Melton Mowbray,
Leicestershire LE13 0HP
Tel: 01664 563563 e-mail: reception@sysonby.co.uk
Fax: 01664 410364 website: www.sysonby.co.uk

Winner of the Best Visitor Accommodation, Leicestershire 2002 and 2003, **Sysonby Knoll Hotel** is a handsome 3 Star Edwardian country house which has been owned and run by the same family since 1965. It stands in its own secluded grounds of 5 acres with a river frontage and carries the highest quality rating of any hotel in the town. The recently refurbished downstairs lounge area is furnished in period style and in winter guests are welcomed by a fire in reception with the owners' dogs in prime position! Your hosts, Gavin and Jenny Howling, have established the hotel's reputation for fine food and exceptional hospitality with the lively restaurant deservedly popular with residents and local people alike. It provides an informal and relaxed atmosphere in which to enjoy some of the creative dishes from the extensive à la carte and table d'hôte menus.

The hotel's 30 bedrooms are equipped with all the facilities you would expect at 3-star level and the more spacious superior and executive bedrooms offer an even higher level of comfort. Most of the bedrooms overlook the quiet central courtyard while the two 4-poster bedrooms both command fine views over the gardens and river. Pets are welcome and the hotel offers special discounted rates for weekend breaks of 2 nights or more.

Manor Oven

40/42 Sherrard Street, Melton Mowbray, Leicestershire LE13 1XJ
Tel: 01664 565920

Manor Oven is a traditional bakery and Richard Greasley is a master baker who trained at Borough Poly in London and in Lucerne, Switzerland. His family has been in the business both in England and Italy. A bakery and coffee shop, Manor Oven was established in 1971 and specialises in breads – with a full range of traditional crusty breads baked on the premises – and a range of pastries that includes a delicious Melton Mowbray cheesecake. Also popular is Stilton and Walnut Bread which, like all the Manor Oven products, is also available in the coffee shop along with hot light meals, toasted sandwiches and filled rolls.

AROUND MELTON MOWBRAY

Grimston

3 miles W of Melton off the A6006

Perhaps because of its unappealing name, Grimston tends to be overlooked by guide books. It is in fact one of the county's most appealing villages. At its centre is a lovely green where a set of ancient stocks stands beneath a chestnut tree. Overlooking the green are two venerable hostelries and the Church of St John the Evangelist. Here the curious custom of "bidding by candle" continued until the early 1900s.

A small stump of candle was lit and buyers would then make their bids for the item being auctioned. Whoever made the last bid before the candle guttered acquired the lot at that price.

Indian Ocean Trading Company

Old Dalby Lodge, Paddys Lane, Old Dalby, Melton Mowbray, Leicestershire LE14 3LY
Tel: 01509 881975 Fax: 01509 889178
e-mail: meltonm@indian-ocean.co.uk website: www.indian-ocean.co.uk

Elegant and durable garden furniture in teak is the speciality of the **Indian Ocean Trading Company** or, as they put it: "For teak, you should drop into Indian Ocean". John and Rosemary Morley have represented the company since 2000 and it now has 20 outlets nationwide "all staffed by people who actually know what they're talking about!" and offers the broadest range of beautifully designed, highly durable, teak garden furniture. There's a choice of 6 luxury sun loungers, 23 different sturdy tables, 27 chairs, 6 parasols, 7 benches and 7 styles of outdoor lighting.

The Morleys believe that their quality control and customer service are unsurpassed – all deliveries are free, the furniture comes fully assembled, will be placed where you want it, and then all the packaging will be taken away by the company's drivers. A free 112-page brochure detailing the company's range of products can be obtained by calling free on 0800 092 0959 or you can shop securely online at www.indian-ocean.co.uk. "And remember" say the Morleys "even if the sun isn't shining today, it will be sooner or later!"

RED LION INN

Red Lion Street, Stathern, Leicestershire LE14 4HS
Tel: 01949 860868 Fax: 01949 861579
e-mail: redlion@work.gb.com

Following their outstanding success in re-opening The Olive Branch pub at Clipsham in Rutland, partners Ben Jones, Marcus Welford and Sean Hope continued their quest to revitalise closed-down village pubs by acquiring the **Red Lion Inn** in Stathern. This charming old inn dates back to 1653 and has a warm rustic appeal with lots of oak beams, two open fires, a log-burning stove and a dining room in what was originally a skittle alley. Chef Phil Lowe – previously sous-chef at Hart's restaurant in Nottingham – offers a daily-changing menu for which he says "We're trying to produce simple, home-cooked food – or at least something you might have a go at in your own kitchen".

He also likes re-introducing dishes that people may not have seen for some time such as potted ham, pease pudding and home-made piccalilli. Great emphasis is placed on sourcing ingredients from local suppliers. A map on the back of the menu shows exactly where the produce comes from – partridges and pheasants, for example, are delivered from the nearby Belvoir Castle estate. As at The Olive Branch, the wine list has been compiled by Marcus Welford and shows the same combination of imaginative selection and affordable prices. In good weather, customers can dine outside in the courtyard garden where there's also a children's play area.

ROYAL HORSE SHOES

Melton Road,
Waltham on the Wolds,
Leicestershire LE14 4AJ
Tel: 01664 464289
Fax: 01664 464022

A delightful country pub in the pleasant village of Waltham on the Wolds, the **Royal Horse Shoes** was so named after Queen Victoria stayed the night here and her horses were re-shod by the local farrier. Dating back to the 1600s, this picturesque thatched hostelry stands in the heart of the village, just across the road from the parish church. It's owned by the Noble family – Alan and Audrey and their son Simon – who also own and run the Rose & Crown at Tilton on the Hill (see separate entry).

The Royal Horse Shoes is noted for its excellent home cooked and freshly prepared food, with a no smoking area, which can be extended throughout the lounge. Sunday lunch is very special and there's also a set lunch for senior citizens, Monday to Saturday. To accompany your meal, there's a choice of at least 4 real ales or a selection of reasonably priced wines. If you are planning to stay in this attractive part of the county, the inn has 4 guest bedrooms – 2 doubles and 2 twins. They all have en suite facilities, are tastefully furnished and decorated and, although they adjoin the pub, are completely self-contained.

EASTWELL
5 miles N of Melton off the A607

Just outside the village, **Crossroads Farm Museum**, in a 17th century barn, is a treasure trove of farming equipment and memorabilia from Victorian times
to the present day.

STATHERN
7 miles N of Melton off the A607

A peaceful village nestling in the Vale of Belvoir, Stathern has a medieval church with a beautifully carved 13th century doorway, an arcaded 14th century font, and some fine modern glass. A one-time resident here was Colonel Hacker who acted as "master of ceremonies" at the execution of Charles I. After the Restoration he, too, was despatched by the executioner's axe.

WALTHAM ON THE WOLDS
5 miles NE of Melton on the A607

Straddling the A607, high up on the Leicestershire Wolds, Waltham is an attractive village with an excellent hostelry, the Royal Horse Shoes *(see separate entry)*, and a tall-spired medieval church. Roman pavements and Saxon stone coffins have been discovered here,

Jousting at Belvoir Castle

testifying to the antiquity of the settlement. The country lane that leads from Waltham to Harby is unusually wide because, it is believed, it was an ancient drovers' road leading to Nottingham.

BELVOIR CASTLE
12 miles N of Melton off the A607

The Leicestershire home of the Duke of Rutland is an imposing mock-medieval building in an equally imposing setting overlooking the pastoral Vale of Belvoir. The present **Belvoir Castle** was completed in the early 19th century after previous buildings had been destroyed during the Wars of the Roses, the Civil War and in the major fire of 1816. In the

BRYN BARN

38 High Street, Waltham on the Wolds, Leicestershire LE14 4AH
Tel: 01664 464783 Fax: 01664 464138
e-mail: glenarowlands@onetel.net.uk

In the conservation village of Waltham on the Wolds in the beautiful Vale of Belvoir, **Bryn Barn** offers high quality accommodation in a barn and stable conversion set in secluded cottage gardens. There are 4 guest bedrooms, (2 doubles; 1 family; 1 twin), all with AA 4-Diamonds ratings. Each has en suite or private facilities and is provided with TV, hospitality tray and many extras. Guests comment particularly on the comfortable beds. Your hosts, Glena and Andrew Rowlands, serve a hearty English breakfast (special diets catered for) and for evening meals there are two good village pubs within walking distance.

stunning interior are notable collections of furniture and porcelain, silks and tapestries, sculptures and paintings. There are works by Van Dyck, Reynolds, Hogarth and, most familiar of all, Holbein's imposing portrait of Henry VIII. Also within the castle is the **Queen's Royal Lancers Museum**. The grounds are as splendid as the castle and are used for medieval jousting tournaments on certain days in the summer.

WYMONDHAM
6 miles E of Melton off the B676

A must for visitors here is the six-sailed **Windmill** (free) dating from 1814 and currently being restored. It is one of only four of its kind in the country and most of its massive machinery is still intact. The mill's former outbuildings have been converted into a **Craft Centre** with workshops for wrought iron work

candle-making, pine furniture, hand-made kitchens, playhouses and architectural antiques. There's a tearoom serving light lunches and home-baked cakes, a free bouncy castle and play area. Bed & breakfast accommodation is also available.

BURROUGH-ON-THE-HILL
5 miles S of Melton off the B6047

Burrough Hill is an Iron Age fort rising to almost 700ft overlooking the Wreake Valley. There are grand views from its flat summit which in Victorian times was used for horse racing.

TILTON ON THE HILL
7 miles S of Melton on the B6047

The highest habitation in the county, some 700ft above sea level, Tilton has a charming little church with some striking Norman gargoyles and stone carvings of human heads and animals,

ROSE & CROWN

Main Street,
Tilton on the Hill,
Leicestershire LE40 9FS
Tel: 0116 259 7234

Standing opposite the 13th century parish church of St Peter's, the **Rose & Crown** is dated 1707 when, it's believed, it was built as an ale house. Inside, there's lots of exposed timbers and some unusual carved timbers over the fireplace. The inn is full of charm and character with a large inglenook fireplace and open fire in the bar, an unusually comfortable pool and darts room complete with settees. An extensive bar menu is available with home-made soup and Mexican Nachos among the starters, and main dishes that range from Steak & Ale Pie to Spinach and Ricotta Tortellini.

In the separate non-smoking restaurant, also heavily beamed, you'll find outstanding cuisine – home cured Gravadlax served on a French Bean and Tomato Salad amongst the starters and appetising main dishes such as Tiger Prawns cooked in white wine or a Crispy cheese pastry tart filled with goats cheese. There's also a children's menu with many more choices than usual. The Rose & Crown is one of two fine inns owned and run by the Noble family: the other is the Royal Horse Shoes at Waltham on the Wolds.

and some impressive monuments to members of the Digby family. About 3 miles east of the village, there's pleasant walking in the Forestry Commission's **Owston Woods** – look out for the 800-year-old lime tree which is still in remarkably good shape.

RUTLAND

Rutland Water

The motto of the county is, appropriately, 'multum in parvo' ('much in little'). It has two delightful market towns, Oakham and Uppingham, and 52 small, unspoilt villages of thatch and ironstone cottages clustered round their churches. The county's central feature is **Rutland Water** which extends over 3,300 acres and is the largest man-made reservoir in Europe. Started in 1971 to supply water to East Midlands towns, it was created by damming the valley near Empingham. There's good walking around its 26-mile shoreline, some great bird-watching (including wild ospreys), excellent trout and pike fishing, and a wide variety of watersports.

The county boasts two leading public schools, Oakham and Uppingham; one of the most striking and best-preserved Norman churches in the country, at Tickencote; a grand 12th century Great Hall and the home of the original 'Tom Thumb', both in Oakham.

Curiously for such a pastoral, peaceful county, it was Rutland men who were prime movers in two of the most dangerous conspiracies in England's history. In a room over the porch of Stoke Dry church, the Gunpowder Plot was hatched with the local lord of the manor, Sir Everard Digby, as one of the ringleaders. Some 75 years later, Titus Oates and his fellow conspirators hatched the anti-Catholic 'Popish Plot' at his home in Oakham.

MARC OXLEY FINE ART

Tel: 01572 822334   e-mail: marc@marcoxleyfineart.co.uk

Marc Oxley Fine Art was established in 1981 by Marc Oxley after leaving Christies where he had worked in the watercolour department for three years. Now operating from his home, Marc deals mainly in watercolours and drawings pre-1940, of which he has a stock of more than 500 originals, and antiquarian maps pre-1850. Another special interest is original animation art – drawings and production cels for films such as *The Pink Panther, The Flintstones* and Walt Disney productions. Marc also deals in anime – the Japanese equivalent of production cels. If you have any requirements in these fields, just phone or e-mail Marc and he'll do his very best to find what you want.

UPPINGHAM

8 miles N of Corby on the A6003

This picturesque stone-built town is the major community in the south part of the county. It has a long, handsome high street and a fine market place where traders have hawked their wares every Friday since 1280. The town is known for its bookshops and art galleries, but whereas other places are dominated by castles or cathedrals, in Uppingham it's the impressive **Uppingham School** that gives the town its special character. The school was founded in 1584 by Robert Johnson, Archdeacon of Leicester, who also founded Rutland's other celebrated public school at Oakham. For more than 250 years, Uppingham was just one of many such small grammar schools, giving rigorous instruction in classical languages to a couple of dozen sons of the local gentry. Then, in 1853, the Revd Edward Thring was appointed

headmaster. During his 43-year tenure the sleepy little school was transformed.

The Old School Building still stands in the churchyard, with trilingual inscriptions around the walls in Latin, Greek and Hebrew – *Train up a child in the way he should go* is one of them. In its place rose a magnificent complex of neo-gothic buildings: not just the traditional classrooms and a (splendid) chapel, but also a laboratory, workshops, museum, gymnasium and the most extensive school playing fields in the country.

Dr Thring wrote extensively on educational matters, championed education for girls and founded the Headmasters Conference. When he retired in 1897 he could look back with pride on the creation of one of the country's most successful public schools, both academically and financially. The old school, the 18th century studies, the Victorian chapel and schoolrooms, and

---

DELIVERANCE COUNTY

25 High Street East, Uppingham, Rutland LE15 9PY
Tel: 01572 820080 Fax: 01572 822893
e-mail: kap61@dial.pipex.com
website: www.deliverancecounty.com

Wendy de Verteuil's career in ceramics was initiated when she took a course in the subject at a local college as a respite from the rigours of bringing up 4 small children. When the course was completed Wendy started

developing her own range of ceramics which she named **Deliverance County**. To begin with she used to hold one day sales in her home, selling teapots, mugs, bowls and kitchen crockery all of which she decorated herself. As her children grew up and Wendy had more time to herself, her output became more prolific and in February 1999 she and her husband bought a small shop in Uppingham's High Street.

Wendy has her own work space in the shop so visitors can watch the delicate process of hand painting in progress. She is surrounded by the whole range of her household ceramics – jugs and mugs in a variety of sizes; teapots, sugar bowls, candle bowls, plates, cups and saucers, lampbases, egg cups, cheese hoods and plates, serving platters and more. There's a choice of attractive themed collections – the Shaker, Antique Rose, Kitchen Garden and Worker Bee for example, and any item can be personalised with a message of your choice. One-offs to your own brief using existing shapes can also be ordered and Deliverance County also has a mail order service.

Uppingham

the 20th century great hall, all Grade I or Grade II listed, can be visited on a guided tour on Saturday afternoons in summer.

AROUND UPPINGHAM

STOKE DRY
3 miles S of Uppingham on the A6003

There are some striking monuments in the church at Stoke Dry to the Digby family, particularly an engraved alabaster slab to Jaquetta Digby who died in 1496. One of her descendants, Sir Everard Digby, was to bring great shame on the family. He was born in the village in 1578 but when the Protestant James I ascended the throne, Sir Everard and his Catholic friends became involved in the conspiracy now known as the Gunpowder Plot. It was in the priest's room over the porch of St Andrew's

Church that the conspirators met. After his conviction in 1609 Sir Everard endured the gruesome ordeal of death by hanging, drawing and quartering. The porch where the plotters met has another macabre story attached to it – it's said that one vicar locked a witch in the room and left her to die by starvation.

Stoke Dry overlooks **Eyebrook Reservoir**, a 300-acre trout fishery in an idyllic location in the Welland Valley, by the border with Leicestershire and Northamptonshire. Good bank and boat fishing from April to October.

LYDDINGTON
3 miles SE of Uppingham off the A6003

A quiet village where English Heritage oversees the **Bede House**, one of the finest examples of Tudor domestic architecture in the country. This house of prayer was once part of a retreat for the Bishops of Lincoln and was later converted to a hospital (bede house) for 12 poor men, 2 women and a warden. It remained in use right up until 1930. The fine 16th century rooms can be visited daily from April to October. The small gardens contain a notable herb garden with over 60 herbs, both culinary and medicinal, and just outside the grounds lie the fish ponds that used to supply the bishop's kitchen.

WING
2 miles NE of Uppingham off the A6003

The little village of Wing is best known for a Maze in which it's impossible to get lost. The medieval **Turf Maze** is made of foot-high turf banks and measuring 40 feet across. Its design is identical to the mosaic patterns in the floors of Chartres Cathedral and other French cathedrals. An old tradition asserts that penitents were required to crawl around the maze on their knees, stopping at various

Continued on page 358

WALK 6

Rutland Water

Start	Upper Hambleton
Distance	4½ miles (7.2 km)
Approximate time	2 hours
Parking	Roadside parking by church at Upper Hambleton
Refreshments	Pub at Upper Hambleton
Ordnance Survey maps	Landranger 141 (Kettering and Corby) and Explorer 15 (Rutland Water)

Rutland Water is man-made; a vast reservoir, one of the largest in the country. It was constructed as a water supply for the local area but also provides a useful recreational and scenic asset in a region lacking natural lakes. The higher ground around Upper Hambleton was left above the water when the area was flooded and now forms a peninsula. The walk follows a track around the shoreline of this peninsula, from where there is a succession of very attractive and ever-changing views across the water. As the route forms part of the Rutland Cycle Way you share the track with cyclists, but that shouldn't be a problem as it is broad and well constructed all the way.

Upper Hambleton occupies the highest land in the area and overlooks Rutland Water and the Vale of Catmose. The church dates mainly from the late 12th century though the tower, crowned with a low spire, is 13th century and the chancel was rebuilt in the 1890s.

Start by the church and walk back along the road, in the Oakham direction. Where the road bends left, turn right on to a track **A** that descends towards the shores of Rutland Water. Follow this gently undulating track which winds along the north side of the peninsula above the lake, at one stage passing through the attractive Armley Wood. Along the way are several cattle-grids beside which there are stiles to climb. Eventually, turn right and descend to Barnhill Creek **B**.

The track now curves right across the end of the peninsula to a road. Cross over, turn right to keep parallel to the road, later rounding a left bend and heading down to the south side of the peninsula. To the left, on the opposite shore, is the early 19th century Normanton church, partly submerged when the reservoir was built and now a museum of the history of Rutland and the construction of the reservoir.

Turn right and continue along the meandering shoreline that is more wooded on this side. After passing

through Hambleton Wood, keep along the left edge of the trees to reach a T-junction of tracks by the Old Hall, a large, stone house by the lake. Turn right **C** along a tarmac lane. At a pair of cattle-grids pass by the right-hand one, here leaving the lakeside cycle track, and follow the lane uphill back into Upper Hambleton.

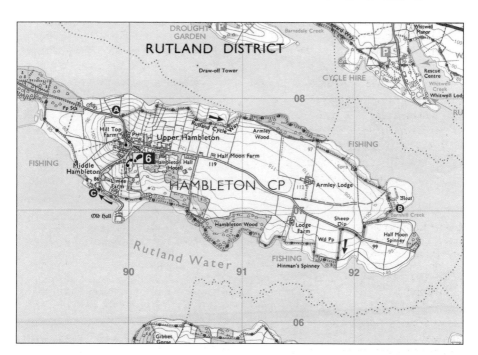

points to say prayers. Once a fairly common sight, only eight such turf mazes are known to still exist in England. They were already falling into disfavour by Shakespeare's time. In *A Midsummer Night's Dream* he wrote:

And the quaint mazes in the wanton green
For lack of tread, are indistinguishable.

OAKHAM

Oakham is one of England's most appealing county towns, a friendly place with many old hostelries, a regular weekly market, a wide variety of family-owned shops, a fine church and a major public school.

Just off the Market Place with its charming market cross and stocks is **Rutland Castle**, a romantic, evocative fortified manor house built between 1180 and 1190, with the earliest surviving example of an aisled stone hall in the country. A unique feature is a collection of over 200 horseshoes hanging all around the walls of the hall. For centuries, any peer of the realm passing through the town has been required to present a horseshoe to the castle. When this custom began isn't clear although one plausible story says that it began in the days of William the Conqueror when his farrier lived here. (The farrier's descendants, the Ferrers family, later built the Great Hall). This unusual tax is still being imposed – amongst the hundreds of horseshoes of every size, some ornately gilded, others rusty, is one presented by Queen Elizabeth II.

All Saints Church is the spiritual centre of town, a fine parish church with a 14th century tower. On the capitals in

---

SWANS ANTIQUES & INTERIORS

17 Mill Street, Oakham, Rutland LE15 6EA
Tel: 01572 724364 Fax: 01572 755094
e-mail: info@swansofoakham.co.uk
website: swansofoakham.co.uk

Housed in a building that dates back to the 1550s, **Swans Antiques & Interiors** offers a unique range of genuine antique furniture along with quality reproductions. At any one time they have more than 150 antique French beds in stock in various styles and sizes – Louis, Henri and Empire styles in walnut and mahogany; lit bateaux and wall beds; and cane, upholstered and painted beds. All have been fully restored and polished, lengthened where necessary, fitted with new upholstered bases and are available with handmade mattresses. Swans also make reproduction beds and specialise in custom-made 4-posters in oak or cherry, often with original posts.

The 12 showrooms also contain a constantly changing stock of complementary furniture – armoires, chests, sofas, dressing and bedside units. Established almost 20 years ago, Swans is owned by Peter and Linda Jones who travel widely to source their unique stock. Tom, their son, and Richard, run the shop. There are also two workshops producing a unique hand-painted range of furniture that includes kitchen dressers, wardrobes, superb bookcases, dining tables and much more. Swans also offers a comprehensive furnishing service and can take all the strain of fully furnishing your house with good quality antique furniture sourced in the UK and Europe.

the nave are striking carvings of traditional subjects, including dragons, the Green Man, Adam and Eve, and Reynard the Fox.

Rutland County Museum (free), housed in a splendid 18th century riding school in Catmose Street, has displays of farm equipment, machinery and wagons, domestic collections and local archaeology. The riding school belonged to the Rutland Fencibles, a volunteer cavalry regiment raised in 1794 and now remembered in a gallery in the museum.

Oakham's Tourist Information Centre is in **Flore's House**, one of the oldest buildings in the town. It dates from the late 1300s and was built by William Flore and his son Roger, who was a wealthy merchant and four times Speaker of the House of Commons.

Notable natives of Oakham include the infamous conspirator Titus Oates who was born here in 1649 and lived in Mill Street. A minor cleric, he played the leading role in fabricating the 'Popish Plot' of 1678. Oates claimed to have uncovered a secret Jesuit plot to assassinate Charles II and return the Catholic church to power. Many innocent Catholics were killed as a result of this alarm, but Oates, when the truth was discovered, did not escape lightly. He was sentenced to yearly whippings and was not freed until 1688; he died in obscurity in 1705.

Another Oakham man involved in Titus Oates' conspiracy was the famed midget Jeffery Hudson, 'the smallest man from the smallest county in England'. He lived in a thatched cottage which still stands on Melton Road opposite the White Lion pub. By the age of 9 Jeffery stood a mere 18 inches high. His father, who was above average height, worked on the Duke of Buckingham's estate at nearby **Burley on the Hill**, a couple of miles north-east of Oakham. The duchess took a fancy to the miniscule lad, dressed him in costly silk and satin, and kept him by her as a kind of mascot. When Charles I and his Queen Henrietta Maria were guests at Burley, a huge cold pie was placed on the table before them and when the pie was cut open out popped Jeffery. The Queen was so delighted with the midget that she took him back to the royal court, where he became a popular figure, was knighted and had his portrait painted by Van Dyck. But Jeffery was an extremely quarrelsome character and on one occasion challenged Lord Crofts to a duel in which the latter was killed. Jeffery was banished for a time but while travelling back to England was captured by Turkish pirates and sold as a slave. Ransomed by the Duke of Buckingham, he returned to Oakham and the house in the High Street. With his usual impetuosity he became involved in Titus Oates' Popish Plot and was imprisoned.

WINGWELL NURSERY

5 Top Street, Wing, Oakham, Rutland LE15 8SE
Tel: 01572 737727 e-mail: sales@wingwellnursery.com
Fax: 01572 737788 website: www.wingwellnursery.com

Recently recommended in Leslie Geddes-Brown's publication *Gardeners' Favourite Nurseries* and by Alan Titchmarsh in his "Nursery Focus" column, **Wingwell Nursery** enjoys an unrivalled reputation for the quality, performance and reliability of its plants. The range includes more than 1,600 varieties available for sale and there are many more under propagation. The owner, Rose Dejardin, specialises in hardy herbaceous perennials but the choice also includes climbers, roses, shrubs and grasses. Open every day, 10am to 5pm, from March 1st to December 23rd.

Oakham School was founded in 1584 by Archdeacon Robert Johnson, who also founded Uppingham School. As at Uppingham, the original single room school building still stands, its walls inscribed with Hebrew, Latin and Greek quotations. Both schools expanded greatly in the 19th century but while the school buildings at Uppingham dominate the little town, at Oakham they are spread across the town centre, partly hidden away off the attractive market place where the ancient Butter Cross still provides shelter for the town stocks. Now co-educational, Oakham School has around 1000 pupils.

On the outskirts of town, the road to Uppingham crosses **Swooning Bridge**, where condemned felons going on their last journey from the town gaol first saw, on top of a small rise called Mount Pleasant, the gallows from which they were about to hang.

AROUND OAKHAM

TEIGH
5 miles N of Oakham on a minor road

Teigh (pronounced 'tea') is one of the 31 'Thankful Villages', those communities where all the men and women who served in World War I survived. A brass inscription in the church gives thanks for the safe return of the 11 men and 2 women from the village who came back.

The **Old Rectory**, which stands next to the Strawberry Hill-style Gothic church, has a delightful partly-walled garden that was first laid out in the 1950s.

COTTESMORE
5 miles NE of Oakham on the B668

The **Rutland Railway Museum** (see panel below) is the big attraction here. The working steam/diesel museum is based on local quarry and industrial

---

RUTLAND RAILWAY MUSEUM

Ashwell Road, Cottesmore, Oakham, Rutland LE15 7BX
Tel: 01572 813203

Located in the pleasant countryside of the ancient county of Rutland, four miles from Oakham, **Rutland Railway Museum** is dedicated to telling the story of railways in industry, especially local ironstone quarrying. It goes back to the days before mass road transport when most freight was carried by rail and factories, works and quarries had their own railway systems.

The Museum's open air steam centre hosts a large collection of steam and diesel locomo-tives, wagons, vans and coaches, together with other related items and artefacts. Train rides and demonstrations are a regular feature of steam days - part of the ongoing development and restoration of the Museum site by volunteer members.

You can relax in comfort at the Visitor Centre where light refreshments are available and the Centre's souvenir shop has a variety of books, videos, souvenirs and low priced children's items on sale. Or why not enjoy a walk in pleasant country alongside the Museum's demonstration line. Watch the trains go by as you walk or picnic, and see the remains of the old Oakham Canal. A leaflet is available giving details of features of natural interest along the way. There are regular displays and exhibitions and the locomotives can be seen being repaired or painted.

railways. Call 01572 813203 for details of steam days and gala days. A little further along the B668 is the village of Greetham on the Viking Way, one of the three long-distance walks that converge on Oakham.

CLIPSHAM
10 miles NE of Oakham off the B668

Just to the east of this small village is one of the most extraordinary sights in the county, **Yew Tree Avenue** (Forest Enterprise, free). In the 1870s Amos Alexander, head forester to the Clipsham Hall Estate, began clipping the yew trees around his lodge into chimerical shapes – a fantastic parade of animals, chess pieces and abstract forms. The Squire of Clipsham admired them greatly and gave Amos a free hand with the 150 yew trees lining the approach to the hall. Along the 700yd avenue appeared a dream-like succession of figures, some

commemorating local or national events, others recording family events.

Amos died in the early 1900s and the trees were left untended until in 1955 the Forestry Commission assumed responsibility for the avenue and renewed the topiary tradition. Each of the trees is between 15 to 20ft high, and each is shaped individually. An elephant looks across to a ballerina; a Spitfire takes off towards a battleship, Diddy-men cavort near a windmill – there's even a Big Mac hamburger in there somewhere!

EXTON
5 miles NE of Oakham off the A606

A charming village in one of the largest ironstone extraction areas in the country with a church set in delightful parkland. The **Church of St Peter & St Paul** is remarkable for its wealth of fine monuments, a sumptuous series

THE OLIVE BRANCH

Main Street, Clipsham, Rutland LE15 7SH
Tel: 01780 410355 Fax: 01780 410000
e-mail: olive@work.gb.com

One of only 3 inns in the country to have been awarded a Michelin star, the story of **The Olive Branch** pub is a heartening one. The pub closed in December 1997 because of lack of trade but almost exactly two years later re-opened thanks to the efforts of three friends, Sean Hope, Marcus Welford and Ben Jones. Sean was particularly enthusiastic about the project since he had started his catering career at The Olive Branch as a washer-up. The success of their venture has surprised even the three partners. Word soon spread of the excellent modern pub food, the fine wines and real ales all at affordable prices, and the traditional atmosphere with open fires and shelves full of books.

In winter, there are roast chestnuts and mulled wine at the bar; in summer, fresh home-made lemonade, Pimms cocktails and barbecues in the garden. Sean is in charge of the kitchen, heading a

team of dedicated young local chefs producing a unique style of traditional pub food using local ingredients. Marcus looks after the front of house and uses his 10 years experience in the wine trade to seek out fine and rare bin ends and other interesting alternatives to the 11 reds and 11 whites featured on the house list. Together with business manager Ben Jones they have formed the Rutland Inn Company to rescue and revive other country pubs. The second of their ventures, The Red Lion Inn at Stathern is also featured in this guide.

RUTLAND FALCONRY & OWL CENTRE

Burley Bushes, Exton Lane, Exton, Rutland LE15 7TA
Mobile: 07778 152814 / 0797 959 5642

Set in 42 acres of unspoilt woodland with glorious panoramic views over Rutland Water, the **Rutland Falconry and Owl Centre** is home to a fascinating variety of birds of prey – owls, hawks, falcons, buzzards and even vultures. Some of the 90-odd birds can be handled (check first with a member of staff!) and others prefer to fly for visitors. There are daily falconry demonstrations, depending on the weather, and the Centre offers a range of Courses ideal for those wishing to get closer to these impressive birds. An introductory "Hands On" day course includes

instruction in how to handle the birds after which participants can actually fly some of the resident birds "to the fist". Advance booking for the course is essential.

Also available on a limited basis are "Hawk Walks" – 30 minute sessions with a hawk, owl or falcon. Chris Lawton and Jan Taylor, who own and run the Centre, also arrange off-site seminars, as well as static and flying displays. They have also introduced a Sponsorship scheme which enables individuals, clubs, groups, schools or companies to sponsor an individual bird of prey, or even an aviary. The Centre is open 7 days a week: in summer from 10am until late; in winter from 10am until 4pm (last admission).

commemorating members of the Noel and Harington families interred here from the early 1500s to the late 1700s. This imposing collection is dominated by a colossal memorial to Baptist Noel, 3rd Viscount Campden, who died in 1683. Sculpted in black and white marble by Grinling Gibbons, it stands 22ft high and 14ft wide, almost filling one wall of the north transept. A lengthy inscription extols Viscount Campden's many fine qualities which had "justly rendered him the admiration of his contemporaries and the imitation of postery".

Barnsdale Gardens (see panel opposite), in The Avenue, offers unusual garden plants and also has a coffee shop. It was designed and owned by the TV gardening presenter Geoff Hamilton.

EGLETON

1 mile E of Oakham on a minor road

Egleton is home to **Anglian Water's**

Birdwatching Centre, located on two storeys on the west shore. It has an osprey platform with CCTV.

EDITH WESTON

5 miles E of Oakham off the A6003

This village takes its name from Edith, wife and then widow of King Edward the Confessor (1042-66), who gave her this part of the county as a gift. A peaceful spot in the heart of really lovely countryside on the south shore of Rutland Water. Near the village, off the A606 and A6121, stands Rutland's best-known landmark. **Normanton Church**, on the very edge of Rutland Water, was formerly part of the Normanton Estate and now houses a display dedicated to the construction of the reservoir by Anglian Water and a history of the area. Open April to September. The estate was the property of the big local landowner Sir Gilbert Heathcote, sometime Lord

Mayor of London, who pulled down the village of Normanton to enlarge his park and moved the villagers to nearby Empingham.

EMPINGHAM

5 miles E of Oakham on the A606

This pleasant little town is dominated by the tower and spire of St Peter's Church, whose interior features include fragments of ancient glass. In a field just outside the village stands a well-preserved **Dovecote** containing 700 nests. It could have been in this very field that one of the bloodiest slaughters of the Wars of the Roses took place, on 12 March 1470 – in all, some 10,000 men were killed. This gory clash of arms became known as the **Battle of Losecoat Field** because the defeated Lancastrians shed their

Normanton Church

uniforms as they fled in the hope of avoiding recognition, capture and certain death.

At Sykes Lane, North Shore, just west of Empingham, is the Rutland Water **Butterfly Farm & Aquatic Centre**. A great place to spend a few hours, with 5,000 square feet of walk-through jungle that is home to free-flying butterflies and

BARNSDALE GARDENS

The Avenue, Exton, Oakham, Rutland LE15 8AH
Tel: 01572 813200 Fax: 01572 813346
e-mail: office@barnsdalegardens.co.uk
website: www.barnsdalegardens.co.uk

Millions of television viewers will be familiar with **Barnsdale Gardens** as the home of BBC2's *Gardeners World* hosted by Geoff Hamilton. The gardens actually comprise 37 individual smaller gardens and features that are blended together by linking borders to form one 8-acre garden. The grounds contain a huge number of different plants in many combinations and provide many useful and practical ideas for any garden. On site there is also a nursery stocked with a wide range of choice and unusual species, many of which were initially propagated from the gardens.

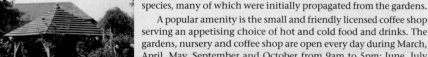

A popular amenity is the small and friendly licensed coffee shop serving an appetising choice of hot and cold food and drinks. The gardens, nursery and coffee shop are open every day during March, April, May, September and October from 9am to 5pm; June, July and August from 9am to 7pm. From November to February the gardens are open from 10am to 4pm; the coffee shop is open at weekends only during this period. Entry for children is free and there is excellent disabled access with two wheelchairs available free – these should be booked in advance. The gardens are licensed for weddings and provide a beautiful backdrop for those precious photographs.

tropical birds. Other creatures at the centre include koi carp, terrapins, iguanas, tarantulas, tropical creepy-crawlies and monitor lizards. Open daily April to October.

TICKENCOTE

8 miles NE of Oakham off the A1

Apart from Canterbury Cathedral there is nothing in England to compare with the astonishing Norman sexpartite vaulting over the chancel of the parish **Church of St Peter** in the tiny village of Tickencote. Equally breathtaking is the chancel arch, a mighty six-layered portal leading to a miniscule nave beyond. Built around 1140, each of the overlapping six arches is carved with a different design – foliage, chevrons, double zig-zags, beak-head ornament or just plain round mouldings. In addition to these masterpieces of Norman architecture, St Peter's also contains a remarkably fine 13th century font and an unusual wooden life-size effigy of a 14th century knight.

LITTLE CASTERTON

9 miles E of Oakham via the A606/A1

Tolethorpe Hall, just off the A1 and close to the Lincolnshire border, is best known as the home of the Stamford Shakespeare Company, which each summer performs three different plays on an open-air stage in an idyllic woodland setting facing a 600-seat covered auditorium. (Call 01780 754381 for details of future performances). The old manor house has another claim to fame as the birthplace in 1550 of Robert Browne, one of the earliest 'congregationalists'. His radical views led to his arrest and it was only through the intervention of his kinsman Lord Burghley that he was released. Browne's religious views mellowed with the passing

of the years – his fiery temper did not. At the age of 80 Browne was consigned to Northampton for an assault on a constable and it was there that he died in 1633.

PICKWORTH

9 miles NE of Oakham off the A1

Pickworth's most famous resident was **John Clare**, surely one of the saddest figures in the pantheon of English poets. Born in 1793 in a village near Peterborough, Clare came to Pickworth as a young man, finding work on a nearby farm. Over the course of a year he managed to save £1 from his meagre wages and used it to publish a prospectus of his poems. The poems were eventually published, in 1820, but did not sell. Poverty, poor health and incipient madness stalked him throughout his life. His happiest years may well have been spent at Pickworth for it was here that he met 18-year-old Patty Turner whom he immortalised in one of his most charming poems:

> *And I would go to Patty's cot,*
> *And Patty came to me,*
> *Each knew the other's every thought*
> *Under the hawthorn tree.*
> *And I'll be true for Patty's sake*
> *And she'll be true for mine,*
> *And I this little ballad make*
> *To be her Valentine.*

They married soon afterwards and eventually had seven children. But Clare was working beyond his strength and gradually his habitual melancholy deteriorated into madness. He spent the last 27 years of his life in asylums. His youngest son went to see him once; Patty could never bring herself to visit.

9 NORTHAMPTONSHIRE

Although this is a relatively small county Northamptonshire has a lot to offer but, as it is crossed by some of the country's major routes, it is also one that is often bypassed. The county town, Northampton, along with other local towns, is famed for its shoe industry although Northamptonshire remains, essentially, a farming county littered with ancient market towns and rural villages. However, it is its long history that is most interesting – the decisive battle of Naseby was fought on its soil and it was at the now ruined Fotheringay Castle that Mary, Queen of Scots was executed.

Northamptonshire is shaped like a laurel leaf, with the River Nene a distinctive feature. Wherever one journeys across the county one is never far from its banks and the reflection of the trees in high summer on its shimmering waters can be quite breathtaking. The alluvial soils and gravel terraces of the Nene Valley have been continuously farmed since Neolithic times and there are remains of many Anglo-Saxon settlements.

Old Stables, Duddington

A county of great landowners, Northamptonshire also has many royal connections. The original Rockingham Castle was built by William the Conqueror; Richard III was born at Fotheringhay Castle, Mary Queen of Scots was beheaded there; Charles I spent several months in captivity at Holdenby Hall, at that time the largest house in England; and in more recent times, Althorp entered the national consciousness as the childhood home of Diana, Princess of Wales, and as her final resting place.

Another royal death is commemorated by the two elaborate Eleanor Crosses erected by a grieving King Edward I to mark the places where the coffin bearing his wife Eleanor to London from Nottinghamshire rested overnight. One is at Geddington, near Kettering; the second on the outskirts of

Northampton; only one other of the original twelve Crosses survives, at Waltham near London.

The county boasts two extraordinary Elizabethan buildings – the Triangular Lodge at Rushton, and Lyveden New Bield near Brigstock, both of them expressing a deeply religious symbolism. The roll-call of outstanding churches in the county includes All Saints at Brixworth, one of the finest Anglo-Saxon churches in England and the only one still in use; the tiny church at Slapton with its glorious medieval wall paintings; and the Church of the Holy Sepulchre in Northampton – the largest and best-preserved Norman round church in the country.

Land-locked though it is, Northamptonshire has an abundance of canals, rivers and lakes. The River Nene is navigable right from the Wash into the heart of Northampton and links up with the Grand Union Canal. The Canal Museum in the popular

Rockingham Castle, Corby

canalside village of Stoke Bruerne provides an insight into 200 years of history and traditions on the county's waterways.

Sporting enthusiasts will find plenty to interest them, including National Hunt racing at Towcester, football (Northampton Town, Rushden & Diamonds), motor racing at Silverstone which has hosted the Formula 1 Grand Prix for the past ten years, drag racing at Santa Pod.....and the world conker championships at Ashton near Oundle!

ADVERTISERS AND PLACES OF INTEREST

LOCATOR MAP

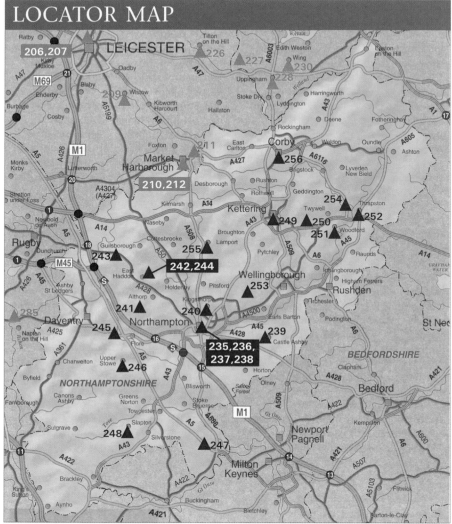

NORTHAMPTON

Much of its face is modern, but the capital of the county has a wealth of history for the visitor to discover. At least 6,000 years ago a camp was set up at **Briar Hill**, and more recent traces of early settlements in the area date from between 700BC and 50AD. The Domesday Book of 1086 shows Northampton as a town of 300 houses, comparable in size to Derby or Nottingham. Richard I granted the town its first charter in 1189, and by the 13th century Northampton had become a major market town, and its market square, dating from that period, is reputed to be the second largest in the country.

For centuries Northampton has been associated with the shoemaking trade. Tradition has it that in 1213 a pair of boots was made here for King John, and the first large order came in 1642 when 4,000 pairs of shoes and 600 pairs of boots were made for the army. The industry grew rapidly throughout the county and by the end of the 1800s, 40% of the population was involved in the shoe trade. People like Philip Manfield and William Barrett were just two of the major players who started their businesses in Northampton and grew them into extensive chains. William Barrett gave his name to the maternity hospital, and Manfield gave his to another of the town's hospitals. St Crispin, the patron saint of shoemakers, is portrayed in several churches, and Northampton Town Football Club are known as the Cobblers. The **Central Museum and Art Gallery** (see panel opposite) has the world's largest collection of footwear, showing shoe fashions down the centuries and the machines that made the shoes. There is also an outstanding collection of British and Oriental ceramics, leathercraft from around the world and some fine paintings including Italian works of the 15th to18th centuries and British art. The **Abington Museum**, set in a 15th century manor house, has a number of interesting exhibits, including a room with 16th century oak panelling, exhibits detailing the county's military history, a 19th century fashion gallery, and a display titled "Northampton Life – from the cradle to the grave".

Northampton has two outstanding churches: All Saints, designed by Henry Bell in the Wren style, with ornate plasterwork by Edward Goudge and two organs by JS Walker; and the wonderful **Church of the Holy Sepulchre**, one of only four remaining round churches in the kingdom. Founded by Simon de Senlis, 1st Earl of Northampton, to

---

BERBAR WOOL & CRAFTS

5 St Peter's Walk, Northampton NN1 1PT
Tel: 01604 622112

Berbar Wool & Crafts is an absolute delight for anyone with an interest in needlecraft. Owned and run by Berenice Wyke and her mother Barbara, the shop is crammed full with a wonderful range of materials – Heritage and Anchor wool and threads, cross-stitch kits, needles, haberdashery and much more. Also on sale are attractive cushions handmade by Berenice, children's kits, baby knitwear, the Gund range of collectors toys, and cuddly animals. Berenice and Barbara are both very knowledgeable and happy to give advice. The shop is open 9.30am to 4.30pm, Monday to Saturday, and there's ample parking close by.

NORTHAMPTON MUSEUM & ART GALLERY
(INCORPORATING NORTHAMPTON TOURIST INFORMATION & VISITOR SERVICES)

Guildhall Road, Northampton NN1 1DP
Tel: 01604 838111 Fax: 01604 838720
e-mail: museums@northampton.gov.uk
website: www.northampton.gov.uk/museums

Fascinating footwear worn throughout the ages is just one of the attractions at the **Northampton Museum and Art Gallery**. The town's national pre-eminence in shoe and boot-making is celebrated in the largest collection of footwear exhibits in the world. Amongst them you'll find the silk wedding shoe worn by Queen Victoria in 1840 as well as some extraordinarily extravagant forms of footwear from all around the world. The Life & Sole Gallery provides insights into Northampton's history as a shoe manufacturing town, including how shoes are made - past and present. The Followers of Fashion Gallery highlights the incredible variety of shoe designs that have adorned

the feet of our forebears. The story of Northampton from the Stone Age to the present day is told with the help of objects, sound and film.

Amongst the decorative arts on display are some outstanding Oriental and British ceramics while the Art Gallery boasts a fine collection of Italian paintings from the 15th to 18th century along with an excellent British collection.

The Museum and Art Gallery is open from 10am to 5pm, Monday to Saturday; 2pm to 5pm on Sunday, and entrance is free.

is certainly the **Guildhall**, a gem of Victorian architecture built in 1864 by Edward Godwin and later extended by Matthew Holding and Arnold Jeffrey. Grand tours of the building take in the old prison cells, the Mayor's parlour, the Great Hall, the Godwin Room and the Council Chamber. The Royal Theatre is another Victorian gem, built in 1884 in opulent Italianate style and home to one of the oldest repertory companies in England. The **Welsh House**, one of the few buildings to survive the disastrous fire of 1675, dates from 1595 and recalls the time when Welsh drovers would bring their cattle to the market. Another striking building is No. 78 Derngate, designed by the Scottish architect Charles Rennie Mackintosh.

In 1290 the funeral procession of Queen Eleanor, wife of Edward I, stopped for the night at Delapre Abbey. In the south of town, at **Hardingstone** on the London Road A508, stands one of the three surviving **Eleanor Crosses** of the twelve originally erected to mark each

commemorate his safe return from the Crusades in 1100, it is often known as the "Soldiers Church" and carried battle scars from the Wars of the Roses. It is the oldest standing building in Northampton and is almost identical to the original in Jerusalem.

The most prestigious building in town

Cave's Furnishers & Antiques

111 Kettering Road, Northampton NN1 4BA
Tel: 01604 638278

Established in 1879, **Cave's Furnishers & Antiques** is still a family business and over the years has established an unrivalled reputation in the county for quality, knowledge and service. They stock both traditional and modern furniture for all household rooms, including mahogany and oak pieces; there's a comprehensive choice of beds in all designs; and a wide range of carpets supported by a high quality fitting service.

Daily Bread Co-operative Ltd

The Old Laundry, Bedford Road,
Northampton NN4 7AD
Tel: 01604 621531
e-mail: northampton@dailybread.co.uk
Fax: 01604 603725 website: www.dailybread.co.uk

Trading since 1980, and open to the general public, Daily Bread Wholefood warehouse stocks 3,000 different products, some 500 of them organic, and is a co-operative dedicated to the proposition "People Before Profit". A sum of money is set aside each year to support various projects in developing countries and the local community. It also aims to supply wholefoods that have good nutritional value and are good value for money. Amongst its products are a variety of dried fruit, nuts, seeds, herbs, spices, beans, pulses, grains, flakes, wholemeal and white flours, and much, much more.

night of the progress of the mournful cortege to London. See under Geddington for more about the Eleanor Crosses.

Northampton boasts more than 150 parks and open spaces, most notably **Abington Park** with lakes, aviaries and the museum mentioned above. Northampton's racecourse is the setting for the International Hot Air Balloon Festival, a summer highlight that attracts visitors from far and wide. Other outdoor attractions include Delapre Park, where the Cluniac Abbey was built in 1145; and **Hunsbury Hill Country Park**, where the Iron Age hill fort can still be seen – this park is also home to the Northamptonshire Ironstone Railway Trust's museum and railway. Northampton's sports and leisure facilities are abundant: two of the best

are Billing Aquadrome with extensive fishing and moorings and, opened in 1999, the **Nene White Water Centre** with facilities for canoeing, rafting, rowing and orienteering.

AROUND NORTHAMPTON

Earls Barton
5 miles NE of Northampton off the A45

A great treasure here is the village **Church of All Saints**, with one of the most impressive Anglo-Saxon towers in the whole country, its surface adorned with purely decorative masonry strips. The tower is 10th century, the south doorway is 12th, the aisles are 13th, the tower arch 14th, the south porch 19th but they all co-exist in great architectural harmony. Beyond the remarkably well-preserved Norman doorway the most amazing sight is the 15ᵗʰ century chancel screen, ablaze with hundreds of dazzling butterflies on the wing; next to it is a wonderful, heavily carved Jacobean pulpit in black oak.

CASTLE ASHBY

6 miles E of Northampton off the A428

Two major attractions for the visitor here. Castle Ashby is a fine Elizabethan mansion, home of the Marquess of Northampton, standing in Capability Brown parkland with Victorian gardens and a lake. The building of Castle Ashby was started in 1574 on the site of a 13ᵗʰ century castle that had been demolished. The original plan of the building was in the shape of an 'E' in honour of Queen Elizabeth I, and is typical of many Elizabethan houses. About sixty years later the courtyard was enclosed by a

screen designed by Inigo Jones. One of the features of Castle Ashby is the lettering around the house and terraces. The inscriptions, which are in Latin, read when translated *"The Lord guard your coming in"* and *"The Lord guard your going out"*. Inside there is some wonderful restoration furniture and paintings of the English and Renaissance schools.

On a much smaller scale the old **Manor House** makes a delightful picture by the church; it has a dungeon and there is a 13ᵗʰ century window with exquisite tracery set in the oldest part of the house near a blocked Norman arch. The poet Cowper loved to wander amongst the trees, some of which are said to have been planted by the Countess Judith herself. The tree that attracts the most visitors is called Cowper's Oak, the branches of which spread twice as far across as the tree is

THE FALCON HOTEL

Castle Ashby, Northants. NN7 1LF
Tel: 01604 696200 Fax: 01604 696673
e-mail: falcon.castleashby@oldenglishinns.co.uk

Six miles southeast of Northampton off the A428 Northamton-Bedford road, Michael and Jennifer Eastick offer a warm welcome at **The Falcon Hotel**. A gracious, intimate hotel dating back to 1594, it has an inviting "country cottage" feel. The Easticks describe The Falcon as a "restaurant with rooms" and the 16 bedrooms combine period charm with up-to-date amenities. All the rooms (9 doubles; 4 twin/doubles; 3 singles) have en suite facilities, a writing desk, TV, radio, telephone, hairdryer, trouser press and tea/coffee makers. Five of the bedrooms are in the main building; the other 11 in a pretty cottage environment next door but one.

Friendly, personal service is a watchword and the hotel also has a great reputation for the high standard of its cooking as well as the range and quality of its wines and beers. Fresh, seasonal produce provides the basis of imaginative à la carte menus; lighter snacks are served in the lovely cellar bar. There's also a very pleasant cocktail bar and in summer drinks can be enjoyed on the garden patio. The Falcon is delightfully situated a short walk from the village green and attractions in or around the village include the Castle itself, standing in Capability Brown parkland; the old manor house by the church, and an interesting craft centre.

high. There is a tradition that it will never die because Cowper stood beneath it one day during a heavy thunderstorm and was inspired to write his famous hymn: *"God moves in Mysterious Ways"*.

Castle Ashby Craft Centre & Rural Shopping Yard is set in an old farmyard and comprises a farm shop and delicatessen, craft shops, pottery, goldsmith's studio, art gallery and tea room.

HORTON

6 miles SE of Northampton on the B526

A mile south of the village a gate leads off the road and across fields to **The Menagerie**, a fascinating garden surrounding the great house (pulled down in 1936) where Lord Halifax once had a private zoo. A lime avenue, water gardens, a rose garden and thatched arbours are among the delights of a garden that is still being developed. A distinguished son of Horton was Ralph Lane, the first Governor of Virginia.

SALCEY FOREST

8 miles S of Northampton off the B526

Reached from the A508 at Roade or the B526 between Horton and Stoke Goldington, the 1,250-acre Salcey Forest has been owned and managed by the Forestry Commission since the 1920s.

Part of the chain of ancient Royal Hunting Forests that stretched from Stamford to Oxford, it produces quality timber while providing a home for a wide variety of animal and plant life, and recreational facilities for the public. There are three circular trails at Salcey, named after the three woodpeckers found there: the Lesser Spotted Trail of a leisurely hour; the Great Spotted Trail of about two miles; and, for the more energetic, the Green Woodpecker Trail of about 2½ hours. The forest is open to visitors all year round.

KINGSTHORPE

2 miles N of Northampton on the A508

Once a small riverside village, Kingsthorpe is now effectively a suburb of Northampton but its ancient church still looks across meadows to the River Nene. Inside, there are some massive Norman arches with varied ornamental carving.

PITSFORD

4 miles N of Northampton off the A508

Off the A508 just north of the village, **Pitsford Water** is an 800-acre reservoir with trout fishing and boats for hire, sailing, a picnic area, nature reserve and information centre. The reservoir is also accessible from the village of Holcot.

THE GERANIUM & PELARGONIUM SPECIALISTS

Cramden Nursery, Harborough Road North, Kingsthorpe, Northampton NN2 8LU
Tel: 01604 842365 Fax: 01604 820440
e-mail: geranium@cramdennursery.fsworld.co.uk
website: www.pelargoniumpromotions.co.uk

One of the top producers and propagators in the country, **The Geranium & Pelargonium Specialists** have been growing these colourful plants since 1964. Over 50,000 plants are grown on site for sale, covering a range of 100 different varieties. Many go to add brilliance to events such as Ascot and Silverstone; others are bought by trade nurseries; many more brighten up gardens all round the country. Pelargoniums of various varieties are displayed from spring to late summer. This family business is run by John Mitchell and his daughter Emily, who are highly respected in British horticultural circles. Phone for opening times.

COTTESBROOKE

9 miles N of Northampton off the A5199

In secluded countryside near the site of the Battle of Naseby, **Cottesbrooke Hall** is one of the finest of all the grand houses in the county. The magnificent Queen Anne house, reputedly the model for Jane Austen's *Mansfield Park*, was begun in 1702 and is home to an impressive collection of pictures, porcelain and furniture. The grounds are quite superb,

Althorp House

featuring the Statue Walk (statues from the Temple of Ancient Virtue, at Stowe), the Dilemma Garden with old roses and rare trees, the Dutch Garden, the Pine Court and many other charming gardens and courtyards. The hall and gardens are open to visitors on certain days in the summer.

CHAPEL BRAMPTON

4 miles NW of Northampton off the A508

Steam train buffs will want to pay a visit to the **Northampton & Lamport Railway**, which is home to an interesting collection of railway-related vehicles. Visitors can enjoy a journey hauled by vintage locomotives; there are heritage displays and special events throughout

the year. Trains run regularly on Sundays and Bank Holiday Mondays, March to November, from Pitsford and Brampton Station. More details on 01604 820327.

ALTHORP

5 miles NW of Northampton off the A428

The home of the Spencer family since 1508, Althorp remains exactly that – a classic family-owned English stately home which the Spencers have stamped with their style ever since John Spencer, a large-scale sheep farmer, acquired the estate. The present house was begun in 1573, and behind the stark tiling of the exterior is a wealth of fine paintings, sculpture, porcelain and furniture. Known widely by connoisseurs for

---

YE OLDE SARACENS HEAD

Little Brington, nr Althorp, Northants NN7 4HS
Tel/Fax: 01604 770640
e-mail: info@yeoldesaracenshead.co.uk
website: www.yeoldesaracenshead.co.uk

The pretty little village of Little Brington boasts an excellent hostelry in **Ye Olde Saracens Head,** owned and run by local man Richard Williams. An expert chef, Richard took over here in 2002 and quickly established a reputation for serving outstanding food with lots of variety and based wherever possible on local produce. The real ales too are local, including Frog Island Natterjack and Greene King IPA, while the wine list is extensive. There's a patio garden at the rear and the inn also offers comfortable and attractive accommodation (3 doubles; 1 twin), all with TV, CD, radio alarm and hospitality tray.

PATCHWORK PALACE

The Stableyard, Holdenby House, East Haddon,
Northants NN6 7DJ
Tel: 01604 771303
e-mail: sales@patchworkpalace.com
website: www.patchworkpalace.com

Set in the lovely grounds of stately Holdenby House,
Patchwork Palace is a treasure trove of fabrics and
haberdashery. Owner Helena Bayfield has filled the
rooms of this converted stable block with some 3000
different bolts of fabric and a huge range of threads,
wadding, books on patchwork and quilting and "notions and potions". Collections featured include
French Garden, Balis, Kaffe Fasset, Moda Marbles and many others.

The "notions" include accessories such as hot-iron transfer pencils, needles of every kind, quilt
backings, piece-makers, stencils – in fact just about
everything you could ever need. Courses are available daily
between 10am and 3pm with special beginners 2-hour
courses on Tuesdays. Patchwork Palace is open from 10am
to 4pm, Monday to Saturday, and knowledgeable and
welcoming staff are on hand to assist in any way they can.
Why not combine a visit to Patchwork Palace with a stroll
through the 20-acre gardens of Holdenby House or inspect
the grandeur of its splendid interior? And Althorp,
childhood home of Diana, Princess of Wales, is just a
couple of miles away.

PAUL HOPWELL ANTIQUES

30 High Street, West Haddon,
Northants NN6 7AP
Tel: 01788 510636 Fax: 01788 510044
e-mail: paulhopwell@antiqueoak.co.uk
website: www.antiqueoak.co.uk

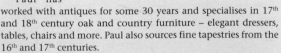

Paul Hopwell Antiques occupies a delightful

thatched
house on the
main street of
West Haddon,
just minutes
from Junction
18 of the M1.

Paul has
worked with antiques for some 30 years and specialises in 17th
and 18th century oak and country furniture – elegant dressers,
tables, chairs and more. Paul also sources fine tapestries from the
16th and 17th centuries.

The shop is open from 10am to 6pm, Monday to Saturday, at
other times by appointment. You can also see his items at 10
different antiques fairs during the year, amongst them the National
Exhibition Centre, Olympia, Chelsea and Buxton.

generations, Althorp is now known across the whole world since the tragic death of Diana, Princess of Wales, in 1997. She lies in peace in the beautiful, tranquil setting of the Round Oval, an ornamental lake, surrounded by her family's ancestral heritage. Visits to the house are strictly by advance booking: call 01604 592020.

HOLDENBY

7 miles NW of Northampton off the A428

The Royal connections go back more than 400 years at **Holdenby Hall**, which was built by Elizabeth I's Lord Chancellor and favourite Sir Christopher Hatton for the purpose of entertaining the Queen. At the time, it was the largest Elizabethan house in England, and, for the diarist John Evelyn, "one of the most pleasing sights that ever I saw". It was visited but once by Elizabeth; it later became the palace and eventually the prison of Charles I, who was kept under guard here for five months after his defeat in the Civil War. The house, which appeared as Limmeridge House in the BBC's *The Woman in White*, stands in magnificent grounds, which contain a falconry

centre, a smaller scale reconstruction of Hatton's original garden, a fully working armoury and a 17th century farmstead that evokes the sights and smells of life in days gone by. There's a museum, a children's farm and a lakeside train ride together with tea in the Victorian Kitchen.

EAST HADDON

7 miles NW of Northampton off the A428

A village of thatched cottages, a village pump protected by a neat thatched cone, a 14th century church and an 18th century hall. It is best known for **Haddonstone Showgardens** (see panel below) which has walled gardens on

HADDONSTONE SHOWGARDENS

The Forge House, Church Lane, East Haddon, Northants NN6 8DB
Tel: 01604 770711 Fax: 01604 770027
e-mail: info@haddonstone.co.uk
website: www.haddonstone.co.uk

Haddonstone's Showgardens provide an exquisite setting for a permanent display from the company's renowned range of garden ornaments and architectural stonework. Urns, seats, fountains, statuary, sundials, pavilions and balustrading are all to be found in the delightful setting of the walled Manor House gardens. These charming gardens, set on different levels, feature old shrub roses, ground cover plants, conifers, clematis and climbers. Devotees of water features will find an amazing array within the Arcadian Garden Features range that includes centrepieces in pebble bowls or on pebble pools; self-contained fountains and wall-mounted fountains; as well as innovate table top and paving water features.

In 2000, the striking Jubilee Garden opened featuring a pavilion, small classical temple and an evocative Gothic Grotto – a recreation of Haddonstone's exhibit at the 1999 Chelsea Flower Show. And in 2002 the

Orangery was constructed in the main Show Gardens. The 5-acre gardens are designed to provide inspiration for gardeners. In particular they show the many and varied opportunities to use ornamental stonework within a garden – whether large or small, terrace or open ground. The garden and showroom is open to visitors from 9am. to 5.30pm, Monday to Friday – public holidays and Christmas period excepted.

different levels and a huge stock of garden ornaments of every kind.

GUILSBOROUGH

9 miles NW of Northampton off the A5199

A handsome, dignified village where Wordsworth came to stay in the vicarage and, it is said, brought with him the yellow Cumberland poppy that is often seen here. The church has lovely windows by William Morris and Burne-Jones, and Guilsborough Grange has a wildlife park and areas for walking and picnicking. A short distance south of the village, in the tiny community of Coton, **Coton Manor Garden** is a traditional garden originally laid out in 1925 and embracing several delightful smaller gardens. Beyond the garden are a wildflower meadow and a magical five-acre bluebell wood. The nursery propagates over 1,000 varieties of plant, and in the stable yard are a restaurant and tea room.

DAVENTRY

Old and new blend intriguingly in this historic market town whose streets are shared by dignified Georgian houses and modern shops. A colourful market is held along the High Street every Tuesday and Friday, and in the Market Place stands the Moot Hall, built in 1769 of ironstone. Originally a private house, it became the moot hall, or town hall, in 1806 after the former town hall was demolished. It is now home to the Tourist Information Centre and to Daventry Museum, which illustrates the social history of the town and its environs. It also shows regularly changing arts and crafts exhibitions and contains archaeological finds from **Borough Hill** and some of the equipment used by the BBC when it had a transmitter station on the hill. The oval hill, which rises to 650 feet above sea level, is more than two miles round and

covers an area of 150 acres. It was the third largest Iron Age hill fort in Britain and in more recent times was topped by the huge radio masts that transmitted the World Service of the BBC.

Daventry was once an important stop on the coaching routes, and it is said that King Charles I spent several days at the Wheatsheaf Inn before the Battle of Naseby, where he lost the battle and his kingdom. Shakespeare mentions the town in *King Henry IV (Part 1)*, when Falstaff tells Bardolph the tale of a shirt stolen from a "red-nose innkeeper". During the coaching era the chief industry of Daventry was whip-making.

Daventry Country Park is a beautiful 133-acre site centred on the old Daventry Reservoir. Coarse fishing, a picnic area, adventure playground, nature trails, nature reserve and visitor centre are among the amenities. Open daily all year.

AROUND DAVENTRY

ASHBY ST LEDGERS

3 miles N of Daventry on the A361

From 1375 to 1605 the manor house at Ashby was the home of the Catesby family, and it was in a room above the gatehouse that Guy Fawkes is said to have met Robert Catesby to hatch the **Gunpowder Plot**. On the 5th of November, 1605, Catesby rode the 80 miles from London in seven hours with the news that the plot had failed. He fled to Holbeach in Staffordshire, where he was shot dead after refusing to surrender. The Church of St Mary & St Leodegarious has much to interest the visitor, including Jacobean box pews, an elaborately carved rood screen, a Norman font, a number of Catesby brasses and, most notably, some medieval wall paintings depicting the Passion of Christ.

SWAN HOUSE

Dodford, Weedon, Northants NN7 4SX
Tel: 01327 341847

Dating back to the 1600s **Swan House** served as an inn until 1955 but is now the home of Alice Chamberlain who after moving here in 1996 has beautifully restored and renovated the charming old property. Boasting a 4-Diamonds rating, the accommodation is approached through a lovely garden and comprises 1 twin and 1 double room with a separate shower and wc. Each room is provided with television and hospitality tray and has a wonderfully relaxing country cottage feeling. There's a choice of English or Continental breakfast with excellent coffee. Pets are welcome – Alice has three dogs of her own!

FLORE

3 miles E of Daventry on the A45

Called *Flora* in the Domesday Book, the village has a wide green that slopes gently down to the River Nene. **Adams Cottage** was the home of the ancestors of John Adams (1797-1801), President of the United States, whose son was also President. In the 13th century church are several memorial windows, one of them dedicated to Bruce Capell, an artillery officer who was awarded the Military Cross at the age of 22 for courage and devotion to his wounded men. A simple wooden cross from Flanders hangs on the wall, and his window depicts the farewell between David and Jonathan.

UPPER STOWE

5 miles SE of Daventry off the A5

A short drive up the A5 from Towcester brings the visitor to the village of Upper

THE OLD DAIRY FARM CRAFT CENTRE

Upper Stowe, nr Weedon, Northants NN7 4SH
Tel: 01327 340525 Fax: 01327 349987
e-mail: Helen.brodie@virgin.net
website: www.old-dairy-farm-centre.co.uk

Blessed with an idyllic rural setting and wonderful vviews, **The Old Dairy Farm Craft Centre** in the picturesque village of Upper Stowe offers a unique shopping experience, showcasing the work of local artists and craft makers. The Centre was established in 1985 by Helen Brodie whose family has farmed here for four generations. Helen's own shop, Classic Clothes Boutique, sells ladies' quality fashions for every occasion from some of the country's top designers. Next door, Tudor Rose Needlecraft stocks everything for the needlework enthusiast from embroidery, needlepoint, crewelwork and cross-stitch to beadwork and ribbon embroidery.

Aladdin's Cave provides a magical experience for anyone interested in antiques and collectables and also offers a wide selection of beautiful and unusual cards. Continuing clockwise around the

courtyard, Cot'n'Togs is a delightful shop for children and adults alike with an exclusive range of hand-crafted girls' clothes together with boys' casual wear and accessories. Dianthus offers a full range of decorative accessories for the home and their hand-made products can be made and finished to suit your requirements. Rosella Silks has flower arrangements for all occasions as well as absolutely everything for dolls' houses; Allsorts stocks a superb selection of unique hand-crafted gifts; Sheer Delights offers a wonderful range of lingerie for special occasions. An Art Gallery and excellent restaurant complete the varied list of attractions.

Stowe and the **Old Dairy Farm Centre**. The community of **Stowe Nine Churches** is very oddly named, particularly as there is only one church, late Anglo-Saxon. The story is that the builders tried eight times to build the church but each time the Devil took away the stones. At the ninth attempt they succeeded – hence the name.

Canons Ashby House

CANONS ASHBY

7 miles S of Daventry off the A361

This pretty village contains the Church of St Mary, once part of the Black Canons' Monastery church and much reduced in size at the time of the Dissolution of the Monasteries. **Canons Ashby House**, built from part of the ecclesiastical building after the Dissolution, is one of the finest of Northamptonshire's great houses. Home of the Dryden family since the 1550s and now in the care of the National Trust, it contains some marvellous Elizabethan wall paintings and sumptuous Jacobean plasterwork. The grounds are equally delightful, with yews, cedars and mulberry trees, terraces and parkland. Open afternoons, April to October, except Thursdays and Fridays.

CHARWELTON

4 miles SW of Daventry on the A361

The chief claim to fame of Charwelton is that it is the spot where the River Cherwell rises, in the cellar of **Cherwell House**. The river forms the county boundary as it travels south into Oxfordshire before joining the Thames. In the village is a lovely old packhorse bridge.

BYFIELD

5 miles SW of Daventry on the A361

The tall tower of the rich-stone 14th century church is one of the major local landmarks. A major leisure attraction just west of the village is **Boddington Reservoir**, a balancing reservoir for the Oxford Canal. A good place to start a walk, or to fish, sail or windsurf on the reservoir itself.

TOWCESTER

A busy little place, Towcester is popular with seekers of antiques – there are at least half a dozen different establishments selling antiques.

In Roman times the town was called Lactodorum and it stood on the major highway Watling Street (now the A5). The Romans improved the road and built a fort to guard their troop movements. During the Civil War it was the only Royalist stronghold in the area and in the following centuries it was an important stop on the coaching route between London and Holyhead. By the end of the 18th century there were twenty coaching inns in the town, servicing up

REINDEER ANTIQUES

Watling Street, Potterspury, Towcester,
Northamptonshire NN12 7QD
Tel: 01908 542200 Fax: 01908 542121
e-mail: nicholasfuller@btconnect.com
website: www.reindeerantiques.co.uk

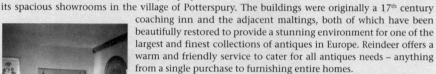

Specialising in fine English furniture from the 17th, 18th and 19th centuries, **Reindeer Antiques** enjoys a reputation for excellence and high quality of service with an unrivalled inventory displayed in

its spacious showrooms in the village of Potterspury. The buildings were originally a 17th century coaching inn and the adjacent maltings, both of which have been beautifully restored to provide a stunning environment for one of the largest and finest collections of antiques in Europe. Reindeer offers a warm and friendly service to cater for all antiques needs – anything from a single purchase to furnishing entire homes.

A member of the respected British Antiques Dealers Association and the Association of Art and Antique Dealers, Reindeer is committed to deal only with authentic pieces and offers clients total security with their purchases. Services include valuations for insurance, sale or probate, restorations by skilled and experienced craftsmen, commissioned purchases, after sales service and worldwide delivery through established professional sources. Clients can even have furniture on approval, giving the opportunity of seeing pieces in situ without commitment. Reindeer also has a London showroom in Kensington Church Street with showrooms arranged on two floors of an elegantly restored Georgian building.

to forty coaches every day. Charles Dickens stayed at the Saracen's Head, then called the Pomfret Hotel, and immortalised it in *The Pickwick Papers*. The parish church of St Lawrence, built on the site of a substantial Roman building, is one of the loveliest in the county, with features from several centuries: the crypt, reached by a doorway from the sanctuary, is 13th century, the arcades 13th and 14th. On the arch of the south chapel is a carved jester's head probably from the 14th century, while the massive tower and the font are from the 1400s. Close to the church is the **Chantry House**, formerly a school, founded by Archdeacon Sponne in 1447.

Towcester Racecourse is set in the beautiful parkland estate of Easton Neston, the family home of Lord Hesketh. The course, which has its entrance on the A5, came into being in 1876, when the Empress of Austria was staying at Easton Neston and attended an Easter steeplechase held in her honour. The course now stages about 16 National Hunt meetings a year, including a couple in the evening.

At Springfields, off the A43 south roundabout, **Towcester Leisure Centre** has a five-lane swimming pool, floodlit tennis court, gymnasium, sports hall and art exhibitions.

AROUND TOWCESTER

GREENS NORTON
1 mile NW of Towcester off the A5

A village at the southern end of the 12-mile **Knightley Way**, one of several mapped walking routes in the county. At this point the Grafton Way takes over, continuing to Cosgrove in the very south of Northamptonshire. The church at Greens Norton is well worth a visit, with its Saxon stonework, Norman font and commemorative brasses of the Green family.

Canal Museum, Stoke Bruerne

BLISWORTH

3 miles NE of Towcester off the A43

The building of the Grand Union and Oxford Canals brought trade and prosperity to the area and now provides miles of quiet, picturesque walks or boat trips. On the Grand Union Canal, the **Blisworth Tunnel** between Blisworth and Stoke Bruerne, opened in 1805, is the longest in England, at nearly two miles. The pretty village of Blisworth is a mass of roses in summer, in the cottage gardens, in the Tudor and Jacobean houses and around the 13th century church. The most significant treasure in the church is a high screen of the 15th century complete with doors. Also of interest is a tablet near the altar which tells of the wife of a sergeant-at-arms to Queen Elizabeth I. The tablet records that she lived a maid for 18 years, was a wife for 20 years and a widow for 61, dying in her 99th year.

STOKE BRUERNE

3 miles NE of Towcester off the A508

A picturesque canalside village at the southern end of the famous Blisworth Tunnel. The canal provides the major attractions, with waterside walks, boat trips to the tunnel and a visit to the fascinating **Canal Museum**. Housed in a converted corn mill, the museum

displays 200 years of canal history and life on the narrow boats (many of which are still in use for pleasure trips). The exhibits include working engines, old photographs, waterway wildlife and the tools used by canal workers and boatmen. The museum, which is open throughout the year, has a tea room and a souvenir shop. The canal has a series of locks at this point, and visitors can stop in the car park at the lower lock on the A508 and walk into the village along the towpath, passing seven locks en route. There are shops, pubs and restaurants at this popular place, which is the perfect location for a family day out and an ideal starting point for a canal holiday.

A private drive on the Stoke Bruerne to Shutlanger road leads to **Stoke Park**, a great house standing in a 400-acre estate. Attributed to Inigo Jones, the house was built in Palladian style (the first in this country) around 1630 for Sir Francis Crane, head of the Mortlake Tapestry Works. The main house burnt down in 1886, and only the pavilions and a colonnade remain; but they are an impressive sight and may be viewed externally on afternoons in August or by appointment (Tel: 01604 862172).

SILVERSTONE

4 miles SW of Towcester on the A43

The home of British motor racing, located off the A43 in the village. The **British Grand Prix** is the highlight of the year, but the circuit hosts a large number of other events, including rounds of the Auto Trader touring car championship and the **International Historic Car Festival**. Members of the public can test their skills in a single-seater racer, a Lotus Elise, a rally car or a 4x4 off-road vehicle. For details call 01327 850206.

Tucked away on country roads northwest of Silverstone are two of the many interesting churches for which Northamptonshire is famous. The **Church of St Mary** at **Wappenham** has a sculpture by Giles Gilbert Scott from the renowned family of architects, who had local connections; two fonts; a clock from the 17th century; and brass memorials to the Lovett family.

SLAPTON

4 miles SW of Towcester off the A43 or A45

Slapton is little more than a hamlet but its tiny **St Botolph's Church**, set on the hillside above the River Tove, contains some of the finest medieval wall paintings in the county. Hidden under limewash for three centuries, the paintings were discovered in the mid-1800s and magnificently restored. Covering almost all of the interior walls, they colourfully depict Bible stories and scenes from the life and works of various saints. Slight variations in style suggest they belong to two separate periods, one in the late 1200s, the other in the mid-1300s.

The village of **Weedon Lois**, a mile or so to the west of Slapton, is the final resting place of Edith Sitwell (1887-1964). Her grave is marked with a restrained memorial by Henry Moore.

BRACKLEY

10 miles SW of Towcester off the A43 or A422

A town of Saxon origins with houses clustered round a tangle of streets. A castle was built here in the early part of the 12th century, which some accounts claim as the meeting place for the rebel barons who drew up the first version of Magna Carta in 1215. King John did not approve of their proposals, and it took almost a year before he relented and signed. Wool brought prosperity in the Middle Ages, allowing the rebuilding of the Church of St Peter with a fine early English west tower and south aisle. A free hospital and chapel which had been built by Robert le Bossu for the benefit of the poor was sold to Magdalen College, Oxford, in 1484 and halfway through

SLAPTON MANOR

Slapton Manor Farm, Slapton, Towcester, Northamptonshire NN12 8PF
Tel: 01327 860344 Fax: 01327 860758
website: www.slaptonmanor.co.uk

Standing in extensive grounds adjacent to Slapton's famous medieval church, Slapton Manor is a 12th century manor house, the home of Rob and Barbara Smith who welcome bed & breakfast guests to this tranquil spot. Visitors stay in an ingeniously converted period carthorse stable and hay loft next to the manor house. There are 3 spacious en suite rooms, all attractively furnished and decorated: one is a family room. A traditional breakfast is served and for an evening meal there's a pub just a mile up the road. There are some lovely walks nearby and the Manor is just 3 miles from Silverstone Circuit with Stowe Gardens, Canons Ashby and Sulgrave Manor all within easy reach.

the following century a school was opened on the site. The buildings have been much altered down the years, but the school exists to this day, now known as **Magdalen College Comprehensive School**. A notable landmark on the High Street is the baroque town hall, with its handsome clock tower, built in 1706 at the instigation of the Duke of Bridgwater. During the 19th century, Brackley was served by two railway companies, the London & North Western and the Great Central, with stations at either end of town. Alas, the lines were axed in the 1960s.

AYNHO

16 miles SW of Towcester on the B4100

A peaceful, picturesque limestone village of leafy lanes and lovely old cottages. The former manor house, **Aynho Park**, is a very grand 17th century country house in the care of the Country Houses Association. It was originally the property of the Cartwright family who, it is said, claimed the rents from their tenants in the form of apricots; some apricot trees can still be seen trained into fan shapes and growing on the walls of cottages. The house was burnt down by Royalist troops during the Civil war but was rebuilt by the Cartwrights, who at the same time rebuilt the village church with the same proportions as the house, so the church too has the appearance of a country villa. Later changes were made to the house by Archer and Soane. Public rooms and the grounds are open to the public on Wednesday and Thursday afternoons from May to September. **The Wharf** at Aynho on the Oxford Canal has holiday boats for hire and a canalside shop.

KING'S SUTTON

15 miles SW of Towcester off the A4260

Located at the southernmost tip of the

county, King's Sutton boasts one of Northamptonshire's finest church towers. The 15th century spire of **Church of St Peter and St Paul** soars almost 200ft towards the heavens and in a county famous for its elegant spires, King's Sutton is unmatched in its beauty. The interior, heavily restored by George Gilbert Scott in 1866, is less inspiring but is worth visiting to see the macabre memorial to Thomas Langton Freke who died in 1769. It represents Christ rising above His own skeleton which is depicted with gruesome realism and has a rib cage moulded in iron.

A famous son of the village was William Lisle Bowles, born in 1762. The poems written by this vicar's son so delighted Samuel Taylor Coleridge that he changed from studying theology to writing poetry himself.

SULGRAVE

10 miles W of Towcester off the B4525

The best-known attraction here is **Sulgrave Manor**, a Tudor manor house built by the ancestors of George Washington, first President of the United States of America. Lawrence Washington,

Sulgrave Manor

sometime Mayor of Northampton, bought the manor from Henry VIII in 1539. In 1656, Lawrence Washington's great-great-grandson Colonel John Washington left England to take up land in Virginia, which later became Mount Vernon. This man was the great-grandfather of George. The Washington family arms, which are said to have inspired the stars and stripes design of the American flag, are prominent above the front door, and the house is a treasure trove of George Washington memorabilia, including documents, a velvet coat and even a lock of his hair. The house is open daily (except Monday) from April to October, and at weekends in March, November and December. A lottery grant has allowed the construction of a series of buildings in the grounds which are part of major educational programmes covering all aspects of Tudor history. The lovely gardens include yew hedges, topiary, herbaceous borders and a formal rose garden planted in 1999. There's a gift shop and a buttery serving light refreshments.

KETTERING

An important town standing above the River Ise, Kettering gained fame as a producer of both clothing and shoes. It was in Kettering that the missionary William Carey and the preacher Andrew Fuller founded the Baptist Missionary Society in 1792, giving a new impetus to the cause of foreign missions all over the world. The parish church of St Peter and St Paul, with its elegant crocketed spire, is one of the finest in the country and a landmark for miles around. Much of the old town has been swallowed up in modern development, but there are still a few old houses in the narrow lanes, and the **Heritage Quarter** around the church gives a fascinating, hands-on insight into the town's past.

The **Manor House Museum**, housed in an 18th century manor house, has impressive collections of social and industrial history, archaeology and geology. Individual items range from a macabre mummified cat to an example of the Robinson car built in Kettering in 1907.

In the adjacent **Alfred East Gallery** a constantly changing programme of exhibitions of paintings, crafts, sculpture, photography and children's work ensures that there will be something new to see on every visit. Among the items on permanent display are works by Alfred East RA and Thomas Cooper Gotch. In between visits to the museum and gallery (both wheelchair-accessible) the Heritage Gardens are a

GLEBE FARM SHOP & TEA ROOMS

Glebe Farm, Rothwell Road, Kettering, Northants NN16 8XF
Tel: 01536 513849 Fax: 01536 410609
e-mail: chrisfarm@hotmail.com website: glebefarmshop.co.uk

Conveniently located on the A14/A6003 roundabout north of Kettering, **Glebe Farm Shop** is owned and run by Chris Holdsworth whose family has been farming hereabouts for more than a hundred years. In addition to local fruit and vegetables the shop sells English meats, cheeses, wines, preserves and jams along with some delicious home-made cakes which can also be enjoyed in the excellent licensed tea room. Here, Chris's wife also offers a choice of 3 daily specials. The shop is also an outlet for Errington Reay salt glazed stoneware of every kind, gifts and some elegant woodturning products.

pleasant place for a stroll or a picnic. The Tourist Information Centre is at the same location.

On the A6, on the outskirts of town, **Wicksteed Park** is a 148-acre site of leisure and pleasure, with 40 rides and attractions, including roller coaster, pirate ship, train ride, Mississippi river boat and pitch & putt. There are several catering outlets, shops, a pottery, a photographic studio and two playground areas. Open daily Easter-September, weekends to November.

Boughton House

AROUND KETTERING

GEDDINGTON
3 miles NE of Kettering off the A43

This attractive village, like many in the county, has known royal visitors: monarchs from the time of William the Conqueror used a summer palace as a base for hunting in the Royal Forest of Rockingham. In the centre of the village is an ornately carved stone cross almost 40 feet high. This is the best preserved of the three surviving **Eleanor Crosses** that marked the funeral procession of Queen Eleanor, who had died at Harby in Nottinghamshire in 1290. Her devoted husband, King Edward I, accompanied the body south to London, and wherever the funeral bier rested, he built a cross. Of all the crosses this, at Geddington, is the most complete. Other crosses were raised at Lincoln (where the Queen's heart was buried), Grantham, Stamford, Hardingstone in Northampton (this still exists), Stony Stratford, Dunstable, St

Albans, Waltham (this still exists), Cheapside and Charing Cross.

Off the A43, on a minor road between Geddington and Grafton Underwood (where there is a monument to the crews of B17 bombers), stands one of the very finest houses in the country. The origins of **Boughton House**, the Northamptonshire home of the Duke of Buccleuch, go back 500 years to a small monastic building. Extended over the years, it was transformed into "a vision of Louis XIV's Versailles". In addition to the wonderful architecture, Boughton is noted for its French and English furniture, its paintings (El Greco, Murillo, 40 Van Dycks) and its collection of armoury and weaponry. The grounds, which include parkland, lakes, picnic areas and woodland play areas, are open May to September, the house in August only.

Large tracts of the ancient woodland of the region have survived, and in the fields by Boughton House are the remains of more recent planting. The 2nd Duke of Montagu, nicknamed **John the Planter**, had the notion of planting an avenue of trees all the way from the

CRANFORD ARTS

The Old Forge, Grafton Road, Cranford St Andrew,
Kettering, Northants NN14 4JE
Tel: 01536 330660 Fax: 01536 330644
e-mail: cranford-arts@btclick.com

Located in the pretty village of Cranford St Andrew,
Cranford Arts is housed in a former forge, a delightful
building with ancient beams, a wood block floor and the
old forge and bellows still in place. Offering a wonderful
range of ceramics, floral art and a wide range of crafts,
Cranford Arts was established in 1998 by Julia Bennie and Jane Stonebridge, both teachers up until
then. Julia looks after the floral side of the business, creating wonderful floral displays whether for

domestic decoration, weddings, churches, receptions, Christmas-
time or wreaths. Clients for Julias' floral decorations include
Castle Ashby House near Northampton.

Jane studied Three-Dimensional Design – Ceramics at
Loughborough University and her lively designs make perfect
gifts as well as brightening up one's own house. Her versatile
skills encompass pottery, tiles, mosaics, murals and 3-D design
and visitors are welcome at their working studio on Sundays
between 11am and 4pm (except during August). Both Jane and
Julia conduct day courses in their respective areas of expertise
so, for example, you could learn how to make a mosaic tray or
sculpt a life-size portrait in terracotta from your favourite
photograph. Just call for details.

house to his London home. The plan hit
immediate trouble when his neighbour,
the Duke of Bedford, refused to let the
trees cross his estate; instead, the Planter
set down many avenues on his own
estate, amounting to the 70 miles of the
distance to London. Dutch Elm disease
destroyed much of his planting, but the
old trees are being replaced with limes
and beeches.

TWYWELL
4 miles E of Kettering off the A14

Twywell (the name means 'double
spring') has a history that includes the
Romans, the Saxons and the Normans,
but the strongest, and most surprising
connection is with Africa. Two African
boys, Susi and Chuma, faithful servants
and companions of David Livingstone,
were with him when he died and carried
his body hundreds of miles to the sea
before accompanying it to Westminster

Abbey. They had saved all Livingstone's
papers and stayed at Twywell as guests of
the explorer's friend Horace Waller while
Livingstone's Journals were being
prepared. In the church are three stones
from Calvary in the window by the altar.
They were sent by the rector's friend,
General Gordon, who wrote a letter
saying that he hoped to visit the Pope on
his way back from Palestine. That letter is
preserved in the church.

WOODFORD
6 miles E of Kettering off the A14

A bizarre story here. A human heart was
found in one of the columns of the
Norman church during restoration work
in the 19th century. It is thought to
belong to one of the Traillys, who died
while fighting in the Crusades; his heart
was brought back by his followers so that
he could rest with the other Traillys, who
were the local lords of the manor at the

THE WHITE HORSE INN

1 Club Lane, Woodford, nr Thrapston, Northants NN14 4EY
Tel: 01832 732646 e-mail: j.Hawkins@tinyworld.co.uk

Located just off the A14 and overlooking the Nene Valley, **The White Horse Inn** is a charming old hostelry built in traditional stone in the mid-1800s. David and Jennifer Cant took over here in 2001 and have earned the inn a reputation for excellent food and well-maintained real ales. Food is served every lunchtime and evening and ranges from traditional pub fayre such as Steak & Ale pie, steaks and grills to an appetising à la carte menu (not available on Mondays). The real ales on tap are Black Sheep and Abbot, supplemented by two guest brews. On Sundays, Jennifer presides over a superb carvery – booking is strongly recommended.

FINISHING TOUCHES

65 High Street, Thrapston, Northants NN14 4JJ
Tel: 01832 731283 Fax: 01832 731379
e-mail: sarah@finishingtouches-thrapston.co.uk
website: www.finishingtouches-thrapston.co.uk

With its extensive stock of gifts and home accessories, Sarah Line's town centre shop promises to provide the **Finishing Touches** for your own décor. In this Aladdin's Cave of desirable objects displayed in a room setting you'll find an exclusive range of exquisite pewter and silver decorated glassware; elegant champagne flutes; candle holders and candles from Price's and others; Bath Bomb cosmetics; lamps; vases; a wonderful range of soft toys and, a speciality of the shop, an extensive selection of wicker baskets in various shapes and sizes – laundry baskets, shopping baskets, trugs, picnic baskets and more. Also available is a range of quality garden furniture.

The shop is open Monday to Saturday from 9.30am to 5.30pm. Just a 10-minute drive away, Finishing Touches has a sister establishment of the same name at 30, High Street, Kimbolton, just across the county border in Cambridgeshire, which specialises in kitchenware, oak furniture and also baskets. Between the two of them you should have no problem finding distinctive items to enhance your own décor or to present as cherishable gifts.

THE ROSE & CROWN

1 High Street, Islip, Thrapston, Northants NN14 3JS
Tel: 01832 733118

Located close to the church and the River Nene, **The Rose and Crown** is a charming old hostelry dating back to 1691. Inside, there are log fires and traditional settles lining the walls of the bar where you'll find 4 real ales on tap including Bishop's Farewell from Oakham Ales. Mine hosts, Leslie and Diane Shiret, also offer appetising food at lunchtimes with a choice of freshly cut sandwiches of home-made bread, soup, ploughmans and a daily dish of the day. The Shirets are keen gardeners so in summer the garden to the rear is a delight and colourful hanging baskets are ranged along the front of the inn. Standing on the Nene Way, the inn is understandably popular with walkers and bird-watchers.

time. Also of note in the church are over 100 carved oak figures, some medieval brasses and a tablet commemorating John Cole, bookseller, schoolmaster and writer on antiquities. He lived from 1792 to 1848, dying in great poverty. Woodford was the home of a certain Josiah Eaton, a man of small stature (5'2") but great stamina. A prodigious walker, he set out in 1815 on a marathon walk around Blackheath, completing a mile every hour for six weeks, without ever stopping. At the end of this amazing feat of endurance he had covered 1,100 miles.

THRAPSTON

5 miles E of Kettering on the A605

The **Medieval Bridge** at Thrapston crosses the **River Nene** on one of its loveliest stretches. The town is surrounded by fine pastureland, created when the flood waters and rich mud subsided after the two Ice Ages. The main attraction in the church is a stone tablet carved with stars and stripes. It is thought by some that this motif was the inspiration for the American flag, being the coat of arms of Sir John Washington, who died in 1624. The church and nearby Montagu House, home of Sir John, are places of pilgrimage for many American tourists.

RAUNDS

7 miles SE of Kettering on the B663

A small town in the Nene Valley with a lofty (183ft) church spire. It was at the heart of the Northamptonshire shoemaking trade, specialising in army boots, and was also known for the manufacture of dolls. In May 1905 Raunds hit the headlines when 200 men marched to London to protest at the poor rates of pay for bootmakers. They were delighted to find on their arrival that a crowd of 10,000 supporters was waiting for them. After ten days, the strikers won concessions and returned victorious.

IRTHLINGBOROUGH

7 miles SE of Kettering on the B571/A6

A small town noted for its leather and iron industries. It boasts two fine bridges across the Nene, one built in the 14th century, the other in the 20th. The medieval bridge has ten ribbed arches, and the arms of an ancient monastery carved into one if its stones, suggesting perhaps that it was built by monks, perhaps from Peterborough. The modern one, running parallel to the old, is an impressive sight, its great arches stretching for half a mile over the low-lying land by the river. Irthlingborough is home to Rushden & Diamond Football Club, whose stadium is located in the magnificent Diamond Centre. Also in the centre is the Doc Shop, selling Dr Martens boots.

HIGHAM FERRERS

10 miles SE of Kettering off the A45

Just off the **Market Place** in this delightful old town a narrow lane leads to a unique group of ecclesiastical buildings. These include the 13th century spired Church of St Mary the Virgin, a chantry and bede house, and a 13th century market cross. Also here is **Chichele College**, a college for secular canons founded in 1422, named in honour of a local worthy called Henry Chichele. Born here in 1362, he progressed from baker's boy to Archbishop of Canterbury, a position he filled for 30 years until his death in 1443.

PYTCHLEY

2 mile S of Kettering off the A509

The location of the old headquarters of the **Pytchley Hunt**. One of the most famous Masters of the Hunt (1827-1834) was Squire Osbaldeston, a man of boundless energy and stamina, who once successfully wagered a thousand guineas that he could ride 200 miles in ten hours, changing horses as necessary. He used 32 horses and completed the 200 miles with more than an hour to spare. No one took up his offer of a vast sum of money if they could achieve the same feat with the same horses. The good squire was a crack shot, a talented underarm bowler and a fine boxer. He was evidently less accomplished at backing horses than riding them, for he ended his days in London in obscurity and comparative poverty.

WELLINGBOROUGH
8 miles S of Kettering off the A509 or A45

This important market and industrial town, known for its iron mills, flour mills and tanneries, sits near the point where the River Ise joins the River Nene. The spire of the medieval All Hallows Church rises among trees in the centre of town, and the other church, whose great tower can be seen on the further bank of the Nene, is the **Church of St Mary.** It was built in the first decades of the 20th century and is regarded as Sir Ninian Comper's masterpiece. He declared St Mary's his favourite church and wished to be buried here with his wife but Comper's fame demanded interment in

Westminster Abbey. Funded by two Anglo-Catholic spinster sisters, St Mary's has been described as "a sort of fantastical King's College, Cambridge", a sumptuous medley of extravagant Gothic features complete with gilded columns and golden angels. Not to be missed!

Wellingborough was granted its market charter in 1201 and markets are still held four days a week. In and around the market square are several interesting old buildings, including the gabled **Hind Hotel**. One of its rooms is called the Cromwell Room because it was being constructed while the Battle of Naseby was in progress.

Another fine building is **Croyland Abbey**, now a Heritage Centre with a wealth of local history, and near it is a splendidly restored old tithe barn originally used for storing the manorial tithes. Stone-walled and thatch-roofed, it is 70 feet long and 22 feet wide. It dates from the 1400s and has two great doorways at either side, one of them 13 feet in height. A recently opened attraction in the centre of town is the Millennium Rose Garden at **Swanspool Gardens**. The Embankment at Wellingborough is a great place for a family outing, where a thriving population of swans lives next to the outdoor paddling pool that dates from the 1930s. South of the town, **Summer**

GAGGINI'S PLANT CENTRE
Glebe Road, Mears Ashby, Northampton NN6 0DL
Tel: 01604 811811 Fax: 01604 812353

Now approaching its third decade in business, **Gaggini's Plant Centre** offers gardeners a very wide choice of vigorous and healthy plants, shrubs and trees. Specialities include showy climbers such as wisteria; ornamental trees; conifers; fruit trees and large tree ferns. Amongst the shrubs are some hardy tropical plants and there's an extensive selection of herbaceous plants all of which have been nourished with tender loving care by the owners, John and Janette Gaggini. Open 7 days a week, the Centre also stocks an extensive range of pots, tubs and garden statuary.

Leys Nature Reserve is a year-round haven for large numbers of birds. Each May, thousands of people visit the town for the **International Waendel Weekend** of walking, cycling and swimming.

IRCHESTER
2 miles SE of Wellingborough off the A45

Originally a Roman settlement, a fortified town whose walls were eight feet thick. A Saxon cemetery was also discovered here, and Norman England is represented by the plinths in the church. The six-arched bridge that crosses the River Nene is 14th century and bears the crossed keys of Peterborough Abbey and the wheel of St Catherine. On the B570 is **Irchester Country Park**, 200 acres of woodland walks, wayfaring course, nature trail, picnic meadows and ranger service in a former ironstone quarry.

PODINGTON
4 miles SE of Wellingborough off the A509

The noisiest place for miles around, this is the location of the **Santa Pod Raceway**, where the fastest motorsport on earth takes place on selected days between March and November. The Top Fuel Dragsters can accelerate from 0 to 100mph in under a second, so put in your ear plugs and don't blink!

BROUGHTON
3 miles SW of Kettering

The lovely, mostly Elizabethan **Broughton Castle** has been lived in by the same family for more than 600 years. The oldest parts of the moated castle date back to a manor house of 1300; it was enlarged in the 1500s. The castle is surrounded by lovely gardens and there's a parapet walk with fine views over parkland. Amenities include a tea room and gift shop. Opening times are limited – for more details telephone 01295 276070.

LAMPORT
8 miles SW of Kettering off the A508

Lamport Hall (see panel below) is a fine 16th century house enlarged in the 17th century by John Webb. Home to the Isham family from 1560 to 1976, it features an outstanding collection of furniture, books, paintings and china. It has gardens and parkland, including the first Alpine garden and the first garden gnomes in England, plus a shop and tea room. It is also the home of the

LAMPORT HALL & GARDENS

Lamport, Northamptonshire NN6 9HD
Tel: 01604 686272 Fax: 01604 686224
e-mail: admin@lamporthall.co.uk
website: www.lamporthall.co.uk

Lamport Hall was the home of the Isham family for over four centuries. The present Hall was started by John Webb in 1655 and completed by Francis Smith of Warwick. In addition to its fine rooms, the Hall contains a wealth of outstanding paintings, books, furniture and china collected by the family, many during a Grand Tour of Europe in the 1670s.

The Hall is set in tranquil gardens originally laid out in 1655 by Gilbert Clark. The 10th Baronet is responsible for the present day appearance including the rock garden, which is 24 feet tall.

The 12th Baronet created the Lamport Hall Preservation Trust to continue the work of completely restoring the house for the benefit of the public. The Hall is open until October. For details of opening times, Fairs and the 'Summerhouse', Season of Arts, programme are available on the above phone number or website.

Hannington Vintage Tractor Club, which houses a wide variety of vintage tractors and other farm machinery. Open certain days Easter-September.

NASEBY

10 miles W of Kettering off the A5199

Two monuments and interpretation panels mark the site of the **Battle of Naseby**, where, in 1645, Oliver Cromwell's Parliamentarian forces defeated King Charles I and determined the outcome of the Civil War, thereby giving the English people the right to rule their own country. Cromwell and Fairfax with 14,000 Roundheads faced the Royalist forces, who advanced outnumbered two to one. The first attack came at 10 o'clock on the morning of June 14 and, after heavy fighting, Fairfax won a decisive victory, capturing all the King's baggage and a fortune in gold and silver. The King surrendered in Newark some months later and the Civil War was at an end. Naseby Battle and Farm Museum, in the village, contains a model layout of the battle, relics from the fight and a collection of bygone agricultural machinery.

Many of the defeated Royalists who fled after the battle were surrounded and killed at the village of **Marston Trussell** on the Leicestershire border. Their remains lie in the churchyard.

KELMARSH

6 miles W of Kettering on the A508

Near Junction 2 of the A14, just outside the village of Kelmarsh, **Kelmarsh Hall** is an early 18th century house designed in Palladian style by an outstanding pupil of Sir Christopher Wren, James Gibbs (who is perhaps best known as the architect of the Church of St Martin in the Fields, London). One of only two surviving houses outside London by Gibbs in this style, it stands in 3,000 acres of farmland, with a lake, beautiful gardens and woodland walks. The Great Hall is the focal point of the house, with many of Gibbs' original features. One of the most attractive rooms is the Chinese Room, where the hand-painted wallpaper, from Kimberley Hall in Norfolk, dates from the 1840s. Open to the public Sunday and Bank Holiday afternoons from Easter Sunday to the end of August. The church opposite the main entrance to the Hall contains fine marble from Rome, some William Morris furnishings and the vaults of the families who have lived at the Hall – the Hanburys, the Naylors and the Lancasters.

RUSHTON

4 miles NW of Kettering off the A6

One mile west of the village, on an unclassified road, stands **Rushton Triangular Lodge**, described as "the purest folly in the country". It was built by Sir Thomas Tresham in 1597 and symbolises the Holy Trinity, with three walls, each with three windows, three gables and three storeys, topped with a three-sided chimney. Thomas Tresham, known as Thomas the Builder, was brought up a Protestant but courageously returned to the Roman Catholic faith of his ancestors. At Rushton Hall, the Tresham family home since the 14th century, he was caught harbouring the renowned Jesuit Edmund Campion and was sentenced to seven years' imprisonment. Responsible for several intriguing buildings, he died soon after proclaiming the first Stuart king and just before his son Francis was arrested as a protagonist in the Gunpowder Plot.

Neighbouring **Rushton Hall**, also dating back 400 years, is described as a "dazzling example of Tudor and Stuart splendour". Built by Sir John Tresham, enlarged by Sir Thomas and completed by the Cockayne family, it now houses a Royal Institute for the Blind school, but is open to the public by appointment and for special events. Tel: 01536 710506

CORBY

6 miles N of Kettering off the A43

A modern industrial town, but one with a history. Taking its name from a Scandinavian chieftain during the Danish occupation, it grew in significance in the mid-10th

Rockingham

century, when King Edgar set up the Corby Hundred, with a local Moot Court governing the affairs of other villages in the area. True industry arrived at Corby in the later years of Queen Victoria's reign, with the building of the **Kettering-Manton railway**. Many of the bricks used in the building of the viaduct at Harringworth were made at Corby brickworks, which closed at the beginning of the 20th century. But Corby was still essentially a small village until the 1930s, when Stewarts & Lloyds built a huge steel-making plant based on the area's known reserves of iron ore. That industry virtually stopped in 1980, but Corby remains a go-ahead modern town, with many cultural and leisure opportunities for young and old alike. It also treasures its heritage, both historic and geographic. 170 acres of woodland have been preserved intact at the very heart of the town, and there is much to interest the visitor in the surrounding villages that make up Corby Borough: Cottingham, East Carlton, Middleton, Rockingham, Stanion and Weldon.

EAST CARLTON

1 mile W of Corby on the A427

East Carlton Countryside Park comprises 100 acres of parkland with nature trails and a steel-making heritage centre with craft workshops, a forge and a cafeteria.

ROCKINGHAM

2 miles N of Corby on the A6003

"450 Years a Royal Castle, 450 years a family home". Nine hundred years of history are contained within the walls of **Rockingham Castle**, built by William the Conqueror on the slopes of Rockingham Hill, overlooking the Welland Valley and the thatched and slate-roofed cottages of the village. The grand rooms are superbly furnished, and the armour in the Tudor Great Hall recalls the Civil War, when the castle was captured by the Roundheads. Owned and lived in since 1530 by the Watson family, the castle was put to atmospheric use by the BBC in the series *By the Sword Divided*, in which it was known as Arnescote Castle. Charles Dickens wrote much of *Bleak House* at Rockingham.

HARRINGWORTH

4 miles N of Corby off the B672

An impressive sight here is the great **Viaduct** carrying the railway from Kettering to Oakham a mile across the Welland Valley. Completed in 1879, it has 82 spans, each 40 feet wide. In the village are a notable village cross and the

Church of St John the Baptist (12ᵗʰ to 14ᵗʰ centuries).

DEENE

4 miles NE of Corby off the A43

Surrounded by beautiful gardens and grounds filled with old-fashioned roses and rare trees and shrub stands **Deene Park** (see panel below). Originally a medieval manor, it was acquired in 1514 by Sir Robert Brudenell and has been occupied by the family ever since. One of the family's most distinguished members was James, 7ᵗʰ Earl of Cadogan, who led the Charge of the Light Brigade at the Battle of Balaclava. Transformed from medieval manor to Tudor and Georgian mansion, Deene Park contains many fine examples of period furniture and some beautiful paintings. The oldest visible part is an arch of about 1300 in the east of the house; the Great Hall was completed in the late 1500s and has a

magnificent sweet chestnut hammerbeam roof. The house is open on certain days between Easter and August.

Also near Deene, in the parish of Gretton, is **Kirby Hall** (English Heritage), one of the loveliest Elizabethan ruins in England. Now only partly roofed, the hall dates from 1570 and was given by Elizabeth I to her Lord Chancellor and favourite courtier Sir Christopher Hatton. Alterations attributed to Inigo Jones were made in the 17ᵗʰ century. The fine gardens with their peacock population are being restored. A version of Jane Austen's *Mansfield Park* was filmed here in 1998.

WELDON

2 miles E of Corby on the A427

This sizeable village is best known for the honey-coloured building stone quarried here. The stone was used to build nearby Rockingham Castle and Great St Mary's

---

DEENE PARK

Corby, Northamptonshire NN17 3EW

A very interesting house which has been developed over six centuries from a typical medieval manor around a courtyard into a Tudor and Georgian mansion. Many of the rooms of different periods can be seen by visitors who enjoy the impressive yet intimate ambience of the family home of the Brudenelts, seven of whom were Earls of Cardigan. The most flamboyant of them was the 7th Earl who led the light Brigade charge at Balaklava and of whom there are some historic relics and pictures.

The present owner is Mr. Edmund Brudenell who together with the Hon. Mrs. Brudenell has carefully restored the house from its dilapidated condition at the end of the last war and also added considerably to the furniture and picture collection.

The gardens have been made over the last thirty years, with long mixed borders of shrubs, old fashioned roses and flowers, a parterre designed by David Hicks fronts the house with long walks under fine old trees by the water which meanders passed the house and out into the lake next to the Parkland

Church in distant Cambridge. An interesting house on the village green is the windowless **Round House**, once used as a lock-up.

BRIGSTOCK
5 miles SE of Corby on the A6116

On the banks of a tributary of the River Nene called Harpers Brook, the Saxon village of Brigstock has many delightful old cottages, a 16th century manor house, and a church with an unusual circular extension to its tower. The village was once deep in Rockingham Forest, and the church bells were rung three times a day to guide travellers. By the little tree-covered village green a quaint Elizabethan cross topped by a ball weather vane stands on four steps. Brigstock has a popular herb centre, **Hill Farm Herbs**, set in an old farm complex, and outside the village is a country park for rambling and enjoying nature.

EASTON-ON-THE-HILL
12 miles NE of Corby on the A43

An attraction here at the far northern tip of the county is the **Priest's House**, a pre-Reformation priest's lodge which is of specialist architectural interest and is in the care of the National Trust. It contains a small museum of village bygones. Visits by appointment only. Tel: 01909 486411 (regional office).

In the village church is a tablet commemorating one Lancelot Skynner, a rector's son, who died in 1799 when the ship *La Lutine*, laden with gold, sank off Holland. The ship's bell was recovered and now hangs in the London headquarters of Lloyd's who had insured the cargo.

OUNDLE

Oundle is a beguiling little town with some fine stone buildings dating from the 17th and 18th centuries, ancient hostelries and a variety of specialist shops. The town is probably best known for its **Public School**, founded by Sir William Laxton in 1556. An inscription to his memory is written above the 17th century doorway in Greek, Latin and Hebrew. The medieval church, with its magnificent tower and 200-feet spire, is an impressive sight, and other notable buildings include three sets of almshouses. The museum paints a picture of local life down the years.

In mid-July, the town hosts the **Oundle International Festival** – ten days devoted to a vibrant mix of classical music, theatre, jazz and film. The festivities include a hugely popular open-air jazz and firework spectacular. On a smaller scale, but generating a wildly competitive spirit, are the **World Conker Championships** held at Ashton, just to the east of the town.

AROUND OUNDLE

LYVEDEN NEW BIELD
4 miles SW of Oundle via the A427

Another of Sir Thomas Tresham's creations, Lyveden New Bield is a cross-shaped Elizabethan garden lodge erected to symbolise the Passion. Begun around 1595 as a garden lodge for his main residence, the Old Bield, it remains virtually unaltered since work on it stopped with the death of Sir Thomas in 1605. An intriguing and haunting roofless shell, it features some interesting exterior frieze work and stands in beautiful open countryside, with the remains of late-Elizabethan water gardens adjoining the site. Owned by the National Trust, it is open Wednesday to Sunday all year during daylight hours.

WALK 7

Oundle and the River Nene

Start	Oundle
Distance	6 miles (9.7 km)
Approximate time	3 hours
Parking	Oundle
Refreshments	Pubs and cafés at Oundle, pub and restaurant by Barnwell Country Park
Ordnance Survey maps	Landranger 141 (Kettering & Corby) and 142 (Peterborough), Pathfinder 939, TL08/18 (Oundle & Sawtry)

Much of this walk is along the banks of the placid River Nene which does a wide loop around Oundle, almost encircling the town. There are fine views across riverside meadows, a walk through an attractive estate village and a visit to Barnwell Country Park, created from old gravel workings by the river that were abandoned in the late 1960s. Its meadows, woods and pools are now a haven for wildlife.

Oundle is a delightful old town with a wealth of dignified 17th and 18th century buildings, mostly constructed from the local creamy-coloured limestone. Dominating the town is the magnificent 13th-century parish church, an unusually large building with a tall, graceful 14th century tower and spire, visible from much of the walk. The town has a notable public school, founded in 1556, with a chapel that was built just after World War I as a memorial to members of the school who died in the conflict. The walk starts in the Market Place in front of the market hall.

Face the market hall and turn right. Follow the main road to the left along North Street, pass to the right of the church and continue to cross North Bridge over the River Nene. Keep ahead over the busy bypass at a traffic island, and on the other side climb a stile at a public footpath sign **A**.

Take the path ahead through a small group of trees and walk along the left edge of two fields. Climb a stile in the corner of the second field and bear right diagonally across the next field to join and keep alongside a wire fence bordering woodland. Where the fence ends, continue in the same direction and turn left over a stile in a churchyard wall. Turn right across the churchyard, passing to the right of the small, early 18th century chapel, and go through gates on to the road in Ashton. This seemingly traditional village of picturesque, thatched houses grouped around a green is deceptive; it is an estate village rebuilt in the Tudor style in 1900 for Charles Rothschild.

Turn right **B** at a Nene Valley Way fingerpost,along a tarmac track, and where it ends, keep ahead along a path to a kissing-gate. Go through, continue downhill across a field, go through another gate and descend steps on to a road. Turn right and at the National Dragonfly Museum, housed in the former Ashton Mill, turn left and take the track that passes to the right of a mill building. Go through a kissing gate, keep ahead across a meadow, then cross an iron footbridge over the Nene and turn left along the riverbank **C**.

Now keep beside the lazily meandering Nene across flat, lush meadows, following the river around a sharp right bend. There are several stiles to climb and regular Nene Valley Way signs. One part of the route is along the edge of an arable field and after passing under the bypass the path goes through a wooded area, followed by a narrow stretch below a hedge and embankment on the right.

Finally, the path emerges into meadows again – on seeing the first houses over to the right, bear right across the meadow to a stile and public footpath sign **D**. Do not climb the stile but turn sharp left and head back across the meadow to cross a metal footbridge over the river. Turn left to another bridge, turn right over it and keep ahead through scrub and trees to cross a foot-bridge by a lock. Turn right alongside the Nene again, climb a double stile and continue along a broad track, between a lake on the left and the river and a marina on the right, to a road. Turn right over Barnwell Mill Bridge and shortly afterwards turn

left along a tarmac drive to the pub and restaurant.

The drive bends left and just before the gates to the pub, turn right **E** through a fence gap – there is a 'Welcome to Barnwell Country Park' sign here – and turn right again on to a path, between a fence and drive on the right and trees and bushes bordering a pool on the left. Follow this pleasant path through trees, continue across an open grassy area and then a car park, and pass in front of the visitor centre.

At a fork, take the right-hand path, alongside another pool on the left, and look out for where you turn right up steps to rejoin the road **F**. Turn left and cross South Bridge into Oundle. At a junction in front of a church turn right along West Street and follow it back to the Market Place. ●

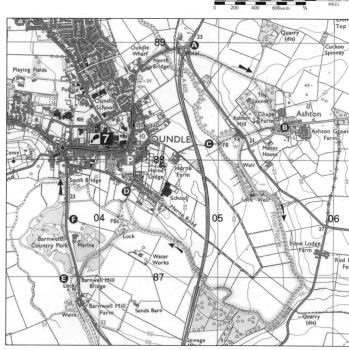

ASHTON

1 mile E of Oundle off the A605

A unique attraction at Ashton Mill is the **National Dragonfly Museum**, the only one of its kind in Europe. It highlights the beauty, the wonder and the plight of dragonflies through habitats, exhibitions and videos, and guarantees a visit with a difference that is both fascinating and educational. The museum is open at weekends and on Bank Holiday Mondays, mid-June to the end of September.

Fotheringay

FOTHERINGHAY

4 miles NE of Oundle off the A605

The first **Fotheringhay Castle** was built around 1100 by the son-in-law of William the Conqueror; the second in the 14th century by Edmund of Langley, a son of Edward III. Richard III was born here; Henry VIII gave the castle to Catherine of Aragon and it later became the prison and place of execution of Mary, Queen of Scots, who was brought here in bands of steel and beheaded in the Banqueting Hall in 1587. Sir Christopher Hatton, a favourite of Elizabeth I whom we have met at Holdenby and Kirkby Hall, was one of the judges who sentenced Mary to death. Following her death, it is said that her jewellery was stolen and hidden in the woodlands around Corby. If so, it lies there still. The castle was pulled down in 1627 and 200 years later a gold ring was found with a lovers' knot entwined around the initials M and D - Mary and Darnley? Perhaps the ring fell from the Queen's finger as she was executed. The evocative site of the castles by the River Nene is rich in atmosphere, and visitors to Fotheringhay should not leave the village without seeing the **Church of St Mary and All Saints**, a 15th century former collegiate church in a prominent position overlooking the Nene Valley.

10 WARWICKSHIRE AND THE WEST MIDLANDS

A rich vein of medieval and Tudor history runs through Warwickshire and the romantic ruins of Kenilworth Castle, the grandeur of Warwick Castle and the elegance of Royal Leamington Spa set the tone for this most delightful of counties. However, it is Stratford-upon-Avon that is most visitors' focal point and, known throughout the world as the birthplace of William Shakespeare, the old part of the town is completely dominated by the exceptional man who died nearly 400 years ago. Along with the various timber-framed houses that are linked with the Bard, Stratford is also the home of the Royal Shakespeare Company and there is a regular programme of performances of his plays held here each year.

Another town that has found fame through one of its young citizens is Rugby as it was a pupil who, in the early 19th century, broke the rules of football during a match and, in so doing, founded the game that bears the name of the town. Close by is the ancient village of Dunchurch that is often dubbed the 'Gunpowder Plot Village' as it was here that the conspirators waited to hear if they had succeeded.

While Stratford will be the obvious focal point for most visitors to Warwickshire, the region boasts any number of attractive and

Warwick Castle

peaceful villages and hamlets well off the beaten tourist track. Warwickshire's waterways form an important and extensive part of the 2,000 miles of Britain's inland network, boasting as it does long stretches of the Oxford Canal, as well as restored lengths of the Stratford Canal and the upper Avon.

Village after village along the Rivers Avon, Arrow or Alne, many relatively untouched since Tudor times, reflect some of the best traditional architecture and scenery to be found in the region. There are also several impressive hilltop views to be had along the way, revealing breathtaking views of the surrounding countryside.

The West Midlands and the extreme north of the county of Warwickshire is dominated by the major cities of Birmingham and Coventry. It often gets overlooked by visitors but repays a closer look. It is an area rich in natural beauty, with a wealth of beautiful gardens, some excellent museums and historic buildings, and a long and distinguished industrial and cultural heritage.

LOCATOR MAP

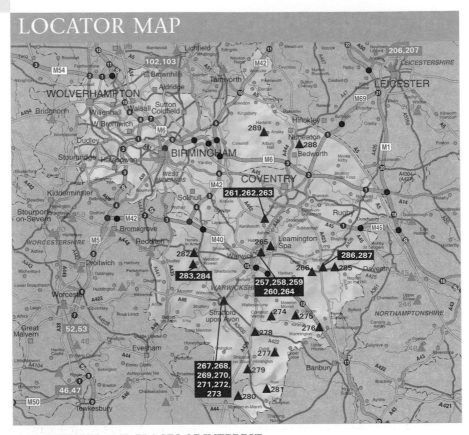

ADVERTISERS AND PLACES OF INTEREST

WARWICK

Over the past ten centuries **Warwick Castle** has witnessed some of the most turbulent times in English history. From the era of William the Conqueror to the grand reign of Queen Victoria, the Castle has left us a fascinating legacy to enjoy today. Dominating the town, it is surely everyone's ideal of a medieval building, one of the country's most splendid castles and certainly one of the most visited. It still serves as a home as well as retaining the greater part of its original masonry. Standing by the River Avon, Warwick is in a good defensive position and became part of Crown lands as recorded in the Domesday Book in 1086.

A tour of this palatial mansion takes you from the grim austerity of the original dungeons with their gruesome torture chambers to the gloomy but sumptuous opulence of rooms later adapted for comfortable living. The castle's magnificent State Rooms, once used to entertain the highest members of the nobility, house some superb art treasures including works by Holbein, Rubens and Velasquez. As the castle is owned by Madame Tussaud's, striking waxworks play their part in the displays. In the castle's Ghost Tower, visitors can learn of the dark and sinister secrets surrounding the fatal stabbing of Sir Fulke Greville who is said to haunt the

Warwick Castle

premises to this day. In the Great Hall visitors come face to face with Oliver Cromwell's death mask. And the armoury houses one of the best private collections in the country.

The castle exterior is best viewed from **Castle Bridge**, where the 14th century walls can be seen reflected in the waters of the River Avon. There is a walk along the ramparts, and much to explore within 60 acres of grounds, including a re-created Victorian formal rose garden, the Peacock Gardens and an expanse of open parkland designed by Capability Brown. Events throughout the year include **Medieval Tournaments**, open-air firework concerts and special entertainment days.

KATE BOATS

Nelson Lane, Warwick CV34 5JB
Tel: 01926 492968 Fax: 01926 419314
e-mail: cheryl@kateboats.co.uk website: www.kateboats.co.uk

Boating holidays continue to grow in popularity and **Kate Boats** offers a choice of beautifully maintained narrowboats from their bases at Warwick and at Stockton Top Marina, a 20-minute drive from Warwick. Owners of this family-run business, Cheryl and Nick Howes, believe their fleet of 12 boats is small enough for them to take care of every detail. The boats are comprehensively equipped with excellent kitchens, en suite facilities, radio and colour television. The Warwickshire Canal Ring passes through some delightful countryside.

SIMPLY DIVINE

60 Market Place, Warwick CV34 4SD
Tel/Fax: 01926 776999
Open 9am-5.30pm Monday-Saturday

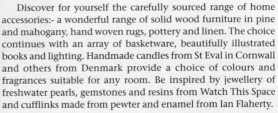

The elegant arched windows of **Simply Divine's** shop-front frame an enticing display of furniture and accessories for the home and garden. This gives an insight into the amazing range of goods to be found in this stylish store. 'Discover and be inspired' is the invitation of owners Christine Fuller and her mother Barbara Essex who opened Simply Divine in the heart of beautiful historic Warwick in 2000.

Discover for yourself the carefully sourced range of home accessories:- a wonderful range of solid wood furniture in pine and mahogany, hand woven rugs, pottery and linen. The choice continues with an array of basketware, beautifully illustrated books and lighting. Handmade candles from St Eval in Cornwall and others from Denmark provide a choice of colours and fragrances suitable for any room. Be inspired by jewellery of freshwater pearls, gemstones and resins from Watch This Space and cufflinks made from pewter and enamel from Ian Flaherty.

All that is offered has been carefully selected for its affordability, usefulness and simple styling so that Simply Divine once discovered will inspire.

FORTH HOUSE

44 High Street, Warwick CV34 4AX
Tel: 01926 401512 Fax: 01926 490809
e-mail: info@forthhouseuk.co.uk website: www.forthhouseuk.co.uk

Forth House was one of the first houses to be burned in Warwick's Great Fire of 1694, but fortunately, most of the 16th century building survived and a new Georgian frontage was added later. It now offers a choice of bed & breakfast or self-catering accommodation and boasts an English Tourism Council Silver Award. B&B guests stay in either the Garden Suite on the ground floor with its own sitting room, or in the Brook Room overlooking the garden. Copes Flat, originally the hayloft and groom's quarters of the stables, overlooks old walled gardens and can accommodate up to 3 guests.

A strong link with the castle is found in the **Collegiate Church of St Mary** in Old Square, a splendid medieval church on the town's highest point. Of pre-Conquest origin, the church contains the magnificent fan-vaulted Beauchamp Chapel, built to house the monuments of Richard Beauchamp, Earl of Warwick, and his family. The chapel contains an outstanding collection of Warwickshire tombs, a chapter house and a Norman crypt (complete with a tumbrel, part of a medieval ducking stool). In summer visitors can ascend the tower to enjoy the excellent views.

The centre of Warwick was rebuilt after a fire in 1694, and though many older buildings survived, the centre is dominated by elegant Queen Anne buildings. A walk around High Street and Northgate Street takes in some of the finest buildings, including **Court House** and **Landor House**. Court House on Jury Street houses the **Warwickshire Yeomanry Museum**, with displays of uniforms, arms, swords, sabres and selected silver, and Warwick Town Museum, which features changing exhibitions.

Some of the town's oldest structures can be found around Mill Street, an attractive place for a stroll, with several antique shops along the way. The **Mill Garden** at the end of Mill Street is home to a delightful series of plantings in a breathtaking setting on the Avon beside the castle. Here visitors will find a herb garden, raised beds, small trees, shrubs and cottage plants including some unusual varieties.

Warwickshire Museum (free) in Market Place occupies an imposing 17th century market hall housing collections that illustrate the geology, wildlife and history of the county. Notable exhibits include giant fossils, live bees, ancient jewellery and the historic Sheldon Tapestry map of Warwickshire. Changing programmes in the ground floor galleries offer exciting exhibitions of acclaimed local and national artists' work.

History of a different kind can be seen at picturesque **Oken's House**, an ancient building once owned by Thomas Oken, a self-made businessman who died childless in 1573 and left his fortune to found almshouses for the poor. This carefully restored Elizabethan house is now home to **The Doll Museum**, displaying hundreds of dolls, teddies and toys from days gone by. Visitors can have a go at hopscotch or spinning tops, or hunt for Teddy's friends, while video bring the exhibits to life, demonstrating how all the mechanical toys on display work.

One of the most important buildings in Warwick is St John's House, dating

---

AROMA GALLERY

26 Swan Street, Warwick CV34 4BJ
Tel: 01926 499770

Seeking inspiration for interior design ideas or looking for interesting gifts? Then the place to make for is Caroline Rowland's **Aroma Gallery** just off the Market Place. Here you'll find an intriguing variety of attractive items – clocks, trinket and jewellery boxes, candles and candle holders, lanterns (a big seller during the summer months), and much more. Caroline also stocks a wide range of aromatherapy products and toiletries, healing crystals, lavender warmers, scented sachets, pot pourris, silk flowers, notelet sets and hand-made greetings cards. And if you enjoy relaxing music, the gallery also sells an extensive selection of CDs from Global Journey.

from 1666 and considered a very good example of the period. Today the building houses a museum where visitors can find out how people lived in the past. Upstairs is the **Museum of the Royal Warwickshire Regiment**.

Two of Warwick's medieval town gateways survive, complete with chapels. Of these, Westgate Chapel forms part of **Lord Leycester's Hospital**, a spectacularly tottering and beautiful collection of 15th century half-timbered buildings enclosing a pretty galleried courtyard. Inside, the main interest is provided by the **Queen's Own Hussars Regimental Museum**. This 600-year-old medieval treasure has a unique chantry Chapel dating back to 1123, a magnificent Great Hall and Guildhall together with other timber-framed buildings, first established by the Earl of Leicester as an old soldiers' home in 1571. The historic Master's Garden, featuring a Norman arch and 2,000 year-old vase from the Nile, is a spectacular summer attraction.

In the heart of Warwick, just 400 yards from the castle, the Lord Leycester Hotel occupies Grade II listed buildings steeped in history: in 1694 they halted the Great Fire of Warwick; in the 1700s they housed the Three Tuns Inn; and by the 19th century they were elegant townhouses.

Warwick Racecourse in Hampton Street offers flat and National Hunt racing throughout the year. This picturesque racecourse makes a good day out for all the family, with a regular programme of 25 meetings throughout the year. The central grandstand incorporates the first stand built in 1809, among the oldest surviving in the country.

AROUND WARWICK

KENILWORTH

4 miles N of Warwick on the A452

Although the town was here before the Domesday Book was compiled, Kenilworth's name is invariably linked with its castle. Today the remains of this castle stand as England's finest and most extensive castle ruins, dramatically ensconced at the western edge of the town.

Kenilworth Castle's red sandstone towers, keep and wall glow with an impressive richness in the sun, particularly at sunrise and sunset. Here you can learn about the great building's links with Henry V (who retired to Kenilworth after the Battle of Agincourt), King John, Edward II and John of Gaunt. The tales of this great fortress, immortalised (if enhanced) in Sir Walter

---

FERNDALE HOUSE

Priory Road, Kenilworth, Warwickshire CV8 1LL
Tel: 01926 853214 Fax: 01926 858336
e-mail: ferndalehouse@tiscali.co.uk

In a peaceful suburb, just 5 minutes from the old town, **Ferndale House** is a spacious Victorian house offering comfortable accommodation which boasts a 4-Diamonds rating from the English Tourist Council. Mike and Su North-Bond provide "home-from-home" hospitality and Mike's home-made breakfast comes with a choice of traditional, vegetarian or Continental with extras such as fresh fruits in summer and a hearty porridge in winter. The 7 en suite bedrooms are all attractively furnished, capturing the Victorian charm of the residence, and are equipped with tea-making facilities and colour television.

Scott's novel *Kenilworth* written in 1821, are many and varied. The marvellous Norman keep, the oldest part of the ruins, was built between 1150 and 1175. John of Gaunt's Great Hall once rivalled London's Westminster Hall in palatial grandeur. After Simon de Montfort's death at the Battle of Evesham in 1265, Kenilworth was held by his son. At that time the castle was surrounded by the Kenilworth Great Pool, a lake covering about 120 acres.

Kenilworth Castle

An audio tour guides you on a revealing journey around the Castle, recounting stories of Kenilworth's turbulent past. There are fine views from the top of Saintlowe Tower, and lovely grounds for exploring and picnicking, as well as beautifully reconstructed Tudor gardens. Special events throughout the year include a festival of Tudor Music, Saxon and Viking exhibitions, medieval

JUTERONOMY & THE ROCKING HORSE COFFEE SHOP

21/22 Talisman Square, Kenilworth, Warwickshire CV8 1JB
Tel: 01926 854721 (Coffee Shop Tel: 01926 856413)
website: www.tearcraft.org

More than 25 years ago, Kath Shortley was one of the early supporters of Tearcraft, a Christian charity dedicated to ensuring that fair prices are paid for the work of craftspeople living in some of the world's poorest communities. Many of their beautiful products are on display in **Juteronomy** in the centre of Kenilworth. Each year, Kath visits craftspeople in developing countries to see them produce a fascinating range of items – exquisitely designed fabrics from Bangladesh, wondrously carved wooden items from Thailand, elegant brass and enamel dishes and trays from India, pan pipes and other

musical instruments from Peru, jewellery from South Africa and India, and much, much more. The full range can be seen in the shop or ordered on the charity's website.

Right next to the crafts shop, **The Rocking Horse Coffee Shop** has been a popular place of refreshment for a quarter of a century. In addition to quality teas and coffees the fare on offer includes home-made cakes and pastries, sandwiches, baked potatoes, tasty salads and hot lunches such as lasagne and chilli dishes. All day breakfasts, ice creams and milk shakes are also available. The coffee shop is open from 9.30am to 5pm, Monday to Saturday.

BRAMBLES OF KENILWORTH

1 Smalley Place, Kenilworth, Warwickshire CV8 1QG
Tel/Fax: 01926 511108

Opened in May 2002, **Brambles of Kenilworth** has quickly
established itself as the premier place for quality gifts and items
for the home. Kim Harris and Jan Corton have selected an
outstanding range of desirable objects, all at realistic prices.
There's Leonardo glass from Germany, English trinket boxes and
jewellery with a Celtic theme, some of it solid silver. Kitchen
items include drizzle olive oil bottles from France, pewter pieces and serviette rings; there's an excellent
range of elegant photo frames, children's soft toys, artificial flowers and much, much more. An ideal
place to visit if there's a birthday – or Christmas – coming up! We have something for everyone.

pageantry, various re-enactments, plays
and operas in the grounds and much
more. The remains of **Kenilworth Abbey**
can be seen in the churchyard of the
Norman parish church of St Nicholas in
the High Street. Much of interest was
discovered during excavations and there
are many relics on display in the church,
including a 'pig' of lead. It is said that
this formed part of the roof at the time
of the Dissolution but was then melted
down and stamped by the
Commissioners of Henry VIII.

ASHOW

4 miles NE of Warwick off the A46

Avon Cottage in Ashow,
at the far end of this
attractive village adjacent
to the church is a
charming cottage garden
surrounding a picturesque
18th-century Grade II
listed building. It
stretches for 1½ acres
with extensive River Avon
frontage. Diverse and
interesting plantings
make for year-round
interest. There is also an
attractive orchard area
with free-range domestic
hens and waterfowl.

HATTON

2 miles NW of Warwick off the A41

Hatton Country World (see panel
below) is a uniquely charming blend of
family fun and country shopping. On
this 100-acre farm, visitors will find the
largest collection of rare breed farm
animals in Britain and the largest craft
village in England with some 35
workshops employing over 100 people.

SHREWLEY

5 miles NW of Warwick off the B4439

Shrewley boasts a marina situated on the
Grand Union Canal. Its well-known

HATTON COUNTRY WORLD

Hatton House, Warwick CV35 7LD
Tel: 01926 843411 Fax: 01926 842023

Hatton Country World consists of two unique attractions side by
side. The Shopping Village at Hatton Country World is home to 25
craft & specialist gift shops, an Antique Centre with 20 dealers and
The Outlet. All housed in a charming cluster of converted Victorian
farm buildings, it is the perfect place for those unique and
unusual gifts.

The Farm Park is a fun
packed paradise for
children and adults, with
a unique mix of animals,
adventure and all out
activity! Where else could
you start the day
cuddling a Guinea Pig
and end it panning for
gold?

landmark is the Hatton flight of 21 locks that stretches for 2½ miles up **Hatton Hill**.

BARFORD

3 miles S of Warwick on the A429

The name of Joseph Arch may not be known to many nowadays, but in his time he was one of the leading figures in the world of farming. Born in a tiny house in 1826 (the house still stands), he was a scare-crower, ploughboy, stable lad and champion hedge-cutter before his radical views led him to found the Warwickshire Agricultural Labourers Union, and later the National Union. He became the first truly working-class Member of Parliament (for North West Norfolk) and was a friend of the prince of Wales, but he never forgot his roots and he died, at the grand old age of 93, in the little house where he was born. A much grander building is the **Regency Barford House**, notable for its giant Ionic columns. The Church of St Peter was mainly rebuilt in 1884 by RC Hussey.

SHERBOURNE

3 miles S of Warwick on the A46

Set in lovely countryside with views over fields to the River Avon, **Sherbourne Park** is one of

the very finest gardens in the county. Highlights of the gardens, which were designed by Lady Smith-Ryland in the 1950s, include a paved terrace covered by clematis, wisteria and a magnolia; an 'orchard' of sorbus trees; a box-edged, rose-filled parterre and the White Garden surrounded by yew hedges. The redbrick house of the Park is early Georgian, and the view is dominated by the parish church, built in 1863 by Sir George Gilbert Scott. Open on certain afternoons and by appointment. Tel: 01926 624255

ROYAL LEAMINGTON SPA

2 miles E of Warwick off the A46

This attractive town boasts a handsome mixture of smart shops and Regency buildings. The Parade is undoubtedly one of the finest streets in Warwickshire. It

Royal Leamington Spa

COUNTRY BUMPKINS DELICATESSEN

53 Warwick Street, Leamington Spa, Warwickshire CV32 5JR
Tel: 01926 425571 Fax: 01926 427312
e-mail: chris@ctrybumpkins.co.spacomputers.com
website: www.countrybumpkinsdeli.co.uk

Country Bumpkins Delicatessen presents a sight to gladden the heart of anyone who appreciates top quality ingredients in their cuisine. This town centre deli offers daily fresh bread and baguettes from local bakeries and the French Boulangerie de Paris; a huge range of cooked meats and pâtés; fresh olives and olive oil; jams, preserves and chutneys; chocolates and confectionery. Owner Chris Atkins is an expert on cheese and the varieties on offer include tasty local Warwickshire cheeses – Fowlers and Berkswell – along with goat's and ewe's milk cheeses.

THE BUTCHERS ARMS

Fisher Road, Bishops Itchington, nr Leamington Spa,
Warwickshire CV47 2RE
Tel: 01926 614161

Mine host David Taylor knows his pub, The Butchers Arms,
very well – he was born in this pretty village some 40 years ago
and remembers when a pint cost 1 shilling and 9 pence (about
9p). He and his wife Geraldine bought this friendly country
pub in 2002 and it's already earned a reputation for good food, real ales (3 or 4 always on tap), and a
value for money wine list. The inn has a cosy bar with an open fire and a separate dining room where
customers have the choice of hearty main meals (a 24oz rump steak, for example); pot meals, jacket
potatoes, vegetarian options and a selection of children's meals.

starts at the railway bridge, dives
between a double row of shops and
comes up again at the place marked with
a small stone temple announcing 'The
Original Spring Recorded by Camden in
1586'. In 1801 very few people knew of
the existence of Leamington, but by
1838 all this had changed. By this time
the famous waters were cascading
expensively over the many 'patients' and
the increasingly fashionable spa was
given the title 'Royal' by permission of
the new Queen, Victoria. **The Pump
Rooms** were opened in 1814 by Henry
Jephson, a local doctor who was largely
responsible for promoting the Spa's
medicinal properties. This elegant spa
resort was soon popularised by the rich,
who came to take the waters in the 18th

and 19th centuries. Immediately opposite
the Spa itself are **Jephson's Gardens**
containing a Corinthian temple which
houses a statue of him. The town's
supply of saline waters is inexhaustible,
and a wide range of 'cures' is available,
under supervision, to this day.

**Warwick District Council Art Gallery
and Museum** in Avenue Road boasts
collections of pottery, ceramics and glass,
as well as some excellent Flemish, Dutch
and British paintings from the 1500s to
the present.

UFTON FIELDS NATURE RESERVE

5 miles E of Leamington Spa off the A425

This haven is open every Sunday from 11
till 4. It boasts an all-weather footpath
and a wealth of butterflies, dragonflies
and wild flowers, as well as a
bird hide.

HARBURY

5 miles SE of Leamington Spa off the B4452

The history of this area goes
back many years – dinosaur
fossils have been found in the
local quarries and the Fosse
Way, a major Roman road,
passes close by. Just outside the
village lies **Chesterton
Windmill**, an unusual mill
built in 1632.

Royal Leamington Spa

STRATFORD-UPON-AVON

After London, many visitors to England put Stratford-upon-Avon next on the itinerary, and all because of one man. William Shakespeare was born here in 1564, found fame in London and then retired here, dying in 1616. Needless to say, the places connected with his life and work have become meccas for anyone interested in the cultural history, not just of these islands, but of the entire world.

Each of the houses associated with the Bard has its own fascinating story to tell, and staff at the houses are happy to guide visitors on a journey encompassing what life might have been like in Stratford-upon-Avon during Shakespeare's day.

With the help of a £300,000 grant, the half-timbered house that is

Dusk over Stratford upon Avon

Shakespeare's Birthplace has been returned to the way it would have looked in his day. Household inventories, books and pictures have been assembled, and a

Montpellier Gallery

8 Chapel Street, Stratford-upon-Avon, Warwickshire CV37 6EP   Tel: 01789 261161
e-mail: peter@montpelliergallery.com
website: www.montpelliergallery.com

Located in the heart of Stratford-upon-Avon since 1991, **Montpellier Gallery** enjoys a strong reputation for the contemporary works it shows – paintings, printmaking, ceramics, studio glass, sculpture and contemporary jewellery. The Gallery is run by Peter Burridge, a trained jeweller/silversmith and an established artist-printmaker in his own right. It is his broad knowledge of the fine arts and his discerning eye for selecting pieces of quality, originality and form which gives the gallery a refreshing breadth of choice. This mix ensures a unique visual excitement of colour and stylistic diversity .

Montpellier gallery regularly features exhibitions of work by individual British artists and craftspeople, or shows a variety of media sharing a common theme. Between exhibitions, the varied displays represent a selection of the finest work by new and recognised makers, "Bringing" says Peter "fresh expectations along with the continuity from earlier traditions". He finds there is a ready responsiveness and enthusiasm for new talent, together with a loyalty and appreciation of established names. With prices ranging from £20 to around £3,500 and a dazzling variety of pieces by more than 300 of Britain's leading makers, many Craft Council Selected, the Gallery offers inspiration for those looking for imaginative and original ideas.

room thought to have been his father John's workshop was been re-created with the help of the Worshipful Company of Glovers.

Further along, on Chapel Street, stands **Nash's House**. This half-timbered building was inherited by Shakespeare's granddaughter, Elizabeth Hall, from her first husband, Thomas Nash. It now contains an exceptional collection of Elizabethan furniture and tapestries, as well as displays, upstairs, on the history of Stratford. The spectacular Elizabethan-style knot garden is an added attraction. Next door, in New Place, Shakespeare bought a house where he spent his retirement years, from 1611 to 1616. Today all that can be seen are the gardens and foundations of where the house once stood. An exhibit in Nash's House explains why this, Shakespeare's final home in Stratford, was destroyed in the 18th century. Opposite New Place is

the **Guild Chapel**, and beyond this is the Grammar School, where it is believed that Shakespeare was educated.

Hall's Croft in Old Town is one of the best examples of a half-timbered gabled house in Stratford. It was named after Dr John Hall, who married Shakespeare's daughter Susanna in 1607. This impressive house contains outstanding 16th and 17th century furniture and paintings. There is also a reconstruction of Dr Hall's 'consulting room', accompanied by an exhibition detailing medical practices during Shakespeare's time. Outside, the beautiful walled garden features a large herb bed; visitors can take tea near the 200-year-old mulberry tree or have lunch in the restaurant here.

Hall's Croft is near **Holy Trinity Church**, an inspiration for many poets and artists because of its beautiful setting beside the River Avon. It is here that

EVERSLEY BEARS

37 Grove Road, Stratford-upon-Avon, Warks. CV37 6PB
Tel: 01789 292334

Teddy bear lovers will be in their element at **Eversley Bears**, an outstanding bed & breakfast establishment with a 4-Diamonds rating from both the AA and the English Tourism Board. A 4-feet high bear stands by the front door to greet guests and many others are scattered around the house, lounging on the landings and there are even little ones on the door handles. This teddy bear sanctuary is the home of Clayton Doherty and Sarah Barker-Doherty, both of whom are professionally involved in theatre production, direction and teacher.

They are joint artistic directors of Stratford's Carpe Diem Theatre

which is dedicated to "developing the human potential in young people through performing arts training and performance opportunities". Naturally, they are happy to give advice on Stratford's theatres and to source tickets if required. Currently, the house has 6 attractively decorated and furnished guest bedrooms, 2 of them en suite (with more to follow), and include 2 family rooms which can sleep up to 4 – cots are available if needed. All rooms have remote control colour TV and hospitality tray. An excellent breakfast is included in the tariff and vegetarians can be catered for.

Shakespeare is buried. Dating partly from the 13th century, it is approached down an attractive avenue of limes. The north door has a sanctuary knocker, used in the past to ensure any fugitive who reached it 37 days' grace. Shakespeare's wife Anne Hathaway and their daughter Susanna and her husband John Hall are also buried here.

Shakespeare is not the only illustrious name to have associations with the town. **Harvard House** in the High Street, dating from 1596, was the childhood home of Katherine Rogers. Her son, John Harvard, went to the American Colonies in the early 1600s and founded the university named after him in 1636. In 1909 Harvard House was restored and presented to Harvard University. It boasts the most ornately carved timbered frontage in the town. Cared for by the Shakespeare Birthplace Trust, it houses the nationally important Neish Collection of Pewter.

There are many fascinating old buildings in Stratford. The old market site in Rother Street has a history dating from 1196, when a weekly market was granted by King John. In the square is an ornate fountain-cum-clock tower, a gift from GW Childs of Philadelphia in the

Bridge over Avon, Stratford

jubilee year of Queen Victoria. It was unveiled by the actor Sir Henry Irving, who in 1895 became the first Knight of the Stage.

Stratford has become a mecca for theatre-lovers, who flock to enjoy an evening at one of the town's three theatres. The first commemoration of Shakespeare's passing was organised by the actor David Garrick (of Garrick Theatre and the Garrick Club fame), 150 years after the Bard's death. People have been celebrating this illustrious poet and playwright's life and times ever since. The **Royal Shakespeare Company** has an unrivalled reputation both in the UK and worldwide, and wherever the RSC perform, the audience are certain of witnessing performances of the highest standard. The

BANCROFT CRUISES

Stratford Moat House, Bridgefoot, Stratford-upon-Avon CV37 6YR
Tel: 01789 269669   e-mail: captain@bancroftcruises.co.uk
Fax: 01789 204483   website: www.bancroftcruises.co.uk

A well-established family business operating from the heart of Stratford-upon-Avon, **Bancroft Cruises** specialises in providing custom-made packages for personal parties, school groups and corporate entertainment. The company's two elegant passenger boats cruise a lovely 4 miles of the river taking in the Royal Shakespeare Theatre, Holy Trinity Church, the hand-operated chain ferry, 15th century Clopton Bridge and passes beautiful riverside gardens. Between April and October, half-hour, one-hour or full day cruises are available and a tour guide is always on board to point out places of interest. Bar and catering facilities are available.

THE VINTNER RESTAURANT & CAFÉ WINEBAR

Sheep Street, Stratford-upon-Avon, Warwickshire, CV37 6EF
Tel: 01789 297259 Fax: 01789 266779
e-mail: info@the-vintner.co.uk
website: www.the_vintner.co.uk

Occupying a charming old building dating back to 1490, **The Vintner Restaurant & Café Winebar** derives its name from the Elizabethan John Smith who traded here as a wine merchant (vintner) in the early 1600s – Shakespeare himself may well have been a customer! The building itself, a genuinely unique example of timber-framed Tudor architecture has remained largely unchanged, still displaying a wealth of oak beams and flagstone floors.

The restaurant has been owned and run since 1989 by Nick Mills who prides himself on offering a fine mixture of traditional English cooking and Pan-European cuisine all day (10am to 10pm), every

day. Each day, special dishes prepared by the team of chefs make imaginative use of fresh, local produce. Whether you are enjoying a long, leisurely brunch, a full Sunday roast dinner or celebrating some special event in the Taittinger Room with its magnificent chestnut dining table capable of seating up to 24 guests, the superb cuisine, meticulous attention to detail and unobtrusive service all combine to make dining at The Vintner an experience to remember. The restaurant is just a 2-minute walk from the River Avon, the Shakespeare properties and the Royal Shakespeare Theatre, making it an ideal venue for a pre-theatre lunch or supper – but booking is essential!

COUNTRY ARTISTS FACTORY SHOP & VISITOR CENTRE

The Mill, Avenue Farm, Stratford-upon-Avon,
Warwickshire CV37 0HS
Tel: 01789 200720 Fax: 01789 200721
website: www.countryartists.co.uk

It was just over 25 years ago that Richard Cooper began making his superb wildlife sculptures and figurines. Today, his company is recognised throughout the world as a market leader in its field. Originally, Richard only featured birds and owls but now the range includes cats and dogs, lions and tigers, horses and humming-birds, all extraordinarily life-like and beautifully detailed. Country Artists also offers the humorous Tuskers range of elephant models, a series for hedgehog lovers, Hedgies, and A Breed Apart, a new sculpted range of species including dogs, cats, domestic and wild animals.

The whole story of the manufacturing process is revealed during a guided tour of the painting studio, at the **Country Artists Factory Shop and Visitor Centre**. Here visitors can also see the artists at work and marvel at their skill and dexterity. Once the tour is complete, visitors are free to browse in the spacious factory shop which display not only sculptures from the current collection but also many pieces from discontinued series. The shop is open daily, 9am-5pm (Sunday: 10am-4pm).

Royal Shakespeare Theatre opened in 1879 with a performance of *Much Ado About Nothing* starring Ellen Terry and Beerbohm Tree. The season was limited to one week as part of a summer festival. It was so successful that, under the direction of FR Benson, it grew to spring and summer seasons, touring the nation in between. In 1925, because of the excellence of the performances and direction, the company was granted a Royal Charter. Sadly, a year later the

Royal Shakespeare Theatre

theatre was destroyed by fire. At the time, playwright George Bernard Shaw sent a one-word telegram: Congratulations! Apparently the building was a bit of an eyesore, but there are few such buildings in today's Stratford. The company, undeterred, continued by giving performances in cinemas while a worldwide fundraising campaign was launched to build a new theatre, which was opened on 23rd April, 1932, the 368th anniversary of the Bard's birth. A tour of the RSC theatre gives visitors the opportunity to discover what goes on behind the scenes and to see the RSC collection of over 1,000 items.

STRATFORD BUTTERFLY FARM

Tramway Walk, Swans Nest Lane, Stratford upon Avon, Warwickshire CV37 7LS
Tel: 01789 299288 Fax: 01789 415878
e-mail: sales@butterflyfarm.co.uk
website: www.butterflyfarm.co.uk

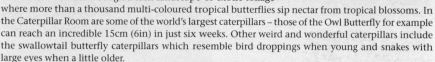

Why not treat yourself to a day trip to the tropics? At **Stratford Butterfly Farm** the temperature is a constant 26° centigrade and visitors can wander through a lush landscape of exotic foliage where more than a thousand multi-coloured tropical butterflies sip nectar from tropical blossoms. In the Caterpillar Room are some of the world's largest caterpillars – those of the Owl Butterfly for example can reach an incredible 15cm (6in) in just six weeks. Other weird and wonderful caterpillars include the swallowtail butterfly caterpillars which resemble bird droppings when young and snakes with large eyes when a little older.

In addition to the caterpillars there's an Insect Room whose fascinating inhabitants include praying mantids, giant beetles, tropical grasshoppers, crabs, giant millipedes and a colony of leaf-cutting ants which trek along a rope carrying their prized bits of leaves. Arachnophobes may be little hesitant about visiting Arachnoland. This spider and scorpion exhibit is home to the largest and most dangerous spiders from across the world – the Goliath bird-eating spider and the Black Widow – and the largest scorpions in the world, the Imperial Scorpions from Africa. Europe's largest farm of its kind, the Butterfly Farm is open daily from 10am to 6pm (summer); 10am to dusk in winter.

THE FALSTAFF'S EXPERIENCE

The Shrieves House, Sheep Street,
Stratford-upon-Avon CV37 6EE
Tel/Fax: 01789 298070
e-mail: info@falstaffsexperience.co.uk
website: www.falstaffsexperience.co.uk

The Shrieve's House is a charming 17th century house whose spacious barn has been imaginatively converted to house Stratford's most unusual attraction, **The Falstaff's Experience**. William Shrieve was the first known tenant of the Shrieves House and was archer to King Henry VIII. Approached by way of a cobbled courtyard, the experience provides visitors with an informative, theatrical and light-hearted glimpse into the pages of history aided by numerous models and costumed actors. Owner Steve Devey promises "all the sights and smells of times gone by.....set within a genuinely haunted building". Open daily from 10.30am to 5.30pm.

Quite apart from the industry that has grown around Shakespeare and his life and times, Stratford boasts a number of other world-class attractions. Stratford's **Butterfly Farm** (see panel on page 411) provides a specially designed and constructed habitat for Europe's largest collection of butterflies. There is also an area devoted to Insect City and, for the brave of heart, Arachnoland where the world's largest spider, rain forest scorpion colonies and other 'spinners' can be seen in perfect safety.

The Royal Shakespeare Theatre Summer House on Avonbank Gardens is home to the **Stratford Brass Rubbing Centre**, which contains a large collection of exact replicas of brasses of knights and ladies, scholars, merchants and priests of the past. Admission is free; a small charge is made for the special paper and wax required.

AROUND STRATFORD-UPON-AVON

SHOTTERY
1 mile W of Stratford off the A422

This was the birthplace of Anne Hathaway, Shakespeare's wife. Here

visitors will find the Elizabethan farmhouse now known as **Anne Hathaway's Cottage**, and can retrace the steps which the courting couple, who married in 1582, might have taken. The epitome of the traditional thatched cottage, this delightful spot was home to Hathaways since the 15th century, up until some 70 years ago when the Shakespeare Birthplace Trust decided it

Anne Hathaway's Cottage

was time to open up the home to the public. The Hathaway bed, settle and other pieces of furniture owned by the family remain, and there is a traditional English cottage garden and orchard – plants and herbs grown by the Shakespeare Trusts' gardeners can be purchased. Other attractions of this handsome village are the Shakespeare Tree Garden, the tranquil Shottery Brook, and well-laid-out Jubilee Walks.

WILMCOTE

3 miles NW of Stratford off the A34

Another notable house connected with the poet is that of his mother, situated here in the village of Wilmcote, slightly off the well-beaten tourist track. **Mary Arden's House** is a striking Tudor farmhouse, now home to the Shakespeare Countryside Museum of farming and rural life. Note in particular the bread oven doors, which are made of bog oak, which never burns, and are seen only very rarely now in England. Special events and demonstrations of traditional sheep shearing, weaving and spinning, crook making and other country crafts are held throughout the year, as well as celebrations and entertainments based on accounts from Shakespeare's plays, in

particular *A Winter's Tale*. Best of all, however, is the dovecote of the house. Robert Arden, who was lord of the manor, was in this capacity the only villager allowed to have one. It has over 600 pigeon holes and, at nesting time, would house about 3,000 birds.

Wilmcote is also one of the few small villages left which retains its Victorian Gothic railway station.

CHARLECOTE

3 miles E of Stratford off the B4086

The National Trust's **Charlecote Park** is a magnificent stately home occupying extensive grounds overlooking the River Avon. Home of the Lucy family since 1247, the present house was built in the mid-1500s. Thomas Lucy was knighted here by Robert Dudley, Earl of Leicester, deputising for Elizabeth I, who spent two nights here in 1572. The house was comprehensively modernised during the 1700s, but when George Hamilton Lucy inherited it in 1823 he took the decision to 'turn the clock back' and create interiors according to rich Victorian 'Romantic' ideals of the Elizabethan era. The house, apart from the family wing which is still used by descendants of these early Lucys, has not been changed since. The lavish furnishings of the house include important pieces from William Beckford's Fonthill Abbey sale in 1823. A treasure-trove of historic works of sculpture and painting, no visitor can fail to be impressed by the house's sheer magnitude, grace and beauty. The park was landscaped by 'Capability' Brown and reflects his use of natural and man-made features

Charlecote Park

complementing each other. The park supports herds of red and fallow deer (in about 1583 the young William Shakespeare is alleged to have been caught poaching Sir Thomas' deer; years later he is said to have taken his revenge by using Sir Thomas as his inspiration for the fussy Justice Shallow in *The Merry Wives of Windsor*), as well as a flock of Jacobs sheep first introduced here in 1756.

Charlecote Mill is situated on the site of an earlier mill mentioned in the Domesday Book, at which time it was valued at six shillings, eight pence (33p). In 1978 this 18th century building was restored with the help of volunteers from Birmingham, and the west waterwheel was repaired at the expense of the BBC for their film of George Eliot's novel, *The Mill on the Floss*.

MORETON MORRELL

7 miles E of Stratford off the B4455

In the **Church of the Holy Cross** (Norman with 14th and 15th century rebuilding) is an effigy of Richard Murden, High Sheriff of Warwickshire in 1635. The village has an American connection. Richard Randolph had seven children baptised in the church, and his third son, William, went to Virginia in 1672. William was an ancestor of Thomas Jefferson, the third President of the USA and the man chiefly responsible for the drafting of the Declaration of Independence. In the same family were John Marshall, America's first Chief Justice, and General Robert E Lee, whose surrender to General Grant in 1865 brought the American Civil War to an end.

ASHORNE

5 miles NE of Stratford off the B4100

Here at Ashorne Hall visitors will find

the 'Mighty Cinema Organ Show' as well as guided tours of the world-famous **Nickelodeon Collection of Mechanical Music**, England's rarest collection of mechanically-played instruments. The collection includes music boxes, demonstrations of self-playing harps, violins, accordions, drums, magic pictures that come to life, fairground organs and life-size automata.

WELLESBOURNE

4 miles E of Stratford off the A429

Wellesbourne Wartime Museum is located on the site of a wartime airfield. On display are tools, ration books and an exhibit in the style of a contemporary battle operations control room. **The Wellesbourne Watermill** is a genuine brick-built working flour mill dating back to 1834. This restored mill on the River Dene, a tributary of the River Avon, is one of the few in the country which visitors can see working as it did when new. A video presentation prepares visitors for the mill itself, providing an insight into this heritage site. Demonstrations of the art and skill of milling stoneground flour are enacted and explained by the miller, and visitors are encouraged to take part. Apart from the working demonstrations, there are guided walks alongside the river and two ponds, tree trails, and coracle boats along the river. There is also a display of antique farm implements, a craft shop, and a tea room in the wonderful 18th century timber-framed barn where teas and lunches are served.

COMPTON VERNEY

6 miles E of Stratford off the B4086

Before crossing the Fosse Way, the Roman road that runs from Exeter to Lincoln passes **Compton Verney Manor House**. For many years closed to the

COMPTON VERNEY GALLERY & FINE ARTS

Compton Verney, Warks. CV35 9HZ
Tel: 01926 645500 Fax: 01926 645501
e-mail: cvhk@comptonverney.org.uk
website: www.comptonverney.org.uk

Destined to become one of Warwickshire's finest art showcases, **Compton Verney Gallery & Fine Arts** is scheduled to open to the public at Easter 2004. It will be housed in a superb 18th century mansion designed by Robert Adam that stands in 40 acres of exquisite parkland landscaped by 'Capability' Brown. The Gallery will display the huge treasury of paintings,

objects and furniture collected by Peter Moores and divided into 5 major collections. The southern European collection is devoted to works from the period 1540 to 1800 and is especially strong on Neapolitan art of that time.

The Northern European collection comes mostly from the period 1500 to 1600, while the Asian collection includes a display of 12 Tang Dynasty (618-907AD) ceramic equestrian figures. Highlights of the British collection include 16th and 17th century portraits of royal figures such as Henry VIII, Edward VI and Elizabeth I as well as leading figures of the time like Thomas Cromwell, the Earl of Essex and the Duchess of Richmond and Lennox. Finally, the British Folk Art collection is devoted to fascinating pieces from the late 1800s to the early 1900s. While the Gallery is being prepared, a programme of outdoor events is being prepared for Summer 2003 – details on the Gallery's website.

public, this magnificent manor has been renovated and is now open to visitors. An exquisite collection of works of art has been assembled, including British portraiture, European Old Masters and modern works, along with a unique collection of British Folk Art. Workshops, evening talks, lectures and special events bring to life the processes and inspiration behind some of these great works. The manor house stands in 40 acres of parkland landscaped by Capability Brown and rich in flora and fauna, with a lake, arbour, stirring stone obelisk, Victorian watercress bed, Cedar of Lebanon, and Adam Bridge. The handsome avenue of Wellingtonias lines what was once the entrance to the estate.

KINETON

8 miles E of Stratford on the B4086

This pleasant old market town is a peaceful retreat with an old Courthouse and several 17th and 18th century houses. To the south-east of the town is the site of the **Battle of Edgehill**, fought here in October 1642. For the Royalists this was the first and one of the most devastating clashes of the Civil War. A year after the battle, Charles I was again in Kineton to meet his wife, Henrietta Maria, who had spent the previous night in Shakespeare's house as the guest of the poet's daughter Susanna.

GAYDON

8 miles E of Stratford off the B4100

The **Heritage Motor Centre** (see panel on page 416) in Gaydon hosts a most impressive collection of historic British cars, and also offers a variety of outdoor activities for the whole family.

This fascinating Centre tells the story of the British motor industry from 1896 to the present day. It boasts about 200 exclusively British vehicles from the world-famous makes of Rover, Austin, Morris, Wolseley, Riley, Standard, Triumph, MG and Austin Healey. The 65-acre site also features a 4 x 4 off-road demonstration circuit.

FENNY COMPTON

11 miles E of Stratford off the A423

This charming village close to **Burton Dassett Hills Country Park** and just half a mile from the **Oxford Canal** provides endless opportunities for scenic walks along the edge of the **Cotswold Scarp**.

Burton Dassett Park itself is distinguished by rugged open hilltops topped by a 14th-century beacon with marvellous views in all directions.

HERITAGE MOTOR CENTRE

Banbury Road, Gaydon, Warwick CV35 0BJ
Tel: 01926 645042 website: www.heritage.org.uk

The Heritage Motor Centre, Gaydon is home to the largest collection of historic British cars in the world. With 200 vehicles on display, the exhibits chart the history of the British car industry from the turn of the century to the present day. Set in 63 acres of grounds, the Centre has activities to appeal to the whole family including a stroll

through the nature reserve, the thrill of the Land Rover off road demonstration course and at weekends and school holidays, children's quad bikes and electric cars. There is a licensed cafe and gift shop and it can be found minutes from junction 12 M40.

FARNBOROUGH

11 miles SE of Stratford off the B4086

The National Trust's **Farnborough Hall** is a lovely honey-coloured stone house

CRANDON HOUSE

Avon Dassett, nr Warwick CV47 2AA
Tel: 01295 770652 Fax: 01295 770632
e-mail: crandonhouse@talk21.com
website: www.crandonhouse.co.uk

Set in 20 acres with beautiful views and surrounded by the peaceful south Warwickshire countryside, **Crandon House** offers an exceptionally high standard of accommodation, comfort and personal service. Guests receive a specially warm welcome from Deborah Lea at this lovely farmhouse, the focal point of a small working farm with a variety of livestock that includes rare British White cattle,

Southdown sheep, and free range poultry, ducks and geese. The beautifully maintained garden with its ornamental pool and the traditional farmland supports an abundance of wildlife.

The house has 3 attractive double and twin-bedded rooms, all with en suite or private bathrooms or shower, colour television, tea and coffee tray, hairdryer and many thoughtful extras to make your stay enjoyable. The Leas have recently converted the former dairy in the garden adjacent to the house into delightful guest accommodation with 2 de luxe en suite bedrooms, one of them on the ground floor. Each has a double and a single bed, colour television, trouser press with iron, hairdryer and tea/coffee tray. All rooms are non-smoking. Guests have the use of two sitting rooms, one with television, and there are some excellent village pubs and restaurants in the locality.

built in the mid-1700s and the home of the Holbech family for over 300 years. The interior features some superb plasterwork, and the delightful grounds include a terrace walk, 18th century temples and an obelisk.

WARMINGTON

10 miles SE of Stratford on the B4100

The **National Herb Centre** enjoys a great location on the northern edge of the Cotswolds on the B4100 close to the Warwickshire-Oxfordshire border. A centre for research and development work for the UK herb industry, the site has been developed with an eye towards providing visitors with a fascinating range of activities and sights. The Plant Centre has one of the widest selections of plants, trees and shrubs with herbal uses in the country. The Herb Shop stocks a range of herbs, health foods and gifts, many produced on site.

OXHILL

8 miles SE of Stratford off the A422

A charming village of brown and redbrick cottages on a tributary of the Stour. The Church of St Laurence is mainly Norman with a unique 12th century font lavishly sculpted and depicting Adam and Eve at the Tree of Life and an impressive Norman doorway decorated with strange faces peering through foliage.

UPTON HOUSE

11 miles SE of Stratford off the A422

Here on the border with Oxfordshire, Upton House is a late 17th century National Trust property built of the

RED HORSE GARDEN PRODUCTS

Banbury Road, Oxhill, nr Stratford upon Avon, Warwickshire CV35 0RL
Tel: 01926 642832 Fax: 01926 642853

For gardeners, **Red Horse Garden Products** really is a "one-stop shop" where they will find virtually anything they could possibly need to maintain and enhance their gardens. Naturally, there's an extensive range of bedding plants, bulbs, grass and vegetable seeds, along with anything from canes to composts, top soil to trellises, water features to well-rotted manure. Also on site is a huge variety of building and fencing materials, greenhouses and cedar gazebos along with pet foods, country clothing, and much, much more. The company also offers a full landscaping and gardening service.

THE WHITE HORSE INN

Banbury Road, Ettington, nr Stratford upon Avon, Warwickshire CV37 7SU
Tel: 01789 740641

Living in the village of Ettington for some 15 years, Kirk and Ali Waller always dreamed of running its classic 16th century pub, **The White Horse Inn,** and now they do. Originally three cottages, the inn now has a cosy lounge/dining area and a lively locals bar with pool and darts. The Wallers are members of the British Institute of Innkeeping which means that their ales, notably Fuller's London Pride and Pedigree, lagers and wines are all very well-maintained. The food too is outstanding, with fresh fish on Tuesday evenings a speciality, and the accommodation (3 doubles, 1 twin), maintains the same high standards.

mellow local stone. The house was remodelled in 1927-9 for the second Viscount Bearsted to house his growing art collection and also to modernise the premises. The collections in the house are the chief attractions, featuring paintings by English and Continental Old Masters including El Greco, Brueghel, Bosch, Hogarth and Stubbs. Brussels tapestries, Sèvres porcelain, Chelsea figures and 18th century furnishings are also on display. In the fine gardens, in summer there can be seen the typically English scene of white-clad cricketers; in winter, the Warwickshire Hunt hold their meet here.

UPPER TYSOE

8 miles SE of Stratford off the A422

From Upper Tysoe there is a lovely walk south over **Windmill Hill** (which actually has a windmill on it), taking you

to the church on the edge of **Compton Wynyates Park**, with views of the attractive Tudor manor below – a refreshing bit of brick building in this Cotswold-edge stone country.

HONINGTON

8 miles SE of Stratford off the A3400

Honington Hall encapsulates the architectural and decorative styles popular in the late 17th and 18th centuries. Opening times are limited but the Hall is well worth a visit, presenting many delightful examples of Regency tastes and refinements.

SHIPSTON-ON-STOUR

9 miles SE of Stratford off the A3400

For centuries, Shipston-on-Stour was an important agricultural centre, in the heart of a rural district known as 'Feldon'. From the 1200s tradesmen and

---

CHURCH STREET GALLERY

24 Church Street, Shipston on Stour, Warks. CV36 4AP
Tel: 01608 662431
e-mail: tonyfield2000@aol.com
website:www.churchstreetgallery.co.uk

At the **Church Street Gallery** you'll find a huge choice of antique maps and prints on sale at realistic prices. Owner Tony Field has some 30 years experience in the business and his stock includes a wide range of topographical prints, late 18th and 19th century oils and watercolours, striking botanical and ornithological prints, all original hand-coloured, hunting and fashion prints, as well as humorous prints from Vanity Fair and Punch. Tony's wife Mary runs the excellent picture framing service, offering hundreds of frames in both traditional and contemporary colours and styles. A cleaning and restoration service is available.

THE FOX & HOUNDS INN

Great Wolford, nr Moreton in Marsh, Warks. CV36 5NQ
Tel: 01608 674220   e-mail: info@thefoxandhoundsinn.com
Fax: 01608 684871   website: www.thefoxandhoundsinn.com

"This pub has it all - the beams, the fire, the faded prints, the characters, fine food and a splendid owner!" Such was the enthusiastic report by the *Sunday Express* on **The Fox & Hounds Inn**, a delightful old hostelry which has been trading since 1540AD. It was Wendy Veale's local for 11 years before she took over as licensee in 2000 and enhanced the inn's reputation for excellent food, with an ever-changing à la carte menu served in the evenings and bar meals only at lunchtimes. Real ales and fine wines are served and three comfortable en suite rooms are available for bed & breakfast guests. Look out for the unique pub sign!

craftsmen helped shape the town that remains to this day a centre for fascinating shops, galleries and antiques shops. The hills that surround the town are perfect for gentle strolls and cycling. This small town has quite a busy shopping centre, but is rewarding to stroll through, with a nice church and many handsome old stone buildings.

Long Compton

12 miles SE of Stratford off the A3400

Just a short distance from the Oxfordshire border, this handsome village lies close to the local beauty spot known as **Whichford Wood**. It is a pleasant Cotswold village of thatched stone houses and some antique shops. A mile or so to the south of Long Compton, straddling the Oxfordshire border, are the **Rollright Stones**, made up of the King Stone on one side of the lane, with the other two stone groupings – known as the King's Men and the Whispering Knights – on the other. Legend has it that this well-preserved stone circle is a king and his men, tricked by a sorceress into falling under her spell, and then petrified.

WEST WARWICKSHIRE

Knowle

1 mile SE of Solihull off the A4141

The Elizabethan **Grimshaw Hall** in Knowle is a fine example of a carefully restored building of great historic significance. Nearby **Chester House** was built in the mid-1300s; it has been successfully refurbished and is today used as a library, thus offering a practical service to today's population.

Whichford Pottery

Whichford, nr Shipston-on-Stour, Warwickshire CV36 5PG
Tel: 01608 684416 Fax: 01608 684833
e-mail: flowerpots@whichfordpottery.com
website: www.whichfordpottery.com

Visit Whichford Pottery and be inspired by their seasonal plantings and watch craftsmen and women throw, mould and transform clay into classic terracotta garden pots.

All Whichford flowerpots are made entirely by hand, and come in all shapes and sizes from Long Toms to Lily pots to huge Urns (which have to be seen to be believed!). Whichford also produce the full range of old-fashioned horticultural ware - seedpans, alpine pots and forcers for seakale and rhubarb. All Whichford pots gain a beautiful, soft patina with age, and are guaranteed for 10 years in any weather, even severe frost. Jim and Dominique Keeling

founded Whichford Pottery in 1976. The partnership has produced five children, a thriving pottery and a range of collectable glazed earthenware. Each piece is entirely individual, decorated by Dominique. There is always a good selection on display in The Gallery Shop, together with jewellery, photography and work by other local artists and craftsmen. There is never a dull moment at the Pottery! Visitors can chat to the potters as they work (weekdays), browse through the full range of terracotta flowerpots and relax in the colourful courtyard garden. The pottery is open - Monday to Friday 9am to 5pm, Saturdays and Bank Holidays 10am to 4pm.

LAPWORTH

5 miles S of Solihull off the A3400

Here where the Grand Union and Stratford Canals meet, handsome Lapworth boasts some characterful old buildings. At Chadwick End, a mile west of the A4141, **Baddesley Clinton** is a romantic, medieval moated manor house which has changed little since 1633. Set against the backdrop of the Forest of Arden, this National Trust-owned property has had strong Catholic connections throughout its history. There is a tiny chapel in the house, and secret priests' holes, used to hide holy fathers during the fiercely anti-Catholic times during the reign of Charles I. The grounds feature a lovely walled garden and herbaceous borders, natural areas and lakeside walks. More modern additions to the site include the second largest ice rink in the country. Lunches and teas are available.

HENLEY-IN-ARDEN

7 miles S of Solihull off the A3400

Possibly the finest old market town in Warwickshire, its mile-long High Street brimming with examples of almost every kind of English architecture from the 15th century onwards, including many old timber-framed houses built with Arden oak. Little remains today of the

Henley-in-Arden

Forest of Arden, the setting adopted by William Shakespeare for his *As You Like It*, as its stocks were diminished in the 1700s by the navy's demand for timber, but nothing could diminish the beauty of Henley itself.

The town emerged initially under the protection of Thurston de Montfort, Lord of the Manor in 1140. **Beaudesert Castle**, home to the de Montfort family, lies behind the churches of St John and

TORQUIL POTTERY & THE GALLERY UPSTAIRS

81 High Street, Henley in Arden, Warwickshire B95 5AT
Tel: 01564 792174

Torquil Pottery occupies a 16th century half-timbered building and is easy to find on the mile long, tree-lined High Street of Henley-in-Arden (A3400). The shop is a treasure trove of pottery, glass and jewellery from makers all over the country as well as that of the two resident potters whose workshop overlooks the garden. Above the workshop is the spacious **Gallery Upstairs**, which hosts two large group exhibitions a year in May and November, displaying paintings, ceramics and sculpture. The gallery has splendid views of the gardens and Henley's famous "Mount". We look forward to your visit

St Nicholas, where remains of the castle mound can still be seen. Famous visitors of the past to this delightful town have included Dr Johnson, his friend James Boswell, and the poet Shenstone.

The 15th century **Church of St John the Baptist** has a tower which dominates the High Street where it narrows near the ancient Guildhall. The roof of the Guildhall is supported by oak beams which were growing at the time of the Norman invasion, and a wooden candelabra hangs from the ceiling. At one end of the hall is a huge dresser displaying a set of pewter plates dating back to 1677. The charter granted to the town has a royal seal embossed in green wax, kept in its own glass case in the Guildhall.

The town's **Court Leet** still meets yearly with the lord of the manor at its head, as it has for centuries. Members of this distinguished grouping have included the High Bailiff, Low Bailiff, Ale-taster (now there's a job!), Butter-weigher, the Mace bearer, the Town Crier, the Town Constable, the Two Affearers and the Two Brook Lockers. Just outside Henley lies **Beaudesert**, a village even older than its near neighbour Henley, with a good few timber-framed cottages and the beautifully restored Norman church of St Nicholas.

WOOTTON WAWEN

9 miles S of Solihull off the A3400

Handy for walks on nearby **Stratford Canal**, Wootton Wawen also contains some fine timber-framed buildings and Warwickshire's oldest church – **St Peter's**, an impressive structure that still has its Saxon tower, now more than a thousand years old. The main building is actually three churches in one; there are three completely separate chapels tacked on to each other with a refreshing

YEW TREE FARM CRAFT CENTRE

Wootton Wawen, Henley in Arden, Warwickshire B95 6BY
Tel: 01564 792701

The Haimes family came to **Yew Tree Farm** following the atrocious winter of 1947. In those days, corn was still stored in the Granary (now home to Palm Spring Interiors), ground up in the Milling Shed and fed to the cows housed in what is now The Heron's Nest Restaurant where visitors can enjoy fresh morning coffee, snacks, delicious home-made light lunches, and mouth-watering afternoon teas with home-made cakes. The farm's dairy, half a century ago, is today's Farm Shop selling locally produced fruit and vegetables, jams, honey, sausages, ice cream, home-made cakes and pies baked on the farm, along with unusual craft and gift ideas, garden ornaments and barrels. In the old days, waste milk and grain was used in the Pig Sty, currently housing Arden Books which sells secondhand and out of print maps, prints, posters, postcards, stamps and stationery.

At the Cart House Stable, the working horses have been replaced by Knot Just Wood producing hand-made furniture, kitchens and bedrooms. Other units are used by everything from bookbinding to Crafty Ideas (craft supplies). Le Grenier Antiques (see separate entry), and The Garden Furniture centre which stocks the largest range of quality garden furniture in the Midlands. It supplies fully assembled pieces ranging from dining suites to loungers and benches, as well as picnic tables, small marquees, gazebos and much more. Bed & Breakfast is available in our Georgian Farmhouse.

WALK 8

Aston Cantlow and Wilmcote

Start	Aston Cantlow
Distance	6½ miles (10.5 km)
Approximate time	3 hours
Parking	Roadside parking at Aston Cantlow
Refreshments	Pub at Aston Cantlow, pubs at Wilmcote
Ordnance Survey maps	Landranger 151 (Stratford-upon-Avon), Pathfinders 997, SP05/15 (Stratford-upon-Avon (West) & Alcester) and 975, SP06/16 (Redditch & Henley-in-Arden)

There is a strong Shakespearian theme to this walk in the countryside of Arden. It starts by the church at Aston Cantlow in which his parents were married and heads across fields to his mother's childhood home at Wilmcote. Then follows an attractive stretch by the Stratford-upon-Avon Canal before tracks and field paths lead back to the start.

Shakespeare's mother and father were married in the 15th century church at Aston Cantlow and went to live in Stratford-upon-Avon where William, the third of their ten children, was born in 1564. Start by the King's Head and turn along Church Lane. Turn left into the churchyard and at a fork, take the left-hand tarmac path to a stile. Climb the stile, walk along an enclosed path, cross a footbridge and keep straight ahead across a field to climb a stile on to a lane **A** .

Climb the stile opposite, walk along a track and where it bends right, keep ahead along the right edge of a field and climb a stile on to a lane **B** . Turn left and after nearly ½ mile (800m), turn left **C** , at a public footpath sign, through a hedge gap to a stile. Climb the stile, keep along the left edge of a field and on joining a track, turn right along it and go through a metal

gate on to a road. Continue along the lane ahead, signposted to Wilmcote, and at a public footpath sign turn right through a metal gate **D** .

Follow a track along the right edge of a field and after passing a redundant stile, turn half-left and walk across the field to a waymarked post at the base of a wooded ridge.

Head uphill through trees and bushes, by a wire fence on the left, and just after passing a shed, turn right over a stile. Turn left along a narrow path which bends right and continues (between fences) to a stile. Climb the stile, turn right along a track and at a public footpath sign, turn left through a metal kissing-gate. Keep ahead to go through another one and continue along the left edge of a succession of fields. In the last field corner, keep ahead along an enclosed path to emerge on to a road on a new housing estate. Turn right, take the first turning on the left and at a T-junction, turn left again into Wilmcote.

By the Mary Arden Inn and a small green, turn right **E**, signposted Stratford and Henley, passing Mary Arden's House. This fine Tudor farmhouse was where Shakespeare's mother was born and lived as a girl. Some of the buildings now house a museum of local farming and rural life. After crossing a canal bridge, turn left over a stile **F** and descend to the towpath of the Stratford-upon-Avon Canal. This was completed in 1816 to provide a link between Birmingham and the River Avon at Stratford. Keep along the towpath as far as the first bridge, turn left over it **G**, climb a stile, turn right along the right edge of a field and climb another stile.

Keep along the right edge of the next field and at a waymarked post, turn left and head across the field to the next post. Now follow a line of posts across a large field, heading gently uphill, climb a stile on the far side and continue along the left edge of the next field. Climb a stile at a crossroads of paths, bear slightly right and walk across the next field to climb another stile. Continue across the next field and near the far corner of the field, climb a stile on to a track.

Turn right to a lane and turn left **H** through the

hamlet of Newnham. Take the left-hand lane at a fork and where it ends, keep ahead along a track and go through a metal gate.

Continue along the left edge of a field, pass through a gap and bear left across the corner of the next field to a stile. Climb the stile, keep along the left edge of a field, climb another stile and continue along a track to a road **J**. Turn left – over the brow of the hill the village and church tower of Aston Cantlow lie ahead.

Where the road bends right, keep ahead through a metal gate, climb a stile and walk along the right edge of a field. Pass through a hedge gap, keep along the right edge of the next field, cross a footbridge over a ditch and turn right along a tarmac track to a road **K**. Turn left along the road and follow it back to the start. ●

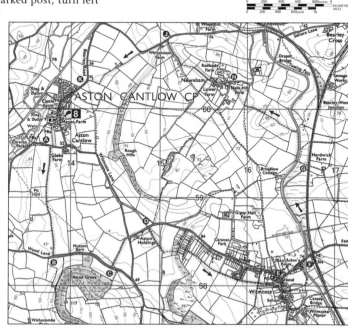

LE GRENIER ANTIQUES

Yew Tree Craft Centre, Stratford Road, Wootton
Wawen, Henley in Arden, Warwickshire B95 6BY
Tel: 01564 795401
e-mail: info@legrenierantiques.com
website: www.legrenierantiques.com

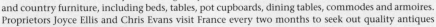

A passion for fine wood and a strong connection with
the south of France are the twin elements behind the
success of **Le Grenier Antiques**, located at the Yew Tree
Craft Centre in Wootton Wawen. In the 2000 square
feet showroom there's always a dazzling array of fine
and country furniture, including beds, tables, pot cupboards, dining tables, commodes and armoires.
Proprietors Joyce Ellis and Chris Evans visit France every two months to seek out quality antiques
which are then shipped out from La Rochelle.

At any one time their stock might include a late 19th
century solid walnut French bed with unique carving to
head and foot, or an early 18th century French armoire in
cherrywood. The complete current range is displayed on
their website. Le Grenier also stocks a range of chairs in
traditional French styles, in walnut or cherrywood, which
are manufactured by a company that has been making
chairs since 1745. Joyce has many years experience in the
restoration of painted furniture, in particular pen work,
and the company is delighted to undertake commissions
and searches at customers' request.

disregard for architectural design which
does not in any way detract from the
church's charm. One of these chapels,
the barn-roofed Lady Chapel, is now **The
Saxon Sanctuary**, a colourful exhibition
that traces the history of 'Wagen's'
woodland village in the Forest of Arden.
It reveals how this small village conceals
a Roman road, two monasteries, an
ancient fort, mysterious underground
passages, a river that changes with
fashion, a disappearing pond and
an aqueduct!

St Peter's stands within a picturesque
churchyard which has won the Diocesan
'Best Kept' award several times. Next to
the church stands **Wotton Hall**, dating
from 1637. Maria Fitzherbert, wife of
George IV, spent her childhood here and
is thought now to return in ghostly form
as the 'Grey Lady' who has been seen
wandering about the Hall.

ALCESTER

15 miles S of Solihull off the A435

Alcester is an ancient Roman market
town built on the **Icknield Street
Encampment**. It boasts several very
pretty cottages on **Maltmill Lane** and a
handsome Norman church. Alcester is
popular for good local walks along the
confluence of the Rivers Alne and Arrow.
The town has been regional winner of a
Britain in Bloom award.

COUGHTON

2 miles N of Alcester off the A435

The parish church of this very pretty
village was built by Sir Robert
Throckmorton between 1486 and 1518.
It has six bells which were restored in
1976 but are still carried in their original
wooden frame. Inside there are some
interesting oddments: a faceless clock,
fish weather vanes and a dole cupboard

from which wheaten loaves were distributed to the needy.

The crowning glory of the village is one of the great Tudor houses, **Coughton Court**, home of the Throckmorton family since 1409. The family were very prominent in Tudor times and were instigators of Catholic emancipation, playing a part in the Gunpowder Plot – the wives of some of the Gunpowder Plotters awaited the outcome of the Plot in the imposing

Coughton Court

central gatehouse. This, and the half-timbered courtyard, are particularly noteworthy, while inside there are important collections of paintings, furniture, porcelain and other family items from Tudor times to the present day. Treasured possessions include the chemise of Mary, Queen of Scots and the Throckmorton Coat; the former was worn by Queen Mary at her execution in 1587. The Coat was the subject of a 1000 guinea wager in 1811. The priest's hole found in the house was constructed by one of the most famous builders of hiding places, Nicholas Owen.

This National Trust property has extensive gardens (a new formal walled garden and bog garden) and grounds, a lake, a riverside walk and two churches to add to the interest. The fountain pool in the courtyard leads out to formal paths of lime trees. Spring heralds a magnificent display of over 100,000 daffodils and other spring blooms. The grounds also boast a walk planted with willows and native shrubs and trees beside the River Arrow, a new bog garden, a formal orchard and a walled garden project opened in 1996 and maturing into a splendid example of

garden 'rooms' set with their own particular plant themes. One herbaceous border is planted with cools blues and yellows, the other with hot reds and orange. Also on site there is the Tudor Restaurant serving coffee, lunches and teas, an attractive gift shop and a plant centre.

A little way east of Coughton, at **Kinwarton** just south of the B4089, there stands another National Trust property in the shape of **Kinwarton Dovecote**. This circular 14th century dovecote still houses doves and retains its 'potence', a pivoted ladder by which access is possible to the nesting boxes. Visitors can home in every day from April to October.

Arrow

1 mile S of Alcester off the A422

The village of Arrow is interesting to stroll around (despite some development) - as is the pretty stream that divides Arrow and Alcester. Though fruit farming around here is much rarer than it used to be, there are still to be found delicious fresh dessert plums for sale in the late summer and early autumn.

Nearby **Ragley Hall** is a genuine 17th century treasure. The Warwickshire home of the Marquess and Marchioness of Hertford, it is a perfectly symmetrical Palladian house set in 400 acres of parkland and gardens landscaped by Capability Brown. One of England's great Palladian country houses, it was inherited by the eighth Marquess in 1940 when he was only nine. During the Second

Ragley Hall

World War the house was used as a hospital, and thereafter became almost completely derelict. In 1956 the Marquess married, and he and his wife set about making the Hall their home. All the main rooms have been redecorated in colours similar to the original ones that would have been used, and the process of restoring and improving continues. This magnificent stately home boasts James Gibb's elegant Baroque plasterwork in the Great Hall, as well as Graham Rust's stunning 20th century mural, 'The Temptation'. A tour takes in Ragley Hall's fabulous collection of treasures from a bygone age, featuring paintings (including some modern art), china, furniture and a goodly assortment of Victorian and Edwardian dolls and toys. The Stables house an impressive carriage collection.

The main formal garden, to the west of the Hall, descends in a series of wide terraces, now entirely occupied by roses. The rest of the garden, covering 24 acres, consists of shrubs and trees interspersed with spacious lawns providing vistas across the 400 acre park. The lake, created in 1625, is now used for fishing, sailing, swimming and water skiing;

there is also a lakeside picnic area. The cricket pitch is in regular use. A country trail of about two miles wends its way through the park and the woods, to end at a very popular adventure playground. The Hall also boasts licensed terrace tea rooms. Special events such as craft fairs, gardeners' weekends, dog trials and outdoor concerts are held throughout the year.

Long Marston

6 miles SE of Alcester off the B4632

Charles I stayed at a house in Long Marston after his flight from the Battle of Worcester. The village's 14th century church has a half-timbered turret and porch. From Long Marston there's access to **The Greenway**, a converted railway line ideal for cycling or walking. This open public greensward boasts two and a half miles of surfaced paths amid beautiful scenery, with picnic areas and a tranquil atmosphere of rural calm.

Ilmington

9 miles SE of Alcester off the B4632

Along the northeastern Cotswolds, at the foot of the Wilmington Downs, you'll

come to the village of Ilmington. This eye-catching place has several lovely old houses. Its part-Norman church, which features oak furnishings by Robert Thompson of Yorkshire, is approached through a Norman arch. This is truly a hidden place and one of the most picturesque one could hope to find. Lying in the valley between the Campden and Foxcote hills, it is surrounded by green fields and Cotswold

Centenary Square, Birmingham

countryside. Here there are fine old stone cottages with roses round the doors, and gardens full of colour. The village's name means *'the elm grown hill'*. It was made famous on Christmas Day 1934, when the first radio broadcast by George V was introduced by Walton Handy, the village shepherd, and relayed to the world from **Ilmington Manor**, the fine Elizabethan house once owned by the de Montfort family. The remains of a tramway, once the main form of transport to the village, can still be seen.

The nearby **Ilmington Downs** are, at 850 feet, the highest point in the county, commanding fine views of the surrounding country. Across the B4632 you will pass **Meon Hill**, where an Iron Age fort stood dominating the valley.

BIRMINGHAM

Birmingham rewards a visit many times over with its wealth of museums, marvellous public spaces, historic buildings and myriad other sights, sounds and attractions. It is a city with a rich and varied industrial history taking in everything from the first steam engine

to button, buckles, clocks and chocolate.

Peter de Bermingham obtained rights of trading in a Market Charter granted in 1166 by King Henry II. By the mid-16th century there were some 1,500 people living in 200 homes, as well as one main street and a number of side-streets, markets for grain and livestock, and mills for tanning. Already the smiths were selling their knives and all manner of tools throughout England. This growth was helped along by the demands of the Parliamentarians, who during the Civil War needed a virtually endless supply of swords, pikes and armour. So it was that Birmingham emerged with a strong reputation as a metal centre.

By the 1750s the population had swelled to over 20,000, and by the time of the Industrial Revolution Birmingham had become the industrial, commercial and cultural capital of the Midlands. This was due in large part to the industriousness of the native 'Brummies'. Today this tradition continues, enhanced by the influx of peoples of differing nationalities and cultures, each adding their own unique gifts and talents to the mix.

The Birmingham Symphony Orchestra, recognised as one of the finest in the world, perform a regular season in the classical Roman-inspired Town Hall, built by Joseph Hansom, of hansom cab fame.

Sporting facilities abound in Birmingham and soccer clubs Aston Villa, Birmingham City and, not far away, Wolverhampton Wanderers, West Bromwich Albion and Walsall all provide opportunities to find

Birmingham Repertory Theatre

a good match in the season. Edgbaston of course, is synonymous with cricket, both county and test.

There are no fewer than 6,000 acres of parkland and open space in Birmingham. **Cannon Hill Park** in Edgbaston is one particular highlight. It has 80 acres of flower and ornamental gardens. Also in Edgbaston, on Westbourne Road, the **Botanical Gardens** comprise 15 acres and boast a Tropical House with lily pond, banana and cocoa trees, the Palm House, Orangery, National Bonsai Collection, Cactus House and the gardens themselves, filled with rhododendrons, azaleas and a good collection of trees. **Birmingham Nature Centre**, not far away on Pershore Road, has British and European wildlife – including wallaby, fallow deer, otters and reptiles – in indoor and outdoor enclosures resembling as closely as possible the creatures' native habitats.

The focus for shopping is the area bounded by New Street and Corporation Street; away from these areas there are some very attractive Victorian arcades which house the smaller speciality shops, including jewellers: Birmingham is traditionally a centre of jewellery, indeed

there is an 18th century church in St Paul's Square known simply as The Jewellers Church. The Jewellery Quarter Discovery Centre is a good place to start if you'd like to learn more about times past and present in the Birmingham jewellery trade. It is located on Vyse Street, centred round the preserved workshops of Smith & Pepper, still much as they were at the end of the 19th century.

The Museum and Art Gallery in Chamberlain Square represents the 17th, 18th and 19th centuries, including the world's finest collection of works by the Pre-Raphaelites. The contemporary art of sculpture is also well represented. Costume, silver, textiles and ceramics as well as works of ethnography from around the world, among which is a large and rare copper Buddha from Sultangani.

The Barber Institute at Birmingham University houses an excellent collection of paintings and sculptures. There is a wealth of Impressionist pieces, as well as the work of European masters.

Birmingham's newest museum is **Soho House**, a handsome Georgian building which has been carefully restored to its

Botanic Gardens, Edgbaston

The Hobbit and *Lord of the Rings*), it was used as a flour mill and also to roll and smooth metal needed during the Industrial Revolution. The present buildings are mainly Georgian, having been rebuilt in the 1760s, and were in commercial use right up to 1919. The mill then fell into disrepair, though it was later carefully restored to working order. Another nearby attraction well worth a visit is Castle Bromwich Hall Gardens, on Chester Road, about four miles east of the city centre. This boasts a collection of plants grown here in the 18th century, including historic herbs and vegetable species, shrubs and border plants, in a classic formal layout popular in the 1700s. Guided tours available.

original elegance. Former home of the pioneering industrialist Matthew Boulton, James Watt's business partner and founder of the Soho Mint, who lived here from 1766 to 1809, it contains some of his original furnishings. Displays relate the story of the man and his times, and offer a chance to see some of the fruits of Boulton's nearby factory – buttons and buckles, ormolu clocks and vases, silver and Sheffield plate tableware – where he and Watt developed the steam engine.

There are some 2,000 listed buildings in Birmingham, dating from the Elizabethan, Jacobean, Georgian and Victorian periods. The 1879 neo-Renaissance Council House is an impressive testament to the city's success and achievements. The Curzon Street Goods Station is a colonnaded building dating from 1838. Built by Philip Hardwick, its Ionic portico celebrates the wonder of the then-new railway industry.

Sarehole Mill in Cole Bank Road in Hall Green is Birmingham's only working water mill. The former childhood haunt of JRR Tolkien (author of

AROUND BIRMINGHAM

ASTON

2 miles N of Birmingham off the A34

Aston Hall was one of the last great Jacobean country houses to be built in

Aston Hall

England. Like Hatfield House and Blickling Hall, it has a highly intricate plan and a dramatic skyline of turrets, gables and chimneys. It is also administered by Birmingham Museum and Art Gallery, who have done much to make it a memorable place to visit. The house was built between 1618 and 1635 by Sir Thomas Holte, and remained the seat of the Holte family until it was sold off in 1817. King Charles I came to Aston Hall in 1642, at the beginning of the Civil War, and it was later besieged and sacked by Parliamentarian soldiers.

KINGSBURY

7 miles NE of Birmingham off the A4097

Kingsbury Water Park boasts over 600 acres of country park, with loads to see and do, including birdwatching, picnic sites, nature trails, fishing and good information centre. There is also a cosy café and special unit housing the park's shop and exhibition hall. Also with the park, **Broomey Croft Children's Farm** makes for an enjoyable and educational day out for all the family, with a wealth of animals housed in renovated early 19th century farm buildings.

YARDLEY

2 miles E of Birmingham off the A45/A4040

Blakesley Hall is Birmingham's finest Elizabethan building. Built in 1590, it is an extremely attractive timber-framed farmhouse which has been carefully restored. Its rich, decorative framing and jettied first and second floors reflect the wealth of its Elizabethan owner and builder, Richard Smallbroke, one of the leading merchants of the time. A diminutive and rare Long Gallery survives, while in Smallbroke's bedroom the original wall paintings were uncovered in 1950. Some of the 12 rooms are furnished to look as they did in 1684, when an inventory of the house's contents was drawn up.

Old Yardley village is one of Birmingham's outstanding conservation areas. Within walking distance of Blakesley Hall, it is truly remarkable for its medieval church and **Trust School**. Of particular note are the pretty Georgian cottages.

BOURNVILLE

4 miles S of Birmingham off the A4040

This planned village built by the Cadbury family, which moved its factory from the city centre in 1879, is a testament to good labour relations. **Cadbury World** is located in the heart of the famous Bournville factory. Here visitors can follow the story of chocolate, from tropical rain forests to 16th century Spain and on to Georgian London and, finally, Victorian Birmingham. Of course, a highlight of any tour here is the chance to sample the modern day product!

Cadbury World

6 miles SE of Birmingham off the A34

Solihull began life as a sparsely populated village in a relatively under-populated part of the country. It did not begin to grow in size, industry and importance until the 1930s. Its motto - 'urbs in rure' (town in country) - is well deserved. Its cottages and houses, since medieval times, have always blended in well with the greenery which covers a large swathe of the surrounding region. Today, Solihull's existing 17th and 18th century houses clearly demonstrate the good planning, which has always been a hallmark of this town's social and architectural design.

Coventry Cathedral

COVENTRY

Although on the fringe of the West Midlands conurbation, Coventry is surrounded by some of the finest scenery and places of historic interest in the country. It claims among many of its famous sons and daughters the novelist George Eliot, who attended boarding school in Warwick Row and lived with her father here between 1841 and 1849 in Floeshill Road, and the poet Philip Larkin, born in the city in 1922.

The three spires of Coventry's Christchurch, Holy Trinity and St Michael's dominate the city skyline. During the terrible bombing inflicted on the city during the Second World War, St Michael's suffered direct hits. Its spire

and ruined windows are all that remains, evoking both the horror and the spirit of reconciliation that arose from those times. Standing in the ruins of these 14th century remains can be a strange and moving experience. The altar is made of broken stones gathered from the night of 15th November 1940. It is surmounted by a cross of charred roof beams and a cross of medieval nails, behind which are inscribed the words from Calvary, 'Father Forgive.'

The new **Cathedral**, designed by Basil Spence, stands by its side, and together they symbolise sacrifice and resurrection. Though unashamedly modern, its vast and striking interior conveys a powerful sense of the past. The **Cathedral Visitor Centre** in the Undercroft tells the story of the momentous events which took place in Coventry, including the Blitz and its aftermath and the Cathedral's role in reconciliation worldwide through the Community of the Cross of Nails.

The city's most famous legend, of course, is that of **Lady Godiva**, who rode the streets naked to protest against taxation on the 11th century town-dwellers. A bronze statue in Broadgate stands in her memory. It was Leofric who started commerce and industry in Coventry as early as 1043, when he chose the small Saxon township as the site for a Benedictine monastery. He gave the monks land on which to raise sheep, laying the basis for the wool trade which made Coventry prosperous for over 500 years. The story has it, though, that this hard-hearted man taxed the people too heavily and Godiva begged him to lessen the burden. She apparently took the advance precaution of sending her messengers to request that everyone stay indoors behind closed shutters before she rode out. One 'Peeping Tom' disregarded her request and was struck blind. The Earl, duly chastened, relented and the taxes were cut.

This modern city has many ancient treasures: Bond's Hospital in Hill Street is a beautiful 16th century Tudor almshouse, now a home for the elderly. The exterior and courtyard are open to the public. **Ford's Hospital** in Greyfriar's Lane is another half-timbered Tudor almshouse, founded in 1509 by Coventry merchant William Ford. Another half-timbered building, Cheylesmore Manor House in New Union Street, was once owned by the Black Prince when he was Lord of the Manor. This attractive half-timbered building is now used as the Register Office, and as such is the oldest in Britain, dating back to 1250. Nearby, in Whitefriars Gate, is the Toy Museum, which houses a collection dating from the 18th century. Near the cathedral is the **Herbert Art Gallery and Museum**, which includes the story of Coventry and reconstructed rooms showing

weaving and other skills that have been associated with the city over the years. In Bayley Lane is **St Mary's Guildhall**, where Kings and Queens have been entertained and Mayors appointed to their office since the 1300s. Its tower once imprisoned Mary, Queen of Scots, and it has a restored 600-year-old crypt. This medieval treasure showcases the city's earliest industrial prosperity, which was founded on wool and cloth. The Guildhall also contains a splendour of old glass, a wealth of carving and a delightful minstrel's gallery with the additional bonus of a unique tapestry. This is one of England's finest Guildhalls, dating back to 1342. Here we see the Arras tapestry, the breathtaking Great North Window, the oak ceiling, and many suits of medieval armour.

The traditional industries of the city – clock-making and silk-weaving – came under threat from Switzerland and France respectively, and during the rapid slump in the city's fortunes many families emigrated to the Americas. It was cycle-making and engineering that ushered in a new wave of prosperity for the city. In 1885 the first modern bicycle was produced, and by 1896 Daimler and Humber had opened Coventry's first automotive factories. It was not long before they were joined by other companies, as Coventry became a magnet for labour from all over Britain. In 1930 a Coventrian, Frank Whittle, patented the jet engine. The **Museum of British Road Transport** in St Agnes Lane, Hales Street, examines the enormous contribution made by the city to the transport industry, spanning over 100 years, from the first cycles to the very latest advances in technology. Over 400 magnificent cars, motorcycles, cycles and commercial vehicles are on display.

A few minutes' walk from the city centre, **Coventry Canal Basin** has a distinguished history. It opened to boat traffic in September 1769, and the warehouses on Leicester Row span the late-18th to early-20th centuries. These warehouses, originally built for unloading and storing bulk goods, have been restored and are now home to artists' studios, boat-builders and specialist craft workshops. Coventry also boasts some outstanding parkland and public spaces. Lady Herbert's Garden in Hales Street lies near two of the town's ancient gates. It is a beautiful secluded garden which incorporates part of the old city wall. Greyfriars Green in Greyfriars Road is a conservation area with attractive open land and two distinct terraces of fine buildings. The War Memorial Park in Kenilworth Road is Coventry's premier park, with beautiful tree-lined walkways, a Peace Garden and Cenotaph. **Coombe Country Park**, a few miles east of the city centre off the B4027, comprises almost 400 acres of beautiful historic parkland with formal gardens, woodland and lakeside walks which make up the grounds of Coombe Abbey, landscaped by 'Capability' Brown.

AROUND COVENTRY

BAGINTON
5 miles S of Coventry off the A444

The **Midland Air Museum** at Coventry Airport in Baginton houses a unique collection of aircraft, engines and exhibits telling the story of the jet engine. In this hands-on museum visitors can sit in the cockpit of a Vulcan Bomber or Meteor, and with over 35 aircraft on display there is something to interest everyone. This very relaxed and informal museum features local aviation history, with a 'Wings Over Coventry' gallery and a wealth of Coventry-

produced aircraft and other exhibits, dominated by the giant Armstrong Whitworth Argosy freighter of 1959. The museum guides are happy to offer information and make all visitors feel welcome.

STONELEIGH
6 miles S of Coventry off the A444

This attractive village has a sandstone Norman church, several timber-framed houses and, nearby, the headquarters of the **Royal Agricultural Society of England**, and the Showground famed for its annual **Royal Show**.

BUBBENHALL
7 miles SE of Coventry off the A445

Between Bubbenhall and Ryton-on-Dunsmore, off the A445, **Ryton Pools Country Park** is a new 100-acre country park with an exciting range of facilities, including a Visitors' Centre, picnic areas, bird hide, numerous footpaths, model railway, fishing site and two adventure playgrounds.

RUGBY

The only town of any great size in north-eastern Warwickshire. Rugby has a **Market Place** surrounded by handsome buildings and a striking Church of St Andrew that was built by the Rokeby family after their castle had been destroyed by Henry II. The old tower dates from the 1400s. With its fireplace and 3 foot-thick walls, it looks more like a fortress and was, indeed, a place of refuge.

Rugby is probably most famous for its **School**, founded in 1567. Originally situated near the Clock Tower in the town, it moved to its present site in 1750. There are many fine buildings, splendid examples of their period, the highlight being the school chapel, designed by William Butterfield. These buildings house treasures such as stained glass believed to be the work of Albrecht Durer, the 15th century German artist and engraver.

There are few places in the world where you can gaze with any certainty over the birthplace of a sport that gives pleasure to millions. The game of Rugby originated here at the school when William Webb Ellis broke the rules during a football match in 1823 by picking up and running with the ball. The **James Gilbert Rugby Museum** is housed in the original building where, since 1842, the Gilberts have been making their world-famous rugby footballs. This Museum is crammed with memorabilia of the game and its development.

Rugby Town Trail is a two-hour walk that brings to life the town's history from its Saxon beginnings to the present day. The walk begins and ends at the **Clock Tower** in Market Place. This edifice was intended to commemorate the Golden Jubilee of Queen Victoria in 1887, yet it was not completed until 1889 because over-indulgent citizens had dipped too deep into the Tower funds to feast and drink at the Jubilee. The Trail takes in many of the town's main tourist attractions, including the house where Rupert Brooke was born, and his statue in Regent Place. Caldecott Park in the centre of town has beautiful floral displays, trees and a herb garden. Picnicking areas and a play area are two more of the highlights of this lovely park, and there are also facilities for bowls, putting, tennis and boules.

Rugby is bounded by two of the greatest Roman roads, Fosse Way and Watling Street, which meet just northwest of Rugby, at **High Cross**, one of the landmarks of the area.

The town is as far inland as it is possible to get in the British Isles, yet Rugby is an excellent centre for all kinds of water sports and aquatic activities. The **Oxford Canal** winds its way through the borough, and the Rivers Avon, Leam and Swift provide good angling, pleasant walks and places to picnic.

Cock Robin Wood is a nature reserve on Dunchurch Road, near the junction with Ashlawn Road. Here the visitor will find extensive areas of oak, ash, rowan, cherry and field maples, as well as grassy areas and a central pond, a haven for insects, frogs and butterflies.

The **Great Central Walk** is a four-mile ramble through Rugby. Along the way visitors will encounter an abundance of wildlife, plants and shrubs, as well as conservation areas and picnic sites.

AROUND RUGBY

DUNCHURCH

1 mile S of Rugby off the A426

'The gunpowder plot village': on November 5th, 1605, the Gunpowder Plot conspirators met at the Red Lion Inn, Dunchurch, to await the news of **Guy Fawkes'** attempt to blow up the English Houses of Parliament. The Red Lion still exists today, as a private residence known as **Guy Fawkes House**. This attractive village with its rows of thatched cottages has a 14th century church built by the monks of Pipewell Abbey, with one of the oldest parish registers in England.

Such was the considerable trade in looking after travellers who stopped over in Dunchurch during the great coaching days (up to 40 coaches a day stopped here), it is said that every property in the centre of the village was at some time an inn or ale house. For centuries

Dunchurch has been a popular stopover point for travellers on the main Holyhead-London road. A coaching stop to take on fresh horses, Dunchurch was also the staging post for pupils, masters, parents and visitors travelling to Rugby School. Many famous and important people have stayed in the village over the centuries, including Princess Victoria, Longfellow, the Duke of Wellington and William Webb Ellis of Rugby Football fame. Today, the village is in a designated conservation area with a lovely village green complete with village stocks and maypole, charming 16th, 17th and 18th century buildings, many of which retain the traditional Warwickshire thatched roofs. In 1996 the village won the prestigious Best Kept Large Village in Warwickshire award.

The Old Smithy which stands on the Rugby Road, is believed to have been the inspiration for Henry Wadsworth Longfellow's poem *Under the Spreading Chestnut Tree*.

DRAYCOTE

4 miles SW of Rugby off the A426

Draycote Water is a centre of watersports, fishing, sailing, birdwatching and attractive walks around the reservoir. Fly fishing permits are available from the Fishing Lodge. **Draycote Country Park**, next to Draycote Water, boasts 21 acres for walks, kite flying, picnicking by the lake, and magnificent hilltop views over Draycote Water, one of the largest reservoirs in the region.

LONG ITCHINGTON

8 miles SW of Rugby off the A423

The picturesque village of Long Itchington straddles the lovely **Grand Union Canal**. The Anglo-Saxon 'Farm by the River Itchen' boasted a population greater than that of Coventry at the time of the Domesday Book. The village **Church of the Holy Trinity** dates in part from 1190. The tower has only the remains of its original spire, which collapsed when struck by lightning during a Sunday morning service in 1762. The carvings in the chancel bear a closer look: one depicts a monkey with her young, another the head and shoulders of what is believed to be a jester.

SOUTHAM

9 miles SW of Rugby off the A426

Southam is an attractive town along the River Itchen. It repays a visit for the lovely rural scenery surrounding the town, and the wealth of good walking in the area. It was here in Southam that Charles I spent the night before the battle of Edge Hill. The Roundheads also came into the town, and Cromwell himself arrived with 7,000 troops in

CALCUTT BOATS

Calcutt Top Lock, Stockton, Southam, Warwickshire CV47 8HX
Tel: 01926 813757 Fax: 01926 814091
e-mail: boats@calcuttboats.com website: www.calcuttboats.com

From the peaceful rural marina at Napton, travellers on **Calcutt Boats** have a great choice of routes leading in all directions across the Heart of England. In business for some 30 years now, this family-run business has hire boats that range from the 4-berth Wild Lavender class to the 8-berth Wild Burdocks which, with a 60ft length, are the longest in the Calcutt fleet. All boats are meticulously maintained and comprehensively equipped, complete with duvets, colour TV, radio/cassette player (bring your own favourite tapes), hairdryer – even a cigar lighter socket for recharging mobile phones!

THE STONEYTHORPE HOTEL

Warwick Road, Southam, Warwickshire CV47 0HN
Tel: 01926 812365 Fax: 01926 817907
website: www.stoneythorpehotel.co.uk

Elegant Regency windows add distinction to **The Stoneythorpe Hotel**, a popular traditional hostelry which has been owned and run by the Hewer family for more than 40 years. Belinda and Les Hewer and their six daughters are all involved in running it. The 23 guest bedrooms include 11 with en suite facilities (more will be upgraded during the course of 2003) – all rooms have remote control TV, hospitality tray and complimentary toiletries. The gracious old building provides a perfect venue for weddings, banquets and conferences – its banqueting room can cater for up to 200 guests.

THE CROWN

Daventry Street, Southam, Warwickshire CV47 0PH
Tel: 01926 810622

What a difference a year makes! In 2002, when local couple Mark and Julie Crowther bought the village inn, **The Crown**, the 400-year-old building was in a deplorable state. Today, it's a lively hostelry with a new, well-appointed restaurant for which it's definitely advisable to book ahead. The menu offers a wide choice of traditional pub food (even including Savoury Suet Pudding); filled jacket potatoes; light bites; filled sandwiches or baguettes; and a selection of children's meals. To accompany your meal, the choice of beverages includes 2 real ales and some excellent wines.

1645. In the main street is the surprisingly named Old Mint Inn, a 14th century stone building taking its name from an occurrence following the Battle of Edge Hill. Charles I commanded his local noblemen to bring him their silver treasure, which was then melted down and minted into coins with which he paid his army.

WOLSTON

5 miles W of Rugby off the A428

The Church of St Margaret is Norman in origin, but was substantially rebuilt after the steeple collapsed into the chancel in 1759. A stone in the churchyard poses the simple question: *'Tell me which is best, the toilsome journey or the traveller's rest?'* Near the 1837 railway bridge are the earthworks of **Brandon Castle**, which was destroyed not very long after it was built in the 13th century.

RYTON-ON-DUNSMORE

6 miles W of Rugby off the A45

This village is home to the **Henry Doubleday Research Association** at Ryton Gardens. This organic farming and gardening organisation leads the way in research and advances in horticulture. The grounds are landscaped with thousands of plants and trees, all organically grown. Also on site are a herb garden, rose garden, garden for the blind, shrub borders and free-roaming animals. **Ryton Pools Country Park** is a 100-acre country park opened in 1996. The 10-acre Ryton Pool is home to great crested grebes, swans, moorhens and Canada geese. There is also an attractive meadow area for strolling or picnicking, a Visitor Centre, shop and exhibition area. **Pagets Pool** near the north-eastern end of the park is one of the most important sites in Warwickshire for dragonflies, with 17 species including the common blue, emperor dragonfly and black-tailed skimmer. Other highlights include guided walks and a model railway run by Coventry Model Engineering Society.

BRANDON

6 miles W of Rugby off the A428

Brandon Marsh Nature Centre is 200 acres of lakes, marshes, woodland and grassland, providing a home and haven for many species of wildlife. There are bird hides, an informative Visitor Centre and a nature trail, as well as guided walks, pond-dipping and changing exhibitions.

STRETTON UNDER FOSSE

5 miles NW of Rugby off the B4112

For a slightly unusual day out, **H M Prison Services Museum** at Newbold Revel, Stretton under Fosse has displays on the history of imprisonment from medieval times to the present. Visits are strictly by appointment; contact the Curator on 01788 834168.

NEWBOLD-ON-AVON

1 mile N of Rugby off the B4112

Newbold Quarry Park affords visitors the opportunity for a country walk just north of Rugby town, with hilly woodland and extensive waterside walks.

This bit of countryside is a haven for birds and wildlife.

ASHBY ST LEDGERS

4 miles SE of Rugby off the A361

The **Gunpowder Plot** conspirators took refuge here in the manor house owned by Robert Catesby. Though not open to visitors, the manor house is close to the road and worth seeing, as it is very evocative of the times. This charming village also rewards a stroll, with some cottages designed by Lutyens. Parts of the handsome village church date back to the early 1500s.

NAPTON ON THE HILL

9 miles S of Rugby off the A425

This attractive village on a rounded hill above a curve in the Oxford Canal - one of the prettiest in this part of the world, with pleasant towpath walks. There are views of seven counties from the hilltop.

NUNEATON

8 miles N of Coventry on the A444

Originally a Saxon town known at Etone, Nuneaton is mentioned in the Domesday Book of 1086. The 'Nun' was added when a wealthy Benedictine priory was founded here in 1290. The Priory ruins left standing are adjacent to the church of St Nicholas, a Victorian edifice occupying a Norman site which

THE CRAFT ROOM

The Arcade, George Street, Attleborough, Nuneaton,
Warwickshire CV11 4LA
Tel: 0244 634 2093   website: www.thecraftroom.co.uk

The Craft Room, located in the pleasant suburb of Attleborough, is much more than an excellent gift and crafts shop, one of the best in the county. Owner Marie Parish is also an accomplished painter and gives art classes of up to 12 people at a time. Participants choose their own ceramic model made from a selection of hundreds of different moulds and then paint them. If you just want to buy a distinctive gift you'll find an incredible choice that takes in porcelain, Pergania parchment craft, sugarcraft, floral displays of every kind, stylish cards and much, much more.

has a beautiful carved ceiling dating back to 1485.

The town has a history as a centre for coal-mining, which began in Nuneaton as early as the 14th century. Other industries for which the town has been famous include brick and tile manufacture and ribbon-making on hand looms. As the textile and hatting industries boomed, the town began to prosper. Today's Nuneaton is a centre of precision engineering, printing, car components and other important trades.

Nuneaton Museum and Art Gallery, located in Riversley Park, features displays of archaeological interest ranging from prehistoric to medieval times, and items from the local earthenware industry. There is also a permanent exhibition of the town's most illustrious daughter, the novelist and thinker George Eliot.

Born to a prosperous land agent at Arbury Hall in 1819, Eliot (whose real name was Mary Ann Evans) was an intellectual giant and free thinker. She left Warwickshire for London in adulthood, and met George Henry Lewes, a writer and actor who was to become her lifelong companion. Lewes, married with three children, left his family so that he and Eliot, very bravely for the time, could set up house together. Eliot's novels return again and again to the scenes and social conventions of her youth, and are among the greatest works of English literature – in particular her masterpiece, *Middlemarch*.

Monks Kirby

9 miles SE of Nuneaton off the A427

The Saxons were the first people to build a church in this ancient settlement, probably a wooden structure originally, being replaced by a stone building later. The Danes arrived about 864 AD as part of their conquest of this part of the country. The field at the rear of the church is still known as the **Denmark Field**.

After the Norman Conquest, a Benedictine Priory was established and a church rebuilt on the old site. Most of the present building dates from the 14th century. The tall spire, built above the tower in the 15th century, could be seen by travellers for many miles around until it was blown down by a great storm on Christmas night in 1701. From its earliest days Monks Kirby grew in size and importance, eventually taking on the full status of a market town. Pilgrims and merchants were accommodated in the Priory's guest house, which probably stood on the site of the current Denbigh Arms public house. This rural, quiet village, dominated by the ancient church, also boasts many pretty cottages along its main streets.

Arbury Hall

3 miles SW of Nuneaton off the B4102

A visit to Arbury Hall fits another piece in the jigsaw of George Eliot's life and times. She was born on the estate, where her father was land agent; in *Mr Gifgil's Love Story* she portrays Arbury as Cheverel Manor, and gives detailed descriptions of many of the rooms in the house, including the Saloon and the Dining Room – comparing the latter, unsurprisingly given its grandeur, to a cathedral. The Hall's grounds include a delightful 10-acre garden with a real air of tranquillity.

Bedworth

3 miles S of Nuneaton off the B4029

This small town was once part of the North Warwickshire coalfield established at the end of the 1600s. Local people were largely responsible for the building of the **Coventry Canal**, running from Coventry to Fradley near Lichfield and completed in 1790, 22 years after work on it began. It was constructed to connect the fast-growing town with the great new trade route, the Grand Trunk – and to provide Coventry with cheap coal from the Bedworth coal field.

French Protestant families fleeing persecution sought refuge here, bringing with them their skill in silk and ribbon weaving. The parish church, completed in 1890, is a good example of Gothic Revival. Its grounds include a scented garden. The open air market and main shopping precinct share the town's central All Saints Square with the splendid Chamberlaine almshouses, founded by a 17th century rector of Bedworth, the Rev. Nicholas Chamberlaine. Close by, the Old Meeting church dates from 1726 and is one of the earliest nonconformist chapels in the region. Bedworth's award-winning **Miners' Welfare Park** contains some of the finest spring and summer bedding layouts in the region, as well as areas devoted to tennis, bowls, pitch and putt, roller skating and cricket.

ANSLEY

5 miles W of Nuneaton off the B4112

Ansley is best known for adjacent **Hoar Park**, which dates back to the 1430s. The existing house and buildings date from 1730, and now form the centrepiece of the 143-acre Park, which contains a handsome **Craft Village** (see panel on page 440). The Park, as well as being a craft, antique and garden centre, is still a working farm.

HARTSHILL

3 miles NW of Nuneaton off the A5

Hartshill Hayes Country Park is an ideal place for exploring the developing rural attractions of this part of Warwickshire. Although surrounded by a network of roads, here visitors find only woodland trails and walks, and magnificent views. The park boasts 136 acres of woodland, meadow and open hilltop. Winner of the Forestry Authority's 'Centre of Excellence Award' in 1996, the park boasts three self-guided walks, an informative Visitors' Centre and truly wonderful views. Hartshill itself was the birthplace of the poet Michael Drayton (1563-1631).

MANCETTER

5 miles NW of Nuneaton off the A5

This former Roman camp is situated on a rocky outcrop overlooking the valley of the River Anker. This camp was once one of a line of forts built by the Romans as they advanced northwards. The village is chiefly associated with the **Mancetter Martyrs**, Robert Glover and Joyce Lewis, both of whom were burnt at the stake for their religious beliefs. The martyrs are commemorated on wooden tablets in the fine **Church of St Peter**, which dates back to the early 1200s. The glory of this church is its rich glass in the east window of the chancel, most of which is 14th century in origin and thought to have been created by John Thornton, builder of the great east window of York Minster. Between the manor and the church are two noteworthy rows of almshouses dating from 1728 to 1822.

ATHERSTONE

5 miles W of Nuneaton off the A5

Atherstone is a small market town situated on the Roman Watling Street at the eastern edge of the Warwickshire Forest of Arden, off the A5 between Nuneaton and Tamworth. Set against the wooded hills of the Merevale Estate, the picturesque town centre dates from

HOAR PARK FARM CRAFT & ANTIQUES CENTRE & CHILDREN'S FARM

B4114 nr Ansley, Coleshill, Warks. CV10 0QU
Tel: 024 7639 4433
e-mail: info@hoar-park.co.uk
website: www.hoar-park.co.uk

Hoar Park Farm Craft & Antiques Centre & Children's Farm provides just about everything you need for a satisfying family day out. Set in the beautiful north Warwickshire

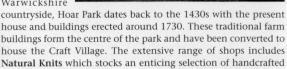

countryside, Hoar Park dates back to the 1430s with the present house and buildings erected around 1730. These traditional farm buildings form the centre of the park and have been converted to house the Craft Village. The extensive range of shops includes **Natural Knits** which stocks an enticing selection of handcrafted garments with designer labels from names such as Rowan, Jaeger, Colinette, Debbie Bliss and Noro. Natural Knits is also the only shop in the Midlands to stock organic dyed wool which can be used for made to measure garments.

Those in search of distinctive jewellery, clothing and accessories will find a dazzling range on offer at **5ᵗʰ Avenue** where an exquisite selection of Italian jewellery, handbags, scarves and belts is constantly updated.

If antiques are your passion you'll enjoy visiting the **Antiques Centre** where regular auctions are held. On site there is a full antique furniture restoration service offering French, oil and wax polishing, cabinet making, veneering, marquetry, carving and releathering. All work is

carried out sympathetically by craftsmen with 35 years experience of restoring the prized possessions of both the trade and the general public. Advice and quotations are given freely.

Other shops include a Saddlery where you'll find everything for the horse and rider, hand made chocolates, soft furnishings and giftware, rattan and pine furniture plus candles, oils and giftware and a garden centre.

When you've completed your shopping, drop into the park's licensed restaurant where home made light refreshments and fine meals are available all day with fine views over the North Warwickshire countryside and The Childrens Farm.

Hoar Park is open all year, Tuesday to Sunday & Bank Holiday Mondays, 10am to 5pm. Admission and parking are free to this friendly working farm craft and garden centre.

medieval times and is unspoiled by modern development. Atherstone's history predates medieval times to the Anglo-Saxons; at the time of the Norman Conquest it belonged to the Countess of Mercia, Lady Godiva. The Domesday Book of 1086 records 14 residents: 11 villagers, two smallholders and one slave. Its importance as a trading centre grew and grew over the ensuing years, so that by 1724 Daniel Defoe could describe it as 'a town famous for a great cheese fair on the 8th September'.

Atherstone's **St Mary's Church** was founded in 1365 as a chapel-of-ease, becoming a parish church in 1835, when Atherstone separated from Mancetter to become a parish in its own right. The tower was rebuilt in 1782 in 'modern Gothic' style. To the rear of the building, the 12th century Baddesley Porch, brought from Baddesley Ensor church when the latter was demolished in 1842, boasts lovely decorative detail.

GRENDON

3 miles NW of Atherstone off the A5

Grendon once boasted its own mint, owned by Sir George Chetwynd of Grendon Hall. It was this same Sir George who fell in love with the actress Lillie Langtry, and who fought Lord Lonsdale in a fist fight to win her favour. He led an extravagant life, spending a lot of time at race meetings and entertaining the Prince of Wales, with the result that his beloved Lillie began a liaison with the Prince, and Sir George lost so much money that Grendon Hall had to be sold off; it was pulled down in 1933.

NEWTON REGIS

6 miles NW of Atherstone off the B5493

One of the most unspoilt villages in Warwickshire, Newton Regis has been voted Best Kept Small Village on numerous occasions. Near the Staffordshire border and between the M42 and B5453, this lovely village is built around an attractive duck pond which was once a quarry pit. The village's name is thought to derive from its former royal ownership, having once been the property of King Henry II. It has in its day also been known as King's Newton and Newton-in-the-Thistles – the latter perhaps referring to the abundance of thistles or specially grown teasels which were used in the carding of flax fibre. Linen looms were worked in the house which is now the Queens Head Inn.

ALVECOTE

6 miles NW of Atherstone off the M42

Alvecote Priory, just on the border with Staffordshire, was founded by William Burnett in 1159, who built it as a penance after having (mistakenly) believed that his wife had been unfaithful during his pilgrimage to the Holy Land. This small Benedictine Priory was founded as a cell to the Great Malvern Priory in Worcestershire. As with many others it was dissolved in 1536, when the buildings were converted into a house, which was pulled down in about 1700 when another house was constructed using some of the old materials. The 14th century remains include a fine moulded doorway and dovecote.

Alvecote Priory Picnic Area boasts canalside picnic spots and a nearby nature reserve. There is also an interesting circular walk that takes in lakes, wildlife, many unusual plants, the old North Warwicks Colliery tip, and handsome canal bridges.

TOURIST INFORMATION CENTRES

DERBYSHIRE

ASHBOURNE

13 Market Place
Ashbourne
Derbyshire
DE6 1EU
Tel: 01335 343666
Fax: 01335 300638

BAKEWELL

Old Market Hall
Bridge Street
Bakewell
Derbyshire
DE45 1DS
Tel: 01629 813227
Fax: 01629 813227

BUXTON

The Crescent
Buxton
Derbyshire
SK17 6BQ
Tel: 01298 25106
Fax: 01298 73153

CHESTERFIELD

Low Pavement
Chesterfield
Derbyshire
S40 1PB
Tel: 01246 345777
Fax: 01246 345770

DERBY

Assembly Rooms
Market Place
Derby
Derbyshire
DE1 3AH
Tel: 01332 255802
Fax: 01332 256137
e-mail: tourism@derby.gov.uk
website: www.visitderby.co.uk

GLOSSOP

The Gatehouse
Victoria Street
Glossop
Derbyshire
SK13 8HT
Tel: 01457 855920
Fax: 01427 855920

MATLOCK

Crown Square
Matlock
Derbyshire
DE3 3AT
Tel: 01629 583388
Fax: 01629 584131

MATLOCK BATH

The Pavillion
Matlock
Derbyshire
DE4 3NR
Tel: 01629 55082
Fax: 01629 56304

RIPLEY

Town Hall
Market Place
Ripley
Derbyshire
DE5 3BT
Tel: 01773 841488
Fax: 01773 841487
e-mail: touristinformation
@ambervalley.gov.uk

HEREFORDSHIRE

BROMYARD

Heritage Centre
1 Rowberry
St. Bromyard
Herefordshire
HR7 4DU

Tel: 01885 482033
Fax: 01432 260053

HEREFORD

1 King Street
Hereford
Herefordshire
HR4 9BW
Tel: 01432 268430
Fax: 01432 342662
e-mail: tic-hereford
@herefordshire.gov.uk

LEDBURY

3 The Homend
Ledbury
Herefordshire
HR8 1BN
Tel: 01531 636147
Fax: 01531 634313

LEOMINSTER

1 Corn Square
Leominster
Herefordshire
HR6 8LR
Tel: 01568 616460
Fax: 01568 615546

QUEENSWOOD

Queenswood Country Park
Dinmore Hill
Leominster
Herefordshire
HR6 0PY
Tel: 01568 797842

ROSS-ON-WYE

Swan House
Edde Cross Street
Ross-On-Wye
Herefordshire
HR2 7JL
Tel 01989 562768
Fax: 01989 565057

LEICESTERSHIRE AND RUTLAND

ASHBY-DE-LA-ZOUCH

North Street
Ashby-de-la-Zouch
Leicestershire
LE65 IHU
Tel: 01530 411767
Fax: 01530 560660

COALVILLE

Snibston Discovery Park
Ashby Road
Coalville
Leicestershire
LE67 3LN
Tel: 01530 813608
Fax: 01530 813608

HINCKLEY

Hinckley Library
Lancaster Road
Hinckley
Leicestershire
LE10 0AT
Tel: 01455 635106
Fax: 01455 251385

LEICESTER

7/9 Every Street
Town Hall Square
Leicester
Leicestershire
LE1 6AG
Tel: 0116 299 8888
Fax: 0116 225 4050
e-mail: tic@leicester
promotions.org.uk

LOUGHBOROUGH

Loughborough Town Hall
Market Place
Loughborough
Leicestershire
LE11 3EB
Tel: 01509 218113
Fax: 01509 240617

MARKET HARBOROUGH

Council Offices
Adam and Eve Street
Market Harborough
Leicestershire
LE16 7AG
Tel: 01858 821270

MELTON MOWBRAY

Melton Carnegie Museum
Thorpe End
Melton Mowbray
Leicestershire
LE13 1RB
Tel: 01664 480992
Fax: 01664 480992

OAKHAM

Flore's House
34 High Street
Oakham
Rutland
LE15 6AL
Tel 01572 724329
Fax: 01572 724329

RUTLAND WATER

Sykes Lane
Empingham
Nr. Oakham
Rutland
LE15 8PX
Tel 01572 653026
Fax: 01572 653027

LINCOLNSHIRE

ALFORD

The Manor House Museum
West Street
Alford
Lincolnshire
LN13 9DJ
Tel: 01507 462143
Fax: 01507 462143
e-mail: enquiries@FunCoast.co.uk

BOSTON

Market Place
Boston
Lincolnshire
PE21 6NN
Tel: 01205 356656
Fax: 01205 356656
e-mail: tourism
bostongb.freeserve.co.uk

BRIGG

The Buttercross
Market Place
Brigg
North Lincolnshire
DN20 8ER
Tel: 01652 657053
Fax: 01652 657053
e-mail: brigg.tic
@northlincs.gov.uk

CLEETHORPES

42-43 Alexandra Road
Cleethorpes
North East Lincolnshire
DN35 8LE
Tel: 01472 323111
Fax: 01472 323112
e-mail: cleethorpes@ytbtic.co.uk

GRANTHAM

The Guildhall Centre
St Peters Hill
Grantham
Lincolnshire
NG31 6PZ
Tel: 01476 406166
Fax: 01476 406166
e-mail: granthamtic@skdc.com

HORNCASTLE

14 Bull Ring
Horncastle
Lincolnshire
LN9 5HU
Tel/Fax: 01507 526636
e-mail: horncastleinfo@e-lindsey.gov.uk

LINCOLN (CASTLE SQUARE)

9 Castle Square
Lincoln
Lincolnshire
LN1 3AA
Tel: 01522 873213
Fax: 01522 873553
e-mail: recreation@lincoln.gov.uk

LINCOLN (CORNHILL)

21 Cornhill
Lincoln
Lincolnshire
LN5 7HB
Tel: 01522 873256
Fax: 01522 544882
e-mail: recreation@lincoln.gov.uk

LOUTH

The New Market Hall
Off Cornmarket
Louth
Lincolnshire
LN11 9PY
Tel: 01507 609289
Fax: 01507 609289
e-mail: louthinfo
        @e-lindsey.gov.uk

MABLETHORPE

Dunes Family Entertainment
Centre
Central Promenade
Mablethorpe
Lincolnshire
LN12 1RG
Tel: 01507 474939
Fax: 01507 474938
e-mail: mablethorpeinfo
        @e-lindsey.gov.uk

SKEGNESS

Grand Parade
Skegness
Lincolnshire
PE25 2UG
Tel: 01754 899887
e-mail: skegnessinfo
        @e-lindsey.gov.uk

SLEAFORD

Advice Centre
"Money's Yard, Carre Street"
Sleaford
Lincolnshire
NG34 7TW
Tel: 01529 414294
Fax: 01529 414294
e-mail: tic@n-kesteven.gov.uk

SPALDING

Ayscoughfee Hall
Churchgate
Spalding
Lincolnshire
PE11 2RA
Tel: 01775 725468
Fax: 01775 762715

STAMFORD

Stamford Arts Centre
27 St Mary's Street
Stamford
Lincolnshire
PE9 2DL
Tel: 01780 755611
Fax: 01780 755611
e-mail: stamfordtic@skdc.com

WOODHALL SPA

Cottage Museum
Iddesleigh Road
Woodhall Spa
Lincolnshire
LN10 6SH
Tel: 01526 353775
Fax: 01526 353775
e-mail: lorraine.leyland
        @e-lindsey.gov.uk

NORTHAMPTON-SHIRE

BRACKLEY

2 Bridge Street
Brackley
Northamptonshire
NN13 7EP
Tel: 01280 700111
Fax: 01280 700157

CORBY

George Street
Corby
Northamptonshire
NN17 1QB
Tel: 01536 407507
Fax: 01536 400200

DAVENTRY

Moot Hall
Market Square
Daventry
Northamptonshire
NN11 4BH
Tel: 01327 300277
Fax: 01327 876684

KETTERING

The Coach House
Sheep Street
Kettering
Northamptonshire
NN16 0AN
Tel: 01536 410266 (01536 534212)
Fax: 01536 534370

NORTHAMPTON

Mr Grant's House
St. Giles Square
Northampton
Northamptonshire
NN1 1DA
Tel: 01604 622677
Fax: 01604 604180
e-mail: tic@pedu.
        northampton.gov.uk

OUNDLE

14 West Street
Oundle
Northamptonshire
PE8 4EF
Tel: 01832 274333 (01832 273326)
Fax: 01832 274333
e-mail: oundletic
        @east-northamptonshire.gov.uk

WELLINGBOROUGH

Wellingborough Library
Pebble Lane
Wellingborough
Northamptonshire
NN8 1AS
Tel: 01933 276412 (01933 225365)
Fax: 01933 442060

NOTTINGHAMSHIRE

NEWARK

The Gilstrap Centre
Castlegate
Newark
Nottinghamshire
NG24 1BG
Tel: 01636 655765
Fax: 01636 655767

NOTTINGHAM (SMITHY ROW)

1-4 Smithy Row
Nottingham
Nottinghamshire
NG1 2BY
Tel: 0115 915 5330
Fax: 0115 915 5323
e-mail: touristinformation
@nottinghamcity.gov.uk

NOTTINGHAM (WEST BRIDGFORD)

County Hall
Loughborough Road
West Bridgford
Nottinghamshire
NG2 7QP
Tel: 0115 977 3558
Fax: 0115 977 3886
e-mail: tic@nottscc.gov.uk

OLLERTON

Sherwood Heath
Ollerton Roundabout
Ollerton,
Nr Newark
Nottinghamshire
NG22 9DR
Tel: 01623 824545
Fax: 01623 822930
e-mail: sherwoodheath
@newark-sherwooddc.gov.uk

RETFORD

40 Grove Street
Retford
Nottinghamshire
DN22 6LD
Tel: 01777 860780
Fax: 01777 860780
e-mail: retford.information
@bassetlaw.gov.uk

WORKSOP

Worksop Library
Memorial Avenue
Worksop
Nottinghamshire
S80 2BP
Tel: 01909 501148
Fax: 01909 501148

SHROPSHIRE

BRIDGNORTH

The Library
Listley Street
Bridgnorth
Shropshire
WV16 4AW
Tel: 01746 763257
Fax: 01746 766625
e-mail: tic@bridgnorth
shropshire.com

CHURCH STRETTON

Church Street
Church Stretton
Shropshire
SY6 6DQ
Tel: 01694 723133
Fax: 01694 723045

ELLESMERE

The Mere's Visitor Centre
The Mere
Ellesmere
Shropshire
SY12 0PA
Tel: 01691 622981
Fax: 01691 622981

IRONBRIDGE

The Wharfage
Ironbridge
Shropshire
TF8 7AW
Tel: 01952 432166
Fax: 01952 432204
e-mail: info@ironbridge.org.uk

LUDLOW

Castle Street
Ludlow
Shropshire
SY8 1AS
Tel: 01584 875053
Fax: 01584 877931

MARKET DRAYTON

49 Cheshire Street
Market Drayton
Shropshire
TF9 1PH
Tel: 01630 652139
Fax: 01630 652139

MUCH WENLOCK

The Museum
High Street
Much Wenlock
Shropshire
TF13 6HR
Tel: 01952 727679

OSWESTRY (HERITAGE CENTRE)

The Heritage Centre
2 Church Terrace
Oswestry
Shropshire
SY11 2TE
Tel: 01691 662753
Fax: 01691 657811
e-mail: osbta@microplus-web.net

OSWESTRY (MILE END SERVICES)

Mile End Services
Oswestry
Shropshire
SY11 4JA
Tel: 01691 662488
Fax: 01691 662883

SHREWSBURY

The Music Hall
The Square
Shrewsbury
Shropshire
SY1 1LH
Tel: 01743 281200
Fax: 01743 281213
e-mail: tic@shrewsbury
tourism.co.uk

TELFORD

The Telford Centre
Management Suite
Telford
Shropshire
TF3 4BX
Tel: 01952 238008 (01952 238009)
Fax: 01952 291723

WHITCHURCH

12 St Mary's Street
Whitchurch
Shropshire
SY13 1QY
Tel: 01948 664577
Fax: 01948 665432

STAFFORDSHIRE

BURTON UPON TRENT

183 High Street
Burton upon Trent
Staffordshire
DE14 1HN
Tel: 01283 516609 (01283 508589)
Fax: 01283 517268
e-mail: tic@burtonwindow.com

LEEK

1, Market Place
Leek
Staffordshire
ST13 5HH
Tel: 01538 483741
Fax: 01538 483743
e-mail: tourism.services
          @staffsmoorlands.gov.uk

LICHFIELD

Donegal House
Bore Street
Lichfield
Staffordshire
WS13 6NE
Tel: 01543 308209
Fax: 01543 308211
e-mail: tic@lichfieldtourist.co.uk

NEWCASTLE-UNDER-LYME

Newcastle Library
Ironmarket
Newcastle-under-Lyme
Staffordshire
ST5 1AT
Tel: 01782 297313
Fax: 01782 297322
e-mail: tic.newcastle
          @staffordshire.gov.uk

STAFFORD

Market Street
Stafford
Staffordshire
ST16 2LQ
Tel: 01785 619619
Fax: 01785 619134
e-mail: tic@staffordbc.gov.uk

STOKE-ON-TRENT

Quadrant Road
Hanley,
Stoke-on-Trent
Staffordshire
ST1 1RZ
Tel: 01782 236000
Fax: 01782 236005
e-mail: stoke.tic@virgin.net

TAMWORTH

29 Market Street
Tamworth
Staffordshire
B79 7LR
Tel 01827 709581
Fax: 01827 709582

WARWICKSHIRE

KENILWORTH

The Library
11 Smalley Place
Kenilworth
Warwickshire
CV8 1QG
Tel: 01926 748900
Fax: 01926 748901

LEAMINGTON SPA

The Royal Pump Rooms
The Parade
Leamington Spa
Warwickshire
CV32 4AB
Tel: 01926 742762
Fax: 01926 742766
e-mail: leamington
          @shakespearecountry.co.uk

NUNEATON

Nuneaton Library
Church Street
Nuneaton
Warwickshire
CV11 4DR
Tel: 024 76 347006 (024 76 384027)
Fax: 024 76 350125
e-mail: nuneatonlibrary
          @dial.pipex.com

RUGBY

The Home of Rugby Football
Visitor Centre
4 Lawrence Sheriff Street
Rugby
Warwickshire
CV22 5EJ
Tel: 01788 534970
Fax: 01788 534979
e-mail: visitor.centre
          @rugby.gov.uk

STRATFORD-UPON-AVON

Bridgefoot
Stratford-upon-Avon
Warwickshire
CV37 6GW
Tel: 01789 293127
Fax: 01789 295262
e-mail: stratfordtic
          @shakespeare-country.co.uk

WARWICK

The Court House
Jury Street
Warwick
Warwickshire
CV34 4EW
Tel: 01926 492212
Fax: 01926 494837
e-mail: warwicktic
          @btconnect.com

WEST MIDLANDS

BIRMINGHAM (ARCADE)

Convention & Visitor Bureau
2 City Arcade
Birmingham
West Midlands
B2 4TX
Tel: 0121 643 2514
Fax: 0121 616 1038
e-mail: ticketshop@bmp.org.uk

BIRMINGHAM (COLMORE)

Visitor Information Centre
130 Colmore Row
Birmingham
West Midlands
B3 3AP
Tel: 0121 693 6300
Fax: 0121 693 9600

BIRMINGHAM (NEC)

Convention & Visitor Bureau
National Exhibition Centre
Birmingham
West Midlands
B40 1NT
Tel: 0121 780 4321
Fax: 0121 780 4260
e-mail: piazza@bmp.org.uk

COVENTRY

Bayley Lane
Coventry
West Midlands
CV1 5RN
Tel: 024 7622 7264
Fax: 024 7622 7255

DUDLEY

39 Churchill Centre
Dudley
West Midlands
DY2 7BL
Tel: 01384 812830
Fax: 01384 815580

MERRY HILL

Merry Hill
Brierley Hill
West Midlands
DY5 1SR
Tel: 01384 487900
Fax: 01384 487910

SOLIHULL

Central Library
Homer Road
Solihull
West Midlands
B91 3RG
Tel: 0121 704 6130
Fax: 0121 704 8224
e-mail: ckelly@solihull.gov.uk

WOLVERHAMPTON

18 Queen Square
Wolverhampton
West Midlands
WV1 1TQ
Tel: 01902 556110 (01902 556112)
Fax: 01902 556111
e-mail: wolverhampton.tic
@dial.pipex.com

WORCESTERSHIRE

BEWDLEY

Load Street
Bewdley
Worcestershire
DY12 2AE
Tel: 01299 404740
Fax: 01299 404740

BROADWAY

1 Cotswold Court
Broadway
Worcestershire
WR12 7AA
Tel: 01386 852937

BROMSGROVE

Bromsgrove Museum
26 Birmingham Road
Bromsgrove
Worcestershire
B61 0DD
Tel: 01527 831809
Fax: 01527 577983

DROITWICH SPA

St Richard's House
Victoria Square
Droitwich Spa
Worcestershire
WR9 8DS
Tel: 01905 774312
Fax: 01905 794226

EVESHAM

The Almonry
Abbey Gate
Evesham
Worcestershire
WR11 4BG
Tel: 01386 446944
Fax: 01386 442348

MALVERN

21 Church Street
Malvern
Worcestershire
WR14 2AA
Tel: 01684 892289 (01684 86234)
Fax: 01684 892872
e-mail: malvern.tic
@malvernhills.gov.uk

PERSHORE

19 High Street
Pershore
Worcestershire
WR10 1AA
Tel: 01386 554262
Fax: 01386 561660

REDDITCH

Civic Square
Alcester Street
Redditch
Worcestershire
B98 8AH
Tel: 01527 60806
Fax: 01527 60806

UPTON UPON SEVERN

4 High Street
Upton Upon Severn
Worcestershire
WR8 0HB
Tel: 01684 594200
Fax: 01684 594185
e-mail: upton.tic
@malvernhills.gov.uk

WORCESTER

The Guildhall
High Street
Worcester
Worcestershire
WR1 2EY
Tel: 01905 726311 (01905 722480)
Fax: 01905 722481

INDEX OF ADVERTISERS

INDEX OF ADVERTISERS

Jarrold
Pathfinder Guides

- Ordnance Survey mapping

- 28 walk routes, graded easy, moderate and challenging

- Introduces you to the area and highlights the most scenic routes

- Details useful organisations, refreshment stops and places to leave your car

- Series covers all of the UK

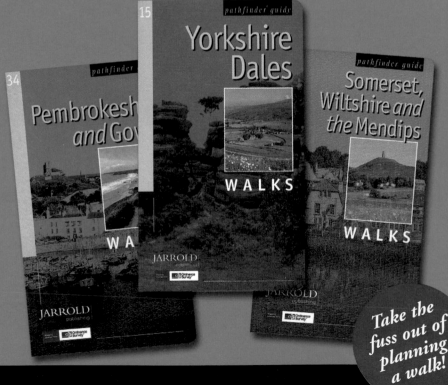

34 · *pathfinder*
Pembrokesh and Gow
W A
JARROLD publishing
Ordnance Survey

15 · *pathfinder guide*
Yorkshire Dales
W A L K S
JARROLD publishing
Ordnance Survey

pathfinder guide
Somerset, Wiltshire *and* the Mendips
W A L K S
JARROLD publishing
Ordnance Survey

Take the fuss out of planning a walk!

Available at tourist outlets,